HANDBOOK OF RESEARCH ON STRATEGIC HUMAN CAPITAL RESOURCES

In memoriam: David P. Lepak

Dave Lepak (1971–2017), former Professor in the Isenberg School of Management at the University of Massachusetts Amherst, USA, was an early contributor to HCR theory and a co-founder of the Strategic Human Capital Interest Group at the Strategic Management Society. He was a co-author, colleague, mentor, and friend to many of the contributors to this volume. We miss you, Dave, and dearly wish you were contributing a chapter on this topic: we know you would have given us something important to think about.

Handbook of Research on Strategic Human Capital Resources

Edited by

Anthony J. Nyberg

Distinguished Moore Fellow, Darla Moore School of Business, University of South Carolina, USA

Thomas P. Moliterno

Earl W. Stafford Professor of Entrepreneurial Studies, Isenberg School of Management, University of Massachusetts Amherst, USA

Edward Elgar PUBLISHING

Cheltenham, UK • Northampton, MA, USA

Published by
Edward Elgar Publishing Limited
The Lypiatts
15 Lansdown Road
Cheltenham
Glos GL50 2JA
UK

Edward Elgar Publishing, Inc.
William Pratt House
9 Dewey Court
Northampton
Massachusetts 01060
USA

A catalogue record for this book
is available from the British Library

Library of Congress Control Number: 2019951630

This book is available electronically in the **Elgar**online
Business subject collection
DOI 10.4337/9781788116695

MIX
Paper from
responsible sources
FSC® C013604

ISBN 978 1 78811 668 8 (cased)
ISBN 978 1 78811 669 5 (eBook)

Typeset by Servis Filmsetting Ltd, Stockport, Cheshire
Printed and bound by CPI Group (UK) Ltd, Croydon CR0 4YY

Contents

Commentary Chapters

Contributors

Rajshree Agarwal, Rudolph P. Lamone Chair and Professor and Director of the Ed Snider Center for Enterprise and Markets, Robert H. Smith School of Business, University of Maryland, USA.

Brittney Amber, Doctoral student, School of Science, Indiana University–Purdue University Indianapolis, USA.

Jay B. Barney, Presidential Professor of Strategic Management and Lassonde Chair of Social Entrepreneurship, David Eccles School of Business, University of Utah, USA.

F. Scott Bentley, Assistant Professor of Strategy and Center for Leadership Studies Fellow, School of Management, Binghamton University, USA.

Y. Sekou Bermiss, Associate Professor, McCombs School of Business, University of Texas at Austin, USA.

Matthew Bidwell, Associate Professor, The Wharton School, University of Pennsylvania, USA.

Flore Bridoux, Associate Professor, Amsterdam Business School, University of Amsterdam, the Netherlands.

Rhett A. Brymer, Assistant Professor, Carl H. Lindner College of Business, University of Cincinnati, USA.

Ben Campbell, Associate Professor, Fisher College of Business, Ohio State University, USA.

Arnaldo Camuffo, Full Professor and Vice Director of Invernizzi Center for Research in Innovation, Organization, Strategy and Entrepreneurship (ICRIOS), SDA Bocconi School of Management, Bocconi University, Italy.

Albert A. Cannella, Jr, Professor and Blue Bell Creameries Endowed Chair, Mays Business School, Texas A&M University, USA.

Clint Chadwick, Professor and Howard Fitch Research Fellow, School of Business, University of Kansas, USA.

Gilad Chen, Robert H. Smith Chair in Organization Behavior, Robert H. Smith School of Business, University of Maryland, USA.

Russell Coff, UW Foundation Chairman Orr Bascom Professor in Business and Senior Associate Dean for Faculty and Research, School of Business, University of Wisconsin–Madison, USA.

Samantha A. Conroy, Associate Professor, College of Business, Colorado State University, USA.

Alia Crocker, Assistant Professor, F. W. Olin Graduate School of Business, Babson College, USA.

Samantha Darnell, Doctoral student, The Wharton School, University of Pennsylvania, USA.

Federica De Stefano, Postdoctoral Research Fellow at Wharton People Analytics, The Wharton School, University of Pennsylvania, USA.

John E. Delery, Professor and Raymond F. Orr Chair, Sam M. Walton College of Business, University of Arkansas, USA.

Rory Eckardt, Assistant Professor and Center for Leadership Studies Fellow, School of Management, Binghamton University, USA.

Spenser M. Essman, Doctoral student in Human Resources, Darla Moore School of Business, University of South Carolina, USA.

Barry Gerhart, Professor and Bruce R. Ellig Distinguished Chair in Pay and Organizational Effectiveness, Wisconsin School of Business, University of Wisconsin–Madison, USA.

John P. Hausknecht, Associate Professor, School of Industrial and Labor Relations, Cornell University, USA.

Michael A. Hitt, Texas A&M Distinguished Professor Emeritus, Mays Business School, Texas A&M University and TCU Distinguished Research Fellow, Neeley School of Business, Texas Christian University, USA.

Kaifeng Jiang, Associate Professor, Fisher College of Business, Ohio State University, USA.

Rebecca R. Kehoe, Associate Professor, School of Management and Labor Relations, Rutgers University, USA.

Steve W. J. Kozlowski, Professor, College of Social Science, Michigan State University, USA.

David Kryscynski, Associate Professor, Marriott School of Business, Brigham Young University, USA.

Ian Larkin, Associate Professor, Anderson School of Management, University of California, Los Angeles, USA.

David Lewin, Professor Emeritus, Anderson School of Management, University of California, Los Angeles, USA.

Alison Mackey, Visiting Assistant Professor and Visiting Scholar, Brigham Young University, USA.

Thomas P. Moliterno, Earl W. Stafford Professor of Entrepreneurial Studies, Isenberg School of Management, University of Massachusetts Amherst, USA.

Shad Morris, Associate Professor, Marriott School of Business, Brigham Young University, USA.

Anthony J. Nyberg, Professor and Distinguished Moore Fellow, Darla Moore School of Business, University of South Carolina, USA.

Tomasz Obloj, Associate Professor, École des hautes études commerciales de Paris (HEC Paris), France.

Robert E. Ployhart, Professor and Bank of America Professor of Business Administration, Darla Moore School of Business, University of South Carolina, USA.

Christopher O. L. H. Porter, Professor, Kelley Venture Fellow, and IUPUI Adjunct Professor of Psychology, Kelley School of Business, Indiana University, USA.

Greg Reilly, Associate Professor and Academic Director of Graduate Programs in Human Resources, School of Business, University of Connecticut, USA.

Christopher I. Rider, Akkaway Term Associate Professor, McDonough School of Business, Georgetown University, USA.

Dorothea Roumpi, Assistant Professor, School of Labor and Employment Relations, Pennsylvania State University, USA.

Scott Snell, E. Thayer Bigelow Research Professor in Business Administration, Darden School of Business, University of Virginia, USA.

J. W. Stoelhorst, Associate Professor, Amsterdam Business School, University of Amsterdam, the Netherlands.

Valerie A. Sy, PhD student and Research Assistant, Mays Business School, Texas A&M University, USA.

David Tan, Associate Professor and Michael G. Foster Endowed Fellow, Foster School of Business, University of Washington, USA.

David J. Teece, Professor and Thomas W. Tusher Chair, Haas School of Business, University of California, Berkeley, USA.

Ernie Wang, Doctoral student, State University of New York at Buffalo, USA.

Ingo Weller, Professor and Director of the Institute for Human Capital Management, Munich School of Management, LMU Munich, Germany.

Margarethe Wiersema, Dean's Professorship in Strategic Management, The Paul Merage School of Business, University of California, Irvine, USA.

Patrick M. Wright, Thomas C. Vandiver Bicentennial Chair in Business, Darla School of Business, University of South Carolina, USA.

Todd Zenger, N. Eldon Tanner Professor of Strategy and Strategic Leadership and Presidential Professor, David Eccles School of Business, University of Utah, USA.

INTRODUCTION

Strategic human capital resources: a brief history, construct definition, and introduction to the *Handbook of Research on Strategic Human Capital Resources*

Thomas P. Moliterno and Anthony J. Nyberg

INTRODUCTION

This volume is about human capital resources (HCRs). Since the HCR construct is a newcomer to a long-standing literature on human capital (Becker, 1964), we begin with a brief historical thumbnail review of the history of research on HCR. We do so to provide a quick orientation to the focus of this volume: it is neither our intention nor hope to be exhaustive in this regard. Over the past 20 years, there has been an increasing convergence of scholarly disciplines exploring the association of human capital and organizational performance. Early gatherings at the Wharton School of the University of Pennsylvania and the University of Utah brought together arrays of scholars from diverse backgrounds who were interested in exploring the organizational effects and antecedents of human capital. As scholarly discourse at the intersection of these fields grew, researchers from strategic human resource management (HRM) and strategy disciplines combined to create the Strategic Human Capital Interest Group that first met in Rome in 2010 and has been one of the faster-growing interest groups of the Strategic Management Society (SMS).

At this point, the HCR construct had not yet been articulated and defined. Its genesis came from the realization that the human capital construct had begun to take on different meanings in different literatures. Many scholars thought of human capital as something specifically owned by workers (i.e., "the individual's human capital"), while others were focused on how workers contributed to organizational performance (i.e., "the firm's human capital"). That is, some researchers (predominantly from the "micro" traditions of organizational behavior, organizational psychology, and human resource management) focused on the "human" and some researchers (predominantly from the "macro" traditions of strategy and economics) focused on the "capital." Hence the term "human capital" was simultaneously being used too broadly, including all firm-level phenomena involving workers, and too narrowly, missing how individual differences in knowledge, skills, abilities, and other characteristics (KSAOs) help define the value of the worker to the firm.

A central cause of this tension also proved to offer a path to resolving it. Early strategic HRM research by Wright and McMahan (1992) invoked macro-level resource-based theory (RBT) from the strategy literature (Barney, 1991) to suggest the strategic value of the firm's human resources and the policies and practices used to manage them. In the macro literature, Hitt et al. (2001) extended this logic by arguing that the firm's human capital was a strategic resource. Thus, the same theoretical perspective and framing were being used in different literatures, but these different literatures rarely spoke to each other. And yet it was this shared theoretical perspective that suggested a path forward for the theoretical integration of multiple levels of analysis in our understanding of human capital. Ployhart and Moliterno (2011) articulated this integration and introduced the term "human capital resource" (HCR) as a unit-level construct.[1] This work posited that important insights flowed from the convergence of "micro" and "macro" perspectives on the relationship between human capabilities and organizational performance, with the lynchpin being the mechanisms by which a firm-level HCR emerges (Kozlowski and Klein, 2000) from a collection of individual-level human resources. Shortly thereafter, Nyberg et al. (2014) undertook a comprehensive review of the strategic HRM and strategy literatures, mapping prior findings onto a new multidimensional and multilevel HCR framework.

Indeed, 2014 was a watershed year for research on HCRs. In addition to the review by Nyberg et al., there was a special issue of the *Journal of Management* (Wright et al., 2014). One of the articles in that issue developed the HCR construct still further. Ployhart et al. (2014) declared "human capital is dead; long live human capital resources" and argued that HCRs could be conceptualized and observed at both the individual and unit level. Importantly, in this article Ployhart et al. formally define "human capital resource" (more on this below), thereby permanently entering the term into the canon. This article attempted to pull from a broad set of theoretical backgrounds to establish a clear definition of HCRs. It further worked to explain and differentiate relevant terms from KSAOs to human capital to HCR to strategic HCR. The paper also went on to describe how each of these constructs can be created, and their relative benefits for individuals and units. Scholars also gathered at the University of South Carolina in 2014 to discuss bridging the language divide between micro and macro perspectives, and an associated special issue publishing the lessons learned (Nyberg and Wright, 2015).

Shortly thereafter, we were approached with the opportunity to edit a volume for the Edgar Elgar Handbook series, and we knew that this provided an opportunity to create a volume that could focus on HCRs: exploring this rapidly evolving field, articulating and illustrating ongoing theoretical tensions, and suggesting research to move the field forward. And so we set out to design a conversation about HCRs that spanned levels of analysis, scholarly disciplines, and theoretical domains. Of course, that presumed that we could ourselves agree on an HCR definition. And this will be no surprise to our colleagues who know us: we couldn't.

DEFINING STRATEGIC HUMAN CAPITAL RESOURCES

The most interesting and fun aspect of developing this book was the tremendous willingness for the leading voices in the field to join the efforts to discuss this topic. One activity involved bringing authors together (hosted by the University of Maryland in May 2018). During this gathering – which was notable for the civil and challenging discourse that occurred, as well as the willingness for extremely successful scholars to truly listen and learn – what emerged was the recognition that many people working in this area differ in how they understand, define, and operationalize the HCR construct. Indeed, we came to realize that even we did not see eye-to-eye about some of the underlying assumptions in an area that we have worked on together and with others for over a decade. Hence, as much as for ourselves as for readers of this volume, we begin by defining the HCR construct.

Figure I.1 The editors, as once photographed by Sekou Bermiss, disagreeing as usual

The main difference between the traditional view of human capital (Becker, 1964) and the perspective on HCRs suggested by Ployhart and Moliterno (2011) is the explicit focus on the organization as the level of theory: "we define human capital as a unit-level resource created from the emergence of individuals' [KSAOs]" (2011: 127–8). As noted above, Ployhart et al. elaborated on this by formally defining HCRs to include the individual level of theory and analysis: "Human capital resources are individual or unit-level capacities based on individual KSAOs that are accessible for unit-relevant purposes" (2014: 374). The most notable difference between these two perspectives is the place of the individual. Ployhart and Moliterno understand the individual as *component* to the unit-level HCR, whereas Ployhart et al. understand the individual as an HCR *sui generis*. This non-trivial difference notwithstanding, these two definitions share a number of areas of similarity. Both recognize that the unit-level resource comprises individual-level components, and both invoke a resource-based theoretical framing.

Most importantly, both papers conclude that HCRs can be "strategic," that is, a source of differentiated unit-level performance outcomes and (ultimately) competitive advantage. In Ployhart and Moliterno, this strategic resource exists only at the firm level. In contrast, Ployhart et al. suggest that the individual-level HCR can *also* be a strategic

HCR. For many years, this has been a point of disagreement between us. Resource-based theory (Barney, 1991) describes how a firm-level resource can be leveraged for competitive advantage: how should we think about applying that theoretical proposition at the individual level? Is this not a "cross-level fallacy" (Rousseau, 1985) as described in Ployhart and Moliterno? In the course of the conversations that lead to this book we have resolved this question to our mutual satisfaction, and find that the answer to this puzzle illuminates an interesting boundary condition to our theorizing.

Before we delve into that, however, it is useful to explore a number of concepts that are important to understand when thinking about HCRs. To summarize briefly, when we think about the individual's KSAOs, then human capital is the correct term. However, when we talk about human capital from the unit's (e.g., firm, team, and department) perspective, then we are talking about HCRs. To the extent that we are tying the HCR to unit-level performance outcomes, then we are considering strategic HCRs (SHCRs). Broadly speaking, and from their own vantage, this is the topic that we asked the leading experts in the field to write about in this book.

The Individual and Unit Level

The HCR is a multilevel construct. Both Ployhart and Moliterno (2011) and Ployhart et al. (2014) agree that at the firm level the HCR comprises aggregations of individuals and their unique configurations of KSAOs. In the initial formulation, Ployhart and Moliterno did not label these individuals "human capital resources" *per se*. Rather, they argued that "the roots of human capital lie at the individual level and exist in the full range of employees' KSAOs" (2011: 132). That is, in their model, the individual employee contributes components of the unit-level HCR by drawing on their respective KSAO endowments, and the unit-level HCR emerges (Kozlowski and Klein, 2000) through the combination of these component KSAOs.

Ployhart et al. (2014) extended this line of thinking to argue that HCRs do not exist only at the unit level as combinations of individual KSAOs. Rather, the individual employee herself could be an HCR. That is, an individual could leverage her KSAOs in such a way that she – as an individual – becomes a resource that can be a source of firm-level performance. Thus, individuals are (or can be) both HCRs and components of HCRs. At the individual level the knowledge within a single domain of a single scientist working in the unit is an example of an individual-level HCR. By this definition, an individual's accessible and relevant KSAOs have potential to be a unit's HCR. The HCR is also the portfolio of complementary skills possessed by a group of individuals. For example, the collection of people working in a marketing department constitute an HCR, as does the shared capability for joint production that can be enacted by a small group of production operators. Hence, although not clearly articulated in Ployhart et al. (2014), the term HCR can be used to describe subparts of a firm's people-related resources (i.e., individual HCRs), the totality of those resources (i.e., unit-level HCRs), or both.

In sum, HCR theory necessarily starts with individuals. The firm comprises a collective of people who individually act – hopefully in a coordinated way – to pursue the organization's goals and objectives. Accordingly, we note that it is important to remember that individual people take action: when we are considering individual HCRs this is obvious. And since it is still individuals who act when we consider the HCR as a unit-level resource, unit-level HCRs should not be thought of as actors *per se*. Individuals act both alone and together with varying degrees of motivation toward a variety of objectives. It is the collection of these actions that lead to firm-level performance, and ideally competitive advantage. We will return to this momentarily.

Accessibility of HCR Capacities

While individuals and the human capital embedded in their KSAOs are at the foundation of all HCRs, it is important to note that it is the productive capacities that the KSAOs make available to the organization – and not the KSAOs *per se* – that associate with firm-level outcomes. This is an important distinction and theoretical extension articulated in Ployhart et al. (2014) that hews closely to Penrose's (1959) early insights regarding the strategically important "services" provided by the firm's human resources. Thus, while HCRs are assets that the firm leverages to produce its products and services in ways consistent with the underlying resource-based theory (Barney, 1991), the *HCR is not just another resource*. The value in HCRs is the useful productive capacities that they make accessible to a unit. Simply put, for the HCR to be a valuable resource, individuals must perform.

Given this, the firm can only leverage the value created by the HCR if it can access their KSAO-based productive capacity; and it can only access that capacity if individuals apply it in service of the firm's strategic priorities and direction. The question then becomes one of the mechanisms by which the firm can access the productive capacities latent in HCRs. Given what we know about the complexity of individuals and groups (e.g., Coff, 1997), it is easy to extrapolate that this complexity will make these mechanisms very important and interesting. Very often, the ability to access these capacities becomes a question of complementarities (Milgrom and Roberts, 1995; Adegbesan, 2009): identifying the other organizational practices or resources that can be combined with the focal HCR to create unique value (also see Morris and Snell, Chapter 12; Crocker, Chapter 13; Wright and Essman, Chapter 14; and Brymer and Hitt, Chapter 15).

At the individual level, human resource management policies and practices can be structured and implemented in such a way as to access these KSAO-based capacities. For instance, Nyberg and Reilly (Chapter 23) argue that pay strategies play a crucial role in the degree to which the capacities described by the HCR are enacted by people to yield performance outcomes for units.

There are also mechanisms for KSAO-based capacity accessible at the unit level. Crocker (Chapter 13) explores how social capital within the unit interrelates with HCR value creation, suggesting a social mechanism for capacity accessibility. In fact, even how the unit-level HCRs are created and structured can affect the accessibility of these capacities: Ployhart and Moliterno (2011) describe an "emergence enabling process," and Ployhart et al. (2014) articulate different "human capital resource combinations." Crocker also examines how "external social capital" can provide access to HCRs outside the firm, suggesting that we should not focus only on mechanisms for accessing KSAO-based capacities provided by people who work in the firm. Accordingly, the HCR construct is broader than it may seem at first glance since it can include the KSAOs of people who do not work inside the unit but whose skills are accessible to the unit.

There is a necessary limiting implication of these thoughts on accessibility. Consider an individual working in a unit who has a particular skill or knowledge that represents a valuable capacity for the firm. The fact that they possess that skill is not enough to describe that individual, or the unit in which they participate, as an HCR. To the extent that the skill of an employee is inaccessible to the unit it cannot be considered an HCR. Thus, just as there are mechanisms that make a KSAO-based productive capacity accessible, so too are there mechanisms that make it inaccessible: a lack of discovery of the capacity by leaders; a lack of motivation to use the capacity by the employee; or the lack of the complementary resources needed to make the capacity usable in a specific context. It is this enactment by people of capacity into reality that is one of the key differences between human capital and other resources. Whereas the prescribed capacity of a machine resource can be expected to be realized regularly (as long as regular maintenance is conducted), we can expect that realization of a human's productive capacity will be more variable.

Unit-Relevant Purposes . . . and a Puzzle

The final dimension of the HCR that merits some discussion is the "unit-level purposes" for which the firm leverages the HCR's productive capacities. Ployhart et al. note that "while specific purposes are idiosyncratic to individual units, most aim to create value for various stakeholders and in many cases by winning in competitive markets" (2014: 379). Thus, in keeping with the underlying RBT (Barney, 1991), our definition of HCRs includes performance outcomes at the unit (i.e., often the firm) level. Ultimately, all the foregoing discussion regarding the individual's KSAOs, capabilities, and accessibility relates to the ability of the HCR to provide some sort of value – usually economic – to the organization.

Of course, this hews closely to the central questions in the strategy discipline: what drives performance differences among firms; and how do firms achieve superior performance (i.e., "competitive advantage") relative to other firms in their industry? RBT (Barney, 1991) suggests that the answers to these questions lie in the firm's resource configuration. A review of this theoretical perspective and its application to the human capital literature is likely unnecessary for readers of this chapter. To oversimplify: RBT's response to the core strategy question is – the firm's resource configuration. Thus a "strategic" resource is one that is associated with firm performance and, ideally, competitive advantage.

Scholars working in the human capital literature have drawn on this RBT scaffolding as the foundation for their work, and Ployhart et al. made the specific connection to HCRs: "[HCRs] can be housed across all levels of an organization. There is a difference between strategic [HCRs] that are relevant for competitive advantage and fit the RBT framework and [HCRs] that can be beneficial for unit performance at all levels" (2014: 390). Inasmuch as they argue that HCRs are created at the individual and unit level, Ployhart and colleagues conclude that "strategic human capital resources can exist at all levels" (2014: 391). That is, both individual- and unit-level HCRs can be associated with unit-/firm-level performance.

As we noted earlier in this chapter, this component of the HCR framework has been central to a disagreement we have had for years. The core of this disagreement concerns how we should think of the levels of theory (Kozlowski and Klein, 2000; Rousseau, 1985) in this context. RBT is a firm-level theory describing how a firm-level resource can be leveraged for competitive advantage – so how should we think about assuming isomorphism and applying that theoretical proposition at the individual level? Do we not create a "cross-level fallacy" (Rousseau, 1985) as described in Ployhart and Moliterno (2011) when we apply the firm-level theory to an individual-level resource, and then argue that the individual-level resource associates with unit-level performance outcomes (let alone firm-level competitive advantage)?

As we prepared this volume, we discussed this on a number of occasions and came to agree that the arguments in Ployhart et al. (2014) apply only if and when we consider the individual-level HCR a unit-level resource. That is, if we consider the individual-level HCR a unit-level resource, we are operating at the same level of theory, and are on solid ground theorizing an association between the individual-level HCR and unit-level performance. This points to an important boundary condition for the insights articulated in Ployhart et al. An individual can be a strategic HCR when they behave as a firm-level construct: for instance, when there is only one of them in the firm and all their actions occur at the firm level. Examples of this are an entrepreneur in a start-up and a CEO of a major corporation. It is also possible that "a star" scientist (e.g., Call et al., 2015; Kehoe et al., 2018) could be thought of in this manner if we are able to attribute their individual output to unit-level outcomes. If such a scientist is part of a team or a research lab, they are then part of a unit and our comments above about complementarities within the unit apply. That is, we have to assume that some part of their productive output is a function of the complementary HCRs in their unit (and perhaps the social capital; Crocker, this volume). We believe that the kernel of this boundary condition is embedded in Ployhart et al. (2014); and with these comments we hope to make that boundary condition explicit. In any event, this has resolved a long-standing disagreement between us.

OUTLINE OF THIS VOLUME

The chapters in this book fall into two broad domains of thinking surrounding HCRs: how we *conceptualize* them and how we *actuate* them in organizations. Within each of these two broad domains are four parts designed to be conversations about an aspect of HCR from both more micro and more macro perspectives. Each of the four parts is further divided by "starter" chapters that are designed to approach the topic in a creative way, and two "commentary" chapters – one each again from the micro and macro perspectives – that use the starter chapters as a means for exploring the issues.

Conceptualizing HCRs

The chapters in this half of the book are focused on fundamental questions surrounding how we think about and understand HCRs. As such, the four parts consider value creation, multilevel perspectives, firm-specificity, and complementarities.

Part I Value creation and value capture: rents

The first part in this half of the book focuses on the value created by HCRs, how that value is captured, and by whom. Conroy (Chapter 1) approaches the topic by considering the role of base pay in understanding the trade-off between the value captured by employees who compose HCR and the value captured by the organization. Bridoux and

Stoelhorst (Chapter 2) take a different approach by considering alternative mechanisms for governing employment relationships. In their commentary chapters (one of two cases in the volume where the micro and macro authors combined forces due to what they viewed as the shared approach between their respective perspectives) Chadwick and Coff (Chapters 3 and 4) pick up and build on both of these ideas to present an integrated discussion as a holistic means for evaluating the role of rent sharing among the organization's critical stakeholders.

Part II Multilevel approaches: emergence

This part establishes both a methodological and theoretical approach to thinking about the multilevel nature of HCR and emergence. In their combined starter chapter, Eckhardt and Jiang (Chapter 5) provide an excellent and exhaustive primer on the theoretical and empirical issues surrounding the multilevel nature of HCRs. In their commentary chapters, Kozlowski (Chapter 6) and Cannella and Sy (Chapter 7) explore these same ideas and raise the critical issue of path dependence. They also note the complexities involved in emergence, the difficulties associated with trying to measure emergence, and the necessity of thinking about emergence over time and as a process.

Part III Isolating mechanisms: firm-specificity

Central to the RBT (Barney, 1991) that is employed in scholarship on HCRs is the notion that the firm-specificity of a resource acts as an isolating mechanism that provides the firm a competitive advantage (Peteraf, 1993). Both of the starter chapters in this section (Weller, Chapter 8; Campbell and Kryscynski, Chapter 9) provide both insights and caution regarding the use and reliance on the construct of firm-specificity in the context of theorizing on HCRs. Weller focuses on the importance of matching as a determinant of firm value, and Campbell and Kryscynski remind us that it may be the system that is responsible for driving value. Commenting on these starter chapters, Delery and Roumpi (Chapter 10) take a broad perspective on thinking about firm-specificity to discuss the (lack of) constraints that firm-specificity may really have and the importance of considering a broader selection of specificities. Lewin and Teece (Chapter 11) tackle this topic from a systems perspective, and introduce the need for involving the dynamic capabilities framework to appreciate how organizations can use HCR to their advantage.

Part IV Complementarities: human and social capital

Much of the extant research on HCRs notes the challenge of determining where human capital ends and social capital begins (e.g., Ployhart and Moliterno, 2011; Nyberg et al., 2014; Wright et al., 2014; Ployhart et al., 2014). Morris and Snell (Chapter 12) explore this question by taking a customer problem-solving perspective to argue for the importance of considering the relationship between human and social capital, while Crocker (Chapter 13) highlights the inherent and reciprocal relationship between HCR and social capital before, during, and after the emergence of unit-level HCRs. Brymer and Hitt (Chapter 15) take a decidedly different approach by acknowledging that social capital can positively influence HCR, and also introduce the idea that social capital can negatively influence HCR. Wright and Essman (Chapter 14) integrate ideas across chapters to remind readers that social capital and HCR, in combination, influence an organization's ability to compete in the market.

Actuating HCRs

This half of the volume moves away from the broad theoretical and nomological network within which HCR theory is embedded, and focuses instead on topics surrounding various manifestations and implications of HCRs in the organizational context. The sections in this half of the volume explore questions surrounding how organizations acquire HCRs, mobilize them as teams, and pay and otherwise incentivize them, and implications of the fact that employees move between organizations.

Part V Building SHCRs: hiring and acquiring

It is trivial to observe that without hiring employees, the organization cannot have HCRs. What is not at all trivial are the complex theoretical questions surrounding, and critical practical implications of, the recruitment and acquisition of "talent." Kehoe and Bentley (Chapter 16) provide a comprehensive scholarly overview of the selection and mobility literatures, and then incorporate ideas surrounding the "vertical" and "horizontal" fit of employees. Writing from the macro perspective, Camuffo and De Stefano (Chapter 17) approach the topic by questioning some of the conceptual premises posited in the selection literature and outlining four broad strategies for acquiring HCRs. Mackey and Barney (Chapter 18) provide the macro commentary on the two starter chapters, and then integrate insights from transaction cost economics and RBT to provide a framework for thinking about when HCRs should be inside or outside the boundary of the firm. There is no micro commentary in this part: one of the great voices in our field fell silent before he was able to write this chapter. Dave Lepak was an early contributor to HCR theory, and a co-founder of the Strategic Human Capital Interest Group at the Strategic Management Society. He was a co-author, colleague, and/or mentor to many of the contributors to this volume. He was a friend to all of them. We miss you, Dave, and dearly wish you were contributing a chapter on this topic: we know you would have given us something important to think about.

Part VI Mobilizing strategic human capital resources: teams

Teams are one of the most common and theoretically interesting units in which the emergent HCR can be found. In their starter chapter on this topic, Porter, Amber, and Wang (Chapter 19) provide new theoretical ideas for how to think about goal alignment within teams. The authors examine the challenge faced when individuals' goals differ from each other's and from the team's, and how these differing goals impact performance outcomes. Taking a perspective on teams that is common in the macro literature, Bermiss and Darnell (Chapter 20) focus on the firm's top management team. Taking a new perspective on this literature, the authors raise interesting questions about how top management teams respond to negative events. Ployhart and Chen (Chapter 21), from the micro perspective, and Wiersema (Chapter 22), from the macro perspective, tie these concepts together and push readers to think more broadly about the role of teams in affecting organizational outcomes. Together, these chapters suggest great new opportunities for pursuing team research relevant to HCRs.

Part VII Compensating strategic human capital resources: incentives

As Coff (1997) notes, the firm's human capital is the only resource that walks out the door every night. Accordingly, the question of incentivizing the HCR to return and remain productive is both theoretically and practically important. Nyberg and Reilly (Chapter 23) begin this part with a model that argues that pay is a critical component in the actualization of HCR. Larkin (Chapter 24) follows this by admonishing researchers studying pay to think about the strategic implications of pay and how pay affects the HCR. Addressing the challenges posed in these two chapters, and providing its own perspective, Gerhart (Chapter 25) provides specific commentary on why research involving pay and HCR has, at times, been stilted. This chapter also provides specific suggestions for future research, particularly the need to examine the relationship between pay and performance within a system over time. In the macro-level commentary, Obloj and Zenger (Chapter 26) push readers in a similar direction by explicating how and why HCR research in general, and the study of pay in relationship to HCR in particular, must take a dynamic approach.

Part VIII Keeping strategic human capital resources: mobility

The concluding part in this half of the book focuses on the organizational reality surrounding the volition of employees to move between organizations. Such mobility necessarily impacts the firm's HCRs. Hausknecht (Chapter 27) provides an exceptional review of the turnover literature, and shows clear connections between mobility and turnover literatures before providing specific guidelines for research that integrates the two. Likewise, Rider and Tan (Chapter 28) challenge the common assumption that turnover equals losses as a mechanism for pointing to how organizational behavior (OB), strategy, and entrepreneurship research can be integrated to advance our knowledge about how inflows and outflows of employees impact the firm's HCR. Bidwell (Chapter 29) builds on the starter chapters to further rethink how we research mobility, and what leaving means for HCR in terms of both disruption and the costs of preventing that disruption. Agarwal (Chapter 30) takes a broader view by looking at how HCR mobility, particularly from an entrepreneurial perspective, is a critical element in understanding firm performance. This chapter argues that we need a stronger connection between micro and macro fields to break down assumptions and to learn from multiple perspectives about the mechanisms at work in employee mobility.

CONCLUSION

The idea of bringing together scholars from different perspectives is not new. Yet, even in academic disciplines where we strive for rigor and true learning, rarely are differing perspectives embraced – but embrace we must. Indeed, scholarship on HCRs necessitates the integration of multiple perspectives inasmuch as the construct is inherently multilevel and interdisciplinary. Accordingly, our approach to studying HCR must be similarly multilevel and interdisciplinary. Only through the combination of knowledge, analytical techniques, and unique perspectives can the HCR field – which draws from fields ranging from psychology to economics and anthropology to sociology – properly address this interdisciplinary construct (Nyberg and Wright, 2015). As can be seen throughout the book, each author in this collection of extraordinary scholars addresses their own specific topic exceedingly well, but also touches on topics relevant to many other chapters as well. This provides an excellent example of the value that can come through combining the knowledge generated across disciplines, allowing scholars to benefit from the leading insights and the most enlightened research available. Through the chapters in this book, which combine the voices of leading scholars from a wide range of disciplinary backgrounds, we can identify commonalities: commonalities that we can use as foundational building blocks and opportunities for advancing the field.

NOTE

1. Consistent with prior work in this literature, we use the term "unit-level" as a generic term to describe any organizational collective. Thus, a firm is a unit, as is a division, a group, or a team.

REFERENCES

Adegbesan, J. A. (2009). On the origins of competitive advantage: Strategic factor markets and heterogeneous resource complementarity. *Academy of Management Review*, *34*(3), 463–75.

Barney, J. (1991). Firm resources and sustained competitive advantage. *Journal of Management*, *17*(1), 99–120.

Becker, G. S. (1964). *Human Capital: A Theoretical and Empirical Analysis, with Special Reference to Education*. Chicago, IL: University of Chicago Press.

Call, M. L., Nyberg, A. J., and Thatcher, S. M. B. (2015). Stargazing: An integrative conceptual review, theoretical reconciliation, and extension for star employee research. *Journal of Applied Psychology*, *100*(3), 623–40.

Coff, R. W. (1997). Human assets and management dilemmas: Coping with hazards on the road to resource-based theory. *Academy of Management Review*, *22*(2), 374–402.

Hitt, M. A., Bierman, L., Shimizu, K., and Kochhar, R. (2001). Direct and moderating effects of human capital on strategy and performance in professional service firms: A resource-based perspective. *Academy of Management Journal*, *44*(1), 13–28.

Kehoe, R. R., Lepak, D. P., and Bentley, F. S. (2018). Let's call a star a star: Task performance, external status, and exceptional contributors in organizations. *Journal of Management*, *44*(5), 1848–72.

Kozlowski, S. W. J., and Klein, K. J. (2000). A multilevel approach to theory and research in organizations: Contextual, temporal, and emergent processes. In K. J. Klein and S. W. J. Kozlowski (eds), *Multilevel Theory, Research, and Methods in Organizations: Foundations, Extensions, and New Directions*, 3–90. San Francisco, CA: Jossey-Bass.

Milgrom, P., and Roberts, J. (1995). Complementarities and fit strategy, structure, and organizational change in manufacturing. *Journal of Accounting and Economics*, *19*(2–3), 179–208.

Nyberg, A. J., Moliterno, T. P., Hale, D. H., and Lepak, D. P. (2014). Resource-based perspectives on unit-level human capital: A review and integration. *Journal of Management*, *40*(1): 316–46.

Nyberg, A. J., and Wright, P. M. (2015). 50 years of human capital research: Assessing what we know, exploring where we go. *Academy of Management Perspectives*, *29*(3), 287–95.

Penrose, E. (1959). *The Theory of the Growth of the Firm*. New York: Wiley.

Peteraf, M. A. (1993). The cornerstones of competitive advantage: A resource-based view. *Strategic Management Journal*, *14*(3), 179–91.

Ployhart, R. E., and Moliterno, T. P. (2011). Emergence of the human capital resource: A multilevel model. *Academy of Management Review*, *36*(1), 127–50.

Ployhart, R. E., Nyberg, A. J., Reilly, G., and Maltarich, M. A. (2014). Human capital is dead; long live human capital resources! *Journal of Management*, *40*(2), 371–98.

Rousseau, D. M. (1985). Issues of level in organizational research: Multi-level and cross-level perspectives. In L. L. Cummings and B. Staw (eds), *Research in Organizational Behavior* (Vol. 7: 1–37). Greenwich, CT: JAI Press.

Wright, P. M., Coff, R., and Moliterno, T. P. (2014). Strategic human capital: Crossing the great divide. *Journal of Management*, *40*(2), 353–70.

Wright, P. M., and McMahan, G. C. (1992). Theoretical perspectives for strategic human resource management. *Journal of Management*, *18*, 295–320.

CONCEPTUALIZING HCRS

PART I

VALUE CREATION AND VALUE CAPTURE: RENTS

1. Setting base pay rates: integrating compensation practice with human capital value creation and value capture

Samantha A. Conroy

Compensating employees is one of the costliest activities for an organization. In fact, the average employee compensation cost is approximately 36 dollars per hour worked; wages and salaries alone account for 68 percent of the money spent on employee compensation (Bureau of Labor Statistics, 2017). Beyond cost, compensation matters to employees. Voluntary turnover has a relationship of $r = -0.15$ with pay satisfaction according to meta-analysis findings (Williams et al., 2006), and the economic status of most individuals is tied to their compensation.

The human capital literature has acknowledged the importance of compensation (e.g., Harris and Helfat, 1997), and compensation has figured prominently in frameworks on human resource configurations (Lepak and Snell, 2002). For example, internally equitable pay, externally equitable pay, and various pay bases have been central factors in empirical work on human resource configurations (Toh et al., 2008). Coff (1997) noted that focusing on employee pay perceptions, such as pay satisfaction and internal comparisons, is a potential human capital retention strategy. Yet, the nuances of compensation relevant to compensation researchers have rarely been sufficiently integrated with the nuances of the strategic human capital literature.

Compensation design involves many strategic choices, such as decisions about job evaluation, merit pay, and market matching (Balkin and Gomez-Mejia, 1987; Gerhart and Rynes, 2003). One strategy of practical importance often neglected by compensation researchers is base compensation determination, i.e., the approaches used to designate "the cash compensation that an employer pays for the work performed" (non-contingent pay; Milkovich et al., 2014: 14). This neglect is in spite of base pay being one of the largest components of compensation for many jobs, especially those jobs of most employees (i.e., non-executives; Bureau of Labor Statistics, 2017). Perhaps this lack of attention is due to a myth that base pay is determined completely by market forces, and thus cannot be a source of competitive advantage (i.e., above average performance, as defined by Barney and Wright, 1998).

Research over the last two decades on strategic human capital militates against the myth that base pay is not relevant to competitive advantage. For example, Coff examined firm coping strategies for human capital management dilemmas. Within this investigation, Coff explained, "pay differentials within the firm may be more important than the pay relative to the labor market. This, in turn, implies that firms can increase pay satisfaction without competing with other employers" (1997: 383). Decisions around base pay are not simply market and cost concerns, and these decisions may relate to competitive advantage through human capital value creation and capture (i.e., respectively, increased use value and decreased costs associated with human capital, as defined by Chadwick, 2017).

Interestingly, when employees are hired for jobs, their use value or potential value creation in the firm is unknown. That is, information asymmetry dominates the hiring process (Chadwick, 2017; Chadwick and Dabu, 2009). Organizations have reasonably clear information on the job that will be filled by the applicant and the context of that job, on the one hand, and somewhat vague information on the potential applicant's knowledge, skills, abilities, and other characteristics (KSAOs), on the other hand. Potential hires have reasonably clear information on their own KSAOs and somewhat vague information on the context of the job they will fill. This means that at the moment a base pay determination is made, both parties lack important information.

The goal of this chapter is to illuminate the process of base pay determination at the entry stages of employment. I integrate strategic human capital and base compensation knowledge to answer the questions: *How do different approaches to base pay determination contribute to competitive advantage through value creation and capture? How can these processes account for the potential of a hire to contribute to unit-level human capital resources?* In order to manage the scope of this endeavor, I focus on the processes that influence individual base pay for external hires upon entering the organization (e.g., job-based pay rates, individual pay adjustments and negotiations), rather than the ongoing process of negotiating and adjusting base pay over time for current employees (e.g., merit pay cycles and other performance-based pay or promotion practices). However, given my goal of addressing competitive advantage, I do note the implications of selected base pay approaches to longer-term value creation and capture.

I begin with a brief overview of the relevant strategic human capital literature. Then, I review the base compensation literature and the primary base pay approaches used by organizations today. The rest of the chapter is devoted to the value creation potential, value capture potential, and problem areas of three main factors that influence base pay setting (i.e., job evaluation, market pricing, and individual job offers). Finally, I discuss the implications and limitations of this integration.

COMPETITIVE ADVANTAGE THROUGH STRATEGIC HUMAN CAPITAL RESOURCES

Human capital has been defined as the knowledge, skills, abilities, and other characteristics of individuals, which can contribute to firm competitive advantage due to difficulty in imitation by other firms (Campbell et al., 2012). In a comprehensive discussion around how to define human capital, Ployhart et al. expanded this definition to consider multiple levels, focusing on the concept of human capital *resources* (HCRs) – "individual or unit-level capacities based on individual KSAOs that are accessible for unit-relevant purposes" (2014: 374). In essence, human capital can contribute to competitive advantage, and these contributions are not simply through individual contributions but also through capacities at higher levels.

Ployhart et al. further distinguished between HCRs that contribute to competitive parity and *strategic* HCRs that contribute to competitive advantage. Competitive parity involves performance meeting that of competitors and the absence of a competitive disadvantage, and exists when a firm has a valuable resource; competitive advantage refers to performance above average, and requires both valuable and rare resources; sustained competitive advantage refers to above average performance over longer periods of time, and requires valuable, rare, and difficult to imitate resources (Barney, 1991; Barney and Wright, 1998).

Another important distinction in the literature exists regarding general and firm-specific skills (Barney and Wright, 1998). This distinction refers to the difference between skills that can be applied across firms (e.g., general skills like accounting knowledge) and those that are specific to the firm (e.g., firm-specific skills like understanding organizational procedures and navigating organizational culture). Much of the literature assumes that firm-specific skills are much more likely to contribute to sustained competitive advantage than general skills; however, Campbell et al. made a compelling case that these models are limited. Specifically, the conditions necessary for this logic to hold include: 1) exchange value equal to or less than use value of human capital; 2) tightly coupled exchange value and firm-specificity of skills; and 3) worker costs to moving greater than the desire to move. Ployhart et al. also questioned the assumption that general skills do not contribute to competitive advantage because combinations of general skills can create difficult to replicate unit-level capacities. Essentially, the firm-specificity of skills may not be the key to explaining how human capital can be a source of sustainable competitive advantage; and in fact, under certain conditions, general skills may be a source of sustained competitive advantage. Altogether, this indicates that an assumption that general skills can be easily priced and move smoothly across organizations is untenable.

Both Coff (1999) and Chadwick explored how firms derive human capital rents – i.e., economic profits drawn from human capital. Two avenues of human capital rent have been central to such theorizing – those associated with value creation and those associated with value capture. Value creation refers to increasing the use value of human capital, and can be increased through worker complementarities (Chadwick, 2017; see also Ployhart et al., 2014). Value capture refers to reducing the costs associated with human capital. A primary avenue to value capture is to prevent employees from taking created value for themselves, i.e., preventing turnover (Chadwick, 2017). Another avenue to value capture is reduction of administrative costs associated with human capital (Chadwick, 2017).

Value creation and capture for firms are complicated by the fact that employees have free will and ownership of their human capital, such that firms cannot be certain that employees will both generate value and maintain membership within the organization (Chadwick, 2017; Coff, 1997, 1999). Chadwick noted that it is because of these issues that firms must consider both the economic and affective aspects of employment. Similarly, Coff (1997) noted that while pay matters in employee decisions to move, loss or gain of *psychic income* matters as well (i.e., the instrumental value of pay is not the only consideration in employee moves).

This brief review summarizes a few key underpinnings to HCRs that will be important to developing an understanding of base pay determination. One, HCRs, which exist at multiple levels, can be used to attain competitive parity or competitive advantage (Ployhart et al., 2014). Two, general skills and firm-specific skills can both contribute to competitive advantage (Campbell et al., 2012; Ployhart et al., 2014). And, finally, the contribution of HCRs to firm rents occurs through value creation and value capture.

HOW DO DIFFERENT APPROACHES TO BASE PAY DETERMINATION CONTRIBUTE TO COMPETITIVE ADVANTAGE THROUGH VALUE CREATION AND CAPTURE?

To have a discussion about base pay determination (i.e., the process of setting base pay rates), we must first establish what is meant by base pay and what the base pay setting process typically looks like. Base pay refers to compensation in exchange for work, i.e., salary and wages. It is not inclusive of incentives or other forms of behavior-dependent pay; nor is it inclusive of benefits. Base pay simply refers to the hourly or annual compensation paid to employees for doing their job (Milkovich et al., 2014).

Base pay is often conceptualized at the organization level as the firm's pay structure – i.e., "the array of pay rates for different work or skills within a single organization" (Milkovich et al., 2014: 72) – or, per Gerhart and Rynes (2003: 81), the "relative pay within organizations." Most research on base compensation has focused on the size of pay differences and the basis of these pay differences within pay structures – i.e., the pay dispersion literature (Conroy et al., 2014; Trevor et al., 2012).

In practice, a typical approach to base pay involves a graded or banded structure where jobs are placed in grades or bands with other equivalently valued jobs. These grades have rates associated with them based on the value assessed for the job, which is based on a job evaluation and/or market price. This value is represented as a minimum, midpoint, and maximum pay amount. That is, each grade or band has a pay range, and individuals placed in jobs are expected to be compensated within these pay ranges.

Individual job offers and negotiated base pay rates for external hires typically incorporate the following steps. First, the job an individual is going to fill has a grade and corresponding range associated with it, so the individual will, in most cases, be offered a base rate within that range. Second, where the individual falls within that range depends on the offer and negotiation process. Organizational representatives (e.g., compensation analysts, human resource generalists, hiring managers) decide on a job offer amount within the grade's pay range adjusted for factors such as the individual's KSAOs and the current market pressure for the specific job. Finally, in some cases, a negotiation process ensues between the applicant and the organization to determine the final base pay for the new hire. Whether or not a firm will negotiate is both firm- and job-specific (Michelacci and Suarez, 2006).

Researchers have separated base pay issues into vertical concerns (i.e., between-job valuation differences) and horizontal concerns (i.e., within-job valuation differences) (Gupta et al., 2012). These foci are often separate areas of study – e.g., horizontal (Shaw and Gupta, 2007) or vertical (DeVaro, 2006). In this chapter, I address both because the processes associated with each ultimately determine the pay rate of an external hire. I separate these processes into different sections (i.e., vertical and horizontal) for conceptual clarity. In what follows, the processes of each are discussed, and then related to value creation and value capture.

Vertical Pay Variations: Job-Based Pay Setting

Most organizations use a job-based system for determining base pay (Lazear, 1992). The bulk of the determinant of a person's pay is the value assigned to their job, defined as the set of work in which they are engaged. For example, a company may assign a value of \$65,000 to the job of manager with a range of pay of \$55,000 to \$75,000. Any employee hired to be a manager would be paid somewhere in this range. So, the largest proportion of an employee's base rate is based on the job that he or she fills. In fact, Lazear (1992) reported that 95 percent of variance in monthly pay was due to the job rather than within-job differences in a sample of over 19,000 employees. Alternatively, some organizations have skill-based pay systems – e.g., pay is based on the number of skills an employee has (Lawler et al., 1993; Mitra et al., 2011), but this approach is much less common. Furthermore, vertical differences are typically viewed as across-job differences based on job evaluations and market forces (Gupta et al., 2012). As such, I focus on setting base pay in job-based pay systems here.

Job-based pay approaches require an assessment of the content and value of work (Milkovich et al., 2014). Any assessment requires that the organization complete a process to clarify what the work entails for each job in the organization (i.e., job analysis) as a starting point. Following this job analysis, two considerations have traditionally gone into this assessment process – job evaluations and market prices. Job evaluation processes focus on internal alignment (i.e., job value in comparison to other jobs within the company), while market pricing processes focus on external alignment (i.e., job value in comparison to the same job in other companies).

There are various methods of job evaluation, including classification, point factor, and ranking. Job evaluation procedures focus on organizational strategy and culture to understand how work should be valued. In the process of job evaluation, "raters typically assign a score that is intended to reflect the relative value of each job to the firm. Because of unique factors such as business strategy or organizational structure, this relative value may differ across employers" (Gerhart and Rynes, 2003: 85). Still, it would be almost impossible for organizations to solely focus on internal value since they must compete with other firms in the labor market to obtain talent. Thus, job evaluation is combined with market pricing to determine a job's base dollar value in an organization. Market pricing involves assessing the value of a job on the market and assigning that value as the "market price" for the work.[1] The process of determining the market price involves an information search to find relevant competitors, equivalent jobs, and the associated pay rates. By engaging in this process, organizations are able to address the importance of the labor market in the flow of talent.

Limited research has been conducted on job evaluation and market pricing (for a recent exception, comparing job-based methods to skill-based pay, see Mitra et al., 2011). In the early 1990s, a conceptual/theoretical debate around base pay setting ensued with a focus on the value of job evaluation, a form of job-based pay, as compared to skill-based pay, a form of person-based pay (Barrett, 1991; Gupta and Jenkins, 1991; Mahoney, 1991). Despite this "raging controversy" (Gupta and Jenkins, 1991: 92), which often leaned toward skill-based pay as a more capable approach to compensation, job-based pay remains the primary and most common approach to compensation.

In a rare empirical study on the topic of job evaluation and market pricing, Weber and Rynes (1991) assessed managerial decision making regarding job valuation. Their primary finding was that market rates were more important than job evaluation information for decision makers. It appears that since the publication of the Weber and Rynes's paper, the trend has accelerated (SHRM, 2012). In particular, many organizations have moved to a market pricing only system, basing their entire job-based pay structure on "external market forces" (Milkovich et al., 2014: 289). A recent WorldatWork survey (2016) indicated that 91 percent of organizations used market pricing in some form to determine the relative value of jobs, while only 44 percent used classification, point factor, or ranking – indicating that a large portion of base pay structures are entirely market-based. Still yet, Gerhart and Rynes note that "organizations seem to have at least some flexibility to set unique internal pay rates, and in fact they often exercise this flexibility" (2003: 87).

The spectrum of job-based pay design emphasis ranges from a system entirely focused on internal worth to a system entirely focused on external worth. Traditionally, systems have fallen somewhere in the middle of this spectrum, combining internal and external factors with varying levels of emphasis. Most base pay systems today are either: 1) a combination of job evaluation and market pricing, in which both internal and external considerations are incorporated; or 2) market pricing only, in which only external considerations are incorporated (Milkovich et al., 2014; WorldatWork, 2016). Almost *no* systems, to my knowledge, are job evaluation focused alone without market consideration.

Given the lack of research on job-based pay design, the significant costs associated with base pay, and the trend toward entirely market-based systems of job pay determination, it is important to take a moment to consider the strategic implications of job-based pay design. Are market-based systems actually ideal for value capture and creation? While very few scholars have addressed this issue, the one place I could find where concerns about the trend toward full market pricing are raised is the textbook *Compensation* (Milkovich et al., 2014) used in many total rewards college classes in the United States. In particular, the authors scratch the surface of the issue by briefly noting that full market pricing prevents the pay structure from being a source of competitive advantage since market pricing removes firm pay structure and organizational strategy alignment. I explore potential explanations for these claims in the following section. I also explore other processes and pitfalls related to job evaluation and market pricing. But first, a few assumptions are noted.

First, my analysis assumes base pay within markets where firms may choose the amounts and levels of pay for those they employ – i.e., not countries where amounts and levels are dictated (Milkovich et al., 2014: 77). Building on the first assumption, my analysis assumes that external factors – such as government policies, laws, and regulations – are held constant. Finally, my analysis is focused on "regular people" pay structures, not executive pay structures or base pay for temporary or contract work.

An internal focus alone (i.e., job evaluation only) is a theoretical, but not practical, concept in that most organizations use some market data in their job pricing models. However, to ensure conceptual clarity, I address the issues of value creation, value capture, and other pitfalls for job evaluation and market pricing separately.

Job Evaluation Approaches

Value creation

Job evaluation is an inherently inward-focused process (Milkovich et al., 2014). Organizational leaders must engage in a process that clarifies exactly what factors are of value to the firm and how important those factors are. The link between the firm's values and the job evaluation process is exemplified in a points method job evaluation system in which organizations identify compensable factors – i.e., "characteristics in the work that the organization values, that help it pursue its strategy" (Milkovich et al., 2014: 145) – and assign these factors weight based on their importance to the firm.

As an example of the value assignment process, a company like Southwest Airlines may develop a job evaluation system with an emphasis on customer relationship building as a key compensable factor that is highly weighted, while another airline may value this factor much less. This emphasis on organizationally valuable factors provides an opportunity for strategic alignment of the compensation system, and potential value creation, by emphasizing and valuing those components of work that are most important to the firm gaining a competitive advantage. When the organization's base pay is aligned with its values and strategy, it can attract the highest-quality applicants for its most strategically relevant functions. Thus, job evaluation is unique to the organization, and can assign value to work based on the extent of strategically required human capital for jobs.

In addition, designing a job evaluation system specific to the organization allows a firm to create and "leverage idiosyncratic advantages with respect to labor market frictions, such as offering an attractive organizational culture that serves as meaningful and unique" (Chadwick, 2017: 504). Because the job evaluation system is unique to the organization, it can contribute to the building of a strong and unique organizational culture. As the values of the organization determine what work will be paid and how limited resources are distributed, this can be a sense-giving process (Ashforth et al., 2008), which serves to inform employees of the organization's culture.

A third avenue to value creation through job evaluation is related to its relationship with internal alignment. Specifically, job evaluation focuses on how to assign value to work based on comparisons to other jobs internally. This focus has the potential to increase employee perceptions of internal equity (i.e., the fairness of the pay system when making internal comparisons), which is important to employees. For example, in a study of salespeople, internal salary equity was a significant predictor of job satisfaction (Livingstone et al., 1995).

Finally, as described by Ployhart et al. (2014), strategic HCRs involve both individual and unit-level capacities. Unit-level capacities require efficient functioning within groups in the organization. When the job evaluation process promotes feelings of fairness and satisfaction with base compensation within organizational groups, individuals within groups are more likely to collaborate and develop relationships within those groups (Conroy and Gupta, 2016; Sinclair, 2003). Ultimately, these improved group dynamics may improve HCRs.

Internally developed job evaluation approaches have the potential to contribute to value creation through strategic alignment, organizational culture, internal equity, and, ultimately, human capital resources. Because the approach is unique to the firm, it is hard to imitate in other organizational contexts.

Value capture

Value capture can occur through reducing turnover and administrative costs (Chadwick, 2017). While the administrative costs of job evaluation will be noted under pitfalls, turnover reduction may be related to job evaluation in two main ways. First, by clarifying value in the work of the firm, organizations can be expected to pay more for the jobs containing the highest levels of strategic human capital. Assuming limited resources, it is not that job evaluation would involve paying all jobs more; it is that job evaluation involves paying jobs requiring higher levels of strategic human capital more than jobs requiring lower levels. Research has shown pretty clearly that higher pay levels are associated with lower turnover (Gerhart and Rynes, 2003; Rubenstein et al., 2018). So, a firm may not reduce turnover in total, but strategically aligned job evaluation may lead to lower turnover in the most important firm roles.

Second, because job evaluation can create internal equity perceptions within the organization and can contribute to the development of organizational culture, the use of job evaluation as part of an overall human resource system may contribute to affective ties to the organization. Chadwick (2017) claimed that such affective ties may be key to leveraging labor market frictions because they cannot be easily imitated by a competitor. Job evaluation systems treat jobs in the organization as unique and specific to the organization, rather than as exchangeable with the market. This means it is possible that organizations are signaling the importance of the most strategically relevant human capital through the job evaluation system in a different way than in a market pricing system.

Related to this, Coff viewed "firm-specific compensation" as a means toward creating a psychic cost to exiting the organization, thus reducing turnover (1997: 384). Employees may develop a preference for how an organization values and designs work, and this preference could influence the required price for the employees to move to another organization. By nurturing a set of organizationally central values (Coff, 1997) in the job evaluation process, the base pay system can differentiate the organization from others.

> *Internally developed job evaluation approaches have the potential to contribute to value capture through strategic alignment and affective ties. Because the approach is unique to the firm, it is hard to imitate in other organizational contexts.*

Pitfalls

Taking an entirely job evaluation-based approach to base pay has a number of downsides, and in fact may be so foolish that almost no companies use this approach alone (Romanoff, Boehm, and Benson, 1986). The primary problem is that job evaluation alone ignores the labor market associated with work. Thus, it is possible that a job evaluation system could become so unhinged from the labor market that an organization could not attract employees to join the firm, or only attract employees within a few very specific jobs. This of course would be an example of under-compensating most employees. Another possibility would be over-compensating employees to such an extent that the firm is not capturing any value at all.

A second problem that arises with a solely job evaluation-based structure is that administrative costs are likely to be high, and administrative costs reduce value capture (Chadwick, 2017). Job evaluation requires a time-intensive process of identifying compensable factors, weighting factors, and then assessing each job according to the developed scale. Often organizations, recognizing the importance of internal equity and fairness of the system, will engage multiple stakeholders in the evaluation process. Given these stakeholders tend to be high in the organizational hierarchy, their time and involvement in the process is an expensive investment by the firm in comparison to market pricing, which can be completed by one or two analysts. Another related concern is the potential for political manipulation in the job evaluation process, such that it may not have the intended alignment with organizational strategy in organizations, and rather may be defined by high levels of politics (Gupta and Jenkins, 1996; Welbourne and Trevor, 2000).

Another variable that could interfere with the value creation and value capture proposition of a job evaluation system would be the implementation of an easily replicable system. In particular, some consulting companies have "off-the-shelf" evaluation systems which firms can buy and implement. In this case, the system no longer connects to the organization strategy in a unique way. Perhaps most importantly, the system becomes highly replicable and, thus, unable to contribute to a sustainable competitive advantage.

Organizations must be wary of extreme over- or under-compensating, administrative management costs, and using easily replicable systems when using job evaluation to set base pay.

Market Pricing Approaches

Value creation

Market pricing is an outward-focused process to assess the value of work. Unlike job evaluation, the primary concern is obtaining information about the value of jobs on the labor market (Barcellos, 2005). Once values are obtained, firms can choose to match, lag, or lead these values (Klaas and McClendon, 1996).

Of course, the greatest strength of a market pricing approach is that firms are more aligned with the labor market. It is a potential means of avoiding over- or under-compensating employees. Any benefit to value creation comes from the perceptions of potential and current employees that the firm is paying fairly as compared to the job market. As external comparisons do relate to pay satisfaction, employees may feel they are treated well by the firm when market pricing accurately values jobs on the labor market (Sweeney and McFarlin, 2005).

It is notable, however, that market pricing is likely to be imitable for a couple of reasons. One, most market data is obtained through surveys provided by third parties. Thus, the data obtained by one firm is likely the same as the data obtained by another firm, and these data may not be modified to match the actual human capital configurations of the focal organization. Two, the goal with market pricing is to assess the "true market price" of each job. While the market price is more a theoretical than an actual concept (Barcellos, 2005), it is noteworthy that all firms are seeking the same value. That is, any firm using a market pricing approach is seeking externally driven information using a common method. This approach can easily be replicated by other firms. At best, a competency in market pricing a job structure would lead to competitive parity; at worst, problems with inaccurate market pricing would lead to a competitive disadvantage. Market pricing is necessary, but unlikely to lead to competitive advantage.

Market pricing approaches have the potential to contribute to value creation due to the pay structure's relationship with external equity. However, this approach is not unique to the firm and is easily replicated in other organizational contexts.

Value capture

Market pricing is likely attractive to many firms because it drives down the administrative costs associated with base pay systems. These administrative efficiencies occur for a few reasons. One, market pricing requires little input from stakeholders. Firm analysts can seek out market information and put a price on each job. This means there is a low time burden for most organizational members associated with the market pricing task.

Two, market pricing processes require relatively little maintenance beyond updating data. While this takes time for the compensation analyst, it does not require full system revisions or the associated processes to get organizational members to accept and agree upon the system. External pricing data is likely to be quickly accepted by organizational members to explain pay decisions, and conversations around the organization's values are not necessary. Thus, the only administrative cost of market pricing appears to be the purchase and management of market survey data, which, in comparison to the costs of job evaluation processes, seems a minor concern.

Again, as with the discussion of value creation using market pricing, the easy replication of this system is problematic. Any organization can access the administrative efficiencies of such a system, making this value capture easily imitable.

> *Market pricing approaches have the potential to contribute to value capture due to the pay structure's lower administrative costs. However, this approach is not unique to the firm and is easily replicated in other organizational contexts.*

Pitfalls

A number of potential problems arise for firms when one considers a fully market-focused approach to base pay. First, market pricing is fully disconnected from anything that makes the firm unique. It is assumed that all work within the firm is the same as work performed outside of the firm. That is, work becomes a commodity despite the reality that organizations are unlikely to configure work in the same way (i.e., jobs are unlikely to be exact human capital matches across organizations). In fact, given that organizations can utilize HCRs for higher performance, external market data cannot accurately assess a job's value to its unit and to the firm. The firm's culture, values, and strategy are, at most, incorporated by the lag, lead, or match pay decision, but are not incorporated in the organization's actual valuation of work. And, as noted earlier, all of these are easily replicated organizational processes.

Second, market pricing is unlikely to create affective ties to an organization. As the work of a job is "priced" on the market rather than with respect to the organization or the individual's human capital, there is the potential for people to feel more like widgets than individuals of relevance and importance to the organization. Thus, little affective connection would be created through a market pricing approach.

Finally, while rarely discussed, market pricing processes are not without problems. The existence of a true market price is mostly theoretical. Each analyst pricing jobs will engage in this process with their own biases and limitations. Bounded rationality prevents perfection in the process (Conlisk, 1996). And, there are information problems throughout the process. In the process of gathering market pay data, firms providing data may limit or alter the information provided, and outliers (i.e., unique incumbents in jobs) may pull prices away from the true market price. Furthermore, the valuation process can never entirely explain human capital value in use as each organization's use of human capital will be different. That is, use value can vary across firms for the same skills based on how skills are used (Campbell et al., 2012: 379; Ployhart et al., 2014). So, while a strength of market pricing is the potential for alignment with external prices, even this cannot be assured due to information problems and bounded rationality.

Organizations must be wary of disconnecting from organizational strategy and culture, weak affective ties, and matching inaccuracies when using a market pricing approach to set base pay.

Horizontal Pay Variations: Person-Based and Within-Grade Pay Setting

The preceding section addressed the process through which organizations determine the pay rate and range for a particular job. Differences in compensation across jobs can be understood based on this analysis; however, differences in compensation rates across people within jobs cannot. This section is intended to address those differences across people upon firm entry. That is, the pay associated with a new external hire combines the job's value with the person's specific value within the job.

I note that the concept of horizontal, i.e., within-job, pay variations in the literature is typically associated with current employees, such that the primary bases for these variations are performance and seniority, among others (Gupta et al., 2012). The bases considered when we look at pay rates assigned upon hire include *anticipated* value creation (i.e., expected performance, productivity within the organizational context). Here, I address the processes related to person-specific new external hire pay rates, so anticipated value creation is the primary concern.

Workers even within a job can be heterogeneous in their contribution to the organization (Lazear, 1992). This heterogeneity depends on a multitude of factors – job content, monitoring, recruiting strategies – and has been noted in prior management work as SDy (i.e., the standard deviation of performance at work; Hunter and Schmidt, 1983). An organization can choose whether to make adjustments to the job-based pay rate as a result of such differences; if adjusting occurs, then the firm can choose whether or not there will be bargaining (i.e., negotiating) in the base pay setting process. The approach an organization takes in deciding the hiring rate for workers is likely to depend on this heterogeneity, with greater heterogeneity associated with a firm's decision to bargain with hires to determine new hire compensation (Michelacci and Suarez, 2006). For example, a retail firm is unlikely to negotiate the rate of pay for a cashier, but may negotiate the rate of pay for a marketing manager. Both the economics and management literatures suggest that organizations will vary in the extent to which they negotiate pay rates at the individual level and that, within organizations, the likelihood of negotiating pay rates will depend on the specific job (Michelacci and Suarez, 2006).

In addition to research on whether or not a firm will bargain, there is a literature on candidate and firm negotiation processes (e.g., Gerhart and Rynes, 1991; Marks and Harold, 2011; O'Shea and Bush, 2002). This work indicates that in a negotiation, there is uncertainty on both sides regarding the other party's "reservation point (the point at which the negotiator is indifferent between reaching a settlement and walking away from the negotiation) and target point (the negotiator's ideal or most preferred outcome)"

(Galinsky and Mussweiler, 2001: 656). As a result the negotiation process is defined by uncertainty, as neither the company nor the potential hire has perfect information.

Controlling for the job-based rate in determining base pay rates for individuals entering a firm, organization leaders and representatives make a few decisions. One, will the job-based pay rate be adjusted to account for the specific potential value creation of a given hire? Two, will bargaining occur at all? Three, what are the reservation and target points if negotiation is to occur? That is, at what point is the firm willing to move on to a next potential hire rather than continue the bargaining process with a candidate, and at what point is the firm paying the ideal rate? To determine acceptable and ideal wage rates, a firm must assess the value of the hire without having certainty of what their use value will be.

One problem associated with this external hiring and pay setting process has been termed the "market for lemons" problem, which essentially proposes that since candidates have more information about their own value than employers, employers will undercompensate new hires to avoid overpaying for a "lemon" (Akerlof, 1970). In turn, the best potential hires will not be available on the market because there is a penalty to job change (Akerlof, 1970; Coff and Kryscynski, 2011). This highlights a few assumptions: 1) candidates have more information about their contribution to value creation; 2) firms will tend toward lower acceptable/ideal rates; and 3) there is a higher proportion of undesirable than desirable candidates as high performers opt out of the search.

Counter to the ideas around the "market for lemons," there is research to show that firms tend to pay more for external hires than internal hires even in the same job, but, in the end, they "pay more to get less" (Bidwell, 2011: 369). This suggests that organizations may not be doing a good job assessing potential value creation in the external pay setting process and/or that they are missing out on value capture with external hires in comparison to internal hires. I will argue below that despite the apparent problems in the pay setting process, given the information firms have about context, firms may be able to gain by accurately assessing candidates' potential value creation and adjusting rates based on this information.

In practice, job offer negotiations are completed by various organizational representatives (Malhotra, 2014), are idiosyncratic to the negotiators and the biases associated with these individuals (Anderson and Thompson, 2004; Olekalns and Smith, 2009), and are controlled by pay ranges (Milkovich et al., 2014). Thus, it seems unlikely then that negotiations are done consistently, meaning the negotiation process itself is heterogeneous. Thus, the value creation and capture for each external hire will be different when bargaining is used.

For the following section, I assume work is such that there is heterogeneity of employee contribution, and discuss how adjustments to base pay rates for individual employees can lead to value creation and capture. I will continue to maintain the organization-level focus as used in the job-based section by focusing on organizational practices around making adjustments and engaging in bargaining with applicants. However, examples at lower levels are inherent in the discussion of individual value assessment. It is also important to note that organizations may vary in the extent to which they adjust pay from the job-based rates depending on the job.

Value creation

One tension between compensation in practice and how the literature tends to treat compensation of human capital is that, in practice, base pay is primarily determined around the job (discussed at length earlier in this chapter). However, there is some leeway in that assignment within pay ranges. Firms with policies that allow for adjustments and/or bargaining have the potential to better narrow in on the actual value creation of the hire.

Coff and Kryscynski noted that individuals have "unique mixes of human capital" (2011: 1433); this uniqueness is inconsistent with the common job-based approach to pay, which assumes that value can be assessed based solely on job content. So, some individual adjustments at hire seem necessary to address the inherent uniquenesses of human capital. But the potential value creation of these processes requires accurate human capital assessments by the firm, which "are difficult to observe and evaluate ex ante" (Coff and Kryscynski, 2011: 1433).

An important question at this point is: what is an accurate assessment of human capital value? Drawing on the concepts of Chadwick (2017), it would be fair to say that an accurate assessment exists when the firm is able to evaluate the actual value creation of an individual. For a new hire this would be an accurate assessment of future value creation of the individual in the job. It seems clear that each person in a job in an organization, given each individual's unique set of skills, will vary. This is especially the case for jobs that are not highly monitored. This variance is accommodated by pay structures as the pay range increases as the grade level of the job increases (Milkovich et al., 2014).

In reality, value creation by any individual cannot be perfectly assessed in most organizations. This is particularly true when you consider the role of time and social complexity in value creation. For example, Coff and Kryscynski suggested that ability and willingness to learn firm-specific skills would increase the value of a hire over time. Should organizations include this in their value assessments and pay extra for those who will invest in these skills? Coff and Kryscynski also noted that individuals who act as boundary spanners have value beyond their role and potential beyond the apparent value at hire. Should firms assess this value and incorporate it into value assessments? And, when we consider HCRs (Ployhart et al., 2014), the value of an individual becomes even murkier. Here organizations have the upper hand in assessing an employee's value to the extent they can assess how this person will fit within the group and organization to contribute to unit-level capacities and potential strategic HCRs (see Kehoe and Bentley, Chapter 16 this volume).

Given the clear difficulties of assessing the value creation of new hires, it appears that firms able to do it well may have a competitive advantage over firms that cannot. These assessments allow the firm to compensate new hires more consistently with their worth and/or derive clear strategies around pay for value creation, potentially attracting the highest contributors and avoiding those with low value creation capacity. It is particularly important that adjustments are made with context as a central consideration. That is, organizations must consider the individual's potential HCR contribution. This requires considering multiple levels of value creation potential, i.e., individual KSAOs that contribute to the unit and how these individual KSAOs complement or detract from the unit-level capacities.

Note that I am not suggesting that alignment of pay and value creation would be equal; the firm could still pay slightly less than value creation. Market inaccuracies occur for human capital, so attracting the best talent with these rates may be possible. Given the firm-specificity of such assessments – i.e., the assessments must incorporate the value of the skills within the firm given the complex social structures of the firm (see Chapter 16) – these assessments cannot be easily copied by other firms.

Individual adjustments to job-based pay rates can contribute to value creation when adjustments are aligned with use value of human capital. Particularly important to the success of individual adjustments is assessment of the individual's contribution to HCRs.

Value capture

As noted earlier, value capture can occur through preventing employees from taking their value with them and through reduction of administrative costs (Chadwick, 2017). The decision of a firm to adjust pay from the job-based rate or to engage in the bargaining process and attempt to accurately assess human capital value prior to employment will be administratively more costly than a decision to pay all hires the same amount. Thus, a decision to bargain does not benefit the firm in terms of administrative efficiencies. Rather, it is other considerations, the roles of individual adjustments and bargaining on potential turnover, that are most relevant.

Accurate assessments of value creation potential allow an organization to choose a strategy around pay and then consistently administer that strategy. Consistency and fairness are important to employees in regard to pay satisfaction and subsequent retention (Williams et al., 2006). That is, the closer a firm can get to accurately assessing value potential, the more consistent their negotiation process can be across hires. It may be that, rather than "bargaining" or "negotiating," "adjusting" base pay offers to be in alignment with expected value creation is the most effective approach since the power of the other party to affect the rate exists when bargaining occurs.

To the extent firms are able to make base pay decisions for external hires in line with the contribution that will occur upon hire, employees are more likely to feel fairly treated – i.e., social comparisons yield fair input/outcome ratios across employees in the job (Adams, 1965). Perceptions of fair treatment increase pay satisfaction (Williams et al., 2006) and ultimately reduce turnover (Rubenstein et al., 2018). Furthermore, if we consider the possibility that contribution to value creation ebbs and flows over time for any individual, individuals who feel they have been treated fairly in the past are more likely to remain, even in moments at which their value creation greatly exceeds that which they individually capture. Thus, a fair and well-aligned rate assigned at hire has the potential to yield greater value capture over time.

Individual adjustments to job-based pay rates can contribute to value capture by preventing excessive payments and reducing turnover.

Pitfalls

Though individual adjustments come with potential upsides of value creation and capture, there are downsides of which firms must be wary when selecting an adjustment strategy. One obvious pitfall is the cost of assessing each employee's potential value creation within the organizational context. Engagement in assessing value and then negotiating with employees can be costly. This may explain why we see broader ranges and more negotiating at higher levels (Milkovich et al., 2014). Firms choose to adjust only when human capital value creation is highly variable within a job (Michelacci and Suarez, 2006).

Beyond administrative costs, there are significant risks to engaging in bargaining. One is that the assessments of value may be incorrect. An organization's capability at assessing human capital value creation potential is critical to the success of this strategy. And, as noted in the value creation section, this assessment involves a great deal of forward-looking and context-dependent assessment (i.e., consideration of HCRs). These assessments are made with significant uncertainty regarding how the individual will integrate with the group. If these assessments are incorrect, the organization runs the risk of compensating good negotiators rather than valuable contributors to the unit's HCRs. Furthermore, inconsistencies in alignment of pay with value creation may create problems within the organization over time, where social comparisons of inputs (e.g., perceived value creation) and outcomes (e.g., base pay) lead to employee frustration with inequity (Adams, 1965).

A second risk is that bargaining or negotiating tends to be done by an organizational representative and is unlikely to be a consistent process. Rather, it is idiosyncratic to the particular negotiators involved. The intention of negotiators is likely to vary significantly (Kimmel et al., 1980). For instance, some negotiators engage in bargaining with the goal of a "win" (i.e., a distributive negotiation strategy), while others engage in bargaining with a more interpersonally focused definition of negotiation success (i.e., an integrative negotiation strategy; Kimmel et al., 1980). Those who enter the process to win may gain by offering a wage significantly lower than the actual value creation potential of the new hire. However, given what we know about the importance of affective connection to the organization impacting employee behaviors (Ashforth et al., 2008), the long-term effects of this strategy may be negative. This is because the employee is being under-compensated such that better alternatives may arise. As these alternatives become apparent to the employee, the fact that the individual may feel negatively toward the organization based on the negotiation experience makes them more likely to exit.

Organizations must be wary of administrative costs, inaccuracy of value creation assessments, and strained negotiations when individual adjustments to job-based pay rates are included in the base pay setting process.

CONCLUSION

The goal of this chapter was to explore base pay setting practices in organizations through the lens of human capital value creation and value capture. This work contributes to the bases of pay variation literature (e.g., Gupta et al., 2012) by addressing rarely considered bases. More often, this literature has focused on performance-based pay concerns. I hope to spur more attention on job evaluation, market pricing, and individual adjustment explanations for differences in pay. This exploration indicates that more work addressing strategic considerations in base pay setting processes is needed for a few reasons. One, clearly the base pay setting process is associated with some of an organization's largest expenditures. Two, the base pay setting process is not simply a process of finding a true market rate and offering that rate. Some jobs may be hard to price, and a true market price does not actually exist in many cases. Furthermore, when we consider use value and unit-level capacities specific to an organization, the importance of organizational assessments of value becomes apparent. Three, value creation and value capture issues are interwoven throughout the base pay setting process, from the job assessment to the individual offer.

While a number of potential factors associated with value creation and capture were identified here, much more work is needed. The factors identified here could benefit from empirical exploration. And, there may be value in investigating specific issues conceptually in more detail. For example, I noted the ebb and flow of value creation over time. How does the base rate set at hire relate to this ebb and flow as far as value appropriation for the organization? Do firms over- and underpay over time for the same employee depending on unit and organizational conditions? This is likely given that base rates are set based on the job more so than on the individual. Pay-for-performance (PFP) may be a way of creating alignment of value creation and pay over time (see Nyberg and Reilly, Chapter 23 this volume). For example, Lazear (2000) described implementation of piece rate plans leading to better firm outcomes and higher pay for the highest-performing employees. Yet, PFP is known to have significant challenges in implementation (Beer and Cannon, 2004), and, as explained earlier in this chapter, makes up a relatively small amount of compensation for most employees as compared to base compensation. Base pay is important to attracting talent (Chapter 23). Moving towards greater emphasis on variable pay is likely to reduce resources available for base pay, so research aimed at understanding how pay mix may relate to value creation and capture over time would address a complex issue.

Another question emerging is whether the administrative burdens associated with job evaluations and individual adjustments are worth the potential value creation benefits. It is possible organizations have moved toward market pricing, in practice, in order to avoid a competitive disadvantage and reduce costs. Perhaps job evaluation is higher risk, leading to competitive advantage or competitive disadvantage depending on multiple factors, including the quality of the process. We know the effectiveness of any pay plan depends on the organizational climate and culture (Mitra et al., 2011), so this factor must also be considered. We need a better understanding of both of these processes in organizations to address these conjectures. Yet, little work has explored base pay setting in the past two decades, especially job-based determinants of pay.

Given that HCRs are person- and unit-specific (Ployhart et al., 2014), I am left wondering why organizations continue to pay by the job. Might base pay need to take a new direction in practice? The skill-based pay versus job evaluation-based pay debate of the 1990s raised this same concern (e.g., Gupta and Jenkins, 1991). Following up on this debate, Mitra et al. demonstrated empirically the superiority of skill-based pay plans to job evaluation and market pricing plans, assuming fit with the organization's culture. Yet, little has changed as most organizations continue to take a market pricing approach to base pay. The changing nature of work from manufacturing to more knowledge-intensive jobs may make traditional skill-based pay difficult to implement in today's organizations. Though skill-based pay may not be the answer, organizations that can figure out how to compensate in alignment with human capital resources may be able to secure a sustainable competitive advantage.

CHAPTER SUMMARY

BOX 1.1 KEY TAKEAWAYS

1. Organizational base pay setting processes are related to strategic human capital as these processes determine the alignment of human capital costs with human capital value creation and capture.
2. Using job evaluation to set base pay has greater potential for competitive advantage than market pricing, while market pricing is necessary to prevent competitive disadvantage. Setting base pay for the job has several limitations regardless of the approach, so adjusting for individual human capital is also a necessary consideration.
3. While organizations lack full information about an external hire's human capital, they have unique information about unit-level human capital resources and the potential of a specific hire to contribute to these resources. Thus, base pay setting processes should include assessment of a new hire's potential to contribute to HCRs.

BOX 1.2 DIRECTIONS FOR FUTURE RESEARCH

1. More research is needed exploring the base pay setting process. In particular, empirical work is needed in addressing how job evaluation, market pricing, and individual base pay adjustments relate to human capital value creation and capture.
2. The relationships between base pay and value creation should be studied over time to understand how ebbs and flows in value creation coupled with relatively unchanging base pay relate to human capital retention and value capture.
3. Models proposing how to compensate employees by moving beyond job-based paradigms and in light of insights on strategic human capital resources are needed.

NOTE

1. Here, the term "market pricing" refers to a well-known approach to base pay in organizations. This is not to be confused with the concept of market pricing as discussed in relational human capital models (Bridoux and Stoelhorst, 2016), though it would be reasonable to propose a market pricing approach to base pay fits with the market pricing relational model.

REFERENCES

Adams, J. S. (1965). Inequity in social exchange. In L. Berkowitz (ed.), *Advances in Experimental Social Psychology* (Vol. 2, pp. 267–99). New York: Academic Press.

Akerlof, G. (1970). The market for lemons. *Quarterly Journal of Economics*, *84*(3), 488–500.

Anderson, C., and Thompson, L. L. (2004). Affect from the top down: How powerful individuals' positive affect shapes negotiations. *Organizational Behavior and Human Decision Processes*, *95*, 125–39.

Ashforth, B. E., Harrison, S. H., and Corley, K. G. (2008). Identification in organizations: An examination of four fundamental questions. *Journal of Management*, *34*(3), 325–74.

Balkin, D. B., and Gomez-Mejia, L. R. (1987). Toward a contingency theory of compensation strategy. *Strategic Management Journal*, *8*(2), 169–82.

Barcellos, D. (2005). The reality and promise of market-based pay. *Employment Relations Today*, *32*(1), 1–10.

Barney, J. (1991). Firm resources and sustained competitive advantage. *Journal of Management*, *17*(1), 99–120.
Barney, J. B., and Wright, P. M. (1998). On becoming a strategic partner: The role of human resources in gaining competitive advantage. *Human Resource Management*, *37*(1), 31–46.
Barrett, G. V. (1991). Comparison of skill-based pay with traditional job evaluation techniques. *Human Resource Management Review*, *1*(2), 97–105.
Beer, M., and Cannon, M. D. (2004). Promise and peril in implementing pay-for-performance. *Human Resource Management*, *43*(1), 3–48.
Bidwell, M. (2011). Paying more to get less: The effects of external hiring versus internal mobility. *Administrative Science Quarterly*, *56*(3), 369–407.
Bridoux, F., and Stoelhorst, J. W. (2016). Stakeholder relationships and social welfare: A behavioral theory of contributions to joint value creation. *Academy of Management Review*, *41*(2), 229–51.
Bureau of Labor Statistics. (2017, December 17). Employer costs for employee compensation [Press release]. Retrieved from https://www.bls.gov/news.release/pdf/ecec.pdf.
Campbell, B. A., Coff, R., and Kryscynski, D. (2012). Rethinking sustained competitive advantage from human capital. *Academy of Management Review*, *37*(3), 376–95.
Chadwick, C. (2017). Toward a more comprehensive model of firms' human capital rents. *Academy of Management Review*, *42*(3), 499–519.
Chadwick, C., and Dabu, A. (2009). Human resources, human resource management, and the competitive advantage of firms: Toward a more comprehensive model of causal linkages. *Organization Science*, *20*(1), 253–72.
Coff, R. W. (1997). Human assets and management dilemmas: Coping with hazards on the road to resource-based theory. *Academy of Management Review*, *22*(2), 374–402.
Coff, R. W. (1999). When competitive advantage doesn't lead to performance: The resource-based view and stakeholder bargaining power. *Organization Science*, *10*(2), 119–33.
Coff, R. W., and Kryscynski, D. (2011). Invited editorial: Drilling for micro-foundations of human capital-based competitive advantages. *Journal of Management*, *37*(5), 1429–43.
Conlisk, J. (1996). Why bounded rationality? *Journal of Economic Literature*, *34*(2), 669–700.
Conroy, S. A., and Gupta, N. (2016). Team pay-for-performance: The devil is in the details. *Group and Organization Management*, *41*(1), 32–65.
Conroy, S., Gupta, N., Shaw, J., and Park, T. (2014). A multi-level approach to the effects of pay variation. *Research in Personnel and Human Resources Management*, *32*, 1–64.
DeVaro, J. (2006). Strategic promotion tournaments and worker performance. *Strategic Management Journal*, *27*(8), 721–40.
Galinsky, A. D., and Mussweiler, T. (2001). First offers as anchors: the role of perspective-taking and negotiator focus. *Journal of Personality and Social Psychology*, *81*(4), 657–69.
Gerhart, B., and Rynes, S. (1991). Determinants and consequences of salary negotiations by male and female MBA graduates. *Journal of Applied Psychology*, *76*(2), 256–62.
Gerhart, B., and Rynes, S. (2003). *Compensation: Theory, Evidence, and Strategic Implications*. Thousand Oaks, CA: Sage.
Gupta, N., Conroy, S. A., and Delery, J. E. (2012). The many faces of pay variation. *Human Resource Management Review*, *22*(2), 100–115.
Gupta, N., and Jenkins Jr, G. D. (1991). Job evaluation: An overview. *Human Resource Management Review*, *1*(2), 91–5.
Gupta, N., and Jenkins Jr, G. D. (1996). The politics of pay. *Compensation and Benefits Review*, *28*(2), 23–30.
Harris, D., and Helfat, C. (1997). Specificity of CEO human capital and compensation. *Strategic Management Journal*, *18*(11), 895–920.
Hunter, J. E., and Schmidt, F. L. (1983). Quantifying the effects of psychological interventions on employee job performance and work-force productivity. *American Psychologist*, *38*(4), 473.
Kimmel, M. J., Pruitt, D. G., Magenau, J. M., Konar-Goldband, E., and Carnevale, P. J. (1980). Effects of trust, aspiration, and gender on negotiation tactics. *Journal of Personality and Social Psychology*, *38*(1), 9–22.
Klaas, B. S., and McClendon, J. A. (1996). To lead, lag, or match: Estimating the financial impact of pay level policies. *Personnel Psychology*, *49*(1), 121–41.
Lawler, E. E., Ledford, G. E., and Chang, L. (1993). Who uses skill-based pay, and why. *Compensation and Benefits Review*, *25*(2), 22–6.
Lazear, E. P. (1992). The job as a concept. In W. J. Bruns (ed.), *Performance Measurement, Evaluation, and Incentives* (pp. 183–215). Boston, MA: Harvard Business School Press.
Lazear, E. P. (2000). Performance pay and productivity. *American Economic Review*, *90*(5), 1346–61.
Lepak, D. P., and Snell, S. A. (2002). Examining the human resource architecture: The relationships among human capital, employment, and human resource configurations. *Journal of Management*, *28*(4), 517–43.
Livingstone, L. P., Roberts, J. A., and Chonko, L. B. (1995). Perceptions of internal and external equity as predictors of outside salespeoples' [*sic*] job satisfaction. *Journal of Personal Selling and Sales Management*, *15*(2), 33–46.

Mahoney, T. A. (1991). Job evaluation: endangered species or anachronism? *Human Resource Management Review*, *1*(2), 155–62.
Malhotra, D. (2014). 15 Rules for negotiating a job offer. *Harvard Business Review*, *92*(4), 117–20.
Marks, M., and Harold, C. (2011). Who asks and who receives in salary negotiation. *Journal of Organizational Behavior*, *32*(3), 371–94.
Michelacci, C., and Suarez, J. (2006). Incomplete wage posting. *Journal of Political Economy*, *114*(6), 1098–123.
Milkovich, G. T., Newman, J. M., and Gerhart, B. (2014). *Compensation* (11th edn). New York: McGraw-Hill.
Mitra, A., Gupta, N., and Shaw, J. D. (2011). A comparative examination of traditional and skill-based pay plans. *Journal of Managerial Psychology*, *26*(4), 278–96.
Olekalns, M., and Smith, P. (2009). Mutually dependent: Power, trust, affect and the use of deception in negotiation. *Journal of Business Ethics*, *85*(3), 347–65.
O'Shea, P. G., and Bush, D. F. (2002). Negotiation for starting salary: Antecedents and outcomes among recent college graduates. *Journal of Business and Psychology*, *16*(3), 365–82.
Ployhart, R. E., Nyberg, A. J., Reilly, G., and Maltarich, M. A. (2014). Human capital is dead; long live human capital resources! *Journal of Management*, *40*(2), 371–98.
Romanoff, K., Boehm, K., and Benson, E. (1986). Pay equity: Internal and external considerations. *Compensation and Benefits Review*, *18*(6), 17–25.
Rubenstein, A. L., Eberly, M. B., Lee, T. W., and Mitchell, T. R. (2018). Surveying the forest: A meta-analysis, moderator investigation, and future-oriented discussion of the antecedents of voluntary employee turnover. *Personnel Psychology*, *71*(1), 23–65.
Shaw, J. D., and Gupta, N. (2007). Pay system characteristics and quit patterns of good, average, and poor performers. *Personnel Psychology*, *60*(4), 903–28.
Sinclair, A. L. (2003). The effects of justice and cooperation on team effectiveness. *Small Group Research*, *34*(1), 74–100.
Society for Human Resource Management [SHRM]. (2012). More organizations shift to market-based pay structures. Retrieved from: https://www.shrm.org/resourcesandtools/hr-topics/compensation/pages/pay-structures-shift.aspx.
Sweeney, P. D., and McFarlin, D. B. (2005). Wage comparisons with similar and dissimilar others. *Journal of Occupational and Organizational Psychology*, *78*(1), 113–31.
Toh, S. M., Morgeson, F. P., and Campion, M. A. (2008). Human resource configurations: Investigating fit with the organizational context. *Journal of Applied Psychology*, *93*(4), 864–82.
Trevor, C. O., Reilly, G., and Gerhart, B. (2012). Reconsidering pay dispersion's effect on the performance of interdependent work: Reconciling sorting and pay inequality. *Academy of Management Journal*, *55*(3), 585–610.
Weber, C. L., and Rynes, S. L. (1991). Effects of compensation strategy on job pay decision. *Academy of Management Journal*, *34*(1), 86–109.
Welbourne, T. M., and Trevor, C. O. (2000). The roles of departmental and position power in job evaluation. *Academy of Management Journal*, *43*(4), 761–71.
Williams, M. L., McDaniel, M. A., and Nguyen, N. T. (2006). A meta-analysis of the antecedents and consequences of pay level satisfaction. *Journal of Applied Psychology*, *91*(2), 392–413.
WorldatWork, The Total Rewards Association. (2016). Compensation programs and practices survey. Retrieved at https://www.worldatwork.org/docs/research-and-surveys/Survey-Brief-Survey-on-Compensation-Programs-and-Practices-2016.pdf.

2. Rents from human capital complementarities: a relational view of value creation and value capture

Flore Bridoux and J. W. Stoelhorst

The strategic human capital literature has its origin in the recognition that human capital (HC) is different from other resources in important respects (Coff, 1997). On the one hand, like any other resource, human capital resources (HCRs) are a potential source of competitive advantage when they are valuable, rare, inimitable, and non-substitutable (Barney, 1991). On the other hand, unlike other resources, firms cannot take full ownership of HCRs: absent slavery, employees can exercise free will and put more or less effort into their work or decide to work elsewhere. This means that a firm's ability to attract, motivate, and retain employees is a strategic issue. Firms with human resource (HR) practices that allow them to better attract, motivate, and retain employees will, *ceteris paribus*, create more value (Coff, 1997).

Such HR practices are especially important when value creation depends on complementarities involving HCRs. While superior HC complementarities are a potential source of competitive advantage and rents (Chadwick, 2017; Ployhart et al., 2014), it may be difficult to motivate employees to develop and exploit the firm-specific and collective HCRs from which these complementarities arise (Klein et al., 2012; Wang et al., 2009). As we explain below, difficulties are especially likely when firms rely on a purely economic rationale to motivate their employees – i.e., when they use pecuniary benefits to appeal to people's self-interest. But if an economic rationale is ill-suited to motivating employees to develop HC complementarities, to which alternative should firms turn instead?

We answer this question by building on relational models theory (Fiske, 1991, 1992, 2004). Relational models theory distinguishes four mental models (Communal Sharing, Authority Ranking, Equality Matching, and Market Pricing) that people use to frame their relationships with others. We specify how these four models relate to value creation and value capture, and link them to the strategic human resource management (SHRM) literature.

Our main message can be summarized in three points. The first is that we need all four relational models to fully understand employees' motivation to contribute to value creation. The four models each imply a different set of norms that simultaneously affect employees' motivation to contribute to value creation and their expectations about how value will be captured. Second, firms' HR practices in large part determine the relational model that their employees will adopt (Mossholder et al., 2011). Importantly, HR practices need to consistently reflect one of the four models to be effective, explaining the configurational nature of HR practices. Third, in shaping their HR practices, firms have three clearly delineated alternatives (Communal Sharing, Authority Ranking, Equality Matching) for the purely economic rationale of motivating people (based on Market Pricing). Moreover, configurations of HR practices based on these alternatives, and on Communal Sharing in particular, are more likely to solve the motivational problems inherent in the process of generating rents from HC complementarities.

VALUE CREATION, COMPLEMENTARITIES, AND RENTS

In this section we define our terms, highlight the main insights on value creation and capture from the strategic human capital (SHC) literature, and make the case for a relational view of value creation and value capture.

Value Creation, Value Capture, and the Firm

Following Brandenburger and Stuart (1996), value creation and value capture (what they refer to as value appropriation) need to be understood as two interrelated processes. In their conceptualization, a coalition of suppliers, a firm, and buyers simultaneously cooperates to create value and competes to capture that value. Value created is defined as the difference between buyers' willingness-to-pay for the firm's products and the sum of suppliers' opportunity costs, which are defined as the payments suppliers would receive in their best outside option. Who appropriates the value created by the coalition of the firm and its buyers and suppliers is determined by the prices paid in product and factor markets. The buyers' share of the value created is the difference (if any) between their willingness-to-pay and the price they pay in the product market. The suppliers' share of the value created is the difference (if any) between the price they receive in the factor market and their opportunity costs. The firm's share of the value created is the difference (if any) between the price paid by buyers in the product market and the sum of the prices paid to suppliers in the factor market (Brandenburger and Stuart, 1996).

An important question raised by Brandenburger and Stuart's approach is how we should understand the firm. On this point, we follow the conceptualization of Coff (1999), who adopts a nexus of contracts view and makes a distinction between internal and external resource suppliers. Coff emphasizes that, on a nexus of contracts view, firms cannot be seen as actors who appropriate value. Firms are legal entities and, as such, can own non-human resources. But firms cannot act, let alone appropriate, value: only individuals do. In addition, Coff makes a distinction between internal resource suppliers (shareholders, managers, and other employees) and external resource suppliers (e.g., a party supplying raw materials). Combining Brandenburger and Stuart with Coff results in Figure 2.1.

This conceptualization has two immediate implications. First, by definition, the value created through a firm's activities equals the value appropriated by all the firm's stakeholders – meaning buyers, internal resources suppliers, and external resource suppliers (Lieberman et al., 2017). Second, the value appropriated by the firm (the firm's share in Figure 2.1) must be equal to the value appropriated by the firm's internal resource suppliers.

Human Capital and Rents

HC can be defined as "an individual's knowledge, skills, abilities, and other characteristics that are relevant for achieving economic outcomes" (Ployhart et al., 2014: 376). The SHC literature starts from the dual recognition that HC is a key strategic resource for firms, but one that differs from other (non-human) resources because it cannot be fully owned by the

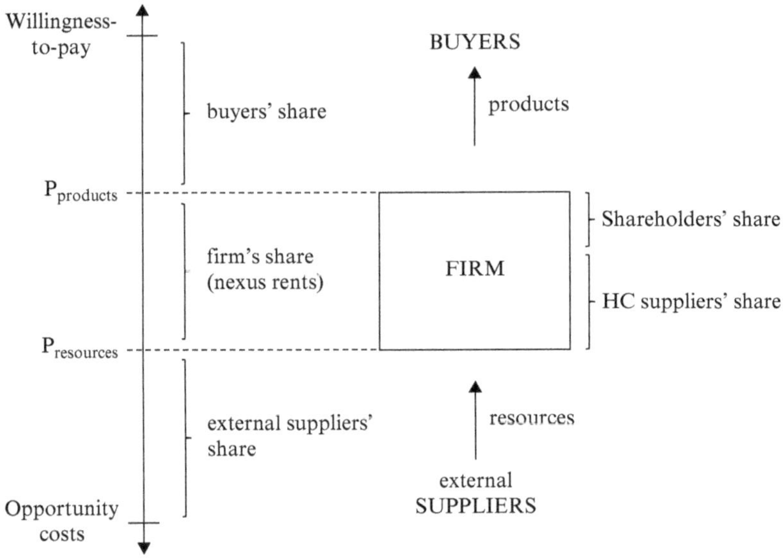

Figure 2.1 Value creation and capture

firm (Coff, 1997). As a result of this, firms cannot buy HC but can only hire it, making employee compensation a perpetually ongoing bargaining process (Chadwick, 2017).

What makes the SHC literature 'strategic' is its interest in the generation and capture of rents, where rents are defined as payments above opportunity costs (cf. Peteraf, 1993; Rumelt, 1987). The particular interest is in the generation and capture of what Coff (1999) refers to as 'nexus rents', which, following the conceptualization in Figure 2.1, equal the firm's share, or the sum of all the rents (if any) paid to internal resource suppliers. Importantly, for a firm to generate nexus rents, it must have some advantage over its competitors (Brandenburger and Stuart, 1996). This then leads to the twin questions that define much of the SHC literature: first, how can HCRs contribute to competitive advantage and, hence, the generation of nexus rents; and, second, who among the internal resource suppliers is likely to capture these rents?

In answering these questions, the SHC literature has distinguished three main types of so-called *strategic* HCRs, i.e., HCRs that are relevant for competitive advantage: heterogeneous generic HCRs (the case of 'star employees'), firm-specific HCRs, and collective HCRs (Ployhart and Moliterno, 2011; Ployhart et al., 2014). In the context of efficient factor markets, the link between value creation and value capture for generic HCRs is easy to understand. Generic HCRs, by definition, can create the same amount of value in multiple organizations. Following the logic of resource-based theory (Barney, 1991; Peteraf, 1993), such HCRs can only be a source of competitive advantage if there is heterogeneity in the HC supplied and limited supply in the factor market: 'star employees', such as a scientific genius in an R&D lab or an All-Star player on a sports team, can give their organizations a competitive advantage because of the superior quality of their HCRs. At the same time, if labor markets are efficient the rents generated by a competitive advantage based on the heterogeneous qualities of star employees will be fully captured by these employees. This is because their HCRs, being generic, have equal value in other organizations, driving up the price for their HCRs in the factor market (in the form of compensation) to the point where the star employees' opportunity costs (their best outside offers) equal the rents that their superior HC generates.

More recently, however, SHC scholars have argued that if we relax the assumption of an efficient factor market and allow for reasonable market frictions, who captures the rents from heterogeneous generic HC is no longer so straightforward (Campbell et al., 2012). In particular, employees may not fully capture the rents their generic HC helps create because they value other things an employer offers besides monetary compensation, such as a specific location (Campbell et al., 2012) or fairness (Bridoux and Vishwanathan, 2018).

Human Capital Complementarities

In contrast to the case of heterogeneous generic HCRs, where competitive advantage results from the superior quality of a stand-alone HCR, in the case of firm-specific and collective HCRs competitive advantage results from superior HC complementarities. Following Ployhart et al. (2014), who adopt the definition of Ennen and Richter (2010: 207), we see complementarities as "the beneficial interplay of the elements of a system where the presence of one element increases the value of others". Firm-specific HCRs involve complementarities between an individual employee's HCRs and other human and non-human resources controlled by the firm (e.g., patents, machines) that are, by definition, superior to the complementarities between generic HCRs and the same resources controlled by the firm (Becker, 1964). If a firm is better than its competitors at motivating employees to make their HCRs firm-specific and to realize the potential value these superior complementarities can create, it can achieve a competitive advantage (Campbell and Kryscynski, Chapter 9 this volume; Chadwick, 2017). To the extent that competitors cannot easily imitate how to motivate employees to make their HCRs firm-specific, this competitive advantage is also sustainable.

A similar argument applies to collective HCRs. The explicit recognition of this category of HCRs stems from the recent interest in investigating HCRs at the unit level – i.e., any organizational level (team, department, or firm) above the individual (Ployhart and Moliterno, 2011; Ployhart et al., 2014). Collective HCRs are defined as unit-level capacities relevant for achieving economic outcomes that result from combinations of individual HCRs, which are typically supplied by multiple individuals (Ployhart et al., 2014). A firm can gain competitive advantage from motivating employees to create such combinations to the extent that these combinations lead to superior HC complementarities. Furthermore, the firm can sustain this competitive advantage if isolating mechanisms such as social complexity protect against imitation of the collective HCRs themselves, the way they are put to use to create value, or the way in which employees were motivated to create them.

While superior HC complementarities may often be the key to the creation of competitive advantage and the generation of nexus rents, it is not at all obvious that employees will be motivated to invest in developing these complementarities because they may question whether they will be adequately compensated for their investment (Wang et al., 2009). This is the case because the link between value creation and value capture is much less straightforward for firm-specific and collective HCRs than for generic HCRs, even before we allow for deviations from the assumption of efficient factor markets, such as reasonable market frictions or more complex employee utility functions that include variables other than purely monetary compensation.

The Need for a Relational View

Firm-specific and collective HCRs complicate the analysis of the link between value creation and capture because they make multiple parties dependent on each other in creating value. As a result of these interdependencies, value capture is 'formally indeterminate' (Brandenburger and Stuart, 1996), which is to say that value capture is determined by non-market factors. In efficient markets competition results in an outcome where each party captures its marginal product (Makowski and Ostroy, 2001), or what Brandenburger and Stuart refer to as 'added value' (defined as the drop in the value created by the coalition without the focal party). But this is only possible in the absence of interdependencies (Makowski and Ostroy, 2001). Without interdependencies, the total value created equals the sum of the added values of all parties involved. But with interdependencies, such as HC complementarities, the sum of the added values of all parties is more than the value created (Brandenburger and Stuart, 1996). As a result, value capture is no longer decided by competition, and parties will have to settle on a division of the value they can jointly create on some other basis than minimizing opportunity costs.

In line with the above, the SHC literature has recognized that governance mechanisms and HR practices are crucial additional variables in explaining the degree to which firms are able to realize the full rent-generating potential of HCRs (Campbell and Kryscynski, this volume; Mahoney and Kor, 2015; Wang et al., 2009). In the case of firm-specific investments, rational employees would not make these investments unless they are reassured that they will not become the victims of the opportunism of some other members of the nexus (the firm's shareholders and other suppliers of HC). In the case of the development of collective HCRs, self-interested employees would recognize that they face a team production situation and would respond by shirking (e.g., Alchian and Demsetz, 1972; Arrow, 1974). Other employees, anticipating this shirking, would also be reluctant to contribute. To repeat, these problems cannot be solved on the basis of the standard economic rationale in which the connection between value creation and value capture takes the form of monetary incentives that appeal to employees' self-interest by promising them payment of their marginal product. This naturally leads to the question: *What are alternative ways of motivating employees to invest in HC complementarities?* To answer this question, we turn to relational models theory, which holds that the economic rationale is but one of four ways to govern relationships.

A RELATIONAL VIEW OF VALUE CREATION AND VALUE CAPTURE

While SHC scholars have a tendency to assume self-interest – in the narrow sense of the exclusive pursuit of personal material outcomes without regard for others' outcomes[1] – there is ample evidence that humans are social animals who actively seek out social interactions with others to satisfy a fundamental need to belong and relate to others, and who have evolved mental structures to deal with the conflicts of interest inherent in cooperating with others (Galinsky et al., 2005; Tomasello, 2016). Disciplines as diverse as psychology, economics, political science, sociology, anthropology, and biology have generated large bodies of literature to explain why and to what extent people cooperate in social interactions despite the temptation to free-ride and the fear of being taken advantage of (Van Lange et al., 2013). One key message from this research is that humans have developed specific mental structures to establish and maintain social relationships. Relational models theory explores these mental structures (Fiske, 1991, 1992, 2004).

Relational Models Theory

On the basis of an exhaustive review of the major work on social relationships in sociology, social anthropology, and social psychology, Fiske argues that we employ four elementary relational models to coordinate nearly all our social interactions (Rai and Fiske, 2011): Communal Sharing, Authority Ranking, Equality Matching, and Market Pricing.[2] The relational models are already familiar to management scholars under other labels, such as coordination mechanisms (market, hierarchy, and clan) and different organizational climates. However, our elaboration on relational models theory below advances our understanding of these more familiar typologies in ways that are especially relevant for the SHC literature. First, relational models theory leads to a configurational view: norms guiding behaviors in the value creation dimension of social interactions go hand in hand with specific norms in the value capture dimension. Second, because, as we explain below, relational models exist at both the individual and at the collective level, relational models theory allows us to link multiple levels of analysis to understand employees' motivation to develop new and exploit existing HC complementarities. Third, the theory enables us to link the SHC literature to the strategic human resource management (SHRM) literature. Specifically, HR practices, through their effect on how employees frame their relationships, can be expected to affect employees' motivation to develop HC complementarities, which in turn affects value creation. These links are shown in Figure 2.2.

At the individual level

At the individual level, relational models are "representations, grammars, or script-like social schemata" (Fiske, 1991: 21) that enable people to internalize relationships as part of their cognitive functioning and translate them into behavior (cf. Haslam, 2001; Turner et al., 1994). People use these relational models (unconsciously) "to plan and to generate their own action, to understand, remember, and anticipate others' action, to coordinate the joint production of collective action and institutions, and to evaluate their own and others' actions" (Fiske, 2004: 3). The relational models are not exclusively cognitive; they also comprise needs, motives, evaluative attitudes and judgments, as well as emotions (Fiske, 1991). The relational models trigger different behaviors in social interactions because they (a) involve different perceptions of who one is in relation to the partner, (b) are associated with different motives, and, therefore, (c) lead to different rules of appropriate behavior for oneself and the partner (Bridoux and Stoelhorst, 2016).

Actions that are inappropriate according to a relational model are evaluated as immoral by individuals using that model, and generate moral emotions such as guilt, shame, disgust, or outrage (Rai and Fiske, 2011). In this latter aspect, relational models are closely related to injunctive norms, namely the perception of what most people approve

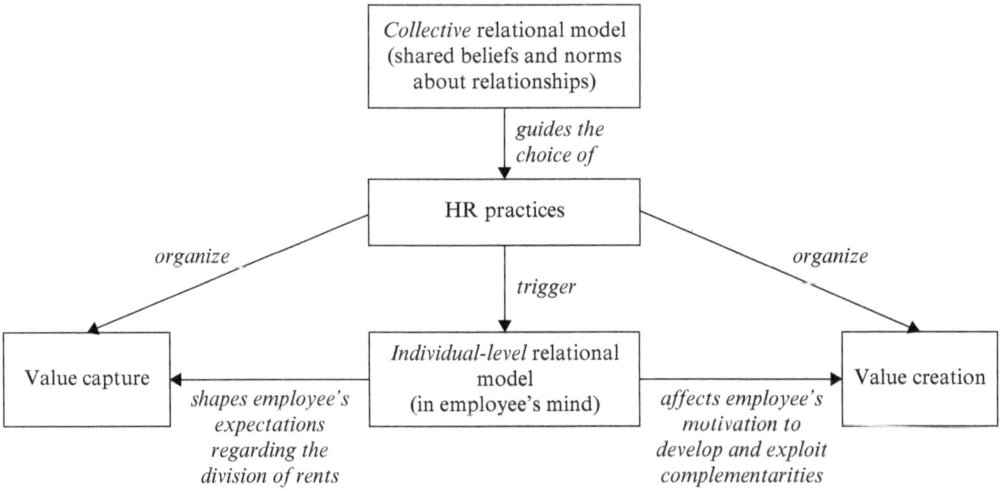

Figure 2.2 Relational models link value creation and capture

or disapprove of (Cialdini et al., 1991). Such norms form an essential mechanism by which human social behavior is directed (Aarts and Dijksterhuis, 2003). When we physically interact with others, others' behavior provides direct input for our own actions. However, successful collective action usually depends on the more indirect social influence provided by social norms because others are not always physically present when we face the choice between pursuing the collective or our own interest. Social norms guide us to select behavior that we believe other people expect from us (Cialdini and Trost, 1998). There is plenty of evidence that self-reported measures of injunctive social norms correlate with, and independently predict, a variety of behaviors, especially when the behavior occurs in social settings (Aarts and Dijksterhuis, 2003).

In relation to a specific partner in a specific role, individuals can only hold one relational model at a time; but different models can follow one another relatively quickly in individuals' minds in response to situational cues, in particular cues about the behavior and intentions of the relational partner(s) (Bridoux and Stoelhorst, 2016). In general, when individuals perceive their relational partner(s) to use the same relational model as they do themselves, they experience the relationship as harmonious because they understand the other's (others') behavior, have similar motivations and expectations, and evaluate actions using the same criteria (Connelley and Folger, 2004; Giessner and van Quaquebeke, 2010). In contrast, when individuals perceive their relational partner(s) to purposefully behave in a way that does not fit the relational model they use, they experience this misfit as a transgression (Fiske, 1991; Giessner and van Quaquebeke, 2010). This transgression triggers negative moral emotions (Fiske, 1991) and may lead individuals to question the relational model they have adopted to frame the relationship. These socio-psychological dynamics imply that, while the relational models are mental representations of relationships in the minds of individual employees, their use is shaped by situational cues.

In order to understand employees' motivation to develop and exploit HC complementarities, it is necessary to consider both employees' relationship with the firm and with other employees. For example, while employees' contributions to collective HCRs are likely to be explained best by studying their relationships with colleagues, their investments in firm-specific HCRs are likely to be better explained by examining their relationship with the firm. On the other hand, it may be justified to consider that the same set of mental representations apply to both the firm and other employees. Employees often anthropomorphize the firm that employs them, selectively ascribing humanlike characteristics, motivations, intentions, and emotions to the organization (Morrison and Robinson, 1997; Sluss and Ashforth, 2008). This is not surprising, as neuroscience research has shown that humans use the same neuronal circuitry to assess and respond to organizations and people (Plitt et al., 2015).

HR practices link the individual level to the collective level

Within a firm or subunit, there may also be a *collective relational model* regarding value creation and capture (see Figure 2.2). Brickson (2005) showed that organizations' members are likely to have a shared representation of how their organization relates to internal and external parties. This shared representation is an aspect of an organization's culture according to some researchers (Brickson, 2005, 2007; Jones et al., 2007) or of a (strong) organizational climate to others (Mossholder et al., 2011).[3]

If such a shared representation of relationships exists, HR practices are likely to be central to how the collective relational model relates to the individual-level relational model that employees hold. First, HR practices are shaped by organizational assumptions and values (Bowen and Ostroff, 2004). The stronger the consensus among organizational members on how employees relate to each other and the firm, the stronger the assumptions and values guiding the design of HR practices and the more consistent the HR practices are likely to be.

Second, HR practices, as a system, are a principal means through which managers can influence how employees perceive relationships with the firm and with other employees (Bowen and Ostroff, 2004; Mossholder et al., 2011; Suazo et al., 2009) because "they send signals to employees that allow them to understand the desired and appropriate responses and form a collective sense of what is expected" (Bowen and Ostroff, 2004: 204). When the HR practices constituting the HR system are coherent, in the sense that they are closely associated with one and only one of the four relational models, they are likely to cause employees to frame their relationships on the basis of the same relational model (Mossholder et al., 2011). In other words, consistency in HR practices will likely foster consensus with regard to how employees relate to each other and to the firm (Bowen and Ostroff, 2004), making social interactions more harmonious (Fiske, 1991). If, on the contrary, the HR practices relate to multiple relational models, they send ambiguous messages to employees about what is important and which behaviors are expected and rewarded. If, as a result, individual employees adopt different relational models to guide their behavior, social interactions within the firm are likely to be problematic, as employees will see others as transgressors, leading to negative emotions.

The Four Relational Models: Value Creation, Value Capture, and HR Systems

The four relational models differ on key features that help explain why they offer very different solutions to the problem of motivating employees to develop and exploit HC complementarities. As summarized in Table 2.1, these key features are: (a) the representation

Table 2.1 Key features of the relational models

	Market Pricing	Communal Sharing	Equality Matching	Authority Ranking	
				Superior (the partner is the subordinate)	Subordinate (the partner is the superior)
Representation of the employee and the partner	Individual actor	Community member	Equal partner	Superior (the partner is the subordinate)	Subordinate (the partner is the superior)
Motivation	Self-interest	Altruism	Reciprocity	Legitimate power	Security from association with a powerful other
Norm for *value creation* behavior in the relationship	Pursue individual interest (i.e., contribute in proportion to individual rewards)	Pursue the collective interest (e.g., pitch in whenever needed)	Reciprocate the partner's behavior (e.g., take into account the partner's interest *as long as* the partner cooperates)	Take into account the partner's interest and use legitimate power to coordinate own and subordinate's actions	Take into account the partner's interest and comply with the superior's directives
Norm for *value capture*	Equity	Need	Equality	In proportion to power	
Relational need the model fulfills	Need for achievement	Need to belong	Need for equality	Need for dominance	Need for deference and security
Decision-making	Individual decisions mediated by the market	Consensus	Equal say	Directives	

of who the employee is in relation to its relational partners, namely the firm and other employees (i.e., relational identity); (b) the motives the employee attributes to the firm and other employees; and (c) the norms regarding how to work together to create value and how to divide this value.

Market pricing (MP)

The MP model closely corresponds to what is known as 'economic exchange' in social exchange theory (Blau, 1964) and to a transactional psychological contract (Rousseau, 1995). It also relates to the traditional view of transactions in economic theory, and is similar to the notion of the market as a governance mechanism in Williamson (1979). Because the MP model makes the individual identities of relational partners salient, employees who adopt an MP model of their relationships perceive themselves, the firm, and other employees as individual actors with their own characteristics and personal goals (Bridoux and Stoelhorst, 2016; Fiske, 1991; Vohs et al., 2006). As a result of this representation, relational partners are seen as motivated by self-interest – pursuing their individual interest with little consideration for others' or the collective interest (Fiske, 1991). In fact, in the context of MP, the pursuit of efficiency and the maximization of one's individual payoffs are accepted as appropriate behaviors (Fiske, 1991). This establishes a clear norm for employees' contributions to value creation, which are expected to be in proportion to individual rewards.

In an MP model, the rule that governs value capture is equity. Applying this distributive rule means allocating value in proportion to merits (Deutsch, 1975). Employees' payoffs (which can include salary, bonuses, gain sharing, or stock ownership programs) should therefore be in proportion to their inputs to productive activities (e.g., effort, time, individual HC) as compared to other employees' inputs (Adams, 1965).[4] In an organizational context, the equity principle is always present to some extent (Colquitt et al., 2001; Kabanoff, 1991) because market forces affect employees' compensations for their HC inputs (Gomez-Mejia et al., 2010). Yet, organizations vary in how much emphasis they put on the equity principle when allocating value.

Mossholder et al. (2011) proposed that the compliance HR system of Lepak and Snell (1999) will lead employees to frame their relationship with the firm and other employees in terms of MP. This compliance HR system is very similar to what Tsui, Pearce, Porter, and Tripoli label the 'quasi spot contract'. Such an HR system assumes short-term and transactional relationships on both the employee's and the firm's side: "the employer offers short-term, purely economic inducements in exchange for well-specified contributions by the employee" and "neither party expects contributions or inducements beyond those specified" (Tsui et al., 1997: 1091–2). By assuming relationships of an arm's-length nature, the HR practices "focus on the work to be done, the results to be accomplished, the terms of the contract, and virtually nothing else" (Lepak and Snell, 1999: 39). This implies little concern for training and development (Mossholder et al., 2011). The focus is on specifying rules and procedures and on aligning employees' interests with the firm's interests through monetary incentives (Arthur, 1994). Compensation practices therefore involve schemes with high-powered individual incentive plans – e.g., piece rates payment, commission systems, and bonus plans (cf. Zenger and Marshall, 2000) – that aim to motivate employees on the basis of the equity principle, but that also tend to generate larger pay dispersion within and across groups of employees (Cobb and Flannery, 2017) and that often encourage competition between employees (Gomez-Mejia et al., 2010).

Communal sharing (CS)

A CS model has a lot in common with, inter alia, the clan of Ouchi (1980), the community of Adler (2001), the communal relationships of Clark and Mills (1979), and the relational psychological contract of Rousseau. If employees perceive their relationships in terms of the CS model, they see themselves and their relational partners as a community and, thus, as members of a collective (Brickson, 2007; Bridoux and Stoelhorst, 2016). This fusion of the identity of employees with the community means that the collective as opposed to the individual identity is psychologically salient. As a consequence, employees see relational partners as equivalent and undifferentiated on the key dimensions that define the community (Turner et al., 1994). They also see them as sharing the same motivation and goals (Fiske, 1991).

The identification with the collective makes employees want to pursue the interest of this collective in order to maintain it (Fiske, 1991, 1992). As a result, the motivation in a CS model is altruism – the pursuit of the collective interest with little regard for the impact on one's individual material payoffs.[5] This claim is supported by research on social identity theory that has repeatedly shown that when a collective identity is salient, individuals assimilate the norms and values of the group (Turner, 1991). Altruism explains how the identification with a collective enables collective action, even in situations where it is clear that the collective action will not succeed (Rowley and Moldoveanu, 2003). Because this altruistic motivation is also ascribed to the relational partners, employees focus on achieving the subset of the partners' goals that have emerged as collective goals. The norm for cooperation in a CS model is to pitch in and do whatever is necessary to achieve the collective goals (Fiske, 1991). In terms of employees' contribution to value creation this would include making investments in HC complementarities.

In a CS model the distributive rule that governs value capture is need: whoever has a greater material need should get more (Deutsch, 1975). At first glance, this may seem a norm that is out of place in the context of firms. Unlike in a family, where the division of food can be ruled exclusively by how hungry the family members are, the need principle is unlikely to fully determine the division of value in firms because factor market forces enforce equity to some extent. Yet, the value created by superior complementarities, which is by definition above and beyond what resource suppliers would get if they moved elsewhere, could well be divided on the basis of the need principle. For example, some of this value can be used to raise the wages of low-paid employees above the minimum wage.

Mossholder et al. (2011) argued that a commitment HR system will lead employees to frame their relationships in terms of CS. Such a system bolsters collective commitment through employment relationships that imply living up to unwritten obligations both on the firm's and on the employee's part (see also Tsui et al., 1997). While unwritten obligations on the employees' side include "to consider the unit's or the organization's interests as important as core job duties," on the firm's side they include full-time and long-term employment (Mossholder et al., 2011; Tsui et al., 1997: 1092). The commitment HR system is also characterized by significant investments in training and by internal career development (Lepak and Snell, 1999) – an emphasis on employees' well-being that complies with the need principle (Ashforth and Johnson, 2001). Selection, the socialization of newcomers, and training emphasize employees' prosocial values and relational skills (Mossholder et al., 2011) and a common identity (Ashforth and Johnson, 2001). An HR commitment system is likely to favor group rewards to divide value. With group rewards an employee's payoffs are contingent on the collective outcomes at the level of the team (e.g., project bonus), business unit (e.g., group sharing), or firm (e.g., profit sharing) (Gomez-Mejia et al., 2010; Nyberg et al., 2018). Group rewards help employees feel interdependent rather than independent or in competition with each other (Gomez-Mejia et al., 2010).

Equality matching (EM)

While the EM model is not included in the traditional triad of hierarchy, market, and clan/community known to strategy scholars, it is closely related to what SHRM scholars know as 'social exchange' (Blau, 1964), the balanced psychological contract (Rousseau, 1995), and the exchange relationship (Clark and Mills, 1979). If employees see their relationships with the firm and other employees as EM, an interpersonal identity is salient: employees perceive the relational partners to be equal (with the same rights and duties) but distinct – with their own characteristics and goals (Bridoux and Stoelhorst, 2016; Fiske, 1991). A representation of the relational partners at the interpersonal level, as opposed to the individual (MP) or collective level (CS), implies that divergent interests are acknowledged and can be explicitly taken into account in decisions; they do not form a threat to the relationship, as they would in a CS relationship. A representation at the interpersonal level also implies that the relational partners are viewed as not only concerned with their personal welfare, but also as having a genuine concern for the welfare of their partner (Brewer and Gardner, 1996; Brickson, 2007) – at least as long as the partners exhibit the same concern, for example by behaving cooperatively.

Parties to an EM relationship are motivated by reciprocity in order to maintain a balance in the relationship (Fiske, 1991, 1992). This positive reciprocity in an EM model implies that employees are ready to reward others' fair or cooperative behavior by creating value in order to increase others' welfare, even if this reward comes at a personal cost (Fehr and Fischbacher, 2003; Fischbacher et al., 2001). An EM model also implies the possibility of negative reciprocity: relational partners are viewed as ready to punish what is interpreted as unfair or uncooperative behavior from others, even if this punishment is costly and will not necessarily pay off in the future (Fehr and Gächter, 2000, 2002). Consequently, in the context of EM, the rule for cooperation is that an actor is expected to reciprocate others' behavior following a tit-for-tat rule (Fiske, 1991), implying that employees are likely to invest in HC complementarities as long as they feel that these investments are reciprocated by the firm and other employees.

In EM relationships value capture is governed by the equality rule: the equality principle prescribes dividing the value created equally among the relational partners (Deutsch, 1975). As in the case of the need principle in CS, equality cannot be the only distributive principle governing the division of value in firms that have to compete in factor markets to attract and retain employees. However, many firms have compensation systems that only relatively weakly reward inputs or behavior, but instead standardize wages between workers doing the same job and minimize wage disparities across jobs, which leads to a wage distribution that is flatter than equity would suggest (Conroy, Chapter 1 this volume; Nickerson and Zenger, 2008). Such compressed pay structures decrease the costs linked to social comparison among employees (Larkin et al., 2012; Zenger and Marshall, 2000). They will also trigger employees to see their relationships with the firm and other employees as EM (Mossholder et al., 2011).

In order to get employees to frame their relationships with the firm and other employees as EM, Mossholder et al. proposed adopting the practices underlying the collaborative HR system of Lepak and Snell (1999) – which combines seeking cooperation from employees with protecting the organization against employee opportunism by incorporating vestiges of instrumental tactics. For example, it involves designing productive tasks so as to generate or make salient reciprocal interdependencies among employees (Mossholder et al., 2011). With regard to value capture, a collaborative HR system involves compressed pay structures and can combine individual and group rewards (Mossholder et al., 2011). In addition, symbolic management should encourage feelings of social obligations and use words like 'partners' or 'friends' to mark reciprocity and equality among the participants.

Authority ranking (AR)

The AR model shares some similarities with the hierarchy of Williamson (1979), and is related to much of the organizational behavior (OB) literature on leadership (Anderson and Sun, 2017; Judge and Piccolo, 2004). If employees perceive their relationships with the firm or other employees as governed by an AR model, they see one of the relational partners as the superior and the other as the subordinate. Importantly, this relationship should be based on a legitimate source of power such as formal authority or expertise (Fiske, 1991, 1992). As in the EM model, an interpersonal identity is salient (Bridoux and Stoelhorst, 2016; Fiske, 1991), which implies that the relational partners are viewed as not only concerned with their personal welfare, but also as having a genuine concern for the welfare of their relational partner (Brewer and Gardner, 1996; Brickson, 2007). The superior is seen as motivated by a desire to exercise power, but in combination with a pastoral care for the subordinates (a motivation to help with personal needs and problems). The subordinates are motivated by the security that associating with a powerful partner bestows. In an AR relationship, appropriate behaviors are linked to an actor's rank: the superior is expected to organize and control the contribution of subordinates, and the subordinates are expected to follow the superior's directives (Fiske, 1991). This establishes a clear norm for value creation and investments in HC complementarities: compliance with managers' orders.

An imbalance in power usually comes from an imbalance in resources – the more powerful actor has greater resources that are highly valued by the less powerful actor (Weitz and Jap, 1995). Yet, not all relationships characterized by power imbalance are governed by an AR model. The legitimacy of the superior's power is an essential characteristic of AR (Fiske, 1991). Legitimacy refers to the subordinate's perception that the partner's authority is appropriate, proper, and just, which leads to voluntarily deference to the partner's decisions (Tyler, 2006). Power coming from reward and coercion may bring compliance of the weakest partner but will not lead the subordinate to see the relationship as AR (Fiske, 1991); the subordinate is then more likely to frame the relationship using an MP model or to shift to a null relationship.

In AR relationships value is divided based on legitimate power: whoever has more legitimate power should capture more value. Legitimate power is not included among the distributive principles listed by key authors in the justice literature, such as Morton Deutsch (1975, 1985). Yet, this may reflect a cultural bias in the justice literature, which has focused on an American context characterized by low power distance, individualism, and low uncertainty avoidance (Gomez-Mejia and Welbourne, 1991). For example, in countries where hierarchical differences are readily accepted and where employees score high on uncertainty avoidance (i.e., they favor predictability and certainty), the use of compensation systems based on seniority is widespread (Schuler and Rogovsky, 1998), which suggests that the power derived from different positions in a hierarchical structure can be seen as a legitimate distributive principle. When legitimate power is grounded in an individual characteristic such as expertise, a distribution of value based on legitimate power or based on equity can be very similar.

A steep hierarchy with clear chains of command and a compensation system that emphasizes a legitimate source of power to divide value are likely to trigger employees to frame their relationships in terms of AR. The study of leadership styles by OB scholars can inform us about the HR practices likely to be associated with AR. For example, the pastoral care that the superior must exhibit for the subordinate to perceive the relationship as AR relates to the 'individualized consideration' of transformational leadership: "the degree to which the leader attends to each follower's needs, acts as a mentor or coach to the follower, and listens to the follower's concerns and needs" (Judge and Piccolo, 2004: 755). Furthermore, to have this pastoral care, it is likely that the superior's span of control must be quite limited: managing many subordinates would not allow for the attention to personal needs and problems pastoral care involves. The legitimacy of the leader that is at the core of the AR model could come from one or two of the three other dimensions of transformational leadership: namely, 'charisma' – i.e., "the degree to which the leader behaves in admirable ways that cause followers to identify with the leader"; and 'inspirational motivation' – i.e., "the degree to which the leader articulates a vision that is appealing and inspiring to followers" (Judge and Piccolo, 2004: 755). Yet, a leader's legitimacy does not have to be linked to a leader's leadership style; it can also come from the legitimacy of the criterion on the basis of which (e.g., seniority, expertise) and procedures through which the leader is selected (e.g., transparent procedures).

Relational Models as Solutions to Motivational Problems

We now return to the motivational problems inherent in the creation of superior HC complementarities that motivated our proposal for a relational view of value creation and value capture. The nature of these problems is best understood in terms of two predictions from standard economic theory: self-interested employees would (1) not make firm-specific investments and (2) would shirk on contributing to the development and exploitation of collective HCRs. Relational models theory suggests, however, that whether or not employees will behave in this way depends on how they frame their relationships with others. Some of the models (MP, as well as the null relationship and asocial relationship mentioned in note 2) revolve around mental frames that will indeed lead to the behaviors assumed in standard economic theory, while other models (EM, AR, and CS) revolve around mental frames that lead to very different behaviors.

We believe that this fundamental insight has important implications for solving the motivational problems related to the creation of superior HC complementarities. Previous work in management on inter-firm relationships (Dyer and Singh, 1998; Madhok and Tallman, 1998) as well as on firm-specific investments by employees (Wang et al., 2009) has already argued that firms can circumvent the motivational problems highlighted in standard economic theory by using a relational rather than a transactional approach to managing relationships. What our elaboration on relational models theory adds to this work is a much finer-grained understanding of why and how such a relational approach might work. For example, an important implication of using relational models theory is that there is not one undifferentiated relational approach, but that there are four different approaches, each with their own specific effects on the motivational problems linked to HC complementarities.

In previous work we have argued that whenever value creation requires team production – in the sense that value creation processes involve multiple parties "who face high task and outcome interdependence in providing mutually supportive contributions to value creation" (Bridoux and Stoelhorst, 2016: 231) – individual stakeholders' motivation to contribute to the joint creation of value will be highest in a CS frame, followed by EM, AR, and finally MP (Bridoux and Stoelhorst, 2016). These arguments also apply to employees' motivation to develop and exploit HC complementarities. Motivation will be lowest in MP because in this frame each party is expected to perform rational cost-benefit calculations in order to obtain the highest individual payoffs in return for the lowest contributions (Fiske, 1991, 1992). As a result, commitment to the relationship will primarily be of a calculative nature. In other words, by making self-interest salient, MP triggers the very source of the motivational problems that may occur in situations of interdependence. In contrast, the other three models trigger mental frames in which self-interest is no longer central.

In an AR relationship, both parties (superior and subordinate) expect the other to take their interests into account. Commitment is based on mutual loyalty: the superior is expected to take pastoral care of the subordinate, who in turn is expected to respect the wishes of the superior. This model can help solve motivational problems because employees defer to the orders of their managers. At the same time, the success of the model in creating value hinges on superiors' intimate knowledge of how value is best created, which is likely to blunt its effectiveness whenever value creation is knowledge-intensive and depends on expert employees.

Such information asymmetries are less likely to be a problem in EM relationships. In these relationships, parties similarly expect the other to take their interests into account. Commitment is based on loyalty to the exchange partner, and this loyalty grows over time as parties reciprocate each other's behaviors. This model can help solve motivational problems because parties trust each other to keep contributing to the common good. At the same time, because partners are perceived as equal yet different, it is accepted that they do have their own goals, meaning that their interests are unlikely to be completely aligned.

Whereas in AR and EM relationships the focus on self-interest that is central to MP is balanced out by taking into account the interests of others, in CS self-interest disappears altogether. This is the case because CS triggers a mental frame in which individuals' identity becomes synonymous with the identity of the group. Loyalty is no longer to a beneficial exchange relationship (as in MP) or to an ongoing personal relationship with others (as in AR and EM), but to the collective. As a result, the collective interest substitutes for and in fact becomes the self-interest: what motivates employees is no longer what is good for themselves and/or for specific others, but what is good for the group. This reverses the predictions of standard economic theory: employees who frame their relationships with the firm and each other in CS terms will happily make firm-specific investments and contribute to the creation and exploitation of collective HCRs.

DISCUSSION AND CONCLUSION

Here we discuss two implications of adopting a relational view of value creation and capture, and conclude by suggesting a number of avenues for future research.

Behavioral Assumptions: From Pecuniary Benefits to Relational Rents

Much of the SHC literature builds on insights from labor economics and, consequently, either implicitly or explicitly starts from standard economic assumptions about human behavior, which is assumed to be rational and self-interested. At the same time, much of the progress in the SHC literature comes from relaxing such assumptions, e.g. by taking into account the trusting and affective as opposed to merely economic nature of human relationships (Chadwick, 2017; Wang et al., 2009). Our work ties in with this strand of theorizing in that it offers an alternative to the economic 'model of man': relational models theory paints a picture of human economic actors as fundamentally social creatures. The upshot is that economic relationships are inherently social and based on norms that guide value creation and capture. This is not to deny that human economic actors never behave as standard economic theory assumes they do. For example, in an MP frame putting one's self-interest first is acceptable behavior. Yet, even in MP, such behavior is only acceptable as long as it is consistent with the norm of equity.

One important implication for the SHC literature of adopting the more realistic behavioral assumptions of relational models theory is that it suggests a broader view of the value that firms create. The prevalent conceptualization of value creation – that the only, or at least the most relevant, value created by a firm is economic value – has been criticized as too narrow (Harrison and Wicks, 2013; Priem, 2007). Alternatively, we could define value creation much more broadly, to include "anything that has the potential to be of worth" to the firm's resource suppliers and customers (Harrison and Wicks, 2013: 101; Priem, 2007). As social animals, humans have a need to form and maintain non-aversive, stable interpersonal relationships, and this need constitutes "a powerful, fundamental, and extremely pervasive motivation" (Baumeister and Leary, 1995: 497). Fulfilling this fundamental need has multiple and strong effects on psychological well-being, while social isolation negatively impacts not just well-being but even health (Baumeister and Leary, 1995). It is therefore clear that, in addition to tangible economic value, employment relationships can also offer intangible value linked to the fulfillment of relational needs.

Relational models theory helps us understand the nature of this 'relational value'. More specifically, it suggests that the four relational models provide quite different psychological benefits because they each fulfill a very specific relational need. MP relationships can help employees fulfill their need for achievement. While people can sometimes feel proud of their achievements outside of relationships (e.g., when one solves a very difficult problem), the need for achievement is best fulfilled in social interactions, as one's own success is usually assessed in comparison to what others have achieved. Similarly, one's self-esteem is nurtured by others acknowledging success. The equity principle at the core of the MP model provides a particularly powerful metric to measure one's success and worth in others' eyes.

A CS model meets individuals' need to belong to a collective. It has long been argued that seeing oneself as a member of an organization – i.e., organizational identification – reflects a perception of belonging to that organization (Ashforth and Mael, 1989). Belonging to a collective supports psychological well-being because it feeds the individual's self-esteem and helps "reduce subjective uncertainty about one's perceptions, attitudes, feelings, and behaviors and, ultimately, one's self-concept and place within the social world" (Hogg and Terry, 2000: 124).

EM fulfills employees' need to be acknowledged as unique, worthy individuals. Individuals have a need to be accepted as different and distinctive (Hornsey and Jetten, 2004; Turner, 1991). Equality, the principle at the core of the EM model, supports individuals' perception of self-worth, as equality means that individual differences are accepted by the relational partner. In line with this, in their search for universal human values Schwartz and his colleagues found that the acceptance of others as equals is a value widely shared across human societies (Schwartz, 1994).

Finally, AR relationships fulfill different needs for superiors and subordinates. The subordinate can fulfill a need for deference and security. Being related to a powerful other who is benevolent provides a sense of control over future outcomes when these outcomes are (partly) under others' control and one is therefore vulnerable to their opportunistic behavior (cf. Thibaut and Walker, 1975). For the superior an AR relationship can meet a need for dominance. It may be difficult for superiors to fulfill this need without destroying the ground of the AR relationship – namely, the subordinate's perception that the superiors' authority is legitimate. Yet, if superiors exercise their power with pastoral care for their subordinates, subordinates will react by liking and trusting their superior more (Colquitt and Rodell, 2011; Yang et al., 2009), which in turn will lead to closer AR relationships (Cropanzano et al., 2001). Ideas about how to exercise power while taking care of subordinates have been developed in the literature on servant leadership (Greenleaf, 1977; van Dierendonck, 2011).

As more realistic behavioral assumptions lead to a broader view of the nature of the value created in economic relationships, the SHC literature should consider adopting a broader view of rents. In keeping with most of the strategy literature, at the outset of this chapter we defined rents as payments above opportunity costs. But this definition only considers the economic value that employees (or any other resource supplier) may capture. On a more sophisticated understanding of human nature, we should also consider the relational value that employees may derive from their relationship with the firm. One way of thinking about this value would be in terms of 'relational rents', which could be defined as the additional relational value that employees derive from their relationship with the firm over and above their best outside option.

The Microfoundations of Rents: Bridging Macro and Micro

Although much of the SHC literature focuses on macro-level dependent variables such as firm performance, it has always had an explicit interest in bridging individual and collective levels of analysis (Ployhart and Moliterno, 2011). In line with this, and in line with the broader microfoundations movement in strategy (Felin and Foss, 2005; Felin et al., 2015), our elaboration on relational models theory helps explain how HR practices at the macro level of the firm affect firm performance through their effect on shaping cognitive and motivational processes at the micro level of the individual. Similarly, although much of the SHC literature builds on economic theorizing, it has always had an explicit interest in linking up with research on strategic human resource management (SHRM), and HR systems in particular (Boon et al., 2018; Ployhart and Moliterno, 2011). In line with this, and in line with the message of Campbell and Kryscynski (this volume) that HR systems are at the core of competitive advantages based on HC, we help further bridge the SHC and SHRM literatures by suggesting that HR systems are crucial determinants of the relational models that employees will adopt to frame their relationships with the firm and each other.

More specifically, our relational view provides an explanation for the configurational nature of HR systems. That HR systems can be understood as configurations of HR practices has long been recognized by the SHRM literature (Delery and Doty, 1996), but relational models theory offers specific insights into the 'why', 'how' and 'when' of these configurations. On the 'why' question, relational models theory suggests that the configurational nature of HR practices derives from a fundamental aspect of human nature: that we structure our social relationships on the basis of four, and only four, relational models that each revolve around specific norms for value creation and capture. On the 'how' question, relational models theory suggests that given this aspect of human nature, combinations of HR practices will only work well if they consistently reflect the set of norms of one of the four relational models. And on the 'when' question, our elaboration on relational models theory in the context of value creation and value capture suggests that a crucial contingency variable in explaining the effect of different configurations of HR practices on firm performance is the degree to which value creation involves interdependencies. In line with this, in their recent review of ways to further integrate the SHC and SHRM literatures, Boon et al. (2018: 53) ask: "do some HR systems create more opportunities for the emergence of complementarities than other systems?" Our answer is 'yes': systems that trigger a CS frame create more opportunities than systems that trigger an EM or AR frame, which in turn creates more opportunities than systems that trigger an MP frame.

Avenues for Future Research

More research is needed in at least two areas. First, we have said very little about the emergence of the collective relational model that guides the choice of HR practices. A collective relational model is not only a contextual factor that, through HR practices, shapes the relational model employees adopt; it also emerges from the interactions among employees. We believe that several factors come into play in the process of emergence, inter alia: (1) the tendency of employees to favor a particular model over other models, which depends on individual-level stable characteristics such as social dispositions (Bridoux and Stoelhorst, 2016); (2) the nature of the interactions among employees (frequency of interactions, face-to-face or virtual, etc.); and (3) the capacity of the firm's leaders to communicate core values and norms. For example, if employees exhibit homogeneous social dispositions – e.g., because of selection and self-selection processes (cf. Bridoux and Stoelhorst, 2014; Jones, 1995) – then they are likely to adopt the same relational model to frame value creation and value capture, which will lead to harmonious relationships and reinforce this model as the collective relational model. As Bryant (2014) has argued for organizational culture, a collective relational model is likely to emerge relatively early in the life of an organization. It is also likely to be a relatively stable feature once it has become embedded in HR practices. Yet, new leaders can change a collective relational model even in larger and older firms, as illustrated by the turnaround in relationships at Continental Airlines that Gordon Bethune was able to effectuate after becoming president in 1994 (Higgins and McAllaster, 2004).

Second, more research is needed to understand the relationships between collective relational models and firm performance. The quality of the solution to the motivational problems inherent in the creation and exploitation of superior HC complementarities is not the only factor that determines the extent to which the firm, as a nexus of relationships, is able to generate rents: a particular relational model can also be more or less adapted to other aspects of the market activities the firm engages in. Importantly, the relational models impose different rules for decision-making (cf. bottom row in Table 2.1). These rules, in turn, imply different trade-offs between the accuracy of decisions, the speed of decisions, and maintaining group cohesion. Ideally, collective decision-making would be fast and accurate, while maintaining group cohesion. However, there is often tension between speed and accuracy of decisions (Beersma et al., 2003; Förster et al., 2003) and between speed and building consensus to maintain group cohesion. In fast-changing environments where firms need to make quick decisions to compete successfully, the trade-off should be solved in favor of speed over accuracy and consensus, whereas in environments where competition is focused on efficient execution, accuracy and consensus are more important than speed (Baum and Wally, 2003; Eisenhardt, 1989; Perlow et al., 2002: 1768).

Decision-making in the hands of legitimate leaders distributed throughout the organization in an AR model can support fast decision-making, but will sacrifice some accuracy as relevant knowledge of lower-level employees is more likely to be ignored than in the decision-making modes of the other models (Bridoux and Stoelhorst, 2016). In an MP model, decisions are made at all levels in the organization by employees who pursue rewards. In this sense, one could see decision-making in an MP model as extremely decentralized. Yet, at the same time, decisions are not guided directly by external markets; top managers decide on which key performance indicators to embed in the pay-for-performance systems.

> Pay-for-individual performance systems cannot automatically reflect changes in the firm's external environment. These systems rely on managers translating the desired firm-level outcomes into desirable individual-level outcomes or behaviors, which are then measured and rewarded. In this translation process, even if they aim to incentivize learning and innovation, managers are likely to be biased toward past successes. (Bridoux et al., 2017: 1768)

As such, we believe that the decision-making mode in MP is typically more centralized and leads to less adaptation to the firm's external environment than often assumed.

In contrast, as illustrated by Southwest Airlines (Gittell, 2003), efficient execution to compete in more mature markets requires a huge commitment of employees at all levels in the organization to foster bottom-up incremental innovations that need to be carefully selected before being rolled out on a larger scale. Such commitment can be obtained with a CS model and its consensus mode. Overuse of the top-down decision-making that characterizes MP (through the incentive system) and AR (leaders' directives) would kill these dynamics.

Finally, characterized by equal say, an EM relationship is conducive to the sharing of distributed knowledge and to the discussion of opposing views in an open-minded and constructive way. Both are important to making accurate decisions in the face of individuals' and groups' tendencies to favor knowledge that supports their initial preferences (Schulz-Hardt et al., 2000), as well as groups' tendencies to favor knowledge that is already held in common before engaging in the decision-making task (Brodbeck et al., 2007; Stasser and Titus, 1985). An EM relationship is conducive to these processes because the relational partners are perceived as different but equally able to contribute, and therefore as having equal say in the decision. Hence, an EM model can be a source of value creation for firms that innovate by combining knowledge distributed among their employees. In contrast, the search for harmony in CS relationships and the power differences in AR relationships are obstacles to knowledge sharing and constructive controversy (Nijstad and De Dreu, 2002).

To conclude, we have argued for a relational view of value creation and capture that explicitly acknowledges that an economic rationale based on self-interest is but one way of framing employment relationships. Moreover, this Market Pricing frame is ill-suited to governing economic relationships aimed at creating and exploiting superior HC complementarities. There are three additional ways of framing relationships that will better motivate employees to create and exploit firm-specific and collective HCRs. Firms can trigger these frames by implementing configurations of HR practices that are consistent with the norms of Authority Ranking, Equality Matching, or Communal Sharing.

CHAPTER SUMMARY

BOX 2.1 KEY TAKEAWAYS

1. How well firms are able to motivate their employees to develop the firm-specific and collective human capital resources that underlie rents from human capital complementarities depends on how employees mentally frame their relationships with the firm and each other.
2. Employees can frame relationships in four different ways: in terms of Market Pricing, Communal Sharing, Equality Matching, or Authority Ranking. Each of these frames triggers a different set of norms that affect both employees' motivation to create value and their expectations with regard to value capture.
3. Firms are more likely to generate rents from human capital complementarities with HR practices that signal an Equality Matching, Authority Ranking, and especially a Communal Sharing model than with HR practices that signal Market Pricing by relying on financial incentives that appeal to employees' self-interest.

BOX 2.2 DIRECTIONS FOR FUTURE RESEARCH

1. How does adopting the behavioral foundations of relational models theory change the SHC literature? How do the predictions and managerial implications of the SHC literature change if rents appropriated by employees are defined to include non-pecuniary relational benefits?
2. How do the collective mental models that guide the choice of specific configurations of HR practices emerge from interactions among individuals and groups in the organization? How do collective mental models change over time?
3. What are the mechanisms through which the different configurations of HR practices affect firm performance? What are boundary conditions to the proposed positive link between Communal Sharing, Equality Matching, and Authority Ranking (as compared to Market Pricing) and value creation?

NOTES

1. Self-interest can be defined much more broadly to include anything that brings utility to the individual (Simon, 1993). On such a broader definition, altruistic actions, which increase another's outcomes at a personal cost, can be classified as self-interested if they come with intangible benefits such as prestige or positive self-image.
2. The four models cover the social interactions among people. Fiske (1991, 1992) also recognizes 'null relationships' (when others are not seen in social terms and treated as if they were objects) and 'asocial relationships' (in which others are seen in social terms but treated as means to non-social ulterior ends).
3. While we acknowledge that culture and climate may be seen as different phenomena (Denison, 1996), this debate is of limited relevance for our arguments.
4. Readers interested in compensation systems that are based on the equity principle will find in Chapter 1 by Conroy in this volume an in-depth discussion of the implications of the choice between internal alignment (i.e., the value of the employee is determined by comparison to other employees) and a market pricing process (i.e., the value of the employee is determined by comparison to what s/he would get from other employers).
5. Altruism is used here to refer to little regard for one's own *material* payoffs. Social identity theory (Ashforth and Mael, 1989; Bergami and Bagozzi, 2000; Tajfel, 1982) suggests that when the community is a part of the employee's identity, pursuing the objectives of the community brings immaterial payoffs to the employee in the form of, for example, higher firm-based self-esteem.

REFERENCES

Aarts, H., and Dijksterhuis, A. (2003). The silence of the library: environment, situational norm, and social behavior. *Journal of Personality and Social Psychology*, *84*(1), 18–28.

Adams, J. S. (1965). Inequity in social exchange. In L. Berkowitz (ed.), *Advances in Experimental Social Psychology*, Vol. 2: 267–99. New York: Academic Press.

Adler, P. S. (2001). Market, hierarchy, and trust: The knowledge economy and the future of capitalism. *Organization Science*, *12*(2), 215–34.

Alchian, A. A., and Demsetz, H. (1972). Production, information costs, and economic organization. *American Economic Review*, *62*(5), 777–95.

Anderson, M. H., and Sun, P. Y. (2017). Reviewing leadership styles: Overlaps and the need for a new "full-range" theory. *International Journal of Management Reviews*, *19*(1), 76–96.

Arrow, K. (1974). *The Limits of Organization*. New York: Norton.

Arthur, J. B. (1994). Effects of human resource systems on manufacturing performance and turnover. *Academy of Management Journal*, *37*(3), 670–87.

Ashforth, B. E., and Johnson, S. (2001). Which hat to wear. In M. A. Hogg and D. J. Terry (eds), *Social Identity Processes in Organizational Contexts*: 32–48. New York: Psychology Press.

Ashforth, B. E., and Mael, F. (1989). Social identity theory and the organization. *Academy of Management Review*, *14*(1), 20–39.
Barney, J. B. (1991). Firm resources and sustained competitive advantage. *Journal of Management*, *17*(1), 99–120.
Baum, R. J., and Wally, S. (2003). Strategic decision speed and firm performance. *Strategic Management Journal*, *24*(11), 1107–29.
Baumeister, R. F., and Leary, M. R. (1995). The need to belong: Desire for interpersonal attachments as a fundamental human motivation. *Psychological Bulletin*, *117*(3), 497–529.
Becker, G. S. (1964). *Human Capital: A Theoretical and Empirical Analysis, with Special Reference to Education*. Chicago, IL: University of Chicago Press.
Beersma, B., Hollenbeck, J. R., Humphrey, S. E., Moon, H., Conlon, D. E., and Ilgen, D. R. (2003). Cooperation, competition, and team performance: Toward a contingency approach. *Academy of Management Journal*, *46*(5), 572–90.
Bergami, M., and Bagozzi, R. P. (2000). Self-categorization, affective commitment and group self-esteem as distinct aspects of social identity in the organization. *British Journal of Social Psychology*, *39*(4), 555–77.
Blau, P. M. (1964). *Exchange and Power in Social Life*. New York: Wiley.
Boon, C., Eckardt, R., Lepak, D. P., and Boselie, P. (2018). Integrating strategic human capital and strategic human resource management. *International Journal of Human Resource Management*, *29*(1), 34–67.
Bowen, D. E., and Ostroff, C. (2004). Understanding HRM–firm performance linkages: The role of the "strength" of the HRM system. *Academy of Management Review*, *29*(2), 203–21.
Brandenburger, A. M., and Stuart, H. (1996). Value-based strategy. *Journal of Economics and Management Strategy*, *5*, 5–24.
Brewer, M. B., and Gardner, W. (1996). Who is this "we"? Levels of collective identity and self representations. *Journal of Personality and Social Psychology*, *71*(1), 83–93.
Brickson, S. L. (2005). Organizational identity orientation: Forging a link between organizational identity and organizations' relations with stakeholders. *Administrative Science Quarterly*, *50*(4), 576–609.
Brickson, S. L. (2007). Organizational identity orientation: The genesis of the role of the firm and distinct forms of social value. *Academy of Management Review*, *32*(3), 864–88.
Bridoux, F., and Stoelhorst, J. W. (2016). Stakeholder relationships and social welfare: A behavioral theory of contributions to joint value creation. *Academy of Management Review*, *41*(2), 229–51.
Bridoux, F., Coeurderoy, R., and Durand, R. (2017). Heterogeneous social motives and interactions: the three predictable paths of capability development. *Strategic Management Journal*, *38*, 1755–73.
Bridoux, F. M., and Vishwanathan, P. (2018). When do powerful stakeholders give managers the latitude to balance all stakeholders' interests? *Business and Society*, https://doi.org/10.1177/0007650318775077.
Brodbeck, F. C., Kerschreiter, R., Mojzisch, A., and Schulz-Hardt, S. (2007). Group decision making under conditions of distributed knowledge: The information asymmetries model. *Academy of Management Review*, *32*(2), 459–79.
Bryant, P. T. (2014). Imprinting by design: The microfoundations of entrepreneurial adaptation. *Entrepreneurship Theory and Practice*, *38*(5), 1081–102.
Campbell, B. A., Coff, R., and Kryscynski, D. (2012). Rethinking sustained competitive advantage from human capital. *Academy of Management Review*, *37*(3), 376–95.
Chadwick, C. (2017). Toward a more comprehensive model of firms' human capital rents. *Academy of Management Review*, *42*(3), 499–519.
Cialdini, R. B., and Trost, M. R. (1998). Social influence: Social norms, conformity and compliance. In D. T. Gilbert, S. T. Fiske, and G. Lindzey (eds), *The Handbook of Social Psychology*: 151–192. New York: McGraw-Hill.
Cialdini, R. B., Kallgren, C. A., and Reno, R. R. (1991). A focus theory of normative conduct: A theoretical refinement and reevaluation of the role of norms in human behavior, *Advances in Experimental Social Psychology*, Vol. 24: 201–34. Burlington: Elsevier.
Clark, M. S., and Mills, J. (1979). Interpersonal attraction in exchange and communal relationships. *Journal of Personality and Social Psychology*, *37*(1), 12–24.
Cobb, J. A., and Flannery, G. S. (2017). These unequal states: Corporate organization and income inequality in the United States. *Administrative Science Quarterly*, *62*(2), 304–40.
Coff, R. W. (1997). Human assets and management dilemmas: Coping with hazards on the road to resource-based theory. *Academy of Management Review*, *22*(2), 374–402.
Coff, R. W. (1999). When competitive advantage doesn't lead to performance: The resource-based view and stakeholder bargaining power. *Organization Science*, *10*(2), 119–33.
Colquitt, J. A., and Rodell, J. B. (2011). Justice, trust, and trustworthiness: A longitudinal analysis integrating three theoretical perspectives. *Academy of Management Journal*, *54*(6), 1183–206.
Colquitt, J. A., Conlon, D. E., Wesson, M. J., Porter, C. O., and Ng, K. Y. (2001). Justice at the millennium: A meta-analytic review of 25 years of organizational justice research. *Journal of Applied Psychology*, *86*(3), 425–45.

Connelley, D. L., and Folger, R. (2004). The influence of relational models on perceptions of fairness in human resource systems. In N. Haslam (ed.), *Relational Models Theory: A Contemporary Overview*: 197–220. Mahwah, NJ: Erlbaum.
Cropanzano, R., Rupp, D. E., Mohler, C. J., and Schminke, M. (2001). Three roads to organizational justice. In G. R. Ferris (ed.), *Research in Personnel and Human Resources Management*, Vol. 20, 1–113. Greenwich, CT: JAI Press.
Delery, J. E., and Doty, D. H. (1996). Modes of theorizing in strategic human resource management: Tests of universalistic, contingency, and configurational performance predictions. *Academy of Management Journal*, *39*(4), 802–35.
Denison, D. R. (1996). What is the difference between organizational culture and organizational climate? A native's point of view on a decade of paradigm wars. *Academy of Management Review*, *21*(3), 619–54.
Deutsch, M. (1975). Equity, equality, and need: What determines which value will be used as the basis of distributive justice? *Journal of Social Issues*, *31*(3), 137–49.
Deutsch, M. (1985). *Distributive Justice: A Social-Psychological Perspective*. New Haven, CT: Yale University Press.
Dyer, J. H., and Singh, H. (1998). The relational view: Cooperative strategy and sources of interorganizational competitive advantage. *Academy of Management Review*, *23*(4), 660–80.
Eisenhardt, K. M. (1989). Making fast strategic decisions in high-velocity environments. *Academy of Management Journal*, *32*(3), 543–76.
Ennen, E., and Richter, A. (2010). The whole is more than the sum of its parts – or is it? A review of the empirical literature on complementarities in organizations. *Journal of Management*, *36*(1), 207–33.
Fehr, E., and Fischbacher, U. (2003). The nature of human altruism. *Nature*, *425*(6960), 785–91.
Fehr, E., and Gächter, S. (2000). Fairness and retaliation: The economics of reciprocity. *Journal of Economic Perspectives*, *14*(3), 159–81.
Fehr, E., and Gächter, S. (2002). Altruistic punishment in humans. *Nature*, *415*(6868), 137–40.
Felin, T., and Foss, N. J. (2005). Strategic organization: A field in search of micro-foundations. *Strategic Organization*, *3*(4), 441–55.
Felin, T., Foss, N. J., and Ployhart, R. E. (2015). The microfoundations movement in strategy and organization theory. *Academy of Management Annals*, *9*(1), 575–632.
Fischbacher, U., Gächter, S., and Fehr, E. (2001). Are people conditionally cooperative? Evidence from a public goods experiment. *Economics Letters*, *71*(3), 397–404.
Fiske, A. P. (1991). *Structures of Social Life: The Four Elementary Forms of Human Relations*. New York: Free Press.
Fiske, A. P. (1992). The four elementary forms of sociality: Framework for a unified theory of social relations. *Psychological Review*, *99*(4), 689–723.
Fiske, A. P. (2004). Relational models theory 2.0. In N. Haslam (ed.), *Relational Models Theory: A Contemporary Overview*: 3–25. Mahwah, NJ: Erlbaum.
Förster, J., Higgins, E. T., and Bianco, A. T. (2003). Speed/accuracy decisions in task performance: Built-in trade-off or separate strategic concerns? *Organizational Behavior and Human Decision Processes*, *90*(1), 148–64.
Galinsky, A. D., Ku, G., and Wang, C. S. (2005). Perspective-taking and self-other overlap: Fostering social bonds and facilitating social coordination. *Group Processes and Intergroup Relations*, *8*(2), 109–24.
Giessner, S., and van Quaquebeke, N. (2010). Using a relational models perspective to understand normatively appropriate conduct in ethical leadership. *Journal of Business Ethics*, *95*, 43–55.
Gittell, J. H. (2003). *Southwest Airlines Way: Using the Power of Relationships to Achieve High Performance*. New York: McGraw-Hill.
Gomez-Mejia, L. R., Berrone, P., and Franco-Santos, M. (2010). *Compensation and Organizational Performance: Theory, Research, and Practice*. Armonk, NY: Sharpe.
Gomez-Mejia, L. R., and Welbourne, T. (1991). Compensation strategies in a global context. *Human Resource Planning*, *14*(1), 29–41.
Greenleaf, R. K. (1977). *Servant Leadership: A Journey into the Nature of Legitimate Power and Greatness*. Mahwah, NJ: Paulist Press.
Harrison, J. S., and Wicks, A. C. (2013). Stakeholder theory, value, and firm performance. *Business Ethics Quarterly*, *23*(1), 97–124.
Haslam, S. A. (2001). *Psychology in organizations*. London: Sage.
Higgins, J. M., and McAllaster, C. (2004). If you want strategic change, don't forget to change your cultural artifacts. *Journal of Change Management*, *4*(1), 63–73.
Hogg, M. A., and Terry, D. J. (2000). Social identity and self-categorization processes in organizational contexts. *Academy of Management Review*, *25*(1), 121–40.
Hornsey, M. J., and Jetten, J. (2004). The individual within the group: Balancing the need to belong with the need to be different. *Personality and Social Psychology Review*, *8*(3), 248–64.

Jones, T.M. (1995). Instrumental stakeholder theory: A synthesis of ethics and economics. *Academy of Management Review*, *20*(2), 404–37.

Jones, T. M., Felps, W., and Bigley, G. A. (2007). Ethical theory and stakeholder-related decisions: The role of stakeholder culture. *Academy of Management Review*, *32*(1), 137–55.

Judge, T. A., and Piccolo, R. F. (2004). Transformational and transactional leadership: A meta-analytic test of their relative validity. *Journal of Applied Psychology*, *89*(5), 755–68.

Kabanoff, B. (1991). Equity, equality, power, and conflict. *Academy of Management Review*, *16*(2), 416–41.

Klein, P. G., Mahoney, J. T., McGahan, A. M., and Pitelis, C. N. (2012). Who is in charge? A property rights perspective on stakeholder governance. *Strategic Organization*, *10*(3), 304–15.

Larkin, I., Pierce, L., and Gino, F. (2012). The psychological costs of pay-for-performance: Implications for the strategic compensation of employees. *Strategic Management Journal*, *33*(10), 1194–214.

Lepak, D. P., and Snell, S. A. (1999). The human resource architecture: Toward a theory of human capital allocation and development. *Academy of Management Review*, *24*(1), 31–48.

Lieberman, M. B., Garcia-Castro, R., and Balasubramanian, N. (2017). Measuring value creation and appropriation in firms: The VCA model. *Strategic Management Journal*, *38*(6), 1193–211.

Madhok, A., and Tallman, S. B. (1998). Resources, transactions and rents: Managing value through interfirm collaborative relationships. *Organization Science*, *9*(3), 326–39.

Mahoney, J. T., and Kor, Y. Y. (2015). Advancing the human capital perspective on value creation by joining capabilities and governance approaches. *Academy of Management Perspectives*, *29*(3), 296–308.

Makowski, L., and Ostroy, J. M. (2001). Perfect competition and the creativity of the market. *Journal of Economic Literature*, *39*(2), 479–535.

Morrison, E. W., and Robinson, S. L. (1997). When employees feel betrayed: A model of how psychological contract violation develops. *Academy of Management Review*, *22*(1), 226–56.

Mossholder, K. W., Richardson, H. A., and Settoon, R. P. (2011). Human resource systems and helping in organizations: A relational perspective. *Academy of Management Review*, *36*(1), 33–52.

Nickerson, J. A., and Zenger, T. R. (2008). Envy, comparison costs, and the economic theory of the firm. *Strategic Management Journal*, *29*(13), 1429–49.

Nijstad, B. A., and De Dreu, C. K. W. (2002). Creativity and group innovation. *Applied Psychology*, *51*(3), 400–406.

Nyberg, A. J., Maltarich, M. A., Abdulsalam, D. D., Essman, S. M., and Cragun, O. (2018). Collective pay for performance: A cross-disciplinary review and meta-analysis. *Journal of Management*, *44*(6), 2433–72.

Ouchi, W. G. (1980). Markets, bureaucracies, and clans. *Administrative Science Quarterly*, *25*(1), 129–41.

Perlow, L. A., Okhuysen, G. A., and Repenning, N. P. (2002). The speed trap: Exploring the relationship between decision making and temporal context. *Academy of Management Journal*, *45*(5), 931–55.

Peteraf, M. A. (1993). The cornerstones of competitive advantage: A resource-based view. *Strategic Management Journal*, *14*(3), 179–91.

Plitt, M., Savjani, R. R., and Eagleman, D. M. (2015). Are corporations people too? The neural correlates of moral judgments about companies and individuals. *Social Neuroscience*, *10*(2), 113–25.

Ployhart, R. E., and Moliterno, T. P. (2011). Emergence of the human capital resource: A multilevel model. *Academy of Management Review*, *36*(1), 127–50.

Ployhart, R. E., Nyberg, A. J., Reilly, G., and Maltarich, M. (2014). Human capital is dead; long live human capital resources! *Journal of Management*, *40*(2), 371–98.

Priem, R. L. (2007). A consumer perspective on value creation. *Academy of Management Review*, *32*(1), 219–35.

Rai, T. S., and Fiske, A. P. (2011). Moral psychology is relationship regulation: Moral motives for unity, hierarchy, equality, and proportionality. *Psychological Review*, *118*(1), 57–75.

Rousseau, D. M. (1995). *Psychological Contract in Organizations: Understanding Written and Unwritten Agreements*. Newbury Park, CA: Sage.

Rowley, T. I., and Moldoveanu, M. (2003). When will stakeholder groups act? An interest- and identity-based model of stakeholder group mobilization. *Academy of Management Review*, *28*(2), 204–19.

Rumelt, R. P. (1987). Theory, strategy, and entrepreneurship. In D. J. Teece (ed.), *The Competitive Challenge*: 137–58. Cambridge, MA: Ballinger.

Schuler, R. S., and Rogovsky, N. (1998). Understanding compensation practice variations across firms: The impact of national culture. *Journal of International Business Studies*, *29*(1), 159–77.

Schulz-Hardt, S., Frey, D., Lüthgens, C., and Moscovici, S. (2000). Biased information search in group decision making. *Journal of Personality and Social Psychology*, *78*(4), 655–69.

Schwartz, S. H. (1994). Are there universal aspects in the structure and contents of human values? *Journal of Social Issues*, *50*(4), 19–45.

Simon, H. A. (1993). Altruism and economics. *American Economic Review*, *83*(2), 156–61.

Sluss, D. M., and Ashforth, B. E. (2008). How relational and organizational identification converge: Processes and conditions. *Organization Science*, *19*(6), 807–23.

Stasser, G., and Titus, W. (1985). Pooling of unshared information in group decision making: Biased information sampling during discussion. *Journal of Personality and Social Psychology*, *48*(6), 1467–78.

Suazo, M. M., Martínez, P. G., and Sandoval, R. (2009). Creating psychological and legal contracts through human resource practices: A signaling theory perspective. *Human Resource Management Review*, *19*(2), 154–66.
Tajfel, H. (1982). Social psychology of intergroup relations. *Annual Review of Psychology*, *33*(1), 1–39.
Thibaut, J. W., and Walker, L. (1975). *Procedural Justice: A Psychological Analysis*. Hillsdale, NJ: Erlbaum.
Tomasello, M. (2016). *A Natural History of Human Morality*. Cambridge, MA: Harvard University Press.
Tsui, A. S., Pearce, J. L., Porter, L. W., and Tripoli, A. M. (1997). Alternative approaches to the employee-organization relationship: Does investment in employees pay off? *Academy of Management Journal*, *40*(5), 1089–121.
Turner, J. C. (1991). *Social Influence*. Milton Keynes, UK: Open University Press.
Turner, J. C., Oakes, P. J., Haslam, S. A., and McGarty, C. (1994). Self and collective: Cognition and social context. *Personality and Social Psychology Bulletin*, *20*(5), 454–63.
Tyler, T. R. (2006). Psychological perspectives on legitimacy and legitimation. *Annual Review of Psychology*, *57*, 375–400.
van Dierendonck, D. (2011). Servant leadership: A review and synthesis. *Journal of Management*, *37*(4), 1228–61.
Van Lange, P. A. M., Joireman, J., Parks. C. D., and Van Dijk, E. (2013). The psychology of social dilemmas: A review. *Organizational Behavior and Human Decision Processes*, *120*(2), 125–41.
Vohs, K. D., Mead, N. L., and Goode, M. R. (2006). The psychological consequences of money. *Science*, *314*(5802), 1154–6.
Wang, H., He, J., and Mahoney, J. (2009). Firm-specific knowledge resources and competitive advantage: The roles of economic- and relationship-based employee governance mechanisms. *Strategic Management Journal*, *30*(12), 1265–85.
Weitz, B. A., and Jap, S. D. (1995). Relationship marketing and distribution channels. *Journal of the Academy of Marketing Science*, *23*(4), 305–20.
Williamson, O. E. (1979). Transaction cost economics: The governance of contractual relations. *Journal of Law and Economics*, *22*(2), 233–61.
Yang, J., Mossholder, K. W., and Peng, T. K. (2009). Supervisory procedural justice effects: The mediating roles of cognitive and affective trust. *Leadership Quarterly*, *20*(2), 143–54.
Zenger, T. R., and Marshall, C. R. (2000). Determinants of incentive intensity in group-based rewards. *Academy of Management Journal*, *43*(2), 149–63.

3. Commentary on "Setting base pay rates: integrating compensation practice with human capital value creation and value capture"

Russell Coff and Clint Chadwick

INTRODUCTION

Pay Setting: Where the Rubber Hits the Road . . . But Still Only Part of the Picture

Russell: Sam really has the right idea here. Strategy scholars tend to ignore processes for setting base pay. However, in order to understand human capital-based competitive advantages, we really must understand the routines by which pay is systematically set.

Clint: Agreed. I think we're going to need to be able to keep a big picture framing along with the nitty-gritty of how pay setting actually works. To me, the big picture opportunities for rents would reflect chances for firms to leverage these pay setting processes in unique ways. For value creation, I expect that uniqueness would, in turn, affect some other construct such as worker motivation on the job, inducements to invest in skills, or coordination amongst workers. In other words, it's hard for me to picture pay setting routines affecting value creation without some significant mediating constructs, and mapping out those mechanisms empirically may be one opportunity to move strategic human capital research forward. Value capture could be simpler if it involves somehow paying workers at a discount relative to their value creation; though that's not the only way that pay setting could affect value capture, as Sam goes into later in the chapter.

Russell: Yes, it isn't pay setting alone. There are clearly complementarities within HR systems as well as with other resources and capabilities. Still, the role of pay setting in this context tends to be glossed over.

Clint: So the big picture takeaway for SHC scholars is that the tactical issues around how firms actually do pay setting (and other key human capital processes) can be strategic. This is a theme that we have heard before from strategic HRM (SHRM) scholars. However, SHRM authors, conceptually, tend to stress how "bundling" HR practices can make those "tactical" HR practices be "strategic" by incorporating them into HR systems where they become mutually enhancing. Our implicit emphasis is, instead, on uniqueness driven by linkages with other contextual variables. Am I reading too much into this here? The difference would be what SHRM scholars describe as internal HR system fit on the one hand and external HR system fit on the other. It would seem that these need to be complementary perspectives, but perhaps SHRM and SHC scholars have inclinations to emphasize one of these more than the other.

The Widely Accepted Best Practice, Market-Based Pay, Eliminates Human Capital Rents

Clint: The point that a market-based compensation approach negates the chances for firms to garner human capital rents (p. 60) has been mentioned before in the SHC literature. However, thinking of Sam's arguments, this point assumes not only that that labor market itself doesn't have imperfections such that the market reflects human capital value in use, but also that the process by which firms translate labor market price and quality signals into workers' compensation is efficient and straightforward. I suppose that if the latter is imperfect, it is really also a market imperfection, but not one we've given a lot of attention to, as this occurs within firms. In other words, can there be exploitable imperfections in how firms translate market signals by running those market signals through managerial systems?

Russell: Yes, there are all kinds of assumptions about efficiency. That said, if the firm is only seeking to reflect the market as opposed to trying to understand (and take advantage of) inefficiencies, the only chance of value creation/capture through this process would be luck. My suspicion is that firms are rarely adept at identifying such inefficiencies. Most probably don't even try.

Clint: Yes, it would seem to require a lot of "organizational introspection" for firms to leverage this kind of imperfection, and perhaps they are just moving too fast to do much of this on purpose. So luck would be a good candidate for advantage in these types of jobs, to the extent that advantage exists, which would seem to be pretty rare. There is another alternative, though, which is *disadvantage*. It's not hard to imagine firms screwing up these complicated pay setting processes. Could a firm have an edge if it isn't screwing up compensation as badly as its competitors are? Maybe firms engage in market-based compensation when they're trying to avoid screwing up more than trying to get an advantage.

Pay Satisfaction Doesn't Explain Much about Turnover

Russell: As an aside, the correlation between voluntary turnover and pay satisfaction is only −0.15. That sure leaves lots of room for other factors that the firm might leverage to retain people at lower pay levels.

Clint: Agreed. Lots of unexplained variance in that relationship, and probably significant, exploitable imperfections, as well.

Renegotiating Pay Poses Exploitable Imperfections, Too

Clint: I can see why Sam simplified her focus to initial wage setting (p. 16) in order to get her hands around the chapter, but that leaves out a really big part of the phenomenon: what do firms and employees do after actual value in use becomes less ambiguous than it was *ex ante* to employment? Mapping out the opportunities for competitive advantage in that renegotiation process is itself an opportunity for value capture, and perhaps can spur value creation, too, in ways that may matter more than the initial pay setting process in some contexts. Some insurance sales functions, for instance, claim that it's not possible to figure out who is going to be a good salesperson prior to hiring, so they hire lots of people and then put a lot of effort into the wage renegotiation process with the successful salespeople after a probationary period. That said, it's interesting to me that firms would rather fire workers whose value in use declines relative to their wage than renegotiate their wages downward. Workers' wages typically are either increasing or stagnant, but they rarely go down.

Russell: It's also common to pay people for previous productivity after it has dropped (thinking of Poppo and Weigelt's, 2000, baseball free agent story). If a firm could figure out how to renegotiate down, it really could be an advantage.

Clint: Interesting point! Why don't firms do downward renegotiations? Are they afraid of losing those workers? Why would they care if those workers' productivity has gone down? Are they afraid of peripheral effects on the rest of the workforce?

COMPETITIVE ADVANTAGE THROUGH STRATEGIC HUMAN CAPITAL RESOURCES

What Should Firms Do with Hard-to-Observe Human Capital Value in Use?

Russell: Firm-specificity and the multilevel nature of complementarities are key attributes of competitive advantage that should affect base pay. Of course it's reasonable to focus on these, and I think they yield some really important insights. One might also want to consider hard-to-observe individual contributions (tacit knowledge, complex expertise, interpersonal knowledge, and informal social networks) that facilitate productivity. These may also have implications for setting base pay.

Clint: Russ, I wonder about the implicit assumption that workers' pay should reflect those hard-to-observe contributions. If the value is hard to observe to the firm, are there occasions where workers don't know how much value they are creating, too? Wouldn't it be better not to let them know so they don't try to bargain with the firm over that value?

Russell: I don't know that they can prevent bargaining over the value. For complex tasks the actual value in use may never quite be apparent to the firm or employees. Valuing sales representatives is relatively easy since they directly generate revenue streams, but other types of positions are much harder to value. So, this raises the question of how people respond when there is ambiguity about their value in use. Some scholars assume that workers don't bargain for that value and it would naturally flow to the shareholders. However, I would guess that there is an upward, self-serving, bias in most people's assessments of their value creation. As such, ambiguity may tend to increase the claims on value created rather than reduce them.

Clint: Your comment, Russ, reminds me of a key point in equity theory, which is that equity evaluations are perceptual. If you're right that the self-serving bias you describe would be more acute as ambiguity about workers' use value grows, then a firm might experience a double whammy, as equity dissatisfaction could be higher in ambiguous circumstances, too.

VERTICAL PAY VARIATIONS: JOB-BASED PAY SETTING

What Happened to ILMs?

Russell: Where have internal labor markets (ILMs) gone? I'm somewhat stunned that so many firms use market pricing for every single position. Perhaps the greatest contribution of job evaluation is that it provides a basis for evaluating idiosyncratic jobs for which there isn't a mature external labor market. This means that some firms rely very little on internal labor markets, while others use poor market proxies to price idiosyncratic jobs. This seems like a real opportunity for firms that are able to manage idiosyncratic jobs within ILMs effectively.

Clint: Yeah, I wondered that, too, especially with Sam's discussion. I see the demise of ILMs as a partial consequence of the increase in relative influence of the finance function and the ideology of efficient markets. Unfortunately, standard finance modeling and the ideology of the market that underlie it values market efficiency over capturing the upside opportunities for human capital Ricardian rents. This can limit efficiency losses for the firm from its human capital, but also forfeit rents. For example, ILMs may be less "efficient" than market pricing in some sense, but they are not less profitable in all conditions. It depends on whether an ILM can exploit a labor market imperfection for the benefit of its firm, such as when it's valuable to induce workers to invest in firm-specific skills. But ILMs are seen as riskier in markets that are dynamic, and that is a big factor in their demise.

Various Forces Reduce Variance in How Firms Pay Workers – Paving over Opportunities for Competitive Advantage

Clint: The discussion has me thinking again about where the opportunities are for firms to differentiate themselves. Much of the discussion to this point suggests that the real action isn't in trying to shape the labor market segment or the firm's positioning in relation to the labor market, but instead in how jobs are evaluated and priced by the firm. In other words, the competitive advantage story to this point is in job evaluation more than in compensation per se.

Russell: Of course, job evaluation often drives compensation, and I do see it as a key strategic element. It seems like job evaluation needs to be quite firm-specific to be a source of advantage – tied to the truly unique aspects of the firm's capabilities and strategy. My sense is that, in practice, it is often more industry-specific. For example, while it doesn't seem like other airlines (than Southwest) value customer service (IMHO), there are some that do – and this, alone, might not promote an advantage if adopted more widely. This leads me to a personal "aha!" moment. Consultants and professional norms (SHRM) facilitate the spread of effective job evaluation, but also may minimize the focus on firm-specific aspects. These can improve performance, but mainly this might promote competitive parity. This also may mean that there are great opportunities for the few that take a firmer specific approach.

Clint: Good point, Russ. In the Dave Ulrich manner of thinking about HR, this is, perhaps, a consequence of a "loss-avoidance" approach to HRM rather than an emphasis on opportunity maximization. So, perhaps professional norms in HRM are also pushing towards uniformity, in addition or even complementary to the power of the market-based approach to pricing HC. We also shouldn't forget the employment law considerations that inform nearly everything that HR does in practice, which can flatten out the variance in how workers are treated within firms.

Russell: How much latitude do firms really have when choosing a pay approach? It seems evident that the approach *should* match the strategy and context (technology, etc.). If a firm has many idiosyncratic jobs and a structured ILM with limited ports of entry, a job evaluation system that focuses internally should be essential. In the absence of such an ILM, pursuing a more internally focused job evaluation system might actually destroy value – the firm would still go to the market to fill most positions, so external equity is critical for every position. To what extent do firms adopt systems that match their context and strategies? Do consultants and professional norms in the field of HR acknowledge these contextual factors to facilitate matching (or do efforts to adopt best practices actually exacerbate the tendency to mismatch)?

Clint: I suspect that the differences that we observe in employee pay are due in part to pay policy (broad approaches to how the firm's pay compares to the market) and, also, to differences in the firm's ability to negotiate and close the deal to recruit an employee. Given the description here, perhaps the action is not as much in the former (which would be translated into pay ranges attached to particular jobs) but in the position on the pay range that a specific employee occupies, which would be primarily a value capture story (discussion on p. 25). Is it more plausible that a firm could have a heterogeneous and inimitable capability to maintain a pay policy position with its workforce generally or to negotiate favorable positions on a pay range across its employees?

Appropriating Value from Firm-Specific Skills May Be a Rare Happy Accident

Russell: In the end, do firms offer any systematic base pay adjustment for firm-specific skills? Job evaluation systems seek to place a value on idiosyncratic jobs that cannot be easily matched in the labor market. In doing so, is there any systematic downward or conservative bias such that more value is captured from idiosyncratic jobs? My sense is that the effort is to create realistic external reference points for such jobs so that it isn't clear that the firm captures more value. However, if such routines existed, that might be important to explore and document.

Clint: Given the lack of conscious interest in firm-specific skill among practitioners that we have been hearing about from our SHRM colleagues, it does make me wonder how much of firm-specific human capital (FSHC) rents are accidental rather than purposeful. And, if a firm were to identify FSHC's value creation, would that give employees more incentive to bargain for a piece of that value? Maybe it would be better for some firms to just not give FSHC rents explicit attention in the compensation system and induce them through less direct mechanisms like norms and culture? That is, do we really want the system to be accurate? That assumption seems to be driving the approaches to job evaluation among HRM practitioners.

HORIZONTAL PAY VARIATIONS: PERSON-BASED AND WITHIN-GRADE PAY SETTING

Firms May Not Capture Value from Stars, But Players around a Star May Allow Firms to Capture Value

Russell: Sam doesn't really talk about red circle pay rates, but that may be an important aspect – especially when there are significant differences in individual capabilities. Of course, merit pay is beyond the scope of her focus, but I think this might still be an element of base pay. Recognizing idiosyncratic individual capabilities (e.g., stars) in setting base pay could carry substantial strategic importance.

Clint: Well, that opens up another interesting angle when we think of value capture, in particular. Could the value capture story be about the observability of workers' value in use (this is becoming a theme)? What your comment has me thinking, Russ, is about whether you might have to pay stars the equivalent of what they contribute because it's clear what their use value is. But with complementary, "B" players whose contributions are less obvious, you can capture more rents relative to their use value because it's not so clear. It would be ironic if the high value in use "stars" aren't where you're getting the human capital rents because you have to pay them too close to their use value.

Russell: So how much does the market for lemons really apply (see p. 26)? Sam points to Bidwell's finding that external hires are often paid more – but may perform at lower levels. Firms do pay more when they poach to coax the person into the market. Of course, poaching occurs to avoid hiring lemons. Digging deeper, did the previous person exit because the pay was low? In other words, did the firm try to appropriate too much so the employee left to capture more of her value? This might force the firm to pay the full value in order to hire externally. Relatedly, where internal hires are paid less but choose to stay, what makes them want to stay? Did they do an external search and still find good reason to stay, or was there no external search? These are all important questions for understanding the link between pay policy and competitive advantage.

Clint: Russ, are you thinking of the market for business professors? I wonder if that dynamic of the market for lemons and human capital poaching is getting too much attention in general in SHC. Obviously, it happens and it matters: e.g., whether LeBron James goes to the Lakers has a big impact on the NBA. But maybe we should examine the *relative* impact of key players on value creation in a particular firm instead of implicitly assuming that star employees have uniformly high value relative to other workers. There are only a few stars, and there are a lot of other workers. Poaching and pay inequality impact value creation from the other, non-star, employees in the firm, and under certain conditions maybe it's not worth it to poach a star when all is said and done.

Who Captures Value from Complementarities? It May Not Go to the Firm

Russell: Who gets the value of complementarities or unit level-value? While this might be a team effort, that might mean that multiple employees take credit for the value created (e.g., self-attribution bias). In this way, team production is expected to result in more claims on the value created rather than fewer. Where there is ambiguity about individuals' contributions, the sum of the claims may well exceed the total value created (Blyler and Coff, 2003). In addition, if firms in an industry experience similar complementarities, some or all of the resulting unit-level value may be reflected in base pay. While these would be unlikely to drive firm-level rents (Chadwick, 2017), it is important to recognize that such complementarities may be rolled into base pay even if they cannot be traced to individuals' contributions. While you point out that *idiosyncratic* complementarities may be the source of human capital rents, more routine complementarities may still be reflected in base pay (as opposed to being captured by shareholders).

Clint: This is a great point. So if you're right about this, Russ, then the strategic story here is about avoiding screwing up in accurately paying people what they're worth. You generally need to pay people what they're worth in order to avoid creating equity concerns in the workforce; but you also need to make sure that you're not overpaying in situations where individuals' contributions are not clear. So in this case, HRM practitioners' emphasis on accuracy may be useful for their firms – not for rent creation or capture, but to avoid human capital losses, which is something we haven't given much attention.

CONCLUSION

Value Creation and Capture are Often Loosely Linked: How Do the Dynamics of Ambiguity Play Out?

Clint: In general, this discussion points to a firm-level capability that may lead to human capital rents: the ability to predict future value in use. But there may be another, less benign one here, as well: the ability to induce workers to underestimate the value of their contributions to the firm. Let's say you were good at that, which is a value capture capability. What would that do to workers' discretionary effort and value creation? I guess I'm questioning the implicit assumption of the need for accuracy in pricing human capital value in use in all cases.

Russell: That said, variations in pay must be perceived as legitimate. Often value is created when there are hard-to-observe individual differences or complementarities create ambiguity about individuals' roles in generating unit-level value. In this case, horizontal variation in pay may be hard to justify as legitimate. However, it may be apparent that the value is created by the team and the loss of any team member might seem to put that value creation in jeopardy. Accordingly, the value might therefore be distributed back to the team evenly to maintain perceptions of equity and fairness.

Clint: Similarly, an issue that I was thinking about throughout Sam's chapter is how much *should* a firm acknowledge and pay for such hard-to-observe/value employee contributions? In terms of value capture, we might prescribe that a firm should pay as little as possible; but if it does that, then it can reduce employees' value creation by decreasing their discretionary effort. So where is the tipping point? How much value capture should a firm take before employees' affective and cognitive reactions make it counterproductive in terms of value creation (note, e.g., the equity discussion on p. 29)? I assume that some of the contingencies at play are whether the employment relationship is long term and how much the work is interdependent (and what types of interdependencies are at play).

Concluding Comments

As the preceding discussion illustrates, we find a lot of value in Samantha Conroy's close look at the pay setting process in firms. Sam's chapter focuses our attention on this process, with implications for both description and prescription. The chapter describes a lot of variance in how firms approach pay setting issues, and our discussion of the points that it raises suggests that there are a variety of strategic approaches that firms could take in addressing those issues. Future research that sorts out the efficacy of firms' various approaches to these issues could significantly advance the strategic human capital research stream (see summary Boxes 3.1 and 3.2). More broadly, this close look at pay setting suggests that many other human capital management processes in firms could also be fruitful places for SHC scholars to explore.

CHAPTER SUMMARY

BOX 3.1 KEY TAKEAWAYS

1. Economists typically assume wages are set equal to the worker's marginal product (use value). However, pay setting is not a straightforward translation of value in use into workers' compensation. There are ambiguities and inefficiencies in this process that offer firms opportunities to capture rents from this process.
2. Pay setting necessarily encompasses other HR activities, such as job design and performance appraisal, which can create advantages (e.g., through HR practice complementarities) and complexity that inhibits operational effectiveness. At the same time, most firms actively seek to match the external market, and efforts to capture value are actually quite limited (e.g., in the case of firm-specific human capital).
3. The process by which firms renegotiate pay with workers has similarities and differences with ex ante pay negotiations, but is generally an under-researched topic in strategic human capital. Ongoing pay adjustments, then, may not track as closely with changes in productivity (value in use) as is often assumed.
4. Ambiguity regarding the accuracy of firms' perceptions of their workers use value poses both descriptive and prescriptive challenges for strategic human capital scholars. The pay setting literature tends to focus more on information asymmetries at the time of hiring, but imperfect information in internal labor markets may also be substantial.

BOX 3.2 DIRECTIONS FOR FUTURE RESEARCH

Compensation issue	Related research question(s)
Ambiguity in valuing workers' value creation	What are workers' bargaining (value capture) reactions to such ambiguity? Do compensation demands regularly exceed value in use? How do firms respond in that case? What are the strategic issues in compensation renegotiation after a period of performance?

	How can firms be significantly better than their competitors at perceiving workers' use value?
Strategic intent in compensation	Which strategic issues influence firms' compensation decisions? To which workers does strategic intent tend to apply most? When is standardized compensation better for unit performance than intra-unit variance in compensation? How does a firm resist the institutional pressures to standardize compensation?
Market-based pay	Which contingencies are most favorable for utilizing market-based compensation? Is the best frame for decision making under this approach human capital loss avoidance or human capital value creation? Does the use of market-based pay for all positions assure that employees capture most of the value created? How/when are complementarities reflected in market-based pay (e.g., if all rivals have similar complementarities)?
Job analysis and compensation for idiosyncratic jobs	Idiosyncratic jobs may be most likely to involve firm-specific human capital. How do firms value those jobs, and how do their valuation approaches affect the portions of that value captured by firms and workers? What would strategically valuable, firm-specific job evaluation capabilities look like?

REFERENCES

Blyler, M., and Coff, R. W. (2003). Dynamic capabilities, social capital, and rent appropriation: Ties that split pies. *Strategic Management Journal*, *24*(7), 677–86.

Chadwick, C. (2017). Towards a more comprehensive model of firms' human capital rents. *Academy of Management Review*, *42*(3), 499–519.

Poppo, L., and Weigelt, K. (2000). A test of the resource-based model using baseball free agents. *Journal of Economics and Management Strategy*, *9*(4), 585–614.

4. Commentary on "Rents from human capital complementarities: a relational view of value creation and value capture"

Clint Chadwick and Russell Coff

THE NEED FOR A RELATIONAL VIEW

The Distinctiveness of the Relational Models is the Big Proposition

Clint: Perhaps the key issue of the chapter is, are these different configurations mutually exclusive, or can you partition the workforce to have different employment relationships? In that respect, this chapter is pointing out a disconnect between the logic epitomized by Lepak and Snell (1999) that allows for such variation in employment relationships within firms, and Bowen and Ostroff's (2004) "strong situation" logic wherein all of the HR practices should be aligned to the same type of employment relation in order for their effects to be mutually reinforcing. Is the relational model approach more consistent with Bowen and Ostroff? More generally, how much variance from these models could one observe within a firm before a particular relational model gets too muddled to work effectively?

Russell: Good point. I imagine some variation may naturally exist across functions, departments and locations. Of course, the "pure types" may be impractical in varying degrees. Most firms would have to be hybrids. Which configurations might be most appropriate for which functions or types of business unit? Is this too close to selective intervention (which Williamson suggested is untenable)?

Clint: So, not to be clichéd, the question may be an empirical one: how much are these pure types reflected in practice, and how inconsistent are they with each other? There is also a prescriptive question here about how much consistency in employment system(s) within firms is best for effectiveness.

Russell: Yes, we tend to assume firms are more homogeneous in their practices than is probably the case. Much of research on HR practices uses single-informant surveys to gauge practices firm-wide. This works for smaller single-business firms with limited geographic scope. However, for most complex organizations, I imagine practices must vary substantially. Why, then, wouldn't the type of configuration also vary? This suggests a need for empirical work on variation in configurations within firms.

Clint: One way I'm thinking about this issue is that there are different types of human capital complementarities, and that these different types of complementarities are connected to different types of employment relationships because they each demand different relational models. So that's a different take on moving the Lepak and Snell framework forward, I suppose. If that is so, then there are two different ways to screw up employment relationships with respect to human capital rents: 1) picking the wrong relational model for the human capital complementarities in question; and 2) mismatching of an ostensibly effective complementarities/HR system pairing to organizational contingencies. This is akin to what SHRM scholars call internal and external HR system fit, respectively. Perhaps a framing around this would allow the tradeoffs discussed on p. 52 to be specified in greater detail, as it might suggest some propositions about the more effective types of matchups on these two dimensions.

Russell: I suspect there are many more ways to screw up (something I have some expertise in). Of course, this is ultimately a very complex problem. My suggestion that a single configuration might work for a simpler firm (single business, etc.) may be off. Even within that environment, there may be many different types of human capital complementarities. Somehow there must be enough nuance to accommodate different relationships. Perhaps this is where individuals come in. Routines may not be terribly flexible, but putting the right individual to manage a function may allow for more variation in the configurations.

Market Pricing (MP)

Wow, no complementarities: what, then, are the necessary conditions for the MP model to be successful?

Russell: The distributive rule is *to each according to her merits* (p. 43). It appears to me that this is very focused on value in use. Do we mean that labor markets are efficient and wage = marginal revenue product? Put another way, the discussion actually suggests a very strong focus on internal equity: "Employees' payoffs . . . should therefore be in proportion to their inputs . . . as compared to other employees' inputs" (p. 43). I guess I was surprised to see that the market pricing model focuses so extensively on internal equity as opposed to an external labor market wage. Maybe I'm misunderstanding.

Clint: I'm actually glad to see this in here as a counterpoint to the other types of relational models discussed elsewhere in the chapter. As Flore and J.W. suggest, the MP approach is going to work best when there are no real complementarities among workers with respect to value creation. This condition is what we might call, in classic organizational theory terminology, pooled interdependence. The key to pooled interdependence is avoiding losses by making sure that the independent efforts of each worker aren't detracting from each other with respect to the outcome, i.e., to make sure that 2+2 isn't adding up to less than 4. That process is going to require aligning workers' efforts in some way (e.g., perhaps by management direction, perhaps by incentives, perhaps by work design), so I would expect such managerial alignment systems to be a requirement of the MP system. That is, despite the orientation towards the market, since we're inside firms, managerial systems are still critical to making this work.

Russell: I hadn't thought of it that way – hard to imagine a firm with no complementarities at all. That might suggest firms that are homogeneous in resource endowments. Of course, this is a theoretical construct, so all worlds can be considered. Another way to look at it is that this requires that individual contributions are easily observable and measurable. Piece rate systems can be very effective but many/most jobs cannot be organized around this pay system. It also can have very negative implications when coordination or team production are required.

Clint: Yes! In fact, the reference in the description of the MP system to equity is intriguing. Per equity theory, workers' assessments of equity are perceptual and typically egocentrically biased. So I expect that worker performance (i.e., value creation) needs to be explicit and easily discernable by all parties or the system will create big motivational problems. This can be a result of having performance like team production that is ambiguously related to individual workers; but I would also expect that the MP system can also break down simply from workers' perceptions going wrong, say, by overestimating their own value in use.

Russell: Indeed, this may be a fairly common pain point for the MP system or a boundary condition for when it can be effectively applied. The firm that can resolve equity problems in the context of moderate ambiguity may effectively enjoy an advantage.

Clint: Aren't there also implicit requirements in the MP system that workers' value creation needs to be observable to external parties and that workers are portable from firm to firm? If so, then is this system an ideal type that we use as a conceptual reference point, but we'd expect to be very rare in practice? (This would be akin to how we treat the concept of perfectly competitive markets.)

Russell: That's how it seemed to me. If so, it's hard to discuss competitive advantage in this context. We need to have some friction to generate rents. Put another way, you need to put the rabbit into the hat before you can pull it out.

Communal Sharing (CS)

CS as a pure type

Clint: As a pure type, I can understand the CS case, but as a practical matter I'm having a hard time thinking of situations in which workers' self-interest disappears completely. Maybe it doesn't have to go all the way to self-interest being gone. I wonder what the practical point would be where CS dynamics start to take over.

Russell: You've attended too many faculty meetings ;-). Of course, all of the "pure types" may be impractical in varying degrees. Most firms would have to be hybrids. Having said that, clearly this is closest to Ouchi's "clan," and we do know that some firms rely more on culture to motivate workers. Even within the academic world, I would argue that culture makes some departments much more effective than others. The question is how to maintain it when you have personnel changes on a fairly regular basis.

Clint: Hmmmm. I'm fuzzy on the distinctiveness of the CS and the EM models in practice. I can see them as pure types, but it seems to me that the orientation of the system towards obligations to others is more distinct as pure types than they would be in practice. The "otherness" orientation in CS is towards the community, while in EM it is more of an implicitly dyadic orientation towards the firm as a partner. Either way, the worker is oriented towards the firm, but "the firm" is a community of colleagues on the one hand, and an anthropomorphized partner on the other. I can see those distinct conceptions blending, however. But it is a distinction that has some similarities with one you have been playing with, Russ, in asking who we're talking about when we say that "the firm" gets human capital rents. The way I read it, that discussion among SHC scholars has largely been about value capture. Are Flore and J.W. suggesting that human capital value creation is also contingent on how workers define "the firm"?

Russell: Ok, now you're going to get me on a rant. We typically use the words "firm" and "organization" interchangeably. However, I think they are distinct and we need to be more precise. *Firm* is generally drawn from an economics perspective and may be considered as a "legal fiction" whose boundaries are defined by the ownership of assets. In contrast, an *organization* is a "system of consciously coordinated activities" (Barnard, 1938) – its boundaries are defined by cooperation rather than ownership. Sometimes we are interested in ownership and we should refer to the firm. However, most of the time we are interested in cooperative efforts, and asset ownership is only one means to influence cooperation. When we use the term *organization*, rents can be generated and/or captured outside of the legal boundaries of a given firm. So, yes, I think that may be what Flore and J.W. are suggesting. Ok, I'd better get off my hobby horse – sorry about that.

Flatter pay structures

Russell: Some firms certainly do have flatter pay structures. I'm not sure if this always reflects workers' needs so much as equity. Also, would group rewards fall under need or is that more about equity in the context of team production?

Clint: Maybe Flore and J.W. are suggesting that the question is more of a performance one: Do flat pay structures that are seen as operationalizing equality across workers lead to more value creation than flat pay structures that are built on the equity of being tied to workers' differing value in use?

Russell: Perhaps we need to tie this more closely to the underlying complementarities. This would be more team production oriented (unlike MP), so individual contributions may not be known. In this context, perhaps equity is closer to equality. In a team production context where a monitor cannot effectively untangle contributions, Alchian and Demsetz (1972) suggest that teams will revert to profit sharing (as opposed to using the residual value to incentivize a monitor).

Equality Matching (EM)

Overlaps with Ouchi's framework

Russell: I struggled with this one a bit since I am so accustomed to Ouchi's markets/hierarchies/clans framework. It seems more focused on norms for reciprocity at a dyadic level as opposed the strong identification with the firm that CS seems to imply.

Clint: Yeah, me too. Back to my earlier comment: to the extent that the CS and EM distinction collapses in practice, we have some congruence between the markets (MP), clan (CS/EM), and hierarchy (AR) approaches. Using a strategic HRM lens, would it be a correct interpretation to say that the CS approach emphasizes organizational capital, while EM emphasizes social capital? Or is it more accurate to say that they leverage different *types* of organizational capital and social capital?

Russell: I think you may have it. They are relying on different mechanisms, but they are both ultimately relational in nature. One may draw on organizational identification (CS) while the other (EM) depends on social networks within the firm and norms for social interaction within those networks. In practice, these norms may be intertwined. That is, organizational identification may motivate workers, but in order to realize value from complementarities they must interact and cooperate. As such, CS cannot operate without norms for social interaction.

Equity and complementarities as key characteristics

Russell: Using Sam Conroy's terms, this would seem to suggest less horizontal pay variation, but there might still be vertical pay variation. As such, the overall pay structure might not appear flat. Of course, this depends on the employees' equity reference points. It may be that other jobs are still relevant for assessing equity.

Clint: I'm also wondering which types of complementarities are best fitted to the EM model. Reversing myself a bit from the earlier comment, perhaps the CS model might be best fitted to complementarities that arise among a group of workers that are related to collective HCR. In contrast, EM can work when the need is for workers' discretionary effort but the interdependencies are lower. One way to put this is that I can see EM influencing value creation, but perhaps it could be used solely as non-financial compensation that supports value capture without influencing value creation much.

Authority Ranking (AR)

Coordination mechanisms

Russell: My first assumption was that this fit Ouchi's (or Williamson's) discussion of hierarchies. The focus on legitimate power derived from positions of authority seems to fit this (or perhaps a Weberian perspective). However, I think the addition of charismatic or transformational leadership puts it in another category. When we add this individual-level factor, I wonder if the compensation practices might reflect the individuals' values. In other words, a charismatic leader might espouse a flat structure emphasizing equality or a steep structure emphasizing individual merit (tournament style).

Clint: In any case, one issue this goes back to is the mechanisms that coordinate workers' efforts, which is an appropriately big topic if the question is how firms induce complementarities. I mentioned earlier that managerial mechanisms have to be part of the MP story. They are clearly part of the AR approach, as well, and I would suggest that there are managerial coordination mechanisms inherent in the CS and EM system, as well. If one is within the firm, there is simply no way to get around managerial systems. If one were able to fully utilize market mechanisms within the firm instead, then the rationale for having a firm in the first place goes away. The real question is, *which* managerial mechanisms are most appropriate in a given circumstance? That points to a contingencies approach that could be usefully mapped out here.

RELATIONAL MODELS AS SOLUTIONS TO MOTIVATIONAL PROBLEMS

Russell: Here, Flore and J.W. argue that the relational models may address individuals' reluctance to invest in firm-specific human capital. In practice, it is rare for employees to resist firm-specific investments. I believe that they may be suggesting that the relational models are efficiently deployed in the wild, and thus help explain why this isn't a problem that we observe more regularly.

Clint: That's an intriguing proposition. I am typically skeptical of the idea that the organizational forms that we observe in practice are the effective ones; the "market" for organizational forms seems to me to often be dramatically inefficient, particularly in the short term (as evidenced by various and future management fads). I wonder if a firm would get beneficial firm-specific human capital investments if it had *any* of these models, as long as the model that it employed had internal fit/alignment, or if the matches between specific models and organizational contingencies are also necessary (i.e., external fit). This seems like a testable proposition to me.

Russell: Good point. I tend also to be skeptical that efficiency reigns supreme out there in the wild. Digging deeper, it seems to me that the CS and EM configurations would rely heavily on workers being socialized into the firm's values and norms. Then, they might subsequently be more willing to invest in firm-specific knowledge and skills. This may be hard to square with the socialization literature which suggests that new employees actively seek firm-specific knowledge and skills upon arrival (Morrison, 1993). As such, very early on, workers may think of firm-specific skills as having a positive utility as opposed to requiring a costly investment. The AR system involves routines (and authority structures) that require employees to make such investments and which they must accept in order to join the organization. This is closer to a zone of indifference in that workers grant the organization a legitimate right to ask them to make such investments. The logic may require assortative matching to identify employees who accept the organization's authority readily or those norms may be embedded in society so they tend to be shared by most workers.

Clint: This is an interesting comment. It suggests a micro-foundations research question: "What are the determinants of employees' reactions to inducements for firm-specific investments?" You and Raffiee recently published some work in this area, and I think it's one of the under-researched areas of big opportunity in strategic human capital.

Russell: Thanks for the shout-out. There is much I feel we don't understand. More broadly, I think the relational models might have important implications for realizing complementarities necessary to create unit level value. These may also have important implications for how much "rent" is captured by employees as opposed to other stakeholders (like shareholders).

Clint: The authors point to HR practices as a way to operationalize different relational models, but underlying the HR practices are different approaches to managerial coordination and, in turn, different managerial ideologies/value systems. Unpacking those linkages could be valuable, and there are empirical findings in HRM that could help flesh this out. One of the things that we know, for instance, is that managerial values regarding relational models can be imprinted early in a firm's history, and then tend to persist and are manifest in organization structures, HR practices, etc. Thus, firms may both consciously decide on different relational models and also inherit them from their pasts in ways that have a lot of inertia.

Russell: Yes, and inherited practices can be functional or dysfunctional. It also occurs to me that firms might outgrow a given configuration. For example, we know that entrepreneurial firms may tend toward the CS configuration – especially if they are driven by a social mission. But when they grow up (think Ben & Jerry's), they require a new configuration (AR?) and this transition creates a great deal of turmoil.

CONCLUDING COMMENTS

As the preceding discussion illustrates, it is intriguing to take a close look at how configurations may be linked to value creation in the context of human capital complementarities. In addition, such configurations may have significant implications for how value is ultimately captured. Flore and J.W.'s chapter focuses our attention on these organizing principles, with implications for both description and prescription. Our discussion of the points that they raise suggests that there is ample room for additional research in this area (see Box 4.2). We see the need for both theoretical and empirical advances to explore various aspects of the configurations and their relationships to value creation and capture.

CHAPTER SUMMARY

BOX 4.1 KEY TAKEAWAYS

1. Theoretic configurations of employment practices can be built around different conceptions of the employment relationship that workers have with firms, which may, in turn, reflect different types of human capital complementarities.
2. The observability of workers' value creation may be a key factor in determining which relational model suits a particular context.
3. Managerial coordination systems are key to successful relational models, even the market pricing model.
4. Relational models have a variety of determinants in addition to strategic choice, and a great deal of inertia.

BOX 4.2 DIRECTIONS FOR FUTURE RESEARCH

Relational models issue	Related research question(s)
1. Distinctiveness of the relational models	To what degree can different relational models exist in the same organization before inconsistencies between them inhibit their effectiveness too much?

2.	Causal mechanisms with performance	Are the mechanisms that influence models' effectiveness motivation, coordination, or affective/identity oriented? Do employees' reactions to opportunities to invest in firm-specific skills vary with the relational system that they are inhabiting?
3.	Specific characteristics of the relational models	What are the different types of human capital complementarities that are operationalized in these different relational models? What are the differences in managerial systems required by different relational models?
4.	Performance contingencies	Do simpler, smaller firms have an advantage in being able to focus on fewer relational models?
5.	Dynamic relational configurations	Do firms outgrow their configurations? Does this help explain transitions firms undergo as they move through the organizational lifecycle? Can there be firm-specific capabilities in managing transitions between relational models?

REFERENCES

Alchian, A. A., and Demsetz, H. (1972). Production, information costs, and economic organization. *American Economic Review*, *62*(5), 777–95.

Barnard, C. (1938). *The Functions of the Executive*. Cambridge, MA: Harvard University Press.

Bowen, D. E., and Ostroff, C. (2004). Understanding HRM–firm performance linkages: The role of the "strength" of the HRM system. *Academy of Management Review*, *29*(2), 203–21.

Lepak, D. P., and Snell, S. A. (1999). The human resource architecture: Toward a theory of human capital allocation and development. *Academy of Management Review*, *24*(2), 31–48.

Morrison, E. W. (1993). Longitudinal study of the effects of information seeking on newcomer socialization. *Journal of Applied Psychology*, *78*(2), 173–83.

PART II

MULTILEVEL APPROACHES: EMERGENCE

5. Human capital resource emergence: theoretical and methodological clarifications and a path forward*

Rory Eckardt and Kaifeng Jiang

INTRODUCTION

The extant work on human capital resource emergence (HCRE), which is defined as the transformation and amplification of individual human capital into a unit-level human capital resource (Ployhart and Moliterno, 2011), has made great contributions to the field of strategic human capital. In particular, it has played a pivotal role in drawing attention to the complex multilevel and social-psychological considerations involved with valuable human capital resources (Barney and Felin, 2013; Nyberg et al., 2014; Ployhart et al., 2014; Wright and McMahan, 2011), thereby providing a platform for integrating micro and macro and other varied perspectives on human capital (Boon et al., 2018; Eckardt et al., 2018a; Felin et al., 2015; Nyberg and Ployhart, 2013; Ployhart, 2015; Ployhart and Hale, 2014). As a result, the work on HCRE has laid the groundwork for a truly integrated and holistic understanding of the development and maintenance of human capital as an important unit-level resource.

There are several aspects of the scholarly work on HCRE that need more attention and clarity before the full impact of HCRE on the field can be realized though. First, while existing work has identified broad categories and considerations with respect to emergence enabling factors, the underlying mechanisms and processes are unclear (cf. Felin et al., 2015; Mathieu and Luciano, 2018). That is, we need more detailed understanding of the actual changes and dynamics that occur during the HCRE process. Second, the specific manner through which HCRE leads toward the development of human capital-based competitive advantage could be more clearly specified (Nyberg et al., 2018). In particular, more attention is needed on how some aspects of HCRE may involve greater interfirm heterogeneity, isolating mechanism, and bargaining positions – factors that have important implications for competitive advantage to be achieved with human capital resources (Campbell et al., 2012; Chadwick, 2017; Coff, 1997; Molloy and Barney, 2015). Third, there is scant advice available on the ways to operationalize and empirically examine HCRE. These challenges stem, in part, not only from lack of precision and traceability in the extant theorizing related to HCRE, but also from the more general limited consideration given to multilevel methods for bottom-up effects and processes (Hitt et al., 2007; Kozlowski and Chao, 2012; Kozlowski et al., 2013; Mathieu and Chen, 2011; Moliterno and Ployhart, 2016).

The purpose of this chapter is to make progress on these aspects of HCRE that need more attention and clarity. The first three sections focus on issues related to the underlying theoretical mechanisms and processes, competitive advantage implications, and methodological considerations and approaches. The final section outlines several needed next steps to advance research on HCRE. Specifically, we call for:

1. more collaborations with strategic human capital and micro-oriented researchers and state-of-the-science reviews of micro-oriented topics related to the HCRE emergence enabling factors;
2. thinking of HCRE as a broad integrating framework for research related to human capital resources;
3. increased use of process-based theorizing with improved traceability;
4. more explicit attention to emergence in aggregation techniques for unit-level human capital resources;
5. greater consideration and use of dyadic perspectives;
6. added clarity and focus with respect to the potential for multiple HCRE processes to simultaneously occur in a firm and vary in magnitude and form of their strategic significance; and
7. more *empirical* research on HCRE.

UNDERLYING THEORETICAL MECHANISMS

Ployhart and Moliterno's seminal paper on HCRE leverages the more general work in management on the concept of emergence (e.g., Kozlowski and Klein, 2000) to describe the processes involved with how individual knowledge, skills, abilities, and other characteristics (KSAOs) are transformed and amplified to result in a valuable unit-level human capital resource. The emergence of unit-level human capital resources is suggested to take a fuzzy composition form (Ployhart and Moliterno, 2011). Fuzzy composition forms of emergence refer to situations where the higher-level construct has a similar meaning to the lower-level construct, but differs in that the higher-level construct has contextual influences (Bliese, 2000). In the context of human capital, this type of emergence means that individual and unit-level human capital both refer to stocks of KSAOs that are relevant for economic value and productive purposes (Ployhart et al., 2014) – however, the unit-level resource involves additional contextual factors that influence the nature of the unit's stock of KSAOs and their deployment in the productive function of the firm.

The contextual influences on both the stock and deployment of KSAOs are thus the crux of the HCRE process. Ployhart and Moliterno (2011) contend that these contextual influences relate to characteristics of, and interplay between, the task and social environment in which unit members are situated. In particular, they identify task complexity and several behavioral (coordination, communication, and regulation), cognitive (unit-climate, unit-memory, and unit-learning), and affective (cohesion, trusting environment, and positive unit affect) unit-level states that are likely to exert direct and interactive effects on the HCRE process. These are referred to as the emergence enabling mechanisms of unit-level human capital resources.

The subsequent sections seek to extend the baseline model of HCRE outlined by Ployhart and Moliterno (2011) by explicating and clarifying the underlying theoretical mechanisms involved with this emergent process. We begin with noting the criticality of considering individual factors when theorizing about this emergence process, then move to clearly define the *transformation* and *amplification* aspects of HCRE and connect these aspects to the previously identified emergence enabling mechanisms.

Criticality of Individual Actions and Changes

The general notion of emergence was put forth by Kozlowski and Klein (2000, p. 55): "A phenomenon is emergent when it originates in the cognition, affect, behaviors, or other characteristics of individuals, is amplified by their interactions, and manifests as a higher-level, collective phenomenon." This definition highlights that while emergence involves moving to a higher-level construct, the mechanisms through which this occurs involve individual factors. In particular, emergent phenomena start from *individual* characteristics and evolve into higher-level phenomena through *individual* actions and interactions. It follows that unpacking the underlying mechanisms and processes of emergent phenomena involves an important focus on individual actions and changes (cf. Felin et al., 2015; Kozlowski et al., 2013; Lang and Bliese, 2018; Lang et al., 2018).

Consistent with this idea, a key factor involved with improving our understanding of HCRE involves giving greater primacy to individual actions and changes. In particular, our theorizing needs to focus on the individual actions and changes that are foundational to and create an emerged unit-level human capital resource. This suggested focus on individual actions and changes does not negate the role of contextual factors that reside at a higher-level analysis. As mentioned above, such factors are the crux of the HCRE process (Ployhart and Moliterno, 2011). Rather, the point is that individuals are a focal level of analysis to understand how these contextual factors drive individual actions, and changes to their characteristics and productive capacities to result in a valuable unit-level resource.

Transformation and Amplification

The HCRE process has been described as involving the transformation and amplification of individual KSAOs into a valuable unit-level human capital resource (Ployhart and Moliterno, 2011). These two aspects, transformation and amplification, are not explicitly defined in the original work on HCRE. That said, a close reading of the HCRE and related work reveals that there are, in essence, two important processes and changes that are going on during HCRE that map to these concepts. The first involves changes to the individual stock of KSAOs that occurs via knowledge transfer and learning from unit-member interactions. That is, through working and interacting with unit members, individual KSAOs are *transformed* during the emergence process. Depending on the nature of the task environment and coordinating factors used, such changes to individual KSAOs could involve increases to the overall stock of KSAOs held by unit members, as well as situations where the nature of KSAOs converge or diverge over time (Ployhart et al., 2014). As described below, this transformation aspect can also refer to the development of colleague-specific knowledge involved with streamlining and sequencing actions, shared mental models, and transactive memory. Additionally, transformation can include learning from the external environment in which a unit is situated.

The second important process involves the *amplification* of the value derived from individual KSAOs. This aspect relates to the concept of complementarities (Ployhart et al., 2014) and refers to the creation of contextual factors that enhance the performance/value that can be generated by a particular stock of individual KSAOs (Crocker and Eckardt, 2014; Ployhart and Cragun, 2017). There are likely to be motivation- and cognitive-oriented mechanisms that allow for amplifying/complementary effects in the

HCRE process. The motivation-oriented mechanisms refer to situations where contextual factors encourage unit members to put forth additional effort, and the cognitive-oriented mechanisms are contextual factors that allow unit members to allocate a greater portion of their limited cognitive capacities on unit tasks (Boon et al., 2018) – both of which can increase the performance derived from a given level of KSAOs (La Pointe and Engle, 1990; Vroom, 1964). The amplification aspects are the underlying synergistic component of HCRE, creating a situation where the performance generated by a unit is larger than that which is solely attributable to the unit's individual KSAO parts.

In sum, the transformation and amplification aspects of HCRE represent contextual influences that improve the overall value derived from an initial stock of KSAOs in a unit. The transformation aspect captures learning from unit members (i.e., augmentation of initial KSAOs of unit members), which can directly improve the efficiency and effectiveness of task-related activities (Hatch and Dyer, 2004; Ployhart et al., 2011), and the amplification aspect captures complementarities that improve the performance derived from a given stock of KSAOs. It is the valued performance improvements that derive from these transformation and amplification aspects (which are driven by contextual influences) that result in an initial stock of KSAOs emerging into a valuable unit-level human capital resource.

Roles in the Emergence Enabling Factors

The HCRE process is influenced by the interrelationship of the task and social environment of a unit (Ployhart and Moliterno, 2011). A valuable unit-level human capital resource does not always emerge from the mere hiring and grouping of individual human capital. Rather, the degree to which HCRE occurs depends on the nature of tasks and presence of particular behavioral, cognitive, and affective states. The remaining part of this section provides background on these important considerations, and describes how the underlying transformation and amplification dimensions of HCRE are associated with the task and emergence enabling states (see Table 5.1 for a summary). For space and consistency reasons, we keep our discussion of the HCRE emergence enabling factors focused on the specific categories and considerations that were mentioned as part of theoretical framework developed by Ployhart and Moliterno (2011).

Task complexity

A unit's task complexity can be characterized along a number of dimensions, but a critical component is the manner in which work flows between individuals (Ployhart and Moliterno, 2011). The most simple task environments are those that involve *pooled* workflow structures. For these environments, individuals complete their tasks separately and involve little interaction or coordination with other members of the unit (Thompson, 1967). These environments tend to be associated with low levels of dynamism and require weak social ties among individuals (Bell and Kozlowski, 2002). The next two task environments that represent increased complexity are *sequential* and *reciprocal* workflow structures. Sequential workflow structures involve situations where work tasks move between individuals in a unidirectional successive manner, whereas reciprocal workflow structures are those that have bidirectional movement of work tasks between people (Thompson, 1967). As these workflow structures involve more

Table 5.1 Summary of transformation and amplification aspects of human capital resource emergence by emergence enabling categories

Emergence Enabling Broad Category	Emergence Enabling Subcategory	Impact on Human Capital Resource Emergence
Task Complexity	Workflow Structure Pooled ↓ Group	Accentuating transformation and amplification effects of behavioral, cognitive and affective enabling states
Behavioral	Coordination	Transformation and Amplification
	Communication	Transformation
	Regulation	Transformation
Cognitive	Unit-climate	Transformation and Amplification
	Unit-memory	Transformation and Amplification
	Unit-learning	Transformation
Affective	Cohesion	Transformation and Amplification
	Trusting Environment	Transformation and Amplification
	Positive Attitude/Mood	Transformation and Amplification

Note: Transformation refers to augmentation of unit-member KSAOs, and amplification refers to enhancing the performance/value derived from a unit's stock of KSAOs.

interaction and interdependence among the individuals in the unit, they often require more coordination and stronger social ties. Additionally, dynamism often increases for these workflow structures as the interdependencies between individuals create the potential for more uncertainty and variability (Bell and Kozlowski, 2002). The final broad category of workflow structures, *group-based*, represents the most complex task environment. In this workflow structure, individuals work together to complete tasks in a simultaneous and multidirectional manner (Van de Ven et al., 1976). This task environment requires considerable coordination, collaboration, and dependence among individuals (Kozlowski et al., 1999). As such, the group-based workflow structure involves significant dynamism and requires strong social linkages between individuals (Van de Ven et al., 1976).

Ployhart and Moliterno (2011) maintain that task complexity influences the potential for a unit-level human capital resource to emerge. Specifically, as the workflow structure results in more task complexity, there is greater within-unit interaction and interdependence that can facilitate the sharing and conveyance of KSAOs among individuals and accentuate the importance of coordination and relational aspects (Ployhart and Hale, 2014). These, in turn, can impact the transformation and amplification aspects of HCRE. It is instructive to note that while task complexity provides the potential for a valuable unit-level human capital resource to emerge, the mere presence of workflow structures that result in high levels of task complexity do not necessitate such emergence. That is, the transformation and amplification aspects will not automatically occur as a function of a unit using a particular task workflow structure. Rather, the degree to which a unit-level human capital resource emerges depends on the presence of appropriate behavioral, cognitive and affective enabling states (Ployhart and Hale, 2014).

Emergence enabling states

As noted above, the emergence enabling states of the unit relate to the behavioral, cognitive, and affective conditions in the unit. These three states influence the emergence of human capital by establishing the social environment in which the unit operates (Kozlowski and Ilgen, 2006). Ployhart and Moliterno (2011, p. 135) refer to these states as influencing how unit members "act, think and feel." In many ways, these social environment factors are the "engine" of the HCRE emergence process.

Behavioral Behavioral processes relate to factors that influence unit members' actions. This potentially can involve a wide array of factors, but is largely influenced by coordination, communication, and regulation considerations (Kozlowski and Ilgen, 2006). Coordination relates to the manner in which unit members interact and work together to complete a focal task. It involves decisions and processes associated with allocating individuals to specific task activities. As these decisions can have a complementary effect by appropriately matching and deploying unit members' KSAOs to tasks (Crocker and Eckardt, 2014), coordination can have an influence on the amplification aspect of HCRE. Coordination can also impact the transformation aspect of HCRE though. In particular, coordination decisions can impact the frequency in which particular unit members work together on tasks, and this can have important implications for the diffusion of knowledge among workers (Argote, 1999; Nonaka and Takeuchi, 1995). Coordination also relates to finding ways to streamline and synchronize interactions and interfaces of individuals and work products. This can be achieved by standardizing work component interfaces and/or individuals developing knowledge about the work practices and preferences of unit members. The latter would be a case of colleague-specific knowledge that develops to improve the efficiency and/or quality of unit outputs (cf. Campbell et al., 2014).

Communication refers to the frequency and openness in which unit members exchange information and ideas. It can help facilitate coordination of actions among unit members, thereby enhancing this dimension of the behavioral enabling state (Kozlowski and Ilgen, 2006). Communication can also aid in the sharing and transferring of knowledge between individuals within the unit (Argote, 1999). While this can obviously relate to explicit knowledge that is easy to transfer between individuals, it also can help facilitate the conveyance of tacit-oriented knowledge. Specifically, frequent and open communication can encourage the sharing of stories that can embody tacit-oriented knowledge (Brown and Duguid, 1991). Additionally, it can allow for the repeated and prolonged discourse needed to convey tacit-oriented knowledge between individuals (Dreyfus and Dreyfus, 1986; Hansen, 1999). As such, communication can help transform the stock of knowledge held by the individuals in a unit.

Behavioral regulation captures the degree to which the unit members' behaviors are guided by explicitly set goals, monitored and corrected for deviation from actions consistent with goals, and involve *ex post* task reflection (Marks et al., 2001). Such regulation can be an important way through which individuals learn and improve over time. For example, the regulation process can help draw an individual's attention to salient situational considerations and redirect actions in ways that improve efficiency and/or quality. As such, the use of behavioral regulation approaches can help transform the individual KSAOs in a unit. Additionally, it can help facilitate open communication and coordination among unit members (Kozlowski and Ilgen, 2006), thereby positively impacting unit-level human capital resource emergence indirectly through its effect on these other behavioral-enabling dimensions.

As a whole, these behavioral factors can aid in the emergence of human capital resources by transforming the individual KSAOs in the unit and amplifying their link with value/performance. These behavioral factors can be beneficial to the emergence of valuable unit-level human capital resources in simple and complex task environments (Ployhart et al., 2014); however, their importance is likely to increase drastically in situations of greater task complexity due to the enhanced need in such settings to have streamlined and synchronized actions between individuals (Ployhart and Moliterno, 2011).

Cognitive Cognitive states at the unit level pertain to shared cognitive structures and orientations (Kozlowski and Ilgen, 2006). Three broad unit-oriented cognitive states have been suggested to be particularly relevant to HCRE: unit-climate, unit-memory, and unit-learning. Unit-climate relates to the degree to which shared norms have been established for the manner in which individuals in the unit interact and communicate (Rentsch, 1990). The development of shared norms requires that individuals in the unit obtain knowledge related to appropriate ways to exchange information and interact. This can be thought of as the accumulation of unit-specific knowledge, and thus can impact the KSAOs of the individuals in the unit (Ployhart and Moliterno, 2011). As such, unit-climate can influence HCRE through the transformation aspect. However, the more salient impact of unit-climate is potentially related to its ability to enhance the performance that can be obtained from a given level of KSAOs. Specifically, the shared norms related to unit-climate provide mental schema or scripts that guide thought processes and actions in a more automatic manner (cf. DiMaggio, 1997). This frees up individuals' limited cognitive and attention resources to focus on the task, which, in turn, can allow for improved utilization of KSAOs to positively impact performance (Crocker and Eckardt, 2014; Schmader and Johns, 2003). In this way, unit-climate can also enable the emergence of unit-level human capital resources by having an amplifying effect on the performance/value obtained from a given stock of KSAOs.

Unit-memory refers to the procedural and declarative knowledge developed by unit members from working together over a period of time (Ployhart and Moliterno, 2011). These shared memories have a task focus and pertain to two broad types of unit-specific knowledge. The first is shared knowledge about the task, or unit-mental models. Such mental models refer to situations where unit members develop considerable overlap in declarative (i.e., know about) and procedural (i.e., know how) knowledge pertaining to tasks (Cannon-Bowers et al., 1993). For example, individuals in a unit may develop similar knowledge with respect to potential approaches or tools that can be used for various aspects of a task, or how to effectively deploy these approaches/tools with the other unit members to complete tasks. The former is declarative-oriented knowledge and context neutral, whereas the latter knowledge involves a procedural orientation and colleague-specific elements regarding work practices and preferences. The second type of shared knowledge is transactive memory. Transactive memory refers to metaknowledge that develops regarding the knowledge endowments held by other members in the unit – i.e., who knows what (Argote and Ren, 2012). As individuals in a unit develop such metaknowledge, it allows for greater coordination and integration of the KSAOs of unit members (Ployhart and Moliterno, 2011). Additionally, transactive memory promotes greater specialization among individuals (Ren and Argote, 2011), and this can also enhance the degree to which members in the unit learn from task-oriented experiences over time. Both types of unit-memory (shared mental models and transactive memory) augment the knowledge held by individuals in the unit. Additionally, such colleague-specific and shared understandings can potentially improve the utilization and deployment of KSAOs in a given unit (Mathieu et al., 2000; Ren and Argote, 2011) and thus also potentially lead to improved value/performance derived from a unit's stock of KSAOs. As such, unit-memory can influence HCRE through the transformation and amplification aspects.

Unit-learning refers to the ability to acquire, internalize, and exploit knowledge from the external environment (Ployhart and Moliterno, 2011). While a considerable amount of knowledge is available in the external environment, research suggests that individuals, groups, and firms vary in respect to their ability to see value in, obtain, and utilize such knowledge (Cohen and Levinthal, 1990; Huber, 1991; Volberda et al., 2010). Units that arc able to effectively learn from the external environment can positively impact the HCRE process by augmenting the KSAOs of unit members. In this way, unit-learning influences HCRE through the transformation dimension.

The unit-level cognitive states contribute to HCRE by transforming individual KSAOs and amplifying the value/performance generated from the KSAOs. While these are potentially important in any task environment, they are likely to have accentuated importance in complex task environments given the enhanced need in such environments for unit-member interaction and coordination (Ployhart and Moliterno, 2011).

Affective Affective states refer to a broad category of factors that can influence how individuals "feel" when they are working in a particular unit. As it relates to the emergence of unit-level human capital resources, three factors have been highlighted as likely to be particularly important: cohesion, trust, and positive emotional orientation (Ployhart and Moliterno, 2011). The first factor, cohesion, pertains to the degree to which unit members: 1) enjoy working with the individuals associated with the unit (Evans and Jarvis, 1980); 2) are committed to the unit members (Hackman, 1987) and mission (Carron, 1982; Goodman et al., 1987); and 3) feel pride for their association with the unit (Festinger, 1950). Cohesion can positively impact HCRE through both the transformation and amplification aspects. In particular, cohesion is likely to help high-quality relationships develop between individuals which can be helpful in the sharing and diffusion of knowledge (Ployhart and Moliterno, 2011; Szulanski, 1996). Additionally, the enjoyment and commitment individuals feel in cohesive environments is likely to motivate individuals to put forth more effort in their task-related activities (Beal et al., 2003). This can create an amplifying impact in the sense that additional effort can allow for greater performance to arise from a given knowledge endowment (Mitchell and Daniels, 2003; Vroom, 1964).

Trusting environments describe those where individuals have a high willingness for vulnerability (Schoorman et al., 2007). Such willingness often stems from positive expectations or confidence regarding the intentions or behaviors of other individuals in the environment (Rousseau et al., 1998). Trust can enable the emergence of a human capital resource by helping to facilitate the sharing and diffusion of knowledge among individuals in the unit (Abrams et al., 2003; Nahapiet and Ghoshal, 1998; Ployhart and Moliterno, 2011). Trust is particularly important in the conveyance of tacit-oriented knowledge as the source may feel vulnerable when attempting to convey knowledge that is not fully clear to them and the recipient may question whether the source is acting in their best interest and has valuable insights to convey (Levin and Cross, 2004). Trusting environments also have the potential to enable HCRE in an amplifying manner. Specifically, trusting environments are likely to lessen feelings of worry or anxiety, and this should allow individuals to devote more of their limited attention and cognitive capacity to the task at hand (Ashcraft and Kirk, 2001; Eysenck and Derakshan, 1998; Klein and Boals, 2001; Sorg and Whitney, 1992). This increased focus, should, in turn, improve the ability of individuals to utilize and derive value from their KSAOs (Crocker and Eckardt, 2014; Schmader and Johns, 2003).

Positive emotional orientation refers to temporary or persistent positive feelings and emotions (moods, attitudes, emotional displays, etc.) among unit members (Kozlowski and Ilgen, 2006). It has the potential to enhance the emergence of a valuable unit-level human capital resource through both the transformation and amplification aspects. As it relates to transformation, positive moods can encourage the sharing of knowledge and helping behavior among individuals in the unit. Additionally, positive emotions can help to facilitate the creation of new knowledge among individuals in the unit (Amabile et al., 2005; Isen et al., 1987). Collectively, these factors associated with positive feelings/emotions can help augment the stock of KSAOs of the unit members (Ployhart and Moliterno, 2011). Positive feelings/emotions can also have an amplifying impact on the performance that can be obtained from a given level of KSAOs. In particular, positive emotions among those in a unit can help to provide a supportive social context that can lessen worry and anxiety (Staw et al., 1994) and allow individuals to allocate a greater portion of their limited cognition and attention to work tasks. Additionally, positive feelings/emotions are thought to aid in the effort that is put forth by individuals (Seo et al., 2004; Staw et al., 1994).

Taken together, these affective-oriented emergence enabling states impact the development of a unit-level human capital resource by transforming the individual KSAOs and amplifying their impact on performance. As with the behavioral and cognitive enabling factors, the importance of the affect-enabling factors increases with higher levels of task complexity. That is, while these affective-oriented enabling factors can help to transform individuals' KSAOs and amplify their link to value/performance in situations of low task complexity, these effects are likely to be most pronounced when workflow structures involve interdependencies that create greater task complexity (Ployhart and Moliterno, 2011).

LINKS TO COMPETITIVE ADVANTAGE

Competitive advantage is achieved with a firm's human capital resources if the gap between the value generated (e.g., increases to product quality or production efficiency) and the cost of these resources (e.g., employee compensation and support structures and practices) exceeds that of competitors[1] (Chadwick, 2017; Coff and Kryscynski, 2011; Lepak et al., 2007; Molloy and Barney, 2015). Moreover, such an advantage can only be sustained over time if there are limits to the diffusion and imitation of the human capital resources to competitors (Campbell et al., 2012). Collectively, this raises important considerations related to interfirm heterogeneity, isolating mechanisms, and bargaining power (vis-à-vis firms and employees). Each of these is discussed below with respect to HCRE and the associated emergence enabling factors and underlying theoretical mechanisms.

Interfirm Heterogeneity

A critical condition of resource-based derived competitive advantage is interfirm heterogeneity (Barney, 1991; Peteraf, 1993). That is, a firm can only realize competitive advantage with a particular resource (human capital included) if there is variation in an industry with respect to their endowments and characteristics of their resources. As firm human capital resources are generated from, and influenced by, the HCRE process (Ployhart and Moliterno, 2011), this implies that the sources of interfirm heterogeneity with respect to human capital resources is largely a function of heterogeneity with respect to the associated emergence enabling factors. In other words, the sources of heterogeneity in human capital resources may be primarily driven by the heterogeneity of the factors that enable the emergence of such resources.

With this in mind, the emergence enabling mechanisms associated with the social environment (e.g., behavioral, cognitive, and affective states) in which employees are situated are likely to be more consequential from an interfirm heterogeneity standpoint than task environment-based considerations (e.g., task complexity). The task environment is largely determined by competitors' industry and therefore has reduced intra-industry heterogeneity (Porter, 1985). In contrast, firms have substantial discretion in and variation among their social environments (cf. Leana and Van Buren, 1999). For example, firms can use a number of different leadership and other human resource management (HRM) practices to impact the emergence enabling factors related to the social environment (Ployhart and Hale, 2014), thereby resulting in more variability in this aspect of the HCRE process. As a result, the social environment emergence enabling factors may be more likely to lead to interfirm heterogeneity and thus be a more critical aspect of the link between HCRE and competitive advantage.

Isolating Mechanisms

Isolating mechanisms refer to factors that limit the degree to which competitors can readily imitate or otherwise obtain a firm's valuable resources (Barney, 1991; Peteraf, 1993). In the context of human capital resources, this could involve the movement of individuals to a competitor or the development of similar resources by a competitor through selection, training, and other HRM practices. Firm specificity, social complexity, path dependence, and causal ambiguity are frequently suggested to be important isolating mechanisms with human capital resources (Coff, 1997; Coff and Kryscynski, 2011). *Firm specificity* refers to the degree to which the underlying KSAOs are only applicable at a particular firm. Increased firm specificity has historically been argued to reduce employee mobility options as competitors see a reduced "use value" at their firm, and thus will likely offer inferior compensation packages to entice such employees to move laterally to their firm (Becker, 1964; Glick and Feuer, 1984; Hashimoto, 1981). Under this traditional view, the firm-specific KSAOs that materialize from the transformation aspect of HCRE (e.g., the colleague-specific knowledge and skills associated with the coordination and unit-memory emergence enabling states) would help to limit employee movement to competitors. However, an alternative perspective has recently been put forth to suggest that competitors may see accumulations of firm-specific KSAOs as a signal of difficult to observe and valuable generic KSAOs, and thus may target and offer equivalent or enhanced compensation packages to entice individuals with high levels of firm-specific KSAOs to move laterally (Campbell et al., 2012; Morris et al., 2017). Under this alternative view, the firm-specific aspect of HCRE may not be fully effective as an isolating mechanism.

Social complexity refers to the degree to which individuals are embedded in a complex network of connections with colleagues and other firm resources; *path dependence* captures the need for resource replication efforts to go through a prolonged process that involves specific historical conditions; and *causal ambiguity* relates to situations where the link between specific actions and outcomes is hard to discern (Barney, 1991). These attributes are inherent to HCRE, and therefore make it difficult for competitors to imitate a firm's human capital resource (Ployhart and Moliterno, 2011; Ployhart et al., 2014). The sources of social complexity, path dependence, and causal ambiguity are more likely to do with the social environment enabling factors of HCRE though. Differences in task environment among competitors (if present) can be relatively easy to discern and diffuse. Thus, it is unlikely that the task environment plays a direct role in HCRE generating or sustaining competitive advantage. Rather, the impact of task environment is likely more indirect via its accentuating impact on the social environment enabling factors of HCRE. That is, the isolating mechanisms associated with the social environment enabling factors of HCRE are likely enhanced in situations of greater task complexity (cf. Dierickx and Cool, 1989).

Bargaining Power

Human capital is a unique firm resource as it has agency to adjust its cost to the firm after it is acquired. In particular, if the individual's underlying unit-level human capital resource plays an important role in improving their "use value" to the firm, they are likely to want an increased compensation package that is commensurate with the increased value they provide the firm (Coff, 2010).[2] If the firm grants the individual increased compensation, they will be reducing the gap between the value and cost of their human capital resources and diminish any associated competitive advantage (Coff, 1999; Chadwick, 2017; Molloy and Barney, 2015). While forgoing the increased compensation could help the firm to capture more of the value generated from their human capital resources, employees have a strong bargaining position as they can reduce work effort and also depart the firm (Coff, 1997). As these employee responses would negatively impact the value generated by the human capital resources, this could also reduce the economic benefits generated from these resources and prospects of competitive advantage.

These inherent bargaining dynamics and value creation and capture tensions with human capital resources have important implications for the transformation and amplification aspects of HCRE. In particular, as both the transformation and amplification aspects of HCRE can enhance the value generated by unit members, it is likely that such members will bargain with the firm to capture a greater portion of the value. As a portion of the KSAOs that result from the transformation aspect of HCRE could be generic and applicable to competitors, unit members have an enhanced bargaining position with their current employer due to their enhanced mobility options (Campbell et al., 2012; Coff, 1997; Coff and Kryscynski, 2011). Firms therefore may need to include commensurate compensation increases for the value creation that is generated from the transformation aspect of HCRE. This would limit the degree to which this aspect of HCRE results in significant net economic improvements and thus reduce its role in HCRE resulting in competitive advantage.

In contrast, the amplification aspect of HCRE provides the firm with an improved bargaining position to retain a portion of the generated value. Specifically, the complementarity orientation of the amplification aspect means that the increased value creation of unit members is dependent, in part, on the contextual factors created by the firm. This provides the firm with a greater claim to the value created by this aspect of HCRE and increased leverage in compensation-oriented negotiations. As a result of this enhanced bargaining position, firms may be more able to limit the degree to which unit members' compensation increases in a commensurate way to their increased value generation at the firm (Chadwick, 2017; Molloy and Barney, 2015). Thus, the amplification aspect of HCRE can potentially have meaningful and substantial improvements to the net economic improvements (i.e., increasing the "use value" of human capital resources but limiting the cost increases associated with such increased value) from human capital resources.

Summary

All aspects of the HCRE process (task and social environment emergence enabling factors, transformation and amplification mechanisms) have the potential to increase the value generated from a firm's initial endowment of KSAOs. However, the notion of competitive advantage requires one to consider the uniqueness and imitability of the underlying drivers of increased value (Barney, 1991; Peteraf, 1993) and the degree to which the firm can capture a portion of the value generated by its human capital resources (Chadwick, 2017; Coff, 1999; Lepak et al., 2007; Molloy and Barney, 2015). When these are considered, it seems likely that the *social environment emergence enabling factors* and *amplification mechanisms* are the most critical aspects linking HCRE to competitive advantage. The social environment emergence enabling factors are important as they increase interfirm heterogeneity and inimitability (due to greater variability and discretion in underlying antecedents and increased path dependence, social complexity, and causal ambiguity); and the amplification mechanisms involve complementarities that provide the firm with an enhanced bargaining position (Molloy and Barney, 2015) to limit the degree to which unit-member compensation moves in lockstep with increased contributions to value creation.

METHODOLOGICAL CONSIDERATIONS AND APPROACHES

Empirical studies related to HCRE are limited and studies of the HCRE process are practically nonexistent. Such scarcity stems, in part, from the general lack of methodological attention and consideration of bottom-up effects and processes (Kozlowski and Chao, 2012; Kozlowski et al., 2013; Moliterno and Ployhart, 2016). However, the lack of empirical studies on HCRE is also likely due to reduced precision and detail on the underlying mechanisms and considerations involved with this phenomenon. Having attempted to outline more detail on these factors in the previous sections, we now discuss a few methodological approaches that can potentially be used to capture and study these aspects and processes involved with HCRE.

Important Principles and Background

Before discussing particular techniques and approaches to examine HCRE, it is important to note two broad guidelines and considerations associated with the focal phenomenon. First, the emergence of a valuable unit human capital resource happens *over time*. Thus, in line with the more general recommendations on studying emergent processes (Kozlowski et al., 2013), empirical examinations of the HCRE process should involve longitudinal data collection and analytical techniques. Second, HCRE involves the manifestation of individual KSAOs into a valuable unit-level human capital resource, a process that involves the influence of a number of task- and social-oriented contextual factors. It should be readily apparent that there are multiple levels of analysis involved with this process. As such, empirical examinations of HCRE should involve data collection at *multiple levels of analysis*, and use analytical techniques that address the unique statistical analysis challenges of such data and allow for the testing of cross-level associations.

There are several potentially useful modeling approaches that could potentially accommodate these guidelines and considerations – e.g., multilevel structural equation modeling (MSEM), within-and-between-analysis (WABA). The following discussion primarily focuses on the application of random coefficient modeling (RCM) – also referred to as Hierarchical Linear Modeling (HLM) – as this technique: 1) is the most commonly used approach for multilevel modeling (Aguinis et al., 2009; Mathieu and Chen, 2011); 2) is well-suited to address the noted longitudinal and multilevel guidelines and considerations (Bliese and Ployhart, 2002; Hofmann, 1997); and 3) has flexibility to be used in novel ways to explore HCRE (Eckardt and Moliterno, 2016). In that there are number of high-quality overviews of RCM (e.g., Aguinis et al., 2013; Bliese and Ployhart, 2002; González-Romá and Hernández, 2017; Hofmann, 1997; Raudenbush and Bryk, 2002), we will not provide detailed background on the analytical technique. However, the general purpose and utility of RCM is to: 1) partition variance in a focal dependent variable into multiple levels of analysis; and 2) add independent variables at the different levels of analysis to explain variation attributed to that level of analysis and examine cross-level interactive effects (e.g., how a lower-level relationship may depend on an attribute at a higher level).

Empirically Capturing HCRE and Analyzing Mechanisms with RCM Growth Models

As mentioned previously, HCRE involves two underlying mechanisms related to the transformation of KSAOs and amplification of the productive value from a given stock of KSAOs. Both of these mechanisms involve changes to unit members over time. In particular, if a valuable unit-level human capital resource is emerging, we should see changes to unit members' KSAOs (transformation) and enhanced links between unit-member KSAOs and performance (amplification). To capture these changes, one could use RCM growth models.

Modeling transformation

For the transformation aspect, the model can be structured such that level 1 represents individual KSAOs over time (with time-varying covariates), level 2 captures stable individual characteristics of unit members (e.g., unit roles and titles, education, and other demographics), and level 3 includes unit-level contextual factors. A generic model specification for such a model is the following:

Level-1 Model (KSAOs at Time t)

$$KSAOs_{tij} = \pi_{0ij} + \pi_{1ij}*(TIME_{tij}) + \pi_{2ij}*(TimeVaryingCovariates_{tij}) + e_{tij}$$

Level-2 Model (Unit Members)

$$\pi_{0ij} = \beta_{00j} + \beta_{01j}*(StableIndividualCharacteristcs_{ij}) + r_{0ij}$$
$$\pi_{1ij} = \beta_{10j} + \beta_{11j}*(StableIndividualCharacteristcs) + r_{1ij}$$
$$\pi_{2ij} = \beta_{20j} + r_{2ij}$$

Level-3 Model (Units)

$$\beta_{00j} = \gamma_{000} + u_{00j}$$
$$\beta_{01j} = \gamma_{010} + u_{01j}$$
$$\beta_{10j} = \gamma_{100} + u_{10j}$$
$$\beta_{11j} = \gamma_{110} + u_{11j}$$
$$\beta_{20j} = \gamma_{200} + u_{20j}$$

(Equation Set 1)

where $KSAOs_{tij}$ is the KSAOs at time *t* for unit-member *i* in unit *j*; $TIME_{tij}$ is the time variable for the growth model; $TimeVaryingCovariates_{tij}$ represent time varying covariates at time *t* for unit-member *i* in unit *j*; $StableIndividualCharacteristcs_{ij}$ refer to stable individual characteristics of unit-member *i* in unit *j*; π_{0ij} is the level 1 intercept; π_{1ij} and π_{2ij} are the slopes for the time variable and time varying covariates, respectively; β_{00j}, β_{10j}, and β_{20j} are the level 2 intercepts; β_{01j} is the level 2 slope relating the stable individual characteristics control variable to the level 1 intercept; β_{11j} is the level 2 slope relating the stable individual characteristics control variable to the level 1 slope for the time variable; γ_{000}, γ_{010}, γ_{100}, γ_{110}, and γ_{200} are the level 3 intercepts; e_{tij} is the residual (error term) at level 1; r_{0ij}, r_{1ij}, and r_{2ij} are the residuals (random effects) at level 2; and u_{00j}, u_{01j}, u_{10j}, u_{11j}, and u_{20j} are the residuals (random effects) at level 3.

A hypothetical graphical depiction of this model is in Figures 5.1–5.4. To ease the space required and complexity of the figures, we only depict a scenario where there are two unit members nested within two units. Such a model would not have adequate observations for a real analysis, but it helps to convey the structure and terms in this hypothetical model. It is important to keep in mind that RCM is conceptually fitting different regression lines to the data for each unit member, and then pooling and explaining the variability in the intercepts and slopes of those regression lines. The figures focus on the relationship between the KSAOs and time variables, as this is the primary association of interest for the transformation aspect of HCRE (e.g., change in unit-member KSAOs over time).

Figure 5.1 provides an illustration of the pooled scatterplot for the raw KSAO data. Unlike a traditional regression approach, RCM essentially fits separate regression lines for each data subset associated with level 2 (unit members). Figure 5.2 depicts the data

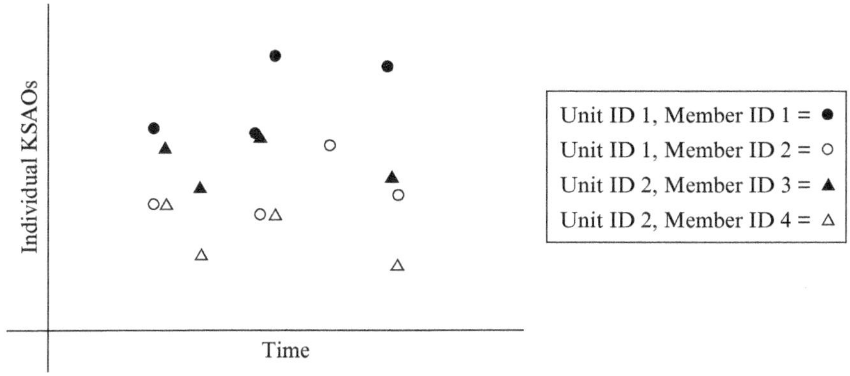

Figure 5.1 *Illustration of pooled scatterplot of individual KSAOs and time for four unit members and two units*

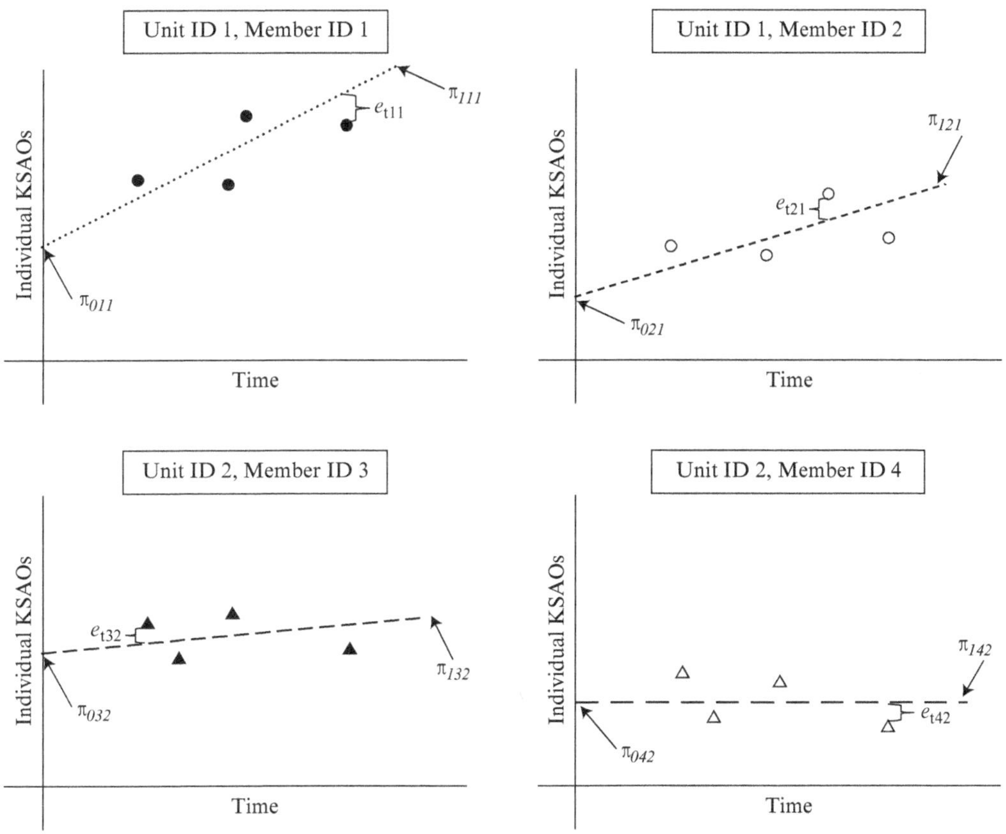

Figure 5.2 *Illustration of RCM level 1 equations for individual KSAOs–time relationship for four unit members and two units*

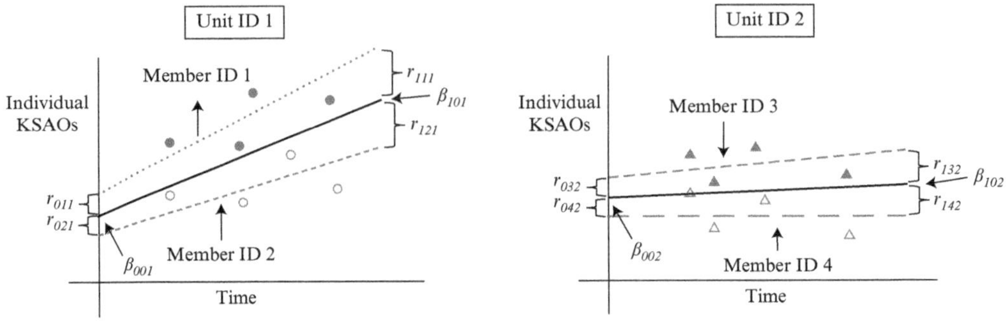

Figure 5.3 Illustration of RCM level 2 equations for individual KSAOs–time relationship for four unit members and two units

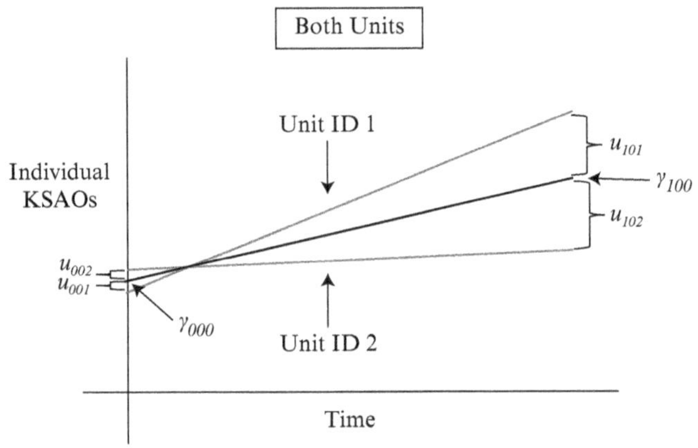

Figure 5.4 Illustration of RCM level 3 equations for individual KSAOs–time relationship for four unit members and two units

and regression lines for each unit member. The level 1 residual (e_{tij}), intercept (π_{0ij}), and slope (π_{1ij}) for each unit member is also indicated on this figure. Figure 5.3 illustrates the level 2 equations, including the mean intercept (β_{00j}) and slope (β_{10j}) for each unit's change in KSAOs over time and the unit-member deviations from those means (r_{0ij}, r_{1ij}). The level 3 equations are represented in Figure 5.4. This diagram depicts the mean intercept (γ_{000}) and slope (γ_{100}) for the overall sample's changes in KSAOs over time and the differences from these mean values for each unit (u_{00j}, u_{10j}).

As the slope residual for the time variable at level 3 (u_{10j}) represents the degree to which a unit's members' KSAOs changed over time, it provides a measure of the transformation aspect. In particular, as this variable increases, it suggests an increase in the rate of change in unit members' KSAOs, and thus a larger degree of the transformation aspect of HCRE. As a result, Unit ID 1 in Figure 5.4 would have more emergence via the transformation aspect than Unit ID 2. With this in mind, variables representing different unit task and social environment-oriented emergence enabling factors (or other relevant unit-level factors – e.g., leadership characteristics and approaches, HRM practices) can then be added at level 3 to explain variation in the these residuals related to the transformation of KSAOs. A generic example of this model specification is the following:

Level-1 Model (KSAOs at Time t)

$$KSAOs_{tij} = \pi_{0ij} + \pi_{1ij}*(TIME_{tij}) + \pi_{2ij}*(TimeVaryingCovariates_{tij}) + e_{tij}$$

Level-2 Model (Unit Members)

$$\pi_{0ij} = \beta_{00j} + \beta_{01j}*(StableIndividualCharacteristcs_{ij}) + r_{0ij}$$
$$\pi_{1ij} = \beta_{10j} + \beta_{11j}*(StableIndividualCharacteristcs) + r_{1ij}$$
$$\pi_{2ij} = \beta_{20j} + r_{2ij}$$

Level-3 Model (Units)

$$\beta_{00j} = \gamma_{000} + \gamma_{001}*(Task\ EEF_j) + \gamma_{002}*(Social\ EEF_j) + u_{00j}$$
$$\beta_{01j} = \gamma_{010} + u_{01j}$$
$$\beta_{10j} = \gamma_{100} + \gamma_{101}*(Task\ EEF_j) + \gamma_{102}*(Social\ EEF_j) + u_{10j}$$
$$\beta_{11j} = \gamma_{110} + u_{11j}$$
$$\beta_{20j} = \gamma_{200} + u_{20j}$$

(Equation Set 2)

where the variable names and model parameters match the previously listed model (Equation Set 1), with several new variables and parameters: *Task* EEF_j represents task environment emergence enabling factors (e.g., task complexity) for unit *j*; *Social* EEF_j represents social environment emergence enabling factors (e.g., emergence enabling states); γ_{001} and γ_{002} are the level 3 slopes relating the task and social environment emergence enable variables to the level 2 intercept; and γ_{101} and γ_{102} are the level 2 slopes relating the task and social environment emergence enabling variables to the level 2 slope for the time variable. It is these last parameters (γ_{101}, γ_{102}) that would provide insight into whether the task and social environment emergence enabling factors had an influence on the transformation aspect of HCRE.

Modeling amplification

Similar RCM growth models could be used to look at the amplification aspect of HCRE over time. However, the measure of amplification is likely to require permutations to the model specification or a series of additional 2-level cross-sectional RCMs to capture the degree to which a unit is deriving additional value/performance from their stock of KSAOs. As indicated in Figure 5.5, there are essentially two ways in which a firm could improve the value/performance obtained from their stock of KSAOs. The first is through increases to the intercept of the relationship between KSAOs, and the second is through increases to the slopes of the KSAO–performance relationship.

An example of the 2-level cross-section RCM specification that could be used to *measure* these intercept and slope aspects associated with the performance/value enhancements from KSAOs is the following:

Level-1 Model (Unit Members)

$$Performance_{ij} = \beta_{0j} + \beta_{1j}*(KSAOs_{ij}) + \beta_{2j}*(IndividualCharacteristics_{ij})\ r_{ij}$$

Level-2 Model (Units)

$$\beta_{0j} = \gamma_{00} + u_{0j}$$

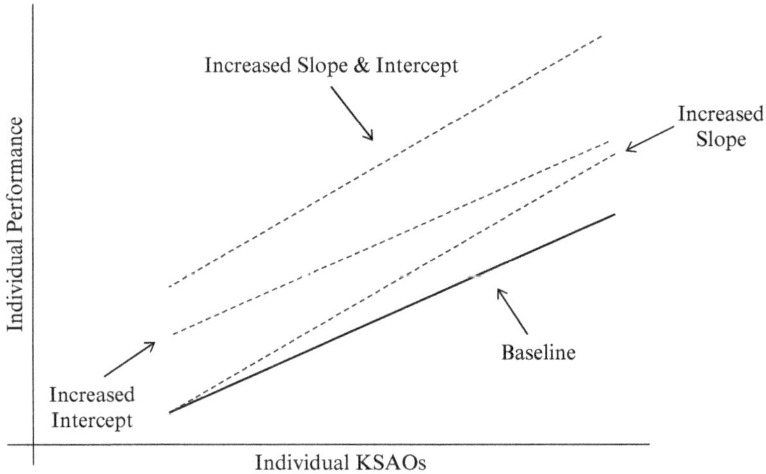

Figure 5.5 Illustration of intercept and slope forms of amplification of the individual performance–KSAOs association

$$\beta_{1j} = \gamma_{10} + u_{1j}$$
$$\beta_{2j} = \gamma_{20} + u_{2j}$$

(Equation Set 3)

where $Performance_{ij}$ is the performance of unit member i in unit j; $KSAOs_{ij}$ is the KSAOs of unit member i in unit j; $IndividualCharacteristics_{ij}$ is the individual characteristics control variable for unit member i in unit j; β_{0j} is the level 1 intercept; β_{1j} is the level 1 slope for the association between unit-member KSAOs and performance; β_{2j} is the level 1 slope for the association between the unit-member individual characteristics control variable and performance; γ_{00}, γ_{10}, and γ_{20} are the level 2 intercepts; r_{ij} is the residual (error term) at level 1; and u_{0j}, u_{1j}, and u_{2j} are the residuals (random effects) at level 2.

In this specification, the β_{0j} and β_{1j} represent the intercept and slope of the unit-member KSAO–performance association for unit j. These parameters are estimated for each unit in these RCM models and available in the residual files for these analyses. As a result, a 2-level model for the unit-member KSAO–performance association could be run at *each time period* to estimate the intercept and slope of this association for each unit. These two parameters (β_{0j}, β_{1j}) could then be standardized and combined to form a composite of the intercept and slope characteristics of the unit-member KSAO–performance relationship. Changes to this composite measure of the amplification aspect of HCRE could then be used to provide an indication of the degree to which the value/performance derived from a unit's KSAOs is increasing over time. This is depicted in Figures 5.6 and 5.7 for a hypothetical scenario where there are three units with multiple unit members each. In these figures, unit 3 has no changes to the slopes or intercepts for the KSAO–performance association over the four time periods, and thus demonstrates no HCRE emergence with respect to the amplification aspect. In contrast, unit 1's intercepts and slopes demonstrate substantial increases over the four time periods and unit 2's increases are more modest.

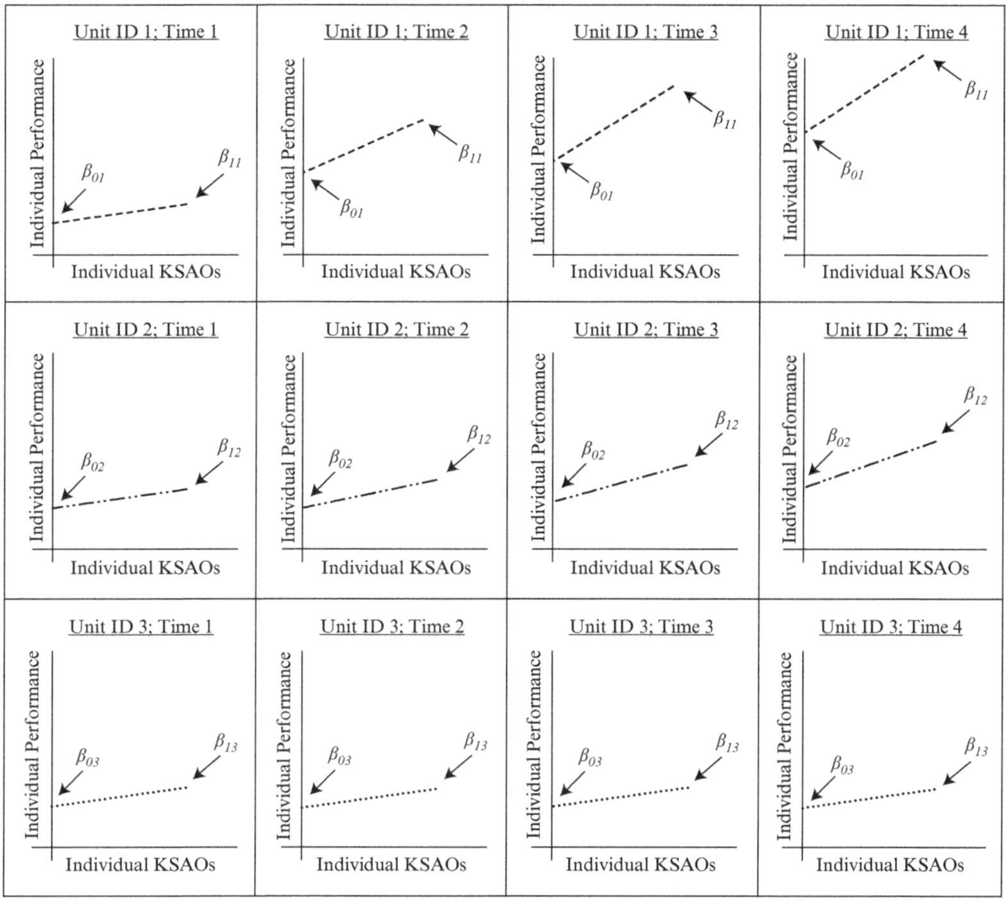

Figure 5.6 Illustration of changes to the cross-sectional 2-level RCM models of the KSAOs–performance association by units and time

The changes to the derived amplification measure could then be model with a 2-level RCM growth model. An example specification is the following:

Level-1 Model (KSAOs-Performance at Time t)

$$KSAOs\text{-}Performance_{tj} = \pi_{0j} + \pi_{1j}{*}(TIME_{tj}) + \pi_{2j}{*}(TimeVaryingCovariates_{tj}) + e_{tj}$$

Level-2 Model (Units)

$$\pi_{0j} = \beta_{00j} + r_{0j}$$
$$\pi_{1j} = \beta_{10j} + r_{1j}$$
$$\pi_{2j} = \beta_{20j} + r_{2j}$$

(Equation Set 4)

where $KSAOs\text{-}Performance_{tj}$ is the composite measure of the KSAOs–performance association for unit j at time t; $TIME_{tj}$ is the time variable for the growth model;

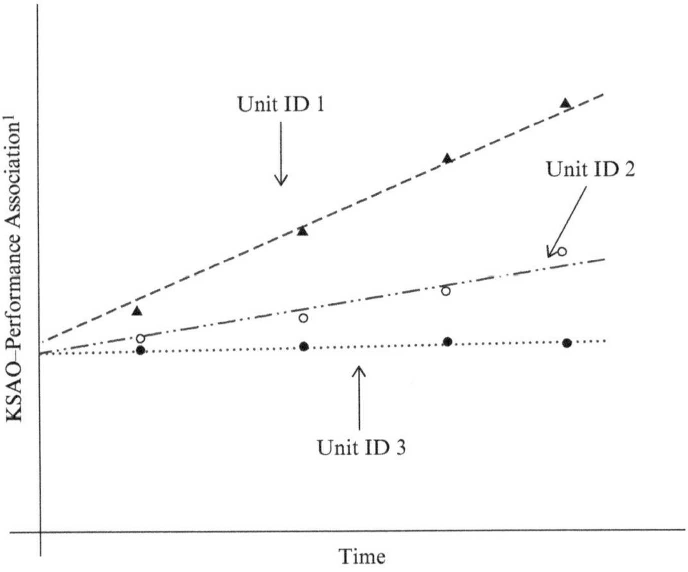

Note: 1. Measured as a composite of the standardized β_{0j} (intercepts) and β_{1j} (slopes) for each unit in a cross-sectional 2-level RCM of the KSAO–performance association at time t (see Figure 5.6).

Figure 5.7 Changes to composite amplification measure by units and time

$TimeVaryingCovariates_{tj}$ represent time varying covariates at time t for unit j; π_{0j} is the level 1 intercept; π_{1j} and π_{2j} are the slopes for the time variable and time varying covariates, respectively; β_{00j}, β_{10j}, and β_{20j} are the level 2 intercepts; e_{tj} is the residual (error term) at level 1; r_{0j}, r_{1j}, and r_{2j} are the residuals (random effects) at level 2.

In this specification, the slope residual for the time variable at level 2 (r_{1j}) represents the degree to which a unit's KSAOs–performance relationship changed over time. It therefore provides a measure of the amplification aspect of HCRE. In particular, as this variable increases, it suggests an increase in the rate of change for the unit members' KSAOs–performance relationship, and thus a larger degree of the amplification aspect of HCRE. Lastly, variables related to the unit's task and social environment emergence enabling factors could be added at level 2 to explain variability in the amplification measure over time. An example model specification with such variables is the following:

Level-1 Model (KSAOs-Performance at Time t)

$$KSAOs\text{-}Performance_{tj} = \pi_{0j} + \pi_{1j}*(TIME_{tj}) + \pi_{2j}*(TimeVaryingCovariates_{tj}) + e_{tj}$$

Level-2 Model (Units)

$$\pi_{0j} = \beta_{00j} + \beta_{01j}*(Task\ EEF_j) + \beta_{02j}*(Social\ EEF_j) + r_{0j}$$
$$\pi_{1j} = \beta_{10j} + \beta_{11j}*(Task\ EEF_j) + \beta_{12j}*(Social\ EEF_j) + r_{1j}$$
$$\pi_{2j} = \beta_{20j} + r_{2j}$$

(Equation Set 5)

where the variable names and model parameters match the previously listed model (Equation Set 4), but have the new variables to represent the unit task and social environment-oriented emergence enabling factors (*Task* EEF_j, *Social* EEF_j) and level 2 coefficients to represent these factors impact on the overall intercept (β_{01j}, β_{02j}) and change in KSAOs–Performance association over time (β_{11j}, β_{12j}). In a similar way to the transformation models described above, it is these last parameters (β_{11j}, β_{12j}) that would provide insight into whether the task and social environment emergence enabling factors had an influence on the amplification aspect of HCRE.

Relating transformation and amplification to unit-level performance outcomes

The modeling approach described in the preceding sections will yield unit-level estimates of the transformation and amplification aspects of HCRE. In particular the residuals at the unit level for the time variables of Equation Set 1 (u_{10j}) and Equation Set 4 (r_{1j}) represent the transformation and amplification aspects of HCRE, respectively. These residuals can be estimated with RCM and extracted from the models' residual files. As both estimates will be on different scales, they should be standardized before being added together to represent the overall emergence of a valuable unit-level human capital resource. This composite measure of HCRE can then be analyzed using traditional regression analyses to assess its impact on competitive advantage-oriented unit-level performance measures – e.g., profitability or proxy for human capital rents (Chadwick, 2017).

It is also possible to analyze the direct and differential effects of the transformation and amplification aspects of HCRE on unit-level performance by including the separate standardized measures of these aspects instead of a composite overall measure of HCRE. Such regression analyses could be coupled with a partial F test to assess the validity of the suggestion above that the amplification dimension/mechanism of HCRE is more critical to competitive advantage than the transformation dimension/mechanism.

Assumptions and Clarifications of Suggested RCM Growth Modeling Approach

The primary purpose of the above modeling approach is to provide an example of how RCM growth modeling could be adapted to examine the transformation and amplification aspects of HCRE. To aid in the conveyance of this approach, we made several simplifying assumptions that are worth explicitly noting, as these may need to be relaxed and/or modified in the context of particular HCRE studies. First, our example assumes linear changes in KSAOs and the KSAOs–performance link over time. As with many aspects of organizational phenomena (Ployhart and Vandenberg, 2010), the changes involved with HCRE may involve nonlinear and discontinuous elements. It may therefore be important for future studies adopting the above general modeling approach to include higher-order versions of the time variable (e.g., $TIME^2$, $TIME^3$) in the model specification to account for nonlinear changes. Additionally, future studies may need to use modified coding of the time variable to accommodate discontinuous change considerations (see Bliese and Lang, 2016).

Second, our example focused on a hypothetical context where an additive view of unit members' KSAOs was assumed appropriate. In particular, the transformation aspect of the above modeling approach relies on an underlying assumption that increases in the stock of KSAOs among all unit members is beneficial from a unit performance standpoint. While this assumption may be valid in a number of settings (e.g., see Hitt et al., 2001; Pil and Leana, 2009; Ployhart et al., 2009), it would not be appropriate in contexts where theory suggests that variability of KSAOs is important to unit outcomes (e.g., see Tzabbar and Margolis, 2017). To accommodate such variability, 2-level RCM growth models with an appropriate diversity criterion could be used (see Biemann and Kearney, 2010 and Harrison and Klein, 2007 for a discussion of diversity constructs and operationalization). In such models, level 1 would be the measure of KSAO diversity for a unit at a particular time (j, t) and level 2 would be units (j). Alternatively, future research requiring a variability of KSAOs perspective could consider the use of mixed effects location-scale models, which explicitly model and predict variability in a multilevel framework (Hedeker et al., 2008), and/or modifications to Lang et al.'s modeling approach to explore temporal dynamics with *divergence-oriented* constructs.

Third, we have glossed over the multidimensionality of KSAOs and presented a simplistic view of their changes in our models. There can be many different types of KSAO (Nyberg et al., 2014; Ployhart et al., 2014) and, as we alluded above, these can be directly related to task completion or more indirectly related to tasks via colleague-specific knowledge and skills (e.g., knowledge and skills related to sequencing and smoothing of workflow interactions on task activities, shared mental models, or transactive memory). Additionally, the changes to certain KSAOs (e.g., cognitive- versus noncognitive-oriented) in the transformation aspect of HCRE may be driven by different emergence enabling factors (cf. Ployhart and Moliterno, 2011). As a result, it is likely that HCRE studies may need to measure and track changes in these different dimensions of KSAOs with multiple RCM growth models. This would mean that, depending on the theoretical focus and study context, there might need to be multiple RCM growth models to capture the multidimensionality of KSAOs (e.g., a different model for each theoretically relevant grouping of KSAOs) in the transformation aspect of HCRE.

It is also possible that different KSAOs may be important to different unit members based on their specific task assignments and roles (Ployhart et al., 2014). This would imply that the link between individual KSAOs and individual performance may vary based on unit-member tasks and roles. In such situations, multiple RCM models may also be needed to capture the different KSAO–performance associations present in a given unit. Alternatively, KSAOs and performance could be converted to standardized values and combined into one model.

Lastly, we have assumed that amplification aspects of HCRE manifest at the individual level of analysis. In particular, we suggested that improvements to the link between a given stock of KSAOs and unit outputs require underlying improvements to the association between individual KSAOs and performance among unit members. This view is consistent with our contention noted in the beginning of this chapter regarding the fundamental role of changes at the individual level in the HCRE process. In taking this position, we acknowledge that collectives are able to accomplish outcomes that individuals are not able to achieve by themselves. However, such situations do not negate the fundamental requirement that collective action is a function of individual actions. That is, if collective action of a unit changes, then it is necessary that the individual actions of the unit's members have also changed in some way. More to the point of the amplification aspect of HCRE, this view implies that if the link between unit-member KSAOs and unit performance improves, then there is likely an underlying enhancement to the link of unit-member KSAOs and unit-member performance. Again, it is hard to imagine how collective action could improve unit outcomes without there being performance improvements of some shape or form at the individual level of analysis.

Although we view this position as valid from a conceptual standpoint, we acknowledge that it may be difficult in some instances to precisely measure the contributions and performance of individuals with respect to unit outcomes. This may be particularly likely in situations of group-based workflow structures where it can be challenging to identify concrete contributions and associated performance assessments (Alchian and Demsetz, 1972). Recent advancements in wearable sensors and other techniques to capture and analyze "digital traces" have potential to lessen these challenges (Kozlowski and Chao, 2018; Kozlowski et al., 2015; Salas et al., 2015); however, there is still much to learn and improve with these methodologies (Chaffin et al., 2017). Thus, there may be instances where measurement challenges require alternatives to the individual KSAO–individual performance amplification modeling approach suggested above. One alternative to consider for such situations is the modified Cobb–Douglas specification developed by Ethiraj and Garg (2012). This approach captures net complementarities among individual human capital in a situation where there is a native performance outcome at a higher level of analysis (e.g., profits of a unit, win–loss ratio of a sports team, publication outcome from a coauthored paper).[3] If required, the modified Cobb–Douglas could be used as an alternative dependent variable in the 2-level RCM growth modeling approach suggested to examine the amplification aspect (Equation Set 4). In these models, level 1 would be the modified Cobb–Douglas derived measure for a unit at a particular time (j, t) and level 2 would be the units (j).

Simultaneity of Transformation and Amplification and Emergent-Oriented Unit-Level Enabling Factors

While we believe the general RCM growth modeling approach and considerations outlined above make important steps to measure, model, and empirically explore the antecedents and consequences of HCRE, it is somewhat limited in that it does not allow for the simultaneous measurement and modeling of the emergence-oriented enabling factors. That is, some of the factors in the social environment category that are thought to be critical to the emergence of HCRE – such as unit-climate, cohesion, or unit-affect – involve emergence processes of their own. There is great advice available on how to measure (e.g., Bliese, 2000; Chan, 1998) and model the consensus-based emergence process (e.g., Lang and Bliese, 2018; Lang et al., 2018) involved with many of these. However, more work is needed on how to simultaneously model the emergence of these enabling factors and the transformation and amplification aspects of HCRE.

There are two potential options for future research to explore the coevolution and simultaneity of the HCRE underlying mechanisms and emergence enabling factors. The first is the use of computational modeling/agent-based simulations (Kozlowski, 2015; Kozlowski et al., 2013, 2016), which allows for the simultaneous specification and modeling of multiple individual, social, and emergence-oriented phenomena, and can be coupled with targeted experimental and other empirical designs to isolate and test important assumptions, associations, and outcomes in the model/simulation (see Grand et al., 2016 for an example). The second option relates to the use of MSEM (e.g., Aguinis and Molina-Azorin, 2015; Preacher et al., 2010; Williams et al., 2009). Such a modeling technique could potentially accommodate simultaneous and cross-level changes and interrelationships among the HCRE emergence enabling factors and underlying mechanisms.

NEEDED STEPS TO MOVE FORWARD

The prior sections sought to make progress on clarifying and extending the extant work on HCRE with respect to understanding of underlying mechanisms, links to competitive advantage, and methodological considerations and approaches. While we believe this helps to advance research on HCRE, there is much work needed on this important area of strategic human capital research. We therefore conclude by describing several of these important next steps and considerations.

More Leveraging and Integrations of Micro-Oriented Research (HRM/HC and Beyond)

Research on HCRE is arguably one of the most micro-macro integrated areas in the broader study of strategic human capital. Much of this integration relates to the general nature of emergent phenomena, which necessitates dual consideration of micro and macro perspectives (Eckardt et al., 2018a; Kozlowski and Chao, 2012). However, it is also one of those rare areas in strategic human capital where the existing theories and perspectives *only* have a micro-macro/multilevel focus (e.g., Nyberg et al., 2014; Ployhart and Moliterno, 2011; Ployhart, 2015; Ployhart et al., 2014; Ployhart and Hale, 2014). That is, there is only a multilevel and micro-macro perspective in research on HCRE. Indeed, it is these two factors (and the general tradition in this research topic of micro-macro collaboration) that led us to request one integrated chapter (as opposed two separate micro and macro chapters) on the topic of HCRE.

While the existing micro-macro traditions and general openness within the strategic human capital literature to such approaches is applaudable, it is critical that such collaborations and integrations continue. We thus believe that it is important for existing strategic human capital researchers to reach out to and interact with micro-oriented researchers in studies of HCRE. As a starting point, there is a natural connection between research on HRM practices and systems and HCRE (Boon et al., 2018). Traditionally, strategic HRM research has focused on the effect of HRM systems on overall human capital of work units (e.g., Jiang et al., 2015; Kehoe and Collins, 2017; Takeuchi et al., 2007). Researchers can extend the work to explore how HRM systems/practices are related to the emergence enabling factors (task environment and the behavioral, cognitive, and affective states) of HCRE. For example, Collins and Smith (2006) have found that commitment-based HRM practices can facilitate social climate (e.g., trust, cooperation, and shared codes and language) and knowledge exchange and combination in subsequence. Other studies have also shown that HRM practices can influence coordination among employees (e.g., Gittell et al., 2010) and help develop employees' shared perceptions (e.g., Chuang and Liao, 2010; Jiang et al., 2015). Those studies suggest that HRM practices play an important role in influencing the behavioral, cognitive, and affective states of HCRE and should be incorporated in future research to understand how specific HRM practices or different components of HRM systems contribute to the HCRE process.

Campbell and Kryscynski (Chapter 9, this volume) also note that a firm's broader

HRM system provides a central source of isolating mechanisms in firms related to the management of human capital. As a result, HRM practices and systems, and the broader management and leadership framework that designs the systems and oversees their implementation (Boon et al., 2018), may reside at the nexus of the critical aspects of HCRE with regard to generating and protecting competitive advantage. That is, it may be essential to include consideration of HRM systems, and the antecedent and contingent effects of managers/leaders associated with such systems, to fully understand how HCRE results in a strategically valuable unit-level resource.

Such collaborations need not be limited to micro-oriented researchers in HRM or human capital though. Rather, there are a vast number of other micro-oriented topics – e.g., leadership, teams, compensation, motivation, job design, perception and decision making, identity, stress, emotions, conflict management (cf. Conroy, Chapter 1 this volume; Porter et al., Chapter 19) – related to the underlying mechanisms and emergence enabling factors of HCRE that can and should be considered and integrated. As a way to encourage these more distal connections with the work on HCRE, we call for more state-of-the-science reviews of existing micro-oriented research related to emergence enabling factors (task environment and the behavioral, cognitive, and affective states) of HCRE. Specifically, such reviews could take stock of an existing body of micro-oriented research through the lens of these factors to identify what is known and unknown about the creation of these states that are important to the HCRE process. These would provide strategic human capital researchers with a great resource to appropriately leverage existing micro-oriented research relevant to HCRE, thereby lessening the chance that strategic human capital researchers "reinvent the wheel" when studying HCRE. Such reviews may also help us to see the HCRE emergence phenomena in a new light, and highlight factors or considerations that only become apparent when looked at through this different perspective (cf. Eckardt et al., 2018a). Lastly, these reviews can provide a natural launching pad for integrations with micro-oriented researchers in non-HR/HC areas as they may identify research areas that are underexplored in the focal micro topic and also relevant to the study of HCRE (i.e., identify research projects that have dual contributions to a specific micro-oriented research area and HCRE).

HCRE as a Broad Integrating Framework for Studying Human Capital Resources

We see HCRE as having potential as a broader integrating framework for much of the research on human capital resources. We have discussed throughout this chapter the important considerations related to the development and deployment of human capital. However, other topics, such as the acquisition and retention of human capital are also inherently relevant to HCRE. For example, research on the acquisition/selection of individual human capital can provide insight about the stock of KSAOs that a unit is working with, and also has implications for critical enabling factors related to the social environment to materialize (Kehoe and Bentley, Chapter 16 this volume). Additionally, research on the acquisition and integration of intact unit-level human capital resources (e.g., team lift-outs, acqui-hiring, mergers and acquisition) has implications for the emergence or disruption of other unit-level human capital resources at the firm (Camuffo and De Stefano, Chapter 17).

With respect to retention of human capital, research on turnover has direct implications for HCRE as the attrition of unit members can disrupt the emergence enabling factors and lead to the disemergence of a valuable unit-level human capital resource (Hausknecht, Chapter 27 this volume; Nyberg and Ployhart, 2013). Moreover, it may simply not be possible for a valuable unit-level human capital resource to emerge in an environment of extremely high rates of employee turnover. It is also important to realize that the effects of turnover need not always be negative (Rider and Tan, Chapter 28). Prior employees can expand the network of current employees, and these can help to enhance certain emergence enabling factors (e.g., unit-learning) associated with HCRE. Additionally, the replacement hires can bring new KSAOs (March, 1991) that can then be diffused to unit members via the transformation aspect of HCRE.

As a result of HCRE's broad applicability to many important topics related to human capital resources (e.g., acquisition, development, deployment, and retention), we believe there is value in considering HCRE as an integrating framework for the field of strategic human capital. Viewing HCRE in this manner would help to tie together the seemingly disjointed research topics on human capital resources, and also improve the chance that any integrate efforts involve both micro and macro perspectives on these topics. This increased emphasis on HCRE would also help to ensure that HCRE stays at the forefront of researchers' attention.

More Process-Oriented Theorizing with Improved Traceability

We have attempted to provide more detail in this chapter on the underlying mechanisms and processes involved with HCRE. While an improvement, there is much still to be done on the specific details, interactions, and dynamics involved in the emergence of valuable unit-level human capital resources. In particular, as we alluded to previously, the HCRE process involves simultaneously emergence processes where there are sub-emergence processes driving the emergence enabling states, which, in turn, are influencing the transformation and amplification mechanisms that result in the emergence of a valuable unit-level human capital resource. This can be complicated further by acknowledging that unit-member actions and interactions can simultaneously influence multiple emergence enabling mechanisms, and that there is the potential for an isolated act or interaction that occupies a short time period to have a profound impact on the trajectory and development of some of the social environment-oriented emergence enabling states. Thus, there is likely to be a substantial amount of complex, discontinuous, and nonlinear theorizing to incorporate into our understanding of the underlying mechanisms and processes involved with HCRE.

To aid in the development of such process-based and detailed theorizing, we echo calls by Kozlowski and colleagues (2012, 2013, 2015, 2016, 2018) for the use of computational modeling and agent-based simulations to explore HCRE. These techniques necessitate an immense amount of precision with respect to specifying the important attributes, parameter estimates, and rules of interactions among unit members, and provide a helpful theorizing tool to add and trim details and complexities to arrive at relatively parsimonious theories of the processes and dynamics involved with complex emergent phenomena (Sayama, 2015; Wang et al., 2016). The improved traceability and precision of theories that can result from these models can also help with developing and identifying methodological approaches to empirically examine these more complex, but likely important, aspects of HCRE.

Better Consideration of HCRE in the Aggregation Techniques for Unit-Level Human Capital Resources

While the transformation and amplification mechanisms help to explain the dynamic process of HCRE and our suggested modeling approaches provide a framework to model and measure these underlying components of HCRE, it is also important to understand how theories related to HCRE may inform aggregations of individual KSAOs in the measurement of unit-level human capital resources at a particular point in time. Indeed, it is not realistic or necessary for all operationalizations of unit-level human capital resources to collect longitudinal data and use an RCM growth modeling approach to measure this constructs; HCRE may simply not be a focal point of some strategic human capital studies. That said, it remains important that any aggregations used in the measurement of unit-level human capital resources be guided by and consistent with an underlying emergence theory (Nyberg et al., 2014).

To help guide the connection between emergence and aggregations, Chan (1998) illustrated several basic emergence forms (additive, direct and referent-shift consensus, dispersion, and process models) and discussed their operationalization. Both additive and consensus models use the summation of the lower-level units to represent a higher-level construct, but the consensus model requires the within-unit agreement to justify the aggregation. In contrast, the dispersion model values the differences among lower-level units and uses the lower-level variance to define the higher-level construct. Lastly, the process model focuses on the changes in lower-level units and explains the process from the lower level of conceptualization to the higher level (this is similar to the approach we focused on in our discussion above on methodological approaches and considerations).

With the exception of the process model approach, these basic emergence forms and operationalizations have been applied and used to support aggregations of individual-level KSAOs in the measurement of unit-level human capital resources. As suggested by Ployhart and Moliterno (2011), task characteristics (e.g., task complexity) may require individual employees to utilize different types of KSAOs. Some tasks may need employees to complete tasks separately and involve little interaction. In this case, employees may use the same types of KSAOs, which can simply be added to represent the unit-level human capital resource. For example, Hitt and colleagues (2001) used the average ranking of the law schools from which all the partners had graduated to represent human capital resources of law firms. In a similar manner, Pil and Leana (2009) used the average of individual teachers' education level, experience, and ability to teach mathematics to represent the stock of human capital among a school's math teachers. Some tasks may require employees to possess the same type of KSAOs at a similar level. For example, Ployhart et al. (2009) used the store-level mean of aggregated individual-level service orientation and justified the aggregation based on inter-rater reliability (i.e., ICC2). In other situations, tasks may require individuals to contribute different types of KSAOs to unit goals. The unit-level human capital resource in such cases may be more appropriately represented by the dispersion or variance of individual-level KSAOs. For example, Tzabbar and Margolis (2017) used educational heterogeneity as a measure of the funding team's human capital of startup companies.

While these prior operationalizations are consistent with a specific theory and approach to emergence, and are thus appropriate, future research could work to improve aggregations of human capital in two general ways. First, researchers could benefit by considering alternatives or additions to the use of simple descriptive statistics (mean and standard deviation) to capture characteristics of aggregated individual human capital. Central tendency and variance can be important ways to characterize the individual KSAOs in a unit; however, each is also limited in its ability to convey the full characteristics and distribution of a unit's stock of human capital (Boon et al., 2018). By developing new ways to account for the varied nature and form of individual KSAOs, we could improve the accuracy and precision of descriptions (and associated understandings) of the various ways in which the unit-level human capital resources emerge.

Second, we need ways to account for the amplification or interaction aspects in aggregation approaches to measure unit-level human capital resources. As we have noted throughout this chapter, these aspects are a central component of emerged human capital resources. In particular, much of what makes unit-level human capital resources different from its lower-level parts are the synergistic factors that result in improvements to the productive capacities realized from the underlying KSAOs of unit members. Additionally, these aspects are likely to be particularly critical to the achievement of human capital-based competitive advantage. Despite their importance, these amplification and interactive aspects are absent from the extant aggregation techniques to measure unit-level human capital resources. There is thus an important need to develop innovative measurement approaches to capture this critical aspect of unit-level human capital resources and incorporate it into extant aggregation approaches.

Greater Consideration of Dyads

The importance of interactions among individuals is regularly noted in the general work on emergence (e.g., Kozlowski and Klein, 2000) and the microfoundations movement (e.g., Felin et al., 2015). Additionally, dyadic relationships are often viewed as the fundamental building block of groups and unit-level phenomena (e.g., Liden et al., 2016). Despite this potential relevance, very little consideration has been given to the dyad level of analysis in extant work on HCRE. This is not particularly surprising, as dyads are often referred to as the "forgotten level of analysis" (Yammarino and Gooty, 2017, p. 239) and have received the least amount of scholarly attention among all the levels of analysis in management research (Gooty and Yammarino, 2011; Kenny et al., 2006; Krasikova and LeBreton, 2012). We contend that the lack of consideration given to dyads in HCRE represents a missed opportunity, and that future research could greatly benefit by giving more attention to this level of analysis and alternative lens to view HCRE. Indeed, the criticality of dyads is likely to become particularly apparent as we begin to unpack the complex and multifaceted mechanisms and processes involved with HCRE.

In calling for more research on HCRE from a dyadic perspective, we believe it is instructive to draw attention to unique theoretical and methodological considerations associated with this level of analysis. Specifically, there is unfortunately a long track record of misalignment among theory and methods for dyads (Krasikova and LeBreton, 2012). To avoid such issues, it is important to ensure that theorizing related to perceptual-oriented aspects of dyads includes consideration of both parties of a dyad, and that methodological approaches measure constructs for both members of the dyad and assess agreement/disparity (Liden et al., 2016). It is also important to remember that since most dyads are nested within groups and other aspects of an organization (Gooty and Yammarino,

2011), it may require researchers to consider: 1) a large number/network of dyads; 2) leverage diffusion, contagion, and other theoretical mechanisms related to inter-dyadic influences; and 3) methodological approaches to account for the nested and interdependent nature of dyads. Lastly, the recent development of exponential random graph models (Kim et al., 2016; Lusher et al., 2013) and their multilevel extensions (Wang et al., 2013; Zappa and Lomi, 2015) provide potentially interesting network-based methodological approaches to study dyadic phenomena within the context of HCRE.

Dealing with Multiple Unit-Level Human Capital Resources

Extant work on HCRE regularly invokes the notion of a unit-level human capital resource to refer to collections of individuals in firms (Nyberg et al., 2014; Ployhart and Moliterno, 2011). The unit-level concept is all encompassing and helpful in initial theorizing and discussions related to HCRE (indeed, we have also leveraged and used the unit level throughout most of this chapter). However, Ployhart et al. (2014) and others in strategic human capital/strategic HRM and related topics (e.g., Crocker and Eckardt, 2014; Delery and Shaw, 2001; Eckardt et al., 2018b; Eckardt et al., 2014; Humphrey et al., 2009; Lepak and Snell, 1999) have noted that firms have multiple unit-level human capital resources and that these can vary with respect to their strategic significance. We believe that the organizational reality of there being multiple unit-level human capital resources in firms has several important implications for future work on HCRE.

First, this means that at any point in time there are likely to be many HCRE processes ongoing in firms. As a result, there is the potential for the simultaneity modeling challenges noted above to be significantly enhanced. Second, it is important that future research on HCRE is clear in theorizing and methodological designs about the focal unit-level human capital resources. There may be an implicit assumption among macro-oriented scholars that the focus is always (and only) on those unit-level human capital resources that play central roles in a firm's economic value generation processes (i.e., the *strategic* unit-level human capital resources). However, it is possible that more micro-oriented scholars operate under different assumptions and see the totality and potential value of all unit-level human capital resources in a firm (Ployhart et al., 2014). This could create subtle, but important, differences in language use, definitions, and understandings (Nyberg and Wright, 2015) and potentially lead to unnecessary confusion and conflict among coauthors, reviewers, and editors. Lastly, while it is understandable that initial research on HCRE may want to focus on *strategic* unit-level human capital resources, it is likely that consideration of less core unit-level human capital resources may provide important performance insights related to the management of a firm's entire portfolio of human capital resources. In particular, such consideration may illuminate the indirect (cf. Nyberg et al., 2018) or interactive (cf. Crocker and Eckardt, 2014; Ployhart and Cragun, 2017; Ployhart et al., 2014) effects of how an emergence process or outcome with fewer core unit-level capital resources may play important roles in the broader links between HCRE and competitive advantage.

More Empirical Research

Although theory building and clarifications are essential to move forward research on HCRE, there is a *strong need* for empirical research in this area. As we note above, there have been very few empirical studies that relate to HCRE, and even fewer that focus specifically on the HCRE process. This is unfortunate as empirical testing is a fundamental part of moving forward any research area. Additionally, there is a risk that the interest among strategic human capital researchers in HCRE and its related processes may wane if empirical studies do not materialize – an outcome that would be detrimental to the potential for this topic area to provide a holistic and integrated (micro-macro) understanding of the multilevel factors involved with the development and deployment of valuable human capital resources.

We have attempted to encourage more empirical research on HCRE by clarifying and explicating the underlying mechanisms of this process and providing guidance on potential approaches and considerations with measuring and modeling HCRE. We have also tried to highlight a few challenges that may arise in modeling HCRE, and made suggestions on possible new methodological directions for researchers in this area. While we hope the guidance and suggestions in this chapter make progress on methodological-oriented aspects of HCRE, we fully acknowledge that they are likely incomplete and need further refinement and clarifications in the context of specific studies. We therefore look forward to hopefully seeing enhancements and extensions of our methodological suggestions and considerations in future empirical studies of HCRE.

CHAPTER SUMMARY

BOX 5.1 KEY TAKEAWAYS

1. The HCRE process involves two underlying mechanisms: transformation of unit-member KSAOs and amplification of unit-member KSAO–performance links. The transformation mechanism can relate to task- and colleague-oriented KSAOs, increases to KSAO stocks, and situations of KSAO convergence and divergence. The amplification mechanism is similar to the notion of complementarities.
2. All aspects of the HCRE process can increase the value generated from a firm's stock of KSAOs. However, considering the other important aspects of competitive advantage (interfirm heterogeneity, isolating mechanisms, bargaining power), the *social environment emergence enabling factors* and *amplification mechanisms* are likely most critical to link HCRE to competitive advantage.
3. Despite the inherent challenges of analyzing bottom-up multilevel processes, many aspects and underlying mechanisms of the HCRE process can be empirically examined using existing multilevel methodologies. The key is to consider the combination of multiple modeling techniques in the same study and to use existing methodological approaches in novel ways.

BOX 5.2 DIRECTIONS FOR FUTURE RESEARCH

1. Greater leveraging and integration of research from micro-oriented perspectives and research into extant HCRE theory. Opportunities exist in proximal areas (e.g., human capital and human resource management) to research on HCRE, as well as more distal areas (leadership, teams, motivation, job design, emotions, conflict, etc.) of the micro-oriented management literature.

2. Development of process and detailed theorizing related to HCRE. There is much to learn about the specific details, interactions, and dynamics involved in HCRE. Computational models/agent-based simulations provide a tool to aid in the development of parsimonious and traceable process-based theories that account for the inherent complexity to HCRE.
3. Empirical research related to HCRE in general and the HCRE process in particular. Empirical testing is fundamental for moving forward any research area. Additionally, there is a risk that the interest among strategic human capital researchers in HCRE and its related processes may wane if empirical studies do not materialize.

NOTES

* The authors of this chapter were originally assigned two separate chapters on the topic of human capital resource emergence (HCRE). In keeping with the general structure of the book, one of these chapters was to be micro-oriented and the other macro-oriented. We requested, however, to write one micro-macro integrated chapter for several reasons: 1) the topic of emergence, in general, *requires* considering and integrating micro-macro perspectives (i.e., we are not sure it is feasible to focus on the broad topic of emergence without attending to and leveraging micro- *and* macro-oriented perspectives); 2) unlike the other topic areas in this book, there are no clear separate micro and macro theories on the topic of HCRE. Rather, the extant work on HCRE draws on one core theoretical perspective (Ployhart and Moliterno, 2011), and this perspective considers multiple levels of analysis and leverages both micro and macro perspectives; and 3) writing one micro-macro integrated chapter would keep with the general tradition in this area of integration and collaboration between micro- and macro-oriented human capital researchers. We thank the editors (Tom Moliterno and Anthony Nyberg) for seeing value in combining our chapters, and for their flexibility and support in the micro-macro integrated view/tradition we seek to maintain for this important area of human capital research.

1. This is also referred to as net economic benefits (Peteraf and Barney, 2003), firm-level value capture (Lepak et al., 2007), and human capital rents (Chadwick, 2017).
2. Our emphasis on monetary compensation as a motivating factor does not negate the idea that employees also value, and can be motivated by, nonpecuniary aspects (see Bridoux and Stoelhorst and Campbell and Kryscynski, Chapters 2 and 9 in this volume). Rather, it is based on the idea that monetary factors are often critical motivators and considerations for employees in work contexts (see Conroy and Nyberg and Reilly, Chapters 1 and 23).
3. A native performance outcome is one that only occurs at a higher level of analysis (e.g., teams, business units) and cannot be decomposed into or otherwise attributed to particular entities at a lower level of analysis (Markham and Markham, 2017).

REFERENCES

Abrams, L. C., Cross, R., Lesser, E., and Levin, D. Z. (2003). Nurturing interpersonal trust in knowledge-sharing networks. *Academy of Management Executive*, *17*(4), 64–77.

Aguinis, H., Gottfredson, R. K., and Culpepper, S. A. (2013). Best-practice recommendations for estimating cross-level interaction effects using multilevel modeling. *Journal of Management*, *39*(6), 1490–528.

Aguinis, H., and Molina-Azorín, J. F. (2015). Using multilevel modeling and mixed methods to make theoretical progress in microfoundations for strategy research. *Strategic Organization*, *13*(4), 353–64.

Aguinis, H., Pierce, C. A., Bosco, F. A., and Muslin, I. S. (2009). First decade of organizational research methods: Trends in design, measurement, and data-analysis topics. *Organizational Research Methods*, *12*(1), 69–112.

Alchian, A. A., and Demsetz, H. (1972). Production, information costs, and economic organization. *American Economic Review*, *62*(5), 777–95.

Amabile, T. M., Barsade, S. G., Mueller, J. S., and Staw, B. M. (2005). Affect and creativity at work. *Administrative Science Quarterly*, *50*(3), 367–403.

Argote, L. (1999). *Organizational Learning: Creating, Retaining, and Transferring Knowledge*. Dordrecht: Springer.

Argote, L., and Ren, Y. (2012). Transactive memory systems: A microfoundation of dynamic capabilities. *Journal of Management Studies*, *49*(8), 1375–82.

Ashcraft, M. H., and Kirk, E. P. (2001). The relationships among working memory, math anxiety, and performance. *Journal of Experimental Psychology: General*, *130*(2), 224–37.
Barney, J. (1991). Firm resources and sustained competitive advantage. *Journal of Management*, *17*(1), 99–120.
Barney, J., and Felin, T. (2013). What are microfoundations? *Academy of Management Perspectives*, *27*(2), 138–55.
Beal, D. J., Cohen, R. R., Burke, M. J., and McLendon, C. L. (2003). Cohesion and performance in groups: A meta-analytic clarification of construct relations. *Journal of Applied Psychology*, *88*(6), 989–1004.
Becker, G. (1964). *Human Capital: A Theoretical and Empirical Analysis, with Special Reference to Education*. Chicago, IL: University of Chicago Press.
Bell, B. S., and Kozlowski, S. W. (2002). A typology of virtual teams: Implications for effective leadership. *Group and Organization Management*, *27*(1), 14–49.
Biemann, T., and Kearney, E. (2010). Size does matter: How varying group sizes in a sample affect the most common measures of group diversity. *Organizational Research Methods*, *13*(3), 582–99.
Bliese, P. D. (2000). Within-group agreement, non-independence, and reliability: Implications for data aggregation and analysis. In K. J. Klein and S. W. J. Kozlowski (eds), *Multilevel Theory, Research, and Methods in Organizations: Foundations, Extensions and New Directions*, 349–81. San Francisco, CA: Wiley.
Bliese, P. D., and Lang, J. W. (2016). Understanding relative and absolute change in discontinuous growth models: Coding alternatives and implications for hypothesis testing. *Organizational Research Methods*, *19*(4), 562–92.
Bliese, P. D., and Ployhart, R. E. (2002). Growth modeling using random coefficient models: Model building, testing, and illustrations. *Organizational Research Methods*, *5*(4), 362–87.
Boon, C., Eckardt, R., Lepak, D. P., and Boselie, P. (2018). Integrating strategic human capital and strategic human resource management. *International Journal of Human Resource Management*, *29*(1), 34–67.
Brown, J. S., and Duguid, P. (2001). Knowledge and organization: A social-practice perspective. *Organization Science*, *12*(2), 198–213.
Campbell, B. A., Coff, R., and Kryscynski, D. (2012). Rethinking sustained competitive advantage from human capital. *Academy of Management Review*, *37*(3), 376–95.
Campbell, B. A., Saxton, B. M., and Banerjee, P. M. (2014). Resetting the shot clock: The effect of comobility on human capital. *Journal of Management*, *40*(2), 531–56.
Cannon-Bowers, J. A., Salas, E., and Converse, S. A. (1993). Shared mental models in expert term decision making. In N. J. Castellan (ed.), *Current Issues in Individual and Group Decision Making*, 221–46. Hillsdale, NJ: Erlbaum.
Carron, A. V. (1982). Cohesiveness in sport groups: Interpretations and considerations. *Journal of Sport Psychology*, *4*(2), 123–38.
Chadwick, C. (2017). Toward a more comprehensive model of firms' human capital rents. *Academy of Management Review*, *42*(3), 499–519.
Chaffin, D., Heidl, R., Hollenbeck, J. R., Howe, M., Yu, A., Voorhees, C., and Calantone, R. (2017). The promises and perils of wearable sensors in organizational research. *Organizational Research Methods*, *20*(1), 3–31.
Chan, D. (1998). Functional relations among constructs in the same content domain at different levels of analysis: A typology of composition models. *Journal of Applied Psychology*, *83*(2), 234–46.
Chuang, C. H., and Liao, H. (2010). Strategic human resource management in service context: Taking care of business by taking care of employees and customers. *Personnel Psychology*, *63*(1), 153–96.
Coff, R. W. (1997). Human assets and management dilemmas: Coping with hazards on the road to resource-based theory. *Academy of Management Review*, *22*(2), 374–402.
Coff, R. W. (1999). When competitive advantage doesn't lead to performance: The resource-based view and stakeholder bargaining power. *Organization Science*, *10*(2), 119–33.
Coff, R. W. (2010). The coevolution of rent appropriation and capability development. *Strategic Management Journal*, *31*(7), 711–33.
Coff, R., and Kryscynski, D. (2011). Drilling for micro-foundations of human capital based competitive advantages. *Journal of Management*, *37*(5), 1429–43.
Cohen, W. M., and Levinthal, D. A. (1990). Absorptive capacity: A new perspective on learning and innovation. *Administrative Science Quarterly*, *35*(1), 128–52.
Collins, C. J., and Smith, K. G. (2006). Knowledge exchange and combination: The role of human resource practices in the performance of high-technology firms. *Academy of Management Journal*, *49*(3), 544–60.
Crocker, A., and Eckardt, R. (2014). A multilevel investigation of individual- and unit-level human capital complementarities. *Journal of Management*, *40*(2), 509–30.
Delery, J. E., and Shaw, J. D. (2001). The strategic management of people in work organizations: Review, synthesis, and extension. In G. R. Ferris (ed.), *Research in Personnel and Human Resources Management*, vol. 20, 165–97. New York: Elsevier.
Dierickx, I., and Cool, K. (1989). Asset stock accumulation and sustainability of competitive advantage. *Management Science*, *35*(12), 1504–11.
DiMaggio, P. (1997). Culture and cognition. *Annual Review of Sociology*, *23*(1), 263–87.

Dreyfus, H. L., and Dreyfus, S. E. (1986). *Mind over Machine*. New York: Free Press.
Eckardt, R., and Moliterno, T. P. (2016). Multilevel empirical research on strategic human capital. *Strategic Human Capital Newsletter*, *5*(1), 6–7.
Eckardt, R., Skaggs, B. C., and Lepak, D. P. (2018b). An examination of the firm-level performance impact of cluster hiring in knowledge-intensive firms. *Academy of Management Journal*, *61*(3), 919–44.
Eckardt, R., Skaggs B. C., and Youndt, M. (2014). Turnover and knowledge loss: An examination of the differential impact of production manager and worker turnover in service and manufacturing firms. *Journal of Management Studies*, *51*(7), 1025–57.
Eckardt, R., Crocker, A., Ahn, Y., Floyd, S. W., Boyd, B. K., Hodgkinson, G. P., Kozlowski, S. W. J., Moliterno, T. P., and Starbuck, W. H. (2018a). Reflections on the micro-macro divide: Ideas from the trenches and moving forward. *Strategic Organization*. https://doi.org/10.1177/1476127018770048.
Ethiraj, S. K. and Garg, P. (2012). The division of gains from complementarities in human-capital-intensive activity. *Organization Science*, *23*(3), 725–42.
Evans, N. J., and Jarvis, P. A. (1980). Group cohesion: A review and reevaluation. *Small Group Behavior*, *11*(4), 359–70.
Eysenck, M. W., and Derakshan, N. (1998). Working memory capacity in high trait-anxious and repressor groups. *Cognition and Emotion*, *12*(5), 697–713.
Felin, T., Foss, N. J., and Ployhart, R. E. (2015). The microfoundations movement in strategy and organization theory. *Academy of Management Annals*, *9*(1), 575–632.
Festinger, L. (1950). Informal social communication. *Psychological Review*, *57*(5), 271–82.
Gittell, J. H., Seidner, R., and Wimbush, J. (2010). A relational model of how high-performance work systems work. *Organization Science*, *21*(2), 490–506.
Glick, H. A., and Feuer, M. J. (1984). Employer-sponsored training and the governance of specific human-capital investments. *Quarterly Review of Economics and Business*, *24*(2), 91–103.
González-Romá, V., and Hernández, A. (2017). Multilevel modeling: Research-based lessons for substantive researchers. *Annual Review of Organizational Psychology and Organizational Behavior*, *4*(1), 183–210.
Goodman, P. S., Ravlin, E., and Schminke, M. (1987). Understanding groups in organizations. *Research in Organizational Behavior*, *9*, 121–73.
Gooty, J., and Yammarino, F. J. (2011). Dyads in organizational research: Conceptual issues and multilevel analyses. *Organizational Research Methods*, *14*(3), 456–83.
Grand, J. A., Braun, M. T., Kuljanin, G., Kozlowski, S. W., and Chao, G. T. (2016). The dynamics of team cognition: A process-oriented theory of knowledge emergence in teams. *Journal of Applied Psychology*, *101*(10), 1353–85.
Hackman, J. R. (1987). The design of work teams. In J. Lorsch (ed.), *Handbook of Organizational Behavior*, 315–42. Englewood Cliffs, NJ: Prentice-Hall.
Hansen, M. T. (1999). The search-transfer problem: The role of weak ties in sharing knowledge across organization subunits. *Administrative Science Quarterly*, *44*(1), 82–5.
Harrison, D. A., and Klein, K. J. (2007). What's the difference? Diversity constructs as separation, variety, or disparity in organizations. *Academy of Management Review*, *32*(4), 1199–228.
Hashimoto, M. (1981). Firm-specific human capital as a shared investment. *American Economic Review*, *71*(3), 475–82.
Hatch, N. W., and Dyer, J. H. (2004). Human capital and learning as a source of sustainable competitive advantage. *Strategic Management Journal*, *25*(12), 1155–78.
Hedeker, D., Mermelstein, R. J., and Demirtas, H. (2008). An application of a mixed-effects location scale model for analysis of ecological momentary assessment (EMA) data. *Biometrics*, *64*(2), 627–34.
Hitt, M. A., Beamish, P. W., Jackson, S. E., and Mathieu, J. E. (2007). Building theoretical and empirical bridges across levels: Multilevel research in management. *Academy of Management Journal*, *50*(6), 1385–99.
Hitt, M. A., Bierman, L., Shimizu, K., and Kochhar, R. (2001). Direct and moderating effects of human capital on strategy and performance in professional service firms: A resource-based perspective. *Academy of Management Journal*, *44*(1), 13–28.
Hofmann, D. A. (1997). An overview of the logic and rationale of hierarchical linear models. *Journal of Management*, *23*(6), 723–44.
Huber, G. P. (1991). Organizational learning: The contributing processes and the literatures. *Organization Science*, *2*(1), 88–115.
Humphrey, S. E., Morgeson, F. P., and Mannor, M. J. (2009). Developing a theory of the strategic core of teams: A role composition model of team performance. *Journal of Applied Psychology*, *94*(1), 48–61.
Isen, A. M., Daubman, K. A., and Nowicki, G. P. (1987). Positive affect facilitates creative problem solving. *Journal of Personality and Social Psychology*, *52*(6), 1122–31.
Jiang, K., Chuang, C. H., and Chiao, Y. C. (2015). Developing collective customer knowledge and service climate: The interaction between service-oriented high-performance work systems and service leadership. *Journal of Applied Psychology*, *100*(4), 1089–106.

Kehoe, R. R., and Collins, C. J. (2017). Human resource management and unit performance in knowledge-intensive work. *Journal of Applied Psychology*, *102*(8), 1222–36.
Kenny, D., Kashy, D. A., and Cook, W. L. (2006). *Dyadic Data Analysis*. New York: Wiley.
Kim, J. Y., Howard, M., Pahnke, E. C., and Boeker, W. (2016). Understanding network formation in strategy research: Exponential random graph models. *Strategic Management Journal*, *37*(1), 22–44.
Klein, K., and Boals, A. (2001). The relationship of life event stress and working memory capacity. *Applied Cognitive Psychology*, *15*(5), 565–79.
Kozlowski, S. W. J. (2015). Advancing research on team process dynamics: Theoretical, methodological, and measurement considerations. *Organizational Psychology Review*, *5*(4), 270–99.
Kozlowski, S. W. J., and Chao, G. T. (2012). The dynamics of emergence: Cognition and cohesion in work teams. *Managerial and Decision Economics*, *33*(5–6), 335–54.
Kozlowski, S. W. J., and Chao, G. T. (2018). Unpacking team process dynamics and emergent phenomena: Challenges, conceptual advances, and innovative methods. *American Psychologist*, *73*(4), 576–92.
Kozlowski, S. W. J., and Ilgen, D. R. (2006). Enhancing the effectiveness of work groups and teams. *Psychological Science in the Public Interest*, *7*(3), 77–124.
Kozlowski, S. W. J., and Klein, K. J. (2000). A multilevel approach to theory and research in organizations: Contextual, temporal, and emergent processes. In K. J. Klein and S. W. J. Kozlowski (eds), *Multilevel Theory, Research, and Methods in Organizations: Foundations, Extensions, and New Directions*, 3–90. San Francisco, CA: Jossey-Bass.
Kozlowski, S. W. J., Chao, G. T., Chang, C.- H., and Fernandez, R. (2015). Team dynamics: Using "big data" to advance the science of team effectiveness. In S. Tonidandel, E. King, and J. Cortina (eds), *Big Data at Work: The Data Science Revolution and Organizational Psychology*, 272–309. New York: Routledge.
Kozlowski, S. W. J., Chao, G. T., Grand, J. A., Braun, M. T., and Kuljanin, G. (2013). Advancing multilevel research design capturing the dynamics of emergence. *Organizational Research Methods*, *16*(4), 581–615.
Kozlowski, S. W. J., Chao, G. T., Grand, J. A., Braun, M. T., and Kuljanin, G. (2016). Capturing the multilevel dynamics of emergence: Computational modeling, simulation, and virtual experimentation. *Organizational Psychology Review*, *6*(1), 3–33.
Kozlowski, S. W. J., Gully, S. M., Nason, E. R., and Smith, E. M. (1999). Developing adaptive teams: A theory of compilation and performance across levels and time. In D. R. Ilgen and E. D. Pulakos (eds), *The Changing Nature of Work Performance: Implications for Staffing, Personnel Actions, and Development*, 240–92. San Francisco, CA: Jossey-Bass.
Krasikova, D. V., and LeBreton, J. M. (2012). Just the two of us: Misalignment of theory and methods in examining dyadic phenomena. *Journal of Applied Psychology*, *97*(4), 739–57.
La Pointe, L. B., and Engle, R. W. (1990). Simple and complex word spans as measures of working memory capacity. *Journal of Experimental Psychology: Learning, Memory, and Cognition*, *16*(6), 1118–33.
Lang, J. W. B., and Bliese, P. D. (2018). A temporal perspective on emergence: Using 3-level mixed effects models to track consensus emergence in groups. In S. E. Humphrey and J. M. LeBreton (eds), *The Handbook of Multilevel Theory, Measurement, and Analysis*. Washington, DC: American Psychological Association.
Lang, J. W. B., Bliese, P. D., and de Voogt, A. (2018). Modeling consensus emergence in groups using longitudinal multilevel methods. *Personnel Psychology*, *71*(2), 255–81.
Leana, C. R., and Van Buren, H. J. (1999). Organizational social capital and employment practices. *Academy of Management Review*, *24*(3), 538–55.
Lepak, D. P., and Snell, S. A. (1999). The human resource architecture: Toward a theory of human capital allocation and development. *Academy of Management Review*, *24*(1), 31–48.
Lepak, D. P., Smith, K. G., and Taylor, M. S. (2007). Value creation and value capture: A multilevel perspective. *Academy of Management Review*, *32*(1), 180–94.
Levin, D. Z., and Cross, R. (2004). The strength of weak ties you can trust: The mediating role of trust in effective knowledge transfer. *Management Science*, *50*(11), 1477–90.
Liden, R. C., Anand, S., and Vidyarthi, P. (2016). Dyadic relationships. *Annual Review of Organizational Psychology and Organizational Behavior*, *3*, 139–66.
Lusher, D., Koskinen, J., and Robins, G. (2013). *Exponential Random Graph Models for Social Networks: Theory, Methods, and Applications*. Cambridge: Cambridge University Press.
March, J. G. (1991). Exploration and exploitation in organizational learning. *Organization Science*, *2*(1), 71–87.
Markham, I. S., and Markham, S. E. (2017). First and second strings: Using entity analytics to contrast core and supporting teams. *Journal of Business and Psychology*, *32*(5), 595–610.
Marks, M. A., Mathieu, J. E., and Zaccaro, S. J. (2001). A temporally based framework and taxonomy of team processes. *Academy of Management Review*, *26*(3), 356–76.
Mathieu, J. E., and Chen, G. (2011). The etiology of the multilevel paradigm in management research. *Journal of Management*, *37*(2), 610–41.
Mathieu, J. E., and Luciano, M. M. (2018). Multilevel emergence in work collectives. In S. E. Humphrey and

J. M. LeBreton (eds), *The Handbook of Multilevel Theory, Measurement and Analysis*. Washington, DC: American Psychological Association.
Mathieu, J. E., Heffner, T. S., Goodwin, G. F., Salas, E., and Cannon-Bowers, J. A. (2000). The influence of shared mental models on team process and performance. *Journal of Applied Psychology*, *85*(2), 273–83.
Mitchell, T. R., and Daniels, D. (2003). Motivation. In W. Borman, D. Ilgen, and R. Klimoski (eds), *Handbook of Psychology*, vol. 12, 225–54. New York: Wiley.
Moliterno, T. P., and Ployhart, R. E. (2016). Multilevel models for strategy research: An idea whose time (still) has come. In C. Cinici and G. B. Dagnino (eds), *Research Methods for Strategic Management*, 51–77. New York: Routledge.
Molloy, J. C., and Barney, J. B. (2015). Who captures the value created with human capital? A market-based view. *Academy of Management Perspectives*, *29*(3), 309–25.
Morris, S. S., Alvarez, S. A., Barney, J. B., and Molloy, J. C. (2017). Firm-specific human capital investments as a signal of general value: Revisiting assumptions about human capital and how it is managed. *Strategic Management Journal*, *38*(4), 912–19.
Nahapiet, J., and Ghoshal, S. (1998). Social capital, intellectual capital, and the organizational advantage. *Academy of Management Review*, *23*(2), 242–66.
Nonaka, I., and Takeuchi, H. (1995). *The Knowledge-Creating Company: How Japanese Companies Create the Dynamics of Innovation*. New York: Oxford University Press.
Nyberg, A. J., and Ployhart, R. E. (2013). Context-emergent turnover (CET) theory: A theory of collective turnover. *Academy of Management Review*, *38*(1): 109–31.
Nyberg, A. J., and Wright, P. M. (2015). 50 years of human capital research: Assessing what we know, exploring where we go. *Academy of Management Perspectives*, *29*(3), 287–95.
Nyberg, A. J., Moliterno, T. P., Hale, D., and Lepak, D. P. (2014). Resource-based perspectives on unit-level human capital A review and integration. *Journal of Management*, *40*(1): 316–46.
Nyberg, A. J., Reilly, G., Essman, S., and Rodrigues, J. (2018). Human capital resources: A call to retire settled debates and to start a few new debates. *International Journal of Human Resource Management*, *29*(1), 68–86.
Peteraf, M. A. (1993). The cornerstones of competitive advantage: A resource-based view. *Strategic Management Journal*, *14*(3), 179–91.
Peteraf, M. A., and Barney, J. B. (2003). Unraveling the resource-based tangle. *Managerial and Decision Economics*, *24*(4), 309–23.
Pil, F. K., and Leana, C. (2009). Applying organizational research to public school reform: The effects of teacher human and social capital on student performance. *Academy of Management Journal*, *52*(6), 1101–24.
Ployhart, R. E. (2015). Strategic organizational behavior (STROBE): The missing voice in the strategic human capital conversation. *Academy of Management Perspectives*, *29*(3), 342–56.
Ployhart, R. E., and Cragun, O. R. (2017). Human capital resource complementarities. In D. G. Collings, K. Mellahl, and W. F. Cascio (eds), *The Oxford Handbook of Talent Management*. Oxford: Oxford University Press.
Ployhart, R. E., and Hale Jr, D. (2014). The fascinating psychological microfoundations of strategy and competitive advantage. *Annual Review of Organizational Psychology and Organizational Behavior*, *1*(1), 145–72.
Ployhart, R. E., and Moliterno, T. P. (2011). Emergence of the human capital resource: A multilevel model. *Academy of Management Review*, *36*(1), 127–50.
Ployhart, R. E., Nyberg, A. J., Reilly, G., and Maltarich, M. A. (2014). Human capital is dead; long live human capital resources! *Journal of Management*, *40*(2), 371–98.
Ployhart, R. E., Van Iddekinge, C. H., and MacKenzie, W. (2011). Acquiring and developing human capital for sustained competitive advantage: The interconnectedness of generic and specific human capital resources. *Academy of Management Journal*, *54*(2), 353–68.
Ployhart, R. E., Weekley, J. A., and Ramsey, J. (2009). The consequences of human resource stocks and flows: A longitudinal examination of unit service orientation and unit effectiveness. *Academy of Management Journal*, *52*(5), 996–1015.
Porter, M. E. (1985). *Competitive Strategy: Creating and Sustaining Superior Performance*. New York: Free Press.
Preacher, K. J., Zyphur, M. J., and Zhang, Z. (2010). A general multilevel SEM framework for assessing multilevel mediation. *Psychological Methods*, *15*(3), 209–33.
Raudenbush, S. W., and Bryk, A. S. (2002). *Hierarchical Linear Models: Applications and Data Analysis Methods*. Newbury Park, CA: Sage.
Ren, Y., and Argote, L. (2011). Transactive memory systems 1985–2010: An integrative framework of key dimensions, antecedents, and consequences. *Academy of Management Annals*, *5*(1), 189–229.
Rentsch, J. R. (1990). Climate and culture: Interaction and qualitative differences in organizational meanings. *Journal of Applied Psychology*, *75*(6), 668–81.
Rousseau, D. M., Sitkin, S. B., Burt, R. S., and Camerer, C. (1998). Not so different after all: A cross-discipline view of trust. *Academy of Management Review*, *23*(3), 393–404.
Salas, E., Tannenbaum, S. I., Kozlowski, S. W. J., Miller, C. A., Mathieu, J. E., and Vessey, W. B. (2015). Teams

in space exploration: A new frontier for the science of team effectiveness. *Current Directions in Psychological Science*, *24*(3), 200–207.
Sayama, H. (2015). *Introduction to the Modeling and Analysis of Complex Systems.* Geneseo, NY: Open SUNY Textbooks.
Schmader, T., and Johns, M. (2003). Converging evidence that stereotype threat reduces working memory capacity. *Journal of Personality and Social Psychology*, *85*(3), 440–52.
Schoorman, F. D., Mayer, R. C., and Davis, J. H. (2007). An integrative model of organizational trust: Past, present, and future. *Academy of Management Review*, *32*(2), 344–54.
Seo, M., Barrett, L. F., and Bartunek, J. M. (2004). The role of affective experience in work motivation. *Academy of Management Review*, *29*(3), 423–39.
Sorg, B. A., and Whitney, P. (1992). The effect of trait anxiety and situational stress on working memory capacity. *Journal of Research in Personality*, *26*(3), 235–41.
Staw, B. M., Sutton, R. I., and Pelled, L. H. (1994). Employee positive emotion and favorable outcomes at the workplace. *Organization Science*, *5*(1), 51–71.
Szulanski, G. (1996). Exploring internal stickiness: Impediments to the transfer of best practice within the firm. *Strategic Management Journal*, *17*, 27–43.
Takeuchi, R., Lepak, D. P., Wang, H., and Takeuchi, K. (2007). An empirical examination of the mechanisms mediating between high-performance work systems and the performance of Japanese organizations. *Journal of Applied Psychology*, *92*(4), 1069–83.
Thompson, J. D. (1967). *Organizations in Action: Social Science Bases of Administrative Theory*. New York: McGraw-Hill.
Tzabbar, D., and Margolis, J. (2017). Beyond the startup stage: The founding team's human capital, new venture's stage of life, founder–CEO duality, and breakthrough innovation. *Organization Science*, *28*(5), 857–72.
Van de Ven, Andrew H., Delbecq, A. L., and Koenig Jr, R. (1976). Determinants of coordination modes within organizations. *American Sociological Review*, *41*(2), 322–38.
Volberda, H. W., Foss, N. J., and Lyles, M. A. (2010). Absorbing the concept of absorptive capacity: How to realize its potential in the organization field. *Organization Science*, *21*(4), 931–51.
Vroom, V. H. (1964). *Work and Motivation*. New York: Wiley.
Wang, P., Robins, G., Pattison, P., and Lazega, E. (2013). Exponential random graph models for multilevel networks. *Social Networks*, *35*(1), 96–115.
Wang, M., Zhou, L., and Zhang, Z. (2016). Dynamic modeling. *Annual Review of Organizational Psychology and Organizational Behavior*, *3*, 241–66.
Williams, L. J., Vandenberg, R. J., and Edwards, J. R. (2009). 12 structural equation modeling in management research: A guide for improved analysis. *Academy of Management Annals*, *3*(1), 543–604.
Wright, P. M., and McMahan, G. C. (2011). Exploring human capital: Putting "human" back into strategic human resource management. *Human Resource Management Journal*, *21*(2), 93–104.
Yammarino, F. J., and Gooty, J. (2017). Multi-level issues and dyads in leadership research. In G. Schyns, R. J. Hall, and P. Neves (eds), *Handbook of Methods in Leadership Research*, 229–255. Cheltenham, UK and Northampton, MA, USA: Edward Elgar Publishing.
Zappa, P., and Lomi, A. (2015). The analysis of multilevel networks in organizations: Models and empirical tests. *Organizational Research Methods*, *18*(3), 542–69.

6. Human capital resource emergence: reflections, insights, and recommendations*

Steve W. J. Kozlowski

The micro–macro divide in organizational science has loomed large for a very long time. Indeed, it is the maximal divide as linking even less drastic differences in system level – micro to meso or meso to macro – represent substantial theoretical and methodological challenges. Scientific progress is being made, but there is still a long way to go. Recent theory and empirical attention devoted to human capital resource emergence (HCRE) holds promise to advance our understanding of linkages across all the levels that comprise organizational systems. HCRE is about processes that drive the transformation and amplification of individual knowledge, skills, abilities, and other characteristics (KSAOs) into the emergence of higher-level human capital resources that provide competitive advantage. It refers to the bottom-up emergence of human capital as a collective phenomenon that originates from the KSAO characteristics of individuals that is transformed and amplified by interaction and exchange process mechanisms – cognitive, motivational, affective, and behavioral – while under the constraints and shaping influence of a higher-level organizational system context (Ployhart and Moliterno, 2011). HCRE represents a scholarly movement that has the potential over the long run to go a long way in bridging the divides across the levels of organizational systems and the disciplines that focus primarily on particular levels within organizations.

The preceding chapter by Eckardt and Jiang is a well-developed, scholarly, and integrative review of the underpinnings of HCRE theory, multilevel modeling approaches that have potential to advance empirical research, and some of the core conceptual and methodological challenges that have to be surmounted going forward. It was particularly astute of Eckardt and Jiang to combine their conceptual foci – micro and macro – into one chapter as an understanding of multilevel phenomena can only be advanced by integration across levels (Roberts et al., 1978). I found their chapter informative and stimulating, with several actionable suggestions for advancing empirical research on HCRE.

The perspective and insights I have to offer in this commentary are primarily focused on encouraging the development of process-oriented theories, directing attention to unpacking emergence process dynamics (i.e., the *process mechanisms* driving emergence as a dynamic process vs. conventional aggregation of *static metrics* to represent an emerged construct), and advancing innovative research methodologies that enable direct investigation of emergence as a process (Grand et al., 2016; Kozlowski, 2015; Kozlowski and Chao, 2012, 2018; Kozlowski et al., 2013, 2016; Kozlowski and Klein, 2000). Although my theory and research efforts directed toward team learning, development, adaptation, and effectiveness are not specifically directed at HCRE, they are nonetheless germane to the core process phenomenon of multilevel emergence – *emergence enabling process mechanisms* – and to core substantive content that is involved in HCRE (Ployhart and Moliterno, 2011). My intent with this commentary is to provide a perspective on the roots and development of multilevel theory (MLT) and the relative inattention in theory and research to emergence as a process. After highlighting and discussing core conceptual and methodological issues focused on emergence as a process phenomenon, I will offer some specific observations stimulated by Eckardt and Jiang and key recommendations relevant to advancing theory and research on HCRE.

THE DEVELOPMENT OF MULTILEVEL THEORY

A Perspective

For perspective, it is useful to trace a bit of history. This is by no means intended to be a comprehensive and dispassionate review of the development of MLT. Rather, my intent is to reflect on the role of MLT in my intellectual evolution, summarize my influence on the development of contemporary MLT, and assert why I think organizational science needs to focus on advancing process-oriented theory and research – with HCRE as a particularly rich and central emergence process target.

When I entered graduate school some years ago, I was interested in studying organizations as dynamic systems. However, I quickly came to realize that organizational psychology and behavior (OPB) – the micro world – treated the concept of *organizational system* as a metaphor and that theory and research were really directed at individuals, with different organizational features (e.g., job characteristics, climate, leadership) serving as perceptual targets for individual reactions (e.g., satisfaction, commitment, performance). I was inspired early in my graduate studies by Roberts et al. (1978) – *Developing an Interdisciplinary Science of Organizations* – which pointed toward bridging system levels. Although the book did not offer a lot of specifics, it provided an aspiration to pursue. My dissertation was an early effort to conduct multilevel research (Kozlowski and Farr, 1988; Kozlowski and Hults, 1987).[1] MLT is what I describe as a meta-theoretical framework – a set of principles for theory building, research design, measurement, and analysis – that can be applied to a wide range of phenomena in organizations. As a new assistant professor, I delved into the limited literature that comprised the underpinnings of what was then "multilevel thinking" (e.g., James, 1982; Rousseau, 1985). I developed a seminar to train graduate students, and honed my understanding of MLT with each successive seminar offering.[2]

By the late 1990s when Katherine Klein and I planned the MLT book, I had developed a deep perspective on the state of multilevel theory and research, which at the time was much plagued by methodological and analytical debates (James et al., 1984, 1993; Klein et al., 1994; Kozlowski and Hattrup, 1992; Schmidt and Hunter, 1989). We had some key goals for the MLT book. First, we wanted to synthesize principles to guide multilevel theory building, research design, and measurement (Kozlowski and Klein, 2000). Beyond principles for theory development, we created a typology to characterize different types of emergent constructs – composition constructs based on convergent forms of emergence and compilation forms based on divergent forms of emergence – to guide measurement and representation. Second, we wanted to clarify and dispel confusion regarding aggregation and analytics that had plagued the literature (Bliese, 2000; Klein et al., 2000). Clarifying the advantages of multilevel random coefficient modeling over other alternative analytic approaches was important. Third, we wanted to sow the seeds of MLT beyond the substantive domains in which it had developed (i.e., climate and leadership). The astute reader will notice that there are no chapters on either of those obvious topics in the book. Instead, four chapters were commissioned to apply MLT to topics that are germane to the current focus on HCRE: selection with respect to influences on the firm (Schneider et al., 2000); performance management and implications for firm performance (DeNisi, 2000); training effectiveness and "vertical" transfer upwards (Kozlowski et al., 2000); and missing links in strategic human resources (Ostroff and Bowen, 2000). I am not asserting that we are responsible for the explosion of MLT research that followed (Gully, 2015), but we did plant seeds that have since flourished quite well.

The Missing Link

The MLT book succeeded in achieving our primary goals, and then some. However, on personal reflection a decade later, there was one target I had for which the needle had not moved much at all. The last section of the opening chapter elaborated theoretical principles underlying *emergent phenomena* in organizations (Kozlowski and Klein, 2000). Much of the theory and research at the time made assumptions about the nature or form of emergence as a means to select an aggregation procedure to represent a higher-level, collective construct using data collected at a lower level (e.g., collective efficacy from individual perceptions). At the time, state-of-the-art representation meant (and still does) a static point estimate. The Chan (1998) measurement typology, which is based on how we in the multilevel seminar viewed aggregation procedures, is consistent with this purpose. My theoretical work at the time was focused on team effectiveness – meso is at the juncture of micro and macro – and, in particular, on *emergence as a process*, not merely an assumption to justify a particular aggregated point estimate (e.g., Kozlowski et al., 1999). However, then (and mostly still now), most multilevel theory and research are top-down (i.e., cross-level contextual effect) and static (i.e., cross-sectional data; Kozlowski, 2012). Emergence is most often assumed to be based on composition/convergent processes, but is inferred (via restricted within unit variance or high agreement) and not observed directly (Kozlowski and Chao, 2012). With rare exceptions (e.g., Kozlowski et al., 1999; Ployhart and Moliterno, 2011), emergence as a dynamic process has been largely ignored.

Taking stock, around 2010 I initiated two multi-year research projects which have produced a series of theoretical and empirical papers with the intent of moving the needle on theory and research methods that enable investigation of emergence process dynamics: *to unpack the black box of team processes.*

EMERGENCE

What is Emergence?

The concept of emergence has been in use for nearly 150 years in philosophy and science. Unfortunately, some of those uses have been contradictory, so it is useful to be clear as to the meaning of emergence.[3] What emergence is not: it is not the mere appearance or growth trajectory of a phenomenon that lacks systems character (e.g., Pickering, 1993). More importantly, it is not about strict holism. General systems theory (von Bertalanffy, 1968), collectivist theories in sociology (Blau, 1987), and classical emergentism in philosophy (Epstein, 1999) treat emergent phenomena as holistic and irreducible. Any effort that attempts to understand emergence as a *micro-macro process* – a consequence of individual interaction and exchange, shaped by the system context, and unfolding over time to manifest as a higher-level phenomenon – is treated as an exercise in reductionism from a holistic perspective.

So, what is emergence as a process? The definition provided by Kozlowski and Klein (2000, p. 55) – "A phenomenon is emergent when it originates in the cognition, affect, behaviors, or other characteristics of individuals, is amplified by their interactions, and manifests as a higher-level, collective phenomenon" – is based on a complexity theory conceptualization. It is the interaction process dynamics among the lower-level system elements, shaped by contextual influences, that give rise to the emergent phenomenon. Similarly, Coleman (1986) stated that system phenomena are "an emergent consequence of the interdependent actions of the actors who make up the system" (p. 1312); Crutchfield (1994) observed that "some of the most engaging and perplexing natural phenomena are those in which highly structured collective behavior emerges over time from the interaction of simple subsystems" (p. 516); Axelrod (1997) asserted that "the large scale effects of locally interacting agents are called 'emergent properties' of the system" (p. 4); and Epstein (1999) described emergent phenomena as "stable macroscopic patterns arising from the local interaction of agents" (p. 53). Thus, one has to be mindful of the relevant levels *and* the process dynamics.

Figure 6.1 captures core concepts in our conceptualization of emergence as a dynamic process (Kozlowski et al., 2013). First, emergence is multilevel in that a phenomenon originates in the KSAOs of individuals – Alpha, Bravo, and Charlie – and transitions to a higher-level construct that may be composition (i.e., convergent/shared) or compilation (i.e., divergent/patterned) in form (Kozlowski and Klein, 2000). Second, the emergence process unfolds dynamically over some time frame. Third, process mechanisms – the engine of emergence – are the "rules" that drive individuals' interactions and exchanges of cognition, affect, motivation, and behavior that undergird the emerged phenomenon (Kozlowski and Ilgen, 2006; Kozlowski and Klein, 2000). Fourth, the operation of the process mechanisms are shaped and amplified by relevant higher-level contextual features that constrain the lower-level unit.

With respect to the notion of holism, Kozlowski et al. (2013) stated that "the issue is not one of reductionism, that is, of deducing the properties of macro phenomena from their micro origins. Rather, the issue is to deduce the *process mechanisms* inherent in *micro interaction dynamics* that yield the higher level phenomenon. . . . The goal is to understand the process of emergence through system dynamics across multiple levels—simultaneously" (p. 585). That means process-oriented theory and research.

Emergence as a Process: Moving the Needle

At their core, most theories in organizational science are about processes. HCRE is a process. However, when the theory is translated into hypotheses and research designs, processes largely give way to a focus on relationships between constructs operationalized as variables. Process becomes an inference. Understanding the process mechanisms that drive HCRE means focusing theory and research on individual KSAOs, contextual influences, and the interaction and exchange processes that undergird HCRE. Once human

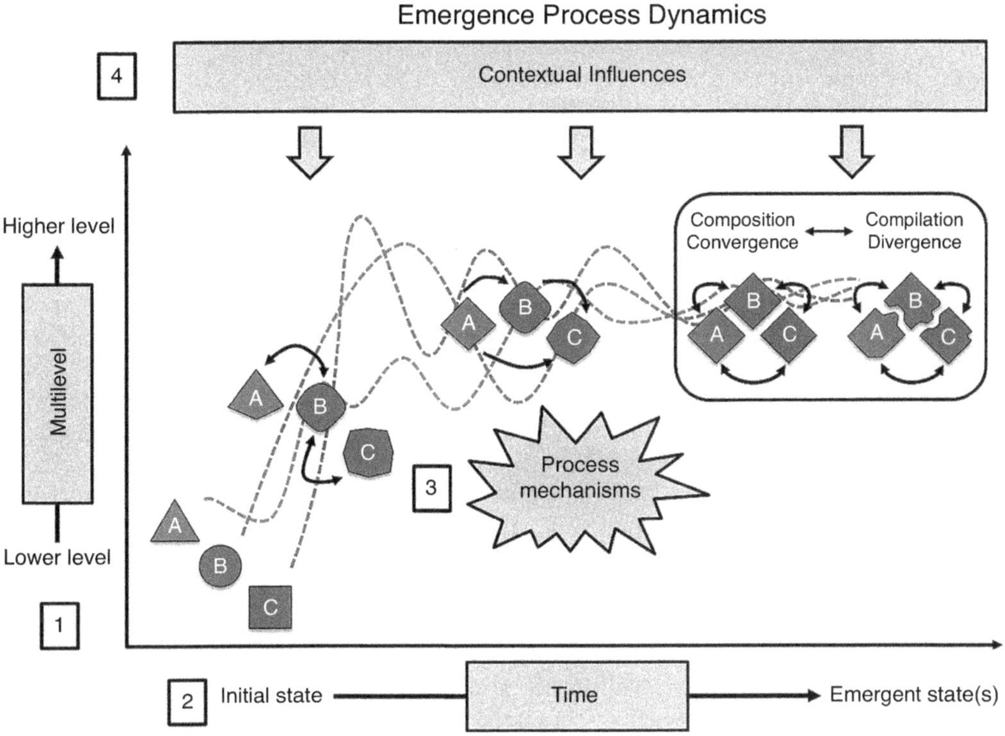

Source: Adapted from Kozlowski et al. (2013). Reprinted with permission.

Figure 6.1 Heuristic illustrating core conceptual foci of emergence

capital resources have emerged at the team, unit, or system level, one will also be interested in how they relate to firm effectiveness and other outcomes. However, these are two very distinct theory and research foci. One focus is on HCRE as a dynamic process. Theory and methods need to be process oriented. The other focus is on relationships between HCRE as a collective phenomenon (aggregation or construct representation) and other meso or macro phenomena. Theory and method need to be relations oriented.

It is very common for scholars to think of theory and methods as distinctly different, but they are intimately related. One can trace the roots of the core disciplines that comprise organizational science (i.e., economics, psychology, and sociology) back a century or more. For example, the oldest journal in the micro area is the *Journal of Applied Psychology*, which celebrated its centennial in 2017 (Kozlowski et al., 2017). Early research published in the journal was wide open and used a range of methods; but over the course of just a decade or so most research began to coalesce around two novel (at the time) methods – the use of multi-item scales to assess constructs (following the success of cognitive ability testing) and the use of correlations to describe linear associations between construct measures. Often, the data were cross-sectional (Cortina et al., 2017).

These basic methodological tools have shaped theorizing and dominated research designs in the organizational sciences for a century. It is the marriage of measurement techniques and the methods of research design – constraining what it is possible to study and how to study it – that drives theorizing, not the other way around. Virtually every theory in organizational science implicates *processes* in its rationale, but hypotheses and research are invariably about *relationships* between and among constructs. Processes by definition are dynamic. Constructs are static. One can string a series of construct measurements out over time to assess changes in the trajectory of the construct. This is often construed as a way to capture processes. It is not. It may provide a basis to draw inferences about a hypothetical process that drives changes in the construct's trajectory, but it is not a direct observation of processes per se. Analysis is often still focused on a relationship between the trajectory of change and some other characteristic, not on the *process mechanisms* that actually drive the changes in construct trajectory and relations. Emergence is largely an inference.

Structural equations modeling (SEM) was developed in the early 1970s (Joreskog and Van Thillo, 1972) and brought with it a major advance to theory building. Box and arrow models – with boxes representing constructs and arrows representing linking "processes" (but really relationships) – took hold as a means to convey theory with more precision than just words in a set of hypotheses. This is theory being shaped by method. Using an explicit model to specify a set of theoretical relations was a major advance in precision because of the improved transparency to assess correspondence among the narrative theoretical rationale (words), model, hypotheses, measures, and analysis. Multilevel analytical techniques have since added even more sophisticated approaches to parse variance across the levels of a system. Multilevel moderated-mediated or mediated-moderated models can be evaluated. Even complicated longitudinal designs can be examined. However, theory is still focused on relationships rather than processes per se, and the dominant methodology is still based on questions and correlations – very sophisticated questions and correlational techniques – but still at the core the same measurement and method technologies that have been in use for a century. If organizational science is going to move the needle on unpacking emergence as a process, it is going to have to use more innovative, process-oriented approaches to do so.

Computational Theory, Modeling, and Process Dynamics

Computational modeling (CM) research is grounded in formal theory and software code that emulates dynamic system behavior of interest. It has been used as a research methodology for decades in weather forecasting (e.g., Lynch, 2008), physics (e.g., Giordano and Nakanishi, 2007; Thijssen, 2007), biology (e.g., Kriete and Eils, 2006), and other hard sciences. Applications of this methodology in organizational science, however, have been very limited (Harrison et al., 2007; Ilgen and Hulin, 2000). That is beginning to change as organizational theory and research are evolving to become more process oriented. CM is uniquely suited to capture and unpack process mechanisms in complex systems.

A computational theory or model is a formal *theoretical* description of system behavior over time realized as a set of interlinked propositional logic statements or functional equations. Unlike narrative theories that typify organizational science generally, the logic/equations specify the theory precisely, making CM more transparent, explicit, and bounded (Ilgen and Hulin, 2000; Wang et al., 2016). As a formal theory, a CM needs to be instantiated in computer software to run simulations and investigations of system dynamics and behavior. There are a variety of CM types, including agent-based, systems dynamics, and cellular automata (Harrison et al., 2007). Individuals are the lowest meaningful unit in human social systems, making agent-based simulation (ABS) particularly useful because software-based agents are coded to emulate human behavior. A CM/ABS describes how virtual individuals or agents interact and collaborate to give rise to the emergence of team and higher-level phenomena (Epstein, 1999; Kozlowski et al., 2013).

An early example of CM/ABS with group behavior is Reynolds' (1987) model of bird flocking. The CM specifies "rules" or process-mechanisms that drive the agent, or "boid," behaviors related to flocking: (1) separation – avoid collisions with other boids; (2) alignment – match speed and heading of the mass of other boids; and (3) cohesion – steer toward the center mass of nearby agents. Boids situated randomly at the start of a simulation will form flocks as the simulation progresses that emulate the behavior of real birds. Flocks emerge as individual boids maximize the simple rules guiding their behavior *in dynamic interaction* with the other boids endeavoring to maximize their rule set. Flocking as a system-level phenomenon emerges over time from these interaction dynamics driven by the process mechanisms. ABS implementations with additional rules can alter the nature of emergence. For instance, adding the view rule (Flake, 1998) – move aside if another boid blocks the view – produces the familiar V-formation of migrating geese.

The boids CM illustrates how computational theory and modeling can identify plausible process mechanisms that can account for emergence as a dynamic process. "So what?" you might think. It is too microscopic and down in the weeds. What is the value of this type of theorizing? The primary value is that one can put one's theory in motion. Current theorizing in organizational science is presented as a snapshot, frozen in time. A CM is a movie – a movie that can be re-played multiple times in the form of *virtual experiments*. For example, one might posit that individual differences in boid sensitivity to the different rules would produce different effects on the emergence of flocking, such as how long it takes the flock to emerge or how robust the flock is to disruptions.[4] One could posit specific hypotheses targeting particular rule combinations in an experimental design or conduct a parameter sweep that explores the effects of a very wide range of parameter combinations. After running the ABS experiments or explorations with hundreds of thousands or millions of entities under different conditions, one could examine how different combinations of agent individual differences relate to outcomes (i.e., emergence of flocking features) in a conventional way. However, what one gains from the CM approach is that one would know *how and why* particular combinations of agent individual differences shaped particular types of emergence in particular ways. One is then equipped with theoretical knowledge to guide interventions that can directly shape the nature and form of emergent phenomena (Grand et al., 2016; Kozlowski et al., 2013). You cannot get that via correlations, even very sophisticated ones.

The basic steps for using CM /ABS include: (a) identify the phenomenon and synthesize the narrative theory; (b) specify substantive content, processes, and mechanisms in a formal CM; (c) operationalize the CM in an ABS with process algorithms (i.e., what, when and how specific entities interact in the system); and (d) evaluate the CM/ABS with virtual experiments (Grand et al., 2016; Kozlowski et al., 2013, 2016; Vancouver and Weinhardt, 2012). Unlike most experimental and correlational studies, CM/ABS research is not constrained by small or non-representative samples, limited variables, and time restrictions. Systems can be heavily stressed and low probability "what if" scenarios can be explored. The full area of a theoretical space – even the dark corners – can be systematically examined. They are ideally suited for studying dynamic behavior in human systems (Epstein, 1999).

My colleagues and I have applied this approach to examine the emergence of team knowledge for decision making (Grand et al., 2016). Teams of different experts who have to acquire unique information about a specific problem, share it with other team members, and then develop a problem solution is a very common scenario across a wide range of domains – management, medical, and military, for example. This problem structure is represented in the voluminous research using the hidden profile paradigm (HPP) in social psychology (Stasser, 1988). The most common finding in HPP research is that teams tend to spend most of their time sharing and discussing common information, and fail to attend to the unique information that is actually diagnostic for an optimal decision. Thus, team decisions within the HPP are typically suboptimal – an observation that has anecdotal support outside of the lab (Janus, 1972). Research on emergence in teams is meso focused, but the principles involved are isomorphic to the core issues involved in studying HCRE – at least for the micro to meso stage of emergence.

Our research involved applying CM to develop and establish the plausibility of a theory of team knowledge emergence. As illustrated in Figure 6.2, Step 1 involved developing a narrative theory to describe the *process mechanisms* involved in individual *learning* (i.e., data selection, encoding, decoding, and integration) and knowledge *sharing* (member selection, retrieval, sharing, and acknowledgement). Step 2 involved formalizing the process mechanisms described by the narrative theory into a computational theory or model that specified the operation of the process mechanisms precisely. This is analogous to specifying the "rules" for the boid CM. Step 3 involved instantiating the CM in an ABS and running a series of virtual experiments that varied input parameters (e.g., team member ability targeted at learning mechanisms, team member propensity to communicate targeted on sharing mechanisms, distribution of common and unique information) and examined how (patterns) and how well (effectiveness) knowledge emerged in agent teams. Step 4 involved interpreting the findings from the virtual experiments from Step 3, generating insights about agent-team knowledge emergence, identifying possible points of intervention in the process mechanisms to improve team knowledge emergence, and then running an experiment with real teams that applied the interventions to improve team knowledge emergence. Because we had insights that targeted specific learning and sharing process mechanisms, we were able to demonstrate experimentally that team knowledge emergence could be improved via those intervention points. This demonstrated both the plausibility of the computational theory and its pragmatic value for *prediction* and *prescription*. That is the value of CM: the focus on process mechanisms rather than relationships for studying emergent phenomena. Understanding *how and why* patterns of emergence unfold as they do allows one to directly intervene to shape the nature of emergence. As illustrated in this example, I believe that a CM-based approach has high potential to advance understanding of the process mechanisms that undergird HCRE.

CM has value for both theory building and application. In a theory-building/refinement mode, an *intellective* CM needs to generate data patterns consistent with the theory or theories and extant research findings (e.g., meta-analyses) on which it is based. This establishes the "generative sufficiency" of the computational theory as a means for investigating phenomena relevant to the underlying theories. This use of an intellective CM is illustrated in the previous example of team knowledge emergence and would be

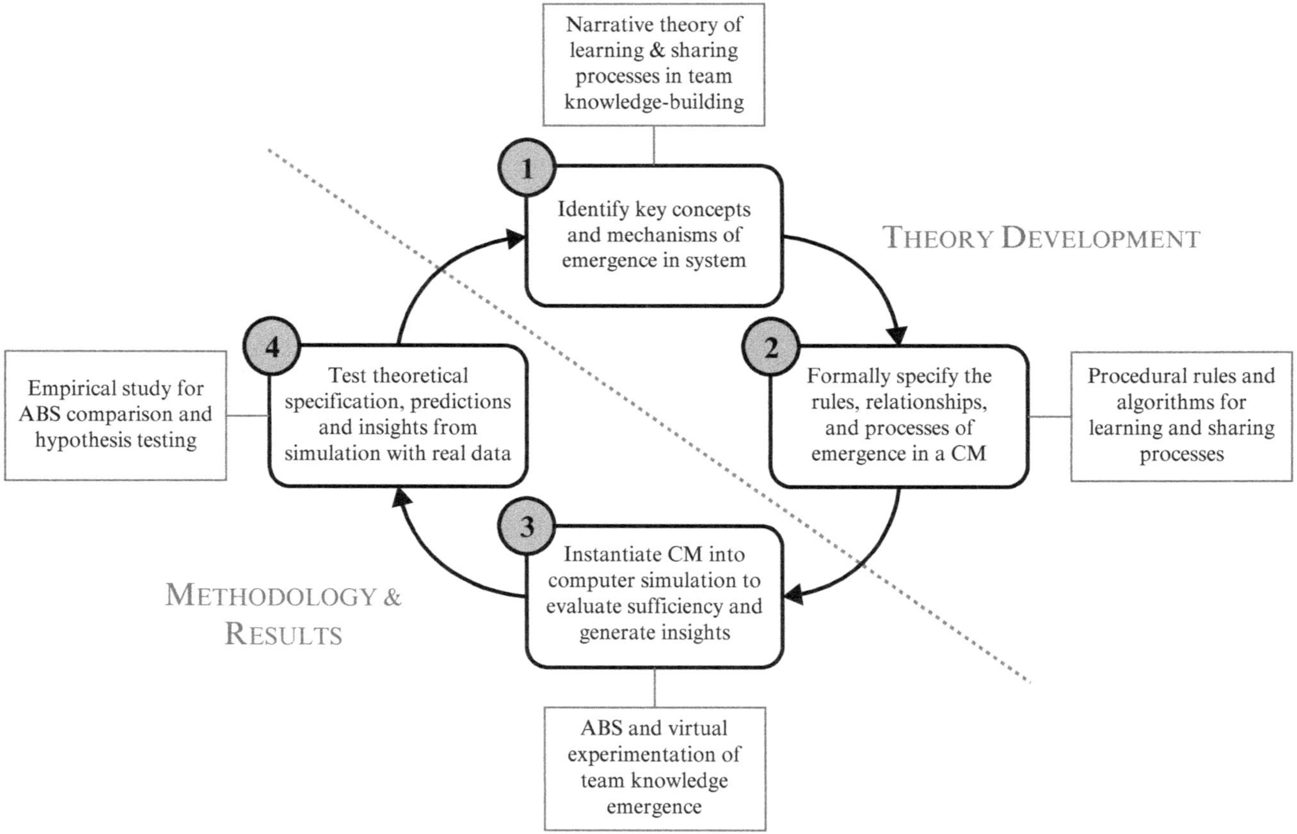

Note: CM = computational model; ABS = agent-based simulation. Descriptions in the light gray boxes summarize the tasks carried out for each step in the present research.

Source: Grand et al. (2016). Reprinted with permission.

Figure 6.2 General framework for developing and evaluating theories of emergence

relevant to building general theoretical principles for the "how and why" of HRCE. In an application mode, an *emulative* CM needs to generate data patterns that align with a specific system. In general, this necessitates very precise parameter estimates and can be very demanding to accomplish because one needs direct observations of the target system. On the other hand, an emulative CM that is tuned to a specific system can be used for prediction and prescription, making it a very powerful tool for prediction and system optimization (Levitt, 2012). This would be relevant to exploring HRCE in a particular organization to examine options and to achieve a particular form of HRCE that aligns with/implements strategy or propels it (Snow and Snell, 2012).

RECOMMENDATIONS FOR ADVANCING HCRE THEORY AND RESEARCH

Behavior in organizational systems is driven by two primary forces: top-down, contextual effects that shape and constrain lower-level phenomena; and bottom-up emergent phenomena that manifest from the interactions among individuals and teams to manifest as higher-level system phenomena. Almost all multilevel organizational research is focused on cross-level contextual effects (Kozlowski, 2012).

For the last decade or so, my colleagues and I have been arguing that multilevel emergence has largely been neglected in the organizational science literature (Kozlowski, 2012, 2015; Kozlowski and Chao, 2012, 2018; Kozlowski et al., 2013). There are a few theories directed toward explicating emergent collective phenomena in teams (e.g., Kozlowski et al., 1999) and higher-level systems (e.g., Ployhart and Moliterno, 2011) and some direct empirical research (Grand et al., 2016). However, to the extent that emergence is considered at all, it is typically used as a theoretical explanation to justify a particular data aggregation procedure – i.e., the use of lower-level data to represent a higher-level phenomenon (Chan, 1998). Emergence is an inference, and not observed directly (Kozlowski and Chao, 2012). Real progress will be made in organizational science when both top-down *and* bottom-up phenomena are investigated and researchers get serious about studying process dynamics over time. I have summarized core principles that advance these points in Box 6.1.

As a scholar who is endeavoring to investigate emergence process dynamics directly, I can tell you that it is very challenging to examine directly micro to meso emergence processes in teams. The intent of research on HCRE is *far more ambitious* because it aims to integrate across all system levels, and it is *far more complicated* because other contextual phenomena that may shape HCRE are also emergent. As Eckardt and Jiang note in Chapter 5 (p. 99):

> factors in the social environment category that are thought to be critical to the emergence of HCRE – such as unit-climate, cohesion, or unit-affect – involve emergence processes of their own . . . [M]ore work is needed on how to simultaneously model the emergence of these enabling factors and the transformation and amplification aspects of HCRE.

There is no question that researching HCRE is very challenging, but I think that by developing a strategy and set of tactics – decomposing HCRE research into meaningful chunks and tackling them systematically – it can be made tractable. I would also highlight that even though I have devoted considerable attention in this commentary to the value of CM for investigating HCRE as a process, CM alone will not be sufficient. It will need to be coupled with coordinated lines of field research.

As a point of departure for broad recommendations, I propose several features (shown below) as a means to organize a systematic research strategy. Broadly speaking, I see the first two features – theoretical focus and methodology – as coupled around research strategy. That is, a focus on building theory aimed at unpacking HCRE process dynamics is more likely to entail the use of CM (vs. field observations) and theory aimed at HCR construct relations as more likely to rely on empirical observations in the field. Similarly, I see the third and fourth features – multilevel scope and organizational state – as coupled around tactics for decomposing the problem, given its many complications. The last feature – time frame – is relevant to how research resources are deployed so as to advance systematically. These features are used to drive a set of three primary recommendations shown in Box 6.2.

- Theoretical focus: HCRC process dynamics vs. emerged (collective) HCR construct relations
- Methodology: CM vs. empirical observations in the field
- Scope: adjacent levels (micro to meso, meso to macro) vs. full system
- Organizational state: new vs. ongoing vs. transforming
- Time frame: near term (next decade) vs. long term (further out).

Recommendation 1: CM should be harnessed to advance theory building targeted at elucidating core HCRE process mechanisms and contextual factors that shape the dynamics of HCRE.

As described in this commentary and elsewhere, CM is uniquely well-suited for theory building and investigation focused on identifying plausible process mechanisms that drive emergent HCR phenomena in organizational systems. My colleagues and I (Grand et al., 2016; Kozlowski et al., 2013) have advanced an exemplar approach for how CM can be harnessed to investigate emergence processes for an important middle-range phenomenon – learning and knowledge building – in teams. We also engaged in a much more ambitious effort to design a CM architecture capable of modeling emergence for system scale phenomena – individuals, teams, and networks of teams – that undergird system robustness, adaptability, and effectiveness (Kozlowski et al., 2014). The CM architecture is sufficiently flexible that it can be used to theorize about and investigate HCRE-relevant process mechanisms, contextual influences, and emergent outcomes. I strongly encourage scholars interested in HCRE to add CM methods to their capability toolbox or to partner with investigators who have CM capabilities.

Recommendation 2: Empirical field research on HCRE should be facilitated as a means to provide critical descriptive information regarding relationships between HCRE constructs and firm outcomes.

It is vital that the research community gains knowledge regarding what clusters of HCRs are associated with relevant firm outcomes. Empirical research aimed at this target not only advances descriptive knowledge; it is also essential for identifying and developing potential CM process mechanisms and for providing parameter values for operationalizing CM mechanisms in an ABS. The last decade has witnessed a substantial upswing of interest in conducting the challenging empirical research that is needed to advance understanding of the microfoundations of firm strategy (Barney and Felin, 2013; Eckardt et al., 2018; Felin et al., 2015) and the emergence of HCR as a core phenomenon for firm effectiveness (Ployhart et al., 2017). A meaningful foundation of empirical research is accumulating that describes the influence of human capital and/or human capital antecedents such as selection and training on unit effectiveness. For example, human resources practices such as selection, training, and others have been associated with unit performance (e.g., Kehoe and Collins, 2017; Kim and Ployhart, 2018; Ployhart et al., 2011; Van Iddekinge et al., 2009). Turnover has been treated as a multilevel, emergent, collective phenomenon (e.g., Call et al., 2015; Nyberg and Ployhart, 2013). Emergent enabling factors such as climate have been linked to unit effectiveness (e.g., Jiang et al., 2015; Ployhart et al., 2009; Schneider and Bowen, 1993). Even core KSAOs, such as personality, have been associated with unit effectiveness (e.g., Hofmann and Jones, 2005; Oh et al., 2015). The recommendations made by Eckardt and Jiang in Chapter 5 are relevant for advancing this line of inquiry. This research is of tremendous value for understanding HCRE, and needs continued encouragement and facilitation.

Going forward, it will be possible to utilize digital traces in the form of technology-mediated interactions (e.g., email, chat, system records) along with team interaction sensors (e.g., Olguín Olguín et al., 2009) to identify, examine, and unpack communication and exchange process mechanisms in the workplace. Although there are some "teething" challenges with these new methodologies, i.e., measurement validation (Chaffin et al., 2017), those challenges can be overcome with careful attention to technology design, algorithm development, and validation (Kozlowski and Chao, 2018; Kozlowski et al., 2015).

Recommendation 3: Theory and research on HCRE should be decomposed to focus on more tractable aspects of the HCRE domain and then systematically advanced to address more complicated aspects as knowledge accrues, theory matures, methods advance, and full integration across levels of the system becomes possible.

One complication has to do with the nature of the organizational state. For investigating emergence via CM, one can design and conduct virtual experiments that examine new systems, new and ongoing systems with specific contextual features (i.e., the emerged social enabling mechanisms), or systems in flux due to one or more disturbances. I suggest starting with the less complicated state and then progressing as knowledge accrues. Thus, one would likely begin with new systems where HCRE is unconstrained by existing contextual features to enable investigation of unconstrained HCRE. One would likely couple this approach with research on systems that have specified contextual features that represent a range of emerged social enabling mechanisms as conditions in an experimental design or as a parameter sweep across a wide range of plausible values for potential contextual features. This would be a very large-scale simulation effort. As one gained understanding, the research could advance to examine HCRE for systems that encounter a range of internal and external disturbances that necessitate adaptation. For empirical field research, one takes what one can get. Any meaningful information will be useful for advancing knowledge and for designing computational theory and research that can tackle the problem more systematically.

Another complication is that there is a much more substantial existing theory and research foundation that is relevant to micro to meso emergence than there is for meso to macro emergence. Thus, it makes sense to first focus most effort to understanding emergence for these closely coupled, adjacent levels of the system. Moreover, unpacking the meso to macro connection is likely to entail more complications (i.e., there are qualitative differences and unique contextual contributions at each successively higher level), multiple echelons (i.e., in-between unit levels that will have to be mapped for particular systems/organizations), and – for real-world data – much longer time frames for emergence to unfold. I think more will be gained by focusing initially on micro to meso emergence and then moving up to the next bracket(s) as knowledge and capabilities accrue. Research that examines a full integration across all system levels – micro, meso, and macro – is a long-term prospect. However, it is a prospect that is achievable and one that is crucial for bridging the disciplinary divides in organizational science and advancing scholarship aimed at enhancing effectiveness across the multiple levels of the organizational system (Ployhart et al., 2017).

CHAPTER SUMMARY

BOX 6.1 KEY TAKEAWAYS AND CORE PRINCIPLES FOR ADVANCING HCRE THEORY AND RESEARCH

1. Emergence is a dynamic process, not merely a conceptual assumption to be used to justify the aggregation of lower-level measures to represent an "emerged" higher-level construct.
2. The key to elucidating emergence as a dynamic process lies in elucidating the process mechanisms that drive HCRE in theory and research, rather than focusing exclusively on relations between "emerged" HCR constructs and higher-level firm outcomes.
3. Computational models and agent-based simulation represent alternative theoretical and methodological approaches for conceptualizing and investigating emergence as a dynamic process relevant to HCRE as a critical phenomenon for organizational effectiveness.

BOX 6.2 DIRECTIONS FOR FUTURE RESEARCH

1. Recommendation 1: CM should be harnessed to advance theory building targeted at elucidating core HCRE process mechanisms and contextual factors that shape the dynamics of HCRE.
2. Recommendation 2: Empirical field research on HCRE should be facilitated as a means to provide critical descriptive information regarding relationships between HCRE constructs and firm outcomes.
3. Recommendation 3: Theory and research on HCRE should be decomposed to focus on more tractable aspects of the HCRE domain and then systematically advanced to address more complicated aspects as knowledge accrues, theory matures, methods advance, and full integration across levels of the system becomes possible.

NOTES

* I gratefully acknowledge the U.S. Army Research Institute for the Behavioral and Social Sciences (ARI; W911NF-14-1-0026, S.W.J. Kozlowski and G.T. Chao, Principal Investigators) for support that in part contributed to the composition of this chapter. Any opinions, findings, conclusions, and recommendations expressed are those of the authors and do not necessarily reflect the views of ARI.

1. I would characterize my dissertation as being on the bleeding edge, rather than the leading edge. It took several efforts to get it published as MLT was by no means mainstream and reviewers did not understand it very well.
2. Teaching grad students is a good way to advance one's knowledge and understanding. Some selected alumni of the MLT seminar include Brad Bell, Mike Braun, Ken Brown, David Chan, James Grand, Stan Gully, Brian Hults, Jeff LePine, Henry Moon, Cheri Ostroff, and Rob Ployhart, to name but a few.
3. See Kozlowski et al. (2013) for a more elaborated treatment.
4. This would be analogous to positing that different combinations of individual KSAOs are likely to have an effect on HCRE – how, how long, what form.

REFERENCES

Axelrod, R. (1997). *The Complexity of Cooperation: Agent-Based Models of Competition and Collaboration*. Princeton, NJ: Princeton University Press.

Barney, J., and Felin, T. (2013). What are microfoundations? *Academy of Management Perspectives*, *27*, 138–55.

Blau, P. M. (1987). Microprocesses and macrostructure. In K. S. Cook (ed.), *Social Exchange Theory* (pp. 83–100). Newbury Park, CA: Sage.

Bliese, P. D. (2000). Within-group agreement, non-independence, and reliability: Implications for data aggregation and analysis. In K. J. Klein and S. W. J. Kozlowski (eds), *Multilevel Theory, Research, and Methods in Organizations* (pp. 349–81). San Francisco: Jossey-Bass.

Call, M. L., Nyberg, A. J., Ployhart, R. E., and Weekley, J. A. (2015). The dynamic nature of collective turnover and unit performance: The impact of time, quality, and replacements. *Academy of Management Journal*, *58*, 1208–32.

Chaffin, D., Heidl, R., Hollenbeck, J. R., Howe, M., Yu, A., Voorhees, C., and Calantone, R. (2017). The promises and perils of wearable sensors in organizational research. *Organizational Research Methods*, *20*, 3–31.

Chan, D. (1998). Functional relations among constructs in the same content domain at different levels of analysis: A typology of composition models. *Journal of Applied Psychology*, *83*, 234–46.

Coleman, J. S. (1986). Social theory, social research, and a theory of action. *American Journal of Sociology*, *91*, 1309–35.

Cortina, J. M., Aguinis, H., and DeShon, R. P. (2017). Twilight of dawn or of evening? A century of research methods in the *Journal of Applied Psychology*. *Journal of Applied Psychology*, *102*, 237–53.

Crutchfield, J. P. (1994). The calculi of emergence: Computation, dynamics and induction. *Physica D: Nonlinear Phenomena*, *75*, 11–54.

DeNisi, A. S. (2000). Performance appraisal and performance management: A multiple-levels approach. In K.J. Klein and S. W. J. Kozlowski (eds), *Multilevel Theory, Research, and Methods in Organizations: Foundations, Extensions, and New Directions* (pp. 121–56). San Francisco: Jossey-Bass.

Eckardt, R., Crocker, A., Ahn, Y., Floyd, S. W., Boyd, B. K., Hodgkinson, G. P., Kozlowski, S. W. J., Moliterno, T. P., and Starbuck, W. H. (2018). Reflections on the micro-macro divide: Ideas from the trenches and moving forward. *Strategic Organization*. https://doi.org/10.1177/1476127018770048.

Epstein, J. M. (1999). Agent-based computational models and generative social science. *Complexity*, *4*, 41–60.

Felin, T., Foss, N. J., and Ployhart, R. E. (2015). The microfoundations movement in strategy and organization theory. *Academy of Management Annals*, *9*(1), 575–632.

Flake, G. W. (1998). *The Computational Beauty of Nature: Computer Explorations of Fractals, Chaos, Complex Systems, and Adaptation*. Cambridge, MA: MIT Press.

Giordano, N. J., and Nakanishi, H. (2007). *Computational Physics*. London: Pearson.

Grand, J. A., Braun, M. T., Kuljanin, G., Kozlowski, S. W. J., and Chao, G. T. (2016). The dynamics of team cognition: A process-oriented theory of knowledge emergence in teams [Monograph]. *Journal of Applied Psychology*, *101*, 1353–85.

Gully, S. M. (2015) (May). Meta-discussant comments. Multilevel Theory and Research Conference, Penn State Center for Teams and Negotiation. State College, PA.

Harrison, J. R., Lin, Z., Carroll, G. R. and Carley, K. M. (2007). Simulation modeling in organizational and management research. *Academy of Management Review*, *32*, 1229–45.

Hofmann, D. A., and Jones, L. M. (2005). Leadership, collective personality, and performance. *Journal of Applied Psychology*, *90*, 509–22.
Ilgen, D. R., and Hulin, C. L. (2000). Lessons learned and insights gained. In D. R. Ilgen and C. L. Hulin (eds), *Computational Modeling of Behavior in Organizations: The Third Scientific Discipline* (pp. 269–89). Washington, DC: American Psychological Association.
James, L. R. (1982). Aggregation bias in estimates of perceptual agreement. *Journal of Applied Psychology*, *67*, 219–29.
James, L. R., Demaree, R. G., and Wolf, G. (1984). Estimating within group interrater reliability with and without response bias. *Journal of Applied Psychology*, *69*, 85–98.
James, L. R., Demaree, R. G., and Wolf, G. (1993). r_{wg}: An assessment of within group interrater agreement. *Journal of Applied Psychology*, *78*, 306–09.
Janus, I. L. (1972). *Victims of Groupthink: A Psychological Study of Foreign-Policy Decisions and Fiascoes*. Boston: Houghton Mifflin.
Jiang, K., Chuang, C. H., and Chiao, Y. C. (2015). Developing collective customer knowledge and service climate: The interaction between service-oriented high-performance work systems and service leadership. *Journal of Applied Psychology*, *100*(4), 1089–106.
Joreskog, K.G., and Van Thillo, M. (1972). *LISREL: A General Computer Program for Estimating a Linear Structural Equation System Involving Multiple Indicators of Unmeasured Variables* (RB-72-56). Princeton, NJ: Educational Testing Service.
Kehoe, R. R., and Collins, C. J. (2017). Human resource management and unit performance in knowledge-intensive work. *Journal of Applied Psychology*, *102*(8), 1222–36.
Kim, Y., and Ployhart, R. E. (2018). The effects of selection practices on firm performance: A new view and test of a long-held assumption. *Academy of Management Journal*, *61*, 46–66.
Klein, K. J., Dansereau, F., and Hall, R. J. (1994). Levels issues in theory development, data collection, and analysis. *Academy of Management Review*, *19*, 195–229.
Klein, K. J., Bliese, P. D., Kozlowski, S. W. J., Dansereau, F., Gavin, M. B., Griffin, M. A., Hofmann, D. A., James, L. R., Yammarino, F. J., and Bligh, M. C. (2000). Multilevel analytical techniques: Commonalities, differences, and continuing questions. In K. J. Klein and S. W. J. Kozlowski (eds), *Multilevel Theory, Research and Methods in Organizations: Foundations, Extensions, and New Directions* (pp. 512–53). San Francisco: Jossey-Bass.
Kozlowski, S. W. J. (2012). Groups and teams in organizations: Studying the multilevel dynamics of emergence. In A. B. Hollingshead and M. S. Poole (eds), *Research Methods for Studying Groups and Teams: A Guide to Approaches, Tools, and Technologies* (pp. 260–83). New York: Routledge.
Kozlowski, S. W. J. (2015). Advancing research on team process dynamics: Theoretical, methodological, and measurement considerations. *Organizational Psychology Review*, *5*, 270–99.
Kozlowski, S. W. J., and Chao, G. T. (2012). The dynamics of emergence: Cognition and cohesion in work teams. *Managerial and Decision Economics*, *33*, 335–54.
Kozlowski, S. W. J., and Chao, G. T. (2018). Unpacking team process dynamics and emergent phenomena: Challenges, conceptual advances, and innovative methods. *American Psychologist*, *73*, 576–92.
Kozlowski, S. W. J., and Farr, J. L. (1988). An integrative model of updating and performance. *Human Performance*, *1*, 5–29.
Kozlowski, S. W. J., and Hattrup, K. (1992). A disagreement about within-group agreement: Disentangling issues of consistency versus consensus. *Journal of Applied Psychology*, *77*, 161–7.
Kozlowski, S. W. J., and Hults, B. M. (1987). An exploration of climates for technical updating and performance. *Personnel Psychology*, *40*, 539–63.
Kozlowski, S. W. J., and Ilgen, D. R. (2006). Enhancing the effectiveness of work groups and teams [Monograph]. *Psychological Science in the Public Interest*, *7*, 77–124.
Kozlowski, S. W. J., and Klein, K. J. (2000). A multilevel approach to theory and research in organizations: Contextual, temporal, and emergent processes. In K. J. Klein and S. W. J. Kozlowski (eds), *Multilevel Theory, Research and Methods in Organizations: Foundations, Extensions, and New Directions* (pp. 3–90). San Francisco: Jossey-Bass.
Kozlowski, S. W. J., Chen, G., and Salas, E. (2017). One hundred years of the *Journal of Applied Psychology:* Background, evolution, and scientific trends. *Journal of Applied Psychology*, *102*, 237–53.
Kozlowski, S. W. J., Chao, G. T., Chang, C.-H., and Fernandez, R. (2015). Team dynamics: Using "big data" to advance the science of team effectiveness. In S. Tonidandel, E. King, and J. Cortina (eds), *Big Data at Work: The Data Science Revolution and Organizational Psychology* (pp. 272–309). New York: Routledge.
Kozlowski, S. W. J., Gully, S. M., Nason, E. R., and Smith, E. M. (1999). Developing adaptive teams: A theory of compilation and performance across levels and time. In D. R. Ilgen and E. D. Pulakos (eds), *The Changing Nature of Work Performance: Implications for Staffing, Personnel Actions, and Development* (pp. 240–92). San Francisco: Jossey-Bass.
Kozlowski, S. W. J., Brown, K. G., Weissbein, D., Cannon-Bowers, J. A., and Salas, E. (2000). A multilevel

approach to training effectiveness: Enhancing horizontal and vertical transfer. In K. J. Klein and S. W. J. Kozlowski (eds), *Multilevel Theory, Research and Methods in Organizations: Foundations, Extensions, and New Directions* (pp. 157–210). San Francisco: Jossey-Bass.
Kozlowski, S. W. J., Chao, G. T., Braun, M. T., Grand, J. A., and Kuljanin, G. (2014). *A Computational Modeling Approach to Organizational Effectiveness: Mapping the Effects of Leadership, Group Structure, and Environmental Shocks*. Army Research Institute for the Behavioral and Social Sciences (W911NF-14-1-0026; May 2014 to December 2019).
Kozlowski, S. W. J., Chao, G. T., Grand, J. A., Braun, M. T., and Kuljanin, G. (2013). Advancing multilevel research design: Capturing the dynamics of emergence. *Organizational Research Methods*, *16*, 581–615.
Kozlowski, S. W. J., Chao, G. T., Grand, J. A., Braun, M. T., and Kuljanin, G. (2016). Capturing the multilevel dynamics of emergence: Computational modeling, simulation, and virtual experimentation. *Organizational Psychology Review*, *6*, 3–33.
Kriete, A., and Eils, R. (eds) (2006). *Computational Systems Biology: From Molecular Mechanisms to Disease* (2nd edn). Cambridge, MA: Academic Press.
Levitt, R. E. (2012). The virtual design team: Designing project organizations as engineer design bridges. *Journal of Organization Design*, *1*(2), 14–41.
Lynch, P. (2008). The origins of computer weather prediction and climate modeling. *Journal of Computational Physics*, *227*, 3431–44.
Nyberg, A. J., and Ployhart, R. E. (2013). Context-emergent turnover (CET) theory: A theory of collective turnover. *Academy of Management Review*, *38*(1), 109–31.
Oh, I.-S., Kim, S., Van Iddekinge, C. H. (2015). Taking it to another level: Do personality-based human capital resources matter to firm performance? *Journal of Applied Psychology*, *100*, 935–47.
Olguin Olguin, D., Waber, B. N., Kim, T., Mohan, A., Ara, J., and Pentland, A. (2009). Sensible organizations: Technology and methodology for automatically measuring organizational behavior. *IEEE Transactions of Systems, Man, and Cybernetics – Part B: Cybernetics*, *39*(1), 43–55.
Ostroff, C., and Bowen, D. (2000). Moving HR to a higher level: HR practices and organizational effectiveness. In K. J. Klein and S. W. J. Kozlowski (eds), *Multilevel Theory, Research and Methods in Organizations: Foundations, Extensions, and New Directions* (pp. 211–66). San Francisco: Jossey Bass.
Pickering, A. (1993). The mangle of practice: Agency and emergence in the sociology of science. *American Journal of Sociology*, *99*, 559–89.
Ployhart, R.E., and Moliterno, T. P. (2011). Emergence of human capital resource: a multilevel model. *Academy of Management Journal*, *36*, 127–50.
Ployhart, R. E., Schmitt, N., and Tippins, N. T. (2017). Solving the supreme problem: 100 years of recruitment and selection research at the *Journal of Applied Psychology*. *Journal of Applied Psychology*, *102*, 291–304.
Ployhart, R. E., Van Iddekinge, C., and MacKenzie, W. (2011). Acquiring and developing human capital in service contexts: The interconnectedness of human capital resources. *Academy of Management Journal*, *54*, 353–68.
Ployhart, R. E., Weekley, J. A., and Ramsey, J. (2009). The consequences of human resource stocks and flows: A longitudinal examination of unit service orientation and unit effectiveness. *Academy of Management Journal*, *52*(5), 996–1015.
Reynolds, C. W. (1987). Flocks, herds, and schools: A distributed behavioral model. *Computer Graphics*, *21*, 25–34. (SIGGRAPH'87 Conference Proceedings).
Roberts, K.H., Hulin, C.L., and Rousseau, D.M. (1978). *Developing an Interdisciplinary Science of Organizations*. San Francisco: Jossey-Bass.
Rousseau, D. M. (1985). Issues of level in organizational research: Multi-level and cross-level perspectives. In L. L. Cummings and B. Staw (eds), *Research in Organizational Behavior* (Vol. 7: 1–37). Greenwich, CT: JAI Press.
Schmidt, F.L., and Hunter, J.E. (1989). Interrater reliability coefficients cannot be computed when only one stimulus is rated. *Journal of Applied Psychology*, *74*, 368–70.
Schneider, B., and Bowen, D. E. (1993). The service organization: Human resources management is crucial. *Organizational Dynamics*, *21*(4), 39–52.
Schneider, B., Smith, D. B., and Sipe, W. P. (2000). Personnel selection psychology: Multi-level considerations. In K. J. Klein and S. W. J. Kozlowski (eds), *Multilevel Theory, Research and Methods in Organizations: Foundations, Extensions, and New Directions* (pp. 91–120). San Francisco: Jossey Bass.
Snow, C. C., and Snell, S. A. (2012). Strategic human resource management. In S. W. J. Kozlowski (ed.), *The Oxford Handbook of Organizational Psychology* (pp. 993–1008). New York: Oxford University Press.
Stasser, G. (1988). Computer simulation as a research tool: The DISCUSS model of group decision making. *Journal of Experimental Social Psychology*, *24*, 393–422.
Thijssen, J. (2007). *Computational Physics*. Cambridge: Cambridge University Press.
Vancouver, J. B., and Weinhardt, J. M. (2012). Modeling the mind and the milieu: Computational modeling for micro-level organizational researchers. *Organizational Research Methods*, *15*(4), 602–23.

Van Iddekinge, C. H., Ferris, G. R., Perrewé, P. L., Perryman, A. A., Blass, F. R., and Heetderks, T. D. (2009). Effects of selection and training on unit-level performance over time: A latent growth modeling approach. *Journal of Applied Psychology*, *94*, 829–43.

von Bertalanffy, L. (1968). *General System Theory*. New York: Braziller.

Wang, X., Zhang, L., Lin, Y., Zhao, Y., and Hu, X. (2016). Computational models and optimal control strategies for emotion contagion in the human population in emergencies. *Knowledge-Based Systems*, *109*, 35–47.

7. Human capital resource emergence: a commentary

Albert A. Cannella, Jr and Valerie A. Sy

INTRODUCTION

We would like to begin by congratulating Eckardt and Jiang on an excellent chapter. We found their discussion complete and detailed. They review the seminal work by Ployhart and Moliterno (2011) and carry the work forward a bit by introducing and clarifying the concepts of transformation and amplification. These concepts represent incremental but important ideas related to how we go from micro-level KSAOs to the macro concept of human capital resources (HCRs) and their emergence. The methodology section was also complete and thorough and, while not adding a lot of new material, it reviewed the state of the science of empirical analysis regarding human capital resource emergence (HCRE). We believe that Eckardt and Jiang's chapter would make an excellent addition to a PhD seminar on conceptualizing and modeling HCRE. It covers a lot of the basic material in one place and couples that material with analytical advice to get the novice up to speed.

We also like very much Eckardt and Jiang's brief discussion linking HCRE to competitive advantage. In particular, the authors explicate that interfirm heterogeneity manifests in the enabling states of HCRE to a greater extent than does task complexity, as well as in the isolating mechanisms of firm specificity, social complexity, path dependence, and causal ambiguity. The authors note that the social environment in which HCRE takes place is one form of competitive advantage as well as the resulting human capital resources. However, we believe the bargaining power issue that they discuss, while important and valuable, is likely to be a troublesome force in the HCRE process when analyzing the phenomenon at a macro level.

Rather than directly commenting further on Eckardt and Jiang, we would like to comment more broadly on the notion of HCRE and several issues that occurred to us related to theorizing about it and measuring it. Our chapter will represent a more "critical review" of the broad concept that extends beyond Eckardt and Jiang. Our purpose is not to stop or even discourage research on HCRE – far from it. Rather, we will highlight some of the key challenges involved in studying the concept as it has been described to date by a variety of authors – challenges that have been (and likely will continue to be) assumed away by researchers. The ultimate objective of empirical research is to generate valid and useful knowledge that can be generalized to other settings and contexts, and our critique is aimed toward that objective.

We will define and describe five key issues that we believe should be considered by any researcher contemplating the study of HCRE. The first issue is the broad concept of emergence – a concept that has a long and deep history in both science and philosophy (Goldstein 1999). When researchers evoke the concept of emergence, it raises very critical issues for both conceptual and empirical analyses. Briefly, as we will describe, emergence ranges from weak to strong in form. While the former is empirically tractable, the latter is not. Much HCRE research in print ignores this distinction, essentially assuming away the stronger form. However, we believe that a number of the issues found in theorizing about emergence move the concept perilously close to the strong form of emergence.

Our second issue is what we perceive to be a lack of consideration for human agency in the approaches taken to study HCRE thus far. Stated differently, if an issue is deemed to be "strategic," human intentionality is typically presumed to be present and active (Hambrick 1989, 2007). However, we find little thought given to issues of human agency in the HCRE concept at this stage of its evolution. Under classical assumptions of rationality, human agency was assumed away as all actors are presumed to behave rationally (and identically). However, the behavioral view of human decisions and actions has been around for many years (March and Simon 1958) and, after growing slowly for several decades (Hambrick and Mason 1984), is now widely applied in the social sciences. The HCRE concept is quite complex, and behavioral theory highlights that human intentionality doesn't fare well under complexity. This issue has close ties to the emergence problem.

The third issue, related to the second, is the notion of bargaining power as put forth by Eckardt and Jiang in Chapter 5 and others (Campbell et al. 2012; Carpenter et al. 2001; Coff 1999). Bargaining power in the strategic management literature is perhaps best described by Porter (1980), and it refers to the organization's capacity to exercise influence vis-à-vis outside organizations – typically suppliers of inputs or buyers of outputs. Needless to say, employees are a major supplier, but it is a bit unusual in strategy studies to treat them as such. A critical concern in the context of HCRE is that there undoubtedly needs to be some sharing of the rents created by the HCR, and there will be conflicts of interest highlighted by the division of rents; and inevitably opportunities will emerge for executives to exchange HCR for short-term gains or just because they simply do not understand how the HCR is created and maintained. This problem is endemic to the HCRE concept because the cause–effect linkages are complex at best and intractable at worst.

The fourth issue is exogenous factors and their roles in the emergence of human capital at the organizational level. Henry Mintzberg has long decried the assumptions of causality in strategy research and the widespread existence of backward-looking inferences about cause and effect (Mintzberg 1973, 1978, 1980). Jay Barney (1986) has similarly argued that luck plays a critical role in the realization of sustained competitive advantage. The concept of path dependence is often evoked in strategy research, often as a catch-all category where we can agree that a competitive advantage exists but cannot specify the precise sequence of events that led to it. In attempts to describe the path-dependence concept, exogenous events (factors from outside the firm and outside the firm's control) feature prominently. Using the logic of path dependence in a forward-looking way can be done, at least in theory, in some situations – but that will not generally be the case in practice. Related to this issue is the concept of resources, defined as semi-permanent tangible and intangible assets which could be thought of as strengths or weaknesses of a given firm (Wernerfelt 1984). The tautology of defining resource value and the relationship to competitive advantage has been discussed by researchers in many areas, including human capital. We will expand upon this discussion.

Finally, for readers who choose to take our critique seriously, we have some methodological suggestions. Our discussion will try to be more specific about criteria for modeling in the Eckardt and Jiang tradition as well as for identifying situations wherein their modeling suggestions are likely to be inappropriate. These suggestions follow the logic of strong emergence to clarify when and how empirical modeling is likely to encounter insurmountable challenges.

The concept of HCRE has come a long way, and we do not wish for our commentary to dampen enthusiasm for its study. We will highlight some particularly important and compelling conclusions and assertions as we go along. For example, the argument that HCRE is a unit-level construct while KSAOs are inherently individual-level constructs is particularly compelling to us. We begin with the concept of emergence.

THE CONCEPT OF EMERGENCE

As we noted in the introduction, the concept of emergence has a long and deep history in science and philosophy, ranging from Aristotle (350 BC [1994]) to John Stuart Mill (1843). Interactions among the parts of an emergent phenomenon result in a whole that is often described as "other than" the sum of the parts. Emergence exists all around us, but can pose deep problems when it is subjected to scientific scrutiny. The term is frequently used to connote processes that cannot be understood or explained. For example, scientists have studied the properties of hydrogen and oxygen atoms, but simply mixing the two gases together does not form water. Water is an emergent phenomenon that cannot be reduced to the sum of its parts. Another example is the creation of nesting structures by insects. From the perspective of ants or bees, the individual insects are doing their part to build a home. From an outsider human's perspective, we observe an intricate and complex structure that emerges from the insects' individual efforts with no intentionality for the outcome on the part of the insects.

The processes involved in emergence can be considered as on a continuum from weak to strong. Weak-form emergence can be specified to such an extent that it can be modeled by computers through the use of algorithms. This is the form that Eckardt and Jiang spend a good deal of time on with respect to empirical analyses. On the other hand, strong-form emergence cannot be specified as to process or modeled with any computer algorithms. Simply put, the processes are unknown and potentially unknowable. In strong-form emergence, as we noted earlier, the product is not merely more than the sum of the parts, but "other than" the sum of the parts. Thus, as long as the theory behind the HCRE is tractable and appropriately specified by the researcher, the emergence is of the weak form. Here, the methodology must be aligned with the levels of analysis (as Eckardt and Jiang go to some lengths to explain), and all is well. However, some of the theory behind HCRE moves us perilously close to the strong form of emergence.

Emergence is also often used to describe a phenomenon that is truly unique, and this form of emergence is also relevant for HCRE. To the extent that a thing is unique, there is nothing else like it anywhere. For such a phenomenon, the rules of science do not apply as one cannot generalize from the singular phenomenon to any other phenomenon. The way that ice crystals stick together to form a unique snowflake pattern is a strong-form emergent phenomenon; the occurrence cannot be modeled. This may seem a bit extreme, but it is a metaphor that is sometimes applicable to HCRE. Specifying the stream of events and occurrences that led to the resource observed in the present is challenging and difficult, and some could be argued as unique enough that they cannot be expected to be replicated. This is the ultimate in path dependence, when the sequence of events that led to the HCRE themselves emerged from a number of exogenous factors and cannot be replicated by rivals. Of course, one reason the sequence cannot be replicated is that it is not fully understood by the parties to it.

Henry Mintzberg (1987) has long advocated that good strategies are emergent. To him, that means that they are created by bottom-up processes rather than top-down processes. They are started by lower-level employees as they are striving to resolve problems that they encounter or satisfy some request made by customers. Such strategies grow like "strategic weeds" until they are noticed by senior executives. Once noticed, they can be nurtured into fully developed strategies that take hold across the business, or they can be cast out of the metaphorical garden altogether. Which one of these occurs depends on the vagaries of the senior executive who notices. To manage this process, Mintzberg draws upon the concept of crafting rather than planning, as the crafting metaphor is more tied to the notions of path dependence and loose connections between outcomes and both actions and intentions. He would not claim that the process could be modeled by a computer.

The Issue of Agency

There are several definitions of agency, and in strategy research it often derives from the separation of ownership and control, where one person delegates authority to another person while retaining an interest in the outcome. Another definition, and one we focus on in this commentary, is (according to Merriam-Webster) "the capacity, condition, or state of acting or of exerting power." Our definition of agency emphasizes how humans might use the HCRE concept to bring about or realize some intended outcomes. This approach to agency is frequently found in the upper-echelons view, which describes how the unique characteristics of individual executives become manifest in firm-level strategies and structures (Finkelstein et al. 2009; Hambrick and Mason 1984).

The upper-echelons approach is intrinsically behavioral in nature, emphasizing how human actors actually act (i.e., "behave"), not how they are "supposed to" act or how some optimal model of decision making concludes that they should act. Human actors face a number of well-known limitations, including when they confront complexity (they simplify it) or information overload (they cut off or ignore information, sometimes critical information) or risk (they may be risk-seeking or risk-averse, depending on how the decision is framed. Both permanent contextual factors and more temporary ones (e.g., the mood of a key actor) are also important.

Agency is required for researching strategy because strategy inherently implies both a set of objectives (such as wealth creation) and some intentions on the part of those who are striving to achieve objectives. Agency is also a critical consideration when discussing emergence. Much emergence (and all strong-form emergence) is completely disconnected from any form of human intention. That is not to say that humans are unable to use emergent processes, even strong-form emergent processes; but they cannot intervene and alter or manage those processes, and the risk of intervention is precisely what the concept of HCRE would seem to imply. Given that HCR has emerged, agents can use those resources to the extent that they understand them; but because the emergence process is ongoing, it can be harmed inadvertently by the agents in charge. This is in some contrast to emergent phenomena like coal or corn, as agents can mine coal or grow corn with no danger of significantly altering the processes that created the coal or corn in the first place.

As noted above, it is well known that humans do not handle complexity well, and they can fall victim to a large number of predictable errors when making decisions under complexity (Ariely 2008). The HCRE concept is just such a complex situation, and it can only be simplified at significant risk. For example, Michael Lewis (2016) describes the selection decision for professional sports teams as "the problem that never goes away." That is, given the list of individual players available, in the form of player prospects or potential trades, how do team managers decide whom to hire? This is clearly an HCRE-focused issue. Even though they have a huge body of information available on virtually every candidate and highly trained professionals running the process, they often (usually) get it wrong and end up disappointed with their choices. Worse, they often make the same mistakes again and again. The challenge in making these decisions is quite difficult – hence "the problem that never goes away."

While we appreciate the work of Eckardt and Jiang, as we noted earlier, their chapter (and much of the HCRE literature in general) is relentlessly optimistic in tone. At every decision point, the right choices are made and every random event breaks in just the right way to facilitate the emergence of the HCRE concept. A parallel concept is that of normal accidents (Perrow 1984; Vaughan 1999), where the breaks go the other way and the result is disastrous. Neither good nor bad outcomes can be predicted, but, given enough time, both are to be expected. This concern also links back to the path-dependence issue we noted in the section on emergence. The path-dependence phenomenon is very complex and frequently outside the authority or influence of any actor or group of actors. To be fortunate enough to have every extraneous event add to the emergence of strong human capital resources seems too much to ask, in our view.

An important factor to consider in the context of path dependence is short-term performance outcomes. Performance at the firm level has a very large stochastic component, but also often has a definitive impact on the interpretations of human actors surrounding and actively creating the emergence process (Levinthal and March 1993). The impact of short-term performance can be positive or negative on the emergence process. A unit leader can make all the right choices about structuring work flows and selecting people and integrating their behaviors, but if short-term performance is poor or declining and it persists in that way, the entire effort will be undercut. Case studies of turnaround situations are replete with stories of strategic leaders who made all the right choices but were felled by persistent poor performance from exogenous sources like the entry of a foreign rival or an economic slowdown.

There are also more than a few examples of strategic leaders who made a number of bad choices, but who were buoyed by good performance despite the mistakes made. Human observers tend to dramatically overgeneralize from performance, good or bad, to processes that they presume were responsible for generating the performance. Given good performance, the choices made must have been the right ones and, given poor performance, the choices made must have been the wrong ones. At the organization level, "performance" is itself emergent, very complex in its origins, and only loosely connected to the choices of actors. For example, it is well understood that in strategy, the outcome of a strategic move, defined as an intentional action taken by a firm to enhance or maintain its position vis-à-vis rivals, depends on the responses that are forthcoming from those rivals (Chen, Smith and Grimm 1992; Derfus, Maggitti, Grimm and Smith 2008). Needless to say, most of the responses are well outside the control of the firm that initiates an attack; and, indeed, the initial attack may be *sui generis* in that it was not the result of any earlier attack but a stand-alone move designed to benefit the attacker at the expense of the attacked. Still, the performance outcome will be treated by observers (and possibly the leaders themselves) as the direct outcome of actions taken internally. Equally important, the inferences made will be used to bolster or hamper the factors that the narrative asserts to be causal in nature.

Humans are also well known to take outcomes and work backwards through the choices in a very selective manner, yielding a plausible (albeit false) narrative about how the outcomes were achieved (Mintzberg 1987). Humans attribute outcomes to all manner of causes, some of them highly improbable. For example, Michael Lewis recounts a story told by psychologist Daniel Kahneman, who, along with his research partner Amos Tversky, created prospect theory (Kahneman and Tversky 1979) and helped bring behavioral economics into being (Thaler 2015).

> [During the Yom Kippur War in 1973] Danny Kahneman had found his way to the Israeli Air Force. Fighter pilots were also dying in unprecedented numbers, because of Egypt's use of new and improved surface-to-air missiles provided by the Soviet Union. One squadron had suffered especially horrific losses. The general in charge wanted to investigate, and possibly punish, the unit. "I remember him saying accusingly that 'one of the pilots had been hit not only by one missile but by four!' as if that was conclusive evidence of his ineptitude," recalled Danny.
>
> Danny explained to the general that he had a sample size problem: The losses experienced by the supposedly inept fighter squadron could have occurred by random chance alone. If he investigated the unit, he would no doubt find patterns in behavior that might serve as an explanation. Perhaps the pilots in that squadron had paid more visits to their families; or maybe they wore funny-colored underpants. Whatever he found would be a meaningless illusion, however. There weren't enough pilots in the squadron to achieve statistical significance. On top of it, an investigation, implying blame, would be horrible for morale. The only point of an inquiry would be to preserve the general's feelings of omnipotence. The general listened to Danny and stopped the inquiry. "I have considered that my only contribution to the war effort," said Danny. (Lewis 2016)

With this example, we do not intend to disparage all executives; but many of us have had experiences that are similar in that the executive in charge has strong opinions about cause–effect relations that are obviously wrong and destructive in terms of HCRE. At best, HCRE is a fragile thing, difficult to create and easy to disrupt.

The narratives that humans generate become the maps and schematics that they subsequently act upon to get things done. While this has positive aspects in that it speeds up the process of logical decision making by providing the (albeit often flawed) logic, it has long-term consequences that tend toward the harmful. As Danny Miller (1993: 116) described it: "over time, the world views, goals, strategies, cultures, and processes of successful organizations will become more pure or 'simple': They will come to focus more narrowly on a single theme, activity, or issue at the expense of all others." As a result, highly successful firms (and individuals) begin to fade and lose their edge. The process Miller describes is a natural outgrowth of the fact that human decision making has well-known and highly documented flaws. We believe that the process of emergence described in the HCRE literature should also confront this concern. The fact that HCRE involves an emergent process that is active and ongoing, and actively managed by human actors, makes its persistence quite tenuous in many instances.

Bargaining Power in the HCRE Context

As we noted earlier, the bargaining power concept has long been a critical issue in strategic management. The concept discussed by Eckardt and Jiang would fall under bargaining power of suppliers. Should the human capital generated lead to a competitive advantage, indicated by sustained profitability, some tension is likely to be caused by disputes regarding who owns the human capital that has emerged (and, by implication, the rents that it generates). On the one hand, employees of the firm should be able to demand higher wages, to the extent that the capital rests with them as individuals. In contrast, should the emergent processes (presumably the property of the firm) be the attributed cause of the capital, the rents would go to the organization and its shareholders.

It is important to note that the process through which all this is sorted out is likely to be (like the Israeli Air Force pilot story above) very damaging to relations and interactions among parties to the process. To be successful in HCR emergence, organizations need to exist in a climate of trust and mutual respect. The very notion of bargaining power is somewhat antithetical to the development of trust and mutual respect. The financial value attributed to a human capital resource at the individual level may not make sense at the aggregate level. Further, as a firm's reputation grows, its employees become more attractive to other firms. As employees come to believe that they are not adequately compensated for their contributions to the HCR, they will tend to exit the firm.

We suspect that a good way to observe these concerns regarding HCRE will be with executive succession or, more specifically, CEO succession. The separation of ownership and control that naturally occurs with publicly traded firms causes immense pressures on managers to create "new" value for shareholders. Nowhere is this pressure greater than with the new CEO. Early in their tenures, new CEOs suffer from low legitimacy inside the firm, coupled with low power to enact their decisions and especially vis-à-vis the board of directors (Shen 2003). They may (rightfully) fear that some of the firm's executive cadre are out to challenge their authority and take their jobs through a process of power contestation (Shen and Cannella 2002). As noted above, poor performance accentuates these problems, and the poor performance might be either relative to the firm's past performance or relative to its rivals. The end result, however, is that new leaders are under immense pressure to deliver to shareholders, and any upward blip in performance releases some of that pressure.

Our concern here is that an easy way to achieve a blip in performance is to make a tradeoff between short-term and long-term performance. By capturing a larger share of the rents generated by HCRE for shareholders, the new leader can unintentionally disrupt the HCRE process in ways that will generate a short-term blip in performance but in the long term undercut the HCRE process, and possibly damage it irreparably. This is especially concerning in the succession context because the new leader can trade on the trust that his or her predecessors built with employees for short-term gains. A similar process was documented by Zhang and Gimeno (2010) as CEOs felt pressure to meet analyst projections, with the result being a long-term decline in their firms' competitiveness.

Shleifer and Summers (1988) describe a similar process as "breach of trust" by executives and explain how it creates a motive for hostile takeovers in the context of firm-specific human capital. Like Eckardt and Jiang (and others), they note that employees are likely to invest in the development of firm-specific human capital only if they trust that managers will reward them for doing so. Therefore, according to Shleifer and Summers, trust is an essential element in firm-specific human capital and, by implication, in HCRE. This trust can be violated in the context of a hostile takeover when managers from outside the firm take control over it by purchasing the traded shares of stock and replacing the executive cadre and the board of directors. As many have noted, takeovers are often followed by layoffs or pay cuts for employees as the new owners try to take charge and consolidate their purchases (Coffee 1988; Magenheim and Mueller 1988). It is easy to imagine how mergers (hostile and otherwise) will facilitate the destruction of HCR.

Finally, many strategic resources are intangible. However, not all intangible resources are equal. Some, like brand loyalty, emerge over time due to special circumstances that are long past but that prevent rivals from copying the resource. For example, the Procter & Gamble corporation has literally dozens of brands that were built when branding was a new practice and not widespread among firms. When the forces of rivalry were weak, the brands were established. The strength of the Procter & Gamble brands is a strong-form emergent phenomenon which cannot be traced back to one particular event or series of events that resulted in the intangible resource. However, since that time (for many decades) the brands have been maintained by the company, and the maintenance of the resource may be a weak-form emergent phenomenon that could be modeled. The key point is that the maintenance of an intangible like brand loyalty does not rely on re-creating it day after day in an emergent process. The case of HCRE is quite different, and the active management that is required of the intangible resource leads us to believe that successful long-term maintenance will be challenging and frequently unsuccessful.

Exogenous Factors and the Definition of Resources

The fourth issue in our commentary is exogenous factors and their roles in the emergence and maintenance of human capital at the organizational level. We couple this with a discussion of the concept of resources. Exogenous factors are ever-present in strategy. Most successful strategies are not planned, but rather evolve (Mintzberg 1973, 1978). Indeed, it is often noted that good strategies often are realized only when plans are ignored as managers respond to external factors like rivals and customer demands. The case of Honda's entry into the US motorcycle market in the 1960s is widely cited, but there are many others (Christiansen and Pascale 1983; Pascale 1996). Honda assumed, as did most observers, that to compete in the US motorcycle market, large and powerful motorcycles were required. Honda designed and built several such motorcycle models and sent them to the US with a team of salespeople who proceeded, without much success, to establish distribution networks. Instead, they discovered quite by accident that it was the small motorcycles sent along only for the convenience of the sales force that were garnering attention. Only after a protracted struggle did the sales force convince their bosses back in Japan that the true resource was the small motorcycle (the Super Cub). The rest, as they say, is history.[1]

As we noted earlier, in attempts to describe the path-dependence concept, exogenous events (factors from outside the firm and outside the firm's control) feature prominently. Using the logic of path dependence in a forward-looking way can be done in some situations but not in others. It is hard for us to imagine, before the story actually unfolded, that Honda's entry into the US would be so successful and different than anticipated. As we noted earlier, firm performance is a prominent factor in the emergence of a lot of issues in organizations, and it is heavily impacted by factors outside anyone's control.

Barney (1991: 101) defines resources as "all assets, capabilities, organizational processes, firm attributes, information, knowledge, etc. controlled by a firm that enable the firm to conceive of and implement strategies that improve its efficiency and effectiveness." Priem and Butler (2001) and others have noted the tautological nature of this definition (and the many other definitions of resources that exist in the published literature). Proposition 4b from Ployhart and Moliterno (2011) illustrates the problem: "As task complexity increases, human capital resources are more likely to emerge if the unit manifests appropriate behavioral states." We see no way to test this proposition, as it is true by definition. The word "appropriate" is the problem. An appropriate behavioral state is one that makes human capital resources more likely to emerge, thus creating the tautology.

This problem seems endemic to the resource-based view because resources are only defined as valuable when they are linked to competitive advantage. Before the resource-based view can qualify as a "theory" it must be able to specify, a priori, what a resource is without reference to its role in competitive advantage. Scholars have long debated considerations for qualifying human capital as resources, and even further for classifying emergence of human capital resources as contributing to competitive advantage (Campbell, Coff and Kryscynski 2012; Hatch and Dyer 2004; Nyberg, Moliterno, Hale and Lepak 2014; Ployhart, Nyberg, Reilly and Maltarich 2014; Wright, Dunford and Snell 2001; Wright, McMahan and McWilliams 1994); and, most recently, Delery and Roumpi (2017) have claimed that the field has been going in circles, thus a full discussion of human capital resources is beyond the scope of our commentary. However, we recognize that the difficulty in studying the emergence of an entity that in and of itself is difficult to define poses challenges from the very start.

Methodological Concerns for Human Capital Resource Emergence Research

As discussed, we commend the effort put forth by Eckardt and Jiang in detailing the random coefficient modeling technique for transformation and amplification concepts of HCRE. While the examples provided by the authors present the multilevel and time-sensitive nature of modeling the emergent phenomena of HCR, we believe that the models may be too simplistic and only applicable for the weak form of emergence, and especially for a unit-level analysis involving a small number of individuals and their aggregated KSAOs. At the macro level, the analysis may become overly complex as researchers roll up multiple levels of multiple units within an organization. The reality of this aggregation is that to model even the weak form of HCRE may be statistically feasible yet the theoretical approach may not be sufficient to explain and predict the aggregation of KSAOs contributing to a competitive advantage at the organization level comprised of tens of thousands or hundreds of thousands of individual employees.

Not only is aggregation an issue at the macro level; we return to the issue of strong-form emergence and the inability to model such a phenomenon. Taking a top-down view, we can see in the very complex and complicated multinational or multidivisional organization that tracking the emergence of the HCR phenomenon across the entire organization may be next to impossible. First, isolating the individual KSAOs to measure transformation could result in a degree of magnitude that is beyond a computer model; and second, the intricacies of modeling the various potential factors contributing to amplification over time, at different times nonetheless, could be beyond the capabilities of a statistical package. Modeling strong-form emergence is not possible, and simplifying the phenomenon into weak forms by choosing certain transformational KSAOs, isolating amplification factors, and arbitrarily assigning a sequence of time to events will result in a perceived understanding of the overall phenomenon that is, at best, a bit perilous.

We do not believe that studying HCRE is a lost cause. We advocate supplementing weak-form models with qualitative research that can provide richness to the interpretations of simplified models. Interviews with employees, managers, and executives at all stages and ranks within the organization during human resource initiatives may allow researchers to better interpret the applicability of the statistical models and extract more meaningful implications from the results. While qualitative approaches may not imply replicability of a particular study or test specific hypotheses about HCRE, the insights gleaned from rich context can give researchers insight into the difficulty in studying how and when the emergence of strategic human capital resources contributes to a competitive advantage for a firm. We also note that several forms of qualitative research draw from philosophical foundations that are much more aligned with emergent phenomena than with the tenets of science (Lincoln and Guba 1985). Ultimately, any cause–effect inferences from HCRE research should be made with great caution.

CONCLUSION

In summary, we commend Eckardt and Jiang for providing a strong starting point chapter on the topic of strategic human capital resource emergence. The concepts of transformation and amplification were well explained, linkages to competitive advantage further discussed, and a full multilevel methodological approach explicated. From our perspective, the topic of emergence should also be examined more broadly in management research about human capital resources and whether the phenomenon can (or should) be modeled for replication. Additionally, scholars should consider the role of agency when developing studies about strategic human capital resource emergence, and refrain from oversimplifying the idea of bargaining power when it comes to human capital resources. Perhaps most importantly, researchers should be cautioned when modeling a strategic phenomenon as emergent; exogenous factors, path dependence, and the tautology in defining the relationships between resource value and competitive advantage may bring challenges to theorizing about and researching human capital processes. Finally, future work may incorporate more qualitative research methods to highlight and uncover the complexity and nuances in the multilevel approaches to strategic human capital resource emergence.

CHAPTER SUMMARY

BOX 7.1 KEY TAKEAWAYS

1.	The concept of emergence	Emergence can vary from weak to strong forms, and these correlate to the degree that a process can be modeled algorithmically. The complexity of unobservable and potentially unknowable processes involved with HCRE may fall perilously close to strong-form emergence.
2.	The issue of agency	"Strategic" HCRE implies intentionality of human decision making with respect to creating, developing, and managing the processes involved with HCRE.
3.	Bargaining power	Specific ownership of human capital (and thus ownership of the emergence processes) is an interesting debate; the term "bargaining power" may be antithetical to mutual trust and respect necessary for successful HCRE.
4.	Exogenous factors and "resources"	The emergence of HCR in a firm may very well result from factors outside the control of humans, and classifying human capital as "resources providing a competitive advantage" suffers from tautological argument.
5.	Methodology	Mathematical models of HCRE may be too simplistic to explain the aggregation of KSAOs of very large organizations – which may ultimately represent the strong-form emergence phenomenon mentioned above.

BOX 7.2 DIRECTIONS FOR FUTURE RESEARCH

1.	Strong form of emergence	Future research should cautiously address the strong-form nature of HCRE. Algorithmic computer models of human processes could be misrepresentative of the HCRE phenomenon.
2.	HCRE and agency	Though current research in this area has loosely considered the issue of agency, attributing strong emergent processes to human intervention must be done with care.
3.	Succession context	Investigating concerns regarding trust and mutual respect in in the CEO succession context could provide new insights to the field regarding management of intangible HC and HCRE processes.
4.	Externalities	Research in this area may benefit from considering factors that occur and impact HCRE externally. Exogenous events or accidental emergence may be of interest to researchers.
5.	Qualitative research	Quantitative models could be supplemented with qualitative information in order to provide clarity and richness to our insights about HCRE.

NOTE

1. The Super Cub has been in production continuously since 1958 and, with over 100 million sold, it is by far the most successful motor vehicle ever produced.

REFERENCES

Ariely, D. (2008). *Predictably Irrational*. New York: Harper-Collins.
Aristotle. (1994). *Metaphysics Books Z and H*. Oxford: Clarendon.

Barney, J. B. (1986). "Strategic factor markets: Expectations, luck, and business strategy." *Management Science*, *32*(10), 1231–41.
Barney, J. B. (1991). "Firm resources and sustained competitive advantage." *Journal of Management*, *17*(1), 99–120.
Campbell, B. A., Coff, R. and Kryscynski, D. (2012). "Rethinking sustained competitive advantage from human capital." *Academy of Management Review*, *37*(3), 376–95.
Carpenter, M. A., Sanders, G. and Gregersen, H. B. (2001). "Bundling human capital with organizational context: The impact of international assignment experience on multinational firm performance and CEO pay." *Academy of Management Journal*, *44*(3), 493–511.
Chen, M., Smith, K. G. and Grimm, C. (1992). "Action characteristics as predictors of competitive responses." *Management Science*, *38*(3), 439–55.
Christiansen, E. T. and Pascale, R. (1983). "Honda (A)." *Harvard Business School Case*, 384-049.
Coff, R. W. (1999). "When competitive advantage doesn't lead to performance: The resource-based view and stakeholder bargaining power." *Organization Science*, *10*(2), 119–33.
Coffee, J. C. (1988). "Shareholders versus managers: Strain in the corporate web." Pp. 77–134 in *Knights, Raiders and Targets: The Impact of the Hostile Takeover*, edited by John C. Coffee, Jr, Louis Lowenstein and Susan Rose-Ackerman. New York: Oxford University Press.
Delery, J. E. and Roumpi, D. (2017). "Strategic human resource management, human capital and competitive advantage: Is the field going in circles?" *Human Resource Management Journal*, *27*(1), 1–21.
Derfus, P. J., Maggitti, P. G., Grimm, C. M. and Smith, K. G. (2008). "The Red Queen effect: Competitive actions and firm performance." *Academy of Management Journal*, *51*(1), 61–80.
Finkelstein, S., Hambrick, D. C. and Cannella, Jr, A. A. (2009). *Strategic Leadership: Theory and Research on Executives, Top Management Teams, and Boards*. Oxford: Oxford University Press.
Goldstein, J. (1999). "Emergence as a construct: History and issues." *Emergence*, *1*(1), 49–72.
Hambrick, D. C. (1989). "Putting top managers back into the strategy picture." *Strategic Management Journal*, *10*, 5–15.
Hambrick, D. C. (2007). "Upper echelons theory: An update." *Academy of Management Review*, *32*(2), 334–43.
Hambrick, D. C. and Mason, P. (1984). "Upper echelons: The organization as a reflection of its top managers." *Academy of Management Review*, *9*, 193–206.
Hatch, N. W. and Dyer, J. H. (2004). "Human capital and learning as a source of sustainable competitive advantage." *Strategic Management Journal*, *25*(12), 1155–78.
Kahneman, D. and Tversky, A. (1979). "Prospect theory: Analysis of decision making under risk." *Econometrica*, *47*(2), 263–92.
Levinthal, D. A. and March, J. G. (1993). "The myopia of learning." *Strategic Management Journal*, *14*(Special Issue), 95–112.
Lewis, M. (2016). *The Undoing Project*. New York: Norton.
Lincoln, Y. S. and Guba, E. G. (1985). *Naturalistic Inquiry*. Beverly Hills, CA: Sage.
Magenheim, E. B. and Mueller, D. C. (1988). "Are acquiring firm shareholders better off after an acquisition?" Pp. 171–93 in *Knights, Raiders, and Targets: The Impact of the Hostile Takeover*, edited by John C. Coffee, Jr, Louis Lowenstein and Susan Rose-Ackerman. New York: Oxford University Press.
March, J. G. and Simon, H. A. (1958). *Organizations*. New York: Wiley.
Mill, J. S. (1843). *A System of Logic*. London: Parker.
Miller, D. (1993). "The architecture of simplicity." *Academy of Management Review*, *18*(1), 116–38.
Mintzberg, H. (1973). *The Nature of Managerial Work*. New York: Harper & Row.
Mintzberg, H. (1978). "Patterns in strategy formation." *Management Science*, *24*, 934–48.
Mintzberg, H. (1980). *The Nature of Managerial Work*. Englewood Cliffs, NJ: Prentice-Hall.
Mintzberg, H. (1987). "Crafting strategy." *Harvard Business Review*, *65*(4), 66–75.
Nyberg, A. J., Moliterno, T. P., Hale, D. and Lepak, D. P. (2014). "Resource-based perspectives on unit-level human capital: A review and integration." *Journal of Management*, *40*(1), 316–46.
Pascale, R. T. (1996). "The Honda effect." *California Management Review*, *38*(4), 80–91.
Perrow, C. (1984). *Normal Accidents: Living with High-Risk Technologies*. New York: Basic Books.
Ployhart, R. E. and Moliterno, T. P. (2011). "Emergence of the human capital resource: A multilevel model." *Academy of Management Review*, *36*(1), 127–50.
Ployhart, R. E., Nyberg, A. J., Reilly, G. and Maltarich, M. A. (2014). "Human capital is dead; long live human capital resources!" *Journal of Management*, *40*(2), 371–98.
Porter, M. E. (1980). *Competitive Strategy: Techniques for Analyzing Industry and Competitors*. New York: Harper & Row.
Priem, R. L. and Butler, J. E. (2001). "Is the resource-based 'view' a useful perspective for strategic management research?" *Academy of Management Review*, *26*(1), 22–40.
Shen, W. (2003). "The dynamics of the CEO-board relationship: An evolutionary perspective." *Academy of Management Review*, *28*(3), 466–76.

Shen, W. and Cannella Jr, A. A. (2002). "Power dynamics within top management and their impacts on CEO dismissal followed by inside succession." *Academy of Management Journal*, *45*(6), 1195–208.
Shleifer, A. and Summers, L. (1988). "Breach of trust in hostile takeovers." Pp. 33–55 in *Corporate Takeovers: Causes and Consequences*, edited by Alan J. Auerbach. Chicago, IL: University of Chicago Press.
Thaler, R. H. (2015). *Misbehaving: The Making of Behavioral Economics*. New York: Norton.
Vaughan, D. (1999). "The dark side of organizations: Mistake, misconduct, and disaster." *Annual Review of Sociology*, *25*, 271–305.
Wernerfelt, B. (1984). "A resource-based view of the firm." *Strategic Management Journal*, *5*(2), 171–80.
Wright, P. M., Dunford, B. B. and Snell, S. A. (2001). "Human resources and the resource based view of the firm." *Journal of Management*, *27*(6), 701–21.
Wright, P. M., McMahan, G. C. and McWilliams, A. (1994). "Human resources and sustained competitive advantage: A resource-based perspective." *International Journal of Human Resource Management*, *5*(2), 301–26.
Zhang, Y. and Gimeno, J. (2010). "Earnings pressure and competitive behavior: Evidence from the U.S. electricity industry." *Academy of Management Journal*, *53*(4), 743–68.

PART III

ISOLATING MECHANISMS: FIRM-SPECIFITY

8. Specific human capital: a matching perspective*

Ingo Weller

INTRODUCTION

Traditional human capital theory (Becker, 1962, 1993) explains that individuals increase their general or firm-specific human capital through education, on-the-job training, medical treatment, and other related activities. General human capital is valuable in many firms and can be traded on competitive labor markets. Perfectly firm-specific human capital produces value in the focal firm, but not in others. When firm-specific human capital is created, workers and firms can benefit from above-average rents.

This logic has long dominated thinking regarding the nature, measurement, and economic value of human capital and is probably the major foundation for most strategic human capital resources (SHCR) discussions in this volume. Firm-specific human capital is the locomotive of SHCR research, just as "asset specificity is the big locomotive to which transaction cost economics owes much of its predictive content" (Williamson, 1985: 56).

More than 50 years after human capital theory was introduced, researchers are taking new looks at firm-specific human capital. In this chapter, I argue that understanding human capital requires a matching lens regarding when and how individuals and firms invest in human capital, when this human capital is specific, or even firm-specific, and how it impacts individuals and firms. The matching perspective should also help the SHCR community reach its longstanding goal to bridge organizational behavior (OB), human resource (HR), and strategy research.

TRADITIONAL HUMAN CAPITAL THEORY

Rather than thoroughly reviewing the literature in the established field of human capital theory, I review selected issues before discussing new looks at firm-specific human capital.

What is Human Capital?

In the original model, human capital was defined as the stock of "knowledge, information, ideas, skills, and health of individuals" (Becker, 2002: 3) built and maintained through investments in "schooling, on-the-job training, medical care, migration and searching for information about prices and incomes" (Becker, 1993: 11). Economics researchers widely accept that definition, but researchers from other disciplines have failed to establish a common human capital language (Nyberg et al., 2014; Nyberg and Wright, 2015).

Human capital has been studied at both individual and firm levels (Nyberg et al., 2014; Ployhart, Nyberg, Reilly, and Maltarich, 2014). Individual-level management scholars "define human capital largely in terms of individual differences in KSAOs" (Ployhart and Moliterno, 2011: 129). Obviously, this definition differs from the economics view focusing on investments. Instead, the definition explains that individuals perform differently because of their attributes, including general cognitive ability, personality, values, and interests (Ployhart and Moliterno, 2011). However, the investment principle is critical for understanding the economic perspective which originated in Becker's vision to "estimate the money rate of return to college and high-school education in the United States" (Becker, 1993: 29). The management view of human capital is more about understanding individual performance differences, sometimes neglecting the costs and economic returns associated with such differences. SHCR scholarship combines the economics focus on investments and rents and the management focus on performance differences.

General and Firm-Specific Human Capital in the Traditional Perspective

Traditional human capital theory distinguishes between general and firm-specific human capital. General human capital is equally valuable in many firms. Given the "embodiment of human capital in people," maximizing agents "must go where their capital goes" (Becker, 1993: 18): Workers maximize their returns from general human capital through mobility on the external labor market. Because many similar firms offer equal pay according to a worker's marginal productivity, a general equilibrium (i.e., competitive parity) results (Becker, 1962). Therefore, individuals, but not firms, will willingly invest in general human capital.

Firm-specific human capital conveys quasi-rents because it cannot be used in other firms (Becker, 1993). Firms and workers both want to gain from firm-specific investments, but fear that the other party may blackmail the investing party after it invests in specific training. Thus, to avoid underinvestment dilemmas, firms and workers need to share investments and rents (Hashimoto, 1981; Lazear, 2009). The result is a win-win situation (technically: a bilateral monopoly), which serves as an effective isolating mechanism of a firm's human resource base.

Consequently, firm-specific human resources are assumed to drive competitive advantage. Accordingly, SHCR researchers highlight (but also question) the role of perfectly firm-specific human capital (Campbell et al., 2012). Human capital theory is similar to all models in making simplified assumptions. Whereas untrue or unrealistic assumptions may still lead to meaningful predictions (Friedman, 1953), critics argue that distinguishing between general and firm-specific human capital causes the traditional human capital model to make seriously false predictions.

Critique of the Traditional Model

The traditional human capital model assumes that training creates human capital, which then enhances employee behaviors, which then enhance individual-level productivity, which then creates firm revenues. However, the model fails to consider that training may fail to create human capital, or that workers may lack motivation, clear perspective, willingness, or ability to use their skills (Ployhart and Moliterno, 2011). Furthermore, firm-level market success is not guaranteed. Obviously, the model is bound to many strong assumptions. For example, OB scholars doubt that training is always effective (Aguinis and Kraiger, 2009; Salas and Cannon-Bowers, 2001), and resource-based view scholars admit that value is created on markets rather than in firms (Barney, 2001; Priem and Butler, 2001a, 2001b).

Consequently, SHCR researchers assert that firms differ in the use value or market value that they can realize from general human capital (Campbell et al., 2012). For example, some firms may excel in strategically exploiting asset or resource complementarities (Helfat et al., 2007; Sirmon et al., 2011) to create more market value from general human capital than others. Thus, general rather than firm-specific human capital may become the basis of a firm's competitive advantage.

Another aspect relates to the binary distinction between general and firm-specific human capital. In the traditional model, workers invest in general or firm-specific training, but not in both; moreover, there is nothing in between. However, there may be different degrees of firm-specificity, "determined by technology" (Acemoglu and Pischke, 1999b: 540). Skills are then no longer general or firm-specific per se, but are more or less general when they overlap with technologies used or production functions applied in a number of firms. For example, some skills can be industry-specific (Mayer et al., 2012; Neffke and Henning, 2013) or occupation-specific (Geel et al., 2011), rather than completely general or firm-specific.

A related implication is that workers face opportunity costs when they invest in general or firm-specific training (Campbell et al., 2012). Furthermore, they may have complex and multifaceted sets of general and firm-specific human capital components rather than one-dimensional human capital (Weller et al., 2019). In this perspective, further firm-specific training changes the ratio of general to firm-specific human capital, but does not make the individual's human capital set entirely general or firm-specific.

SHCR scholars also criticize human capital theory for its atomistic focus on the relationship between a single firm and a single agent, although firms orchestrate complex workforces of many employees (Nyberg et al., 2014; Ployhart et al., 2014) where optimal investments in one employee may constrain investments for others (Weller et al., 2019). Another assertion is that real employees and employers seem to be unaware of firm-specific human capital. In support, employees were found to have biased perceptions of their firm-specific human capital, which "may drive behavior in ways unanticipated by existing theory" (Raffiee and Coff, 2016: 766). Indeed, interviews of managers revealed a lack of knowledge about firm-specific human capital and an inability to list KSAOs that employees "could not readily apply at a new job if they moved tomorrow" (Kryscynski and Ulrich, 2015: 361).

NEW APPROACHES TO FIRM-SPECIFIC HUMAN CAPITAL

Despite the criticisms outlined, I view the human capital literature positively. I agree that the traditional human capital model has deficits, especially when applied to SHCR, but that is expected because models naturally simplify assumptions to manage complexity. That is, they fix elements of the referent object, and vary others systematically to identify causal mechanisms, all else equal. Given that the human capital model was developed specifically to estimate economic returns from education, OB, strategy, and HR scholars naturally struggle with the original assumptions because they are focused on competitive advantage, between-individual performance differences, and HR activities that drive individual- and firm-level performance. Consequently, we may need alternative assumptions to model these phenomena.

I further believe that many criticisms have been answered in extant literature. For example, in contrast to the traditional human capital model, firms may be willing to pay for general training because they learn about employees' hidden KSAOs, such as personality, and leverage those advantages during future job assignments (Acemoglu and Pischke, 1999b; Ortega, 2001). Also, labor market frictions are critical for understanding when general training is virtually firm-specific, worth the investment, and yields rents (Acemoglu and Pischke, 1998, 1999a). These and related models eloquently complement current SHCR thinking (e.g., Campbell at al., 2012; Chadwick, 2017; Chadwick and Dabu, 2009), but are hardly noticed in the SHCR field. In fact, no unifying framework has integrated the many developments of the traditional human capital model. I suggest a matching framework.[1]

Specific Human Capital

The traditional human capital model assumes that firm-specific training ties workers to a single employer, whereas general training leads to human capital that can be transferred to many firms. More recent human capital models play with these assumptions. My discussion starts with Lazear's skill-weights model of human capital, and then extends this perspective further.

The skill-weights model assumes that most firm-specific "human capital is actually general human capital" (Lazear, 2009: 915). In the skill-weights model an individual has two skill types (e.g., manual and cognitive). Both are general in having the same utility in many firms. The model restricts the analysis to two skills, which simplifies the mathematical notation but ignores the fact that in reality most human capital bundles include a complex and broad array of KSAOs. Second, abundance in one skill is thought to imply deficits in other skills, in a necessary tradeoff "to avoid a situation in which all workers enter the same occupation" (Yamaguchi, 2012: 6). The skill-weights model has been extended to situations where the skill-weights are additive rather than substitutive (Yamaguchi, 2012), and has been partly tested empirically (Gathmann and Schönberg, 2010). These initial arguments lead to three propositions:

P1: Human capital consists of bundles or sets of one or more human capital component(s) (KSAOs).

P2: All human capital components (KSAOs) are general.

P3: Human capital bundles or sets are created by potentially complex aggregation logics, and human capital components (KSAOs) are not necessarily substitutes in these bundles or sets.

The skill-weights model assumes that an employee with the skill set (A,B) produces output at firm i defined as $\lambda_i A+(1-\lambda_i)B$, with $0 \leq \lambda_i \leq 1$. In the formula, lambda is a random variable with density $f(\lambda)$ that varies across firms, such that between-firm heterogeneity is modeled by differences in the skill-weights. To fix ideas, we can think of lambda as approximately normally distributed, implying that most firms have balanced skill needs, and only a few firms require much of one skill and little of the other. The same may hold for individuals. A normal distribution also implies that in balanced areas of the distribution, both parties have a reasonable number of alternatives. Even if we accept the limiting assumption that firms and/or workers are perfectly unique, reasonably similar alternatives occur in dense areas of the lambda and skill distributions, so switching costs should be minimal in the direct neighborhood of the status quo.

Initially, workers are randomly endowed with skills, and land in random matches. Then, based on the current match, they invest in skills. Without specifying initial skill endowments, we can imagine situations in which individual *i* has more of all KSAOs than individual $j, A_i > A_j \wedge B_i > B_j$. The skill-weights model solves the human capital problem when the ratio of the skills *A* and *B* matches the technology indicated in the lambda skill-weights. Individuals with abundant but identical skill ratios have the same degree of match quality but may be conceptualized as occupying higher ranks in the firm, thus realizing stronger productivity and higher wages. The skill-weights model neglects within-firm heterogeneity, but such heterogeneity may be assumed if it complies with the general production technology. In other words, the skill-weights model assumes a constant lambda for firms, which are thus holistic entities with one production function or technology, offering one type of job. That view may be broadened, though, and Lazear admits this possibility:

> We can think of the λ as being not only firm-specific but job- and perhaps industry-specific. For modeling purposes, virtually nothing is changed by expanding the view to include jobs. [. . .] Once we begin to think of λ as being tied to jobs, the approach of Gibbons and Waldman (2004) becomes relevant. They model "task-specific" human capital and argue that different jobs in the firm use different amounts of it. Promotions are performed in a way to minimize underutilization of task-specific skills. (Lazear, 2009: 929–30)

In reality, alternative jobs in firms, whether on the same or on different ranks, are associated with new KSAO weights and different KSAO sets. For example, promotions to higher ranks typically go along with increased leadership responsibilities (Gibbons and Waldman, 2004), such that KSAO demands are likely to change across hierarchies. Based on this more realistic and flexible conception of firms, I assume:

P4: Firms are heterogeneous, both within and between.

The skill-weights model assumes that good matches lead to productivity, where good matches result when an individual's KSAO set is closely aligned with a firm's production function. Similarly, psychologists refer to strong person–situation fit or person–environment fit (Edwards, 2008) that enhance attitudes and performance while lowering stress and withdrawal behaviors (Kristof-Brown et al., 2005). As defined here, "good match" implies a somewhat stricter assumption on fit than in psychology: KSAOs must meet the firm's economically relevant technology or production function rather than some undefined situation or environment. The term *relevant* person–situation fit thus indicates economic relevance (Ployhart et al., 2014). Psychology and OB researchers have focused mostly on person–situation fit, but rarely look at economic relevance explicitly.

P5: The better an individual's human capital matches a firm's technology or production function (i.e., the stronger the relevant person–situation fit), the higher the individual's productivity.

The skill-weights model assumes that all KSAOs are general, and their "uses are specific to the firm" (Lazear, 2009: 915). Although Becker's original model implies a similar logic, Lazear's model states more explicitly that whether human capital is specific is always a match property. Moreover, specificity is continuous rather than binary in this model. General human capital becomes more specific, but not necessarily firm-specific, the more it is aligned with a firm's technology, or the stronger the relevant person–situation fit.

P6: Human capital specificity is a continuous construct equaling match quality or the degree of the relevant person–situation fit; specificity is zero when individuals lack or do not use human capital that firms need; otherwise, some specificity occurs.

How is Specific Human Capital Created?

Lazear's model argues that adaptation (learning) and selection (turnover) cause human capital to become specific. Adaptation reflects the traditional human capital logic arguing that training and education investments generate KSAOs that contribute to individual productivity. The turnover mechanism mirrors the view that some matches are better than others, and that mobility is sometimes more effective than learning for improving match quality. In the skill-weights model, individuals first land in a random match; this reflects labor economics theory according to which job seekers search for jobs randomly (Ehrenberg and Smith, 2016). Based on the quality of this match, they invest in skills to improve it. Their enhanced skills may lead to another external offer, and, consequently, they can bargain for increased wages with their current employer. Based on the bargaining outcome, they tend to stay with the "initial firm during the second period whenever the inside value exceeds the outside output value. [. . .] This condition makes clear that the skill-weights model is a particular kind of matching model, where workers choose jobs that best suit their strengths" (Lazear, 2009: 918).

Integrating human capital and matching theories has many advantages (Weller et al., 2019). For my purposes here, the most important insight is that matching – or the "process by which individuals are dynamically aligned with organizations and the situations (roles, jobs, tasks, etc.) within them" – generates specific human capital. Matching activities harmonize an individual's human capital and a firm's KSAO needs, creating specific human capital and increasing average productivity. Thus:

P7: Matching creates specific human capital by aligning an individual's human capital with an organization's technology or production function (i.e., KSAO needs).

Matches and match quality are altered whenever persons or situations change, and accordingly match quality is not a constant. Training (adaptation) and turnover (selection) are two potential activities for achieving or regaining match quality and specific human capital, but more activities exist. The "dynamic matching lifecycle model"

(Weller et al., 2019) identifies four matching stages that each comprise various activities: the *create* and *terminate* stages follow selection logic; the *develop* and *reconfigure* stages follow adaptation logic. In the create stage, firms attract and select individuals with specific KSAOs that match a firm's KSAO demands. In the develop stage, employees undergo training to develop the KSAOs needed to perform their jobs. However, jobs may also be redesigned or crafted to better use the employee's KSAOs. In the reconfigure stage, firms improve person–situation allocations through internal mobility, using horizontal transfers and vertical promotions. In the terminate stage, separations terminate matches that cannot be improved (push) or are challenged by outside options (pull).

The matching lifecycle model crucially implies that both individuals and firms can create better matches through investments and change. In Lazear's model, as in most human capital models, the individual is the primary change agent who must adapt, learn, or move to a better matching employer, whereas the firm maintains stable, exogenously given skill-weights or a fixed production technology. However, firms and situations within them can also change to improve matches. This integrative perspective leads to the next proposition:

P8: Matching activities occur along a dynamic matching lifecycle: create, develop, reconfigure, terminate. Any one activity or combinations of activities (i.e., matching systems) potentially improve matches and create specific human capital.

When is Specific Human Capital Firm-Specific?

To reiterate, KSAOs are always general in the extended human capital and matching model, and become specific when aligned with a firm's KSAO needs. Specific human capital becomes *firm*-specific in two general ways, which I elaborate on below: In the first case, specific human capital becomes firm-specific when no other firm has the same KSAO demands or skill-weights (uniqueness); in the second case, firms are potentially similar, but specific human capital becomes quasi firm-specific.

In the first case, perfectly firm-specific human capital may be defined according to the relative number of alternative firms that have reasonably similar KSAO demands. With this definition, firm-specificity is "endogenous. As markets become very thick, investments that would otherwise be viewed as firm specific become more general" (Lazear, 2009: 925). That definition broadly aligns with the traditional human capital model. For example, when job alternatives are non-existing, "all training, no matter what its nature, would be specific to the firm" (Becker, 1993: 50).[2] The definition implies that individuals willingly invest in specific KSAO sets when the labor market has plentiful and identical KSAO demands, as is common with balanced skill sets, but relatively seldom with idiosyncratic skill sets in the tails of the lambda distribution. A related implication is that if we assume within-firm heterogeneity along with flexible internal labor markets, even unique employers can motivate or initiate investments in firm-specific human capital because internal labor markets provide employees with at least limited hedging.[3] An example occurs when multi-business firms close one of their businesses, but are able to move the affected workers to surviving parts of the firm.

P9: Availability of comparable outside alternatives determines when specific human capital is firm-specific. When no alternatives are available, specific human capital is perfectly firm-specific. Specificity is a necessary but insufficient condition for firm-specificity.[4]

In the second case, quasi firm-specific human capital emerges. It is quasi firm-specific because, in principle, alternatives exist. However, impediments to imitation prevent rival firms from realizing the same human capital advantages (Barney, 1991; Dierickx and Cool, 1989). For example, labor markets may have restricted mobility for various reasons, including supply-side and demand-side constraints (Campbell et al., 2012). Furthermore, employees and employers may be willing but fail to invest in good matches. For example, recruitment and hiring efforts often generate initial mismatches, partly because of opportunistic behaviors (Bangerter, Roulin, and König, 2012; Spence, 1973). Finally, complex production technologies may cause poor understandings and management of matches, such that good matches are virtually unique and thus firm-specific.

P10: Human capital quasi firm-specificity impedes imitation because of labor market constraints, matching capabilities, and match complexity.

How is Firm-Specific Human Capital Created?

The first case I described mirrors the traditional human capital model, where uniqueness, found in the tails of the lambda distribution, generates firm-specific human capital. In other words, unique firms exploit unique technologies, and unique technologies demand alternative KSAO sets relative to all other technologies used across industries and settings. For instance, uniqueness is possible when firms realize early mover advantages (Besanko et al., 2013) resulting from fundamental shocks that propel a more or less random firm into a beneficial competitive position. Such shocks include "process or product innovations, discoveries of new sources of consumer value or market segments, shifts in demand or tastes, or changes in regulatory policy" (Besanko et al., 2013: 420). From this perspective, differences in learning curves, network effects, buyer uncertainty, and buyer switching costs (Besanko et al., 2013) are endogenous and exogenous mechanisms that help firms realize early mover advantages and potentially exploit rents from firm-specific human capital.

P11: Firms that enjoy an early mover advantage for endogenous or exogenous reasons potentially create firm-specific human capital.

Some situations evoke quasi firm-specific human capital. For example, labor market frictions (e.g., mobility constraints or imperfect knowledge of alternatives) allow firms to exploit matching and human capital advantages even when alternatives are available. Human capital researchers (e.g., Acemoglu and Pischke, 1999b) and SHCR scholars (e.g., Brymer et al., 2016; Campbell et al., 2012; Chadwick, 2017) assume that labor market frictions are important for understanding firm-specific human capital. For example, non-compete clauses (e.g., Conti, 2014; Marx et al., 2009) prevent workers from moving to competitors with similar KSAO demands. Patent enforcement is similar in that it "can restrict the rights of exiting employees (and their new employers) to use technologies" without permission (Ganco et al., 2015: 662).

P12: Firms that effectively exploit labor market frictions (e.g., mobility constraints, incomplete information) potentially create quasi firm-specific human capital.

Matching expertise is another explanation. Some firms may be particularly well equipped to solve matching and human capital challenges. For example, some firms have sophisticated talent systems allowing them to integrate relevant information from various talent agents such as HR managers, line managers, peers, and focal employees (Weller et al., 2018). In combination, these sources assist in matching attempts, resulting in quasi firm-specific human capital. From this perspective, matching expertise is a dynamic firm capability (Eisenhardt and Martin, 2000; Teece et al., 1997) reflecting the firm's ability to create, develop, reconfigure, and terminate matches to address external and internal changes. This view resonates well with recent extensions of the resource-based view of the firm, such as managerial entrepreneurship (Chadwick and Dabu, 2009), asset orchestration (Helfat et al., 2007), resource management (Sirmon et al., 2007), or resource orchestration (Sirmon et al., 2011). All of these extensions argue that the combination of resources, capabilities, and managerial acumen "ultimately results in superior firm performance" (Chadwick et al., 2015: 360).

P13: Firms that effectively exploit matching capabilities potentially create quasi firm-specific human capital.

Match and matching complexity is a further explanation for quasi firm-specific human capital. The complexity logic relates to uniqueness because technologies are likely to be unique when they require many and different KSAOs. However, the focus here is on manageability rather than uniqueness. The greater the complexity of a match or matching process, the more difficult will be its management. Managers and talent agents may find it difficult or impossible to optimize matches when KSAO weights are surrounded by ambiguity (Coff, 1997) and uncertainty. Thus, luck and repeated trials rather than deliberate and one-time matching activities may be necessary for perfect matches.

P14: Firms that successfully circumvent the complexity of matches potentially create quasi firm-specific human capital. Complexity includes ambiguity and uncertainty, such that quasi firm-specific human capital may also result from luck.

When Can Firm-Specific Human Capital Rents be Sustained?

I have suggested and briefly outlined four processes that potentially result in firm-specific human capital: uniqueness, market frictions, matching capabilities, and luck. These processes resonate with the resource-based view of the firm (Barney, 1991; Barney and Wright, 1998) stating that resources must be valuable, rare, inimitable, and enmeshed in the organization's structures and management system to generate sustained competitive advantage. That is, KSAOs are valuable when they match a firm's production function.[5] They are rare when they are unique. They are inimitable when they exploit market frictions and luck; finally, when they are enmeshed in the organization's structures and management system, matching capabilities support a firm's competitive advantage.

Specific human capital leads to productivity. However, from a competitive and resource-based view perspective, specific human capital leads to competitive parity. Firm-specific human capital may allow above-average returns. However, not all these rents are sustainable. Rivals often quickly imitate uniqueness resulting from early mover advantages. Likewise, given that matches are inherently unstable (Weller et al., 2019), quasi firm-specific human capital stemming from lucky moves may also vanish soon and potentially cause regression-to-the-mean (Besanko et al., 2013), or changes in legislation may offset market frictions. Thus, quasi firm-specific human capital from matching capabilities has potentially the most sustainable consequences. For example, matching capabilities often spring from a path-dependent process of constant investments in matching and talent management, and thus impede instant imitation (Besanko et al., 2013; Dierickx and Cool, 1989).

However, such sustainability sources may also erode in the long run. For instance, exogenous technology shocks may offset advantages from path dependencies, such as when digital technologies replace headhunter expertise. Along the same lines, firms may lose matching capabilities when a few key individuals with critical expertise leave. Critical human capital outflows (Reilly et al., 2014) may be avoidable, such as through non-compete clauses, but are sometimes unavoidable, for instance when employees retire or die.

P15: Quasi firm-specific human capital from matching capabilities is most likely to generate sustained competitive advantage (relative to other sources of firm-specificity).

CONCLUSION

In this chapter, I have summarized the extant SHCR research regarding the traditional human capital model. I advance SHCR research by developing a model of firm-specific human capital based on a number of propositions: Human capital consists of KSAO sets where all KSAOs are general. Specific human capital results from aligning KSAO sets and firm technologies through matching. Specificity is a necessary but insufficient condition for firm-specificity. Firm-specific human capital potentially generates competitive advantage.

A matching focus is key to this model. Individuals and firms may use various matching activities to create quality matches and specific or even firm-specific human capital. Although prior SHCR research has mentioned this possibility, it has not consistently considered the competitive advantage effects occurring when KSAOs are all general, and when KSAO sets are specific and firm-specific according to their use in heterogeneous firms.

CHAPTER SUMMARY

BOX 8.1 KEY TAKEAWAYS

Takeaway	Explanation
1. KSAO sets	Human capital consists of sets or bundles of KSAOs. Each KSAO is general.
2. Matching	When KSAO sets are aligned with a firm's production logic, human capital becomes specific. Alignment is achieved through matching.
3. Firm-specificity	Specificity is a necessary but insufficient condition for the firm-specificity of human capital. Labor market thickness (uniqueness), labor market frictions, superior matching capabilities, or luck determine whether specific human capital is firm-specific or quasi firm-specific.

BOX 8.2 DIRECTIONS FOR FUTURE RESEARCH

Ideas	Explanation
1. Specificity and firm-specificity	To test the logics of specific and firm-specific human capital, research could observe when human capital is mobile within but not across firms with similar production logics.
2. Matching and value creation	Matching research should be aligned with SHCR research to analyze when matching efforts generate firm performance and competitive advantage through human capital mechanisms.
3. Causal evidence	Research could observe how exogenous shocks (e.g., legislation, technology breakthroughs) causally impact the firm-specificity of human capital and firm performance.

NOTES

* I thank Florian Englmaier for providing insightful discussions and helpful comments.

1. The next sections draw freely on Weller et al. (2019).
2. March and Simon (1958) also embraced the idea of complex skill sets and specificity, arguing that long-term employees tend to have increasingly specialized skills tied to the organization and will perceive fewer extra-organizational alternatives. Thus specialization decreases the demand and supply for a particular bundle of abilities until "we have an organization that can find a replacement only at prohibitive cost and an employee who can find another job only at prohibitive loss" (p. 102).
3. Internal labor markets thicken the total labor market, but do not necessarily solve the employer-related hold-up problem associated with firm-specific investments.
4. I should note that some human capital bundles may dominate other bundles in that some individuals have more of any one KSAO in their human capital bundle than other individuals. Specificity and firm-specificity, as defined here, may be achieved through a change of KSAOs, including improving but also diminishing or forgetting certain KSAOs. This leads, in some cases, to interesting implications, for instance when a gain in match quality overcompensates a loss in the pure KSAO value. In other words: Employees with less human capital in perfect matches (which are then specific or firm-specific) may be better off than employees with more human capital in imperfect matches (with a lower degree of specificity or firm-specificity).
5. Again, we must assume that firms are successful on the product market.

REFERENCES

Acemoglu, D., and Pischke, J.-S. (1998). Why do firms train? Theory and evidence. *Quarterly Journal of Economics*, *113*(1), 79–119.

Acemoglu, D., and Pischke, J.-S. (1999a). Beyond Becker: Training in imperfect labour markets. *Economic Journal*, *109*(453), F112–42.

Acemoglu, D., and Pischke, J.-S. (1999b). The structure of wages and investment in general training. *Journal of Political Economy*, *107*(3), 539–72.

Aguinis, H., and Kraiger, K. (2009). Benefits of training and development for individuals and teams, organizations, and society. *Annual Review of Psychology*, *60*, 451–74.

Bangerter, A., Roulin, N., and König, C. J. (2012). Personnel selection as a signaling game. *Journal of Applied Psychology*, *97*(4), 719–38.

Barney, J. B. (1991). Firm resources and sustained competitive advantage. *Journal of Management*, *17*(1), 99–120.

Barney, J. B. (2001). Is the resource-based "view" a useful perspective for strategic management research? Yes. *Academy of Management Review*, *26*(1), 41–56.

Barney, J. B., and Wright, P. M. (1998). On becoming a strategic partner: The role of human resources in gaining competitive advantage. *Human Resource Management*, *37*(1), 31–46.

Becker, G. S. (1962). Investment in human capital: A theoretical analysis. *Journal of Political Economy*, *70*(5), 9–49.

Becker, G. S. (1993). *Human Capital: A Theoretical and Empirical Analysis, with Special Reference to Education* (3rd edn). Chicago, IL: University of Chicago Press.

Becker, G. S. (2002). The age of human capital. In E. P. Lazear (ed.), *Education in the Twenty-First Century*, 3–8. Stanford, CA: Hoover Institution Press.

Besanko, D., Dranove, D., Shanley, M., and Schaefer, S. (2013). *Economics of Strategy* (6th edn). Hoboken, NJ: Wiley.

Brymer, R., Molloy, J. C., and Chadwick, C. (2016). Strategic human capital. *Oxford Bibliographies in Management*, online resource [DOI: 10.1093/OBO/9780199846740-0082].

Campbell, B. A., Coff, R., and Kryscynski, D. (2012). Rethinking sustained competitive advantage from human capital. *Academy of Management Review*, *37*(3), 376–95.

Chadwick, C. (2017). Toward a more comprehensive model of firms' human capital rents. *Academy of Management Review*, *42*(3), 499–519.

Chadwick, C., and Dabu, A. (2009). Human resources, human resource management, and the competitive advantage of firms: Toward a more comprehensive model of causal linkages. *Organization Science*, *20*(1), 253–72.

Chadwick, C., Super, J. F., and Kwon, K. (2015). Resource orchestration in practice: CEO emphasis on SHRM, commitment-based HR systems, and firm performance. *Strategic Management Journal*, *36*(3), 360–76.

Coff, R. W. (1997). Human assets and management dilemmas: coping with hazards on the road to resource-based theory. *Academy of Management Review*, *22*(2), 374–402.

Conti, R. (2014). Do non-competition agreements lead firms to pursue risky R&D projects? *Strategic Management Journal*, *35*(8), 1230–48.

Dierickx, I., and Cool, K. (1989). Asset stock accumulation and sustainability of competitive advantage. *Management Science*, *35*(12), 1504–11.

Edwards, J. R. (2008). Person-environment fit in organizations: An assessment of theoretical progress. *Academy of Management Annals*, *2*(1), 167–230.

Ehrenberg, R. G., and Smith, R. S. (2016). *Modern Labor Economics: Theory and Public Policy* (12th edn). Abingdon: Routledge.

Eisenhardt, K. M., and Martin, J. A. (2000). Dynamic capabilities: What are they? *Strategic Management Journal*, *21*, 1105–21.

Friedman, M. (1953). The methodology of positive economics. In M. Friedman (ed.), *Essays in Positive Economics*, 3–43. Chicago, IL: University of Chicago Press.

Ganco, M., Ziedonis, R. H., and Agarwal, R. (2015). More stars stay, but the brightest ones still leave: Job hopping in the shadow of patent enforcement. *Strategic Management Journal*, *36*(5), 659–85.

Gathmann, C., and Schönberg, U. (2010). How general is human capital? A task-based approach. *Journal of Labor Economics*, *28*(1), 1–49.

Geel, R., Mure, J., and Backes-Gellner, U. (2011). Specificity of occupational training and occupational mobility: An empirical study based on Lazear's skill-weights approach. *Education Economics*, *19*(5), 519–35.

Gibbons, R., and Waldman, M. (2004). Task-specific human capital. *American Economic Review*, *94*(2), 203–07.

Hashimoto, M. (1981). Firm-specific human capital as a shared investment. *American Economic Review*, *71*(3), 475–82.

Helfat, C. E., Finkelstein, S., Mitchell, W., Peteraf, M. A., Singh, H., Teece, D. J., and Winter, S. G. (2007). *Dynamic Capabilities: Understanding Strategic Change in Organizations*. Malden, MA: Blackwell.
Kristof-Brown, A. L., Zimmerman, R. D., and Johnson, E. C. (2005). Consequences of individuals' fit at work: a meta-analysis of person-job, person-organization, person-group, and person-supervisor fit. *Personnel Psychology*, *58*(2), 281–342.
Kryscynski, D., and Ulrich, D. (2015). Making strategic human capital relevant: A time-sensitive opportunity. *Academy of Management Perspectives*, *29*(3), 357–69.
Lazear, E. P. (2009). Firm-specific human capital: A skill-weights approach. *Journal of Political Economy*, *117*(5), 914–40.
March, J. G., and Simon, H. A. (1958). *Organizations*. New York: Wiley.
Marx, M., Strumsky, D., and Fleming, L. (2009). Mobility, skills, and the Michigan non-compete experiment. *Management Science*, *55*(6), 875–89.
Mayer, K. J., Somaya, D., and Williamson, I. O. (2012). Firm-specific, industry-specific, and occupational human capital and the sourcing of knowledge work. *Organization Science*, *23*(5), 1311–29.
Neffke, F., and Henning, M. (2013). Skill relatedness and firm diversification. *Strategic Management Journal*, *34*(3), 297–316.
Nyberg, A. J., and Wright, P. M. (2015). 50 years of human capital research: Assessing what we know, exploring where we go. *Academy of Management Perspectives*, *29*(3), 287–95.
Nyberg, A. J., Moliterno, T. P., Hale, D., and Lepak, D. P. (2014). Resource-based perspectives on unit-level human capital. *Journal of Management*, *40*(1), 316–46.
Ortega, J. (2001). Job rotation as a learning mechanism. *Management Science*, *47*(10), 1361–70.
Ployhart, R. E., and Moliterno, T. P. (2011). Emergence of the human capital resource: A multilevel model. *Academy of Management Review*, *36*(1), 127–50.
Ployhart, R. E., Nyberg, A. J., Reilly, G., and Maltarich, M. A. (2014). Human capital is dead; long live human capital resources! *Journal of Management*, *40*(2), 371–98.
Priem, R. L., and Butler, J. E. (2001a). Is the resource-based "view" a useful perspective for strategic management research? *Academy of Management Review*, *2*(1), 22–40.
Priem, R. L., and Butler, J. E. (2001b). Tautology in the resource-based view and the implications of externally determined resource-value: Further comments. *Academy of Management Review*, *26*(1), 57–66.
Raffiee, J., and Coff, R. (2016). Micro-foundations of firm-specific human capital: When do employees perceive their skills to be firm-specific? *Academy of Management Journal*, *59*(3), 766–90.
Reilly, G., Nyberg, A. J., Maltarich, M., and Weller, I. (2014). Human capital flows: Using context-emergent turnover (CET) theory to explore the process by which turnover, hiring, and job demands affect patient satisfaction. *Academy of Management Journal*, *57*(3), 766–90.
Salas, E., and Cannon-Bowers, J. A. (2001). The science of training: A decade of progress. *Annual Review of Psychology*, *52*, 471–99.
Sirmon, D. G., Hitt, M. A., and Ireland, R. D. (2007). Managing firm resources in dynamic environments to create value: Looking inside the black box. *Academy of Management Review*, *32*(1), 273–92.
Sirmon, D. G., Hitt, M. A., Ireland, R. D., and Gilbert, B. A. (2011). Resource orchestration to create competitive advantage. *Journal of Management*, *37*(5), 1390–412.
Spence, M. (1973). Job market signaling. *Quarterly Journal of Economics*, *87*(3), 355–74.
Teece, D. J., Pisano, G., and Shuen, A. (1997). Dynamic capabilities and strategic management. *Strategic Management Journal*, *18*(7), 509–33.
Weller, I., Hymer, C., Nyberg, A. J., and Ebert, J. (2019). How matching creates value: Cogs and wheels for human capital resources research. *Academy of Management Annals*, *13*(1), 188–214.
Williamson, O. E. (1985). *The Economic Institutions of Capitalism: Firms, Markets, Relational Contracting*. New York: Free Press.
Yamaguchi, S. (2012). Tasks and heterogeneous human capital. *Journal of Labor Economics*, *30*(1), 1–53.

9. What are we isolating? Why human capital-based competitive advantage may not be so much about human capital*

Ben Campbell and David Kryscynski

Several years ago we co-authored with Russ Coff a theory paper on human capital and isolating mechanisms that was fortunate enough appear in the *Academy of Management Review*. The thrust of our paper was that strategy theory had become too focused on firm-specific human capital as a source of human capital-based competitive advantage and that we needed to consider a broader perspective on different isolating mechanisms, what we called mobility constraints, that might allow firms to retain the human capital embedded in individual employees. We argued that there are many supply- and demand-side mobility constraints that may facilitate human capital-based competitive advantages, and that firm-specific human capital was only one of many constraints. We also laid out several formal boundary conditions to traditional theory on the effects of firm-specific human capital and value capture. Underlying this chapter is the idea that strategic human capital theory is fundamentally a story about isolating mechanisms. If isolating mechanisms are a necessary condition for creating and capturing economic value from human capital, then the field should elevate the primacy of firms' abilities to create and leverage market frictions.

Like all papers, developing the ideas and insights and seeing them through the review process was very challenging, and we are particularly grateful to the many friendly reviewers and seminar participants who helped us hone our ideas. One particularly impactful insight came from Heli Wang. She brought to our attention that if we are seeking to shift research focus away from the nature of the human capital and towards various mobility constraints and isolating mechanisms, then where does the competitive advantage come from? In other words, if we focus on the various factors that isolate human capital – such as human resource (HR) systems and practices, non-compete agreements, incentives, and so forth – then are the advantages really *human capital* based, or are they more appropriately ascribed to other aspects of the business?

As the paper evolved, this concern took a back seat and we were able to successfully convince each other that this issue was beyond the scope of the paper. But Heli's question haunts us. We frequently type or say the phrase "human capital-based competitive advantage," and every time we do we think of Heli. The phrase is easy for us to use, but when we use it, we too often ignore where the advantage really comes from. We see this issue gaining more attention in recent years, especially from our colleagues in HR who have been studying these same phenomena for years using different terms and, at times, different assumptions. For these scholars, isolating mechanisms, labor market frictions, and mobility constraints have long been studied under different names and using different theoretical frameworks. Delery and Roumpi (2017) nicely argue that supply- and demand-side mobility constraints studied by strategic human capital scholars likely arise from and/or are leveraged by the firm's HR system. If this is true, then does the locus of a human capital-based competitive advantage and the ability of firms to capture value from individual employees belong more with the HR system than with the human capital itself?

Our objective in the rest of this chapter is to start down the path of exploring the implications of this question. We see our contribution as a companion to the work of Delery and Roumpi. They start from a traditional HR perspective and develop a rich framework for understanding how HR practices create isolating mechanisms that in turn shape value creation and value capture in the employer–employee relationship. In other words, they start from the HR perspective and argue that HR underlies the isolating mechanisms studied by strategists. In contrast, we start from a traditional strategy perspective to explore several pathways through which firms can create and capture value from the human capital embedded in specific individuals. While we do not develop a complete list of all possible human capital isolating mechanisms, we focus on the pathways that are most prevalent in the extant literature. Exploring these pathways from the traditional strategy perspective reveals that each key isolating mechanism ties back to the HR system and, therefore, points to the primacy of human resource management. In other words, we argue that the locus of human capital-based competitive advantage is more often found in the HR system than in the human capital itself. Accordingly, we call for strategy scholars (especially ourselves) to more explicitly draw upon the tools of HR scholarship in order to better understand the sources of human capital-based competitive advantage.

DEFINING HUMAN CAPITAL RENTS

To have a human capital-based competitive advantage a firm must capture more human capital rents than the breakeven competitor (Peteraf and Barney, 2003). In our conceptualization, we adopt the standard conventions in the extant strategy literature and focus on the ability of firms to create and capture value through specific individuals, and thus our treatment is at the individual level and not the unit level. Through this perspective, *human capital rents* associated with an employee are defined as the gap between the employee's use value and the economic costs of achieving that use value. The *use value* captures the amount of value that an employee creates for the employer (i.e. marginal revenue product) and the *economic costs* capture the minimum real costs the firm must incur to persuade the employee to actually come to work and deliver that use value on a recurring basis (Chadwick, 2017).

It is useful to be precise in considering what these economic costs mean from the employee's perspective. Since employees are agentic assets and not oil fields (Coff, 1997), firms must continually persuade them to come to work each day and contribute their human capital in ways that actually generate their use value. Firms persuade employees to contribute by offering them positive utility, which could come through wages, benefits, and other material payoffs, as well as altruism, equity, power, and so forth (Bridoux and Stoelhorst, 2019). When employees receive a sufficient bundle of positive utility from the firm vis-à-vis their alternative labor market options, then they contribute their human capital and effort to the focal firm (Simon, 1945). When the total utility from the focal firm drops below some threshold level, then the employee will withhold effort at work, and thus not produce the desired use value, and/or quit. Just as economists have used the term "reservation wage" to capture the minimum wage level required to hold employees in place, we use the term *reservation utility* to capture the minimum total utility required to keep employees in place and functioning in the firm.

Economic costs, then, are the real costs the firm must incur to create the necessary reservation utility for employees. In practice, the firm may incur more than the minimum required economic cost, through offering higher wages, delivering a more pleasing work environment, enhancing the organizational culture, providing non-monetary rewards and incentives, and so forth; but doing so does not alter the amount of human capital rents created, it simply alters who captures those rents. If the firm incurs higher than the minimum economic costs necessary to generate an employee's reservation utility, then employees may capture a portion of those human capital rents by receiving higher total utility than their reservation utility.

Additionally, we note that in practice there need not be a one-to-one ratio between the firm's economic costs of human capital and the employee's reservation utility. It is entirely possible that some firms can create significant positive employee utility for employees at lower real costs than other firms. In other words, two firms may be able to offer identical levels of total utility to their employees, but one firm may be able to do so at a lower real cost. Thus, one firm realizes higher human capital rents than the other firm despite both firms offering identical levels of total utility to employees (Chadwick 2017).

ISOLATING THE ISOLATING MECHANISMS

Isolating mechanisms are factors that facilitate the creation of human capital rents. In Campbell et al. (2012), we highlight the importance of isolating mechanisms (also called labor market frictions and/or mobility constraints) in creating sustained human capital-based competitive advantage. If labor markets are perfectly competitive, meaning there are many identical buyers and identical sellers and there are low transaction costs, then we can quickly deduce that the firm's real costs of creating positive utility for individual employees will equal the use value they derive from those employees. In other words, the invisible hand pushes human capital rents to zero in perfectly competitive labor markets.

Thus, the only way that some firms can create human capital rents is if there are some market imperfections, or isolating mechanisms, that prevent the invisible hand from squeezing out the rents. While we fully acknowledge the rich agentic nature of humans who can choose who to work for and how much effort to exert while at work (Bridoux and Stoelhorst, Chapter 2 this volume; Coff, 1997; Simon, 1945), we present a variety of simplified conditions (or states of the world) that frequently appear in the strategic human capital literature. For each condition, we articulate the key assumptions that underpin the condition. In turn, this leads us to explore how the key assumptions lead to specific isolating mechanisms and an associated taxonomy of human capital-related rents. Thus, through exploring a variety of conditions and their associated assumptions, we are able to isolate specific human capital isolating mechanisms and their effects. We summarize this discussion in the left-hand columns of Table 9.1.

Table 9.1 An incomplete typology of human capital-related rents

Conditions			Human Capital Rent Type	Pathway to Rents	Locus of Advantage
Condition 1: Employees are fully productive once in place	*Condition 1.1: rival firms have similar production technology*		Employer attractiveness rents	Employers have superior value propositions such that employees receive reservation utility at lower economic costs	Firm systems and characteristics underlying the value proposition
			Employer collusion rents	Employers collude to hold down employee reservation utility. Firms can retain employees at lower economic costs	Ability to collude with labor market competitors
			Legal constraint rents	Employers create legally binding agreements that separate humans from their human capital – rents come from employees' lower reservation utility due to limited labor market options	Ability to persuade employees to sign and honor legal agreements
	Condition 1.2: rival firms have different production technologies	Condition 1.2.1: firms have advantageous technologies that are independent of their human capital	Superior technology rents	Some firms have superior technology such that similar human capital has greater use value	Ability to create superior technology
		Condition 1.2.2: firms have advantageous technologies that are co-specialized with their human capital	Firm-specific human capital rents	Some firms have human capital that is co-specialized to technology in a manner that enhances the use value of the human capital	Ability to create superior technology and provide appropriate skill acquisition and development
Condition 2: Employees can choose their level of effort			Motivational rents	Some firms are better able to motivate effort from the workforce – rents come from the higher use value created from the higher employee effort	HR systems that ensure higher motivation and effort
Condition 3: Employee efforts vary in alignment			Alignment rents	Some firms are better able to align employee effort with firm outcomes – rents come from the higher use value created from the better employee alignment	HR systems that ensure higher alignment between effort and firm objectives

Condition 1: Employees are Fully Productive Once in Place

Building on our fundamental assumption of human agency over employment choices, we begin our thoughts in a simplified state of the world where humans are fully productive and functioning once in place. In this state of the world (which is the dominant perspective in much of the strategic human capital literature), individuals choose which firms to work for and which firms to leave, but they are not able to scale their efforts or adjust the direction of their efforts. They simply choose whether or not to work for the firm; and if they choose to work at a firm, they are fully motivated to engage with full effort and their effort is perfectly aligned with desired firm outcomes. In this state of the world, we explore two additional constraining assumptions which allow us to isolate the potential pathways to firms capturing rents from human capital.

Condition 1.1: rival firms have similar production technology

If firms have similar technologies, then firms can derive similar use value from otherwise similar human capital. If so, then the only pathway to the firm capturing rents from human capital is if the firm has lower economic costs than its rivals, i.e. firms have some way of providing the same level of reservation utility as a rival, but at economic discounts relative to competitors (Chadwick and Dabu, 2009; Chadwick, 2017). We see at least three pathways in the extant strategic human capital literature through which firms in this state of the world may be able to provide employees with their reservation utility at an economic discount.

First, firms may have superior employer attractiveness (Delery and Roumpi, 2017) or a superior employee value proposition. This superior employee value proposition might arise from well-designed HR practices and systems, but could also arise from other firm attributes such as the firm's reputation (Turban and Cable, 2003), status (Bidwell et al., 2015), who else works for the firm (Campbell et al., 2012), and so forth. In other words, the firm may have some firm-specific aspects of its employee value proposition that allow it to offer more utility to workers than competitor firms at lower real costs than competitors (Chadwick and Dabu, 2009; Coff, 1997; Kryscynski, 2016). When this happens, the firm creates *employer attractiveness rents*, meaning that the gap between employee use value and economic costs is greater in this firm than alternative firms because of some element of the employer's attractiveness to employees that is relatively low cost for the focal firm to create.

Second, firms may engage in labor market collusion by tacitly (or explicitly) agreeing not to hire employees away from each other. This artificially reduces the reservation utility of employees by reducing the number of potential employers willing to bid for any particular employees' human capital and or capping the utility available to employees at rivals. This type of collusion certainly represents a labor market friction and effectively isolates the human capital rents by restricting employees' outside options, which in turn reduces the economic costs that firms must pay to attract and retain employees. So, collusion is an isolating mechanism that supports the creation of human capital rents – even if all firms have similar technologies and generate similar use value from employees. When this happens, the firm creates *employer collusion rents*, meaning that there is a gap between an employee's use value and economic costs because colluding firms in the labor market hold down the employee's reservation utility.

Third, firms may leverage legal constraints such as non-compete agreements (Marx et al., 2009; Prescott et al., 2016). These kinds of agreements may restrict where an employee can work and what type of work activities an employee can engage in after leaving the focal firm. These kinds of agreements effectively isolate the human from the human capital, meaning that the person can leave the firm but the human capital is legally bound to the focal firm. In other words, the person can leave but cannot apply her human capital elsewhere without legal repercussions. Because employees cannot transfer their full portfolio of human capital to an alternative employer, their reservation utility is reduced since they are less valuable to other firms. The focal firm can thus retain employees with these non-compete agreements with lower total compensation, which, in turn, reduces the firm's economic costs of holding the employee in place. When this occurs the firm creates *legal constraint rents*, meaning that the gap between an employee's use value and economic costs is due to the employer's ability to legally restrict how and where the employee can deploy her human capital.

Condition 1.2: rival firms have different production technologies

If firms have different technologies, then all of the isolating mechanisms and associated types of rents outlined above are still available, but there are additional potential isolating mechanisms. We further subdivide this condition into two categories: 1.2.1 where firms have advantageous technologies that are independent of their human capital; and 1.2.2 where firms' advantageous technologies are co-specialized with their human capital. In the first case, if technologies differ independent of human capital, then otherwise identical human capital could generate heterogeneous use value. In other words, identical human capital might be more valuable in one firm than in alternative firms because the focal firm has some unique technology that disproportionally takes advantage of that human capital. For simplicity in presentation, we contrast this point from the previous section and assume that all firms can provide the same utility to their employees at the same economic costs. When similar human capital has greater use value in the focal firm than in alternative firms, then the focal firm can compensate at the same economic cost as their competitors but realize greater use value from the human capital, thus creating *superior technology rents*.

In the second case, firms' technologies and their human capital are co-specialized. In other words, firms' technologies are not advantageous without access to the appropriate human capital, and the focal human capital is not advantageous without the corresponding technology. In this scenario, we see similar dynamics as in the prior scenario. Employees with co-specialized and/or firm-specific human capital are unable to provide as much use value elsewhere, thus their reservation utility is low. However, they have performance advantages in the focal firm, thus leading to *firm-specific human capital rents*.

Condition 2: Employees Can Choose their Level of Effort

We now shift to a state of the world where, in addition to being able to choose whether or not to work for a firm, we assume that employees are able to choose their level of effort. In this state of the world, employees exert some percentage of their effort towards the firm's goals, and firms vary in the average effort they get from employees. In other words, employees in some firms may exert a much larger percentage of their effort than employees in competitor firms. In this state of the world, we still assume that employee effort is perfectly aligned with the firm's objectives.

This state of the world is consistent with Chadwick's (2017) logic that there can be a gap between the actual value created from human capital and the potential value human capital could create. He argues that some firms may be better than others at closing the gap between potential and realized value, effectively increasing the potential use value and corresponding rents the firm can create from human capital. Importantly, under this condition, the levers the firm can pull in order to enhance employee motivation and effort are the classic levers of HR systems. Firms can create incentive systems that include appropriate measurement of performance outcomes and allocation of financial rewards. Firms can manage total rewards so that employees derive the right balance of both monetary and non-monetary utility (Gerhart and Rynes, 2003). Firms can engage in fair processes to ensure trust and commitment among the workforce (Folger and Konovsky, 1989). In other words, as Chadwick has pointed out, firms are able to increase human capital use value through superior employee motivation and effort; and, if they are able to do so at the same or lower cost than their rivals, then firms can generate *motivational rents*. In this case, some firms are able to enhance the use value of their human capital without a corresponding increase in the economic costs that they bear in order to attract, motivate, and retain the focal employee.

Condition 3: Employee Efforts Vary in Alignment

In the next set of conditions, we assume a state of the world where employees, again, are fully functioning when in place but where employee effort is not necessarily perfectly aligned with the strategy of the employer. In this scenario, employees exert their maximum effort but their effort may or may not be well aligned with their employers' goals. We also assume that firms are heterogeneous in their ability to align employee effort with their strategy, thus some firms achieve higher alignment between employee effort and firm outcomes than others.

This state of the world corresponds to the theories proposed by Gottschalg and Zollo (2007) and Bridoux and Stoelhorst, who articulate the different types of employee motivations and argue that some firms are better able to align employee efforts by pulling the right motivational levers. Firms with advantages in motivating employees to the desired activities can increase the use value of the human capital without simultaneously increasing the economic cost of the human capital. As a result, firms with these advantages can generate *alignment rents*, meaning that these firms can generate higher rents than competitors through their greater ability to align employee efforts.

WHERE DO ISOLATING MECHANISMS COME FROM?

In the prior sections we described a variety of conditions that are common in the extant strategic human capital literature. Each condition is built on several key assumptions, and under these key assumptions there are a variety of pathways through which human capital rents can be created. We now focus our attention on examining the isolating mechanisms that support the creation of the different types of human capital rents. In so doing, we explore the source of the underlying isolating mechanisms, which is summarized in the right-hand column of Table 9.1.

In the dominant perspective in the extant strategic human capital literature, captured as Condition 1 above, we highlighted several different types of human capital rents. Under Condition 1.1, where firms have similar production technologies, we highlighted the availability of employer attractiveness rents, collusion rents, and legal constraints rents. Focusing first on employer attractiveness rents, the ability to create rents from human capital through this pathway lies not in the characteristics of the human capital, but in the firm's ability to offer a superior value proposition. In other words, the ability to provide utility to employees for lower cost than rivals is an isolating mechanism that does not necessarily depend on the quality and/or productivity of human capital: it is a generalizable channel that can apply regardless of the use value of the individual. Thus, to better understand the true source of this pathway to human capital rents, we need to look beyond the human capital that employees bring to the firm. Instead, we need to focus on why some firms can offer superior employee value propositions and why some firms can better select employees who get high utility from such a value proposition. In other words, the isolating mechanism that supports the creation of employer attractiveness rents resides not within the employees, but within the firm's hiring and acquisition of individuals. Thus, the existence of human capital rents is attributable to HR selection practices (Kehoe and Bentley, Chapter 16 this volume). While the magnitude of the rents is shaped by the quality and scarcity of the human capital, the existence of rents is independent of these factors. This point is in line with Chadwick's insight that if all firms create similar value from the human capital, then firms that can attract and retain workers at lower costs have access to human capital rents.

Next, collusion rents arise from the suppression of the employee's reservation utility. Again, the underlying source of the creation of such rents is ultimately unrelated to the human capital: the ability to create rents comes from the firm's ability to collude with other employers in the labor market. This ability is independent of all attributes of human capital. Firms can generate human capital rents by colluding in the market for employees with high use value as well as they can for employees with low use value. Like before, the magnitude of the rents reflects the underlying human capital, but the existence of rents is independent of human capital characteristics. Ultimately, collusion rents are attributable to the firm's management practices and ability, and so the genesis of the rent lies outside the focal human capital. Regardless of whether we consider these rents legal and/or ethical, it is clear that the origin of these rents does not reside in the human capital itself.

Legal constraint rents are categorically similar to collusion rents. The creation of these rents lies in the ability of firms to persuade employees to sign and honor legal agreements that restrict the employee's external market value, thus reducing the employee's reservation utility. Here again, the existence of these rents is independent of the attributes of the focal human capital: the rents are created by the firm's legal and HR management abilities.

Under Condition 1.2, where firms utilize different production technologies that may or may not be independent of human capital, we suggest that superior technology rents and firm-specific human capital rents are available respectively. The pathway to superior technology rents is, by definition, independent of any attributes of the underlying human capital. Here, the source of the human capital rents is that the firm has access to technology that creates more use value from human capital than market rivals. Thus, the genesis of the rent resides in the firm's ability to create and protect technological advances rather than in the focal human capital that uses the superior technology.

Next, we focus on firm-specific human capital rents, or co-specialized human capital rents. On the surface, these rents behave similarly to superior technology rents in that they both require access to technologies that labor market rivals cannot imitate, but the source of the rents has an important distinction. The source of firm-specific human capital rents is the interaction of the firm's technology and an individual's distinct human capital. In other words, the source of the rent is not only human capital. Further, the existence of firm-specific human capital is most likely generated through the training and development systems of the focal firm. It would be very unlikely for individuals to invest in human capital that is specific to a firm if they are not currently employed at that firm, and it would be very unlikely for individuals employed at a firm to make investments in firm-specific human capital without incentives and systems that facilitate them doing so (Wang and Barney, 2006; Wang et al., 2009). So, the existence of firm-specific human capital and the corresponding creation of rents is likely driven by a firm's HR management practices, and thus is distal from the characteristics of the firm's endowment of human capital.

Under Conditions 2 and 3, the role of HR management as the source of human capital rents is clearer. If a firm can generate human capital rents through a differential ability to elicit effort from its employees, then two firms with identical human capital can exhibit differential levels of motivation rents. In other words, the existence of this category of rents is not dependent on the underlying human capital – it is entirely dependent on the firm's HR ability to motivate the employee, which reflects the firm's complementary resources and the preferences of the individual employee (Chapter 2). Thus, cost-effective HR systems that provide advantages in motivating employees are likely a source of human capital rents. These rents come directly from the creation of the appropriately designed and aligned HR systems.

This point is important for our discussion of isolating mechanisms because it highlights an important distinction regarding what is actually being isolated. The HR system in this case is not isolating the human, or even the human capital: employees are free to leave and take their knowledge skills and abilities with them. Instead, the HR system is isolating the *rents* that are generated from the superior effort exerted by employees.

Similarly, the existence of alignment rents is not reflective of the employee's human capital: alignment rents are generated by the focal firm's ability to focus employee effort in the most production tasks. Again, when we explore the details of how firms are able to increase alignment we find that the most important levers are part of the traditional HR system. So, in both cases, the source of the rent is not in the human capital; it is in the HR and management systems of the focal firm. As before, it is important to note that the magnitude of the rents might reflect characteristics of the underlying human capital, but the existence is independent of the focal human capital.

While we have presented a typology of human capital rents that is far from complete, we have tried to focus on the conditions and associated human capital rents that are most common in the extant strategic human capital literature. We find it telling that among our list of seven exemplar human capital rent types, the importance of the characteristics of the underlying human capital is weak. Instead, the focus should be on the management systems that create the isolating mechanisms that allow for the creation of such rents. In summary, it seems that most of the advantages we ascribe to human capital as a strategic asset may actually reside in the HR system, and this means we need to pay more attention to the rich history of HR scholarship.

CONCLUDING THOUGHTS

In conclusion, as we examine the ways that isolating mechanisms lead to human capital-related rents, we are struck by the relative unimportance of the human capital itself. Examining carefully where the rents come from highlights the critical importance of the firm's HR systems and practices. There is no question in our minds that human capital is critical to firm outcomes, and we clearly acknowledge that human capital presents unique management dilemmas that firms do not face with other asset types (Coff, 1997). However, our analysis suggests that human capital-*related* rents, meaning rents that are created through the firm's individual employees, are more appropriately attributable to the firm's systems and practices than the employees themselves. We certainly acknowledge the possibility that some firms may have extremely rare human capital resources like Steve Jobs, Elon Musk, or LeBron James – but this seems the exception rather than the rule; and if these rare talents can appropriate the full value that they generate, then they are not a source of rents anyway.

We suggest that most human capital-related rents arise from well-designed HR systems and practices within the firm, not from the underlying human capital. This suggestion is in line with Chadwick's insight on the strategic implications of cost-effective human capital administration and Delery and Roumpi's argument that HR systems and practices are a *sufficient* source for the development of human capital isolating mechanisms as well. Accordingly, we call for future research to explore whether HR systems and practices are not just sufficient for creating human capital rents, but also *necessary* for the creation of human capital rents.

Also, the extant strategy literature's focus on the role of individual employees in value creation and value capture for the firm ignores much of the complexity in aggregating individual human capital into unit-level human capital resources (Ployhart et al., 2014; Ployhart and Moliterno, 2011). While we presume that many of the paths to human capital rents identified also apply to unit-level human capital resources, a richer and more careful discussion of how isolating mechanisms impact human capital resources is in order. Accordingly, we call for an examination of how market frictions impact the value creation and value capture at the unit level.

Finally, it is also important to note that in the realm of strategic human capital research, we need to carefully articulate what our isolating mechanisms actually isolate. As our comments above illustrate, human capital isolating mechanisms are not about isolating the human or the human capital (i.e. preventing employee mobility); isolating mechanisms are about directly isolating the *rents*. Thus, there is a level of abstraction that is often confounded in the extant strategy literature which gives primacy to mobility constraints that isolate the person. Thus, we call for a shift from this person-focused primacy to a rents-focused scholarship which ultimately provides a bridge that links the traditions of HR-based research and strategy-based research.

CHAPTER SUMMARY

BOX 9.1 KEY TAKEAWAYS

1. The origins of human capital-related rents may lie more in HR systems than in the human capital itself.
2. Isolating rents from human capital resources may be less about what human capital you have and more about what you do with your human capital.
3. "Human capital isolating mechanisms" and "strategic HR systems" may be synonymous.

BOX 9.2 DIRECTIONS FOR FUTURE RESEARCH

1. Future research on human capital and rents could examine the explicit connections between the isolating mechanisms studied by strategists and the HR systems studied by traditional HR scholars.
2. Future strategy work could explicitly bring insights from HR scholarship to better capture paths to human capital value creation and capture.
3. Future work could more explicitly address how isolating mechanisms impact human capital resources.

NOTE

* Equal co-authors listed alphabetically.

REFERENCES

Bidwell, M., Won, S., and Barbulescu, R. (2015). I used to work at Goldman Sachs! How firms benefit from organizational status in the market for human capital. *Strategic Management*, *36*(8), 1164–73.

Campbell, B. A., Coff, R. W., and Kryscynski, D. (2012). Rethinking sustained competitive advantage from human capital. *Academy of Management Review*, *37*(3), 376–95.

Chadwick, C. (2017). Toward a more comprehensive model of firms' human capital rents. *Academy of Management Review*, *42*(3), 499–519.

Chadwick, C., and Dabu, A. (2009). Human resource management, and the competitive advantage of firms: Toward a more comprehensive model of causal linkages. *Organization Science*, *20*, 253–72.

Coff, R. W. (1997). Human assets and management dilemmas: Coping with hazards on the road to resource-based theory. *Academy of Management Review*, *22*(2), 374–402.

Delery, J. E., and Roumpi, D. (2017). Strategic human resource management, human capital and competitive advantage: Is the field going in circles? *Human Resource Management Journal*, *27*(1), 1–21.

Folger, R., and Konovsky, M. A. (1989). Effects of procedural and distributive justice on reactions to pay raise decisions. *Academy of Management Journal*, *32*(1), 115–30.

Gerhart, B., and Rynes, S. L. (2003). *Compensation: Theory, Evidence and Strategic Implications*. Thousand Oaks, CA: Sage.

Gottschalg, O., and Zollo, M. (2007). Interest alignment and competitive advantage. *Academy of Management Review*, *32*(2), 418–37.

Kryscynski, D. (2016). The strategic implications of firm-specific incentives: Explaining human capital based competitive advantages. Working Manuscript.

Marx, M., Strumsky, D., and Fleming, L. (2009). Mobility, skills, and the michigan non-compete experiment. *Management Science*, *55*(6), 875–89.
Peteraf, M. A., and Barney, J. B. (2003). Unraveling the resource-based tangle. *Managerial and Decision Economics*, *24*(4), 309–24.
Ployhart, R. E., and Moliterno, T. P. (2011). Emergence of the human capital resource: A multilevel model. *Academy of Management Review*, *36*(1), 127–50.
Ployhart, R. E., Nyberg, A. J., Reilly, G., and Maltarich, M. A. (2014). Human capital is dead; long live human capital resources! *Journal of Management*, *40*(2), 371–98.
Prescott, J. J., Bishara, N., and Starr, E. P. (2016). Understanding Noncompetition Agreements: The 2014 Noncompete Survey Project. *Michigan State Law Review*, *2016*(2), 369–464.
Simon, H. (1945). *Administrative Behavior*. New York: Macmillan.
Turban, D. B., and Cable, D. M. (2003). Firm reputation and applicant pool characteristics. *Journal of Organizational Behavior*, *24*(6), 733–51.
Wang, H. C., and Barney, J. B. (2006). Employee incentives to make firm-specific investments: Implications for resource-based theories of corporate diversification. *Academy of Management Review*, *31*(2), 466–76.
Wang, H. C., He, J., and Mahoney, J. T. (2009). Firm-specific knowledge resources and competitive advantage: The roles of economic- and relationship-based employee governance mechanisms. *Strategic Management Journal*, *30*(12), 1265–85.

10. Retaining valued human capital: a commentary on the role of firm-specificity as a mobility constraint

John E. Delery and Dorothea Roumpi

One of the basic premises of human capital theory is that organizational survival and success are determined, at least to some extent, by a firm's ability to accumulate valued firm-specific human capital (e.g., Dess and Shaw, 2001; Strober, 1990) that is directly involved in value creation and capture. The distinction between general (or generic) and firm-specific human capital is typically based on answers to questions such as: Can the knowledge, skills, abilities, and other characteristics (KSAOs) of the individual generate rents only for a specific firm or are they generalizable across firms?; and, Is the individual's human capital valued more by the focal firm than the external labor market? (e.g., Becker, 1993, 1996; Brymer et al., 2015; Dierickx and Cool, 1989; Pil and Leana, 2000; Wang et al., 2009; Wright and McMahan, 2011).

This distinction between general and firm-specific human capital is often considered important for a variety of reasons, and research has offered support for the positive relationship between firm-specificity of resources and the creation of value for organizations (e.g., Dutta et al., 2005; Hitt et al., 2001). Specifically, even though the relationship between human capital resources and various organizational-level outcomes has received ample support (e.g., Combs and Ketchen, 1999; Takeuchi et al., 2007), the nature of human capital (general or firm-specific) is argued to influence the strength of this relationship. For instance, Crook et al.'s (2011) meta-analysis results indicate that when human capital is firm-specific, the positive relationship between human capital and performance is 71 percent stronger than when human capital is general. The underlying logic behind these results is simple: *as an individual's human capital becomes more idiosyncratic over time to a firm due to path dependency, the individual's ability to create value in the specific competitive context increases* (see also, e.g., Grant, 1996; Mahoney and Kor, 2015; Penrose, 1959). This rationale also equates human capital firm-specificity with the notions of uniqueness and rarity of the resource-based view (RBV), explaining why human capital resources have the potential to generate competitive advantage (e.g., Barney, 1991; Barney and Wright, 1998; Coff, 1997; Dierickx and Cool, 1989; Wang and Barney, 2006; Wright and McMahan, 2011).

The goal of for-profit organizations, however, is not to just achieve competitive advantage, but to be able to *sustain* this competitive advantage. An important question that emerges then is: *How can organizations transform their human capital-led competitive advantage into sustainable competitive advantage?* At a surface level, the answer to this question is simple. Organizations can turn their human capital-led competitive advantage into sustainable advantage by retaining their valued human capital responsible for this advantage. At a deeper level, this question is much more complex. As several authors have emphasized, human capital does not belong to organizations (e.g., Castanias and Helfat, 2001; Coff, 1997; Ganco et al., 2015); it belongs to employees, and employees are free to terminate their employment relationships at will and move their human capital to other organizations, even rivals (unless bound by a contractual arrangement). This is where isolating mechanisms – such as firm-specificity, social complexity, and resource complementarities – play a role in allowing the firm to capture more of the rents from value creation than they would if firm resources were freely able to exit the firm (at least in theory) (Barney, 1991; Coff and Kryscynski, 2011; Ployhart, 2012).

Conveniently, it can be argued that firm-specificity doubles as a mechanism that, as described earlier, enables organizations to create value but can also be effective as a mobility constraint, leading to the greater capture of rents by the firm. The effectiveness of firm-specificity as a mobility constraint rests on the argument that employees and employers share the cost and the return on investment of firm-specificity and, as such, both parties are less likely to willingly terminate the employment relationship (e.g., Hashimoto, 1981). In other words, by definition, firm-specific human capital has less value outside the organization where this specificity has been developed (e.g., Becker, 1964; Lazear, 2003; Wernerfelt, 1984), and employees should, therefore, be less likely to switch employers (e.g., Pennings et al., 1998).

Having this dual mission of firm-specificity in mind, Roumpi (2018: 99) interviewed a seasoned executive search consultant, who, after being introduced to the concept of firm-specificity as a mobility constraint, laughed and said: "I do not think that firm-specificity is effective, because unless you have learned how to work with unicorns in your current company, there is another firm that could put in use your skills and abilities."

This response aligns with the opinion of several authors who challenge, to some extent, the effectiveness of firm-specificity as an employee mobility barrier, either due to the imperfections of the labor market (e.g., Campbell et al., 2012) or due to the unclear distinction between what constitutes firm-specific and general human capital (e.g., Nyberg and Wright, 2015). For us, this comment gave rise to a series of questions, such as: What truly is firm-specificity? Is firm-specificity an effective employee mobility barrier? If so, is it effective both as a supply- and demand-side mobility barrier? Or is it merely a researchers' "obsession," with little or no value for practitioners (e.g., Kryscynski and Ulrich, 2015)?

On these grounds, we start this commentary by acknowledging that we are not sure that we or anyone can provide definitive answers to the aforementioned questions. We decided, therefore, to take a step back and try to define firm-specificity in more practical terms. As it will be discussed in the next paragraphs, we believe that the term "specificity" is rather broad and encompasses various types of specificity with ill-defined boundaries. Having this framework of various types of specificity as our basis, we then set out to explore on a theoretical basis their effectiveness as employee mobility constraints. Our goal with this commentary is not to provide an exhaustive map of all types of human capital specificity and their levels of effectiveness, but rather to set a framework for both micro and macro scholars to engage in a discussion regarding the specificity of human capital and its role in the external labor markets.

DEFINING FIRM-SPECIFICITY: HOW SPECIFIC IS SPECIFIC?

Human capital, at an individual level, can be defined broadly as a set of individual differences or KSAOs, such as general mental ability and personality traits (e.g., Ployhart and Moliterno, 2011). Although the distinction between general and firm-specific human capital is unclear in practice (e.g., Nyberg and Wright, 2015), as purely general or firm-specific human capital are arguably just figments of the imagination (e.g., Wright and McMahan, 2011), and despite the fact that individuals are likely to possess a combination of both firm-specific and general human capital (e.g., Campbell et al., 2012; Lazear, 2009; Wright et al., 2014), scholars suggest that aspects of human capital can be conceptualized as a continuum that ranges from purely general to purely firm-specific (e.g., Castanias and Helfat, 2001). The former end of the spectrum, namely general human capital, is viewed as a set of characteristics that "are useful across a broad range of economic settings" (Molloy and Barney, 2015: 310).

At the latter end of the spectrum, most scholars discussing the concept of firm-specificity take two routes in defining it. The first approach is associated with the ability of firm-specific human capital to create value for the focal organization (e.g., Becker, 1964). For instance, Sturmam et al. (2008: 291) defined human capital specificity as "the degree to which an individual's knowledge, skills, and experiences are so rare or unique they generate above average rents for the firm." The second approach in defining firm-specific human capital rests on arguments regarding the marketability and, in general, the value of this human capital in the external labor market (e.g., Dierickx and Cool, 1989; Kor and Leblebici, 2005). Wang et al. (2009: 1266), for example, defined firm-specific human capital as an individual's set of KSAOs that "is imperfectly redeployable, or is valued less in the external labor market than within the firm." Such definitions, however, are likely too broad and do not capture the complexity inherent in this concept.

To gain a better understanding of firm-specificity it is important to understand both how firm-specific human capital is created and its basic components. Firm-specific human capital emerges through social, behavioral, and affective processes (e.g., Ployhart and Moliterno, 2011; Wright et al., 2014) and is likely to develop over time through learning-by-doing and socializing (e.g., Mahoney and Kor, 2015; Hatch and Dyer, 2004). In other words, employees develop over time knowledge and expertise that are learned through the interactions with the unique set of constituents of the focal firm (e.g., coworkers, managers, subordinates, customers, suppliers, and other stakeholders), as well as by working with the unique tangible and intangible resources of the firm (e.g., organizational culture, organizational processes, routines, and systems, and physical resources such as customized equipment) (e.g., Døving and Nordhaug, 2002; Mahoney and Kor, 2015; Pennings et al., 1998; Wang and Barney, 2006; Wang et al., 2009).

On this basis, Mahoney and Kor suggested that firm-specific human capital has three basic components. The first, "the experiential knowledge of idiosyncratic resources and capabilities of the firm," refers to the knowledge gained through experience regarding the routines, the resources, the capabilities, and the systems of the firm. The second component of firm-specific human capital they define as "the experiential knowledge of the people employed at the firm" (Mahoney and Kor, 2015: 297). This component entails developing a deeper understanding of other employees' abilities, strengths, limitations, and collaboration and working habits which enables the focal employee to achieve better teamwork results or even make better decisions when it comes to delegating tasks. The last component of firm-specific human capital identified is "the experiential knowledge of the firm's stakeholders and constituents" (2015: 298), which refers to the knowledge built over time regarding the various firms' constituents needs and preferences. It is important to note that Mahoney and Kor, in their effort to identify the components of human capital, focused mainly on knowledge-related aspects. Human capital, however, by definition, entails also skills and abilities (and other individual characteristics). This is rather important when considering the transferability of human capital because some aspects of knowledge might not be transferable, but the skills and the ability required to develop such knowledge may be transferable across organizations. Developing, for example, knowledge regarding the working habits and the strengths and weaknesses of a specific group of coworkers might not be valuable for other organizations. The abilities and skills, however, that are required for the individual to be able to develop this knowledge are likely to be valued by other organizations also.

Given the proposed complexity of human capital specificity (as demonstrated by its components and its emergence process), several authors have created sub-categories of human capital. One such effort is the distinction between required and discretionary firm-specific human capital and co-specialized human capital (Morris et al., 2014; Molloy and Barney, 2015). Required firm-specific human capital refers to the task-related KSAOs that are necessary for individuals to perform their job-related responsibilities, whereas discretionary firm-specific human capital emerges when an employee engages in extra-role behaviors (e.g., socializing with coworkers) but the knowledge that is gained has value for the focal firm (e.g., better decision making) (Molloy and Barney, 2015). Finally, the co-specialized human capital emerges over time while the employee develops expertise working with other employees and/or organizational resources (e.g., financial and physical resources) (Molloy and Barney, 2015).

Other scholars emphasize that even general human capital can be "disguised" as firm-specific human capital. For instance, Lazear (2009) suggests that, in reality, most of the human capital that is often labeled as firm-specific is actually general. According to the skill-weights approach (e.g., Lazear, 2003, 2009; Weller, Chapter 8 this volume), general human capital appears to be firm-specific because the combination of general KSAOs required and utilized is idiosyncratic to the firm. In other words, even when the KSAOs an individual possesses are general, their "uses are specific to the firm" (Lazear, 2009: 915) because not all industries and firms assign the same weights to an individual's general KSAOs. As Weller emphasizes, firm-specificity may emerge when the organization engages in "matching activities." Such activities ensure the alignment between an employee's KSAOs and the organization's technology, or, more broadly, the organization's production function.

Summary: A Broad Typology of Specific Human Capital

As this brief overview of the literature regarding the concept of firm-specificity suggests, there are multiple sources and labels that can be attributed to firm-specific human capital. As it can be derived from the above discussion regarding the definition of firm-specificity, it can be argued that inherent in the concept of firm-specificity is the notion that the unique value these KSAOs have for the focal firm emerges over time through deliberate (e.g., training) and non-deliberate organizational activities (e.g., informal socialization process) and, most importantly, through the interactions among employees with the organizational environment that includes the focal firm's resources and its constituents (internal and external). Through the emergence process, complementarities are created that enhance the value of the human capital for the focal firm. Drawing on this literature, we identify three types of firm-specific human capital we believe can influence the external mobility of employees, and thus influence competitive advantage. These three types of firm-specific human capital are: firm-specific human capital stemming from the interaction with organizational resources; relational firm-specific human capital stemming from interactions with internal constituents of the firm; and relational firm-specific human capital stemming from interactions with external constituents of the firm. Below is a brief description of each of these.

Firm-specific human capital stemming from the interaction with organizational resources

As several scholars have noted, firm-specificity can emerge through the interaction of an employee with a firm's resources (e.g., Mahoney and Kor, 2015; Pennings et al., 1998; Wang and Barney, 2006; Wang et al., 2009), including physical (e.g., customized machinery) and non-physical resources (e.g., organizational culture and processes). Firm-specificity, for example, is created when an employee develops expertise in operating customized machinery and equipment (Døving and Nordhaug, 2002). In addition, an employee who has developed a good understanding of the organizational culture of the focal firm will be able to make more informed decisions that will better align with the specific organizational context (Kor and Mahoney, 2005). This conceptualization of firm-specificity aligns with the concept of person-organization fit (P-O fit) and is discussed further in this volume by Weller in terms of matching. The relevant research suggests that when the KSAOs of an employee have a good "fit" with the organization (e.g., organizational culture), positive organizational outcomes – such as higher performance, more organizational citizenship behaviors, and lower turnover – will emerge (e.g., Kristof-Brown et al., 2005; Podsakoff et al., 2000; Verquer et al., 2003) than if the employee were in a different firm with less fit. By extension, it can be argued that the individual has more value for the focal firm, and the firm might be able to capture greater value.

Relational firm-specific human capital stemming from interactions with internal constituents of the firm

Regardless of whether an employee interacts with other employees of the firm due to job-related demands (required firm-specific human capital) or due to extra-role behaviors (discretionary firm-specific human capital) (Molloy and Barney, 2015), this interaction generates human capital that is unique to the focal firm. Specifically, as an employee interacts with his/her coworkers, superiors, and subordinates (either on or off the job), he/she constantly develops a better understanding of their abilities, limitations, and way of thinking. Consequently, he/she can be more productive in collaborating with these individuals. For instance, a manager who knows the abilities and the interests of other employees is enabled to make better decisions in terms of projects (e.g., What should the synthesis of the team be? Who will work well with whom? Who has strengths that can compensate for someone else's weaknesses?) and resource allocation (e.g., Given the strengths, the weaknesses, and preferences of this employee, what are the required resources to maximize his/her performance?). This form of human capital is firm-specific because the individual develops expertise that has value only within the specific group of other employees.

Relational firm-specific human capital stemming from interactions with external constituents of the firm

An employee's coworkers, superiors, and subordinates are not the only constituents of the firm with whom the individual interacts. An employee can be required, to some extent, to interact with the focal firm's external constituents (e.g., customers, suppliers, and contractors). In a similar manner to the relational firm-specific human capital stemming from interactions with internal constituents, in this case the employee over time develops expertise regarding the best ways of interacting with and handling the focal firm's external constituents by gaining a better understanding regarding their needs and preferences. The firm-specificity of this set of KSAOs is associated with two elements. First, the individual is unlikely to have been exposed and "forced" to form relationships with the exact same set of external constituents outside of the context of the focal firm. Second, the nature of the relationships formed and, by extension, the nature of the KSAOs developed is again contingent on the focal firm. For instance, even when two firms are served by the same supplier, employees in each firm will develop different relationships with the supplier that are associated with a variety of firm-specific factors, such as firm-specific processes and the longevity of the relationship between each firm and the specific supplier.

In addition, we suggest that, by expanding the boundaries of firm-specificity, two more types of human capital specificity should be included: industry-specific human capital and occupation-specific human capital. Although these types of human capital do not fit the traditional definitions of firm-specificity, requiring this set of KSAOs to be of value only for the focal organization, in our opinion they belong in this typology because elements of these forms of specificity, as it will be described in the next paragraphs, emerge gradually through the experience and the interactions an individual has in the context of the focal organization.

Industry-specific human capital has been broadly defined as the KSAOs that are relevant and valuable only within a specific (or at least very similar) industry or sector of the economy (e.g., Castanias and Helfat, 1991; Neal, 1995). An employee working in a specific industry develops knowledge associated with this unique setting or domain and, as such, this knowledge is only redeployable across organizations operating in a similar setting or domain (e.g., Mayer et al., 2012). It can be argued that industry-specific human capital constitutes a rather unique form of human capital. As Sturman et al. (2008) aptly noted, industry-specific human capital is a combination of both firm-specific and general/broadly transferable human capital. In other words, an employee gains an understanding of the workings of a specific industry by working for the focal firm. This industry-specificity, however, is not necessarily generalizable across all firms in the industry because it is developed through the "lens" and the processes of the focal firm. This industry-specificity has been developed to "match" the unique characteristics of the focal firm, and reflects the way the focal firm views and operates in the specific industry.

Finally, *occupation-specific human capital* "refers to knowledge and skills relating to a profession or field of knowledge (e.g., law, accounting, software engineering)" (Mayer et al., 2012: 5). Although occupation-specificity implies that these KSAOs are readily redeployable across organizations for the same occupation, it can be argued that, similar to industry-specificity, some of the occupation expertise an employee has developed is contingent on the idiosyncrasies of the organizations where he/she gained that expertise.

SPECIFITY AND EMPLOYEE MOBILITY

A long line of research exists that suggests the importance of human capital firm-specificity as a mobility barrier in external labor markets. The underlying assumption of this research is that, given that firm-specific human capital by definition has less value for other employers, an employee possessing firm-specific human capital is less attractive in the external labor marker and, consequently the rents he/she will receive for his/her human capital will be lower outside of the focal firm (e.g., Becker, 1964; Hashimoto, 1981; Klein et al., 1978; Parsons, 1972; Pennings et al., 1998; Peteraf, 1993). Thus, neither employees possessing firm-specific human capital nor other employers (besides the firm where the firm-specific human capital has been developed) are motivated to create a new employment relationship. Of course, this is just an oversimplified way of approaching the issue. The question of who creates and who captures the rents of the firm-specificity is rather important and complicated (e.g., Chadwick, 2017). If the focal firm tries to capture "too much," then issues of low distributive justice may emerge. In such a case, the employee has a broad range of potential reactions (e.g., Bartol and Locke, 2000), including leaving (both the employee and the focal firm will lose the opportunity to capture the value stemming from the employee's firm-specificity) or lowering performance (until the employee perceives that the performance levels match the compensation levels).

The effectiveness of firm-specificity as an employee mobility constraint, however, has been questioned in some of the most recent literature. First, in order for firm-specificity to serve as an employee mobility barrier, we need to assume the labor market is working without any imperfections, thus allowing employees and other firms to appropriately evaluate the human capital employees possess. In reality, however, external labor markets are less than perfect and are characterized by information asymmetries (e.g., Campbell et al., 2012), forcing all involved parties (employees and potential future employers) to base their evaluations on perceptions and signals (e.g., Coff and Raffiee, 2015; Delery and Roumpi, 2017; Raffiee and Coff, 2016). Second, this approach is oversimplified in that it does not take into account the complexity of the portfolio of KSAOs that each individual possesses. As Campbell et al. (2012) and Lazear (2009) note, employees do not just possess firm-specific or general human capital; they possess a combination of both forms of human capital. Finally, even under the extreme scenario where other firms are able to accurately evaluate the human capital of an employee as firm-specific, it can be argued that firm-specificity will not necessarily be perceived as an undesirable attribute (e.g., Campbell et al., 2014; Morris et al., 2017). Other firms might actually view an employee's firm-specificity as a signal of the ability and willingness of this individual to develop firm-specific human capital when placed in a different context.

Although we recognize the validity of these concerns regarding the effectiveness of firm-specificity as a mobility constraint, the focus of this section is not to add to these concerns. In this section we aim to theoretically explore the effectiveness of specificity and raise questions for future research for each of the types of human capital we identified in the previous section.

Firm-Specific Human Capital Stemming from the Interaction with Organizational Resources

As described earlier, this type of firm-specificity emphasizes the dependence between an employee's human capital and organizational physical and non-physical resources. When considering this form of specificity as an employee mobility constraint its effectiveness will depend on the perceptions the employee and the external labor market hold regarding transferability of the KSAOs and the extent to which these KSAOs are viewed as value-creating due to complementarities with other resources (e.g., Delery and Roumpi, 2017). First, on the supply side of the labor market (where employees are considering leaving the focal firm) an important question arises: Do employees believe they will be able to generate and capture similar or higher levels of value in organizations with different sets of available resources? For example, employee A works as a market trend analyst for one of the biggest retailers in the world. His current employer has an enormous database of relevant information, and also has the financial resources to purchase the products of consultancy firms to assist him in his decision making. When employee A considers moving to a smaller company for a similar position, he will take into consideration the resources that will be available there and may come to the conclusion that he would not be able to perform at the same level, create as much value for that firm, and, consequently, the value he will be able to capture may be lower than with his current employer.

On the demand side (potential employers considering hiring an employee from the focal firm), it can be argued that the potential new employer relies on signals and the reputation of the focal firm in regards to its resources in order to answer the following question: Given the different set of resources we offer, will we be able to capture the same or higher levels of value by hiring this individual? Using the previous example, the fact that employee A was such a successful market trend analyst could be attributed to the broad range of resources he had at his disposal at the specific firm, and does not guarantee his success at a firm with more limited resources.

As we have discussed earlier in this chapter, it can be argued that even though some aspects of the firm-specificity an individual has developed cannot be transferred from one firm to another, other aspects, such as the ability to create and develop firm-specificity, could be transferred. Thus, a potential new employer needs to respond to a second question: Will an employee who has developed firm-specificity in a firm with significantly different processes and/or organizational culture manage to be effective in the context of our organization? Consider, for instance, the example of an architect who worked for a major social enterprise that built houses for underprivileged families. If the potential new employer is one of the nation's biggest commercial and residential engineering firms, it needs to be considered whether this architect could adjust to an organizational culture that aligns with the more competitive nature of the business.

Relational Firm-Specific Human Capital Stemming from Interactions with Internal Constituents of the Firm

As this type of firm-specificity is embedded in the social interactions among the various internal constituents of the focal firm, both involved parties (the employee and the potential new employer) need to consider whether any parts of this set of KSAOs are transferable and whether the employee will manage to be effective outside of the specific group of coworkers. Thus, both on the demand and the supply side, employees and potential employers need to evaluate the extent to which the created value is attributable on the employee or the complementarities among a group of employees (e.g., Delery and Roumpi, 2017). For example, knowing who the right person is to talk to when you encounter a technical issue or knowing that employee A and employee B do not get along and, as such, should not be put on the same project is knowledge that is not useful outside of the borders of the focal firm.

In addition, on the supply side it can be argued that an employee who has managed to accumulate over time such knowledge and develop strong social ties within an organization will be less willing to consider switching employers. This is associated with the concept of job-embeddedness (e.g., Holtom et al., 2008; Mitchell et al., 2001), which has been linked to lower turnover (e.g., Crossley et al., 2007). Likewise, employees working with a group of people who have managed over time to be high functioning and complement each other's KSAOs would be less likely to consider leaving their current employer for fear that their performance may decline along with their ability to capture value.

Relational Firm-Specific Human Capital Stemming from Interactions with External Constituents of the Firm

Building this type of human capital requires employees to invest a lot of time and effort. On the supply side, when considering switching employers, employees with this type of firm-specific human capital will consider whether or not they will be able to utilize these connections and ties (e.g., with customers) at a different firm. For instance, an employee considering switching to a competitor might hope that he will be able to retain his value emerging from this type of firm-specificity by taking his clients or customers with him. The specific employee will need to evaluate the extent to which this is a plausible scenario on the basis of whether or not his current clients/customers will be interested in his new employer's products or services.

Similarly, on the demand side a potential employer will need to consider whether this social network the employee has developed with external constituents of at the focal firm will be transferable and would have any value for the employer. Even if such firm-specific human capital is perceived to be valuable and transferable by the potential new employer, an additional consideration is associated with whether or not the employee is contractually bounded (e.g., with a noncompete agreement) and, consequently, unable to utilize this network of external constituents outside the limits of the focal firm.

Industry-Specific Human Capital

Extant literature suggests that industry-specificity, unlike other forms of human capital specificity, can be something that is valued and sought after by some firms (e.g., Coff and Raffiee, 2015). For instance, Sturman et al. (2008) showed that executives moving to similar firms received compensation premiums. It can be argued, however, that even within the same industry, this type of human capital can be a mobility constraint for employees. Specifically, within each industry we can observe a lot of variation in the performance of the firm, which is indicative of the different strategies and processes these firms follow and, in turn, signals that the employees of these firms have developed, at least to some extent, firm-specificity. Thus, operating in the same industry, besides offering a better understanding of the workings of the specific industry, does not automatically guarantee the transferability of the human capital. For this case, the example that Wang, Zhao, and Chen offer is indicative of how industry-specific human capital is not necessarily valuable across all organizations within the same industry. The authors, focusing on the petroleum industry, argue that "[d]ue to the different geographical features of each reservoir in the petroleum industry, the innovation of new ways to extract additional crude oil from existing reservoirs is often not transferable across firms, and thus, has firm-specific components" (Wang et al., 2017: 1877). In other words, the resources of and the processes followed by the focal firm are unique for the industry, and the firm-specific element of industry-specificity might influence the perceptions regarding the transferability of the KSAOs both on the supply side (perceptions of the employee who is considering switching employers) and the demand side (perceptions of the potential new employer).

Occupation-Specific Human Capital

Similar to industry-specificity, it is reasonable to assume high levels of transferability of occupation-specific human capital. Working, for instance, as an accountant at a company would equip someone with task-related KSAOs valuable at virtually any other company that would hire this individual as an accountant. Even though we generally agree with this statement, it can be argued that in some cases occupation-specificity, when seen as a set of KSAOs developed at a specific firm (besides the formal occupational training an employee has received), can pose mobility barriers. To better understand the potential of occupation-specificity to act as an employee mobility constraint, we need to consider whether an occupation or a job title has the same meaning across all firms. For example, let's consider employee A and employee B, who have the same job titles; but employee A currently works for one of the biggest firms in the industry, whereas employee B is employed by a small firm. Given the difference in the size of the companies, these two employees, despite the fact they have the same occupation, are likely to develop different KSAOs. Employee A, given the size of his employer, might work along with a big team of individuals with the same occupation and be exposed only to a rather narrow segment of the responsibilities typically associated with his occupation. On the other hand, employee B might be the only one holding the specific title in the firm and, as such, be exposed to the entire spectrum of job responsibilities associated with his occupation.

CONCLUDING REMARKS

Acknowledging the accumulating evidence regarding the importance of firm-specificity in value creation (e.g., Crook et al., 2011), as well the most recent doubts that have been cast regarding the effectiveness of firm-specificity as an employee mobility barrier, in this chapter we took a step back and attempted to offer a better understanding of the concept of human capital specificity. The taxonomy of types of human capital specificity we offer is not an exhaustive list of potential forms firm-specificity can take. It serves, however, our second purpose, which was to theoretically explore the effectiveness of firm-specificity as a mobility constraint. Though the critique of firm-specificity as a mobility constraint may be valid, we believe that firm-specificity, under some conditions, could effectively prevent employees from switching employers. Additional empirical research, however, is needed that will directly capture employee and employer perceptions regarding firm-specificity.

It is also important to note that attributing effectiveness or lack of effectiveness to firm-specificity as an isolating mechanism might not be the most appropriate approach. Given the imperfections of the labor market (e.g., Campbell et al., 2012) and the heavy reliance on signals (e.g., Coff and Raffiee, 2015), it is important for future research to focus additionally on the mechanisms, such as the human resource management (HRM) practices, that create signals to the external labor market. As Campbell and Kryscynski (Chapter 9) and Delery and Roumpi (2017) suggest, HRM systems and practices could be the key in creating, capturing, and retaining human capital rents.

CHAPTER SUMMARY

BOX 10.1 KEY TAKEAWAYS

1. Human capital firm-specificity is a rather complex concept. In order to evaluate the effectiveness of firm-specificity as an employee mobility constraint, it is important to define firm-specificity in more practical terms.
2. We identified three main forms of firm-specificity: firm-specific human capital stemming from the interaction with organizational resources; relational firm-specific human capital stemming from interactions with internal constituents of the firm; and relational firm-specific human capital stemming from interactions with external constituents of the firm.
3. By expanding the boundaries of firm-specificity, it can be argued that industry-specific and occupation-specific human capital also have elements of firm-specificity because they are developed and learned within a specific firm (e.g., following firm-specific processes and viewing the industry and the occupation through the lens of the specific firm).
4. It is important to keep in mind that human capital at an individual level constitutes a set of knowledge, skills, abilities, and other characteristics. Consequently, even when an individual develops some firm-specific knowledge that is neither transferable to nor valued by other organizations, the ability to develop such knowledge might be transferable and valued.

BOX 10.2 DIRECTIONS FOR FUTURE RESEARCH

1. Future research should focus on empirically testing the effects of each of the forms of firm-specificity on the perception employees hold regarding their employability (supply-side mobility constraints) and the perceptions the external labor market holds (demand-side mobility constraints).
2. Future work could explicitly address how organizations can signal the firm-specificity of their valued employees.

REFERENCES

Barney, J. B. (1991). Firm resources and sustained competitive advantage. *Journal of Management*, *17*, 99–120.

Barney, J. B., and Wright, P. M. (1998). On becoming a strategic partner: The role of human resources in gaining competitive advantage. *Human Resource Management*, *37*, 31–46.

Bartol, K.M., and Locke, E.A. (2000). Incentives and motivation. In S. Rynes and B. Gerhart (eds), *Compensation in Organizations: Progress and Perspectives*. San Francisco, CA: Jossey-Bass.

Becker, G. S. (1964). *Human Capital*. New York: Columbia University Press.

Becker, G. S. (1993). *Human Capital: A Theoretical and Empirical Analysis with Special Reference to Education* (3rd edn). Chicago, IL: University of Chicago Press.

Becker, G. S. (1996). *The Economic Way of Looking at Behavior: The Nobel Lecture*. Essays in Public Policy, No. 69, Hoover Institution, Stanford University, Palo Alto, CA.

Brymer, R., Molloy, J., and Chadwick, C. (2015). Strategic Human Capital. *Oxford Bibliographies in Management*. DOI: 10.1093/obo/9780199846740-0082.

Campbell, B. A., Coff, R., and Kryscynski, D. (2012). Rethinking sustained competitive advantage from human capital. *Academy of Management Review*, *37*(3), 376–95.

Campbell, B. A., Saxton, B. M., and Banerjee, P. M. (2014). Resetting the shot clock: The effect of comobility on human capital. *Journal of Management*, *40*(2), 531–56.

Castanias, R. P., and Helfat, C. E. (1991). Managerial resources and rents. *Journal of Management*, *17*(1), 155–71.

Castanias, R. P., and Helfat, C. E. (2001). The managerial rents model: Theory and empirical analysis. *Journal of Management*, *27*(6), 661–78.

Chadwick, C. (2017). Toward a more comprehensive model of firms' human capital rents. *Academy of Management Review*, *42*(3), 499–519.

Coff, R. W. (1997). Human assets and management dilemmas: Coping with hazards on the road to resource-based theory. *Academy of Management Review*, *22*(2), 374–402.

Coff, R., and Kryscynski, D. (2011). Invited editorial: Drilling for micro-foundations of human capital–based competitive advantages. *Journal of Management*, *37*(5), 1429–43.

Coff, R., and Raffiee, J. (2015). Toward a theory of perceived firm-specific human capital. *Academy of Management Perspectives*, *29*(3), 326–41.

Combs, J. G., and Ketchen Jr, D. J. (1999). Can capital scarcity help agency theory explain franchising? Revisiting the capital scarcity hypothesis. *Academy of Management Journal*, *42*(2), 196–207.

Crook, T. R., Todd, S. Y., Combs, J. G., Woehr, D. J., and Ketchen Jr, D. J. (2011). Does human capital matter? A meta-analysis of the relationship between human capital and firm performance. *Journal of Applied Psychology*, *96*(3), 443–56.

Crossley, C. D., Bennett, R. J., Jex, S. M., and Burnfield, J. L. (2007). Development of a global measure of job embeddedness and integration into a traditional model of voluntary turnover. *Journal of Applied Psychology*, *92*(4), 1031–42.

Delery, J. E., and Roumpi, D. (2017). Strategic human resource management, human capital and competitive advantage: Is the field going in circles? *Human Resource Management Journal*, *27*(1), 1–21.

Dess, G. G., and Shaw, J. D. (2001). Voluntary turnover, social capital, and organizational performance. *Academy of Management Review*, *26*(3), 446–56.

Dierickx, I., and Cool, K. (1989). Asset stock accumulation and sustainability of competitive advantage. *Management Science*, *35*(12), 1504–11.

Døving, E., and Nordhaug, O. (2002). *Learning Firm Specific Knowledge and Skills: Conceptual Issues and Empirical Results*. 3rd European conference on organizational knowledge, learning and capabilities. Athens, Greece.

Dutta, S., Narasimhan, O. M., and Rajiv, S. (2005). Conceptualizing and measuring capabilities: Methodology and empirical application. *Strategic Management Journal*, *26*(3), 277–85.

Ganco, M., Ziedonis, R. H., and Agarwal, R. (2015). More stars stay, but the brightest ones still leave: Job hopping in the shadow of patent enforcement. *Strategic Management Journal*, *36*(5), 659–85.

Grant, R. M. (1996). Prospering in dynamically-competitive environments: Organizational capability as knowledge integration. *Organization Science*, *7*, 375–87.

Hashimoto, M. (1981). Firm-specific human capital as a shared investment. *American Economic Review*, *71*(3), 475–82.

Hatch, N. W., and Dyer, J. H. (2004). Human capital and learning as a source of sustainable competitive advantage. *Strategic Management Journal*, *25*(12), 1155–78.

Hitt, M. A., Bierman, L., Shimizu, K., and Kochhar, R. (2001). Direct and moderating effects of human capital on strategy and performance in professional service firms: A resource-based perspective. *Academy of Management Journal*, *44*(1), 13–28.

Holtom, B. C., Mitchell, T. R., Lee, T. W., and Eberly, M. B. (2008). 5 turnover and retention research: A glance at the past, a closer review of the present, and a venture into the future. *Academy of Management Annals*, *2*(1), 231–74.
Klein, B., Crawford, R. G., and Alchian, A. A. (1978). Vertical integration, appropriable rents, and the competitive contracting process. *Journal of Law and Economics*, *21*(2), 297–326.
Kor, Y. Y., and Leblebici, H. (2005). How do interdependencies among human-capital deployment, development, and diversification strategies affect firms' financial performance? *Strategic Management Journal*, *26*(10), 967–85.
Kor, Y. Y., and Mahoney, J. T. (2005). How dynamics, management, and governance of resource deployments influence firm-level performance. *Strategic Management Journal*, *26*(5), 489–96.
Kristof-Brown, A. L., Zimmerman, R. D., and Johnson, E. C. (2005). Consequences of individuals' fit at work: A meta-analysis of person–job, person–organization, person–group, and person–supervisor fit. *Personnel Psychology*, *58*(2), 281–342.
Kryscynski, D., and Ulrich, D. (2015). Making strategic human capital relevant: A time-sensitive opportunity. *Academy of Management Perspectives*, *29*(3), 357–69.
Lazear, E.P. (2003), Firm-specific human capital: A skill-weights approach. IZA Discussion Paper 813, Institute for the Study of Labor, Bonn, Germany.
Lazear, E. P. (2009). Firm-specific human capital: A skill-weights approach. *Journal of Political Economy*, *117*(5), 914–40.
Mahoney, J. T., and Kor, Y. Y. (2015). Advancing the human capital perspective on value creation by joining capabilities and governance approaches. *Academy of Management Perspectives*, *29*(3), 296–308.
Mayer, K. J., Somaya, D., and Williamson, I. O. (2012). Firm-specific, industry-specific, and occupational human capital and the sourcing of knowledge work. *Organization Science*, *23*(5), 1311–29.
Mitchell, T. R., Holtom, B. C., Lee, T. W., Sablynski, C. J., and Erez, M. (2001). Why people stay: Using job embeddedness to predict voluntary turnover. *Academy of Management Journal*, *44*(6), 1102–21.
Molloy, J. C., and Barney, J. B. (2015). Who captures the value created with human capital? A market-based view. *Academy of Management Perspectives*, *29*(3), 309–25.
Morris, S., Alvarez, S., Barney, J., and Molloy, J. (2014). Discretionary firm-specific investments. (Marriott School of Business Working Paper). Provo, UT: Brigham Young University.
Morris, S. S., Alvarez, S. A., Barney, J. B., and Molloy, J. C. (2017). Firm-specific human capital investments as a signal of general value: Revisiting assumptions about human capital and how it is managed. *Strategic Management Journal*, *38*(4), 912–19.
Neal, D. (1995). Industry-specific human capital: Evidence from displaced workers. *Journal of Labor Economics*, *13*(4), 653–77.
Nyberg, A. J., and Wright, P. M. (2015). 50 years of human capital research: Assessing what we know, exploring where we go. *Academy of Management Perspectives*, *29*(3), 287–95.
Parsons, D. O. (1972). Specific human capital: An application to quit rates and layoff rates. *Journal of Political Economy*, *80*(6), 1120–43.
Pennings, J. M., Lee, K., and Witteloostuijn, A. V. (1998). Human capital, social capital, and firm dissolution. *Academy of Management Journal*, *41*(4), 425–40.
Penrose, E. (1959). *The Theory of the Growth of the Firm*. New York: Wiley.
Peteraf, M. A. (1993). The cornerstones of competitive advantage: A resource-based view. *Strategic Management Journal*, *14*(3), 179–91.
Pil, F. K., and Leana, C. R. (2000). Free-agency versus high-involvement approaches to skill development. In C. R. Leana and D. M. Rousseau (eds), *Relational Wealth: The Advantages of Stability in a Changing Economy*, 116–29. Oxford: Oxford University Press.
Ployhart, R. E. (2012). The psychology of competitive advantage: An adjacent possibility. *Industrial and Organizational Psychology*, *5*(1), 62–81.
Ployhart, R. E., and Moliterno, T. P. (2011). Emergence of the human capital resource: A multilevel model. *Academy of Management Review*, *36*(1), 127–50.
Podsakoff, P. M., MacKenzie, S. B., Paine, J. B., and Bachrach, D. G. (2000). Organizational citizenship behaviors: A critical review of the theoretical and empirical literature and suggestions for future research. *Journal of Management*, *26*(3), 513–63.
Raffiee, J., and Coff, R. (2016). Micro-foundations of firm-specific human capital: When do employees perceive their skills to be firm-specific? *Academy of Management Journal*, *59*(3), 766–90.
Roumpi, D. (2018). Retaining valued human capital: Investigating the demand side of the labor market (PhD dissertation). Theses and Dissertations 2839. Retrieved from https://scholarworks.uark.edu/etd/2839.
Strober, M. H. (1990). Human capital theory: Implications for HR managers. *Industrial Relations: A Journal of Economy and Society*, *29*(2), 214–39.
Sturman, M. C., Walsh, K., and Cheramie, R. A. (2008). The value of human capital specificity versus transferability. *Journal of Management*, *34*(2), 290–316.

Takeuchi, R., Lepak, D. P., Wang, H., and Takeuchi, K. (2007). An empirical examination of the mechanisms mediating between high-performance work systems and the performance of Japanese organizations. *Journal of Applied Psychology*, *92*(4), 1069–83.
Verquer, M. L., Beehr, T. A., and Wagner, S. H. (2003). A meta-analysis of relations between person–organization fit and work attitudes. *Journal of Vocational Behavior*, *63*(3), 473–89.
Wang, H. C., and Barney, J. B. (2006). Employee incentives to make firm-specific investments: Implications for resource-based theories of corporate diversification. *Academy of Management Review*, *31*(2), 466–76.
Wang, H. C., He, J., and Mahoney, J. T. (2009). Firm-specific knowledge resources and competitive advantage: the roles of economic- and relationship-based employee governance mechanisms. *Strategic Management Journal*, *30*(12), 1265–85.
Wang, H., Zhao, S., and Chen, G. (2017). Firm-specific knowledge assets and employment arrangements: Evidence from CEO compensation design and CEO dismissal. *Strategic Management Journal*, *38*(9), 1875–94.
Wernerfelt, B. (1984). A resource-based view of the firm. *Strategic Management Journal*, *5*(2), 171–80.
Wright, P. M., and McMahan, G. C. (2011). Exploring human capital: putting "human" back into strategic human resource management. *Human Resource Management Journal*, *21*(2), 93–104.
Wright, P. M., Coff, R., and Moliterno, T. P. (2014). Strategic human capital: Crossing the great divide. *Journal of Management*, *40*(2), 353–70.

11. Human resource management strategy and practice: from individual motivation to dynamic capabilities*

David Lewin and David J. Teece

INTRODUCTION

We've been asked to provide a chapter for this book that provides a macro perspective on the firm's use of strategic human capital resources in response to the chapter on "isolating mechanisms" by Ben Campbell and David Kryscynski. Whereas those authors ground their argument in certain basic assumptions, we contend that the firm's use of human capital resources can best be understood from the perspective of the dynamic capabilities framework, a comprehensive strategic management approach that links resources to outcomes. This framework makes explicit some of the mechanisms within the "black box" that stands between the firm's human resources architecture and its subsequent performance (Becker and Huselid, 2006: 899).[1]

The "isolating mechanisms" approach, while intellectually coherent, effectively isolates human resource (HR) practices by merely positing that some firms are better able to motivate employees and to align their efforts with company objectives. This is in keeping with the tendency in economics to model firm capabilities (or productivity) as a random distribution (e.g., Hopenhayn, 1992). These approaches essentially ignore the specific characteristics of firms—including their HR practices, culture, signature organizational routines, and leadership—that contribute to (or detract from) company performance.

What makes great firms distinctive is how their managers combine and orchestrate the human capital and other resources at their command into a unique system for creating and capturing value. We address this by gradually broadening the lens from individually focused HR practices to strategic human resources management to dynamic capabilities. The following section briefly discusses theories of employee motivation and organizational climate. The next section then broadens the focus to explore one source of climate, namely, how bundles of HR practices link to company performance. We then discuss how HR practices need to support innovation by employees that possess specialist expertise. The subsequent section broadens the focus again to present the dynamic capabilities framework as a system-level approach to thinking about strategic, enterprise-wide issues of alignment. This is followed by a brief conclusion that summarizes and looks to a future in which independent contractors and non-employee customers will increasingly need to be part of management's thinking.

HR PRACTICES AND EMPLOYEE MOTIVATION

As Campbell and Kryscynski note, a firm's ability to motivate its employees is an important element of its specificity. They leave motivation as a black box. In this section, we briefly review how thinking about motivation has evolved and how it is currently understood. The extant literature suggests several answers to the question of how employees can be motivated to give their best.[2]

Early in the 20th century, Frederick Taylor (1911) pioneered the scientific management movement by applying industrial engineering principles to the design of work. In the role of organizational consultants, Taylor and his disciples (Gilbreth and Gilbreth, 1917) observed employees, typically manufacturing workers, performing their work, used those observations to identify the key elements of each job, and then redesigned the jobs such that they could be performed most efficiently. Businesses that adopted Taylor's principles of scientific management experienced twofold and even threefold increases in productivity with the same factor inputs.

Accompanying the newly redesigned (and more specialized) jobs was a more hierarchical organizational structure in which supervisors and managers tightly controlled the work performed by employees. In this high-control system, employees were conceived of as "economic men" motivated to perform their work to high levels of productivity and quality by the enhanced monetary rewards they would receive from doing so. Hence, inherent in scientific management was a theory of money as a—even *the*—motivator.

Later in the 20th century, Elton Mayo (1933) and his colleagues (Rothlisberger and Dickson, 1939) at the Harvard Business School proffered a substantially different theory of motivation, one in which employees' social needs rather than economic needs were paramount. These researchers studied the behavior and performance of employees who assembled telephones at the Hawthorne manufacturing plant of the Bell Telephone Company and discovered that, when employees developed strong, cohesive group norms and bonds, their productivity and product quality increased greatly. Further, these norms and bonds developed largely informally rather than through management dictates. Hence, these researchers identified the informal work group as a key factor/variable influencing employee performance, which led in turn to the Human Relations theory of management and motivation.[3]

On the basis of this theory of motivation, companies quickly came to adopt a variety of employee assistance and psychological counseling programs aimed at meeting employees' noneconomic needs, and also instituted new incentive and reward programs to motivate industrial work groups.[4] Personnel departments bore major responsibility for designing and assisting their companies to implement these new human relations-based programs. As a result, the importance and status of these departments rose markedly.

Still later in the 20th century, a broader theory of motivation emerged and gained widespread attention, namely, expectancy theory. As propounded by Vroom (1964), this theory considers the employee's expectation that effort expended leads to performance, the instrumentality that links performance to (intrinsic and extrinsic) rewards, and the valence the employee attaches to the rewards, which leads to attitudes. These linkages are depicted in Figure 11.1, where attitudes constitute the dependent variable. However, the figure also shows feedback from attitudes to effort in the next period, which provides the dynamics of motivation. It is a theory upon which company HR practices aimed at motivating employees to perform are or can be based.[5]

On the basis of expectancy theory, many companies (and other organizations) began to conduct employee satisfaction surveys, generating a satisfaction metric that attracted widespread attention. Indeed, the heads of personnel departments were often held accountable for such satisfaction, and their own performance and consequent pay

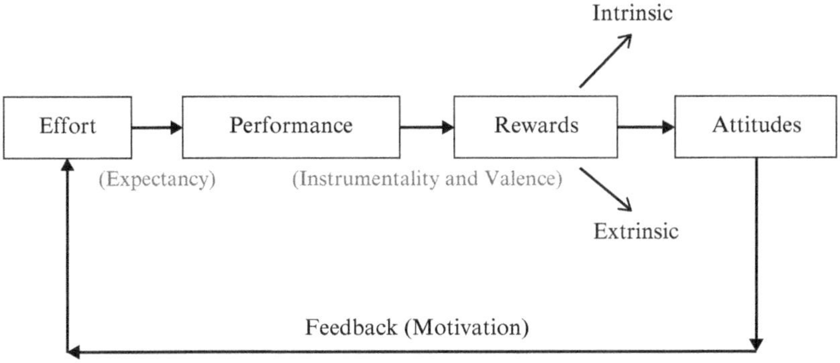

Figure 11.1 Expectancy theory

and other rewards became partially dependent upon employee satisfaction scores. The underlying notion was that a satisfied or "happy" employee was and would be a motivated employee.

Companies' interest in and concern about their employees' satisfaction and motivation persisted throughout the remainder of the 20th century, though the phrase "employee satisfaction" became displaced by "employee morale" and, later, by the phrase "organizational climate" (e.g., Litwin and Stringer, 1968). The latter phrase signaled that the level or unit of analysis in companies' concern about this matter shifted from that of the individual employee and that employee's relationship with his or her manager to that of the group, work unit, department, division of a multi-divisional company, and/or to the company as a whole.

In the later years of the century, companies became relatively more concerned with the satisfaction of another constituency, namely, customers. Company after company instituted one or more customer satisfaction surveys, often published the results of those surveys in their annual reports, and incorporated customer satisfaction into their customer relationship management (CRM) programs (Ngai, 2005; Parvatiyar and Sheth, 2001). In fact, companies generally became relatively more concerned about the motivation of their customers than of their employees.

During the 21st century to date, employee satisfaction has been recast once more, this time by the phrase "employee engagement." Although engagement is still typically determined and measured through surveys of employees, engagement implies more than satisfaction. The intrinsic motivation of employees and their willingness to realize organizational goals can be enhanced by the company's purpose, values, and principles (Kanter et al., 2015). An employee's "engagement score" is used to measure the employee's commitment to the company, and especially an employee's internalization of company norms, values, beliefs and expectations—in other words, an employee's fit with the company's organizational culture (Albrecht, 2010).[6]

The engagement of employees has been linked to reduced turnover (e.g., Harter et al., 2002) and thus can be thought of as an "isolating mechanism" for employees, as Campbell and Kryscynski suggest. However, as we will show in the remainder of this chapter, making strategic use of human capital resources requires a systemic approach that goes beyond the rents that employees generate in isolation.

HRM BUNDLES AND COMPANY PERFORMANCE

The management of human capital resources has of course expanded beyond "climate" and individual satisfaction to encompass a more systemic view. Bundles of practices have been identified that lead to better firm-level outcomes by supporting the firm's strategy implementation.

While motivation theory may have contributed to the design and implementation of contemporary human resource management (HRM) practices, so too has labor economics research (Lewin, 2001; Lewin and Mitchell, 1995). Early on, this institutionally oriented research focused on unionization, particularly the effects of unions on businesses. Scholars analyzed and documented the effects of unions on certain aspects of management, including hiring and staffing practices, work shifts and assignments, discipline and due process, compensation practices, and layoff practices—or, in the language of that era, terms and conditions of employment (e.g., Chamberlain, 1948). The main conclusion drawn from this research was that unions narrowed the scope of management's decision-making authority and control, and to some extent shared that authority and control. Related research analyzed the effects of unions on productivity (e.g., Hartman, 1969). A main conclusion from this research was that unions for the most part had positive impacts on business productivity.

Another body of research, however, focused squarely and more narrowly on the union impacts on wages. Unlike the union impacts on management literature, this research was grounded in a strong, widely accepted theoretical base, namely, neo-classical price theory. Guided by well-known microeconomic assumptions about product and labor market competition, factor mobility, information availability, and especially market equilibrium, labor economists produced substantial quantitative research estimating the effects of unions on wages (Rees, 1977). In some industries, such as supermarkets and apparel, this "union effect" was found to be relatively small, while in other industries, such as construction and steel manufacturing, it was found to be relatively large. Later, labor economists expanded their studies to measure the effects of unions on fringe benefits, and still later on businesses' capital expenditures, research and development (R&D) expenditures, and profitability. The main findings from this research were that unions had positive effects on fringe benefits, meaning that, as with wages, they raised benefit costs to employers, and had negative effects on capital expenditures, R&D expenditures, and profitability (Hirsch, 2007). These findings were then used to explain the subsequent large decline in private sector unionization in the U.S. and other nations.

This labor economics research had an additional impact, however, which was to spur other researchers to focus on quantitatively measuring the impacts of HRM practices on business performance, especially because these practices were increasingly applied to non-union workforces.[7] Key to this research was the development of indices of HRM practices that measured the extent to which such practices were of the so-called "high involvement" type. Operationally, HR indices were constructed on the basis of responses to questions (i.e., items) that were included in surveys of samples of business firms and/or establishments, with a typical establishment being a manufacturing plant. These samples were drawn from populations of publicly traded firms because data on the financial performance of these firms were available from secondary sources, thereby permitting analyses of the relationships between HR practices and business performance. In this research, one or another measure of business performance served as the dependent variable, similar to the way in which wages (or wages plus benefits) served as the dependent variable in labor economists' studies of union impacts on pay. In place of unionism as the main independent variable, HRM research used one or more indices of HR practices.

Company financial performance, measured by return on investment (ROI), return on assets (ROA), and even stock price and/or market value, was often modeled as the dependent variable (Huselid, 1995; Huselid et al., 1997). In other studies, the financial performance of individual business units of conglomerate or diversified companies, measured by ROI, ROA, and/or revenue per employee, was used (Mitchell et al., 1990). The bulk of this research, however, focused on manufacturing plants (i.e., establishments) in which the main business performance measures—dependent variables—were productivity, product quality, plant (or line) up time, and labor costs (Appelbaum et al., 2000; Ichniowski et al., 1997; Dunlop and Weil, 1996; MacDuffie, 1995; Arthur, 1992). The automobile, steel, and apparel industries were prominently featured in this strand of HRM research. A relatively small number of HRM studies focused on service-type establishments, typically field sales and service offices of large companies in the telecommunications and insurance industries (e.g., Batt, 1999). In these studies, revenue growth, quality of service, and customer satisfaction often served as the business performance metrics. Hence, an important contribution of contemporary HRM research is its multi-level, multi-faceted modeling and measurement of business performance.

Another important contribution of contemporary HRM research is the extensive use of primary research methods to develop indices of HR practices. Unlike much business performance data, which can readily be gleaned from a variety of secondary sources, systematic data on the HR practices of business (and non-business) firms are unavailable from secondary sources and must therefore be obtained directly from businesses. For this purpose, HR researchers have designed numerous survey questionnaires and interview protocols and administered them to within-industry and cross-industry samples of firms and establishments, with executives and managers serving as the main survey respondents (e.g., Delaney et al., 1989). While these samples have been developed in bottom-up fashion and have not been synthesized into an overriding nationwide survey or database comparable to national databases on firms' financial performance, they nevertheless have enabled HRM researchers to produce quantitative estimates of the effects of HR practices on business performance in a wide variety of industry, company, and establishment settings. Moreover, this research has been conducted in North American, European and Asian nations (e.g., Boxall and Macky, 2009; Lee and Johnson, 1998; Morishima, 1991), meaning that it has a strong global reach. In this respect, contemporary HRM research is broader and deeper than the research conducted in prior eras by industrial relations specialists and labor economists.

For researchers, a finding rarely stands alone and is typically subject to caveats about sampling and generalization, the moderating effects of other variables, and the limitations of extant research designs and analytical methods (Lewin, 2011a; Kaufman, 2010). For practitioners, by contrast, a key finding from a particular body of research is often taken as dominant, without qualification, and used to shape policy and practice (Rynes et al., 2007; Lewin, 2008).

The main finding of contemporary HRM research is that certain "high involvement" (or "high participation," "high commitment," "high performance," or "empowerment") HR practices are positively associated with—contribute to—business performance. To illustrate, Huselid (1995: 667) concludes that "a one-standard deviation increase in [High Performance Work Practices] is associated with . . . $27,044 more in sales and $18,641 and $3,814 more in market value and profits, respectively." This and related empirical findings have been taken by HR practitioners in particular—and by business executives and managers more broadly—to mean that there is a set of HR "best practices" that, when applied, will enhance business performance (Lewin, 2003). These are: 1) employment security, 2) selective hiring, 3) teamwork and organizational decentralization, 4) high pay contingent on organizational performance, 5) extensive training and development, 6) reduction of status differences, and 7) information-sharing with employees (e.g., Pfeffer, 1998, 1994).

These HR practices are claimed to have their strongest positive effects on business performance when treated and applied as a set (or bundle or package) rather than individually. Indeed, some researchers argue that any one of these practices applied alone will have little to no effect on business performance (Pfeffer and Veiga, 1999). Furthermore, say these researchers, a short-term application of the full set of HR "best practices" will also be unlikely to have positive effects on business performance. Only when these practices are applied together and sustained for the longer term are they likely to enhance business performance. Apparently, however, only a relatively small minority of businesses follows this long-term HR best practices application, either because their executives and managers don't believe the HR–performance connection or because they are too strongly oriented toward the short-term performance of their businesses (Pfeffer and Veiga, 1999). This implies that the large majority of businesses have the potential to enhance their performance if they can overcome the factors that inhibit or prevent them from adopting and sustaining the full set of HR best practices.

AMBIDEXTROUS HRM: MANAGING EXPERTS

"Best practice" implies a level of stability that can lead to imitation by rivals. While not all firms will imitate the best-practice leaders, enough will do so to drive competition. In other words, generic best practices cannot be a basis for competitive advantage.

However, HR best-practice bundles are not applied uniformly within a firm (this section) or identically across firms (next section). Here we consider one of the ways in which HR architectures become differentiated as they are made responsive to "employment mode," such as knowledge-based versus task-based (Lepak and Snell, 2002).

Maintaining a multi-dimensional HR architecture requires a form of organizational ambidexterity, a concept developed in the strategic management field that is usually applied to the simultaneous management of both day-to-day operation of an ongoing business and the more exploratory work of an internal start-up operation. The two types of activities require different management styles, which can lead to two separate subunits with different cultures yet linked by shared company-wide values and by senior managers with an overarching view (O'Reilly and Tushman, 2004, 2008).

A similar condition can occur in a company's HRM system because many of the employees most central to value creation require different handling from operational staff, even if they all work in close proximity. The high-value employees will be referred to here as "experts," people with a high level of specialized knowledge derived from a mix of education and experience.

A large firm's stock of experts will be a mix of those who have been hired for their expertise, those who have developed expertise within the organization, and others who are independent contractors. The most valuable experts are "T-shaped," with a deep understanding in their primary discipline (the vertical trunk of the T) and "also capable of interacting with and understanding specialists from a wide range of disciplines and functional areas" (IfM and IBM, 2008: 11). Collaboration among experts with diverse backgrounds is critical to certain activities, including innovation, product development, and strategy formulation. This, in turn, requires organizational norms of interaction and knowledge sharing (Subramaniam and Youndt, 2005).

Expert human capital alone does not provide competitive advantage. Rather, it is the combination of expert human capital with tacit organizational knowledge and management's dynamic capabilities that creates the possibility of building a quasi-sustainable competitive advantage (Teece, 2011).

Experts, especially those who were hired or contracted externally, tend to be highly productive and highly mobile. While they may develop some firm-specific knowledge over time, they are often contractually limited from using it elsewhere.[8] To take one prominent current example, Doug Field was recently hired by Apple, where he had worked previously, to be the second highest manager in a unit developing autonomous vehicle technology.[9] Field started his career at Ford as a development engineer, and earned dual mechanical engineering and business degrees in 1992. He worked at two other companies during the 1990s then joined Segway, a personal transportation start-up, where he remained for nine years. In addition to developing the hardware for the first self-balancing personal mobility device, his projects at Segway included joint development work with General Motors (GM) on a two-person autonomous pod that reached the prototype stage just as GM ran into serious financial difficulty in 2009. Field then spent three years at Apple as Vice-President of Product Design, where he was second only to Jony Ive. His next stop was at Tesla where he worked for five years, helping to oversee the challenge of turning the $70,000 Model S into the $35,000 Model 3 while maintaining range and performance, before returning to Apple. Field's career path is not atypical of the many talented people who tackle a challenge at one company and then move on after the work has culminated in success or failure, picking up valuable knowledge along the way. In Field's case, his work with electric and autonomous transportation at several companies honed his hardware design skills.

Experts thrive under a different management approach than is needed for operational efficiency. They are unlikely to be productive and satisfied in a traditional hierarchical structure where they are compensated in traditional ways that depend on events beyond their control.

The management style required to get the best out of expert employees involves a light touch. Top talent generally does not need to be told what to do, particularly by a manager with little familiarity with the expert's area of knowledge. Strategic goals and strategy linkages must not be defined so narrowly that real innovation is impossible. Management should foster collaboration, provide adequate resources, and allow enough slack to permit creative ferment and lateral thinking to take place. It's also important to prevent creativity from descending into chaos. Takeuchi and Nonaka (1986) label this "subtle control," which involves a monitoring function that leads to intervention (e.g., eliminating a problematic team member) only when absolutely necessary.

The creative work of experts is also generally best supported in an environment where productive dissent is encouraged (Nemeth, 2012). In other words, identification with the firm and its values should not turn into an emphasis on maintaining group-level harmony, which can devolve into group-think (Goncalo and Staw, 2006). Conflict is a necessary element in collaborative innovation, and a culture that can allow this needs to be established—and modeled— by the firm's leaders (Gelfand et al., 2012).

Managers must also hold experts accountable to the challenge at hand and to alignment with strategy. Autonomy and accountability go together; the more easily performance can be measured, the greater the autonomy that can safely be permitted.

Not only is the management style for experts different from that for other employees, so is the compensation system. Experts must generally be paid more and differently than other employees. But experts also value the chance to grow in their job. To illustrate, Lepak, Takeuchi, and Snell (2003) found that an emphasis on developing employee expertise over time was associated with positive firm-level performance, particularly in firms with a high R&D-to-sales ratio. This suggests that a firm can develop ways of appropriately compensating exceptional talent without undermining the morale of other employees. Put another way, the human capital rents from one set of employees must be considered in terms of its interaction with the rents from the others. In economic terms, the firm must simultaneously optimize its various HRM practices across all employee subsets.

THE DYNAMIC CAPABILITIES FRAMEWORK: FULLY ALIGNING HRM

So far, we have discussed how HRM can be used to improve employee productivity. But HRM is one system among many that must all be co-aligned in order to create sustainable competitive advantage. The key here is to design a unique and differentiated HR architecture that provides the human capital required for an organization's strategic business processes (Becker and Huselid, 2006). It is within this larger perspective, captured by the dynamic capabilities framework, that a company's strategic human capital resources can achieve their highest (firm-specific) value.

The dynamic capabilities framework takes a system-level approach to all the resources, capabilities, and strategic management of the firm (Teece, 2018a). An early definition of dynamic capabilities was "the firm's ability to integrate, build, and reconfigure internal and external competences to address rapidly changing environments" (Teece et al., 1997: 516). That still applies, although the speed of change in the environment may be less relevant than the prevailing degree of uncertainty (Teece et al., 2016).

As described by Teece (2014), the capabilities framework incorporates managerial decision-making as well as organizational routines. The longer an organization has been around and the larger it grows, the less its capabilities are likely to depend on particular individuals; routines (i.e., "the way we do things") become established. A company's unique history gives it the possibility to develop differentiated capabilities that will be hard for rivals to replicate. Managerial leadership adds another source of uniqueness and creates the potential to make changes in direction when necessary.

In this section, we begin by relating dynamic capabilities to the other capabilities of the firm. After that, we discuss the broader capabilities framework that encompasses resources, strategy, and employees.

The Capabilities Hierarchy

Capabilities form a hierarchy. At the top, in strategic terms, are high-order dynamic capabilities consisting of three bundles of ongoing activities:

- sensing (identification and calibration of opportunities and challenges);
- seizing (development of capabilities and business models to exploit opportunities); and
- transforming (implementation of changes large and small in a manner that maintains motivation, flexibility, and alignment).

All firms, from new entrepreneurial ventures to large, well-established firms, have dynamic capabilities, but these capabilities can be weak or strong. A firm may also be stronger in some capabilities than others. For example, it might be great at sensing (e.g., selecting promising R&D initiatives) but poor at seizing (e.g., designing a profitable business model).

At the next level of the capability hierarchy are the components of dynamic capabilities, intermediate activities that have been labeled "microfoundations" (Teece, 2007). These include organizational processes for alliance formation, new product development, and so on. They have elements of repeated routines, and they allow the firm to integrate, reconfigure, add, or subtract resources, which makes them dynamic-like capabilities (Eisenhardt and Martin, 2000). However, they are oriented toward following an existing plan and may be replicable by rivals, which makes them more like ordinary capabilities.

Ordinary capabilities form the base of the hierarchy, providing the foundation on which the strategic superstructure can be built. They are processes, such as hiring routines, that deploy people, facilities, and equipment to carry out the current business of the firm efficiently in the near-term. Ordinary capabilities lend themselves to being documented, measured, and benchmarked, which makes them easier for others to replicate. Since they are therefore unlikely to provide a unique advantage, strong ordinary capabilities need to be accessed but not necessarily owned.

The Broader Framework

The capabilities hierarchy is at the core of the dynamic capabilities framework, which links a firm's resources, capabilities, and strategy to its long-run performance. The framework emphasizes system-level analysis because many moving parts need to approach some degree of alignment if they are to be effective (Teece, 2018a). For example, the elements of a business model (value proposition, revenues, costs) must be internally aligned and coherent, and the business model must be aligned with the organizational structure and overall management model of the company (Teece, 2018b). The subsystems that make up the enterprise, including human resources management, must be congruent with each other and with business strategy (Nadler and Tushman, 1980).

Alignment must extend beyond internal elements to the external environment. For example, Williamson (1991) describes the prototypical Japanese manufacturer of the 1980s as a coherent system of relations with employees, subcontracting suppliers, and banks that are tightly integrated. The companies were, in turn, closely aligned with the government; all major Japanese corporations had one or more former government officials as board members if not executives (Schaede, 1995). This set of interlocking institutions made it difficult for non-Japanese companies to replicate whatever advantages accrued, although it may also have made the system less flexible when problems arose. Alignment should not be an end in itself but, rather, one consideration among others as plans develop and evolve.

Strategy, which is different from dynamic capabilities, is nevertheless an integral part of the dynamic capabilities framework. Dynamic capabilities provide inputs to, and then help to enact, a strategy. Taken together, the exercise of dynamic capabilities and the formulation of strategy create a plan for the future and enable its implementation. The HR architecture mobilizes the strategic human capital resources needed to achieve the plan. When dynamic capabilities are strong and strategy is sound, the enterprise has a good chance of maintaining continued (evolutionary) fitness vis-à-vis the external business environment.

Strong dynamic capabilities and good strategy depend on entrepreneurial management, which is a combination of transformational leadership and an ability to recognize untapped possibilities (Teece, 2016). Entrepreneurial managers, at whatever level of the firm they operate, assemble and deploy resources in pursuit of fresh opportunities, while imparting their vision of the future to the employees within their purview. They must (collectively, but not necessarily individually) excel at the scanning, learning, and interpreting required to sense, test, and seize new technological and market opportunities.

The top management team's ability to make quality decisions is critical to organizational success (Linden and Teece, 2014). This decision-making needs to happen at a speed suited to that of the business environment (Eisenhardt, 1989). Strong dynamic capabilities also require an organizational design that promotes innovation and flexibility. The organizational design must be complemented by a culture and incentive system that promotes initiative, sharing, and organizational identification (Augier and Teece, 2009), such as the "pro-entrepreneurship organizational architecture" advocated by Ireland et al. (2009).[10]

Entrepreneurial managers permit experimentation and a wide search for solutions, but they must be able to support promising paths and close down foolish ones. It is vital to have leadership at the team level or higher that knows which ideas can be rejected out of hand. Such rejections should be handled as transparently as possible and in a way that doesn't discourage future entrepreneurial efforts (Birkinshaw et al., 2011).

It is the combination of a company's unique capabilities, astute management, and strategic human capital resources that creates and captures value. HRM is a vital, boundary-spanning function that helps keep this complex system operating smoothly and successfully. This success creates a virtuous cycle because successful companies are able to pay and reward all their workers better, improving motivation and commitment. In this regard, a recent study found that high-paying firms retain staff over longer periods than organizations that don't—or can't—offer high pay (Abowd et al., 2018).

CONCLUSION

In this chapter, we've attempted to counter the narrow isolating mechanisms approach by building up from the fundamentals of employee motivation through bundles of HRM practices to the overall dynamic capabilities framework. It's within a well-managed and well-aligned system that human capital rents are most likely to be created.[11]

Campbell and Kryscynski are quite conservative about the sources of firm-specific human capital rents. They posit that firm-specific human capital can only be attributed to training provided by the firm. They seem resistant to the notion that some firms are simply better at retaining the best employees by providing a compelling vision, a collegial environment, and challenging work.

Inter-firm differences in this regard are most critical where experts are concerned. HRM practices may generate their biggest rents from expert employees because their work often increases the value that all the firm's employees can generate. Certain fields, such as artificial intelligence (AI) currently, may be in such high demand that salaries offset the rents generated for the individual employee, but the retention of the employee may be vital for raising overall productivity.

Additional research is needed to shed more light on the linkages between individual employee motivation, HR practices, and dynamic capabilities. Specifically, such research should address the following questions: How does expectancy theory apply in a setting that encourages individual entrepreneurship and the freedom to fail? What different bundles of HR practices support sensing, seizing, and reconfiguring? What board-level governance system is needed to select and support executives who make high-quality decisions that keep the enterprise in sync with new technology and market realities?

Another increasingly important area for future research is looking beyond the boundaries of the firm. The isolating mechanisms logic of Campbell and Kryscynski, the human capital matching perspective advocated by Weller in Chapter 8, and our own dynamic capabilities-grounded HRM framework all assume that labor services are rendered by employees. However, in the modern economy, multitudinous "labor services" are provided by independent contractors (Lewin, 2018, 2016), and consumers/customers perform unpaid "work" that was previously done by paid employees.

Examples of the latter include customers who purchase their airline tickets and download their boarding passes on-line, track on-line the packages and other items they ship via overnight delivery companies, check out of and (increasingly) check into hotels without physically stopping at a hotel reservation or check-out desk, and diagnose and repair their electronic equipment/devices using on-line software programs. Each of these activities can be considered an ordinary capability, but they pose the challenge of whether or not such customer-provided labor services can be managed in any meaningful way. This challenge, in turn, should be a key topic of contemporary strategic human capital research.

CHAPTER SUMMARY

BOX 11.1 KEY TAKEAWAYS

1. Employee motivation depends on a combination of expected extrinsic rewards (compensation, responsibility, etc.) and intrinsic rewards (sense of purpose, identification with the organization, etc.).
2. A company's bundle of human resources (HR) practices determines the behavior of employees and shapes organizational "climate."
3. A specific bundle of HR practices is associated with high performance: 1) employment security, 2) selective hiring, 3) teamwork and organizational decentralization, 4) high pay contingent on organizational performance, 5) extensive training and development, 6) reduction of status differences, and 7) information-sharing with employees.
4. The HR management of a company's experts should include a light touch, a collaborative environment, toleration of dissent, and "subtle control."
5. The dynamic capabilities framework provides a system-level view of the company's capabilities, resources, and strategic management, which can assist with prioritizing important alignments such as that between human capital resources and strategic business processes.

BOX 11.2 DIRECTIONS FOR FUTURE RESEARCH

1. How does expectancy theory apply in a setting that encourages individual entrepreneurship and the freedom to fail?
2. What different bundles of HR practices support sensing, seizing, and reconfiguring?
3. What board-level governance system is needed to select and support executives who make high-quality decisions that keep the enterprise in sync with new technology and market realities?
4. Can and should customer-provided services (e.g. airline passengers printing their boarding passes) be managed within a human resources management framework?

NOTES

* The authors are grateful to Greg Linden for helpful suggestions and support.

1. For a comprehensive treatment of human resource management (HRM) research, see Lewin et al. (1997).
2. For elaboration, see Lewin (2001, 2011b).
3. This research provided the intellectual foundation for the substantial amount of theory development and practice regarding team-based work. See, for example, Katzenbach and Smith (1993).
4. This research also became one of the intellectual prongs for the related work of McGregor (1960) and Zaleznik (1989).
5. Expectancy theory has also been used for the development of leadership theory and practice (Vroom and Jago, 1988; Isaac et al., 2001).
6. From a more macro perspective, organization culture is one among a few key elements of organizational alignment theories and models (Galbraith, 2014).
7. An additional factor contributing to the rise of quantitative assessments of the effects of HRM practices on business performance was an emerging popular literature on management that often claimed that "the management of people (employees)" was *the* differentiator between very high-performing firms and other firms. See, for example, Peters and Waterman (1982).
8. See Weller (Chapter 8) for a more thorough discussion of the firm-specificity of human capital resources.

9. The following account of Doug Field's career is reconstructed from various published sources, including his own LinkedIn profile.
10. The intellectual foundations of organizational design in a business enterprise can be traced to Chandler (1962).
11. This is similar to Chadwick's (2017) proposition that "Idiosyncratic firm complementarities increase human capital value in use" but takes an even broader view of complementarities (e.g., with strategy).

REFERENCES

Abowd, J. M., McKinney, K. L., and Zhao, N. L. (2018). Earnings inequality and mobility trends in the United States: Nationally representative estimates from longitudinally Linked employer-employee data. *Journal of Labor Economics*, *36*(S1), S183-300.

Albrecht, S. L. (2010). *Handbook of Employee Engagement: Perspectives, Issues, Research and Practice*. Cheltenham, UK and Northampton, MA, USA: Edward Elgar Publishing.

Appelbaum, E., Bailey, T., Berg, P. and Kalleberg, A. (2000). *Manufacturing Advantage: Why High-Performance Work Systems Pay Off*. Washington, DC: Economic Policy Institute.

Arthur, J. (1992). The link between business strategy and industrial relations systems in American mini-mills. *Industrial and Labor Relations Review*, *45*, 488–506.

Augier, M. and Teece, D. J. (2009). Dynamic capabilities and the role of managers in business strategy and economic performance. *Organization Science*, *20*(2), 410–21.

Batt, R. (1999). Work organization, technology, and performance in customer service and sales. *Industrial and Labor Relations Review*, *52*, 539–64.

Becker, B. E. and Huselid, M. A. (2006). Strategic human resources management: Where do we go from here? *Journal of Management*, *32*(6), 898–925.

Birkinshaw, J., Bouquet, C., and Barsoux, J. L. (2011). The 5 myths of innovation. *MIT Sloan Management Review*, *52*(2), 43–50.

Boxall, P., and Macky, K. (2009). Research and theory on high-performance work systems: Progressing the high-involvement stream. *Human Resource Management Journal*, *19*(1), 3–23.

Chadwick, C. (2017). Toward a more comprehensive model of firms' human capital rents. *Academy of Management Review*, *42*(3), 499–519.

Chamberlain, N. W. (1948). *The Union Challenge to Management Control*. New York: Harper & Bros.

Chandler Jr, A. D. (1962). *Strategy and Structure: Chapters in the History of the American Industrial Enterprise*. Cambridge, MA: MIT Press.

Delaney, J. T., Lewin, D. and Ichniowski, C. (1989). *Human Resource Policies and Practices in American Firms*. BLMR 137. Washington, DC: Bureau of Labor-Management Relations and Cooperative Programs, U.S. Department of Labor.

Dunlop, J. T. and Weil, D. (1996). Diffusion and performance of modular production in the U.S. apparel industry. *Industrial Relations*, *35*, 334–55.

Eisenhardt, K. M. (1989). Making fast strategic decisions in high-velocity environments. *Academy of Management Journal*, *32*(3), 543–76.

Eisenhardt, K. M., and Martin, J. A. (2000). Dynamic capabilities: what are they? *Strategic Management Journal*, *21*(10–11), 1105–21.

Galbraith, J. R. (2014). *Designing Organizations: Strategy, Structure and Process at the Business Unit and Enterprise Levels*, 3rd edn. San Francisco: Jossey-Bass.

Gelfand, M. J., Leslie, L. M., Keller, K., and de Dreu, C. (2012). Conflict cultures in organizations: How leaders shape conflict cultures and their organizational-level consequences. *Journal of Applied Psychology*, *97*(6), 1131–47.

Gilbreth, F. B., and Gilbreth, L. M. (1917). *Applied Motion Study: A Collection of Papers on the Efficient Method to Industrial Preparedness*. New York: Sturgis and Walton.

Goncalo, J. A., and Staw, B. M. (2006). Individualism–collectivism and group creativity. *Organizational Behavior and Human Decision Processes*, *100*(1), 96–109.

Harter, J. K., Schmidt, F. L., and Hayes, T. L. (2002). Business-unit-level relationship between employee satisfaction, employee engagement, and business outcomes: A meta-analysis. *Journal of Applied Psychology*, *87*(2), 268–79.

Hartman, P. (1969). *Collective Bargaining and Productivity: The Longshore Mechanization Agreement*. Berkeley, CA: University of California Press.

Hirsch, B. M. (2007). What do unions do for economic performance? In J. T. Bennett and B. E. Kaufman (eds), *What Do Unions Do? A Twenty-Year Perspective*, 193–237. New Brunswick, NJ: Transaction.

Hopenhayn, H. A. (1992). Entry, exit, and firm dynamics in long run equilibrium. *Econometrica*, *60*(5), 1127–50.
Huselid, M. A. (1995). The impact of human resource management practices on turnover, productivity, and corporate financial performance. *Academy of Management Journal*, *38*, 635–72.
Huselid, M. A., Jackson, S. E., and Schuler, R. S. (1997). Technical and strategic human resource management effectiveness as determinants of firm performance. *Academy of Management Journal*, *40*, 171–88.
Ichniowski, C., Shaw, K., and Prennushi, G. (1997). The effects of human resource management practices on productivity: A study of steel finishing lines. *American Economic Review*, *87*, 291–313.
IfM and IBM. (2008). Succeeding through service innovation. Cambridge: University of Cambridge Institute for Manufacturing. https://www.ifm.eng.cam.ac.uk/uploads/Resources/Reports/080428cambridge_ssme_whitepaper.pdf.
Ireland, R. D., Covin, J. G., and Kuratko, D. F. 2009. Conceptualizing corporate entrepreneurship strategy. *Entrepreneurship Theory and Practice*, *33*(1), 19–46.
Isaac, R. G., Zerbe, W. J., and Pitt, D. C. (2001). Leadership and motivation: The effective application of expectancy theory. *Journal of Managerial Issues*, *13*(2), 212–26.
Kanter, R. M., Bird, M., Bernstein, E. S., and Raffaelli, R. (2015). How leaders use values-based guidance systems to create dynamic capabilities. In D. J. Teece and S. Heaton (eds), *The Oxford Handbook of Dynamic Capabilities*. Oxford: Oxford University Press. https://doi.org/10.1093/oxfordhb/9780199678914.013.002.
Katzenbach, J., and Smith, D. K. (1993). *The Wisdom of Teams: Creating the High-Performance Organization*. Boston, MA: Harvard Business School Press.
Kaufman, B. E. (2010). SHRM theory in the post-Huselid era: Why it is fundamentally misspecified. *Industrial Relations*, *49*(2), 286–313.
Lee, M. B., and Johnson, N. B. (1998). Business environment, high-involvement management, and firm performance in Korea. In D. Lewin and B. E. Kaufman (eds), *Advances in Industrial and Labor Relations*, Vol. 8, 67–87. Greenwich, CT: JAI Press.
Lepak, D. P., and Snell, S. A. (2002). Examining the human resource architecture: The relationships among human capital, employment, and human resource configurations. *Journal of Management*, *28*(4), 517–43.
Lepak, D. P., Takeuchi, R., and Snell, S. A. (2003). Employment flexibility and firm performance: Examining the interaction effects of employment mode, environmental dynamism, and technological intensity. *Journal of Management*, *29*(5), 681–703.
Lewin, D. (2001). IR and HR perspectives on workplace conflict: What can each learn from the other? *Human Resource Management Review*, *11*(4): 453–85.
Lewin, D. (2003). Human resource management and business performance: Lessons for the 21st century. In M. Effron, R. Gandossy, and M. Goldsmith (eds), *Human Resources in the 21st Century*. Hoboken, NJ: Wiley.
Lewin, D. (2008). Human resources management in the 21st century. In C. Wankel (ed.), *21st Century Management: A Reference Handbook*, Vol. 2, 56–64. Thousand Oaks, CA: Sage.
Lewin, D. (2011a). High performance human resources (HPHR). In A. Wilkinson and K. Townsend (eds), *The Future of Employment Relation: New Paradigms, New Developments*, 11–29. London: Palgrave Macmillan.
Lewin, D. (2011b). The historical development of human resource management in the United States. Paper presented at the 71st Academy of Management Annual Meeting, San Antonio, TX (August).
Lewin, D. (2016). Resolving workplace conflicts through litigation: Evidence, and implications. In D. B. Lipsky, A. C. Avgar, and J. R. Lamare (eds), *Managing and Resolving Workplace Conflict*, Advances in Industrial and Labor Relations, Vol. 22, 31–67. London: Emerald.
Lewin, D. (2018). No poaching and independent contractor versus employee status disputes: Definition, analysis, and resolution. In S. L. Hayford (ed.), *Arbitration 2017: The New World of Work*, 329–45. Arlington, VA: Bloomberg Law.
Lewin, D., and Mitchell, D. J. B. (1995). *Human Resource Management: An Economic Approach*, 2nd edn. Cincinnati, OH: South-Western.
Lewin, D., Mitchell, D. J. B., and Zaidi, M. A. (1997). *The Human Resource Management Handbook, Parts I–III*. Greenwich, CT: JAI Press.
Linden, G., Teece, D. J. (2014). Managing expert talent. In P. Sparrow, H. Scullion, and I. Tarique (eds), *Strategic Talent Management: Contemporary Issues in International Context*, 87–116. Cambridge: Cambridge University Press.
Litwin, G. H., and Stringer Jr, R. A. (1968). *Motivation and Organizational Climate*. Boston, MA: Graduate School of Business Administration, Harvard University.
MacDuffie, J. P. (1995). Human resource bundles and manufacturing performance: Organizational logic and flexible production systems in the world auto industry. *Industrial and Labor Relations Review*, *48*, 197–221.
Mayo, E. (1933). *The Human Problems of an Industrial Civilization*. London: Routledge.
McGregor, D. (1960). *The Human Side of Enterprise*. New York: McGraw-Hill.
Mitchell, D. J. B., Lewin, D., and Lawler, E. E. III. (1990). Alternative pay systems, firm performance, and productivity. In A. S. Blinder (ed.), *Paying for Productivity: A Look at the Evidence*, 15–94. Washington, DC: Brookings Institution.

Morishima, M. (1991). Information sharing and firm performance in Japan. *Industrial Relations*, *30*, 37–61.

Nadler, D. A., and Tushman, M. L. (1980). A model for diagnosing organizational behavior. *Organizational Dynamics*, *9*(2), 35–51.

Nemeth, C. J. (2012). Minority influence theory. In P. Van Lange, A. Kruglanski, and T. Higgins (eds), *Handbook of Theories of Social Psychology*, Vol. 2, 362–78. New York: Sage.

Ngai, E. W. T. (2005). Customer relationship management research (1992–2002): An academic literature review and classification, *Marketing Intelligence and Planning*, *23*(6), 582–605.

O'Reilly, C. A., and Tushman, M. L. (2004). The ambidextrous organization. *Harvard Business Review*, *82*(4), 74–81.

O'Reilly, C. A., and Tushman, M. L. (2008). Ambidexterity as a dynamic capability: Resolving the innovator's dilemma. *Research in Organizational Behavior*, *28*, 185–206.

Parvatiyar, A., and Sheth, J. N. (2001). Customer relationship management: Emerging practice, process and discipline, *Journal of Economic and Social Research*, *3*(2), 1–34.

Peters, T. J., and Waterman Jr, R. H. (1982). *In Search of Excellence: Lessons From America's Best Run Companies*. New York: Harper & Row.

Pfeffer, J. (1994). *Competitive Advantage Through People*. Boston, MA: Harvard Business School Press.

Pfeffer, J. (1998). *The Human Equation*. Boston, MA: Harvard Business School Press.

Pfeffer, J., and Veiga, J. F. (1999). Putting people first for organizational success. *Academy of Management Executive*, *13*, 37–48.

Rees, A. (1977). *The Economics of Trade Unions* (revised edn). Chicago: University of Chicago Press.

Roethlisberger, F., and Dickson, J.W. (1939). *Management and the Worker*. Boston, MA: Harvard University Press.

Rynes, S., Gilul, T., and Brown, K. (2007). The very separate worlds of academic and practitioner periodicals in human resource management: Implications for evidence-based management. *Academy of Management Journal*, *50*, 987–1008.

Schaede, U. (1995). The "old boy" network and government-business relationships in Japan. *Journal of Japanese Studies*, *21*(2), 293–317.

Subramaniam, M., and Youndt, M. A. (2005). The influence of intellectual capital on the types of innovative capabilities. *Academy of Management Journal*, *48*(3), 450–63.

Takeuchi, H., and Nonaka, I. (1986). The new product development game. *Harvard Business Review*, *64*(1), 137–46.

Taylor, F. W. (1911). *The Principles of Scientific Management*. New York: Harper & Bros.

Teece, D. J. (2007). Explicating dynamic capabilities: The nature and microfoundations of (sustainable) enterprise performance. *Strategic Management Journal*, *28*(13), 1319–50.

Teece, D. J. (2011). Human capital, capabilities and the firm: Literati, numerati, and entrepreneurs in the 21st-century enterprise. In A. Burton-Jones and J.-C. Spender (eds), *The Oxford Handbook of Human Capital*, 527–62. Oxford: Oxford University Press.

Teece, D. J. (2014). The foundations of enterprise performance: Dynamic and ordinary capabilities in an (economic) theory of firms. *Academy of Management Perspectives*, *28*(4), 328–52.

Teece, D. J. (2016). Dynamic capabilities and entrepreneurial management in large organizations: Toward a theory of the (entrepreneurial) firm. *European Economic Review*, *86*, 202–16.

Teece, D. J. (2018a). Dynamic capabilities as (workable) management systems theory. *Journal of Management and Organization*, *24*(3), 359–68.

Teece, D. J. (2018b). Business models and dynamic capabilities. *Long Range Planning*, *51*(1), 40–49.

Teece, D., Peteraf, M., and Leih, S. (2016). Dynamic capabilities and organizational agility: Risk, uncertainty, and strategy in the innovation economy. *California Management Review*, *58*(4), 13–35.

Teece, D. J., Pisano, G., and Shuen, A. (1997). Dynamic capabilities and strategic management. *Strategic Management Journal*, *18*(7), 509–33.

Vroom, V. H. (1964). *Work and Motivation*. New York: Wiley.

Vroom, V. H., and Jago, A. G. (1988). *The New Leadership: Managing Participation in Organizations*. Englewood Cliffs, NJ: Prentice-Hall.

Williamson, O. E. (1991). Strategizing, economizing, and economic organization. *Strategic Management Journal*, *12*(S2), 75–94.

Zaleznik, A. (1989). *The Managerial Mystique: Restoring Leadership in Business*. New York: Harper & Row.

PART IV

COMPLEMENTARITIES: HUMAN AND SOCIAL CAPITAL

12. How employees can better solve customer problems: a use value approach to human and social capital

Shad Morris and Scott Snell

How can employees better identify customers' dissatisfaction and then invent solutions on their behalf? Two key resources employees draw from to solve customer problems are found in the knowledge gained through experience, education (human capital), and affiliatory networks (social capital) (Wright et al., 2001). The ultimate value of these employee-developed solutions is determined by the customers through their willingness to pay. However, the value of the actual knowledge used to identify customer problems and develop corresponding solutions is somewhat unclear. For example, scholars have developed measures to value the human and social capital of an employee (Hatch and Dyer, 2004), but valuing how those accumulated knowledge stocks are actually used in problem identification and solution development adds a level of complexity that has yet to be fully explored (see Morris et al., 2018).

To help determine the value of the knowledge used to solve customer problems, we ask two questions. First, what is the underlying path for building knowledge stocks that enables a firm to create value for its customers? Second, how are these stocks interconnected with the employee in a way that prescribes how valuable knowledge is in the first place, before it reaches the customer? In answering these questions, we introduce a framework that examines the value of specific knowledge stocks for the indivual users themselves. To do this we incorporate a "use value" perspective, where knowledge flows and inefficiencies are seen as benefits and costs, respectively (Bowman and Swart, 2007; Priem, 2007).[1] In this context, flows represent the movement of knowledge by individuals inside a firm. Knowledge stocks represent aggregate levels of human capital (experience and education) and social capital (networks). While often examined at the aggregate level, knowledge stocks are ultimately drawn upon at the individual level in ways that allow employees to invent and deliver customer solutions (Morris et al., 2006; Wright et al., 2014). However, drawing upon these stocks does not come without individual efficiency costs. Such costs can be identified in how much time and money are consumed by emlpoyees in these activities (Davenport, 2005).

A use value perspective helps us look at the utility of resources in relation to how useful they are perceived to be in trying to provide a customer-based solution. Such an understanding might contribute to theoretical discussions trying to link macro-level phenomena, such as firm-level knowledge stocks and performance, with micro-level processes and people (e.g., Coff and Kryscynski, 2011; Nyberg et al., 2014; Ployhart and Moliterno, 2011). From a practical perspective, examining use value in terms of costs and benefits allows firms to predict and align human and social capital stocks to create customer value.

CREATING CUSTOMER VALUE

Value creation for customers is often measured in one of two ways: (1) financial performance of the firm itself, or (2) customer satisfaction. Both measures assume market characteristics in terms of monetary exchange. Because most firms are neither publicly traded nor under any requirement to report profits, most scholars use revenues per employee (R/P) as a proxy for financial performance (e.g., Lorsch and Tierney, 2002). Such measures can then be linked to a firm's aggregate levels of knowledge. For example, Greenwood et al. (2005) found that the benefits of optimizing knowledge transfer between partners and nonpartners led to greater performance—performance being measured as R/P.

On the other hand, customer satisfaction (though rarely used) is seen as a more appropriate alternative for realizing value created by firms. While profits increase a firm's ability to compete and continue to win bids, ultimately the value of services provided by a firm can be determined by the customer. If customers are not satisfied with a firm they may not return or refer others to the firm. Hence, a company can do well financially one year, but be providing poor service. It is not until later when customer resells are down and referrals are low that the company begins to realize that it had not been creating value for the customer. Hence, customer satisfaction is an important measure in understanding how to create value before it is too late. As recommended by Greenwood et al. (2005), including more dynamic models closer to the customer–employee model, will help scholars expand the definition of performance for firms.

Of course, this is no easy task. The measure of value may be different for each customer, creating a challenge in assessing the value of knowledge resources on the firm's performance. Goods and services rendered, for example, can differ in their customization, cultural adaptation, extent to which customers coproduce them, and ambiguity of specification (Whitley, 2006). What adds value for one customer may not do so for another. This is largely because many firms in a knowledge-based economy have outputs that are "*intangible* applications of *complex* knowledge, making it difficult for consumers to weigh the relative competence of suppliers.[2] Customers are thus dependent on the [employees] delivering these services" (Greenwood et al., 2005: 663). Because of the intangibility and complexity of these outputs, it is not enough to examine the knowledge stocks present in a firm (e.g., aggregate levels of experience, education, social networks) and regress those variables on customer satisfaction or performance. We also need to understand the underlying processes and factors that make that knowledge valuable in the first place, before it reaches the customer.

CREATING USE VALUE

Arguing that individuals are the primary locus of value creation, Sirmon, Hitt and Ireland (2007) call for research using a knowledge-based perspective to take into account the underlying processes and people within an organization. Turning to the individual employees inside a firm, we can better understand how knowledge stocks must first and foremost create value for the user (the employee) before they can be transformed into a solution or product that is valuable to the customer. Such a microfoundations

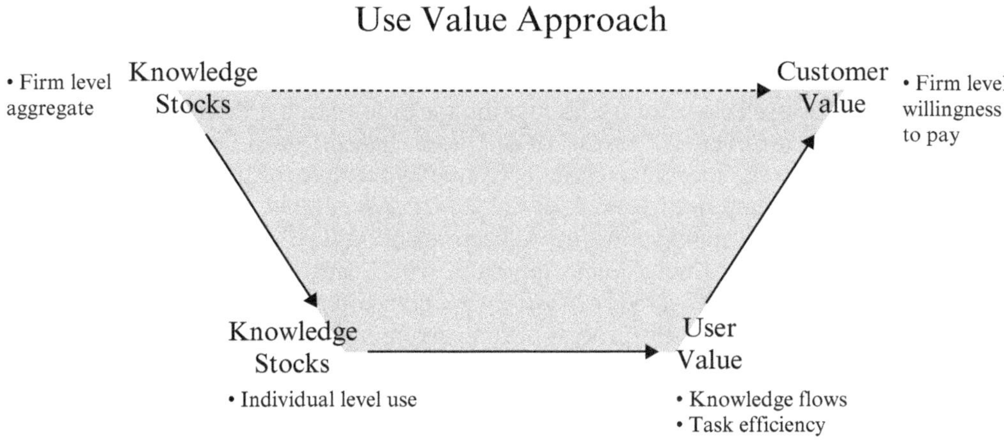

Figure 12.1 Extending the value creation model

approach offers a contingency perspective that allows us to understand the processes of how knowledge is used to create customer value (cf., Morris et al., 2014). For example, a firm may have extensive social networks developed from onboarding programs; but if these networks are not drawn upon extensively by the individuals to help come up with customer solutions, then little value will be created for the customer. Hence, to understand how stocks create customer value, we must first understand how they can be used differently and how the differences in use first create value for the employee at an individual level (see Figure 12.1).

According to Abbott (1988) and Mills and Moberg (1982), much of the knowledge work within firms can be viewed in terms of a process whereby trained experts temporarily come together to draw upon different knowledge stocks or resources that allow them to offer a solution to a customer's problem. Such examples include consulting, accounting, advertising, healthcare, retail, education, technology, engineering, and law firms that must engage with a customer to understand their problem(s) and then develop a solution to that problem. In these settings, the nature of work becomes much more fluid, and oftentimes the proposed path of delivering a solution will change mid-stream, requiring employees to exhaust multiple sources of knowledge (e.g., turning to colleagues in other offices who may have experienced similar customer problems, drawing on personal experience, or even flying people out who have the appropriate background to help with a customer's problem). Because of the knowledge intensity and variability found in knowledge use, such firms provide a rich context for theorizing about how resources create value. As Penrose (1959) explains, "It is never the resources themselves that are the inputs in the production process, only the services that the resources can render" (25). This means that it is more important to look at the usefulness of various stocks to the employees rather than just an aggregate measure of stocks found within the firm. In line with this, Barney (1991) suggests that resources are valuable "when they enable a firm to conceive of or implement strategies that improve its efficiency and effectiveness" (106). In other words, the use of these knowledge stocks should create value by improving the efficiency and effectiveness of employees. This is consistent with resource- and knowledge-based views to say that knowledge stocks have value in relation to their ability to meet users' knowledge flow needs (see Aaker, 1989; Aharoni, 1993; Prahalad and Hamel, 1990, 1994; Williams, 1992). To examine performance from this perspective requires that the value of knowledge be measured closer to the user within the process rather than when the service is rendered to the customer (cf., Arrow, 1974; Glazer, 1998).

Use value refers to the specific qualities perceived by the users of the service or product in relation to what they need (Lepak et al., 2007). As pointed out by Bowman and Ambrosini (2000), such perceptions are subjective and individual-specific. In contrast, much research takes an exchange value approach, which captures the monetary amount realized when a service is delivered to a customer, and is often measured at the firm level. A use value perspective views the process of drawing upon specific knowledge stocks as a labor process that produces value through the knowledge flows needed by the employees; if the resource helps to meet specific needs, then it provides a "benefit" to the employee. But the degree of that benefit is contingent upon the relative "costs" involved in turning to other possible resources that might be more efficient for the person. From the standpoint of value creation, if we conceive of value as the benefits derived over costs incurred, use value presents a suitable framework for analyzing value at the indivual level of a firm.

What this means is that to understand the customer value created by knowledge stocks, we must first understand how the use of those stocks can add more benefit than costs to the individual employees themselves who are responsible for mobilizing knowledge toward providing a solution to a customer problem. Here we see that individuals can actually create value by taking the appropriate steps to create new knowledge, share existing knowledge, and integrate knowledge in order to produce better products and services that can then appropriate value for the firm. Such measures point to the importance of knowledge flows and their antecedents.

KNOWLEDGE FLOWS AND USE VALUE

Earlier, we noted the importance of knowledge flows as a source of internal value creation. Nevertheless, confusion still exists on how to conceptualize and determine the ways that different forms of knowledge flows are linked and simultaneously managed in firms. Kogut and Zander (2003) admit to a lack of understanding of the complex interactions of different forms of knowledge flows. Others argue that more work is needed on these complex relationships and how they are linked (e.g., Brymer et al., 2014). From a problem-solving perspective, knowledge flows represent problem identification and solution development (Nickerson and Zenger, 2004).

The problem-solving process can be divided into two primary phases that follow each other in logical sequence (Abbott, 1988: 35–52). In practice, these two phases may be repeated or iterative. In the first phase, employees search for and obtain information to identify the nature of the customer's problem. In the second phase, the employee searches for and combines knowledge to help develop a solution to the problem.

In the problem identification phase, uncertainty stems from the variability of the problems that must be handled (Daft and Macintosh, 1981; Perrow, 1967). Generally, a person's ability to identify value-creating problems (i.e., problems that provide improved or new market opportunities) depends on the person's ability to understand the local market and link that knowledge with prior experience. During the solution-development phase, employees are likely to reach out to others for help in solving these localized problems (Morris et al., 2015), as well as draw upon experiences.

The greatest barrier to both problem identification and solution development is getting employees to search beyond their existing functions or teams (Rosenkopf and Almeida, 2003). Employees are most likely to turn to their existing knowledge base or those of close network ties—people likely to be part of their local unit or team (McPherson et al., 2001)—whereas effective problem-solving requires interaction with customers and other members of the company outside the local functional team (Abbott, 1988).

The significant component of these two types of knowledge flows is that, while they are interdependent and mutually enabling in the process of providing customer solutions, they are probably distinct enough to be managed separately. Facilitating the different types of knowledge flows may require different levels and kinds of investment. In the next section, we look at how knowledge stocks might influence knowledge flows, and the value in use of supporting certain knowledge stocks toward meeting employees' needs. This means that the value of a firm's knowledge stocks must be assessed by examining how useful they are to employees in terms of both costs and benefits—in other words, how knowledge stocks are "used." This evaluation consists of examining how different knowledge stocks can result in benefits and costs to the flow of knowledge.

KNOWLEDGE STOCKS AND KNOWLEDGE FLOWS

Scholars have noted the importance of the configuration of knowledge stocks (Berry, 2015; Colakoglu et al., 2014; Roper and Hewitt-Dundas, 2015; Yang et al., 2015), and previous research has identified two that are most critical: human capital and social capital (Kang et al., 2007). While specific context will influence the value in use of stocks on different types of knowledge flows, what do existing theories tell us about how knowledge stocks might create benefits and costs? How should these benefits and costs be examined when firm-level outputs are difficult or inapropriate to measure? At what level should these relationships be examined? And how can they be understood from an individual management perspective?

Some researchers have found that strong levels of local market savvy and experience with customers helps in a person's quest to identify customer problems, but the benefits of local market knowledge may not be as great for solving customer problems as it is for identifying them (Morris et al., 2018) (see Figure 12.2). Likewise, when people reach out to distant knowledge networks, they are more likely to come up with beneficial solutions to solve customer problems; but if they rely upon these same types of networks to identify customer problems, then the coordination costs go up.

Below, we present a framework to help understand how the use of human and social capital stocks will lead to differences in value created for employees as they try to solve problems for customers. Such a framework helps to further the knowledge stock and flow research while offering valuable insight on how a firm might more effectively manage its people.

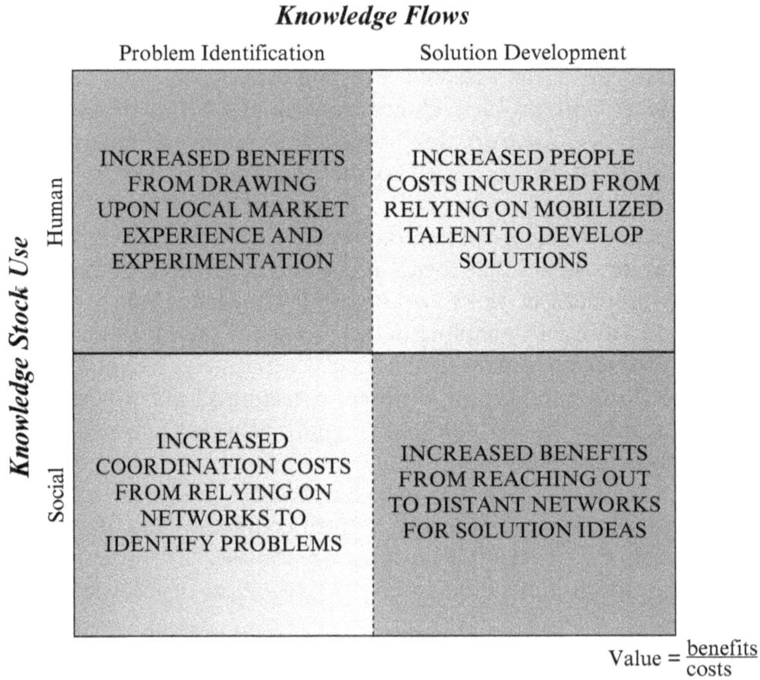

Figure 12.2 Knowledge stocks and flows

Human Capital

Human capital is often defined in terms of the aggregated knowledge, skills, and experience of individuals within the organization, with experience being the key predictor in human capital theory (Becker, 1967: 94–117; Ployhart and Moliterno, 2011). It is often manifested in past experience and formal training. Human capital plays a strong role as the firm's key resource in solving customer problems. We discuss how human capital is perceived in terms of value to meet individual problem-solving needs on the basis of the type of knowledge flow that is most important.

Problem identificiation

Researchers such as Argyris and Schön (1978) and Grant (2001) point out that organizations themselves do not create or produce knowledge—people do. The basic assumption is that ideas new to the firm come from individuals who possess education, skills, and experience—not organizations (Nonaka and Takeuchi, 1995; Simon, 1991). Identifying customer problems is often seen to require experience, experimentation, and reflection by the individual members (Argyris and Schön, 1978; Leonard-Barton, 1995; Snell et al., 1996). Some of these ideas in response to the environment may not be new per se, but they can be considered new for the firm. That is why researchers such as Luo and Peng (1999), March (1991), and Moorman and Miner (1998) claim that exposure to the external environment stimulates the identificiation of relevant problems by individual employees.

In particular, drawing from local market experience, experimentation, and reflection are often seen as key forces that might help employees identify unique problems to be solved.

Employees possessing large amounts of experience, education, and training should be able to effectively create ideas on their own in response to the complexities of unique customer needs. This localized experience helps them understand the needs of local customers and markets, which allows them to develop solutions that are unique to each contextual environment and hence heterogeneous across the firm. Likewise, creative intuition allows them to uniquely frame challenges to identify challenges customers didn't yet know they had. Firms that draw upon human capital tend to rely on the experimentation, inspiration, and experience of individuals to identify a problem.

In identifying customer problems, human capital probably will be a more beneficial resource than reliance upon information from others inside the firm. It is the individual's creative license that allows for more creative thinking and for thinking what is different from what has occurred in the firm so far. The "costs" of such activities are also likely to be lower than if the company were to spend time turning to social networks. The transaction costs in terms of time and money associated with interacting with others and interfacing with technology and processes tend to be greater than those generated by people cognitively identifying problems. By turning to human capital, the firm is required to manage fewer resources or points of information.

Solution development

As pointed out by Morris and colleagues (2018), solution development focuses on the relationships of people, such as across geographical locations or reporting managers, rather than on the human capital attributes of the people themselves. But human capital can also be employed as a resource for developing customer solutions (Skaggs and Youndt, 2004). For example, many firms depend on rotation programs, exchanges, and deployments to move knowledge around the firm that in a way that helps the firm draw upon multiple experiences that can help solve a customer problem (Hatch and Dyer, 2004). Such methods might prove "beneficial" in terms of ensuring that solution ideas come from one part of the organization to another. The level of contextual complexity that is transferred is high, as the individuals bring all their experience and knowledge with them.

While using human capital to share knowledge can be beneficial, it is probably not very "cost"-effective. Depending on individuals' experiences for developing customer solutions means that people must be mobilized to get the knowledge from one place to another. If a firm is in the stage of a project where getting knowledge from other parts of the firm is crucial, relying on human capital to leverage it may require that people be moved to the project to make their contributions, leading to travel and living expenses, time away from their own jobs, and so on. While this is a contextually rich way to develop innovative solutions to customer problems, it is very costly in comparison to social capital. As a result, when solution development is most important, human capital's value to the firm most likely decreases.

Of all the resources drawn upon in firms, human capital is probably the one most used. This is good when the group is working on a particular phase of the project where problem identification is most important. However, overdependence on human capital for other necessary knowledge flows, such as solution development, may be more of a cost than a benefit to the firm, in which case the value of this resource is likely to decrease.

Social Capital

Social capital is the knowledge embedded within, available through, and derived from social networks (Coleman, 2000). Kang and colleagues (2007) pointed out the importance of combining social capital with our understanding of human capital used by firms. In particular, they examined how an employee drawing on social capital might benefit the firm in terms of knowledge exploration and exploitation. Moreover, Adler and Kwon (2002) found that social capital can be beneficial for certain activities and detrimental for others. Below, we explore how social capital can either enhance or diminish value in the problem-solving activities of employees.

Problem identification

Nickerson et al. (2007) argue that problem search is often created through interactions among and between individuals and their environment. While Hansen (2002) maintains that social networks provide an important conduit for solution development, he also contends that such networks contribute to problem identification because they inform network members about the existence, location, and significance of customer dissatisfaction. Burt (1982) found that networks comprising a broader range of contacts are able to draw from a more heterogeneous base of information and knowledge. Though such contacts may not always facilitate a deep understanding of customer problems, they offer different reference points for employees to make comparisons and explore new ideas related to what might be making customers unsatisfied.

A firm's ability to identify problems is likely to be a function of multiple local contacts. Employees often have critical links with local businesses, governments, and customers that allow them to identify local opportunities (Bartlett and Ghoshal, 1989; Hedlund, 1986). Birkinshaw (1997) refers to these as relationships within the "local market." In that setting, an employee is likely to be embedded in different types of relationships (Ghoshal and Bartlett, 1990). McEvily and Zaheer (1999) argue that, because each part of the firm maintains different local patterns of network linkages, the firm is exposed to new problems and opportunities.

Despite being time- and resource-demanding, local contacts act as creative inputs in the problem identification process. However, the high "benefits" of social capital may be offset by high "costs" that come from maintaining multiple relationships. If social capital is based on internal contacts, there is the same risk of incurring high costs from managing multiple relationships, but without the associated benefits. Problem identification is likely to be hindered by internal contacts, as they may create overdependence on social interactions with similar others inside the firm. Such examples are given by Granovetter (1984) and by Hansen (1999), with both arguing that people in a close internal network who are more likely to interact frequently with just a few others may be stuck with similar opportunities that do not allow for the identification of customer opportunities. Similarly, Uzzi (1997) asserts that companies that interact only with similar others (e.g., internal employee members) can become mired in existing ways of seeing things. Part of the reasoning behind this is that, as employees continually turn to similar sources of knowledge, they will be less likely to have access to or contact with different problem sets from customers, thereby driving benefits down and costs up.

Solution development

In a study with multiple Fortune 500 firms, Morris and colleagues (2018) found that when trying to come up with solutions to customer problems, more beneficial solutions came from individuals who would reach out to others both outside and inside the firm. However, they found that the types of knowledge most beneficial were more complex forms of "know-how." Transferring this knowledge requires, first and foremost, social capital. Szulanski (1995) found that one of the biggest obstacles to sharing knowledge in firms is the poor relationship between sources and recipients of information. Ghoshal et al. (1994) also showed the importance of social interactions consisting of both subsidiary-headquarters and intersubsidiary communication in knowledge sharing.

Drawing upon social capital to develop solutions would likely be most beneficial in terms of providing deeper knowledge to solve complex and context-specific problems. Part of the reason is that, through personal contact, two-way or double-loop learning can occur (Argyris and Schön, 1978) whereby a series of feedback loops can be achieved as complex ideas and problems are discussed. The "benefits" of this type of interaction within a firm are greater than those obtained by relying on single-loop processes and systems found in databases, routines, and templates. In terms of cost, turning to people for knowledge that has a much higher likelihood of being useful is potentially more efficient than wasting time with insufficient resources, such as past experience or experimentation.

When employees are reaching out to others for help to solve customer problems, they uncover principles that allow them to combine dispersed knowledge and insight to create a unique solution for the problem. Baden-Fuller and Winter (2007) point out that principles tell *why* operations function how they do, enabling knowledge users to apply their understanding of causal relationships to new contexts and situations. Principles prioritize rationales for institutional operations, leaving the finer details to the individual user (e.g., Baden-Fuller and Winter, 2007; Eisenhardt et al., 2010; Sutter et al., 2014). When reaching out, an employee might draw upon experiential stories from other employees providing the knowledge. For example, an employee reaching out to another distant employee might ask for an explanation of why what he or she did in his or her own project worked or did not work. The story would explain the unique context they were in, while conveying underlying rules or principles behind decisions. These stories do not tell someone the specific steps that need to be taken, but rather prioritize rationales for institutional operations, leaving the finer details to the individual user.

In summary, by examining how knowledge stocks are used by individuals to facilitate different phases of the problem-solving process, we can better understand how value is created within the firm. Some stocks are more useful, depending on the type of flow needed, and ironically, some that enhance one type of flow might hinder another.

DISCUSSION

This framework offers a contingency perspective allowing us to better understand the value of knowledge for the user, the employee. As we understand the microprocesses underlying macro-level phenomena, this framework not only offers greater insight for researchers, but also expands existing research using resource- and knowledge-based views of the firm, which tend not to take into account process contingencies at the micro level. Because the overarching customer value creation process in a firm has been shown to consist of multiple interrelated but distinct forms, it is important to understand the relative value of specific knowledge stocks on each type of knowledge flow for the employees themselves. A particular knowledge stock may help, hinder, or offer no value to employees, depending upon their specific problem-solving needs. Such value is realized through the actual use of knowledge by employees in solving customer problems. This theoretical discussion carries implications for both practical applications for today and future research for tomorrow.

Implications

The goal of this chapter was to facilitate a better understanding of how to valuate human and social capital before it reaches the customer. The implications are quite consequential. If managers are not able to determine the value of employees' activities, they will not know how to generate superior use value. They may inadvertently change something that is critical or be unable to respond to poorly used resources. Through downsizing, restructuring, and shifting strategies, they may eliminate some effective resource channels or incentivize incorrect behaviors. Conversely, managers who understand the value of different knowledge resources to employees will be better equipped to invest in practices that will enable them to offer more unique solutions to customers. Understanding how to value knowledge resources during the problem-solving process can also lead to better customer solutions. While a firm can measure the value of the knowledge once it has been exchanged with a customer, only through measuring knowledge-use interactions with employees can we understand where to make resource changes in the process.

To shed light on this process, this human and social capital framework helps firms understand how they might facilitate different forms of learning on the basis of their specific customer needs. Such a framework will be useful to both academics and practitioners in helping them to develop a better understanding of the costs and benefits of different human and social capital investments according to the learning needs presented to employees. When firms are confronted with novel problems that present a great deal of uncertainty and there is a need for problem-solving, the framework could help them identify which resources to invest in as well as the potential costs and benefits involved in their use.

Another implication of this chapter has to do with the area of use value for knowledge resources. Traditional cost/benefit analysis is an important technique for project appraisal, involving the weighing of costs against benefits for one or more actions in order to choose the best or most profitable option. It is often used to assess the value of activities that are more difficult to express in financial or monetary terms. Inevitably, the benefits and costs that are identified are quite subjective (Brealey and Myers, 2003). Therefore, it is optimal to capture value measures from those who best understand the knowledge being delivered—the employees (Glazer, 1998).

Discussions of use value have purported that, when considering the value of resources, it is best to determine the benefits of those resources to the consumer. Typically, such value is measured by how much the consumer is willing to pay for the resource. In the case of most firms, the initial consumer of knowledge resources is the employee, who decides which resources to draw upon to solve a problem (Adler and Posner, 2006: 24–76;

Maister, 1993). Hence, the employee becomes the most informed source for determining knowledge resource benefit (Glazer, 1998). Because of the complexity and uniqueness of each individual project, it is the worker, and only the worker, who knows exactly how beneficial a resource will be to a project. Costs, on the other hand, can be calculated by individuals or measures removed or partially removed from the employee. Part of the reason is that employees may show some bias in how they represent costs. For example, drawing upon a particular network may require little effort in terms of cost but exact a high efficiency cost from the organization. The reverse is not true; if drawing on a resource is extremely time-consuming and costly for the worker, it will also be costly for the organization in terms of labor.

Most current thinking about how employee activities should be structured to meet the demands of customers seems to center mainly on knowledge workers and the creation of so-called knowledge organizations. A challenge in this effort is how to make the knowledge work process more effective. As stated by McGee (2003):

> The fatal flaw in thinking in terms of knowledge management is in adopting the perspective of the organization as the relevant beneficiary. Discussions of knowledge management start from the premise that the organization is not realizing full value from the knowledge of its employees. While likely true, this fails to address the much more important question from a knowledge worker's perspective of "what's in it for me?"

It may be more useful to turn our attention from the resources of the firm to those of the employee.

The main factor in improving how work is done is to improve how employees solve customers' problems. Taking a look around at today's firms, it is apparent that this is not as easy as it sounds. A key problem with this value proposition has to do with how one determines the value that comes from better-managed human and social capital. How do you measure the value of people accessing their personal experience and training? How do you know if the knowledge benefit received from an internal network will exceed the costs incurred? And how can you determine whether the time it takes to access a database will be worth the benefit to your project as well as the firm? The framework presented will allow firms and scholars to better understand how such situations might be handled with greater value added.

However, the reality is that sometimes these investments in human and social capital have long lead times. Rapid responses are often infeasible. Hence, we also suggest using this framework to analyze a FIRM's performance in light of a) where previous investments and capabilities are made, and b) the type of customers with which the firm engages. Given that framing, a FIRM could decide to make changes in its various capital investment levels to alter future capital; alternatively, it could change the types of customers or projects it services.

Future Research

While the purpose of this chapter is to theoretically discuss how knowledge resources create differences in value for employees, it should also consider how future research might test this framework. Building upon work by King and Zeithaml (2003), an approach specifically geared to studies measuring firm knowledge from a resource-based perspective is proposed. These steps are not only useful for scholars in improving knowledge valuation research; they have practical implications in terms of how firms might better measure the value of their knowledge management activities.

Porac et al. (1995) noted that, when conducting research on knowledge, it is important to first define the boundaries of the industry being studied. Establishing a context with defined boundaries helps reduce potential confounding variables that arise when an industry's dynamics are influenced by diverse configurations of knowledge. This control increases the likelihood of identifying a relatively comprehensive inventory of knowledge stocks or flows. Therefore, ensuring that managers in firms are able to evaluate their perceptions of resources is important. To identify an inventory of organizational knowledge resources, King and Zeithaml (2003) recommend that leaders of firms be interviewed. This method of qualitative data collection should be employed because it allows for the delineation and isolation of some essential qualities of complex social phenomena (Langley, 1999; Dougherty, 2002).

Another factor to consider in testing this framework is how we measure use value. According to Hunt (1995), use value "depends on (a) the tastes and preferences of consumers in the segment and (b) the resources that produce the offering." This means that use value for knowledge is determined by the resources drawn upon by project leaders and by how much their knowledge needs are met. Surveying employees on how useful or "beneficial" the specific resources are in meeting their customer needs could help determine use value.

To understand the "costs" involved in using these resources, the impact that they have on a project in terms of efficiency of time, money, and talent must also be measured. Taking a qualitative approach to understand the behavioral and cognitive dimensions of knowledge stocks and flows in firms could be useful since the relationships between stocks and flows is complex, deep, and historical, and hence difficult to operationalize or capture with archival data (Godfrey and Hill, 1995). An example of the challenges posed by archival data is found in patent and citation counts, which are restricted in industries that are technology- or science-based. Such counts do not address the wide disparity in the usefulness of patents or the different stances that firms take in their degree of aggressiveness toward patenting (Spender and Grant, 1996; DeCarolis and Deeds, 1999).

CONCLUSION

Knowledge stocks present a key source of value for employees. This value is realized in the solutions provided to customers. But something as intangible as knowledge can be a major source of misunderstanding and mismanagement, especially where knowledge activities are the main source of value creation for customers. The knowledge stock and flow framework in this chapter explores the underlying path of how knowledge stocks create customer value. This path required that we examine the microprocesses of how knowledge stocks are used by individuals for knowledge flow needs. For employees, this activity consists of examining how different knowledge stocks can result in benefits and costs to knowledge flows, before a solution is delivered to the customer.

CHAPTER SUMMARY

BOX 12.1 LESSONS LEARNED FROM A USE VALUE APPROACH

Lesson #1	A use value perspective helps examine the utility of resources in relation to how useful they are perceived to be in providing customer solutions.
Lesson #2	Linking macro-level phenomena such as firm-level knowledge stocks and performance with micro-level processes and people can help firms to more effectively solve customer problems.
Lesson #3	Examining use value in terms of costs and benefits allows firms to predict and align human and social capital stocks to create customer value.

BOX 12.2 FUTURE RESEARCH TIPS

Tip #1	When studying human and social capital, scholars should first define the boundaries of the industry being studied. Establishing a context with defined boundaries helps reduce potential confounding variables that arise when an industry's dynamics are influenced by diverse configurations of knowledge. This control increases the likelihood of identifying a relatively comprehensive inventory of knowledge stocks or flows.
Tip #2	When studying human and social capital as it relates to value creation, scholars should not only examine exchange value; they should also examine use value. Use value for knowledge is determined by the resources drawn upon by project leaders and by how much their knowledge needs are met. Surveying employees on how useful or "beneficial" the specific resources are in meeting their customer needs could help determine use value.
Tip #3	When studying human and social capital it is important to consider the costs of these resources, and not just the benefits. To understand the "costs" involved in using these resources, the impact that they have on a project in terms of efficiency of time, money, and talent must also be measured.

NOTES

1. Traditionally, organizations use "exchange value" to determine the value of their knowledge stocks on the basis of whether the attainment costs are less than the benefits generated in terms of market value achieved. This is a typical value capture model for assessing the impact of intangible assets (cf., Arrow, 1974). However, this model fails to examine how different stock investments might lead to different flows depending upon the knowledge flow needs of the workers themselves.
2. While a large part of knowledge-based work is standardized and routine, customers rely on firms to deliver solutions to their unique problems—giving unique aspects to most customer solutions.

REFERENCES

Aaker, D. (1989). *Strategic Marketing Management*. New York: Wiley.

Abbott, A. (1988). *The System of Professions: An Essay on the Division of Expert Labor*. Chicago: University of Chicago Press.

Adler, M. D., and Posner, E. A. (2006). *New Foundations of Cost–Benefit Analysis*. Cambridge, MA: Harvard University Press.
Adler, P. S., and Kwon, S. W. (2002). Social capital: Prospects for a new concept. *Academy of Management Review*, *27*(1): 17–40.
Aharoni, Y. (1993). Globalization of professional business services. In Y. Aharoni (ed.), *Coalitions and Competition: The Globalization of Professional Business Services*, 1–19. London: Routledge.
Argyris, C., and Schön, D. (1978). *Organizational Learning*. Reading, MA: Addison-Wesley.
Arrow, K. J. (1974). Limited knowledge and economic analysis. *American Economic Review*, *64*(1), 1–10.
Baden-Fuller, C., and Winter, S. (2007). Replicating knowledge practices: Principles or templates? Working Paper, Cass Business School, City University, London.
Barney, J. B. (1991). Firm resources and sustained competitive advantage. *Journal of Management*, *17*(1), 99–120.
Bartlett, C., and Ghoshal, S. (1989). *Managing Across Borders: The Transnational Solution*. London: Hutchinson Business Books.
Becker, G. S. (1967). *Human Capital and the Personal Distribution of Income*. Ann Arbor: University of Michigan Press, 1975.
Berry, H. (2015). Knowledge inheritance in global industries: The impact of parent firm knowledge on the performance of foreign subsidiaries. *Academy of Management Journal*, *58*(5), 1438–58.
Birkinshaw, J. (1997). Entrepreneurship in multinational corporations: The characteristics of subsidiary indicatives. *Strategic Management Journal*, *18*(3), 207–29.
Bowman, C., and Ambrosini, V. (2000). Value creation versus value capture: Towards a coherent definition of value in strategy. *British Journal of Management*, *11*, 1–15.
Bowman, C., and Swart, J. (2007). Whose human capital? The challenge of value capture when capital is embedded. *Journal of Management Studies*, *44*(4), 488–505.
Brealey, R. A., and Myers, S. C. (2003). *Principles of Corporate Finance*. Seventh edn. Boston, MA: McGraw-Hill/Irwin.
Brymer, R.A., Molloy, J.C., and Gilbert, B.A. (2014). Human capital pipelines: Competitive implications of repeated interorganizational hiring. *Journal of Management*, *40*(2), 483–508.
Burt, R. S. (1982). *Toward a Structural Theory of Action*. New York: Academic Press.
Coff, R., and Kryscynski, D. (2011). Drilling for micro-foundations of human capital-based advantages. *Journal of Management*, *37*, 1299–315.
Colakoglu, S., Yamao, S., and Lepak, D. P. (2014). Knowledge creation capability in MNC subsidiaries: Examining the roles of global and local knowledge inflows and subsidiary knowledge stocks. *International Business Review*, *23*(1), 91–101.
Coleman, J. S. (2000). Biases of social policy and consequences of micro-macro problems. In R. Boudon and M. Cherkaoui (eds), *Central Currents in Social Theory*, 8–257. London: Sage.
Daft, R. L., and Macintosh, N. B. (1981). A tentative exploration into the amount and equivocality of information processing in organizational work units. *Administrative Science Quarterly*, *26*(2), 207–24.
Davenport, T. H. (2005). *Thinking for a Living: How to Get Better Performance and Results from Knowledge Workers*. Boston: Harvard Business School Press.
DeCarolis, D. M., and Deeds, D. L. (1999). The impact of stocks and flows of organizational knowledge on firm performance: An empirical investigation of the biotechnology industry. *Strategic Management Journal*, *20*, 981–68.
Dougherty, D. (2002). *Grounded Theory Research Methods*. Oxford: Blackwell.
Eisenhardt, K. M., Furr, N. R., and Bingham, C. B. (2010). Crossroads—microfoundations of performance: Balancing efficiency and flexibility in dynamic environments. *Organization Science*, *21*(6), 1263–73.
Ghoshal, S., and Bartlett, C. A. (1990). The multinational corporation as an interorganizational network. *Academy of Management Review*, *15*(4), 603–25.
Ghoshal, S., Korine, H., and Szulanski, G. (1994). Interunit communication in multinational corporations. *Management Science*, *40*, 96–110.
Glazer, R. (1998). Measuring the knower: Toward a theory of knowledge equity. *California Management Review*, *40*(3), 175–94.
Godfrey, P. C., and Hill, C. W. (1995). The problem of unobservables in strategic management research. *Strategic Management Journal*, *16*, 519–33.
Granovetter, M. (1984). Small is bountiful: Labor markets and establishment size. *American Sociological Review*, *49*(3), 323–34.
Grant, R. M. (2001). New directions in strategic management. *Business Strategy Review*, *12*(1), 61–7.
Greenwood, R., Li, S. X., Prakash, R., and Deephouse, D. L. (2005). Reputation, diversification, and organizatinal explanations of performance in employee service firms. *Organization Science*, *16*(6), 661–73.
Hansen, M. T. (1999). The search-transfer problem: The role of weak ties in sharing knowledge across organization subunits. *Administrative Science Quarterly*, *44*(1), 82–111.

Hansen, M. T. (2002). Knowledge networks: Explaining effective knowledge sharing in multiunit companies. *Organization Science*, *13*(3), 232–48.
Hatch, N. W., and Dyer, J. H. (2004). Human capital and learning as a source of sustainable competitive advantage. *Strategic Management Journal*, *25*(12), 1155–78.
Hedlund, G. (1986). The hypermodel MNC: A heterarchy? *Human Resource Management Journal*, *25*(1), 9–35.
Hunt, S. D. (1995). The resource-advantage theory of competition towards explaining productivity and economic growth. *Journal of Management Inquiry*, *4*(4), 317–32.
Kang, S. K., Morris, S. S., and Snell, S. A. (2007). Relational archetypes, organizational learning, and value creation: Extending the human resource architecture. *Academy of Management Review*, *32*(1), 236–56.
King, A. W., and Zeithaml, C. P. (2003). Measuring organizational knowledge: A conceptual and methodological framework. *Strategic Management Journal*, *24*(8), 763–72.
Kogut, B., and Zander, U. (2003). Knowledge of the firm and the evolutionary theory of the multinational corporation. *Journal of International Business Studies*, *34*(6), 516–29.
Langley, A. (1999). Strategies for theorizing from process data. *Academy of Management Review*, *24*, 691–710.
Leonard-Barton, D. (1995). *Wellsprings of Knowledge: Building and Sustaining the Sources of Innovation*. Boston: Harvard Business School Press.
Lepak, D. P., Smith, K. G., and Taylor, M. S. (2007). Value creation and value capture: A multilevel perspective. *Academy of Management Review*, *32*(1), 180–94.
Lorsch, J. W., and Tierney, T. J. (2002). *Aligning the Stars: How to Succeed when Professionals Drive Results*. Boston: Harvard Business School Press.
Luo, Y., and Peng, M. W. (1999). Learning to compete in a transition economy: Experience, environment, and performance. *Journal of International Business Studies*, *30*, 269–96.
Maister, D. H. (1993). *Managing the Employee Service Firm*. New York: Free Press.
March, J. G. (1991). Exploration and exploitation in organizational learning. *Organization Science*, *2*(1), 71–87.
McEvily, B., and Zaheer, A. (1999). Bridging ties: A source of firm heterogeneity in competitive capabilities. *Strategic Management Journal*, *20*(12), 1133–56.
McGee, J. (2003). From managing knowledge to coaching knowledge employees. Available from http://www.mcgeesmusings.net/2003/08/19.html.
McPherson, M., Smith-Lovin, L., and Cook, J. M. (2001). Birds of a feather: Homophily in social networks. *Annual Review of Sociology*, *27*(1), 415–44.
Mills, P. K., and Moberg, D. J. (1982). Perspectives on the technology of service operations. *Academy of Management Review*, *7*(3), 467–78.
Moorman, C., and Miner, A. S. (1998). Organizational improvisation and organizational memory. *Academy of Management Review*, *23*, 698–724.
Morris, S., Hammond, R., and Snell, S. (2014). A microfoundations approach to transnational capabilities: The role of knowledge search in an ever-changing world. *Journal of International Business Studies*, *45*(4), 405–27.
Morris, S. S., Snell, S. A., and Wright, P.M. (2006). A resource-based view of international human resources: Toward a framework of integrative and creative capabilities. In G. K. Stahl and I. Björkman (eds), *Handbook of Research in International Human Resource Management*, 433–48. Cheltenham, UK and Northampton, MA, USA: Edward Elgar Publishing.
Morris, S. S., Zhong, B., and Makhija, M. (2015). Going the distance: The pros and cons of expanding employees' global knowledge reach. *Journal of International Business Studies*, *46*(5), 552–73.
Morris, S., Oldroyd, J., Allen, R., Chng, D., and Han, J. (2018). Individual paths of exploratory and exploitative innovation in and emerging economy. Working Paper, Brigham Young University, Global Management Center, Provo, USA.
Nickerson, J. A., and Zenger, T. R. (2004). A knowledge-based theory of the firm: The problem-solving perspective. *Organization Science*, *15*(6), 617–32.
Nickerson, J. A., Silverman, B. S., and Zenger, T. R. (2007). The "problem" of creating and capturing value. *Strategic Organization*, *5*(3), 211–25.
Nonaka, I., and Takeuchi, H. (1995). *The Knowledge Creating Company: How Japanese Companies Create the Dynamics of Innovation*. New York: Oxford University Press.
Nyberg, A. J., Moliterno, T. P., Hale Jr, D., and Lepak, D. P. (2014). Resource-based perspectives on unit-level human capital: A review and integration. *Journal of Management*, *40*(1), 316–46.
Penrose, E. T. (1959). *The Theory of the Growth of the Firm*. White Plains, NY: Sharpe.
Perrow, C. (1967). A framework for the comparative analysis of organizations. *American Sociological Review*, *32*(2), 194–208.
Ployhart, R. E., and Moliterno, T. P. (2011). Emergence of the human capital resource: A multilevel model. *Academy of Management Review*, *36*(1), 127–50.
Porac, J. F., Thomas, H., Wilson, F., Paton, D., and Kanfer, A. (1995). Rivalry and the industry model of Scottish knitwear producers. *Administrative Science Quarterly*, *40*(2), 203–27.

Prahalad, C. K., and Hamel, G. (1990). The core competence of the corporation. *Harvard Business Review*, *68*(3), 79–91.
Prahalad, C. K., and Hamel, G. (1994). Competing for the future. *Harvard Business Review*, *72*(4), 122–9.
Priem, R. L. (2007). A consumer perspective on value creation. *Academy of Management Review*, *32*(1), 219–35.
Roper, S., and Hewitt-Dundas, N. (2015). Knowledge stocks, knowledge flows and innovation: Evidence from matched patents and innovation panel data. *Research Policy*, *44*(7), 1327–40.
Rosenkopf, L., and Almeida, P. (2003). Overcoming local search through alliances and mobility. *Management science*, *49*(6), 751–66.
Simon, H. A. (1991). Bounded rationality and organizational learning. *Organization Science*, *2*, 125–34.
Sirmon, D. G., Hitt, M. A., and Ireland, R. D. (2007). Managing firm resources in dynamic environments to create value: Looking inside the black box. *Academy of Management Review*, *32*(1), 273–92.
Skaggs, B. C., and Youndt, M. (2004). Strategic positioning, human capital, and performance in service organizations: A customer interaction approach. *Strategic Management Journal*, *25*(1), 85–99.
Snell, S. A., Youndt, M. A., and Wright, P. (1996). Establishing a framework for research in strategic human resource management. *Human Resource Management*, *14*, 61–90.
Spender, J.-C., and Grant, R. M. (1996). Knowledge and the firm: Overview. *Strategic Management Journal*, *17*, 5–10.
Sutter, C. J., Kistruck, G. M., and Morris, S. (2014). Adaptations to knowledge templates in base-of-the-pyramid markets: The role of social interaction. *Strategic Entrepreneurship Journal*, *8*(4), 303–20.
Szulanski, G. (1995). Unpacking stickiness: An empirical investigation of the barriers to transfer best practices inside the firm. *Academy of Management Journal*, *1*, 437–42.
Uzzi, B. (1997). Social structure and competition in interfirm networks: The paradox of embeddedness. *Administrative Science Quarterly*, *42*(1), 35–67.
Whitley, R. (2006). Project-based firms: New organizational form or variations on a theme? *Industrial and Corporate Change*, *15*(1), 77–99.
Williams, J. R. (1992). How sustainable is your competitive advantage? *California Management Review*, *34*(3), 29–52.
Wright, P. M., Coff, R., and Moliterno, T. P. (2014). Strategic human capital: Crossing the great divide. *Journal of Management*, *40*(2), 353–70.
Wright, P. M., Dunford, B. B., and Snell, S. A. (2001). Human resources and the resource-based view of the firm. *Journal of Management*, *27*(6), 701–21.

13. Social capital and human capital co-emergence: a socialized view of emergent human capital resources

Alia Crocker

INTRODUCTION

Granovetter made a theoretical observation that may now seem obvious, when he noted that, "Actors do not behave or decide as atoms outside a social context, nor do they adhere slavishly to a script written for them by the particular intersection of social categories that they happen to occupy" (1985: 487). However, this observation on individual actions as related to larger social systems has profound implications for our current understanding of human capital resources (HCRs). Namely, unit outcomes based in HCRs inherently require the consideration of social relations and context.[1] Indeed, human capital scholars have argued for, and started to take, "a more socialized view of human capital" (Wright et al., 2014: 14). Value from human capital is likely derived from individual and firm combinations, with many human capital-based outcomes related to social factors (Coff and Kryscynski, 2011; Hollenbeck and Jamieson, 2015; Tzabbar et al., 2008). Social capital and human capital share common challenges in value appropriation in that the firm does not fully own these resources and there is an inherent uncertainty with respect to tacit nature, motivation, and time horizons (Coff, 1997; Adler and Kwon, 2002). To this end, various research on unit-level complementarities, high-performing individuals in context, and collective emergence have started to expand our understanding of the social aspects of human capital-based advantages (Campbell et al., 2012; Crocker and Eckardt, 2014; Oldroyd and Morris, 2012; Ployhart and Moliterno, 2011).

However, little attention has been given to how the interconnections between human and social capital transcend levels of analysis or relate to the broader notion of human capital resource emergence (HCRE). Scholars have long accepted that an individual's experiences in social contexts (e.g., community, school, work organizations) shape knowledge, skills, abilities, and other characteristics (KSAOs) (Becker, 1964). Not surprisingly, then, researchers have called for scholarship that examines how the social interactions that occur in those settings shape those KSAOs (Nyberg et al., 2014; Wright et al., 2014; Soltis et al., 2018). Consideration of the social elements of human capital-based advantages aligns with ideas surrounding emergence of multilevel HCRs (Ployhart and Moliterno, 2011; Ployhart et al., 2014), and has implications for other questions central to human capital research. What is the source of a synergistic productive capability observed in a unit-level HCR (uHCR)? How traceable is complementarity among resources? What parts of HCRE and outcomes are firm-specific? Who appropriates the created value in a unit-specific context? Furthermore, how might being a part of a specific unit shape future value capture beyond the immediate context? All of these questions are informed by taking a more socialized understanding of HCRE.

In this chapter, I take an expanded perspective on these questions by developing an integrated view of human and social capital at multiple levels to describe aspects that are critical to valuable uHCRs. I argue that social capital is embedded in the emergence of a uHCR. This entails not only the creation of collective social capital in the emergent resource internal to the firm, but also social capital linking each individual unit member to external resources (Adler and Kwon, 2002; Payne et al., 2011). I further explain that although social capital and human capital are distinct concepts, the complexity associated with identifying the boundary where one ends and the other begins increases when taking a multilevel view, and note that much confusion can come from not considering the source and flow of these resources. The HCR coexists with, and is shaped by, the social capital that exists in the unit among members as well as individual member-sourced external social capital. To this end, I unpack several aspects that influence the combined co-emergent resource: task interdependence, time sequence, complements, substitutes, and mobility. These factors are in some ways opaque in that value is captured from the combined coexistence of human and social capital across multiple levels. Understanding these sub-processes can help alleviate some of the challenges in disentangling specific points of valuable interaction or sources of value in a co-emergent human and social capital resource.

In developing this socialized view of HCRs, I follow Ployhart and Moliterno (2011) and Ployhart et al. (2014) in defining the HCR as a multilevel construct, based on an individual's KSAOs, and comprising both individual and unit-level manifestations. Further, I follow established definitions that social capital is the access to resources through relationships (Lin, 2001), which is a source of information and opportunities (Burt, 1997) in addition to a basis for shared norms and expectations (Coleman, 1988). My model also builds on Chadwick's (2017) emphasis on the importance of human capital-related resources and capabilities in firm value creation and capture. Building on this view, social capital is an essential human capital-related resource in that it is a critically important driver of firm value founded on HCRs. Integrating these perspectives provides support for exploring a socialized view of the firm-specificity of emergent HCRs, the value they create, and the appropriation of that value over time.

In what follows, I build on extant theory to explore a recursive model whereby the social capital that inheres in uHCRs both shapes and is shaped by the individual HCRs (iHCRs) it comprises. That is, there is ongoing, shared influence from both human and social capital at multiple points in the emergence process that relates to outcomes. Essential to this recursive model is the notion that human and social capital often have reciprocal associations that flow not just across levels, but across contexts. Exploring this model helps us understand how the "ongoing systems of social relations" mentioned by Granovetter (1985) relate to our studies of strategic human capital. As such, I explain the co-emergence of human and social capital in the unit-level resource. In doing so, it becomes apparent that there are multiple sub-processes that have the potential to influence the unit-specific co-emergence process and have impact on longer term outcomes for the individuals as well as the collectives involved in the unit-specific combination well after the focal aggregation. Therefore, I further highlight points on time sequence, task interdependence, complements, substitutes, and mobility as opaque sub-processes of co-emergence that associate with value over time.

THEORETICAL BACKGROUND

Emergent Human Capital Resources

Theory on HCRs builds on a multilevel understanding of human capital (Ployhart and Moliterno, 2011; Ployhart et al., 2014) and combines insights from micro- and macro-level scholarship (Nyberg et al., 2014; Wright and McMahan, 2011). The HCR construct captures the individual variation that is foundational to, and a component of, higher-level strategic outcomes. Central to this departure from traditional definitions of human capital in economics, sociology, or psychology (Molloy, Ployhart, and Wright, 2011) is the role of emergence, or the processes through which lower-level phenomena combine to create a higher-level construct (Kozlowski and Klein, 2000).

Ideas surrounding emergence are central to HCR theory because they describe the processes through which a collection of individual-level HCRs come together to form a unit-level HCR (Ployhart and Moliterno, 2011).[2] It is helpful to think of uHCRs as a portfolio of KSAOs (Lepak and Snell, 1999; Nyberg et al., 2014) since individuals contribute to the collective in many different ways (Wright et al., 2014). Emergence, then, is the conceptual mechanism through which this portfolio is constituted (see Eckardt and Jiang, this volume). Despite these conceptualizations, emergence processes are challenging to articulate for a variety of reasons. Variation in the contextual influences and the nature of lower-level elements means that there is no "universal" emergence process (Kozlowski and Klein, 2000). Moreover, while the dynamic interaction among individuals embedded in a particular context can be simplified and depicted for illustrative purposes (e.g. Kozlowski et al., 2013), in practice it is challenging to measure since the process is not directly observable (Kozlowski and Chao, 2012). This is illustrated by a simple example such as occurs when watching two or more people lift heavy cargo without the ability to determine marginal productivity (Alchian and Demsetz, 1972). That is, in this joint production scenario, the following conditions add complexity: the deployment of multiple resources at the same time; the outcome is not clearly dependent on separate inputs from each individual; and the multiple resources deployed belong to multiple parties (Alchian and Demsetz, 1972: 779). The processes through which the unit coalesces from individual members in this case is not just challenging to disentangle, but likely not generalizable in describing another context with increased complexity or further opaque qualities over an extended time period. For example, in the case of knowledge-intensive settings where the output is often less tangible than what results from physical inputs in the lifting example, there may be increased complexity in combining resources that associate with valuable outcomes (cf. Kor and Leblebici, 2005), thereby increasing the complicated nature of human capital-based value.

One avenue to understanding uHCRs is through an appreciation of the social complexity embedded in the unit, inasmuch as emergence involves the actions and interactions of individuals over time. This focuses our attention on more than the variety, or *ex ante* perceived value, of individuals in the unit: the connections between these individuals become particularly salient in understanding emergent processes and resultant outcomes (Kozlowski and Chao, 2012). Moreover, the ties that individual members have outside the unit, whether to others in the firm or across an industry or ecosystem (Adler and Kwon, 2002), may also become accessible for strategic use. Once we have turned our attention to these interactions, we are solidly in the domain of social capital theory.

Social Capital in the Unit-Level Resource

Social capital includes the value that inheres in social relationships, as well as the ability to access that value. For example, college roommates build social capital through living together: the trust, shared values, and reliance that can result from interacting over time have latent value. Many years later, when one roommate contacts the other to help with securing an internship for a family member, we observe that they have social capital and leverage the connection for beneficial outcomes. In this example, we note the bonding component of social capital that manifests through a period of sharing living space, as well as the bridging component demonstrated in establishing the connection for a family member to a potential employer (Burt, 1997; Coleman, 1988). Another manifestation of a different aspect of social capital can occur in this example if, while searching for internships, the family member is steered towards firms affiliated with the alma mater of the roommates. These types of influence often occur as a result of a halo effect or favorable global judgment placed on others due to social affiliations, even in the absence of direct experience (Cummings and Cross, 2003; Lin, 2001). In this way, we see how various aspects of social capital are demonstrated through bonding, bridging, or even due to perceptions as individuals leverage various affiliations in accessing resources.

In the vast literature on social capital, it is important to highlight a few points for our purpose here in linking to HCRE. First, scholars frequently observe the fuzzy boundary between human and social capital. Coleman (1988) discusses the role of social capital in creating human capital, while Nahapiet (2011) notes commonalities between human and social capital related to how it can be challenging to distinguish between the two resources over time due to coevolving reciprocal associations. Second, and relatedly, it is important to underscore the delineation between internal and external components of social capital (Adler and Kwon, 2002; Granovetter, 1973). That is, individuals and groups often deploy social capital through different paths and for different reasons to access resources through relationships within a bounded group, such as a team or firm, as well as to those outside the group, whether it be an individual expert or a collective (Payne et al., 2011). Building on these points, researchers have investigated a variety of connections such as those between social capital and human resource management (Youndt et al., 2004; Soltis et al., 2018), in addition to knowledge creation (McFadyen and Cannella, 2004). Further, human and social capital are combined in empirical studies of boards or CEOs (Johnson et al., 2013; Krause et al., 2016; Stevenson and Radin, 2009; Miller et al., 2015), while the dynamic managerial capabilities perspective (Helfat and Martin, 2015) calls for an integrated examination of human and social capital, along with managerial cognition. Despite these contributions, a review of the social capital literature (Payne et al., 2011) suggests that the link to human capital remains underexplored.

Two pieces of scholarship stand out among the body of research on social capital, particularly when it comes to conceptualizing collectives and the association to the individual level, which is essential in theorizing on the unit-level HCR. First, Oh and colleagues introduce the concept of "group social capital" as a metaconstruct defined as "the set of resources made available to a group through group members' social relationships within the social structure of the group itself, as well as in the broader formal and informal structure of the organization" (Oh et al., 2006: 570). This is an informative perspective to take on social capital as we investigate the association with strategic HCRs in that these authors advocate for a move "beyond treating a group exclusively as a whole unit or, as is more typical, as merely the sum of its individual parts, by explicitly considering individuals as embedded simultaneously in the social structure of subgroups, groups and the overall organization" (Oh et al., 2006: 569). Second, Tasselli and colleagues, in exploring micro foundations of organizational social networks, make note of a "coevolution perspective suggesting that people, in their idiosyncrasies, and networks, in their differentiated structures, coevolve" (Tasselli et al., 2015: 1361). The utility of a dynamic and reciprocal coevolution perspective over a traditional top-down or bottom-up approach to understanding collective outcomes is in line with a socialized view of HCRE. To the extent that the unit-level resources emerges from simultaneous influence from individual characteristics and contextual constraints as well as collective processes (Ployhart and Moliterno, 2011), this coevolution perspective can provide additional explanations beyond examining either component in insolation.

Indeed, by conceptualizing group social capital as seemingly more than "the sum of its individual parts" (Oh et al., 2006), and in recognizing that individuals cannot be understood without considering the network context and nor can organizations be understood without understanding the embedded individuals (Tasselli et al., 2015), these works track very closely the original arguments surrounding HCRs (Ployhart and Moliterno, 2011). That is, Ployhart and Moliterno's multilevel model of human capital includes individual and collective characteristics as well as contextual factors in explaining the emergent unit-level resource. Not surprisingly, Oh et al.'s arguments surrounding group social capital map very neatly onto our conceptual understanding of uHCR. Since their definition of "group" is largely consistent with ours of "unit," for our current purposes we will use the term "unit social capital" (uSC). Further, we align with Tasselli et al. in considering multiple levels along with unit context in the situation of a broader environmental structure. Ultimately, when considering group social capital or the coevolution of individuals and networks over time in organizations, it becomes apparent that social capital coexists alongside human capital in unit-level resources. This notion leads us to questions around how human and social capital coexist.

HUMAN AND SOCIAL CAPITAL COEXISTING IN THE UNIT-LEVEL RESOURCE

Combining Human and Social Capital in the Unit Context

To appreciate how human and social capital coexist in the unit, it is worth reviewing some interrelationships between the two resources at different levels. For an individual, human and social capital may be antecedent, consequential, reciprocal, or simultaneous in development or deployment (Coleman, 1988; Nahapiet, 2011). At a dyadic level, the same associations can hold but are made more complex by the interaction of two individuals, each with respective experience, relationships, and motivations that then have pair-specific properties in terms of the social capital that coheres between them as well as potential overlap or distinctive breadth of human capital (cf. Gooty and Yammarino, 2011). Furthermore, at a larger collective level, the complexity builds because an aggregate human capital resource encompasses individual characteristics but also has unit-level

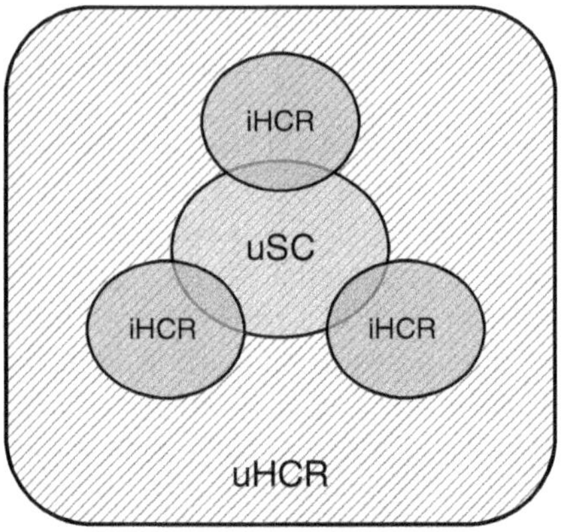

Figure 13.1 Individual and unit-level human capital resources and unit-level social capital

properties with respect to social capital (Oh et al., 2006; Ployhart and Moliterno, 2011). Moreover, there are continual social influences from other non-focal unit collectives on individual members and from other non-unit individuals on the unit (cf. Payne et al., 2011). For simplicity, and since my focus is on the unit-level resource in a firm, I will not go into detail on the myriad cross-level influences and external factors at this point, but it is important to note that these interrelationships exist. A simplified visualization is presented in Figure 13.1, where we observe individual-level resources nested within the unit-level resource. Unit-level social capital separately exists within the collective resource yet is shared by each individual.

To the extent that individuals combine to create an emergent uHCR, social capital is embedded in this process and, as a result, uSC co-exists with the uHCR. However, it is not merely that social ties emerge between individuals in the unit, or that individuals bring access to past and current external ties into the unit with them; rather, a coherent view includes the dynamic unit-specific combination of human and social capital available for strategic use. That is, uSC is an essential part of human capital-based advantages in that human and social capital combine in the unit in various ways. Integrating learning theory helps us better illustrate and understand the multilevel reciprocal nature of human and social capital in the unit-level resource.

A Broadened Perspective from Organizational Learning

The social capital embedded and integrated in individual- and unit-level HCRs can be illustrated through a review of March's (1991) concepts of mutual learning and the organizational code. Mutual learning, or the simultaneous influence between individuals and organizations, deepens our understanding of what happens during human capital resource emergence. March describes that when individuals join an organization they influence the current "code" or embedded qualities of the collective. At the same time, the code influences the individuals through modifications related to salient organizational qualities. Mutual learning is part of the social context in the firm and exemplifies reciprocal exchange and influence over time: each member has a unique set of knowledge and beliefs, while the code contains cumulative knowledge, norms, and processes as a result of different members and contextual changes over time. The organizational code is continually evolving as it can affect and be affected by individual and collective factors such as mobility, speed of learning, or strength of principles. In this way, March's conceptualization of the reciprocal relationship between the individuals and the collective aligns well with our current notions of emergent multilevel HCRs coexisting with social capital.

To explain further, Figure 13.1 depicts individual and unit-level human capital with unit-level social capital at one point in time; but HCRE is a dynamic process. Different individual resources will differentially influence HCRE. For example, each individual brings with them a unique past and current stock of human and social capital. Furthermore, each individual is changed idiosyncratically – whether through development or deployment – via the organizational code, due to assimilation, speed of learning, and other contextual factors. Additionally, the uSC and uHCR reflect traces of past individual members that influenced the organizational code as well as the flow of new members and influence. That is, the components of Figure 13.1 are not static and continually change over time as a result of interrelated sub-processes. Although the unit-level resource may be illustrated at one point in time and explained as starting at an individual level, in practice the process is concurrently ongoing.

In sum, as demonstrated in the mutual learning analogy, HCRE encompasses many context specific sub-processes (Ployhart and Moliterno, 2011) that are difficult to disentangle yet from a strategic standpoint importantly relate to unit-specific combinations that include social capital components. Whereas human capital includes relatively stable cognitive and non-cognitive factors, those that are more malleable and situationally based are outside the concept of human capital (Ployhart et al., 2014). In this way, the salience of unit-level social capital is elevated in that relational aspects shed light on valuable parts of HCRE that are not adequately explained through an exclusive focus on human capital. The multilevel nature of uSC and HCRE thereby necessitates a perspective on social capital emergence that is equitable to that of human capital emergence. As such, I note the unit-specific co-emergence of the HCR and uSC.

Proposition 1: Unit-level human capital and unit-level social capital co-emerge in the context of the firm and include interrelated sub-processes that simultaneously alter both the individual and unit characteristics.

The co-emergence of the uHCR and uSC is depicted in Figure 13.2, and it is important to note that both contribute to outcomes and value creation. Further, we do not assume that all uSC is the same or that it is all equally valuable; just as there are variations in uHCRs, with some leading to strategic parity and others to strategic advantage (Ployhart et al., 2014), so too all uSC is not the same. Variations occur for a range of reasons. Starting at the bottom left side of Figure 13.2 we see how, at an individual level, a unit member's contribution to outcomes and value is derived from both human capital and social capital, as well as integrated associations between the two. Over time, as the uHCR and uSC co-emerge towards a valuable unit-level resource, we see how contributions come not just from individual action in terms of human and social capital, but also from the interaction of those with that of other unit members. The dashed lines in Figure 13.2 represent the malleability and permeability of the resource and influence. That is, the

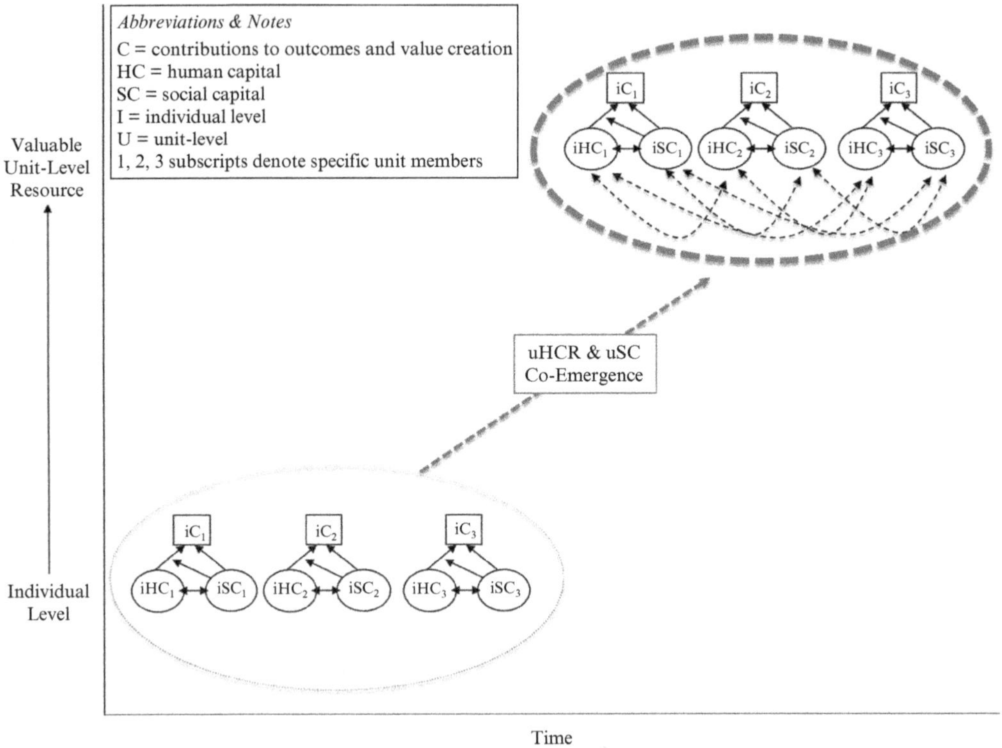

Figure 13.2 Co-emergence of unit-level human capital resources and social capital

co-emergence process may change as a result of the actions of individuals contained in the unit; individual contributions may change as a result of interactions at a unit level; and, subsequently, the overall combined value of the unit may change based on these coexisting actions and interactions over time. Moreover, at each conceptualized step in HCRE there may be influential flows into or out of the emergent unit-level resource due to factors such as resource mobility or external social capital. Further, the dashed lines connecting dyads at the unit level could represent a variety of interdependencies or complementary associations that might range from required or strong to almost non-existent. Similarly, the co-emergence timeline from individual to unit is likely to be less straightforward in practice, potentially further compounded by contextual constraints.

To build on the illustration in Figure 13.2, there are several sub-processes that relate to unit-specific aggregations and context that are important in understanding HCR and uSC co-emergence. Importantly, the human capital nesting arrangement can include a broad range of constraints and enablers at the individual, group, subunit, organizational, interorganizational network, and environmental levels (Hitt et al., 2007). The complexity of this multilevel nesting, along with human capital dilemmas such as individual motivation and mobility (Coff, 1997), can result in varying advantages generated within and for the firm. As such, I delve into some of the salient, yet often not readily apparent, sub-processes that relate to the valuable co-emergence of uHCR and uSC in the next section.

OPAQUE SUB-PROCESSES THAT INFLUENCE VALUABLE CO-EMERGENCE

Understanding the co-emergence of uHCRs and uSC requires an examination of additional considerations with respect to the longitudinal sequence of resource emergence, the unit-level task environment, the presence of valuable resource complementarities or substitutes, and mobility. Furthermore, in the same way that not all human capital constitutes a strategic resource for the firm (Ployhart et al., 2014), not all social capital will provide value as a strategic resource for the firm. I present these features below in order to shed light on the derived value of human and social capital in combination in the unit.

Time Horizon and Sequence

The first opaque sub-process concerns time and the sequence in which action and interaction occur. In HCRE, the presence of reciprocal or simultaneous, rather than clearly antecedent or consequential, associations between individual and unit-level human and social capital complicates our understanding of resource co-emergence. Indeed, Granovetter's sentiment that action is embedded in ongoing social systems, as well as Tasselli and colleagues' observation that network coevolution rather than people making the network or networks making the people, supports the notion that co-emergence cannot be easily separated into distinct and sequential segments. Further, revisiting the comparison to mutual learning, although it may be possible to understand individual characteristics and organizational code attributes beforehand, it is challenging to determine how quickly (or slowly) valuable modifications to both the individual and code will occur. In this way, the co-emergence over time depicted by the line in Figure 13.2 is not so straightforward. In addition, it is often impractical to disentangle incremental origins of value during the co-emergence of uHCR and uSC. That is, the sequence of human and social capital development may not always be clearly observable in the unit context due to the dynamic process of emergence that happens over time (cf. Kozlowski and Klein, 2000; Barney and Felin, 2013). To put it simply, sometimes resources "must be considered jointly, rather than sequentially" when attempting to discern performance variations (Tzabbar et al., 2008: 380); hence the depiction of coexisting contributions from both human and social capital in Figure 13.2. Kozlowski explains how emergence inherently goes against the traditional depictions of models with boxes and arrows (Eckardt et al., 2018a). Although relationships are part of the emergence process (Kozlowski et al., 2013), it is challenging to determine or prescribe an optimized sequence: some social capital may be antecedent to the unit, while some human capital deployment may lead to social capital development; and still other situations might see a concurrent build of the two.

Indeed, the value derived from the emergent HCR depends on the uSC. However, the bonding relationships, norms, and expectations within the unit, as well as the bridging to outside the unit, are not statically available as foundational or fixed resources. That is, uSC-related inputs are not necessarily antecedent to human capital-related factors as might be expected in a traditional process timeline. On one hand, there are conditions present during HCRE that create social ties between individuals, while on the other hand, there are factors rooted in social capital that facilitate HCRE. For example, if two individuals in a unit at a firm played the same sport in college, might this past affiliation-based social capital enable human capital in the form of mentoring? Or perhaps overlapping human capital, such as the past development of a particular skill, makes it easier to develop social capital in the dyad? Scholars have been hesitant to characterize the association between human and social capital as clearly antecedent or consequential (Coleman, 1988; Nahapiet, 2011), a task made more complex by multilevel conceptualizations. As such, although human and social capital are distinct concepts (Nahapiet, 2011; Ployhart et al., 2014), the process by which they cohere under dynamic contextual influences in the unit is not transparent, especially in light of unpredictable, incomplete, or unobservable time horizons.

Proposition 2: A valuable uHCR co-emerges with uSC in the presence of unpredictable time horizons and non-linear sequences.

Task Environment

The second opaque sub-process concerns the nature of the task environment. While Ployhart and Moliterno (2011) discuss the importance of the unit-level task environment to HCRE, assumptions on co-production or task interdependency may initially seem obvious, especially when considering Coleman's points on the role of dependence and bonding in the social group. However, interdependence or co-production is not a necessary requirement for the emergence of the HCR or uSC; not every strategic unit is organized as a traditional team or held together as a closed group through bonding. Although a team is an example of a unit-level HCR, not all unit-level resources are teams (but see Ployhart and Chen, this volume, for a differing perspective). That is, although the definition of teams includes interdependencies, shared goals, social interaction, and the performance of organizationally relevant tasks (Kozlowski and Bell, 2003), there are other collective resources that do not follow the traditional team definition (Ployhart and Moliterno, 2011; Ployhart et al., 2014). This is an important point in terms of the task environment, especially under the context of uSC. For example, there may be a strategic unit that includes individuals with similar occupational roles yet no direct co-production. In this case, the dashed lines at the unit level in Figure 13.2 may be reduced or non-existent at times.

What happens in a unit where there is no task interdependence but conditions of co-location or overlapping occupational conditions or comparisons? Professors in an academic department that do not co-teach classes or co-author research together continue to exist in a unit-level HCR with uSC, despite a lack of obvious social connections. That is, there is still an 'organizational code' (March, 1991) that may not always include a requirement of co-production. In this way, we observe social capital in a unit derived from interaction in the absence of interdependence (Bourdieu, 1986; Nahapiet and Ghoshal, 1998). Thus, the absence of co-production or interdependence does not preclude uSC from emerging during HCRE. Rather, under certain conditions, the lack of interdependence may add value; for example, co-production under the context of toxic or negative interactions could be destructive to uSC, and in this way advantages could result from reduced interdependence. While in many cases task complexity may be assumed to facilitate the creation of valuable social capital, the destruction of value is also possible, and may have an even more powerful impact (cf. Labianca and Brass, 2006). Although social interaction may increase with interdependence, it does not always result in valuable uSC. That is, increased required interaction that can come with interdependence may lead to destruction of social capital under certain conditions. Meanwhile, lack of interdependence does not equate to lack of interaction, and valuable social capital can emerge. In sum, uSC remains a salient factor in valuing HCR regardless of task interdependence.

Proposition 3: A valuable uHCR co-emerges with uSC in the presence of varying degrees of task interdependence or co-production.

Complementarities and Substitutes

Human capital-based advantages rooted in complementarities have received increasing attention in strategy research and, as such, are an important sub-process to consider. Unit-level social capital plays a role in these complementarity-based performance outcomes in that studies have shown that colleague quality, relationship strength, and overlapping tenure relate to performance outcomes (Crocker and Eckardt, 2014; Cross and Cummings, 2004; Harris et al., 2012). Adegbesan (2009) describes complementarities as performance advantages resulting from the combination of resources that would not be possible for component resources in isolation. Novel knowledge or skills are sourced and combined in a strategic manner where the presence of one resource increases advantages from another; the non-redundancy of resources can positively impact performance (Hess and Rothaermel, 2011; Milgrom and Roberts, 1995) and there may a synergistic effect from multiple iHCRs (Ployhart and Cragun, 2017).

While the notion of complementarities has gained traction, less attention has been paid to two important factors that are closely intertwined with uSC: negative impacts from perceived resource complements and positive impacts from unforeseen substitutes are both important to unit-level value. That is, it is essential to consider how strategic uHCRs emerge in practice when compared to the original intended strategy for human capital. The notion of an intended strategy and the importance of emergent alternatives that result in the actual realization of strategic outcomes was championed by Mintzberg and colleagues (Mintzberg, 1978; Mintzberg and Waters, 1985). These ideas align with recent strategic human capital theory in that "the difference between potential value in use and actual human capital value in use represent as yet unrealized opportunities to generate increased value in use" (Chadwick, 2017: 10) and that HCR capacity does not always align with performance enhancing unit activities (Nyberg et al., 2014; Nyberg and Reilly, this volume). Indeed, unrealized and emergent components are important to understanding actual value. For example, in some situations social capital might not accentuate but neutralize human capital (Hollenbeck and Jamieson, 2015: 371), while in other cases superior social capital can overcome voids in other resources by substituting for human capital (Adler and Kwon, 2002: 21). Thus, we can better understand value creation through investigating, first, human capital complementarities that are not realized as intended and, second, substitutes that, although not deliberate, emerge to add value.

Intended and realized complementarities

There may be instances where resources that are perceived, or predicted to be complementary, are in practice not as valuable in tandem or even result in negative effects on the unit.

Indeed, merely combining resources does not lead to valuable complements (Somaya et al., 2007; Tzabber et al., 2008), and active orchestration of resources is often essential in deriving advantages (Sirmon et al., 2011). The uSC plays a role in our understanding of neutralized, negative, or less than synergistic human capital combinations (Hollenbeck and Jamieson, 2015; Labianca and Brass, 2006). Simply sharing the same social context does not equate to sharing the same values (Whitley and McKenzie, 2005), and the shared or influential affective and cognitive components of the unit are central to HCRE (Ployhart and Moliterno, 2011). For example, there may be differences in the levels of competence trust or interpersonal trust that unit members have for one another that, in turn, impact collaboration (Gardner, 2016); whereas competence trust is akin to favorable assessments of human capital, interpersonal trust is more indicative of social capital between unit members. Negative effects, that may be difficult to observe or predict, can result from issues around conflicting goals, unethical behavior, and power imbalances (Brass et al., 1998; Brass et al., 2004) on one side, and perhaps too little conflict or new ideas linked to groupthink or lack of innovation on the other side (Janis, 1972; Leana and Van Buren, 1999).

Alternatively, there may be even more extreme negative consequences from perceived complementarities in other cases, such as when star employees are overwhelmed by colleagues who seek them out due to perceived high levels of human capital or well-intentioned, yet unproductive, collaboration (Oldroyd and Morris, 2012; Cross and Gray, 2013). Further, dysfunctional or other prohibitive behaviors spill over from one context or affiliation to the unit, such as might be the case in family firms (Arregle et al., 2007). These scenarios highlighting intended and unrealized complements, which can arise in settings ranging from lab scientists to construction workers, have the potential to move the value of an iHCR from optimistically positive along the spectrum to not just neutral impact but perhaps negative implications for the unit. In sum, complementarities originally intended to provide value, including those deliberately selected for strategic combination, can emerge as value stunting or destroying under certain conditions of uSC.

Proposition 4: Neutral or negative value may be realized from intended complementarities due to uSC and are embedded in uHCR value.

Unrealized complementarities and emergent substitutes

Substitutive relationships among resources entail redundancy and an interchangeable function within the task environment (Hess and Rothaermel, 2011; Rothaermel and Hess, 2007; Tzabbar et al., 2008). Although different from traditional complementary value, these substitutive resources can have a positive impact on value, especially in the context of over-reliance on rare resources or when predicted complements go unrealized. Social capital outside of the HCR, whether to another part of the organization or externally linking to elsewhere in the environment, can also yield substitute benefits. That is, unit members can leverage external social capital linking them to other individuals or collectives (Payne et al., 2011) to access context-specific resources for unit value creation since employees leverage networks in addition to experience and education in solving problems (Morris and Snell, this volume): accessing resources through social ties is analogous to leveraging their own respective KSAOs (cf. Nyberg et al., 2014). In this way, social capital is leveraged to "borrow" human capital from outside the uHCR, thereby working as a substitute resource since it is used in place of, and compensating for a lack of, their own human capital (cf. Grigoriou and Rothaermel, 2014) or complementary contribution.

To illustrate the role of substitutive resources in adding value to the unit-level HCR, consider the case of a new hire that must complete specific tasks within the unit. It is possible that this employee was hired based on the perception that they possessed the requisite KSAOs to get the job done on their own, or that they would complement an existing resource. However, in the same way that social connections might help overcome a void of financial capital, the same can be leveraged in place of human capital (Adler and Kwon, 2002). The employee may rely on connections to others in the occupation or industry yet from a different firm, thereby filling a gap in their own knowledge and skills towards unit-level performance outcomes. Although this was not the intended strategy, deploying human capital as initially planned goes unrealized, either due to lack of skill or complementary human capital contribution, and instead the actual value emerges from social capital. For this reason, it may be beneficial to screen potential unit members on not only attributes of human capital but also on access to external knowledge via social capital or status (Kehoe and Bentley, this volume). For example, pharmaceutical sales representatives might consult with other sales personnel at a biotechnology or medical device firm, and social capital in the external ecosystem, and not in the immediate unit, might result in valuable outcomes. There is a fuzzy area of this substitutive association that could evolve into a complementary relationship if the external social capital develops internal human capital (see Eckardt and Jiang, this volume on HCRE transformation). Nonetheless, the iHCR may access resources without internalizing them and contribute to unit value due to accessible uSC.

Proposition 5: External social capital embedded in uSC, outside the unit or firm, can substitute for human capital and is embedded in uHCR value.

Mobility Events

There is one last additional sub-process to consider, both because it shapes the co-emergent uSC and uHCR and because it associates with the appropriation of value. Dess and Shaw observe that "The long-term performance consequences of voluntary turnover may be less attributable to a skill (human capital) deficit than to the accumulated social capital lost through voluntary turnover" (2001: 449). Rider and Tan (this volume) provide another important perspective in that mobility that might help the individual could hurt the firm, while mobility that hurts the individual could help the firm. Indeed, mobility influences outcomes at the individual, unit, and firm levels (Campbell et al., 2014; Eckardt et al., 2014; Groysberg et al., 2008); and there is a growing body of literature focusing explicitly on collective emergent turnover, investigating the quality, quantity, and dispersion of mobile HCRs (Nyberg and Ployhart, 2013; Call et al., 2015). Although social capital can often help in the retention of firm human capital (Dess and Shaw, 2001), to the extent that emergence happens over time there will be changes in the stock of human capital in the uHCR and the flow of iHCRs (cf. Dierickx and Cool, 1989), thereby impacting uSC.

Given the nature of how uSC and the uHCR co-emerge over time, any direct firm-specific value that is created at one point in the unit-specific context can have longer-term, indirect impact on future value capture from social and human capital of the individual, or unit, as well as subsequent units that the individual joins. For, example, in revisiting Figures 13.1 and 13.2 we can imagine how this process gets repeated over time, with individuals joining different firms (and experiencing diverse uSC conditions) while simultaneously interacting with additional organizations, thereby building external social capital to be strategically leveraged in the unit (cf. Oh et al., 2006). Past uSC exposure is converted into future human capital or external social capital to be deployed in a new uHCR as a function of iHCR mobility. Various aspects of human capital – such as firm-, industry-, or occupation-specific experience – can result in different manifestations of competitive capabilities for the firm (Mayer et al., 2012) and thus be valued accordingly depending on the competitiveness of the market (Molloy and Barney, 2015). In this way, the iHCR takes knowledge and skills that they have learned in the unit with them, which may have value in the labor market as general human capital, in addition to social connections to be deployed in, and influence the develop of, future uHCRs and uSC.

Due to the absence of unit-specific aggregate social capital and HCRs it is possible that the cumulative benefit to an individual or unit under conditions of mobility will be a fraction of the context-specific value created. Indeed, this is a complicated part of HCRE, especially considering that depreciation of social capital due to context change is unpredictable (Adler and Kwon, 2002: 22) and that value is dependent on idiosyncratic combinations with human capital-related resources (Chadwick, 2017). Alternatively, new idiosyncratic combinations could yield exponential benefits in future units under fortuitous contexts; human capital is often acquired to be recombined, and value often results from what the firm does with the resource more so than the individual resource itself (Camuffo and De Stefano, this volume; Campbell and Kryscynski, this volume). Nonetheless, this is an important observation when considering the dynamic nature of HCRE and the resultant impact that may be felt not only by a mobile individual but also on source and destination collective resources (Mawdsley and Somaya, 2016; Slavova et al., 2016). A simplified depiction of this recursive model with respect to the flow of an individual stock of human capital from the context of unit-level HCRE is shown in Figure 13.3.

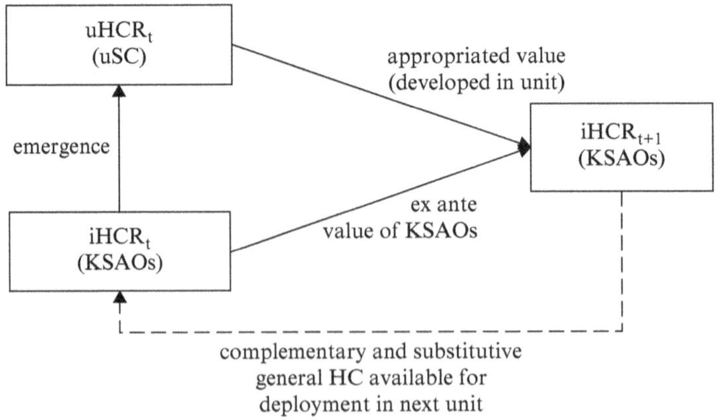

Figure 13.3 Individual-level human capital over time and across units

Although social capital cannot be owned by one individual, there is a latent value of the uSC that is appropriated by the individual (Coleman, 1988; Oh et al., 2006). Figure 13.3 illustrates how a component iHCR preserves a piece of the uSC that will be retained once they leave the organization. This may be in the form of social capital bridging to what will then be an external connection or human capital development from lessons learned during time at the prior firm, to include task- or industry-specific knowledge or skills related to developing social capital. These benefits are different from the direct value derived from the firm-specific uSC, as that joint value is only retained in the event that a unit leaves together (Campbell et al., 2014; Groysberg et al., 2008). As shown in Figure 13.3, the uSC the individual appropriates adds to the *ex ante* value of their previous stock of KSAOs before further development in the unit. The individual may become more valuable to the new firm and appropriate value that is complementary in the next unit based on past uSC converted to general human capital or external social capital. As such, the individual may experience more benefits or higher levels of performance in the new firm context.

Proposition 6: Mobility provides an opportunity for iHCRs to deploy newly developed human capital or previously acquired social capital in new contexts, thus accruing value to the individual.

In the same way that an individual might appropriate pieces of uSC over time as part of different units, units experience cumulative changes to the uSC from mobility of different members. Mobility changes the firm-specific aggregation of individuals, thereby influencing the co-emergence of uHCRs and uSC. On the side of a source firm, the individual (or collective) leaving can diminish the uSC, and thus the value the firm derives from the uHCR is likely to decrease in many cases (Nyberg and Ployhart, 2013). However, value could increase if mobility reduces negative contributors, inadequate or mismatched human capital, or damaging social capital in the unit since failure to retain an individual may not always signify a loss (Hausknecht, this volume; Labianca and Brass, 2006). On the side of an acquiring firm, there is a dynamic effect from how an individual is incorporated in HCRE. Faster assimilation within the firm-specific context may result in more overlap more quickly, while slower learning could result in the retention of diverse KSAOs (March, 1991); the speed of acclimation may differ for the same individual, depending on context-specific attributes such as uSC. Additionally, different sources and destinations of iHCRs can differentially influence value (cf. Mawdsley and Somaya, 2016); for example, mobility to competitors will have a different impact on firm performance compared to mobility to cooperators (Somaya et al., 2008).

Furthermore, from the perspective of the acquiring firm there are issues with perceptions of value regarding the mobile iHCR. That is, how does the new unit understand what is attributable to the social capital versus the human capital, and does the distinction matter (Lester et al., 2008)? Due to information asymmetries, it is often challenging to understand resource quality (Hitt et al., 2001), and certain extracurricular activities or past employers are used as a signal (Bidwell et al., 2015; Rivera, 2011). However, many signals of human capital resource value may be confounded with social capital. Individuals are likely to be judged based on holistic evaluations rather than subsets of specific characteristics (Nisbett and Wilson, 1977). The *ex ante* evaluation of iHCR value may help the unit in getting a head start on uSC and impact value appropriation. For example, firms may develop talent pipelines and repeatedly hire from the same sources over time (Brymer et al., 2014) or strategically practice cluster hiring in intentional acquisitions of HCRs central to the value-creation process (Eckardt et al., 2018b).

Proposition 7: Mobility influences the quality and nature of uSC, and thus the value appropriated by the firm from the uHCR.

MOVING FORWARD

uHCR and uSC co-emergence broadens our understanding of human capital-based value creation and capture in light of task interdependence, time sequence, complementarities, substitutes, mobility, and longer-term outcomes for individuals as well as units. When we examine the productive output of a unit we are seeing the value created by that specific combination of iHCRs and the value created through uSC. Human and social capital simply always coexist at the unit level. As strategic human capital scholarship evolves to include not just individual and collective levels but also internal and external factors over time, the need for a socialized view is increasingly important to comprehensive investigations and in providing alternative explanations. In this way, we can better understand emergent HCRs and uSC and how the reciprocal relationship between these sub-resources can reproduce in different contexts over time.

There are several areas of future research, focused on the intersections of individual and unit-level human capital with internal or external social capital. For example, future studies could examine how unit-specific combinations of human and social capital balance tensions between developing a strong depth of expertise with accessing the requisite breadth of external knowledge in the firm environment. This notion highlights the importance of general human capital in a competitive context that can benefit from specific task, occupation, industry, or ecosystem knowledge and skills. Additionally, other factors, such as opportunity and motivation that can be linked to social factors, may have a cumulative, path-dependent impact on the development and deployment of uSC and HCRs across contexts over time. Similarly, perceptions of human capital and the subsequent influence on acquisition or valuation are important areas of study; closing the gap between perceived potential of iHCRs and realized outcomes related to social capital is a timely topic for practitioners. This is exemplified in our discussion around substituting social capital for lack of human capital, as well as in the notion of negative or neutralized impact from intended complements in the unit. These broad areas are a sampling of under-researched topics that could shed light on the vast associations between human and social capital that can inform practice and theory.

Future research should also include enriched analysis and measures. For example, focusing on the dyad or other ways of incorporating network studies can be beneficial to understanding HCRs. Many studies using social network analysis (SNA) take a perspective of internal social networks of individuals (Cross and Cummings, 2004) or external social networks of collectives (Payne et al., 2011), but it would be useful to examine iHCR networks across firms or uHCR networks within an ecosystem. Additionally, more studies with longitudinal components will help us to better understand HCRE and important sub-processes in emergence (Hollenbeck and Jamieson, 2015; Soltis et al., 2018). There have been multiple calls to improve measurement of human capital (Wright and McMahan, 2011) and make progress to separate those that are better used for either human or social capital (Nahapiet, 2011), yet the shift to thinking about human capital as a multilevel resource in the presence of social capital further complicates these efforts. Indeed, disentangling where human and social capital begin and end across levels and settings continues to be a theoretical challenge which spills over into conceptions of measurement, thereby warranting qualitative studies, simulations, or mixed methods approaches.

Although the literature on strategic human capital resources has grown in many ways since earlier mentions of the nuance of social complexities in accessing value from human capital (Coleman, 1988; Coff, 1997), the extent to how and why social factors matter in human capital-based advantages has not been fully explored. I am hopeful that some of the ideas in this chapter will encourage research on the many interesting facets of HCR and social capital co-emergence.

CHAPTER SUMMARY

BOX 13.1 KEY TAKEAWAYS

1. Unit-level social capital co-emerges with strategic human capital resources in a firm. The unit-level resource incorporates the KSAOs of individual members, the internal social capital among those in the unit, and external social capital accessible to those in the unit, thereby collectively influencing value for the firm.
2. Co-emergence relates to firm value in a complex way through opaque sub-processes: task interdependence (not always necessary for valuable uSC); time sequencing/horizons (simultaneous, reciprocal, or non-linear – not always simple antecedent/consequential); complementary and substitutive relationships (intended, emergent, realized from internal and external sources); and mobility (influencing individual and source/destination units).
3. Disentangling where HC and SC begin and end is challenging. Measurement issues are exacerbated when combined in a single study due to overlap, and even more challenging from a multilevel perspective. Acknowledging inseparability in some cases may be key in identifying the origin, maintenance, and future of human capital-based value.

BOX 13.2 DIRECTIONS FOR FUTURE RESEARCH

1. Further insight into how firms access strategically relevant KSAOs over time is needed. For example, how do firms balance deep expertise with broad access to new and necessary KSAOs in the ecosystem? What are the implications of accessing strategically relevant KSAOs via human capital, social capital, or both resources?
2. Additional research is needed on the social context of strategic human capital. For example, situational factors surrounding combinations of HCRs or perceptions of human capital that are related to social capital are important areas of inquiry.
3. Incorporating a social capital lens and social network analysis into HC studies will shed light on the overlap or delineation between these two resources and clarify associated resource valuation.

NOTES

1. I follow others in the strategic human capital literature (Nyberg et al., 2014; Ployhart and Moliterno, 2011) and use "unit" as the generic term to refer to any aggregation of individuals such as a work group, team, or firm.
2. While these points relate to how individual human capital is transformed and amplified during unit-level HCRE, a detailed account is beyond the scope of this chapter (see Eckardt and Jiang, this volume).

REFERENCES

Adegbesan, J. A. (2009). On the origins of competitive advantage: Strategic factor markets and heterogeneous resource complementarity. *Academy of Management Review*, *34*(3), 463–75.

Adler, P. S., and Kwon, S. W. (2002). Social capital: Prospects for a new concept. *Academy of Management Review*, *27*(1), 17–40.

Alchian, A. A., and Demsetz, H. (1972). Production, information costs, and economic organization. *American Economic Review*, *62*(5), 777–95.

Arregle, J. L., Hitt, M. A., Sirmon, D. G., and Very, P. (2007). The development of organizational social capital: Attributes of family firms. *Journal of Management Studies*, *44*(1), 73–95.

Barney, J., and Felin, T. (2013). What are microfoundations? *Academy of Management Perspectives*, *27*(2), 138–55.

Becker, G. S. (1964). *Human Capital* (3rd edn). Chicago, IL: University of Chicago Press.

Bidwell, M., Won, S., Barbulescu, R., and Mollick, E. (2015). I used to work at Goldman Sachs! How firms benefit from organizational status in the market for human capital. *Strategic Management Journal*, *36*(8), 1164–73.

Bourdieu, P. (1986). The forms of capital. In J. Richardson (ed.) *Handbook of Theory and Research for the Sociology of Education*, 241–58. New York: Greenwood.

Brass, D. J., Butterfield, K. D., and Skaggs, B. C. (1998). Relationships and unethical behavior: A social network perspective. *Academy of Management Review*, *23*(1), 14–31.

Brass, D. J., Galaskiewicz, J., Greve, H. R., and Tsai, W. (2004). Taking stock of networks and organizations: A multilevel perspective. *Academy of Management Journal*, *47*(6), 795–817.

Brymer, R., Molloy, J., and Gilbert, B. (2014). Human capital pipelines: Competitive implications of repeated interorganizational hiring. *Journal of Management*, *40*(2), 483–508.

Burt, R. S. (1997). The contingent value of social capital. *Administrative Science Quarterly*, 339–65.

Call, M. L., Nyberg, A. J., Ployhart, R. E., and Weekley, J. (2015). The dynamic nature of collective turnover and unit performance: The impact of time, quality, and replacements. *Academy of Management Journal*, *58*(4), 1208–32.

Campbell, B. A., Coff, R., and Kryscynski, D. (2012). Rethinking sustained competitive advantage from human capital. *Academy of Management Review*, *37*(3), 376–95.

Campbell, B. A., Saxton, B. M., and Banerjee, P. M. (2014). Resetting the shot clock: The effect of comobility on human capital. *Journal of Management*, *40*(2), 531–56.

Chadwick, C. (2017). Toward a more comprehensive model of firms' human capital rents. *Academy of Management Review*, *42*(3), 499–519.

Coff, R. W. (1997). Human assets and management dilemmas: Coping with hazards on the road to resource-based theory. *Academy of Management Review*, *22*(2), 374–402.

Coff, R., and Kryscynski, D. (2011). Invited editorial: Drilling for micro-foundations of human capital–based competitive advantages. *Journal of Management*, *37*(5), 1429–43.

Coleman, J. S. (1988). Social capital in the creation of human capital. *American Journal of Sociology*, *94*, S95–120.

Crocker, A., and Eckardt, R. (2014). A multilevel investigation of individual- and unit-level human capital complementarities. *Journal of Management*, *40*(2), 509–30.

Cross, R., and Cummings, J. N. (2004). Tie and network correlates of individual performance in knowledge-intensive work. *Academy of Management Journal*, *47*(6), 928–37.

Cross, R., and Gray, P. (2013). Where has the time gone? Addressing collaboration overload in a networked economy. *California Management Review*, *56*(1), 50–66.

Cummings, J. N., and Cross, R. (2003). Structural properties of work groups and their consequences for performance. *Social Networks*, *25*(3), 197–210.

Dess, G. G., and Shaw, J. D. (2001). Voluntary turnover, social capital, and organizational performance. *Academy of Management Review*, *26*(3), 446–56.

Dierickx, I., and Cool, K. (1989). Asset stock accumulation and sustainability of competitive advantage. *Management Science*, *35*(12), 1504–11.
Eckardt, R., Skaggs, B. C., and Lepak, D. P. (2018b). An examination of the firm-level performance impact of cluster hiring in knowledge-intensive firms. *Academy of Management Journal*, *61*(3), 919–44.
Eckardt, R., Skaggs, B. C., and Youndt, M. (2014). Turnover and knowledge loss: An examination of the differential impact of production manager and worker turnover in service and manufacturing firms. *Journal of Management Studies*, *51*(7), 1025–57.
Eckardt, R., Crocker, A., Ahn, Y., Floyd, S. W., Boyd, B. K., Hodgkinson, G. P., Kozlowski, S., Moliterno, T.P., and Starbuck, W. H. (2018a). Reflections on the micro–macro divide: Ideas from the trenches and moving forward. *Strategic Organization*. https://doi.org/10.1177/1476127018770048.
Gardner, H. K. (2016). *Smart Collaboration: How Professionals and their Firms Succeed by Breaking Down Silos*. Boston, MA: Harvard Business Review Press.
Gooty, J., and Yammarino, F. J. (2011). Dyads in organizational research: Conceptual issues and multilevel analyses. *Organizational Research Methods*, *14*(3), 456–83.
Granovetter, M. (1973). The strength of weak ties. *American Journal of Sociology*, *78*, 1360–80.
Granovetter, M. (1985). Economic action and social structure: The problem of embeddedness. *American Journal of Sociology*, *91*(3), 481–510.
Grigoriou, K., and Rothaermel, F. T. (2014). Structural microfoundations of innovation: The role of relational stars. *Journal of Management*, *40*(2), 586–615.
Groysberg, B., Lee, L. E., and Nanda, A. (2008). Can they take it with them? The portability of star knowledge workers' performance. *Management Science*, *54*(7), 1213–30.
Harris, C., McMahan, G., and Wright, P. M. (2012). Talent and time together: The impact of human capital and overlapping tenure on unit performance. *Personnel Review*, *41*(4), 408–27.
Helfat, C. E., and Martin, J. A. (2015). Dynamic managerial capabilities: Review and assessment of managerial impact on strategic change. *Journal of Management*, *41*(5), 1281–312.
Hess, A. M., and Rothaermel, F. T. (2011). When are assets complementary? Star scientists, strategic alliances, and innovation in the pharmaceutical industry. *Strategic Management Journal*, *32*(8), 895–909.
Hitt, M. A., Beamish, P. W., Jackson, S. E., and Mathieu, J. E. (2007). Building theoretical and empirical bridges across levels: Multilevel research in management. *Academy of Management Journal*, *50*(6), 1385–99.
Hitt, M. A., Bierman, L., Shimizu, K., and Kochhar, R. (2001). Direct and moderating effects of human capital on strategy and performance in professional service firms: A resource-based perspective. *Academy of Management Journal*, *44*(1), 13–28.
Hollenbeck, J. R., and Jamieson, B. B. (2015). Human capital, social capital, and social network analysis: Implications for strategic human resource management. *Academy of Management Perspectives*, *29*(3), 370–85.
Janis, I. L. (1972). *Victims of Groupthink: A Psychological Study of Foreign-Policy Decisions and Fiascoes*. Boston, MA: Houghton Mifflin.
Johnson, S. G., Schnatterly, K., and Hill, A. D. (2013). Board composition beyond independence: Social capital, human capital, and demographics. *Journal of Management*, *39*(1), 232–62.
Kor, Y. Y., and Leblebici, H. (2005). How do interdependencies among human-capital deployment, development, and diversification strategies affect firms' financial performance? *Strategic Management Journal*, *26*(10), 967–85.
Kozlowski, S. W., and Bell, B. S. (2003). Work groups and teams in organizations. In W. C. Borman, D. R. Ilgen, and R. J. Klimoski (eds), *Handbook of Psychology, Vol. 12: Industrial and Organizational Psychology*, 333–75. New York: Wiley-Blackwell.
Kozlowski, S. W., and Chao, G. T. (2012). The dynamics of emergence: Cognition and cohesion in work teams. *Managerial and Decision Economics*, *33*(5–6), 335–54.
Kozlowski, S. W., and Klein, K. J. (2000). A multilevel approach to theory and research in organizations: Contextual, temporal, and emergent processes. In K. J. Klein and S. W. J. Kozlowski (eds), *Multilevel Theory, Research, and Methods in Organizations: Foundations, Extensions, and New Directions*, 3–90. San Francisco, CA: Jossey-Bass.
Kozlowski, S. W., Chao, G. T., Grand, J. A., Braun, M. T., and Kuljanin, G. (2013). Advancing multilevel research design: Capturing the dynamics of emergence. *Organizational Research Methods*, *16*(4), 581–615.
Krause, R., Semadeni, M., and Withers, M. C. (2016). That special someone: When the board views its chair as a resource. *Strategic Management Journal*, *37*(9), 1990–2002.
Labianca, G., and Brass, D. J. (2006). Exploring the social ledger: Negative relationships and negative asymmetry in social networks in organizations. *Academy of Management Review*, *31*(3), 596–614.
Leana III, C. R., and Van Buren, H. J. (1999). Organizational social capital and employment practices. *Academy of Management Review*, *24*(3), 538–55.
Lepak, D. P., and Snell, S. A. (1999). The human resource architecture: Toward a theory of human capital allocation and development. *Academy of Management Review*, *24*(1), 31–48.

Lester, R. H., Hillman, A., Zardkoohi, A., and Cannella Jr, A. A. (2008). Former government officials as outside directors: The role of human and social capital. *Academy of Management Journal, 51*(5), 999–1013.
Lin, Nan (2001). *Social Capital: A Theory of Social Structure and Action.* Cambridge: Cambridge University Press.
March, J. G. (1991). Exploration and exploitation in organizational learning. *Organization Science, 2*(1), 71–87.
Mawdsley, J. K., and Somaya, D. (2016). Employee mobility and organizational outcomes: An integrative conceptual framework and research agenda. *Journal of Management, 42*(1), 85–113.
Mayer, K. J., Somaya, D., and Williamson, I. O. (2012). Firm-specific, industry-specific, and occupational human capital and the sourcing of knowledge work. *Organization Science, 23*(5), 1311–29.
McFadyen, M. A., and Cannella Jr, A. A. (2004). Social capital and knowledge creation: Diminishing returns of the number and strength of exchange relationships. *Academy of Management Journal, 47*(5), 735–46.
Milgrom, P., and Roberts, J. (1995). Complementarities and fit strategy, structure, and organizational change in manufacturing. *Journal of Accounting and Economics, 19*(2–3), 179–208.
Miller, D., Xu, X., and Mehrotra, V. (2015). When is human capital a valuable resource? The performance effects of Ivy League selection among celebrated CEOs. *Strategic Management Journal, 36*(6), 930–44.
Mintzberg, H. (1978). Patterns in strategy formation. *Management Science, 24*(9), 934–48.
Mintzberg, H., and Waters, J. A. (1985). Of strategies, deliberate and emergent. *Strategic Management Journal, 6*(3), 257–72.
Molloy, J. C., and Barney, J. B. (2015). Who captures the value created with human capital? A market-based view. *Academy of Management Perspectives, 29*(3), 309–25.
Molloy, J. C., Ployhart, R. E., and Wright, P. M. (2011). The myth of "the" micro-macro divide: Bridging system-level and disciplinary divides. *Journal of Management, 37*(2), 581–609.
Nahapiet, J. (2011). A social perspective: Exploring the links between human capital and social capital. In A. Burton-Jones and J.-C. Spender (eds), *The Oxford Handbook of Human Capital*, 71–95. Oxford: Oxford University Press.
Nahapiet, J., and Ghoshal, S. (1998). Social capital, intellectual capital, and the organizational advantage. *Academy of Management Review, 23*(2), 242–66.
Nisbett, R. E., and Wilson, T. D. (1977). The halo effect: Evidence for unconscious alteration of judgments. *Journal of Personality and Social Psychology, 35*(4), 250–56.
Nyberg, A. J., and Ployhart, R. E. (2013). Context-emergent turnover (CET) theory: A theory of collective turnover. *Academy of Management Review, 38*(1), 109–31.
Nyberg, A. J., Moliterno, T. P., Hale, D., and Lepak, D. P. (2014). Resource-based perspectives on unit-level human capital a review and integration. *Journal of Management, 40*(1), 316–46.
Oh, H., Labianca, G., and Chung, M. H. (2006). A multilevel model of group social capital. *Academy of Management Review, 31*(3), 569–82.
Oldroyd, J. B., and Morris, S. S. (2012). Catching falling stars: A human resource response to social capital's detrimental effect of information overload on star employees. *Academy of Management Review, 37*(3), 396–418.
Payne, G. T., Moore, C. B., Griffis, S. E., and Autry, C. W. (2011). Multilevel challenges and opportunities in social capital research. *Journal of Management, 37*(2), 491–520.
Ployhart, R. E., and Cragun, O. R. (2017). Human capital resource complementarities. In D. G. Collings, K. Mellahl, and W. F. Cascio (eds), *The Oxford Handbook of Talent Management*, 134–49. Oxford: Oxford University Press.
Ployhart, R. E., and Moliterno, T. P. (2011). Emergence of the human capital resource: A multilevel model. *Academy of Management Review, 36*(1), 127–50.
Ployhart, R. E., Nyberg, A. J., Reilly, G., and Maltarich, M. A. (2014). Human capital is dead; long live human capital resources! *Journal of Management, 40*(2), 371–98.
Rivera, L. A. (2011). Ivies, extracurriculars, and exclusion: Elite employers' use of educational credentials. *Research in Social Stratification and Mobility, 29*(1), 71–90.
Rothaermel, F. T., and Hess, A. M. (2007). Building dynamic capabilities: Innovation driven by individual-, firm-, and network-level effects. *Organization Science, 18*(6), 898–921.
Sirmon, D. G., Hitt, M. A., Ireland, R. D., and Gilbert, B. A. (2011). Resource orchestration to create competitive advantage: Breadth, depth, and life cycle effects. *Journal of Management, 37*(5), 1390–412.
Slavova, K., Fosfuri, A., and De Castro, J. O. (2015). Learning by hiring: The effects of scientists' inbound mobility on research performance in academia. *Organization Science, 27*(1), 72–89.
Soltis, S., Brass, D., and Lepak, D. (2018). Social resource management: Integrating social network theory and human resource management. *Academy of Management Annals, 12*(2), 537–73.
Somaya, D., Williamson, I. O., and Lorinkova, N. (2008). Gone but not lost: The different performance impacts of employee mobility between cooperators versus competitors. *Academy of Management Journal, 51*(5), 936–53.
Somaya, D., Williamson, I. O., and Zhang, X. (2007). Combining patent law expertise with R&D for patenting performance. *Organization Science, 18*(6), 922–37.
Stevenson, W. B., and Radin, R. F. (2009). Social capital and social influence on the board of directors. *Journal of Management Studies, 46*(1), 16–44.

Tasselli, S., Kilduff, M., and Menges, J. I. (2015). The microfoundations of organizational social networks: A review and an agenda for future research. *Journal of Management*, *41*(5), 1361–87.
Tzabbar, D., Aharonson, B. S., Amburgey, T. L., and Al-Laham, A. (2008). When is the whole bigger than the sum of its parts? Bundling knowledge stocks for innovative success. *Strategic Organization*, *6*(4), 375–406.
Whitley, R., and McKenzie, K. (2005). Social capital and psychiatry: Review of the literature. *Harvard Review of Psychiatry*, *13*(2), 71–84.
Wright, P. M., and McMahan, G. C. (2011). Exploring human capital: Putting "human" back into strategic human resource management. *Human Resource Management Journal*, *21*(2), 93–104.
Wright, P. M., Coff, R., and Moliterno, T. P. (2014). Strategic human capital: Crossing the great divide. *Journal of Management*, *40*(2), 353–70.
Youndt, M. A., Subramaniam, M., and Snell, S. A. (2004). Intellectual capital profiles: An examination of investments and returns. *Journal of Management Studies*, *41*(2), 335–61.

14. The missing construct in strategic human capital research: humans

Patrick M. Wright and Spenser M. Essman

In John Steinbeck's 1941 book *The Log from the Sea of Cortez* he describes two views of the Mexican Sierra, a much sought-after sport fish. He describes how when the fish strikes on the line it nearly burns the fisherman's hands. He notes the exhilarating beauty of the pulsing colors and tail beating the air when the fisherman has brought it in over the rail. But he then notes that the way to get a specific description of the fish is to pull a dead fish out of a formaldehyde solution and count the spines and describe it. However, he notes that this latter approach misses the relational reality the fisherman experienced. He writes, "It is good to know what you are doing. The man with his pickled fish has set down one truth and recorded in his experience many lies. The fish is not that color, that texture, that dead, nor does he smell that way" (Steinbeck 1941, pp. 2–3, taken from Weick, 1979). We contend in this chapter that by trying to describe the details, the field of Strategic Human Capital (SHC) has ignored the relational reality that comes with understanding what it means to be truly human.

Few would argue with the fact that the field of SHC has grown in both popularity and importance over the past 15 years. As a mechanism to connect researchers in strategy, Human Resources (HR), and related fields, the domain has brought together people from different disciplines (Molloy et al., 2011), resulting in communication issues across disciplines (Wright et al., 2014). While contributions have come from multiple disciplines, economics has tended to dominate the conversation, likely due to origins in Becker's seminal work (1964: 15–28). Some of the most vocal debates within this literature, such as generic vs. specific human capital (e.g. Campbell et al., 2012; Coff and Raffiee, 2015) and value creation and capture (e.g. Chadwick, 2017; Sirmon et al., 2007), are rooted in economics.

While economics has become the underlying discipline within the field, more recent issues may not easily be resolved within its paradigm. As the quote above illustrates, often when looking at phenomenon through a specific scientific lens, we may miss the reality of the phenomenon-in-real-life. The chapters we are commenting on by Morris and Snell (Chapter 12) and Crocker (Chapter 13) exemplify this problem. While both are interesting and provide unique contributions, they seem to exhibit the same "missing constructs" problem in that they treat the phenomenon of interest as a laboratory examination while missing the reality of what it means to be human. Our point is not to level this criticism at these two chapters, as they are completely consistent with the paradigm prevalent in the SHC literature. Rather, we intend to use them to illustrate how the SHC literature, while not wrong, may be missing important constructs.

OVERVIEW OF THE TWO CHAPTERS

Chapters 12 and 13 both focus largely on links between human capital and social capital, albeit with different points of emphasis. Crocker seeks to understand the value of human capital resources primarily through a detailed examination of the co-emergence of human and social capital. She proposes that human capital can impact the emergence of social capital, and vice versa. She also argues that opaque sub-processes such as task interdependence, time sequence, complementary/substitutable relationships, and mobility impact the co-emergence of valuable human capital resources.

Morris and Snell similarly bring together human and social capital, but with an emphasis on how employees can solve customer problems. They note that employees can leverage both their human capital and social capital in the problem identification and solution development process for value creation in relation to customers. They develop both a multilevel "use value" approach to value creation and 2 × 2 matrix based on knowledge stocks (human and social capital) and knowledge flows (Problem Identification and Solution Development).

Both of these contributions expand our understanding of some of the phenomena related to the interface of human and social capital, and do so in a manner that is consistent with the SHC literature; however, as we argue throughout this chapter, the SHC literature often fails to consider what it means to be human. To support this assertion, we first explore the major constructs that serve as the focus within this literature, and then the implicit and explicit assumptions of the SHC literature. Subsequently, we offer insights that we believe can add to the SHC conversation in the future.

MAJOR CONSTRUCTS

Human Capital

Citing Becker (1967) and Ployhart and Moliterno (2011), Morris defines human capital as "the aggregated knowledge, skills, and experience of individuals within the organization, with experience being the key predictor in human capital theory." Crocker similarly treats human capital resources as "a multilevel construct, based on an individual's knowledge, skills, abilities and other characteristics (KSAOs) and comprising both individual- and unit-level manifestations."

These authors' treatment of the multilevel nature of human capital recognizes that the unit-level human capital resources are in part determined by the nature of aggregation and/or emergence of the individual-level human capital. Crocker focuses on exploring specifically how social capital impacts individuals' human capital, and vice versa; and that both influence the unit-level human capital provides a thorough examination of this potential aggregation process.

Social Capital

Regarding social capital, Morris and Snell and Crocker all agree on its importance, but do not agree 100 percent on its definition. As Morris and Snell define it, "Social capital is the knowledge embedded within, available through, and derived from social networks" (Coleman, 1988). Crocker, on the other hand, proposes that "social capital is the access to resources through relationships (Lin, 2001), which is a source of information and opportunities (Burt, 1997) in addition to a basis for shared norms and expectations" (Coleman, 1988). While not opposed to one another, this illustrates the problem we have found inherent in the social capital literature, i.e., that while all authors use the same vocabulary, they often use different dictionaries.

However, let us focus on the commonalities across these definitions. First, the authors agree that individuals possess KSAOs and that there are interactions and processes that determine how effectively the KSAOs of the individuals meld to create a unit-level human capital construct. Second, they emphasize the idea that an individual employee need not have all information or knowledge, but that their value is increased to the extent that they have relationships with others who do have the requisite information and/or knowledge. Third, they note the importance of these relationships both for the individual and the organization, but do not specifically address how and why these relationships emerge. These commonalities in definitions lead to identifying some of the foundational assumptions of their arguments. Again, we note that these assumptions are not unique to these chapters, but rather common to this literature.

EXPLICIT AND IMPLICIT ASSUMPTIONS

Whether explicit or implicit, the authors address a set of assumptions common in the SHC literature. Let us address these briefly.

Rational-Economic Man

Implicit in their treatment of the phenomena is an economist's assumption of the ratio-economic man. Such assumptions consist of the idea that employees are rational actors who seek to maximize their outcomes and make choices consistent with what they believe will result in the maximum benefit. This translates in the SHC literature specifically regarding choices to invest in developing human and/or social capital. This literature assumes such choices stem from individuals making choices that maximize their outcomes, particularly financial outcomes.

People as Repositories of Human Capital

The authors also focus on human capital and, as the definitions noted above, they refer to knowledge, skills, abilities, experiences, and other characteristics. Such a view treats employees as repositories of a set of characteristics of potential value to firms, suggesting that the major challenge for firms is how to manage the composition of the characteristics in a way that creates value for the firm (or for the firm, via the customer – Morris and Snell).

Value

While the authors consider the concept of value, their treatment of value seems external to the individual. In other words, just as Barney et al. (2001) note that value must be defined external to the firm (i.e., in the minds of customers who buy products or services), similarly the value of any human capital characteristic is defined by its ability to create value for the customer (Morris and Snell) or the firm (Crocker).

Instrumentality of Relationships

As previously discussed, both sets of authors define social capital in terms of the information and knowledge that is available to an individual through her relationships. They, consistent with the SHC literature, assume that relationships provide instrumental good to the individuals by increasing their value, and to the firm by increasing the overall flow of knowledge within it.

We note that these assumptions are consistent with the extant SHC literature. We do not suggest that they are wrong, but perhaps incomplete. Just as one might refer to a statistical model as "underspecified" if it fails to account for relevant variables, our reliance on economic theories in SHC underspecifies the constructs that impact the behaviors and decisions of those we seek to study. In order to examine this, we first note an additional assumption that has recently been recognized in this literature, and then explore some of the implications of this assumption.

Free Will

First, while none of the authors mention the construct of free will, they present models that suggest that employees make choices, be they to seek out others in their social network or to engage in certain behaviors with co-workers or customers. The concept of free will recognizes that employees can choose whether or not or how much to exert effort toward some end (Chadwick, 2017; Wright et al., 2001). As Chadwick notes: "One implication of free will is that workers' utility functions encompass both financial and affective dimensions" (p. 500).

However, much of the SHC literature focuses almost solely on the financial drivers and outcomes, ignoring aspects of human choice that may serve as more influential drivers. For instance, a number of authors have distinguished between those who view their work as a job, a career, or a calling (Wrzesniewski et al., 1997). Those who view work as a job focus on the material benefits from work. Those who view work as a career show less concern for monetary gain, but more concern for advancement. Those whose work serves as a calling view their work as socially valuable – i.e., an end in and of itself. For example, Bunderson and Thompson (2009: 32) studied zookeepers' view of work and found that:

> a neoclassical calling is both binding and ennobling. On one hand, zookeepers with a sense of calling strongly identified with and found broader meaning and significance in their work and occupation. On the other hand, they were more likely to see their work as a moral duty, to sacrifice pay, personal time, and comfort for their work, and to hold their zoo to a higher standard.

Clearly, current SHC views of work do not account for such data. Similarly, Allan et al. (2018) conducted a meta-analysis of the consequences of "meaningful" work. They defined meaningful work as "a global judgement that one's work accomplishes significant, valuable, or worthwhile goals that are congruent work with one's existential values." Their results showed that meaningful work impacted self-rated performance, organizational citizenship behaviors, and withdrawal intentions through its more proximal impact on work engagement, commitment, and job satisfaction.

Thus, the SHC literature, by solely focusing on financial drivers of employee choices, misses the complexity of human motivation. Similarly, by solely focusing on instrumentality of human capital to organizational success, the SHC literature actually devalues the phenomenon of interest. We suggest that by broadening our view of human capital to encompass humanity, the SHC literature might provide a more comprehensive view of the relationship between human capital and organizations.

PUTTING THE "HUMAN" IN STRATEGIC HUMAN CAPITAL

From Rational-Economic to Spiritual Man

This section does not suggest the veracity of any specific religion, or religion in general, but seeks to point out that people live as if they are more than information processors. A purely materialistic worldview (i.e., all that exists is matter) requires that individuals are no more than an accidental co-location of atoms, and that all their behavior is determined by material processes such as chemical reactions and electronic impulses (Crick, 1994). Whether or not this is true, we know that people do not believe it to be true. They believe that they are in some sense a spirit that possesses the ability to make choices, and not a "wet robot" programmed to behave in certain ways. Miller and Thoreson (2003: 27) note that usually spirituality is defined:

> in distinction from material reality as experienced by the physical senses . . . generally understood to transcend ordinary physical limits of time and space, matter, and energy . . . Some view spirituality as primarily relational – a transcendent relationship with that which is sacred in life . . . or with something divine beyond the self.

Ashmos and Duchon (2000) write: "To understand spirituality and work is to recognize that workers are spiritual beings whose souls are either nurtured or damaged by their work" (p. 136). The SHC literature fails to hold such a view of humanity, and current models cannot account for any transcendent view or transcendent motivation that might impact behavior of those studies. To not account for this limits our ability to understand human behavior in organizations.

Miller and Thoreson make a similar point that research on health that ignores the spiritual/religious nature of man may miss important determinants of health. They conclude their review by stating:

> Most people want to live with better health, less disease, greater inner peace, and a fuller sense of meaning, direction, and satisfaction in their lives. Increasing levels of affluence and materialism have failed to bring such changes (Myers, 2000). Scientific investigation of this neglected aspect

> of human nature may lead to important new clues for helping people live together with better health, richer positive experiences, and greater meaning and satisfaction in life. (p. 33)

Few SHC researchers have ventured to examine constructs such as health, peace, meaning, and direction, but much has centered on affluence and materialism. Thus, SHC research treating people as purely material rational outcome maximizers may miss more important determinants of human behavior.

From Repositories to Complex Beings

First, we do not intend to argue that employees do not have KSAOs that can potentially provide value to firms. Certainly the entire recruitment, selection, development, and retention process is aimed at ensuring the firm has people with the requisite skills (Ployhart et al., 2017). However, the SHC literature tends to ignore the fact that, in addition to these KSAOs, employees also possess bundles of expectations, aspirations, goals, and values, all of which influence a number of behaviors examined within this literature. People in general, and millennials in particular, have expectations for how a firm will help them develop their skills, and neither know about, nor care about, the distinction between specific and general skills (Kryscynski and Ulrich, 2015). They have aspirations for their careers and status, and firms that obstruct these goals may see employees leave. Finally, they have values regarding work and family, the culture of the organization, and the firm's social reputation that can similarly attract or repel them. Terkel (1995) interviewed a number of workers, hearing their stories and criticisms of their workplaces. This led him to conclude that work must be "about a search, too, for daily meaning as well as daily bread, for recognition as well as cash, for astonishment rather than torpor; in short for a sort of life rather than a Monday through Friday sort of dying" (p. xiii).

We point to the debate over which types of skills, specific or general, enable firms and/or employees to capture rents. The debate began with the idea that general skills cannot be a source of competitive advantage (Wright et al., 1994) and that specific skills can be. However, because employees cannot capture the rents from specific skills, the argument shifted to understanding why employees invest in gaining them. As Campbell and colleagues described, the willingness to gain specific skills signals a desire to learn that may be attractive to other firms and that general skills could be sources of competitive advantage under certain conditions (Campbell et al., 2012). This debate ignores the complexity of human motivation such that most, if not all, seek to grow through constant learning. While marketability may be one aspect of the motivation, it may also be the least important. Our models of SHC need to account for the intrinsic desire of people to grow and learn rather than treat their skill acquisition as a financial calculation.

From Extrinsic Value to Inherent Value

As noted previously, the SHC literature focuses on the value of KSAOs where that value stems from the usefulness of the skills to provide value to customers, shareholders, or other stakeholders. Certainly, the "strategic" part of SHC requires emphasizing the value gained by the firm, but limits the value measurement to a financial criterion. The SHC literature treats people as "objects" whose value stems from what they can do for the firm, rather than as "subjects" whose dignity and worth exists independent of the firm. They are fathers, mothers, children, friends, community members, etc. who are valued for more than the skills they bring to the firm.

This does not suggest that studying the value of human capital (individual) or human capital resources (unit) from the standpoint of the firm has no merit. Rather, it only points to the warning that such a view can result in people being treated as property. Johnny Taylor, the President and CEO of the Society for Human Resource Management (SHRM), spoke at a local SHRM meeting recently. He mentioned that he was using the term "human capital" frequently in a previous talk, and afterward was approached by some African-American members of the audience who asked him not to use that term. When he asked why, they responded that in the era of slavery, slaves were referred to and treated as "capital" – i.e., property that someone owned. While the SHC literature frequently proposes the caveat that human capital differs from other types of capital in that the firm can never own it, many treatments still imply that employees be treated as other types of capital, i.e., based on their value to the firm. The firm cannot "own" people; but it can exploit them, manipulate them, and discard them if their value stems only from the utility they provide the firm.

From Instrumental Relationships to Community

Much of the SHC literature's treatment of social capital focuses on the value that individuals bring to the firm through their relationships and, to some extent, the value that they capture from those relationships. These arguments implicitly assume that relationships serve as instrumental resources to capture value for either the firm or the individual. Again, because the literature emphasizes the "strategic" nature of the construct, this makes sense. But also, again, such a focus on one aspect may ignore other, even more important aspects of human behavior.

Do people view their relationships solely as instrumental resources, or could their motivation be broader? According to Ashmos and Duchon (2000: 136): "Spirituality at work is also about the notion that spiritual being not only express inner life needs by seeking meaningful work but that part of being alive is living in connection to other human beings." They noted that people want to feel connected to each other at work. This suggests that people seek and develop relationships as part of their search for meaning and connection in the workplace, rather than just as an instrumental way of increasing their value. Such connection supersedes a financial motivation, but rather points to an inherent human need for relationships, particularly in what can often be a cold and impersonal bureaucracy. In fact Vaill (1998) noted: "fellowship helps both the leaders and members to confront the loneliness, disappointment, and pain of the modern organization and to decide that these conditions should not continue to rot the spirit of the organization and the people in it" (p. 227).

CONCLUSION

This chapter does not seek to argue that the SHC literature is wrong, or without any value. It has provided insights into the value that employees potentially bring to firms, and the ways in which firms can seek to manage them to provide maximal value (Nyberg et al., 2014; Ployhart et al., 2014; Wright et al., 2014). However, we do suggest that this quest has been limited by its obsession with economic models to explain specifically human phenomena. To be human is to be complex: motivated by multiple goals and values; being far more complicated than the aggregation of knowledge and skills; having intrinsic dignity and worth regardless of knowledge and skills; and inherently social beings. To paraphrase Steinbeck, the SHC researcher with his/her pickled employee has set down one truth and recorded in his experience many lies. The person is not that constrained, not that one-dimensional, his behavior not that determined; nor does he think, act, and feel that way. In taking such an approach, the strategic human capital literature seemingly misses its central construct: humans.

CHAPTER SUMMARY

BOX 14.1 KEY TAKEAWAYS

1. The field of Strategic Human Capital, partially because of its economic roots, often fails to consider what it means to be human.
2. Integrating human capital and social capital requires greater acknowledgement of the complexities of humans.
3. Taking a more holistic view of humans will challenge underlying assumptions of the Strategic Human Capital literature and may lead to greater insights.

BOX 14.2 DIRECTIONS FOR FUTURE RESEARCH

1. To better understand employee behavior, research is needed to understand how humans' desire for meaning and community contradicts their economic rationality.
2. Our models of SHC need to account for the intrinsic desire of people to grow and learn rather than treat their skill acquisition as a financial calculation.

REFERENCES

Allan, B., Batz-Barbarich, C., Sterling, H., and Tay, L. (2018). Outcomes of meaningful work: A meta-analysis. *Journal of Management Inquiry*, doi:10.1111/joms.12406.

Ashmos, D., and Duchon, D. (2000). Spirituality at work: A conceptualization and measure. *Journal of Management Inquiry*, *9*(2), 134–45.

Barney, J., Wright, M., and Ketchen Jr, D. J. (2001). The resource-based view of the firm: Ten years after 1991. *Journal of Management*, *27*(6), 625–41.

Becker, G. S. (1964). *Human Capital: A Theoretical and Empirical Analysis with Special Reference to Education* (3rd edn). Chicago: University of Chicago Press.

Becker, G. S. (1967). *Human Capital and the Personal Distribution of Income*. Ann Arbor: University of Michigan Press.

Bunderson, J., and Thompson, J. (2009). The call of the wild: Zookeepers, callings, and the double-edged sword of deeply meaningful work. *Administrative Science Quarterly*, *54*, 32–57.

Burt, R. (1997). The contingent value of social capital. *Administrative Science Quarterly*, *42*(2), 339–65.

Campbell, B. A., Coff, R., and Kryscynski, D. (2012). Rethinking competitive advantage from human capital. *Academy of Management Review*, *37*, 376–95.
Chadwick, C. (2017). Towards a more comprehensive model of firms' human capital rents. *Academy of Management Review*, *42*(3), 499–519.
Coff, R., and Raffiee, J. (2015). Toward a theory of perceived firm-specific human capital. *Academy of Management Perspectives*, *29*(3), 326–41.
Coleman, J. (1988). Social capital in the creation of human capital. *American Journal of Sociology*, *94*, S95–120.
Crick, F. (1994). *The Astonishing Hypothesis: The Scientific Search for the Soul*. New York: Touchstone.
Kryscynski, D., and Ulrich, D. (2015). Making strategic human capital relevant: A time-sensitive opportunity. *Academy of Management Perspectives*, *29*(3), 357–69.
Lin, N. (2001). *Social Capital: A Theory of Social Structure and Action*. Cambridge: Cambridge University Press.
Miller, W., and Thoreson, C. (2003). Spirituality, religion, and health. *American Psychologist*, *58*(1), 24–35.
Molloy, J., Ployhart, R., and Wright, P. (2011). The myth of the macro–micro divide. *Journal of Management*, *37*, 581–609.
Myers, D. G. (2000). *The American Paradox: Spiritual Hunger in an Age of Plenty*. New Haven, CT: Yale University Press.
Nyberg, A. J., Moliterno, T. P., Hale, D. H., and Lepak, D. P. (2014). Resource-based perspectives on unit-level human capital: A review and integration. *Journal of Management*, *40*(1), 316–46.
Ployhart, R. E., and Moliterno, T. P. (2011). Emergence of the human capital resource: A multilevel model. *Academy of Management Review*, *36*(1), 127–50.
Ployhart, R. E., Schmitt, N., and Tippins, N. T. (2017). Solving the supreme problem: 100 years of recruitment and selection research at the *Journal of Applied Psychology*. *Journal of Applied Psychology*, *102*, 291–304.
Ployhart, R. E., Nyberg, A. J., Reilly, G., and Maltarich, M. A. 2014. Human capital is dead; long live human capital resources! *Journal of Management*, *40*, 371–98.
Sirmon, D., Hitt, M., and Ireland, D. (2007). Managing firm resources in dynamic environments to create value: Looking inside the black box. *Academy of Management Review*, *32*(1), 273–92.
Steinbeck, J. (1941). *The Log from the Sea of Cortez*. New York: Viking.
Terkel, S. (1995). *Working*. New York: Ballantine.
Vaill, P. (1998). *Spirited Leading and Learning*. San Francisco: Jossey-Bass.
Weick, K. (1979). *The Social Psychology of Organizing* (2nd edn). New York: McGraw-Hill.
Wright, P., Coff, R., and Moliterno, T. (2014). Strategic human capital: Crossing the great divide. *Journal of Management*, *40*(2), 353–70.
Wright, P., Dunford, B., and Snell, S. (2001). Contributions of the resource-based view of the firm to the field of strategic HRM: Convergence of two fields. *Journal of Management*, *27*, 701–21.
Wright, P.M., McMahan, G.C., and McWilliams, A. (1994). Human resources as a source of sustained competitive advantage: A resource-based perspective. *International Journal of Human Resource Management*, *5*, 301–26.
Wrzesniewski, A., McCauley, C., Rozin, P., and Schwartz, B. (1997). Jobs, careers, and callings: People's relations to their work. *Journal of Research in Personality*, *31*, 21–33.

15. Agonistic relations, social capital, and (dis)complementarity in the emergence of human capital resources

Rhett A. Brymer and Michael A. Hitt

Several management scholars have acknowledged that the least explored and most promising area for new, compelling theory in our field can be found in the "great divide," the gulf between our knowledge of individuals and the organizations they constitute (Molloy et al., 2011; Wright et al., 2014). While much is understood about the behavior of individuals in workplace settings, we know little about how resources controlled by individual employees are combined – often tens of thousands of them – in ways that help firms to compete. Likewise, although we understand how a firm's strategies and capabilities drive its competitiveness, we need a better understanding of how individual workers' knowledge and behaviors are integrated to contribute to this end. This includes both the ways that workers help and hinder each other.

At the forefront of recent theory development to bridge the gap noted above has been work on the emergence of human capital resources (Ployhart and Moliterno, 2011; Ployhart et al., 2014). Essential in this theorizing is the concept of complementarity among individuals' human capital within the organization, wherein there is the potential for "an increase in the *value of a combined whole*, compared to its constituent units" (Adegbesan, 2009: 465, emphasis in original). The nature of how individually held resources are combined and serve as complements, thus, is critical to our understanding of how and the extent to which human capital resources emerges.

Building on the chapters by Morris and Snell and Crocker, we contend that social capital among individual employees is a substantial determinant of value-adding complementarities among individually possessed human capital resources. Additionally, the nature of social capital can create a variety of complementarity types, ranging from the value-creating emergent synergies often cited by resource-based scholars (e.g. Adegbesan, 2009; Peteraf, 2005; Sirmon et al., 2007) to the less explored deleterious combinations, i.e. negative synergies among workforce members, that harm combined value-in-use (Chadwick, 2017), potentially leading to organizational disadvantage and lower performance.

Finally, we contend that most salient complementarity in human capital occurs through enacted social relations, presenting opportunities for a broad variety of new organizational research. Scholarly work on a host of strategy and organizational theory foci can be conceived to better understand how firms create conditions for social capital among workforce members to develop and evolve. The foci include but are not limited to organizational structure, governance, diversification, executive compensation, collective turnover and hiring, acquisitions, alliances, and internationalization. Human capital research has opportunities to integrate insights from these assorted areas to enhance our understanding of how complementarities contribute to the development of knowledge resources in organizational contexts. Such insights can provide a platform that contributes to more holistic understanding of how organizations compete effectively (Cascio and Boudreau, 2010; Fulmer and Ployhart, 2014).

COMPLEMENTARITIES, HUMAN CAPITAL, AND SOCIAL CAPITAL

Complementarity involves the relationship between multiple inputs or activities where positive interdependencies result (Milgrom and Roberts, 1990; Tzabbar et al., 2008). This implies that one resource enhances the outcomes of other resources. Applied to firms that bundle resources in order to create value for customers (Morris, 2019), complementarity can be as simplistic as two discrete assets that are co-specialized to work together, or as complex as the degree of fit between two firms, each with a complex set of resources the firms use to work jointly to produce outcomes (Makri et al., 2010).

Applied to human capital, complementarity's scale can likewise have a wide range. In the most basic example, a tangible asset might be paired with an individual worker such that the capabilities of both paired together produce outcomes that surpass the sum of the two operating independently. Take for instance a worker and her computer that are co-specialized (via passwords, file organization, applications, etc. specific to that worker). While this example certainly suggests complementarity, it is unlikely that this pairing would generate any advantage for an organization, as such enabling technologies are common and typically easy to imitate.

From a firm-competitiveness perspective, the far more intriguing set of complementarities is how human capital is bundled through a complex set of relationships, and how it combines and is integrated with other firm capabilities, structures, and systems. Human capital is never isolated, but instead is part of a complex web of firm resources that are constantly and dynamically being structured, bundled, and leveraged within and at the boundaries of the organization (Colbert, 2004; Sirmon et al., 2007). The value-in-use – the realized utility of a resource's services (Penrose, 1959) – of a firm's human capital, then, is subject to complementarities with the firm's HR capabilities (Chadwick, 2017), its HR practices, its design (Ennen and Richter, 2010), and its interfirm alliances (Hess and Rothaermel, 2011), among other firm attributes.

The vast majority of these strategically relevant complementarities with human capital involve individuals (or groups) interacting with a host of other individuals and groups in order to execute firm practices, routines, and competitive actions in order to implement the firm's strategy. Human capital is embedded in these dense networks of social interactions, creating social capital between individuals and groups. These bundles of social capital constitute social complexities that are challenging to assess by observant rivals, providing potential isolating mechanisms that can prevent imitation by competitors (Barney, 1991). Knowledge work in the dynamic structures of modern organizations (Ranson et al., 1980) provides rich contexts within which individuals and groups must constantly relate and cooperate with several other individuals and groups in the course of business. The nature of these ties determines how effectively human capital can be complementary to other employees or stakeholders with resources that have the potential to bundle with that human capital to create its value-in-use.

Based on the arguments presented, we conclude that *social capital provides the basis for virtually all strategically relevant human capital complementarities*. Social capital, as the shared relations between human entities (Adler and Kwon, 2002), provides the means by which knowledge can be exchanged and combined, by which entities are motivated to cooperate, and by which cooperation yields greater outcomes. Organizing a firm involves continuously bundling human capital to leverage effective relationships and combinations of knowledge dispersed throughout the firm (Grigoriou and Rothaermel, 2014). Thus, organizing involves creating contexts in which social capital can be developed in ways that the configurations and bundles of human capital resources are complementary (cf. Ployhart and Moliterno, 2011).

A BROADER SPECTRUM OF COMPLEMENTARITIES

Managers of these living, complex systems of human and social capital resources have significant opportunities for value creation. Indeed, literature describing complementarities overwhelmingly focuses on the accretive aspects of resource combination (e.g. Alchian and Demsetz, 1972; Chadwick, 2017; Milgrom and Roberts, 1990). Adegbesan (2009: 465) positively frames complementarities, noting that "a more diverse variation [exists] in resource complementarity than [the] bipolar" extremes of zero and idiosyncratic bilateral synergy.

This is particularly true when human capital is bundled with complementary intent. Human capital is a notoriously complex resource (e.g. Lazear, 2009; Ployhart et al., 2014) that ultimately is controlled by agentic individuals (Coff, 1997). The complexity of human capital creates heterogeneity in the potential to complement other resources; what might originally seem to be an appropriate profile of human capital may not have as high a value-creating potential as deemed *ex ante*. For instance, research on selection has long recognized the low validities of various singular candidate attributes in their ability to predict future performance in a firm (Schmidt and Hunter, 1998), underlining the asymmetric information challenges with acquiring new human capital. Assessing fit of human capital with a firm or its nested resources is difficult. Poor fit with other human capital and organizational idiosyncrasies creates a gap between what Chadwick (2017) deemed intended and realized value for those human capital resources.

Likewise, the complexities of the relationships between units (groups, teams, divisions, or firms) provide ample opportunities for complementarity realization, or lack thereof, between sets of human capital. While social capital can indeed be developed through repeated interactions between parties, in Chapter 13 Crocker points out that there are countless examples where the opposite is true. Relationships within organizations can be negative based on power disparities, moral hazards, personal conflicts, and competitive career-oriented conflict in which individuals take actions that are harmful to others (Brass et al., 1998; Brass et al., 2004; Hollenbeck and Jamieson, 2015). Thus, repeated interactions between parties typically lead to enhanced social capital, and this largely has dominated our assumptions of human interactions in and between firms. Yet it is clear that those interactions can be negatively charged, leading to ill will between the parties, potentially destroying value in what otherwise would be productive human capital combinations. Such relationships are not simply low in social capital – instead they can be conceived of as having "negative social capital."

Stated differently, social capital has (similar to complementarity) been almost universally conceived as having a minimum value of zero, suggesting a neutral relationship between parties (i.e., no social connection). Yet, if relationships between units are counterproductive, the relations are likely to produce worse outcomes than if the units have a neutral relationship, i.e. zero social capital. The connotation of the term "capital" is limiting, as capital is thought of as a means of production, not a foil to production. However, scenarios exist in which collaborative effort between parties might produce less than what would have been created independently. While substitution – or the reduction of the value of one resource in the presence of another due to redundancy – is often held as the opposite of complementarity, substitutes do not cause devaluation of the other's output in an absolute sense. Further, evidence exists that human capital redundancies provide strategic value in the event of unforeseen rival action and/or human capital loss (e.g., Brymer and Sirmon, 2018).

If social capital is the basis for the strategically relevant complementarities composed of human capital, then it is logical that "negative complementarities" can exist as well. As with capital, however, complementarity has been defined only in an accretive sense, where the theoretical minimum is a state of zero or neutral complementarity. In situations where ill will, unethical conflict, or cases of poor fit exists between the possessors of human capital, value destruction can potentially occur. Consider these examples: 1) two rivalrous C-level executives both vying for succession to the elderly CEO's spot; 2) redundant divisions created with a merger of like-sized firms with a high likelihood of imminent layoffs; and 3) two vicious competitor firms in the same multi-firm alliance to determine a new standardized technology platform. In each of these cases, employees or units have motivations to outcompete their rivals. And, in each case, despite a presumed spirit of cooperation between them, sabotage and antagonistic behavior are possible or even likely. Accordingly, our conceptions of complementarity are too narrow for the complex social contexts of human behavior (and human capital).

Attending to this theoretical and semantic shortcoming, we should consider these specific yet ubiquitous conditions of negative relationships and their effects on the human capital bundling (Soltis et al., 2018). Network scholars label individuals working against each other as "negative ties" (Labianca, 2014). Though negative ties between star employees or top management team members may affect the human capital resources of the firm most noticeably, a broader collection of these negative relationships is more likely to stem from social ties between the more voluminous middle management and individual employee contributor layers of organizations. Despite relatively little research concerning the firm performance effects of these lower-level employees, agonistic relations at these levels can have meaningful strategic consequences by blocking potential emergence of more valuable human capital resources (Ployhart et al., 2014).

To more effectively understand the impact of social relationships on the realized value of human capital resources, the agonistic aspects of social interactions – those that are marked by aggressive or defensive social engagement – must be considered. Whereas social capital provides a means of production, *agonistic relations* erode those means through contentious exchanges between individuals possessing human capital. Figure 15.1 provides an illustration of the traditional conceptualization of social capital

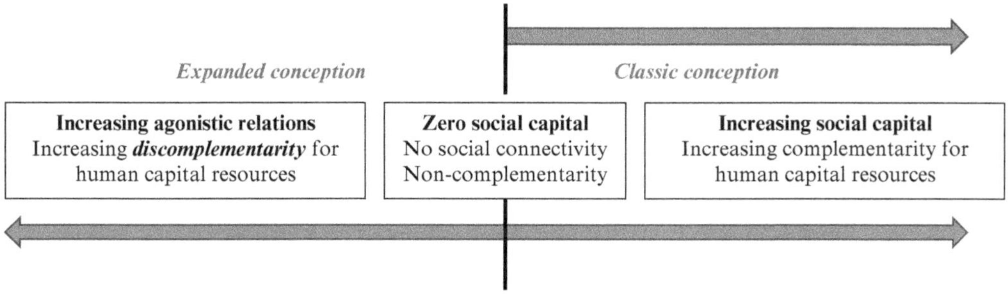

Figure 15.1 Spectra of relational value

value (top), and contrasts that with the spectrum of relational value that includes agonistic relations and their associated discomplementarities (Sav, 2004) for human capital.

To extend our understanding of discomplementarity, agonistic relations, and how social capital connects human capital within firms, consider the assorted types of relationships depicted in Table 15.1. From the top (mapping onto the extreme right of the above figure), catalytic complementarity involves one individual (or small set of individuals) that draw excess value from a wide range of employees through transformational leadership or extraordinary support. We argue that this is the highest form of complementarity, as an individual (or small unit) can provide resources that inspire others across a division or organization. Catalytic complementarity is rare because it involves the combination of someone (or unit) with extraordinary human capital, structurally at the top of the organization or central to its network, along with the ability to generate high degrees of social capital with all those in their sphere of influence.

The next type is classically conceived as synergistic complementarity, upon which most scholarship has focused. The notion that cooperators are able to accomplish more together than they would be able to do separately has been a common refrain accepted in most organizational scholarship (e.g. Alchian and Demsetz, 1972; Milgrom and Roberts, 1990). Social capital is needed for such synergy to function over time in any meaningfully stable manner.

Pairing units where no social capital exists, but also no agonistic relationship, is simplest as such pairing results in no emergent state. In this case, perhaps those involved can start developing social capital in order to build complementarity and create synergy. This may require some time to accomplish, however, and thus the joint work is unlikely to produce the outcomes desired by the organization in the interim. The parties must work to ensure that the relationship does not deteriorate such that positive complementarity cannot be achieved.

If relationships deteriorate, as they can in organizations, human capital value can be destroyed should the parties continue to interact with each other. The milder form of such discomplementarity is exploitative in nature, what we term as "exploitative complementarity," as one party extracts benefits similar to complementarity from a relationship but does not reciprocate. Instead, that party destroys the potential value of the paired entities in order to disproportionately capture value at the expense of the paired units. While that focal party may indeed provide value above what might have been provided alone, it is at the expense of the value created by other human capital. For example, in a multi-firm, non-equity technology alliance it is often an implicit understanding that all firms operate in good faith with an intent to contribute roughly equally to build one or more shared resources that all can use in the future. Any given firm, however, can free ride and exploit the complementarities of the alliance without commensurate resource contribution. The overall output of the alliance could have been better with the resources of the free riding firm(s). The firms that did contribute realized no value from the potential complementarities of the free rider, while the free rider exploited complementarities between the other firms in the alliance for its own gain.

The more extreme version of an agonistic relationship between parties is that of pugilism, where all parties are intent on hurting the others, even at their own expense. Though presumably rare due to the fact that such relationships cannot be sustained, these situations nonetheless do occur. Examples include negative politicking for promotions (e.g., between competing candidates), integration turf wars post-merger, or rivalry in a non-equity alliance. Avoiding pugilistic discomplementarity should be a priority to every manager. Insights regarding the motives, histories, and relationships among parties that are both routinely paired or will be bundled and deployed together are particular crucial for managers to consider when structuring their organization and creating project teams.

Table 15.1 presents these types, ranging from highest social capital to highest agonistic relations, with stylized interactions that sum the nature of the (dis)complementarity and descriptions of how it is achieved.

While a more complete conception of (dis)complementarities increases our understanding of the value created (or not) between any dyad of individuals or units, dyads rarely exist in isolation. Relationships typically are compositional of a broader network of human capital resources and particular individuals or units participating in dozens of ties with other resources of the firm. This social complexity provides the basis for

Table 15.1 Human capital (dis)complementarity typology

Complementarity Type	Stylized Interaction	Description
Catalytic Complementarity	1 + 3 = 6, certain human capital resources activate others to be more productive on their own	Transformational leadership or unit that raises the performance of everyone they are around through inspiration and/or widespread capability enhancement
Synergistic Complementarity	2 + 2 = 5, classically conceived complementarity	Cooperative workers that are more productive together than apart
Neutral or Non-Complementarity	2 + 2 = 4, no benefits from connectedness	Either substitution effects counteracting any complementary interactions, or simply no marginal benefit in the relational value from the cooperation (i.e., no social capital)
Exploitative Discomplementarity	2 + 2 = 3, one party extracts value from the other without reciprocation	Due to substitution (redundancy) or opportunistic behavior on one party's part; the free rider problem
Pugilistic Discomplementarity	2 + 2 = 1, defeating the value of both parties' human capital	Active resistance and aggressive behavior from both parties

emergence to occur, as unique, rare, and inimitable human capital resources result from particular configurations of complementarities (Barney, 1991; Conroy, Chapter 1 this volume; Methot et al., 2018).

Discomplementarities can also exist in these networks, along with the possibility that any particular individual or unit might hinder the formation of more useful complementarities. In these circumstances, the loss of a resource (e.g., individual employee turnover) may provide the opportunity for more fruitful complementarities to form among remaining individuals and/or units. Examples of these "addition by subtraction" events are employee turnover that may help their legacy unit perform more effectively, or the spin-off of a subsidiary where both parent and child organization create more value apart than together. Our field would benefit from more nuanced conceptions of relationships – be they valuable social capital or accretive agonistic relations – and how they are orchestrated to create emergent resources (Sirmon et al., 2007). This draws our attention to the various levers that firms have to manage these emergent processes (Brymer et al., 2011).

MANAGING (DIS)COMPLEMENTARITIES FOR HUMAN CAPITAL RESOURCE EMERGENCE

Scholars have made the case that the management of human capital resources drives up to 80 percent of firm value (Pfeffer, 1998; cf. Fulmer and Ployhart, 2014). Understanding how to create complementarities between individuals and units lies at the heart of this value creation. We cannot provide a comprehensive list of considerations and actions managers as it would require much more space than allowed for a chapter (perhaps a book). Nonetheless, with this volume as a guide, we provide examples pertaining to the most direct disruption of complementarities in employee mobility, as workers sever and create ties when switching organizations (Mawdsley and Somaya, 2016). We conclude with a general discussion of broader firm policies and actions that can provide the structures within which relationships across the firm provide a context for the emergence of human capital resources.

Employee Mobility and (Dis)complementarities

Managing the retention, hiring, and turnover of employees is essential to orchestrating firm resources in general (Sirmon et al., 2007), and in understanding firm-level performance outcomes in particular (Campbell et al., 2017). Maintenance of existing networks through employee retention keeps value-creating complementarities among individuals in the firm, potentially forming a basis for between-firm heterogeneity and human capital advantages (Campbell et al., 2012; Chadwick, 2017). The particular configurations of human capital that create these networks provide the social aspect to the firm-specificity, an oft-cited attribute of the firm's aggregate employee base that is theorized to contribute to or largely provide the barriers to imitation underlying such advantages (Brymer et al., 2015; Chadwick, 2017). For these reasons, managers should strive for stability in the value-generating configurations between individuals in a firm by identifying and working to retain not only star employees (Kehoe et al., 2018) but also average employees who create value through exceptional complementarities.

It is helpful for firms to avoid turnover of employees who generate social capital value. Turnover cannot be avoided altogether, as every organization deals with some degrees of voluntary employee exit. The costs of turnover vary considerably with different temporal, professional, industry, and organization contexts (Hausknecht and Holwerda, 2013; Nyberg and Ployhart, 2013). Skilled managers can contain costs by acting to ensure that complementarities lost are minimized: for instance practices, such as increased pay for assumption of more work tasks, that can spread the employee exits so that they do not happen simultaneously (Call et al., 2015), and to avoid the loss of clusters of connected individuals (Campbell et al., 2014). Such practices can limit damage to social capital structures and the complementary of the human capital left in the legacy firm. Creating redundant concentrations of social capital and human capital may also mitigate turnover damage (Brymer and Sirmon, 2018). Exiting employees starting new ventures often do so with high degrees of social capital. Their loss is particularly damaging to the firm (Campbell et al., 2012; Rocha et al., 2018), so monitoring sudden changes in the value of complementarities controlled by these nascent entrepreneurs may help retain their services (Byun et al., in press).

Though most research on turnover shows a general negative effect, one compelling possibility is that turnover may at times actually produce positive outcomes for firms (Hausknecht, Chapter 27; Rider and Tan, Chapter 28 this volume). Employees that do not create greater value – through their human capital and complementarities – than their remuneration represent economic losses for their firms, and losing them then is likely to produce performance benefits. This logic underlies layoffs in mergers and acquisitions where employee redundancies are eliminated. When employees have agonistic relations, discomplementarities that they cause can impede the emergence of human capital resources in units (e.g., Sutton, 2007). Employees with those agonistic relations who exit essentially eliminate the value destruction due to these discomplementarities, providing another avenue for performance improvement. Finally, though any employee in isolation might create value for the firm, turnover of that employee could reshuffle the relationships surrounding that individual in ways that create higher complementarities than previously realized.

Hiring employees typically has more uncertainty than turnover because of multiple information asymmetries. Additionally, immediate search, socialization, and integration costs cause an initial drag on the value of any new hires. Firms hope that these hiring investments pay off over time, as new hires can create complementarities derived from new knowledge bundles as they develop (Sirmon et al., 2007). Anticipating how and when these bundles will create complementarities worthy of investment may be difficult. Poaching star employees from competitors, presumably for their extraordinary human capital, often produces less than expected returns for the hiring firms because of the underperformance and/or lack of fit of those well-compensated new workers (Groysberg et al., 2008; Raffiee and Byun, 2018). The potential for agonistic relations may be quite high between these new hires and legacy employees, as legacy employees frequently are protective of their knowledge domains and may be resentful of the highly compensated newcomer. This threat increases when new hires come from rival companies or have knowledge and skills that risk changing the status quo of legacy workers.

Firms engage in social capital enhancing hiring practices to ameliorate these issues to improve the chances of complementarities for the new hires. Focusing on prior social ties or capital via prior affiliations can provide primed complementarities for new hires (Garbuio et al., 2011; Oyer and Schaefer, 2016). Pipelines to particular source organizations or affinity-based labor pools improve the quality of information on potential candidates (reduces the information asymmetries for the firm) and the complementarities with existing employees they can foster (Brymer et al., 2014; Brymer et al., 2019; Rocha and Brymer, 2018). Likewise, firms can engage in co-mobility (Campbell et al., 2014; Marx and Timmermans, 2017), cluster (Eckardt et al., 2018), or boomerang hiring (Swider et al., 2017) to improve the social connections between new hires and/or legacy employees. Evidence suggests that such hiring based on prior affiliations provides more complementarities with those hired. Agonistic relations might also be minimized with affiliation hiring because information *ex ante* is of higher quality for the employee, and potentially for the new firm as well. One caution for hiring too much from the same affiliation is the possibility of faultlines developing between in- and out-groups for those affiliation social circles (Thatcher and Patel, 2011). The modes and patterns of hiring clearly play critical roles in systematically building a firm's basis of human capital resources (Camuffo and De Stefano, Chapter 17; Kehoe and Bentley, Chapter 16 this volume).

CONCLUSION

Strategic human capital scholars have observed that while conceptions of human capital resources are theoretically rich (Ployhart and Moliterno, 2011; Ployhart et al., 2014), our measurements of these resources are by contrast overly simplistic and often unidimensional, thus not adequately capturing their complexity nor their richness (Campbell and Kryscynski, Chapter 9 this volume; Nyberg et al., 2014). When we consider complementarities and how they enable emergence of human capital resources, operational shortcomings are particularly problematic. More sophisticated methods to capture these complexities, such as those described by Eckardt and Jiang in Chapter 5, can more fully extend our most basic understanding of how human-based resources can account for so much firm value.

While we highlighted employee mobility as enabling or eroding employee relationships, firms' human capital (dis)complementarities can also be realized by interactions of individual- and firm-level combinations (Crocker and Eckardt, 2014). In particular, specific firm policies or practices and strategies can produce different combinations. Examples include firm governance practices (Bridoux and Stoelhorst, Chapter 2 this volume), internationalization strategies (Brymer et al., 2018), acquisition strategy (Uhlenbruck et al., 2017), and corporate diversification strategy (Hoskisson and Hitt, 1990), to name a few. We have much to learn about human capital complementarities, how they are formed, and why they work (or do not). Recognizing and avoiding the to-date underexplored agonistic relations and the discomplementarities that they engender is a fertile area for future research. With this chapter, we hope to provoke more thought on (dis)complementarities and provide some ideas on avenues forward.

CHAPTER SUMMARY

BOX 15.1 KEY TAKEAWAYS

1. Human capital complementarities rely predominantly on social relations between individuals and/or units.
2. The prevailing and largely unchallenged assumption about social relations is that their outcomes range from no social capital/no complementarities to high social capital/high complementarities.
3. We contend that agonistic relations, those marked by aggressive or defensive social engagement, must be considered to understand the nature of human capital *dis*complementarities.
4. Applying a broader notion of (dis)complementarities and social relations, human capital mobility is explored for a more nuanced understanding of the firm-level effects of hiring, retention, and turnover.
5. Firm-level strategies, policies, and actions can create (dis)complementarities that drive human capital resource emergence processes.

BOX 15.2 DIRECTIONS FOR FUTURE RESEARCH

1. What are the mechanisms and types of human capital (dis)complementarities driven by social relations?
2. What are the antecedents, prominence, and effects of agonistic relations in organizations?
3. How do (dis)complementarities drive the emergence of human capital resources?
4. To what extent can human capital (dis)complementarities explain the performance implications of employee mobility?
5. What firm strategies and actions promote social capital and human capital complementarities? What firm strategies and actions promote agonistic relations and human capital discomplementarities?

REFERENCES

Adegbesan, J. A. (2009). On the origins of competitive advantage: Strategic factor markets and heterogeneous resource complementarity. *Academy of Management Review*, *34*(3), 463–75.

Adler, P. S., and Kwon, S. W. (2002). Social capital: Prospects for a new concept. *Academy of Management Review*, *27*(1), 17–40.

Alchian, A. A., and Demsetz, H. (1972). Production, information costs, and economic organization. *American Economic Review*, *62*(5), 777–95.

Barney, J. (1991). Firm resources and sustained competitive advantage. *Journal of Management*, *17*(1), 99–120.

Brass, D. J., Butterfield, K. D., and Skaggs, B. C. (1998). Relationships and unethical behavior: A social network perspective. *Academy of Management Review*, *23*(1), 14–31.

Brass, D. J., Galaskiewicz, J., Greve, H. R., and Tsai, W. (2004). Taking stock of networks and organizations: A multilevel perspective. *Academy of Management Journal*, *47*(6), 795–817.

Brymer, R. A., and Sirmon, D. G. (2018). Pre-exit bundling, turnover of professionals, and firm performance. *Journal of Management Studies*, *55*(1), 146–73.

Brymer, R., Hitt, M., and Schijven, M. (2011). Cognition and human capital: The dynamic relationship between knowledge and behaviour. In A. Burton-Jones and J.-C. Spender (eds), *The Oxford Handbook of Human Capital*, 120–44. Oxford: Oxford University Press.

Brymer, R., Molloy, J., and Chadwick, C. (2015). Strategic human capital. *Oxford Bibliographies in Management*. DOI: 10.1093/obo/9780199846740-0082.

Brymer, R. A., Molloy, J. C., and Gilbert, B. A. (2014). Human capital pipelines: Competitive implications of repeated interorganizational hiring. *Journal of Management*, *40*(2), 483–508.
Brymer, R. A., Boss, D. S., Uhlenbruck, K., and Bierman, L. (2018). Internationalization's effect on mobility and firms' employee-based resources. *Academy of Management Perspectives*. https://doi.org/10.5465/amp.2016.0179.
Brymer, R. A., Chadwick, C., Hill, A., and Molloy, J. (2019). Pipelines and their portfolios: A more holistic view of human capital heterogeneity via firm-wide employee sourcing. *Academy of Management Perspectives*, *33*(2), 207–33.
Byun, H., Raffiee, J., and Ganco, M. (in press). Discontinuities in the value of relational capital: The effects on employee entrepreneurship and mobility. *Organization Science*.
Campbell, B. A., Coff, R., and Kryscynski, D. (2012). Rethinking sustained competitive advantage from human capital. *Academy of Management Review*, *37*(3), 376–95.
Campbell, B. A., Kryscynski, D., and Olson, D. M. (2017). Bridging strategic human capital and employee entrepreneurship research: A labor market frictions approach. *Strategic Entrepreneurship Journal*, *11*(3), 344–56.
Campbell, B. A., Saxton, B. M., and Banerjee, P. M. (2014). Resetting the shot clock: The effect of comobility on human capital. *Journal of Management*, *40*(2), 531–56.
Campbell, B. A., Ganco, M., Franco, A. M., and Agarwal, R. (2012). Who leaves, where to, and why worry? Employee mobility, entrepreneurship and effects on source firm performance. *Strategic Management Journal*, *33*(1), 65–87.
Call, M. L., Nyberg, A. J., Ployhart, R. E., and Weekley, J. (2015). The dynamic nature of collective turnover and unit performance: The impact of time, quality, and replacements. *Academy of Management Journal*, *58*(4), 1208–32.
Cascio, W., and Boudreau, J. (2010). *Investing in People: Financial Impact of Human Resource Initiatives*. Upper Saddle River, NJ: FT Press.
Chadwick, C. (2017). Toward a more comprehensive model of firms' human capital rents. *Academy of Management Review*, *42*(3), 499–519.
Coff, R. W. (1997). Human assets and management dilemmas: Coping with hazards on the road to resource-based theory. *Academy of management review*, *22*(2), 374–402.
Colbert, B. A. (2004). The complex resource-based view: Implications for theory and practice in strategic human resource management. *Academy of Management Review*, *29*(3), 341–58.
Crocker, A., and Eckardt, R. (2014). A multilevel investigation of individual-and unit-level human capital complementarities. *Journal of Management*, *40*(2), 509–30.
Eckardt, R., Skaggs, B. C., and Lepak, D. P. (2018). An examination of the firm-level performance impact of cluster hiring in knowledge-intensive firms. *Academy of Management Journal*, *61*(3), 919–44.
Ennen, E., and Richter, A. (2010). The whole is more than the sum of its parts – or is it? A review of the empirical literature on complementarities in organizations. *Journal of Management*, *36*(1), 207–33.
Fulmer, I. S., and Ployhart, R. E. (2014). "Our most important asset": A multidisciplinary/multilevel review of human capital valuation for research and practice. *Journal of Management*, *40*(1), 161–92.
Garbuio, M., King, A. W., and Lovallo, D. (2011). Looking inside: Psychological influences on structuring a firm's portfolio of resources. *Journal of Management*, *37*(5), 1444–63.
Grigoriou, K., and Rothaermel, F. T. (2014). Structural microfoundations of innovation: The role of relational stars. *Journal of Management*, *40*(2), 586–615.
Groysberg, B., Lee, L. E., and Nanda, A. (2008). Can they take it with them? The portability of star knowledge workers' performance. *Management Science*, *54*(7), 1213–30.
Hausknecht, J. P., and Holwerda, J. A. (2013). When does employee turnover matter? Dynamic member configurations, productive capacity, and collective performance. *Organization Science*, *24*(1), 210–25.
Hess, A. M., and Rothaermel, F. T. (2011). When are assets complementary? Star scientists, strategic alliances, and innovation in the pharmaceutical industry. *Strategic Management Journal*, *32*(8), 895–909.
Hollenbeck, J. R., and Jamieson, B. B. (2015). Human capital, social capital, and social network analysis: Implications for strategic human resource management. *Academy of Management Perspectives*, *29*(3), 370–85.
Hoskisson, R. E., and Hitt, M. A. (1990). Antecedents and performance outcomes of diversification: A review and critique of theoretical perspectives. *Journal of Management*, *16*(2), 461–509.
Kehoe, R. R., Lepak, D. P., and Bentley, F. S. (2018). Let's call a star a star: Task performance, external status, and exceptional contributors in organizations. *Journal of Management*, *44*(5), 1848–72.
Labianca, G. (2014). Negative ties in organizational networks. In D. J. Brass, G. Labianca, A. Mehra, D. S. Halgin, and S. P. Borgatti (eds), *Contemporary Perspectives on Organizational Social Networks*, 239–59. Bingley, UK: Emerald.
Lazear, E. P. (2009). Firm-specific human capital: A skill-weights approach. *Journal of Political Economy*, *117*(5), 914–40.
Makri, M., Hitt, M. A., and Lane, P. J. (2010). Complementary technologies, knowledge relatedness, and invention outcomes in high technology mergers and acquisitions. *Strategic Management Journal*, *31*(6), 602–28.

Marx, M., and Timmermans, B. (2017). Hiring molecules, not atoms: Comobility and wages. *Organization Science*, *28*(6), 1115–33.
Mawdsley, J. K., and Somaya, D. (2016). Employee mobility and organizational outcomes: An integrative conceptual framework and research agenda. *Journal of Management*, *42*(1), 85–113.
Methot, J. R., Rosado-Solomon, E. H., and Allen, D. G. (2018). The network architecture of human capital: A relational identity perspective. *Academy of Management Review*, *43*, 723–48.
Milgrom, P., and Roberts, J. (1990). The economics of modern manufacturing: Technology, strategy, and organization. *American Economic Review*, *80*(3), 511–28.
Molloy, J. C., Ployhart, R. E., and Wright, P. M. (2011). The myth of "the" micro-macro divide: Bridging system-level and disciplinary divides. *Journal of Management*, *37*(2), 581–609.
Nyberg, A. J., and Ployhart, R. E. (2013). Context-emergent turnover (CET) theory: A theory of collective turnover. *Academy of Management Review*, *38*(1), 109–31.
Nyberg, A. J., Moliterno, T. P., Hale Jr, D., and Lepak, D. P. (2014). Resource-based perspectives on unit-level human capital: A review and integration. *Journal of Management*, *40*(1), 316–46.
Oyer, P., and Schaefer, S. (2016). Firm/employee matching: An industry study of US lawyers. *ILR Review*, *69*(2), 378–404.
Peteraf, M. A. (2005). Research complementarities: A resource-based view of the resource allocation process model (and vice versa). In J. L. Bower and C. G. Gilbert (eds), *From Resource Allocation to Strategy*, 409–26. Oxford: Oxford University Press.
Pfeffer, J. (1998). *The Human Equation: Building Profits by Putting People First*. Boston: Harvard Business School Press.
Ployhart, R. E., and Moliterno, T. P. (2011). Emergence of the human capital resource: A multilevel model. *Academy of Management Review*, *36*(1), 127–50.
Ployhart, R. E., Nyberg, A. J., Reilly, G., and Maltarich, M. A. (2014). Human capital is dead; long live human capital resources! *Journal of Management*, *40*(2), 371–98.
Raffiee, J., and Byun, H. (2018). Revisiting the portability of performance paradox: A use value theory of human and social capital resources. University of Southern California working paper.
Ranson, S., Hinings, B., and Greenwood, R. (1980). The structuring of organizational structures. *Administrative Science Quarterly*, *25*(1), 1–17.
Rocha, V., and Brymer, R. (2018). Founder pipeline hiring in young firms. Copenhagen Business School working paper.
Rocha, V., Carneiro, A., and Varum, C. (2018). Leaving employment to entrepreneurship: The value of co-worker mobility in pushed and pulled-driven start-ups. *Journal of Management Studies*, *55*(1), 60–85.
Sav, G. T. (2004). Higher education costs and scale and scope economies. *Applied Economics*, *36*(6), 607–14.
Schmidt, F. L., and Hunter, J. E. (1998). The validity and utility of selection methods in personnel psychology: Practical and theoretical implications of 85 years of research findings. *Psychological Bulletin*, *124*, 262–74.
Sirmon, D. G., Hitt, M. A., and Ireland, R. D. (2007). Managing firm resources in dynamic environments to create value: Looking inside the black box. *Academy of Management Review*, *32*(1), 273–92.
Soltis, S., Brass, D., and Lepak, D. (2018). Social resource management: Integrating social network theory and human resource management. *Academy of Management Annals*, *12*(2), 537–73.
Sutton, R. I. (2007). *The No Asshole Rule: Building a Civilized Workplace and Surviving One That Isn't*. New York: Business Plus.
Swider, B. W., Liu, J. T., Harris, T. B., and Gardner, R. G. (2017). Employees on the rebound: Extending the careers literature to include boomerang employment. *Journal of Applied Psychology*, *102*(6), 890–909.
Thatcher, S., and Patel, P. C. (2011). Demographic faultlines: A meta-analysis of the literature. *Journal of Applied Psychology*, *96*(6), 1119–39.
Tzabbar, D., Aharonson, B. S., Amburgey, T. L., and Al-Laham, A. (2008). When is the whole bigger than the sum of its parts? Bundling knowledge stocks for innovative success. *Strategic Organization*, *6*(4), 375–406.
Uhlenbruck, K., Hughes-Morgan, M., Hitt, M. A., Ferrier, W. J., and Brymer, R. (2017). Rivals' reactions to mergers and acquisitions. *Strategic Organization*, *15*(1), 40–66.
Wright, P. M., Coff, R., and Moliterno, T. P. (2014). Strategic human capital: Crossing the great divide. *Journal of Management*, *40*(2), 353–70.

ACTUATING HCRS

PART V

BUILDING SHCRS: HIRING AND ACQUIRING

16. Building human capital resources: hiring and acquiring

Rebecca R. Kehoe and F. Scott Bentley

INTRODUCTION

While it has long been accepted by strategy and strategic human resource management (SHRM) scholars that the quality of a firm's human capital can be an important source of competitive advantage (Campbell et al., 2012; Wright et al., 2014), the implications of this wisdom for hiring and acquiring human capital are less straightforward. Indeed, the topics of hiring and acquiring human capital have been addressed in multiple literatures, through a variety of lenses, and with a wide range of conclusions. There are sizable literatures, for instance, that focus on the consequences of: *how* organizations attract and select employees – using what recruitment methods (e.g., Uggerslev et al., 2012) and selection processes (e.g., Schmidt and Hunter, 1998); for *what* specific human capital attributes organizations select among new hires – e.g., general mental ability (Schmidt and Hunter, 1998) and specific types of knowledge (Song et al., 2003); and from *where* organizations source their human capital – e.g., internal vs. external labor markets (Bidwell, 2011), through talent pipelines (Brymer et al., 2014).

While these streams of research are valuable – and practical – in their implications, at the heart of any effective strategy for building strategic human capital resources must be an identification of what the ideal human capital pool of an organization looks like. Accordingly, we suggest there is a need for research on hiring and acquiring human capital rooted in a strategic human capital lens to more explicitly begin from the question: *On what employee attributes can, do, and should organizations focus their selection efforts?* We aim to advance this agenda in the present chapter in two ways: by considering a broader array of attributes through which employees might create value in organizations; and by proposing the more explicit assessment of the fit of prospective employees' attributes relative to other organizational characteristics in the hiring process. We contend that this latter aim is an especially critical – and heretofore largely missing – piece in the puzzle of understanding the building of human capital resources, as individuals do not work in organizations in isolation (Ployhart, 2015; Ployhart and Hale, 2014). Indeed, an important and fundamental notion underlying the concept of human capital resources (HCRs) is that the individual and collective availability and relevance of employees' human capital for value creation at the unit level are likely to vary – not only on the basis of differences across individuals, but also due to their interactions and differential fit with the formal resources, structures, practices, processes, and the informal norms and states characterizing the unit context (Ployhart and Hale, 2014; Ployhart and Moliterno, 2011).

To achieve our first aim, we explicate three broad categories of employee attributes – knowledge, skills, and abilities (KSAs); personality, values, and interests; and status and social capital – that represent potential sources of value creation for organizations. We highlight research – some within and some outside the literatures on selection and mobility – that offers insights into how each of these categories of attributes contributes to an organization's value-creation efforts, acknowledging value creation defined both narrowly at the individual level (e.g., task performance), and, consistent with the perspective of HCRs, more broadly as it relates to higher-level outcomes which may not be traceable to a single individual. In pursuit of the second aim, we highlight the importance of how employee attributes fit with other resources and organizational characteristics in determining the likelihood of actual value creation. In this discussion, we review work on resource complementarities and redundancies in the strategy literature, as well as the concepts of horizontal and vertical fit and the behavioral perspective in the SHRM literature. We discuss the implications of these insights and provide recommendations for future research on building human capital resources.

FOCAL EMPLOYEE ATTRIBUTES FOR THE SELECTION AND ACQUISITION OF HUMAN CAPITAL

Scholars have advanced a variety of conceptual boundaries on the human capital construct, with some suggesting that the definition ends with KSAs – i.e., knowledge, skills, and abilities (e.g., Crook et al., 2011) – and others embracing the more recently introduced label KSAOs to include a variety of "other" attributes, such as personality, in their definitions (e.g., Nyberg et al., 2014; Ployhart and Moliterno, 2011). Scholars have also differed on the boundary conditions that they identify surrounding when the human capital of a firm's employees is likely to serve as a source of sustained competitive advantage (SCA) (Campbell et al., 2012; Ployhart et al., 2014). We do not concern ourselves with either of these questions in the present chapter for two reasons. First, there are employee attributes that are potentially relevant to value creation in organizations – in some cases (e.g., with status or social capital) based on their amplification of the benefits of other employee attributes – irrespective of their classification within or outside the human capital construct; we therefore include these attributes in our consideration here. Second, the creation of value – and therefore the achievement of sustained competitive advantage – rooted in any employee attribute (or for that matter, any resource) depends on its fit within the broader context of the organization in which it is embedded. It is far beyond the scope of our chapter to determine the specific conditions under which every possible employee attribute is likely to be the source of an SCA. Rather, in the present chapter we limit our focus to: a) (here) identifying a range of employee attributes that have been shown to be relevant for value creation; and b) (later) considering several key organizational factors against which the fit of employee attributes might be assessed in predicting the likelihood that they will create value in a particular organizational context. In particular, within this section we review research considering the value-creating potential of employees' a) KSAs; b) personality, values, and interests; and c) status and social capital.

KSAs

(General mental) ability

An expansive literature on selection, reporting on research conducted primarily by industrial and organizational (I-O) psychologists, suggests that individuals with higher cognitive ability are more capable of acquiring job-specific knowledge through training and development and, as a result, achieve higher job performance (Behling, 1998; Schmidt and Hunter, 1998). In their review of this literature, Schmidt and Hunter found that, of all selection procedures, tests of general mental ability have the second highest predictive validity (r = .51) in the context of individuals' overall job performance – ranking second only to work sample tests (r = .54) – and the highest predictive validity (r = .56) in the context of individuals' performance in training programs, and has been proven valuable across a wide range of job functions and occupational contexts (Behling, 1998; Hunter and Hunter, 1984; Ree and Earles, 1992).

Notwithstanding the broad support for the predictive validity of tests of general mental ability, there are a variety of reasons for practitioners and scholars to continue to explore the value of other individual attributes in the context of hiring and acquiring human capital. First, it may not always be possible for organizations to evaluate applicants' general mental ability as part of the selection process. Second, if there is not significant variance on general mental ability in an applicant pool, this attribute will have limited value as a screening criterion. Third, even when testing general mental ability is possible and when there is significant variance in the potential applicant pool, organizations may lack information on general mental ability across the entire relevant labor market, such that this attribute lacks value in the identification of individuals for recruitment into the selection process and is helpful only once an initial applicant pool is isolated. Fourth, as the research of Schmidt and Hunter and others has highlighted, organizations can reap additional benefits from combining the consideration of multiple individual attributes in their selection processes. Finally, while individual job performance and learning outcomes in training programs are certainly relevant to the question of creating value through people in organizations, they are not the only meaningful measures of value creation. Indeed, individuals contribute to organizations in a multitude of other ways, often reflected at higher levels (e.g., by supporting their colleagues, by providing an organization with access to relevant external resources); and different types of contributions – including those made interdependently with other employees and which depend on individuals' fit with other organizational resources – may indeed be better supported by distinct individual attributes that have heretofore received less attention in the micro-oriented selection literature.

Knowledge

Scholars have employed various distinctions in classifying knowledge along different dimensions, including tacit vs. explicit, firm-specific vs. general, etc. (Crook et al., 2011; Mayer et al., 2012). Here, we focus broadly on knowledge that is deemed relevant to the focal organizational context for two reasons (though we address the notion of firm-specificity later in this section). First, while scholars have debated the likelihood that employees' possession of different types of knowledge will serve as the basis for a firm's knowledge-based competitive advantage, as we previously stated, our focus in this chapter is on employee attributes that may create value in some (though not necessarily all) organizational contexts, and serving as a stand-alone basis for competitive advantage is not a prerequisite for inclusion on this basis. Indeed, building on the idea that employees create value in large part in their roles within a unit's higher-level HCR (Ployhart et al., 2014), as we elaborate in greater depth in the latter half of the chapter which focuses on different types of fit, it is more likely the case that complementarities between individual employees' attributes and other organizational resources – rather than individual employees' human capital alone – will form the basis for a firm's competitive advantage. Second, employees are multifaceted, and even within individual employees it is often through the combination of multiple attributes – and in some cases multiple types of knowledge – that individuals make meaningful contributions to an organization's goals.

Scholars of the knowledge-based view have defined firms as "organizations that represent social knowledge of coordination and learning" (Kogut and Zander, 1996). At the heart of knowledge-based competitive advantage, according to this view, is the integration of the specialized knowledge residing in the firm's employees. Employees' knowledge can be applied to a broad array of value-creating activities across organizational contexts, including the generation of patents (Kehoe and Tzabbar, 2015; Rothaermel and Hess, 2007), the innovation of new products (Collins and Smith, 2006; Smith et al., 2005), and the customization and delivery of services (Groysberg and Lee, 2008; Hitt et al., 2001).

In addition to these context-specific, direct applications of knowledge to firms' productivity, individual employees can use their knowledge to contribute to organizational goals less directly. For example, employees with unique expertise can help improve the performance of their colleagues by sharing their knowledge, such as through collaboration or helping behaviors (Azoulay et al., 2010; Oettl, 2012), as well as in mentoring relationships (Noe, 1988). Additionally, employees who are recognized as being particularly knowledgeable can use their expert power (French and Raven, 1959) to positively influence the work behaviors and norms practiced by others throughout an organization (Burke et al., 2007; Lacetera et al., 2004).

In light of our decision to not discuss firm-specific knowledge as a distinct knowledge category, two points on firm-specificity are worth noting here. First, firm-specificity occurs on a spectrum, and some types of knowledge have a greater proportion of firm-specific components than others. For example, as Mayer et al. (2012) note, to the extent that an R&D initiative in a technology firm relates closely to one of the firm's existing products, successful contributions to this effort are more likely to require not only know-how of the R&D and patenting process (i.e., relevant general knowledge), but also an understanding of the product's market position, complementary technologies, and competitive history. Second, some general knowledge is more easily utilized when it is paired with relevant firm-specific knowledge. For example, culture, routines, and language vary across organizational contexts; and to the extent that employees' work requires them to draw on other organizational resources and members, those who understand these nuances within a particular firm may perform their work more effectively (Groysberg et al., 2008; Huckman and Pisano, 2006). We suggest that, rather than treating firm-specific knowledge as a distinct category of knowledge in the hiring realm, a more useful way to think about firm-specificity in the selection context is to identify the particular firm-specific components of a job and then to determine how essential these knowledge components are to the job, and whether it is necessary that they be held by a single individual in the role (i.e., or whether it is possible to structure an employee's role to facilitate greater interdependence with someone who possesses the requisite firm-specific knowledge that he/she lacks). Through this process, organizational decision makers may better equip themselves to give firm-specific knowledge (and, by extension, internal candidates) the appropriate weight in their hiring decisions.

Skills

Skills refer to an individual's level of proficiency in and capabilities to perform specific tasks (Ployhart et al., 2014). As with knowledge, different skills are relevant across tasks and organizational contexts (Maurer et al., 2003). For instance, scholars have demonstrated the value of customer service skills in retail sales (Hogan et al., 1984; Liao and Chuang, 2004; Ployhart et al., 2009) and call center contexts (Batt, 1999); technical and quantitative skills in the investment banking context (Groysberg et al., 2011; Whitwell et al., 2007); and task- and sport-specific skills in professional sports contexts (Crocker and Eckardt, 2014; Ethiraj and Garg, 2012; Sirmon et al., 2008).

Skills that are less directly related to the core tasks of an employee or unit may also be applied to create value for a firm less directly. For instance, employees who possess an understanding of the requirements for effective task performance can create value by employing leadership and mentoring skills that can influence the abilities of their colleagues to perform (Allen et al., 2000; Kram, 1988; Mumford et al., 2000; Noe, 1988). In the context of academia, for example, mentoring by senior faculty can be instrumental in the development of junior faculty (Bullard and Felder, 2003) and doctoral students (Paglis et al., 2006). Academic mentors must possess not only the knowledge of how to achieve performance across a variety of tasks that are unique to the academic context (e.g., publishing research, teaching) but also the skills to communicate and develop protégés to achieve their potential across these tasks (Kirchmeyer, 2005; Tenenbaum et al., 2001). In this process, mentoring may positively influence both the immediate productivity of less experienced individuals, while simultaneously contributing to the long-term development of a university's (or organization's) human capital resources.

Integrating insights on KSAs

In sum, a large body of research both within and outside the selection domain has demonstrated the value of employees' cognitive (i.e., KSA-based) attributes in organizations. This work has largely adopted a "more is better" perspective on KSAs, with some consideration of contextual factors shaping the value-creating potential of different types of knowledge. In our assessment, future research examining KSAs in the realm of firms' hiring activities has greater room to benefit from more deeply exploring the specific KSAs that are particularly relevant to the creation value in a given context than in replicating prior research to reinforce the value of employees' general mental abilities. Moreover, we believe there is an important need to advance our understanding of the many less direct ways in which employees use their KSAs to contribute to value creation in organizations.

Personality, Values, Interests

Personality

Personality has been another major focus of selection research conducted by I-O psychologists (Ployhart et al., 2017), with much of this work focusing on the "Big Five" dimensions of personality: extraversion, emotional stability, agreeableness, conscientiousness, and openness to experience (Barrick and Mount, 1991; Hurtz and Donovan, 2000). Of the Big Five, *conscientiousness* has been shown to be the best predictors of both job performance and training outcomes across a variety of job types, organizational contexts, and industries (Barrick and Mount, 1991; Hurtz and Donovan, 2000; Vinchur et al., 1998), which, as a result, has led to its use as one of the primary personality dimensions used in personnel selection (Behling, 1998; Hurtz and Donovan, 2000). Conscientiousness reflects the extent to which an individual is organized, reliable, hardworking, determined, self-disciplined, and achievement-oriented (Barrick et al., 2002; Costa and McCrae, 1992; Goldberg, 1992). Conscientious employees are inclined to exercise better self-control and more consistently fulfill their job obligations (Barrick et al., 2002; Costa and McCrae, 1992).

While conscientious employees demonstrate superior performance across employment contexts, the importance of other Big Five traits appears to depend more on their fit with the characteristics of the employment setting. For example, *extraversion* has been established as a strong predictor of job performance for jobs characterized as competitive as well as for those which offer performance-based compensation (Barrick and Mount, 1991; Barrick et al., 2002), whereas *agreeableness* has been linked to superior job performance in organizational settings requiring interpersonal interactions (Mount et al., 1998).

Integrity

Scholars have also examined the value of assessing integrity in selection tests. Individuals with greater integrity are more likely to perform according to an organization's rules and to follow guidance provided by superiors, as well as to demonstrate better job performance across organizational contexts relative to their peers (Ones et al., 1993; Schmidt and Hunter, 1998). In the selection context, organizations have more often used tests of integrity to mitigate counterproductive work behaviors such as sabotaging others, fighting, and unethical behavior (Schmidt and Hunter, 1998) rather than as a gauge of candidates' potential to create value for the organization.

Values and interests

Values and interests represent two additional non-cognitive individual attributes that are likely to be stable over an individual's adult life (Deng et al., 2007; Kanfer, 1990) and are important in understanding the fit between an individual and his or her job (Tinsley, 2000). Holland et al. (1969) proposed the RIASEC (Realistic, Investigative, Artistic, Social, Enterprising, and Conventional) model for matching individual interests and occupations. This framework uses these six vocational interest types and matches them with parallel work environments to establish fit between one's interests and organizational settings. Extending this logic, some scholars have integrated insights from the literature on fit with Schneider's (1987) attraction–selection–attrition framework to suggest that greater fit between the values and interests of an individual and his or her organizational setting may increase helping behaviors and job performance (Kristof, 1996).

Integrating insights on personality, values, and interests

A large body of research points to the relevance of personality to individuals' success at work, with some traits (e.g., conscientiousness) linked to superior performance across contexts, and others (e.g., agreeableness) holding particular relevance for specific types of work (e.g., jobs requiring significant interpersonal interactions). Research has also highlighted the role of fit between individuals' values and interests with those of the hiring organization, suggesting that individuals thrive in employment settings where they experience a closer match to their own values and interests. One clear path for future research in this vein would be an examination of how individuals' personalities, values, and interests – which influence their affective states in organizations – shape the value they create through the employment of their cognitive attributes (i.e., KSAs) both on their own and in collaboration with other employees.

Status and Social Capital

Although status and social capital are distinct attributes, both represent potential pathways connecting individuals to relevant stakeholders and other resources outside an organization (Kehoe et al., 2018). Hence, we discuss them together in a single section. Status has been defined as the amount of respect, influence, and admiration an individual enjoys in the eyes of others (Anderson et al., 2001; Magee and Galinsky, 2008). Social capital can be viewed as those tangible and intangible benefits available to an individual as a function of his or her interpersonal relationships and group memberships (Adler and Kwon, 2002; Nahapiet and Ghoshal, 1998). Individuals' status and social capital may be related in a variety of ways (e.g., with status providing an individual with greater opportunities to form interpersonal relationships, or connections to well-positioned social actors leading to increased status) or may be independent of one another.

In the subsections that follow, we draw on extant research to explicate how individuals' status and social capital can aid in the creation of value in organizations. It is worth acknowledging that, with a few noted exceptions, the work we review in these discussions has been conducted largely outside the selection context. That is, rather than examining the predictive validity of assessments of applicants' status or social capital in the selection process, this work has tended to explore the benefits of these attributes when possessed by an organization's incumbent employees.

Access to external stakeholders

The status and social capital of an individual employee can provide an organization with preferential access to relevant external stakeholders, who may be more attracted to and supportive of the organization because of its employment of the individual. For instance, research has demonstrated that employees with high levels of status or social capital can draw higher ticket prices for their teams in the professional sports context (Lucifora and Simmons, 2003), attract more clients to their firms in the investment banking context (Groysberg and Lee, 2008), and help technology firms realize higher proceeds in their initial public offerings (IPOs) (Higgins et al., 2011). Additionally, scholars have pointed out that stars' broad status can help attract new talent to an organization, with new employees in some cases accepting lower compensation for the opportunity to work alongside a star (Coff and Krysynski, 2011; Groysberg et al., 2011). Importantly, the status benefits just described are in part due to the use of status by external stakeholders as a signal of the quality associated with the products or services or general work environment with which a star is involved. We point this out not to downplay the value of status, but rather to highlight its value in complementing other employee attributes that contribute to value creation.

Scholars have also highlighted the value of employees' external social capital in increasing and improving organizations' connections to relevant external stakeholders. For example, Dokko and Rosenkopf (2010) demonstrated that organizations that hired employees with unique interpersonal connections within an external governing body responsible for setting industry standards enjoyed greater influence in the setting of these standards than did other organizations. Research by Broschak (2004; Broschak and Block, 2014) in the context of advertising agencies provides evidence for the value of dyadic ties between managers in advertising agencies and advertisers (i.e., their clients), demonstrating that the departure of managers on either side of these ties increases the likelihood of tie dissolution. Finally, establishing the mobility of individuals' external social capital across firms, Somaya et al. (2008) found that firms hiring employees from potential clients gained more business from those clients, and that firms hiring employees from competitors gained more business from the clients of those competitors.

Access to external knowledge

Status and social capital have also been shown to be important predictors of individuals' access to knowledge. Oldroyd and Morris (2012) developed arguments consistent with this idea in their consideration of information overload experienced by star employees, wherein they suggest that the extremely large number of network connections held by stars (which itself is a function of stars' status as knowledgeable individuals) subjects stars to disproportionate information flows relative to other employees. In Chapter 12 in this volume, Morris and Snell point more directly to the value of employees' network connections in the context of accessing knowledge concerning customers' concerns and unmet needs. Adopting a focus on access to external knowledge in the innovation context, Rothaermel and Hess (2007) note that star scientists' preferential boundary-spanning positions in professional networks in the scientific community position them to filter valuable information into their organizations. Importantly, the authors argued that the *combination* of stars' broad status, key network positions, and expert knowledge is particularly beneficial in this regard as it enables them to not only access but also to "translate coding schemes" in order to evaluate and organize technical knowledge that flows into the organization from external sources (see also Hess and Rothaermel, 2011). Other scholars have demonstrated that both the presence and the characteristics (e.g., structural, cognitive, and relational dimensions) of individuals' dyadic relationships influence the transfer and creation of knowledge within and between organizational boundaries (Argote et al., 2003; Inkpen and Tsang, 2005; Uzzi and Lancaster, 2003).

Integrating insights on status and social capital

Research on status and social capital has pointed to the importance of individuals' professional networks and reputations in providing organizations access to external resources, opportunities, and influence. Interestingly, this research has been conducted largely outside the selection context, pointing to a clear need for future research to strengthen our understanding of: a) how organizations factor these attributes into their hiring decisions; and b) how prospective employees' status and social capital interact with their other human capital attributes and with other organizational resources in determining their value-creating potential in a hiring organization.

Integrating Insights on Employee Attributes

Looking across the extant research explicating the multitude of ways in which different employee attributes may contribute to value creation in organizations, we believe there is a clear need for scholars (and perhaps practitioners) to take a broader perspective in defining relevant selection criteria based on the specific organizations, occupations, and jobs for which they are hiring. That is, while selection research has traditionally focused on the value of individuals' cognitive ability and personality traits, a quick survey of research outside the selection literature points to the value of a variety of other individual attributes (e.g., mentoring skills, social capital), several of which we have discussed here. We contend that there is little value to be gained from additional research examining the relationship between individual attributes – in isolation – and subsequent task performance. Instead, by expanding the focus of selection research to account for *additional* individual attributes connected to *alternative* sources of value creation by individuals (i.e., that extend beyond individual task performance), selection scholars could more accurately tap into the microfoundations of human capital emergence and of the unit-level HCR, and develop a better understanding of how the selection of individuals influences value creation and competitive advantage at the unit or organization level.

While we acknowledge that not all of the attributes discussed above are likely to be relevant to selection decisions in all hiring contexts, we would also note that the aforementioned attributes do not constitute an exhaustive list. That is, there are likely to be additional employee attributes that are integral to value creation within and outside the contexts studied in the research discussed above. Indeed, we contend that by more carefully considering the multiple types of fit, both in terms of form (e.g., complementarities, redundancies) and content (e.g., fit with resources, practices, strategic goals), that may be relevant in different employment contexts, scholars and practitioners will be better positioned to identify the employee attributes that are most relevant – and most likely to combine with other organizational resources and attributes – in the creation of value in a particular setting. Thus, the goal of the following section is to unpack the concept and role of fit in building human capital in this way.

EXPLICATING THE ROLE OF FIT IN BUILDING HUMAN CAPITAL RESOURCES

While in our discussion above we called for a more thorough consideration of the various attributes through which prospective employees *might* create value in an organization, in this section we suggest that an explicit consideration of how different employee attributes fit in the broader organizational context is essential in the estimation of how much value a particular attribute or combination of attributes is actually likely to create. Specifically, as a subset of factors on which fit should be assessed, we consider the role of fit of employee attributes with other organizational resources, the organization's HR system, and the organization's strategy.

Attributes' Fit with Other Unit or Organizational Resources

Many of the contributions through which individuals employ their human capital to create value involve interdependencies with other unit or organizational resources. Thus, the nature of interaction – in particular, the complementarities and redundancies – between different resources is central to the question of potential value creation. We follow Kehoe et al.'s (2018: 15) articulation that complementarities between resources exist "when the resources create greater value in combination than the sum of the value they would create in isolation (Adegbesan, 2009), or the resources together create more value in one context than they would in other contexts (LeBreton-Miller and Miller, 2015; Schmidt and Keil, 2013)." Complementarities represent a particularly noteworthy form of fit among human capital resources both because complementarities themselves tend not to have efficient factor markets and because the individual subcomponents of complementarities tend to be undervalued outside the firm (Denrell et al., 2003; Ployhart, 2015). In contrast to complementarities, redundancies refer to extreme similarity or overlap in the qualities or functions of multiple resources. In general, redundancies between two resources are expected to decrease the unique value created by either resource – though, as we discuss, there are reasons that some resource redundancies can be beneficial for organizations to foster and maintain. Following our discussions of complementarities and redundancies, we consider different forms of compositional fit, a notion drawn from the team literature (e.g., Mathieu et al., 2014) which refers to the mix of attributes characterizing a team's members.

Complementarities

Complementarity can take a variety of forms and may emerge between the same or entirely different types of resources. For example, complementarities between employees may be seen when organizations hire individuals who differ on particular attributes (e.g., work experience, education), where such differences allow employees to integrate and build on one another's distinct perspectives to better perform their jobs (Prat, 2002). In this context, distinct knowledge can enable colleagues to provide one another alternative, creative options for understanding and addressing problems or completing job tasks (Eisenhardt and Schoonhoven, 1990; Horwitz and Horwitz, 2007). In possible support of this view, Carpenter and Fredrickson (2001) found that firms whose top management teams include individuals with different, but complementary, international experience and education are more successful in constructing and implementing successful strategic positions internationally. Second, complementarities may emerge between employees who possess qualitatively different attributes altogether. For example, one individual's broad status might complement the KSAs possessed by other employees who lack the status required to garner visibility and credibility in their work (Fuller and Rothaermel, 2012). For example, Simcoe and Waguespack (2011) found that scholars' publication rates increase when a coauthor team's publishing skills are complemented by the addition of a high-status coauthor. Finally, complementarity may emerge between specific employee attributes and the physical (i.e., non-human) resources owned by the firm (Cross and Thomas, 2008). For example, Hess and Rothaermel (2011) describe how star scientists (who provide pharmaceutical firms with strong research capabilities and foundations in basic science) complement such firms' downstream strategic alliances, which are leveraged in bringing such firms' innovations to market.

Redundancies

Whereas complementarities are by definition value-enhancing, redundancies may improve or inhibit value creation. Scholars have identified a variety of conditions under which firms are likely to benefit from redundancies within their workforce (Ployhart et al., 2014).

First, for some attributes that are conducive to value creation, more truly is better. For instance, in a meta-analysis examining the effect of personality traits on performance in organizational contexts where interpersonal interactions are required, Mount and colleagues (1998) found that agreeableness and emotional stability among employees are particularly important for collective performance in jobs that involve teamwork. Second, redundancies among employees can help buffer organizations against the potential loss of employees possessing those attributes by reducing an organization's dependence on key employees and mitigating disruptions in the case of their turnover (LeBreton-Miller and Miller, 2015; Tzabbar and Kehoe, 2014). Lastly, firms can benefit from redundancies in the context of succession planning, where overlapping knowledge between an incumbent and successor can help ensure the continuity of leadership throughout the succession process (Rothwell, 2010).

In other cases, redundancies can inhibit or reduce the value created by employees, either by contributing to unfavorable social dynamics in the work context or by limiting the uniqueness of contributions made by individual employees. Additionally, the selection of individuals possessing similar levels of status or expertise can foster dysfunctional interpersonal dynamics and work environments as individuals may undermine one another as they compete for dominance in the workplace (Magee and Galinsky, 2008; Overbeck et al., 2005). For example, Groysberg and colleagues (2011) found that the number of high-status, high-performing star equity analysts on a team has an inverted U-shaped effect on team performance. The authors suggest that this finding was likely due to the diminishing returns associated with the (redundant) status and visibility spillovers of multiple stars, as well as the fact that when multiple individuals who are accustomed to being at the top of social hierarchies are brought together they are likely to experience conflict and competition for local status, which could diminish the quality of decision making and other critical team processes.

Interestingly, the role of redundancies in reducing an organization's dependence on particular employees can be simultaneously beneficial and limiting for organizations. For instance, while an employee is less likely to create unique value for a firm through his or her social capital when such social capital is comprised of social ties that are also maintained by one or more other employees (Burt, 1997; Dokko and Rosenkopf, 2010), the accumulation and maintenance of such ties by multiple employees can reinforce an organization's relationships with key external stakeholders as well as protect the firm from the loss of the relationship due to a single employee's turnover (Shaw et al., 2005). For example, Dokko and Rosenkopf found that the positive effect of new hires' external network ties on telecommunications firms influence in an industry standard-setting committee was reduced when a new hire's ties were redundant to relationships already maintained by the firm's incumbent employees.

Fit as composition

Research focusing on team composition points to several additional factors and perspectives that are relevant to the idea of fit in the context of interdependent collectives within organizations (Mathieu et al., 2014). For instance, this work highlights the importance of team members' generic team-oriented competencies that facilitate positive dynamics in team functions, enabling teams to realize the interdependent and collective value-creation potential of the team as a whole. In Chapter 19 in this volume, Porter, Amber, and Wang propose that different patterns of alignment and/or misalignment within and across team and member goals may influence teams' performance by fostering the motivation needed to lubricate teams' interdependent processes.

Other work in this area recognizes the importance of the broader distribution of focal human capital attributes across a team's members, and underscores that a particular member's human capital ought to be evaluated not only in the absolute sense but also relative to the distribution of focal human capital attributes across other team members. This work has been relevant in examining the effects of different types of diversity on team outcomes (e.g., Lau and Murnigham, 1998; Polzer et al., 2006), the consequences of different distributions of personality traits among team members (e.g., Barry and Stewart, 1997), and in the context of *team requisite KSAOs*, which represent one or more specific attributes (e.g., ability to speak a specific language, boundary spanning capability) that a team needs to be possessed by *someone* – or a particular portion of members – but not everyone on the team (Mumford et al., 2000). For such attributes, once the attribute is possessed by the minimum number of required members on the team, its possession by additional members may be less beneficial – or even detrimental (Mathieu et al., 2014).

Another stream of research in this vein acknowledges the disproportionate influence of particular team members on team outcomes, pointing to the potential value in differentially weighting the competencies of particular team members (Kozlowski and Klein, 2000). This work is consistent with research in the star literature highlighting the significant weight that the contributions and behaviors of stars carry in organizations (e.g., Call et al., 2015; Kehoe et al., 2018) as well as research in the strategic human resource management literature on workforce differentiation (e.g., Lepak and Snell, 1999). Finally, team composition research has underscored the critical role of time in the relationship between team composition and team functioning, suggesting that different compositional mixes among team members are likely to vary in their implications for team performance, depending on the life stage of the team in question as teams' development, interactions, and tasks change over time (Mohammed et al., 2009).

Attributes' Fit with an Organization's HR System

While typically SHRM scholars work from the perspective that HR systems shape the attributes characterizing an organization's workforce, we suggest that there is value in also considering how the attributes of prospective employees fit with the HR system that a hiring organization has in place. Although this represents a different starting point than that taken in most SHRM research, it is wholly consistent with the theoretical underpinnings of the SHRM literature and the notion that HR systems are likely to be more effective in supporting firm performance to the extent that they are characterized by strong horizontal fit. Horizontal fit is defined as the internal consistency and congruence of the practices within an HR system (e.g., Delery and Doty, 1996; Wright and McMahan, 1992). Strong horizontal fit is achieved when an organization's HR practices complement one another in supporting a consistent set of goals (Baird and Meshoulam, 1988). Pointing to Osterman's (1994) finding that firms valuing commitment are less likely to make use of temporary employment arrangements, Huselid (1995) noted that such firms are also likely to achieve greater returns from investments in training because they are more likely than other firms to maintain a stable core of employees.

By the same token, we suggest that to the extent that a particular employee attribute is supported and rewarded by multiple complementary HR practices within an organization's HR system, prospective employees who possess that attribute and who are selected into the organization will be better positioned to create value. For instance, scholars have established the horizontal fit of a High Commitment HR system where employees are selected into the organization based in part on the congruence of their values with those of the organization (Baron et al., 1996) and where additional HR practices (e.g., organization-sponsored social events) reinforce this value congruence, while others (e.g., reliance on peer feedback, high levels of employee autonomy and discretion in job design) leverage employees' value congruence in the coordination of work (Collins and Kehoe, 2017; Collins and Smith, 2006). Based on the complementary support provided by multiple High Commitment HR practices, we would expect value congruence to be the source of greater value creation in organizations using a High Commitment HR system than in other organizations. In a similar vein, Liao et al. (2009) demonstrated the horizontal fit of a service-quality-oriented High Performance Work System in which organizations invest in training programs to develop employees' service skills and where other HR practices (e.g., self-managed teams) create structures for employees to use these skills, while others (e.g., performance appraisals based on service quality, compensation based on service quality) reward employees for effectively employing these skills to create value. In sum, we suggest that the value that any employee attribute is likely to create in an organization will be enhanced or diminished based on the inherent worth accorded to the attribute by the practices within the organization's HR system.

Attributes' Fit with an Organization's Strategy

While the concept of horizontal fit in the SHRM literature refers to the internal coherence of the multiple elements or practices within an HR system, vertical fit refers to the alignment of an organization's HR system with other characteristics of the organizational environment (Baird and Meshoulam, 1988; Wright and McMahan, 1992), especially the organization's strategy. The assumption that underpins the value of vertical fit is that the achievement of competitive advantage in different contexts (particularly in the pursuit of different strategies) requires distinct attributes and behaviors within a firm's workforce (Miles and Snow, 1984). In support of this premise, the behavioral perspective of SHRM suggests that an HR system can aid in the creation of competitive advantage to the extent that its HR practices elicit the specific role behaviors required by a firm's strategy (Schuler and Jackson, 1987; Jackson et al., 2014).

SHRM scholars have demonstrated strong support for the behavioral perspective in the study of HR systems. For example, Schuler and Jackson found that firms pursuing innovation versus quality-enhancement versus cost reduction strategies require their employees to engage in different role behaviors to achieve these various strategic goals. Similarly, Miles and Snow demonstrated that different HR systems vary in their alignment with three distinct strategies (i.e., defender, prospector, and analyzer). More recently, Collins and Kehoe (2017) showed that different HR systems support distinct knowledge search and combination behaviors among employees, such that each of the three HR systems they studied exhibited different levels of alignment with two distinct innovation strategies (i.e., exploration and exploitation) pursued by software firms in their sample.

Integrating these insights with the discussions on complementarities and redundancies and horizontal fit above, we can conclude that organizations' selection processes are most likely to result in employees exhibiting value-creating attributes and behaviors to the extent that the attributes on which selection is focused: a) positively interact with the attributes of other employees or other resources in the organization; b) are also rewarded and reinforced through the organization's other HR practices (i.e., reflecting horizontal fit); and c) are well aligned with the behavioral requirements implied by the organization's strategic goals (i.e., reflecting vertical fit).

Integrating Insights on Fit

Scholars have conceptualized and operationalized fit in a variety of ways, suggesting that the interface between employees and the broader organizational contexts in which they are employed is both multidimensional and complex. In the context of human capital resources, the importance of fit has been examined with respect to organizations' HR systems, strategies, and other resources. However, much of the research in these areas has been conducted outside the selection context. Thus, we suggest an important overarching goal for future research should be to more explicitly incorporate the notion of fit in assessing the extent to which attributes of prospective employees are indeed likely to create value in the hiring context.

DISCUSSION

In this chapter we have sought to integrate theory and findings from disparate research streams to offer insights related to two issues that are central to the challenge of building strategic human capital resources: the identification of employee attributes that may be relevant in the hiring context; and the role of fit between employee attributes and other organizational characteristics in estimating the value-creating potential of prospective employees – both as individual contributors and as members of teams, departments, or other relevant aggregates within organizations in which employees work interdependently toward the attainment of collective goals. Rather than attempting to provide an exhaustive review of research related to each of these topics, our goal in this effort has been to highlight relevant insights from various streams of research that are relevant for further exploration of these issues.

Our goal with this chapter is for scholars focusing on building strategic human capital resources to more fully embrace the importance of fit in the hiring context. In particular, we believe this requires two commitments. First, it is essential that we more thoroughly consider the full range of employee attributes that may be relevant to value creation in a particular job or organizational setting. From this standpoint, we would urge scholars examining selection through an HR or I-O psychology lens to focus less narrowly on assessing the validity of a small range of selection tools in the prediction of task or job performance. While valuable in determining the extent to which specific attributes relate to employees' effectiveness in performing the tasks included in the job for which they are hired, this focus may be problematic in that: a) it largely limits this research to the examination of employee attributes that can be precisely assessed through standardized selection tests; and b) fails to account for the importance of employees' potential value-creating activities (e.g., mentoring, attracting external stakeholders), which may not be captured in ratings of individual employee task or job performance.

Likewise, we would encourage strategy scholars focusing on employee mobility to focus less narrowly on the traditional measures of human capital (e.g., experience, characteristics of specialized knowledge) that are most readily available in archival datasets. These scholars have tended to rely less on traditional measures of job performance, and instead have often examined outcomes that are closely tied to the attributes studied: e.g., knowledge flows and knowledge utilization in the study of specialized knowledge (Almeida et al., 2003; Song et al., 2003); clients' rankings of securities analysts' performance in the study of analysts hired based on their high client rankings (Groysberg and Lee, 2008; Groysberg et al., 2008). This approach has been beneficial in relating employee attributes to the specific forms of value creation to which they are most relevant and which may fall outside traditional measures of task or job performance often employed by HR scholars. However, the reliance on measures of attributes available in archival datasets in this research has often come at the expense of examining other relevant individual attributes that can only be collected through other methods (e.g., observation or the administration of a test or survey).

Ideally, scholars focusing on hiring in the context of building human capital resources would step outside their disciplinary, theoretical, and methodological traditions and begin from the question of how individuals do or might create value in the focal organizational context. Thus, our aim in the first half of the chapter was to offer a survey of employee attributes – both within and outside our conceptualizations of human capital – that might serve as a useful starting point in this process. We contend that it is only after a more careful and thorough consideration of the multiple forms that value creation may take that scholars can determine the range of employee attributes that are *potentially valuable* when selected into an organization.

A second – and related – commitment that we would invite from scholars focusing on the building of human capital resources is to engage in a more comprehensive consideration of how specific employee attributes that are deemed *potentially valuable* actually fit in the broader context of other resources, systems, and strategic goals in an organization (Ployhart and Hale, 2014). It is for this purpose that we have allocated a portion of this chapter to highlighting relevant scholarship on resource complementarities and redundancies in the strategy literature, and the concepts of horizontal and vertical fit and the behavioral perspective in the SHRM literature. Importantly, we believe that it is through the explicit consideration of employees' fit in the broader organizational context that research on selection and hiring has the greatest potential to contribute to our understanding of how organizations build strategic human capital resources – as it is the unique combination and interdependencies between employees and other organizational resources (including other employees) that form the basis for the emergence of a strategic human capital resource (Ployhart et al., 2014).

Just as we do not claim to have identified all of the employee attributes that represent potential sources of value creation in the first half of the chapter, we highlight the need for scholars to think through additional sources, aspects, and implications of fit beyond those that we reviewed in the second half of the chapter. For instance, the implications of complementarities and redundancies among resources are likely to depend not only on the characteristics of the resources in question (Coff, 1997) but also on patterns of resource deployment (Sirmon et al., 2007), the nature of interdependence in workflows (Bowman and Swart, 2007), and the extent to which an organization's HR system fosters and rewards the activities where employees' redundant and/or complementary attributes are most relevant. Moreover, scholarship rooted in the resource orchestration perspective points to the importance of considering resources' potential to create value both in the present *and* future of the organization, requiring not only an assessment of the fit between prospective employee attributes with current organizational resources and strategic goals, but also a forecast estimate based on an organization's anticipated resource portfolios and strategic trajectories in the longer term (Sirmon et al., 2007).

While we hope this chapter offers useful insights for future research on building human capital resources – particularly through organizations' hiring efforts – we acknowledge that our recommendations raise some new questions as well as highlighting the continued relevance of others. First, *how can scholars most effectively push past the traditional methodological limitations of their disciplines (i.e., particularly those noted above) to identify and measure the employee attributes that are most relevant in the focal hiring context in their research?* We will echo but not harp on the value of interdisciplinary research in addressing challenges like this, though we would also acknowledge the likely case that there may be alternative solutions that might gain more traction in practice.

Second, while we have focused our attention in this chapter on the relevance of different employee attributes for value creation, an important related question is *what are the implications of different employee attributes and their relative fit with various organizational characteristics for value capture?* While the question of value capture has been addressed elsewhere in the strategic human capital literature (e.g., Coff, 1997; Ethiraj and Garg, 2012; Kehoe et al., 2018), the hiring process represents a unique temporal context during which value capture is negotiated on the basis of potential (versus actual) value creation; and when the nature of prospective employees' eventual intraorganizational interactions (e.g., local status competitions, mentoring activities) – which may be the source of additional value creation or destruction – have not yet been observed. Thus, we suggest this issue warrants additional consideration situated more specifically in the hiring context.

Third, while we have identified a variety of targets against which we can assess the fit of employee attributes, a key question is *how can organizations determine the most appropriate target of fit in the hiring process?* Given the contingencies and interdependences associated with value creation that we have discussed, the fact that organizations' strategies, competitive environments, and workforce compositions are not static and that new hires may enter the organization in one role (or in one unit) and move to another after some time makes the estimation of value creation associated with specific employee attributes uncertain. Thus, the question of the target(s) against which the fit of candidates' attributes ought to be assessed and the question of whether this fit should be assessed with respect to the state of the organization today or the projected state of the organization in the future are important.

CONCLUSION

In this chapter, we have underscored the need for scholars to be more comprehensive in their identification and consideration of employee attributes that may be relevant for value creation in the particular organizational contexts they are studying, as it is only from this starting point that scholars can effectively determine how hiring on the basis of specific attributes relates to subsequent performance and value-creation outcomes. We have sought to lay a foundation for future research to address this need in the context of building strategic human capital resources in two ways. First, we have explicated the many ways in which a variety of different employee attributes may contribute to employee performance directly and to organizations' value-creation efforts more broadly. In doing so, our aim was not to provide an exhaustive review of all attributes that have possible relevance in hiring, but rather to highlight the breadth of attributes and activities through which individuals may create value in organizations. With this in mind, we urge scholars to take a more open-minded stance as they approach research seeking to understand how hiring contributes to the building of organizations' strategic human capital resources. Second, we have discussed the role and importance of fit between employee attributes and other organizational resources, the organization's HR system, and the organization's strategy in shaping the value-creating potential of particular attributes or employees. With this insight, we encourage scholars to evaluate the potential of employee attributes not in isolation, but with respect to the characteristics of the broader organizational context in which they are (or could ultimately be) employed. We believe the integration and application of the ideas presented here could provide a strong foundation for thinking about how micro-level hiring decisions are likely to contribute to (or detract from) the building of strategic human capital resources at the organization level.

CHAPTER SUMMARY

BOX 16.1 KEY TAKEAWAYS

1. We identify a broader array of attributes through which employees might create value in organizations (e.g., to include social capital, status, etc.), arguing that a larger variety of relevant individual attributes should be explicitly accounted for in the study of organizations' hiring processes and outcomes.
2. We embrace a more encompassing perspective on how employees contribute to value creation in organizations, extending our view of individuals' contributions beyond individual task performance to account for activities such as mentoring, knowledge sharing, connecting firms to external resources and opportunities, etc. that create value at a more macro level.
3. We discuss the importance of fit between prospective employees' human capital attributes and characteristics of the hiring organization, including complementarities, redundancies, and compositional fit with other resources, fit with the organization's HR system, and fit with the organization's strategy.

BOX 16.2 DIRECTIONS FOR FUTURE RESEARCH

1. Expand the inventory of employee attributes examined in the study of selection to reflect the full range of attributes through which employees create value, recognizing that relevant attributes are likely to vary across industry, organizational, and occupational contexts.

2. Embrace a more comprehensive conceptualization of value creation in defining relevant outcomes in the study of hiring to account for employees' less direct contributions (e.g., mentoring, knowledge sharing) which are not always reflected in traditional measures of individual task performance.
3. Identify more appropriate (and perhaps more nuanced) approaches to assessing the role of different types of fit between prospective employee attributes and relevant organizational characteristics in the study of organizations' hiring processes and outcomes.

REFERENCES

Adegbesan, J. (2009). On the origins of competitive advantage: Strategic factor markets and heterogeneous resource complementarity. *Academy of Management Review*, *34*, 463–75.
Adler, P. S., and Kwon, S. W. (2002). Social capital: Prospect for a new concept. *Academy of Management Review*, *27*, 17–40.
Allen, T. D., Poteet, M. L., and Russell, J. E. (2000). Protégé selection by mentors: What makes the difference? *Journal of Organizational Behavior*, *21*, 271–82.
Almeida, P., Dokko, G., and Rosenkopf, L. (2003). Startup size and the mechanisms of external learning: Increasing opportunity and decreasing ability. *Research Policy*, *32*, 301–15.
Anderson, C., John, O. P., Keltner, D., and Kring, A. M. (2001). Who attains social status? Effects of personality and psychical attractiveness in social groups. *Journal of Personality and Social Psychology*, *81*, 116–32.
Argote, L., McEvily, B., and Reagans, R. (2003). Managing knowledge in organizations: An integrative framework and review of emerging themes. *Management Science*, *49*, 571–82.
Azoulay, P., Graff Zivin, J. S., and Wang, J. (2010). Superstar extinction. *Quarterly Journal of Economics*, *125*, 549–89.
Baird, L., and Meshoulam, I. (1988). Managing two fits of strategic human resource management. *Academy of Management Review*, *13*, 116–28.
Baron, J. N., Burton, M. D., and Hannan, M. T. (1996). The road taken: Origins and evolution of employment systems in emerging companies. *Industrial and Corporate Change*, *5*, 239–75.
Barrick, M. R., and Mount, M. K. (1991). The Big Five personality dimensions and job performance: A meta-analysis. *Personnel Psychology*, *44*, 1–26.
Barrick, M. R., Stewart, G. L., and Piotrowski, M. (2002). Personality and job performance: Test of the mediating effects of motivation among sales representatives. *Journal of Applied Psychology*, *87*, 43–51.
Barry, B. and Stewart, G. L. (1997). Composition, process, and performance in self-managed teams: The role of personality. *Journal of Applied Psychology*, *82*, 62–78.
Batt, R. (1999). Work organization, technology, and performance in customer service and sales. *Industrial and Labor Relations Review*, *52*, 539–64.
Behling, O. (1998). Employee selection: Will intelligence and conscientiousness do the job? *Academy of Management Executive*, *12*, 77–86.
Bidwell, M. (2011). Paying more to get less: The effect of external hiring versus internal mobility. *Administrative Science Quarterly*, *56*, 369–407.
Bowman, C., and Swart, J. (2007). Whose human capital? The challenge of value capture when capital is embedded. *Journal of Management Studies*, *44*, 488–505.
Broschak, J. P. (2004). Managers' mobility and market interface: The effect of managers' career mobility on the dissolution of market ties. *Administrative Science Quarterly*, *49*, 608–40.
Broschak, J. P., and Block, E. S. (2014). With or without you: When does managerial exit matter for the dissolution of dyadic market ties? *Academy of Management Journal*, *57*, 743–65.
Brymer, R. A., Molloy, J. C., Gilbert, B. A. (2014). Human capital pipelines: Competitive implications of repeated interorganizational hiring. *Journal of Management*, *40*, 483–508.
Bullard, L. G., and Felder, R. M. (2003). Mentoring: A personal perspective. *College Teaching*, *51*, 66–9.
Burke, M. A., Fournier, G. M., and Prasad, K. (2007). The diffusion of a medical innovation: Is success in the stars? *Southern Economic Journal*, *73*, 588–603.
Burt, R. S. (1997). The contingent value of social capital. *Administrative Science Quarterly*, *42*, 339–65.
Call, M. L., Nyberg, A. J., and Thatcher, S. (2015). Stargazing: An integrative conceptual review, theoretical reconciliation, and extension for star employee research. *Journal of Applied Psychology*, *100*, 1–18.
Campbell, B. A., Coff, R., and Kryscynski, D. (2012). Rethinking sustained competitive advantage from human capital. *Academy of Management Review*, *37*, 376–95.

Carpenter, M. A., and Fredrickson, J. W. (2001). Top management teams, global strategic posture, and the moderating role of uncertainty. *Academy of Management Journal*, *44*, 533–45.
Coff, R. W. (1997). Human assets and management dilemmas: Coping with hazards on the road to resource-based theory. *Academy of Management Review*, *22*, 374–402.
Coff, R., and Kryscynski, D. (2011). Invited editorial: Drilling for micro-foundations of human capital-based competitive advantage. *Journal of Management*, *37*, 1429–43.
Collins, C., and Kehoe, R. R. (2017). Examining strategic fit and misfit in the management of knowledge workers. *Industrial and Labor Relations Review*, *70*, 308–35.
Collins, C., and Smith, K. G. (2006). Knowledge exchange and combination: The role of human resource practices in the performance of high-technology firms. *Academy of Management Journal*, *49*, 544–60.
Costa, P. T., and McCrae, R. R. (1992). Four ways five factors are basic. *Personality and Individual Differences*, *13*, 653–65.
Crocker, A., and Eckardt, R. (2014). A multilevel investigation of individual- and unit-level human capital complementarities. *Journal of Management*, *40*, 509–30.
Crook, T. R., Todd, S. Y., Combs, J. G., Woehr, D. J., and Ketchen, D. J. (2011). Does human capital matter? A meta-analysis of the relationship between human capital and firm performance. *Journal of Applied Psychology*, *96*, 443–56.
Cross, R. L., and Thomas, R. J. (2008). *Driving Results through Social Networks: How Organizations Leverage Networks for Performance and Growth*. New York: Wiley.
Delery, J. E., and Doty, D. H. (1996). Modes of theorizing in strategic human resource management: Tests of universalistic, contingency, and configurational performance predictions. *Academy of Management Journal*, *39*, 802–35.
Deng, C. P., Armstrong, P. I., and Rounds, J. (2007). The fit of Holland's RIASEC model to US occupations. *Journal of Vocational Behavior*, *71*, 1–22.
Denrell, J., Fang, C., and Winter, S. G. (2003). The economics of strategic opportunity. *Strategic Management Journal*, *24*, 977–90.
Dokko, G., and Rosenkopf, L. (2010). Social capital for hire? Mobility of technical professionals and firm influence in wireless standards committees. *Organization Science*, *21*, 677–95.
Eisenhardt, K. M., and Schoonhoven, C. B. (1990). Organizational growth: Linking founding team, strategy, environment, and growth among US semiconductor ventures, 1978–1988. *Administrative Science Quarterly*, *35*, 504–29.
Ethiraj, S. K., and Garg, P. (2012). The division of gains from complementarities in human capital-intensive activity. *Organization Science*, *23*, 725–42.
French, J., and Raven, B. (1959). The basis of social power. In D. Cartwright (eds), *Studies in Social Power*. Ann Arbor: University of Michigan Press.
Fuller, A. W., and Rothaermel, F. T. (2012). When stars shine: The effects of faculty founders on new technology ventures. *Strategic Entrepreneurship Journal*, *6*, 220–35.
Goldberg, L. R. (1992). The development of markers for the Big-Five factor structure. *Psychological Assessment*, *4*, 26–42.
Groysberg, B., and Lee, L. (2008). The effects of colleague quality on top performance: The case of security analysts. *Journal of Organizational Behavior*, *29*, 1123–44.
Groysberg, B., Lee, L. E., and Nanda, A. (2008). Can they take it with them? The portability of star knowledge workers' performance. *Management Science*, *5*, 1213–30.
Groysberg, B., Polzer, J. T., and Elfenbein, H. A. (2011). Too many cooks spoil the broth: How high-status individuals decrease group effectiveness. *Organization Science*, *22*, 722–37.
Hess, A. M., and Rothaermel, F. T. (2011). When are assets complementary? Star scientists, strategic alliances, and innovation in the pharmaceutical industry. *Strategic Management Journal*, *32*, 895–909.
Higgins, M. J., Stephan, P. E., and Thursby, J. G. (2011). Conveying quality and value in emerging industries: Star scientists and the role of signals in biotechnology. *Research Policy*, *40*, 605–17.
Hitt, M. A., Bierman, L., Shimizu, K., and Kochhar, R. (2001). Direct and moderating effects of human capital on strategy and performance in professional service firms: A resource-based perspective. *Academy of Management Journal*, *44*, 13–28.
Hogan, J., Hogan, R., and Busch, C. M. (1984). How to measure service orientation. *Journal of Applied Psychology*, *69*, 167–73.
Holland, J. L., Whitney, D. R., Cole, N. S., and Richards, J. M. (1969). An empirical occupational classification derived from a theory of personality and intended for practice and research. Act Research Report. Iowa City: American College Testing Program.
Horwitz, S. K., and Horwitz, I. B. (2007). The effects of team diversity on team outcomes: A meta-analytic review of team demography. *Journal of Management*, *33*, 987–1015.
Huckman, R. S., and Pisano, G. P., (2006). The firm specificity of individual performance: Evidence from cardiac surgery. *Management Science*, *52*, 473–88.

Hunter, J. E., and Hunter, R. F. (1984). Validity and utility of alternative predictors of job performance. *Psychological Bulletin*, *96*, 72–98.
Hurtz, G. M., and Donovan, J. J. (2000). Personality and job performance: The big five revisited. *Journal of Applied Psychology*, *85*, 869–79.
Huselid, M. A. (1995). The impact of human resource management practices on turnover, productivity, and corporate financial performance. *Academy of Management Journal*, *38*, 635–72.
Inkpen, A. C., and Tsang, E. W. K. (2005). Social capital, networks, and knowledge transfer. *Academy of Management Review*, *30*, 146–65.
Jackson, S. E., Schuler, R. S., and Jiang, K. (2014). An aspirational framework for strategic human resource management. *Academy of Management Annals*, *8*, 1–56.
Kanfer, R. (1990). Motivation theory and industrial/organizational psychology. In M. D. Dunnette and L. Hough (eds), *Handbook of Industrial and Organizational Psychology*, vol. 1, 75–170. Palo Alto, CA: Consulting Psychologists Press.
Kehoe, R. R., and Tzabbar, D. (2015). Lighting the way or stealing the shine? An examination of the duality in star scientists' effects on firm innovative performance. *Strategic Management Journal*, *36*, 709–27.
Kehoe, R. R., Lepak, D. P., and Bentley, F. S. (2018). Let's call a star a star: Task performance, external status, and exceptional contributors in organizations. *Journal of Management*, *44*, 1848–72.
Kirchmeyer, C. (2005). The effects of mentoring on academic careers over time: Testing performance and political perspectives. *Human Relations*, *58*, 637–60.
Kogut, B., and Zander, U. (1996). What firms do? Coordination, identity, and learning. *Organization Science*, *7*, 502–18.
Kozlowski, S. W. J., and Klein, K. J. (2000). A multilevel approach to theory and research in organizations: Contextual, temporal, and emergent processes. In K. J. Klein and S. W. J. Kozlowski (eds), *Multilevel Theory, Research, and Methods in Organizations: Foundations, Extensions, and New Directions*. San Francisco: Jossey-Bass.
Kram, K. E. (1988). *Mentoring at Work: Developmental Relationships in Organizational Life.* Glenview, IL: Scott.
Kristof, A. L. (1996). Person-organization fit: An integrative review of its conceptualizations, measurement, and implications. *Personnel Psychology*, *49*, 1–49.
Lacetera, N., Cockburn, I. M., and Henderson, R. (2004). Do firms change capabilities by hiring new people? A study of the adoption of science-based drug discovery. *Advances in Strategic Management*, *21*, 133–59.
Lau, D. C., and Murnighan, J. K. (1998). Demographic diversity and faultlines: The compositional dynamics of organizational groups. *Academy of Management Review*, *23*, 325–40.
LeBreton-Miller, I., and Miller, D. (2015). The paradox of resource vulnerability: Considerations for organizational curatorship. *Strategic Management Journal*, *36*, 397–415.
Lepak, D. P., and Snell, S. A. (1999). The human resource architecture: Toward a theory of human capital allocation and development. *Academy of Management Review*, *24*, 31–48.
Liao, H., and Chuang, A. (2004). A multilevel investigation of factors influencing employee service performance and customer outcomes. *Academy of Management Journal*, *47*, 41–58.
Liao, H., Toya, K., Lepak, D. P., and Hong, Y. (2009). Do they see eye to eye? Management and employee perspectives of high-performance work systems and influence processes on service quality. *Journal of Applied Psychology*, *94*, 371–91.
Lucifora, C., and Simmons, R. (2003). Superstar effects in sport: Evidence from Italian soccer. *Journal of Sports Economics*, *4*, 35–55.
Magee, J. C., and Galinsky, A. D. (2008). Social hierarchy: The self-reinforcing nature of power and status. *Academy of Management Annals*, *2*, 351–98.
Mathieu, J. E., Tannenbaum, S. I., Donsbach, J. S., and Alliger, G. M. (2014). A review and integration of team composition models: Moving toward a dynamic and temporal framework. *Journal of Management*, *40*, 130–60.
Maurer, T. J., Wrenn, K. A., Pierce, H. R., Tross, S. A., and Collins, W. C. (2003). Beliefs about "improvability" of career-relevant skills: Relevance to job/task analysis, competency modelling, and learning orientation. *Journal of Organizational Behavior*, *24*, 107–31.
Mayer, K. J., Somaya, D., and Williamson, I. O. (2012). Firm-specific, industry-specific, and occupational human capital and the sourcing of knowledge work. *Organization Science*, *23*, 1311–29.
Miles, R. E., and Snow, C. C. (1984). Designing strategic human resources systems. *Organizational Dynamics*, *13*, 36–52.
Mount, M. K., Barrick, M. R., and Stewart, G. L. (1998). Five-factor models of personality and performance in jobs involving interpersonal interactions. *Human Relations*, *11*, 145–65.
Mumford, M. D., Zaccaro, S. J., Harding, F. D., Jacobs, T. O., and Fleishman, E. A. (2000). Leadership skills for a changing world: Solving complex social problems. *Leadership Quarterly*, *11*, 11–35.
Nahapiet, J. and Ghoshal, S. (1998). Social capital, intellectual capital, and the organizational advantage. *Academy of Management Review*, *23*, 242–66.

Noe, R. A. (1988). An investigation of the determinants of successful assigned mentoring relationships. *Personnel Psychology*, *41*, 457–73.
Nyberg, A. J., Moliterno, T. P., Hale, D., and Lepak, D. P. (2014). Resource-based perspectives on unit-level human capital: A review and integration. *Journal of Management*, *40*, 316–46.
Oettl, A. (2012). Reconceptualizing stars: Scientist helpfulness and peer performance. *Management Science*, *58*, 1122–40.
Oldroyd, J. B., and Morris, S. S. (2012). Catching falling stars: A human resource response to social capital's detrimental effect of information overload on star employees. *Academy of Management Review*, *37*, 396–418.
Ones, D. S., Viswesvaran, C., and Schmidt, F. L. (1993). Comprehensive meta-analysis of integrity test validities: Findings and implications for personnel selection and theory of job performance. *Journal of Applied Psychology*, *78*, 679–703.
Osterman, P. (1994). How common is workplace transformation and who adopts it? *Industrial and Labor Relations Review*, *47*, 173–88.
Overbeck, J. R., Correll, J., and Park, B. (2005). Internal status sorting in groups: The problem of too many stars. *Research on Managing Groups and Teams*, *7*, 169–99.
Paglis, L. L., Green, S. G., and Bauer, T. N. (2006). Does advisor mentoring add value? A longitudinal study of mentoring and doctoral student outcomes. *Research in Higher Education*, *47*, 451–76.
Ployhart, R. E. (2015). Strategic organizational behavior (STROBE): The missing voice in the strategic human capital conversation. *Academy of Management Perspectives*, *29*, 342–56.
Ployhart, R. E., and Hale, D. (2014). The fascinating psychological microfoundations of strategy and competitive advantage. *Annual Review of Organizational Psychology and Organizational Behavior*, *1*, 145–72.
Ployhart, R. E., and Moliterno, T. P. (2011). Emergence of the human capital resource: A multilevel model. *Academy of Management Review*, *38*, 127–50.
Ployhart, R. E., Schmitt, N., and Tippins, N. T. (2017). Solving the supreme problem: 100 years of selection and recruitment at the *Journal of Applied Psychology*. *Journal of Applied Psychology*, *102*, 291–304.
Ployhart, R. E., Weekley, J. A., and Ramsey, J. (2009). The consequences of human resource stocks and flows: A longitudinal examination of unit service orientation and unit effectiveness. *Academy of Management Journal*, *52*, 996–1015.
Ployhart, R. E., Nyberg, A. J., Reilly, G., and Maltarich, M. A. (2014). Human capital is dead; long live human capital resources! *Journal of Management*, *40*, 371–98.
Polzer, J. T., Crisp, C. B., Jarvenpaa, S. L., and Kim, J. W. (2006). Extending the faultline model to geographically dispersed teams: How collocated subgroups can impair group functioning. *Academy of Management Journal*, *49*, 679–92.
Prat, A. (2002). Should a team be homogeneous? *European Economic Review*, *46*, 1187–207.
Ree, M. J., and Earles, J. A. (1992). Intelligence is the best predictor of job performance. *Psychological Science*, *1*, 86–89.
Rothaermel, F. T., and Hess, A. M. (2007). Building dynamic capabilities: Innovation driven by individual-, firm-, and network-level effects. *Organization Science*, *18*, 898–921.
Rothwell, W. (2010). *Effective Succession Planning: Ensuring Leadership Continuity and Building Talent from Within.* New York: Amacom.
Schmidt, F. L., and Hunter, J. E. (1998). The validity and utility of selection methods in personnel psychology: Practical and theoretical implications of 85 years of research findings. *Psychological Bulletin*, *124*, 262–74.
Schmidt, J. and Keil, T. (2013). What makes a resource valuable? Identifying the drivers of firm-idiosyncratic resource value. *Academy of Management Review*, *38*, 206–28.
Schneider, B. (1987). The people make the place. *Personnel Psychology*, *40*, 437–53.
Schuler, R. S., and Jackson, S. E. (1987). Linking competitive strategies with human resource management practices. *Academy of Management Executive*, *1*, 207–19.
Shaw, J. D., Duffy, M. K., Johnson, J. L., and Lockhart, J. L. (2005). Turnover, social capital losses, and performance. *Academy of Management Journal*, *48*, 594–606.
Simcoe, T. S., and Waguespack, D. M. (2011). Status, quality, and attention: What's in a (missing) name? *Managerial Science*, *57*, 274–90.
Sirmon, D. G., Gove, S., and Hitt, M.A. (2008). Resource management in dyadic competitive rivalry: The effects of resource bundling and deployment. *Academy of Management Journal*, *51*, 919–35.
Sirmon, D. G., Hitt, M. A., and Ireland, D. R. (2007). Managing firm resources in dynamic environments to create value: Looking inside the black box. *Academy of Management Review*, *32*, 273–92.
Smith, K. G., Collins, C. J., and Clark, K. D. (2005). Existing knowledge, knowledge creation capability, and the rate of new product introduction in high-technology firms. *Academy of Management Journal*, *48*, 346–57.
Somaya, D., Williamson, I. O., and Lorinkova, N. (2008). Gone but not lost: The different performance impacts of employee mobility between cooperators versus competitors. *Academy of Management Journal*, *51*, 936–53.
Song, J., Almeida, P., and Wu, G. (2003). Learning-by-hiring: When is mobility more likely to facilitate interfirm knowledge transfer? *Management Science*, *49*, 351–65.

Tenenbaum, H. R., Crosby, F. J., and Gliner, M. D. (2001). Mentoring relationships in graduate school. *Journal of Vocational Behavior*, *59*, 326–41.
Tinsley, H. E. (2000). The congruence myth: An analysis of the efficacy of the person-environment fit model. *Journal of Vocational Behavior*, *56*, 147–79.
Tzabbar, D., and Kehoe, R. R. (2014). Can opportunity emerge from disarray? An examination of exploration and exploitation following star scientist turnover. *Journal of Management*, *40*, 449–82.
Uggerslev, K. L., Fassina, N. E., and Kraichy, D. (2012). Recruiting through the stages: A meta-analytic test of predictors of applicant attraction at different stages of the recruiting process. *Personnel Psychology*, *65*, 597–660.
Uzzi, B., and Lancaster, R. (2003). Relational embeddedness and learning: The case of bank loan managers and their clients. *Management Science*, *49*, 383–99.
Vinchur, A. J., Schippmann, J. S., Switzer, F. S., and Roth, P. L. (1998). A meta-analytic review of predictors of job performance for salespeople. *Journal of Applied Psychology*, *83*, 586–97.
Whitwell, G. J., Lukas, B. A., and Hill, P. (2007). Stock analysts' assessments of the shareholder value of intangible assets. *Journal of Business Research*, *60*, 84–90.
Wright, P. M., and McMahan, G. C. (1992). Theoretical perspectives for strategic human resource management. *Journal of Management*, *18*, 295–320.
Wright, P. M., Coff, R., and Moliterno, T. P. (2014). Strategic human capital: Crossing the great divide. *Journal of Management*, *40*, 353–70.

17. Getting access to strategic human capital resources: a multiple strategic factor market approach*

Arnaldo Camuffo and Federica De Stefano

HUMAN CAPITAL RESOURCES: A WORKING DEFINITION

In the past decade, scholars have increasingly adopted a multi-level approach to the study of human capital (Ployhart and Moliterno, 2011). In this transition, they shifted their attention from the individual-level construct of human capital to the multi-level definition of human capital resources (HCRs) (Ployhart et al., 2014), which are "individual or unit-level capacities based on individual KSAOs that are accessible for unit-relevant purposes" (Ployhart et al., 2014: 374). These capacities are "created from the emergence of individuals' knowledge, skills, abilities, and other characteristics (KSAOs)" (Ployhart and Moliterno, 2011: 128) but encompass multiple levels: micro, intermediate, and macro (Ployhart and Moliterno, 2011).

The HCRs framework has thus extended our understanding of how human capital affects organizational performance beyond an individual-level approach (Ployhart et al., 2014). First, HCRs vary in their *structure* more than the traditional classification of human capital as general or firm-specific (Ployhart et al., 2014): not only there are many different HCRs, but also a wide array of potential combinations of HCRs. Second, these resources manifest themselves both at the individual and at the unit level, and their combinations occur both within and across levels (Nyberg et al., 2014). Third, the combinations of HCRs differ in their functions, that is, that they vary in their performance outcomes (Ployhart et al., 2014).

However, the existing framework used to interpret how organizations build these capacities still prevalently adopts an individual-level approach: organizations acquire human capital at the individual level through hiring, and then develop HCRs by training, socialization, and experience of individuals on the job (Ployhart et al., 2011). This hiring framework challenges "the extent to which strategic factor markets exist for these complex strategic human capital resource combinations" (Ployhart et al., 2014: 393). In this chapter, we argue that these markets exist, and we propose a framework to explain how organizations use them to build HCRs.

GETTING ACCESS TO HCRS: THE CASE OF NOVARTIS

In order to illustrate how firms might get access to HCRs through multiple channels and sourcing markets, we will consider the case of Novartis, the pharmaceutical multinational headquartered in Basel, Switzerland.

Novartis offers a diversified portfolio of innovative medicines, eye care and cost-saving generic pharmaceuticals with revenues in excess of US$50 billion and R&D investment of approximately $9 billion. In the last 15 years, and especially after the acquisition in 2015 of the GlaxoSmithKline (GSK) oncology division, Novartis has significantly grown its oncology business, becoming the #2 player worldwide thanks to a broad pipeline and portfolio of treatments that includes breakthrough innovations like Kymriah – an investigational chimeric antigen receptor T cell (CAR-T) therapy for the treatment of relapsed or refractory pediatric and young adult patients with B-cell acute lymphoblastic leukemia. Oncology is one of the fastest growing therapeutic categories in the pharma industry and will more than double in the next decade, with an expected 15–20 million new patients per year and an average estimated treatment cost of $120,000–150,000 per patient. As cancer treatment has changed dramatically in 15 years, moving from chemotherapy to targeted therapy to immunotherapy, Novartis has significantly adapted its knowledge base and capabilities accordingly. While adapting, it has explicitly acknowledged, even in its financial statements and communication to investors, that its strategy is highly dependent on human capital and that there is a potential related risk to mitigate, as the inability to attract and retain qualified personnel could adversely affect its business. This challenge stems from a variety of concurring factors:

- The potential turnover of key senior members of the scientific and management teams, high-quality researchers and development specialists, and skilled personnel in emerging markets.[1]
- A tight market for talent, especially in emerging markets like Russia and China. Shifting demographics reducing the number of students and graduates in the Western world in the next ten years, with evident talent gaps for some professions and some countries (e.g., engineers in Germany).
- Reduced geographic mobility of talent due to: a) talented individuals in developed and emerging countries anticipating ample career opportunities closer to home; and b) anti-immigrant sentiments in many countries, and laws discouraging immigration.
- Increased competition from numerous pharmaceutical and biotechnology companies, universities, governmental entities, other research institutions, other companies seeking to enter the healthcare space, and companies in other industries.

Novartis has built its human capital resources, first of all through hiring, i.e., trying to address these labor market challenges with stronger investment and renewed efforts in HR, and therefore better supporting the business in transforming cancer care.[2] This implied a major organizational redesign, the identification of ten emergent capabilities[3] (change agility and adaptability, purpose-driven leadership, strategic thinking and action, enterprise leadership, commercial excellence, diagnostics and solutions, market access pricing and oncology policy, portfolio prioritization and management, medical expertise, business development and licensing), and a comprehensive mapping of the capabilities gap to be filled by a variety of HR initiatives including talent acquisition and development and tighter selection criteria.

However, Novartis has also gained access to HCRs in oncology through interorganizational relations, for example emphasizing cancer treatment in the development of a network of collaborations with research institutions and universities, largely hinging on the Novartis Institutes for BioMedical Research. NIBR employs 6000 people in six locations around the globe and represents the innovation engine of the company, collaborating across scientific and organizational boundaries to identify and develop new technologies that have the potential to help produce therapeutic breakthroughs for patients.

Interestingly, NIBR provides opportunities for its associates to pursue multidisciplinary projects and collaborate with investigators inside and outside the company. For example, it recently launched a new research concept called the Genesis Labs, where employees together with external collaborators can explore transformative ideas that fall outside the scope of existing departments at NIBR. Multidisciplinary teams pitch ideas to a panel of scientists, who decide which projects are most promising. In 2017, teams submitted 90 proposals, and five projects ultimately received funding. Members of the selected teams step away from their day jobs to focus on their new project for 6–18 months. They are partnered with NIBR or academic mentors with relevant experience. These cross-organizational teams potentially constitute units in which cross-level HCR combinations are embodied and accessible for NIBR purposes.

Finally, Novartis has built HCRs in oncology, also recently purchasing (in 2017), for approximately $4 billion, Advanced Accelerator Applications (AAA), a radiopharmaceutical company that develops, produces and commercializes Molecular Nuclear Medicines. This acquisition not only complements Novartis's oncology portfolio with treatments like Lutathera®, a first-in-class RLT product for neuroendocrine tumors, but also grants access to a high-quality team of managers, scientists, and technicians. In 15 years AAA has grown from a small team of ten people to a specialty nuclear pharmaceutical organization with over 600 employees across 20 production and R&D facilities in 13 countries. Also in this case, the HCRs embodied in AAA have become accessible through the acquisition by Novartis.

The case of the Novartis oncology division illustrates how a firm can access different HCR combinations, directly and/or indirectly, through different "channels" largely corresponding to different strategic choices, with different sourcing markets (labor markets, supply markets, product markets, financial markets, etc.) operating as acquisition interfaces. Table 17.1 summarizes the HCR acquisition strategies discussed in this chapter.

This chapter offers some reflections on how firms can orchestrate these options in getting access to strategic human capital resources through a multiple strategic factor market approach. It does so by focusing on three interrelated aspects. The first is how the concept of HCRs challenges the way we think about attracting and harnessing people's ingenuity in an organization. The second is how HCRs can be built by organizations and, more specifically, the different ways in which organizations can think about getting access to the HCRs they believe they need to pursue their strategy and achieve a competitive advantage (strategic HCRs) (Barney and Wright, 1998). The third aspect is a specific angle to the process of "emergence" of HCRs – that, is how different HCR acquisition strategies enable different emergence processes.

The main goal of this chapter is to use the emerging theory on HCRs to challenge the assumption (still widespread among scholars and practitioners alike) that firms can build strategic HCRs exclusively by hiring individuals and then developing or combining the human capital embedded in them. Rather, we contend that scholars and practitioners could usefully adopt the HCR perspective and address the problem of how HCRs are

Table 17.1 HCR acquisition strategies

HCR acquisition strategy	Sub-types	Sourcing market	HCR level	HCR combination	Prevalent locus of HCR emergence	HCR acquisition interface
Hiring	Employment Contingent work "Gig-work"	Labor markets	Individual	Hybrid-cross level (individual-unit)	Internal	Jobs
Sourcing through interorganizational relations	Buyer-supplier-seller partner (alliances)	Supply chains Product markets	Unit	Hybrid-cross level (unit-firm) and cross-firm	External	Contracts (buy-sell-ally)
"Acqui-hiring"		Markets for control Financial markets	Unit/firm	Hybrid-cross level (unit-firm) and cross-firm	External	M&As (equity-property rights)
Problem solving Crowdsourcing		Two-sided markets for knowledge/ open innovation	KSAOs	Hybrid-cross level (individual-unit-firm) and cross-firm	Internal-external	Platform technology Strategy/ problem modular decomposition

built from a different, broader standpoint that conceptually hinges on the combinatory, collective, and unit-level nature of HCRs.

The framework that we propose has four major implications. First, it weakens the association "human capital–individuals–hiring–HR." Second, it questions whether firms should allocate the responsibility of building HCRs primarily to the HR function. If hiring individuals is not the only channel to build HCRs, then the firm needs a stronger cross-functional integration to access relevant strategic factor markets for these resources, as well as a fundamental rethinking of the role of the HR function. Third, our framework calls for a tighter integration of strategic human resource management (SHRM) and strategic human capital (SHC) research to extend our understanding of how firms build strategic HCRs. Fourth, we challenge SHC and SHRM scholars to think of labor markets, supply chains, platforms/ecosystems, and financial markets as potentially functional equivalent sources of HCRs (strategic factor markets) characterized, under different conditions, by different comparative static and dynamic efficiency.

BUILDING STRATEGIC HUMAN CAPITAL RESOURCES: HIRING AND ACQUIRING

Based on the above definition and its articulation, we posit that firms can strategize about how to build HCRs, and that there is a variety of (potentially equifinal) ways in which they can: a) acquire the individual and collective components of HCRs; and b) enable the process of "emergence" of HCRs at the unit level.

On the one hand, these ways obviously pertain to the traditional domain of SHRM (Lepak and Snell, 1999). Staffing decisions (recruiting, selection and hiring of individuals) result from HR practices. These practices are the logical antecedents to HCRs (Nyberg et al., 2014) and are therefore "classic" enablers of the HCR emergence process. Adopting "best practices" in hiring leads to higher-quality individual-level HCRs, facilitates the emergence of valuable unit-level HCRs, and eventually enhances unit-relevant performance.

On the other hand, if we take into consideration the "combinatory/collective/unit" level nature of HCRs, then these ways also pertain to other areas of strategic management. If HCRs at the unit level are not the mere sum of the individual HCRs, firms might think about acquiring them in a variety of ways that do not necessarily involve hiring individuals.

Therefore, the acquisition of HCRs (or, more precisely, the possibility of getting access to them) might be thought of at the macro level as the acquisition of an aggregate and already combined unit-level capacity. This unit-level acquisition might thus leverage on all sorts of interorganizational relationships, such as buyer–supplier relations in supply chains and alliances. For example, setting up a contract with a supplier of products or services enables access to the HCRs embodied in the supplier. Moreover, the firm might utilize mergers and acquisitions (M&As) to build unit-level capacities: the acquisition of a firm or of a business unit implies acquiring the HCRs embodied in the target firm or business unit (Coff, 1999, 2002). Furthermore, the firm can access strategic human capital resources through ecosystems, platforms, and industrial clusters. For instance, adopting a business model based on a platform intermediating between suppliers and customers also implies leveraging the HCRs embodied in the actors on the two sides of the platform.

Similarly, choosing to locate operations in a specific region or territory, embedding it in the corresponding industrial cluster or district, also implies the possibility of accessing the HCRs embedded in the cluster (firms and institutions) and its community (Camuffo and Grandinetti, 2011).

In other words, firms can build strategic HCRs by orchestrating an array of acquisition strategies. They can do so from the bottom up by acquiring individual-level KSAOs through hiring and then using the different types of employment modes available to make the strategic HCR combinations emerge. Alternatively, firms can directly acquire HCRs at the collective/unit level, using formal contracting, relational contracting, or property rights to access and utilize the HCR combinations embodied in the target outside units or firms.

This concept is not completely novel to the SHC/SHRM literature. For example, the literature on cluster hiring (Eckardt et al., 2018), lift-outs (Groysberg and Lee, 2009), and pipeline hiring (Brymer et al., 2019) challenge the assumption that firms access human capital through individual, one-off hiring. Even more interestingly, Mawdsley and Somaya (2016) argue that, in the presence of labor market imperfections that impede employee mobility, alternative competing channels like alliances, networks and geographic spillovers, and acquisitions can work as functional equivalents to employee mobility. Coff (2002) makes a similar point from a corporate acquisition perspective, arguing that when human capital cannot be acquired in efficient labor markets but knowledge is critical to firms building a strategic capability, firms will resort to "acqui-hiring" (Chatterji and Patro, 2014), paying the potential price of over-bidding and suffering from all sorts of post-acquisition problems (e.g., turnover of key people in the acquired firms). However, these contributions offer only a partial, not unified, view of how firms can strategize to get access to human capital. We believe that the HCR concept offers an interesting opportunity in this sense.

Finally, a fundamental question is whether practitioners think of the acquisition of HCRs in this way. For sure, firms intentionally and deliberately try to align their hiring strategies to acquire the HCRs (or, at least, the individuals) they think they need to pursue their strategies. However, it is less clear if and to what extent the acquisition of HCRs substantially informs and shapes other strategic decisions regarding organizational boundaries, supply chain design and management, business model architecture, and M&As. We believe that this chapter challenges not only strategic human capital and human resource management scholars to address the issue of how firms get access to HCRs, but also practitioners to broaden their view about how to build and acquire HCRs.

GETTING ACCESS TO HCRS: AN INTERPRETATIVE FRAMEWORK

The premise of the framework that we propose is that HCR acquisition can have two, often intertwined, meanings and goals: HCRs can be acquired "to be used" or "to be developed/recombined." When firms acquire "to use" they have relatively low uncertainty about what HCRs they need and how they will integrate these resources into the business model supporting their strategy. In this case HCRs have already emerged by the time they are acquired or, at least, it is clear how they will after the acquisition. When firms acquire "to develop/recombine" instead, HCR acquisition is only the first step in a more complex and uncertain process of emergence. This process requires further action after the acquisition to ensure that HCRs actually become "individual or unit-level capacities based on individual KSAOs that are accessible for unit-relevant purposes" (Nyberg et al., 2014: 376).

The distinction between getting access "to use" and "to develop/recombine" HCRs is critical as it underlies potentially different strategic intents and human capital strategies. Building on this distinction, we use the HCR typologies proposed by Nyberg et al. (2014) and Ployhart et al. (2014) as the starting point to understand how firms can build strategic HCRs. Specifically, we use those scholars' levels, types, functions, context, and antecedents of HCRs as the bases of our interpretative framework. Our goal is to use these typologies to explain how and why firms vary in the way they get access to HCRs. We believe these are powerful interpretative frameworks because how firms get access to HCRs varies with the levels and the types of resources that the firm needs, with the performance objectives that it pursues, and with the organizational context and practices involved in transforming HCRs in a strategic firm-level asset. In order to extend our analysis of HCR acquisition beyond hiring (Ployhart et al., 2011), we connect the strategic human capital and human resource management literature on HCRs (Ployhart and Moliterno, 2011) to the research areas that have traditionally explored alternative acquisition channels, such as corporate strategy (Capron and Guillén, 2009), supply-chain management (Mahapatra et al., 2010), and open innovation (Belenzon and Schankerman, 2015).

Levels

Our framework builds on the distinction between the two levels at which human capital resources manifest themselves (Ployhart et al., 2014: 380): individual and unit. We use this categorization to interpret the alternative ways to acquire HCRs. If we focus on individual-level HCRs, we might think that hiring individuals with the required portfolios of KSAOs (by the strategy/business model) is a necessary condition to build strategic HCRs at the unit level and achieve unit-level performance. Similarly, if we focus on unit-level HCRs, we might think that buying the products/services of an external supplier/firm/unit or purchasing such firm/unit is another way to get access/use/acquire the HCRs embodied in that unit/firm.

However, the situation is conceptually more nuanced because firms can acquire hybrid combinations of individual- and collective-level human capital resources. Overall, firms might opt for different strategies of acquisition of HCRs that can be conceptually located within a continuum characterized by two extremes. At one extreme of the continuum, the firm builds the HCRs from the bottom up, focusing on hiring individuals. This acquisition strategy is based on the assumptions that the firm designs processes and jobs correctly, and it correctly identifies the KSAOs of different individuals that are necessary to optimally perform the tasks associated with each job. This strategy also implies having knowledge of or at least clear assumptions about the HCR emergence process and the HR system that supports it (Becker and Gerhart, 1996; Lepak et al., 2006). At the other extreme, the firm accesses HCRs at the collective level through interorganizational relationships, such as informal ties, contracts, alliances, equity agreements, and even acquisitions. This strategy creates value under two conditions. First, when the HCRs embodied in the target unit are redeployed in the focal unit, their value exceeds the cost of the unit acquisition. Second, the cost of the acquisition is lower than that of alternative acquisition strategies such as building a unit and hiring the necessary individuals with the necessary skills (Barney, 1986).

Firms can build HCRs by combining or mixing the two acquisition strategies just described. For example, firms might build unit-level HCRs through cluster hiring (Eckardt et al., 2018) or lift-outs (Groysberg and Lee, 2009) – i.e., acquiring team-level HCRs by hiring all the individuals who work in the same team in another unit/firm. By hiring the team, the firm has already observed how unit-level HCRs emerged from team members' KSAOs in another unit (Ployhart et al., 2014). The uncertainty surrounding how the unit-level HCRs will emerge in the future will thus be lower and any potential risk/cost mitigated.

Alternatively, firms might build individual-level HCRs by contracting or acquiring specific firms/units. For instance, a firm might acquire a firm or unit with the ultimate and exclusive goal of accessing the KSAOs of specific individuals employed in such units. This might happen because hiring these individuals is impossible (e.g., due to non-compete agreements) or too costly (individual compensation). This might also happen when a given firm wishes to hire a "star" performer but acknowledges that her star performance is contingent on other contextual factors (Groysberg et al., 2008) or embedded in a team (Oettl, 2012) so that, in order to ensure the individual-level strategic HCRs, it is necessary to acquire collective HCRs. This acquisition strategy requires that the unit-level HCRs embodied in the target unit can be decomposed in sub-unit- and individual-level HCRs that can be effectively redeployed elsewhere in the acquiring organization. A typical example of this approach is to be found in some segments of the fashion/apparel industry, where flagship firms achieve style and design excellence by keeping the design activities in house while, at the same time, collaborating with experienced external designers and stylists (Brun et al., 2008; Djelic and Ainamo, 1999).

Furthermore, a focal firm might indirectly build *its* HCRs by helping its business partners build *their* HCRs. For example, the HR department of the focal firm can help its suppliers, customers, and partners to build *their* HCRs, which are then embodied in the products and services these firms supply to the focal firm or sell on its behalf. This might entail transferring best practices in hiring, as well as providing consulting services (on recruiting, selection, etc.) to the HR departments and/or line managers of suppliers, customers, and partners so that they can hire the best-fitting *individuals*. Interestingly, this directly relates to two separate literatures that explicitly address the potential role of HR practices in fostering the global performance of extended supply chains: supply chain management (Koulikoff-Souviron and Harrison, 2008; Othman and Abdul Ghani, 2008) and human resource management (Hunter et al., 1996; Lengnick-Hall and Lengnick-Hall, 1999; Lengnick-Hall et al., 2013; Scarbrough, 2000).

Overall, distinguishing between the individual and unit level of HCRs is key in understanding how firms might build strategic HCRs and what HCR acquisition strategy they might want to rely on. As discussed later in this chapter, this implies that the characteristics of different HCR sourcing markets shape the firm's acquisition choices, with labor markets, financial markets, and industries/supply chains working as strategic factor markets, partly functionally equivalent sources of HCRs.

Types

The different types (Nyberg et al., 2014: 321) or structures (Ployhart et al., 2014: 376) of HCRs also provide some ground to understanding how and why firms acquire HCRs in multiple ways. One promising avenue of reflection on this topic derives from Ployhart et al.'s call for disambiguating unit-level HCRs (2014: 329): when the firm targets the human capital resources to acquire, it should distinguish between knowledge, skills, abilities, and other characteristics at the individual level (Barney and Felin, 2013) and, correspondingly, specify the precise nature of a given unit's HCR. In theory as well as in practice, knowledge-based HCRs are structurally different from skill-based HCRs and ability-based HCRs (Nyberg et al., 2014: 328). The business models and the strategies hinging on these different types of HCRs might thus require different HCR acquisition strategies.

One area in which this distinction becomes particularly relevant is that of competency modeling (Campion et al., 2011). We believe this is an exemplary case of how confusing different types of HCRs impairs the firm's ability to develop adequate hiring strategies, and to even understand when alternative acquisition strategies are needed.

Firms widely use competency models to elicit or envision the KSAOs they consider necessary or critical to perform specific jobs, families of jobs or, more generally, to fit the organizational culture and align it with the strategy (Shippmann et al., 2000). These models (repertoires of KSAOs) are then used to guide and inform hiring. However, many of these competency models can be misleading in guiding how to identify the HCRs to acquire and how to make them emerge after acquisition. The major potential flaw of these tools is that they perpetuate the widespread tendency, of both practice and human capital research (Nyberg et al., 2014: 328), to treat knowledge, skills, abilities, and other characteristics as interchangeable and/or undifferentiated ways to operationalize HCRs.

In practice – but sometimes also in theory – competency models tend to conflate KSAOs, often confusing them so that it is unclear how these different HCR types map onto individual and unit performance (Lievens et al., 2004). Besides, often with the excuse of keeping them simple and applicable to the entire organization, they tend to be "one-size-fits-all" models: a relatively short list of general attributes that are hardly actionable in hiring (Camuffo and Gerli, 2007; Camuffo et al., 2009). Finally, they tend to be more the result of political processes than the outcome of a real understanding of the firm's human capital structure and dynamics (Kochanski and Ruse, 1996). Therefore, the different types of human capital resources are seldom operationalized with valid and reliable metrics, and their presence and relevance is hard to capture.

The oversimplification underlying most of the competency models that firms develop is grounded on the naïve assumption that HCR combinations are additive and within-level (Nyberg et al., 2014). Firms that try to acknowledge the combinatory, cross-level nature of HCRs, sticking to the "competency repertoire" approach, try to build multiple competency sub-models (by job family, by business unit, by competency type) – making the system too complex and impossible to act upon. Again, what lacks in competency modeling literature and practice is recognition of the multilevel nature of HCRs and of the role of KSAOs and individual interactions in the emergence process (Barney and Felin, 2013). This interestingly pairs with Nyberg et al.'s observation that the vast majority of the human capital literature focuses on only one type of human capital resource and, in some cases, does not even identify a specific KSAO underlying the HCRs. Only a few studies examine multiple KSAO types.

Both scholars and practitioners need to move from human capital conceptualized as indistinct and/or single-type KSAOs to differentiated, complex HCR combinations. These combinations lie at the heart of how KSAOs and HCRs work interdependently within or across levels to create value (Campbell et al., 2012). Therefore, unpacking them theoretically and empirically is the premise to: a) inform decisions on what type of resource the firm should acquire, what type of acquisition channel it should select, and how it should turn the acquired resources into strategic HCRs for competitive advantage; and b) design and implement differentiated and evidence-based practices for hiring and acquisition.

Functions

Firms acquire HCRs to achieve their desired performance outcomes. Ployhart et al. (2014: 379) argue that HCRs have two main functions: the firm can use them to generate more economic value than "the marginal breakeven" competitor (competitive advantage) or the same value that the "marginal breakeven" competitor generates. Human capital resources that allow the firm to achieve competitive advantage are rare, inimitable, and non-substitutable (Peteraf and Barney, 2003), and as such they are strategic HCRs. Instead, the HCRs necessary for competitive parity may well be abundant, imitable, and substitutable, and could be even considered commodities (Ployhart et al., 2014). Therefore, the intended function of these resources affects the type and the level of the HCRs the firm acquires, and in turn the acquisition channel the firm selects.

If the firm acquires HCRs for competitive advantage, then it should focus on acquiring and developing idiosyncratic combinations of activities, practices, and individual-level KSAOs that competitors cannot replicate (Ployhart and Moliterno, 2011). In order to do so, the acquisition process should have two major characteristics: high level of control over the resource and sustainability over time. Since HCRs are different from other capital resources because the individuals in which they are embedded can leave the firm (Coff, 1997), the ability to control the resource and to sustain superior value creation over time derives from the extent to which the firm can constrain the mobility of human capital (Campbell et al., 2012; Chadwick, 2017).

One way to achieve this goal is by hiring individuals and investing in training and development of firm-specific skills that they cannot transfer outside the focal firm, and of idiosyncratic combinations of general skills that cannot be replicated by other employers (Campbell et al., 2012). This way of acquiring HCRs enables the emergence of firm-level strategic human capital resources from individual-level KSAOs (Ployhart and Moliterno, 2011; Ployhart et al., 2011). It is thus not surprising that individual-level hiring dominates the theoretical frameworks on the acquisition of HCRs (Ployhart et al., 2011). However, the firm could achieve this goal using other ways to reduce the likelihood of undesired talent mobility, such as including non-compete agreements in hiring (Marx et al., 2009; Marx, 2011). Furthermore, similar levels of sustainable control over strategic HCRs can be pursued through alternative acquisition modes, such as long-term exclusive relationships with suppliers (Narasimhan et al., 2009; Wuyts and Geyskens, 2005) and acquisitions of other firms/units (Coff, 1999, 2002).

If the firm acquires HCRs for competitive parity, then sustained control over the resource is less central to the selection of the acquisition mode. For example, the firm might acquire these human capital resources by contracting them out to external service providers. While these resources are necessary to achieve "normal" performance levels (Barney and Wright, 1998), they are comparable to one-size-fits-all best practices shared by all the competitors (Ployhart et al., 2014).

In all the cases analyzed above (i.e., interorganizational relations, acquisitions, and contractors), the emergence of strategic HCRs (Ployhart and Moliterno, 2011) will probably differ from the case of hiring. How these alternative emergence processes unfold and how they compare to existing theoretical frameworks remain open and relevant questions. Addressing these questions is necessary to extend our understanding of the causal relationships between the acquisition of HCRs and the firm-performance outcomes (Ployhart et al., 2011).

Context

The organizational context in which the firm acquires and combines HCRs is a relevant driver of how these resources emerge (Nyberg et al., 2014) and of the acquisition mode that the firm selects. For instance, buyer–supplier relationships vary in the power and governance structures across industries: in some contexts, firms can develop strategic HCRs through their suppliers because their relationship is exclusive and long term (e.g., the automotive industry), while in others these relationships are more transactional and short term (Mahapatra et al., 2010). Similarly, the nature of jobs varies across units (Nyberg et al., 2014): cluster hiring from another organization may be unnecessary in units with tasks requiring little coordination, while it may be a source of competitive advantage in units where tasks are highly interdependent. Another example is the stability of the context in which the firm operates: firms operating in very dynamic contexts might prefer the use of contractors over direct hiring to be more flexible in the face of environmental uncertainty (Kalleberg, 2000).

Nyberg et al. (2014: 323) identify two context sub-dimensions that are particularly relevant to how the firm acquires HCRs: "global context" and "organizational activities." The global context is the country in which the firm operates, and encompasses elements such as cultural norms, the legal system, and labor market conditions and institutions. These factors are central to the acquisition strategy that the firm selects to develop HCRs because they determine their productivity and cost (Freeman, 2007) as well as their potential mobility. Moreover, the global context significantly constrains the firm's ability to use the HCRs of a target firm/unit after a corporate acquisition (Capron and Guillén, 2009). Finally, the sub-dimension of organizational activities encompasses strategic actions through which the firm can acquire HCRs, such as corporate mergers and acquisitions (Coff, 1999, 2002; Nyberg at al., 2014). Overall, all these examples of context-related factors highlight that the organizational context is an important moderator of the costs and benefits of different HCR acquisition strategies and should be considered in analyzing the firm's incentives to select one acquisition mode over another.

Antecedents

Finally, we consider the antecedents of HCRs, i.e. the "organizational activities that shape and affect the nature of the unit-level HCR" (Nyberg et al., 2014: 324). Specifically, we argue that the studies on these antecedents of HCRs should also embrace a broader and multidisciplinary perspective on how the firm acquires these resources.

Our argument builds on results from Nyberg et al.'s literature review on unit-level HCRs. In their comprehensive review, the authors find that most of the studies on the practices that enable HCRs to emerge focus on human resource management practices and policies in areas such as staffing, training, and performance appraisal (Nyberg et al., 2014: 324). This finding is highly consistent with the dominant assumption in this literature that HCRs emerge from individual-level hiring, followed by training and development (Ployhart et al., 2011).

However, when firms acquire HCRs through alternative channels they also leverage practices and policies that are often outside the HR functional domain, such as governance practices for mergers and acquisitions (Capron and Guillén, 2009) or supply-management practices for buyer–supplier partnerships (Mahapatra et al., 2010). How these practices "shape and affect" (Nyberg et al., 2014: 324) HCRs and how they interact with HR policies and practices are important and open questions. If the organizational activities leading to the acquisition of HCRs fall outside the domain of the HR function, then the firm should reallocate responsibilities across functions and promote cross-functional integration in the activities that concern human capital acquisition and development (De Stefano et al., 2018).

MARKETS AND STRATEGIC HCRS

The theoretical argument underlying this chapter is that the concept of HCRs, as originally proposed by Ployhart and Moliterno (2011), might help scholars and practitioners adopt a broader, innovative view about how to source human capital. From a theoretical standpoint, it advocates a stronger integration of the strategy (strategic human capital, vertical integration, alliances, M&As) and HR literatures, highlighting how HCR combinations, at the individual or unit level, can be sourced strategically in a variety of ways. From a practical standpoint, it unveils different possible ways in which firms can strategize about the acquisition of human capital other than the standard HR-strategy alignment paradigm so deeply rooted in the strategic HRM literature (Wright and Snell, 1998). In line with the knowledge view (Grant, 1996) and part of the strategic human capital literature, strategic decisions about organizational boundaries, supply chain design and management, external growth, business model design, and ecosystem configuration could be fruitfully viewed and analyzed as decisions about acquiring, building, and retaining HCRs.

From this standpoint, all business transactions that embody HCRs can be considered potential HCR acquisition channels. Consequently, beside labor markets, other markets could be considered as potential HCR sources (Barney, 1986) – including upstream and downstream markets in supply chains (Lengnick-Hall et al., 2013), markets for technologies (Arora and Gambardella, 2010), platforms (Baldwin and Woodward, 2009), and financial markets (for control/ownership) (Coff, 2002).

Hiring: Internal and External Labor Markets

The first, obvious source of HCRs is labor markets. Since the nineteenth century firms have used direct hiring of employees as the primary channel to acquire and control human capital (Hamori et al., 2011). Consistently, the frameworks describing the emergence of HCRs from individuals' KSAOs identified hiring as the first step in the process (Ployhart and Moliterno, 2011; Ployhart et al., 2011): firms acquire individual-level human capital by hiring employees, and then develop them internally to build strategic human capital resources.

Contingent on unit task characteristics (Ployhart and Moliterno, 2011), organizations design processes and jobs, identify the necessary KSAOs to perform them, and recruit and select individuals with best horizontal and vertical fit (Wright and Snell, 1998). Business processes are "modularized" into jobs that often represent the interface between the firm/ unit and the labor market together with hiring practices.

The HR department and HRM practices play a critical role ensuring optimal fit through staffing best practices and enabling the HCR emergence process. Using an HCR perspective sheds new light on human capital acquisition. More specifically, understanding levels, types, and functions of HCRs emphasizes the need to consider how individuals not only match job specification requirements, but also to what extent they (and their KSAOs) are complementary and how they combine. Furthermore, as highlighted by context-emergent turnover theory (Nyberg and Ployhart, 2013; Reilly et al., 2014), it allows us to better appreciate the dynamics of human capital (accrual and depletion) as a function of inflows and outflows. From this standpoint, HCR theory nicely complements both high-performance human resource management practices (Jiang et al., 2012) and internal labor market theories (Waldman, 2013).

Three major phenomena dramatically changed how modern organizations approach hiring and, consequently, the HCR context: 1) the diffusion of alternative work arrangements; 2) the increase in external hiring for non-entry level positions; and 3) the use of technological platforms to intermediate labor supply and demand (the rise of online labor markets).

Hiring workers with alternative work arrangements

Since the 1980s, firms have departed from the "traditional build model of acquiring and developing human capital" (Hamori et al., 2011: 1) to achieve efficiency and flexibility in the face of a more uncertain and competitive economic environment (Kalleberg, 2000). Firms hire employees with traditional employment arrangements and then develop human capital resources within the firm's internal labor market to a lesser extent than in the past (Hamori et al., 2011). Instead, they increasingly rely on the external labor market to acquire human capital and hire individuals through alternative work arrangements, such as part-time, temporary, and contract work (Kalleberg, 2000). These contracts are not based on the expectation of a long-term employment relationship, and vary in the extent to which the firm is able to control and dispose of the supply of human capital (see Cappelli and Keller, 2013, for a typology of alternative work arrangements). Importantly, these alternative arrangements are used not only for peripheral jobs but also for jobs that are core to the firm's value-creation strategy (Bidwell, 2009).

Not only employment relationships shifted from the "build" model to a transaction- and market-based model; this shift also increased the number of entities involved in these relationships (Bonet et al., 2013). Labor market intermediaries such as search firms, employment agencies (Hamori et al., 2011), and online platforms (Friedman, 2014) are increasingly involved in the acquisition and development of human capital. Sometimes they even "own" the HCRs that the firms develop (e.g., temporary employees who work for the firm but are employed by an employment agency).

In this landscape of arrangements and intermediaries, understanding how HCRs emerge and how HR practices should vary across employment groups is particularly complex. Workers with alternative work arrangements are not direct full-time employees who expect to remain in the firm in the long term. Therefore, incentivizing them to invest in the development of firm-specific human capital that they cannot use outside the focal firm might be particularly challenging. This challenge might be costly to firms since the development of idiosyncratic HCR combinations is a key mechanism through which they build strategic HCRs (Ployhart et al., 2014). Moreover, "triangular employment relationships" in which firms and labor market intermediaries share control over the workers' KSAOs (Bonet et al., 2013) raise questions on who should manage the development of HCRs and capture the value deriving from them (Camuffo and De Stefano, 2016).

We argue in favor of extending the models of how HCRs emerge from individual-level KSAOs (Ployhart and Moliterno, 2011) by considering the nature of the work arrangement that the firm uses to acquire human capital. We believe this to be important because the nature of these arrangements shapes the process through which HCRs emerge. They change the nature of employment relationships and the way in which firms can motivate and incentivize workers (Kuhn and Maleki, 2017). Therefore, we should broaden our conceptualization of the types of HCRs that the firm can acquire by considering alternative types of hiring (Nyberg et al., 2014; Ployhart et al., 2014).

External hires

The increase in external hires for positions above the entry level is another factor that challenges the traditional "build" model of acquiring and developing human capital (Hamori et al., 2011). In that model, firms hire individuals for entry-level positions and fill higher-level positions by promotions and transfers within the internal labor market (Doeringer and Piore, 1985). However, workers are now increasingly entering these higher positions through external hires (Royal and Althauser, 2003).

This trend results from how people move across jobs (Bidwell, 2011). On the one hand, workers increasingly build their careers across organizations (Bidwell and Briscoe, 2010) and mix multiple internal and external moves to achieve their career objectives (Bidwell and Mollick, 2015). On the other hand, organizational hierarchies are flatter than in the past, and it is thus harder for organizations to retain and develop HCRs through internal promotions (Hamori et al., 2011). The average tenure of individuals by a single employer is thus lower than it used to be, and there is evidence that external hires are paid more than those who are promoted from within in the same position (Bidwell, 2011).

This increase in workers' interorganizational mobility is a major disruptive factor in how firms acquire and develop their HCRs. Employee turnover depletes the stock of HCRs of the unit and disrupts remaining employees' work, attitudes, and turnover

(Nyberg and Ployhart, 2013; Trevor and Nyberg, 2008). Moreover, external hires take time to get up to speed (Bidwell, 2011) and to integrate with other workers (Reilly et al., 2014).

It is thus important for both researchers and practitioners to understand the boundary conditions of the existing models of how organizations acquire and develop HCRs (Ployhart and Moliterno, 2011; Ployhart et al., 2011) in different contexts (Ployhart et al., 2014), such as organizations whose hierarchy is too flat to offer opportunities for internal promotions (Hamori et al., 2011) and industries where employees earn premiums for changing multiple employers over their career (Bidwell, 2011).

Markets for HCRs

All the cases presented so far support the argument that firms can access HCRs not only by hiring individuals on the labor market but also by using alternative channels and sourcing markets. To introduce and clarify our argument, we consider the example of automotive design.

There is no doubt that, in the global auto industry, car style and design are formidable sources of competitive advantage (Jacobides et al., 2016). All the original equipment manufacturers (OEMs) in the sector strive to design good-looking cars that can attract and/or retain customers. But the capability to design and engineer cars that satisfy the functional and aesthetic needs of ever more sophisticated customers – incorporating the newest technologies and meeting the highest performance and safety standards – is difficult, costly, and takes time to acquire and develop. One might think that the main road to building this capability (HCRs) would be to hire capable engineers with the required KSAOs, and then develop and motivate them into one or more teams till the desired engineering and design capabilities are in place (the HCR emerges). However, this is not the only way of building such HCRs. For example, many automotive OEMs got access to the HCRs necessary to design appealing vehicles by contracting with external third parties. From this standpoint, Italian car designers have been key players in the industry. For example, the Idea Institute contributed to the success of car makers like Hyundai and Tata, while many emerging Chinese automakers have turned to designers like Pininfarina or Icona to design both traditional (ICE) and electric vehicles. The story of Giorgetto Giugiaro – one of the most famous auto designers in the world, and of his company, Italdesign – well illustrates how HCRs emerge, starting from the KSAOs of one or a few individuals, and how other organizations might access the HCRs they need to pursue their strategy through interorganizational relations.

After beginning his career at Fiat in the late 1950s, Giugiaro quit and started working on his own, establishing a car design house, Italdesign, in 1968. In 1974, as external contractor, he designed the VW Golf, which became a global success. Since then he has successfully developed 200 models for various carmakers, including VW, FCA, BMW (for which it developed the Mini in 2006), Hyundai, and Mitsubishi. In 2010 VW bought 90.1 percent of Giugiaro-Italdesign equity and completed the acquisition in 2015. (Interestingly, VW kept Giugiaro on the board of directors, and designed special contractual arrangements for his son and some other key people to prevent their departure.)

Nowadays, Giugiaro-Italdesign, as part of the VW Group, employs 1000 people, mostly engineers, and offers a variety of services and solutions in the transportation industry, including styling, VRC, Engineering, Pre-Series, Testing and Validation, Benchmarking,

Quality, Project Management, IT, 3D Printing and Industrial Design. Undoubtedly, the VW Group got access to and acquired the HCRs it needed to design and engineer innovative, stylish models, especially for its top brand (Audi), initially through collaborations (repeated, long-term contracts embodying hand-in-glove relations) and then through acquisition.

The VW–Giugiaro-Italdesign case well illustrates how companies, while making strategic decisions about their business models and organizational boundaries, are also making decisions about HCR acquisition. This might happen implicitly (in most cases) or intentionally and deliberately. Intentional decisions are more likely to take place in labor- or knowledge-intensive industries (Coff, 2002), or in units/industries where the emergence of HCRs is relatively observable because it results from an additive process of individual-level contributions that the firm is able to identify, such as sports (Chadwick, 2017; Crook et al., 2011).

Accessing SHCRs through interorganizational relationships

As illustrated by the example above, one way of acquiring HCRs is to establish vertical or horizontal interorganizational relationships. When a buyer signs a contract with a supplier for the provision of a product or service, when a seller entrusts a dealer or distributor to sell its products or services, when two or more firms ally, or when a company acquires a competitor, supplier or customer, it also gets access to the HCRs embodied in the partner.

Benetton's original distribution system was one of the first documented examples of deliberate HCR acquisition through interorganizational relationships (Camuffo and Costa, 1993). As the company grew and went international during the 1980s, it contracted with entrepreneurs to act as regional managers. These agents usually supervised and held an interest in a number of Benetton stores in a given area. Luciano Benetton himself assumed responsibility for managing the agents, recruiting and selecting them from among the store owners, evaluating their performance and potential, managing their mobility across geographical areas, and designing their incentive/compensation packages. Interestingly, one of the first and most successful of Benetton's agents and multiple store owners, Antonio Percassi, was selected in 2001 to bring the Zara brand into the Italian market, and signed a joint venture agreement with the Inditex Group. Indeed, this is an interesting example of HCR mobility which is not individual mobility on the labor market, but mediated by changing interorganizational relationships.

In some cases, the firm accesses these HCRs as a by-product of the relationship, and this access might not be intentional. However, the buyer might also explicitly and deliberately establish a relationship with a supplier, a customer, or other organization to get access to the HCRs embodied in them. One way to assess the extent to which the acquisition of HCRs is an intended outcome of these interorganizational relations would be to analyze how the contracts underlying them rule issues concerning employees and intellectual property (IP). Similarly, if the relationship/contract or the supplier/client/partner evaluation and selection system (e.g., vendor rating system) explicitly includes clauses concerning the partner's employees, their selection criteria, and practices or other HR practices, it is more likely that the focal firm is deliberately considering the interorganizational relationship a source of HCRs.

Firms that intentionally/deliberately consider interorganizational relationships as potential sources of HCRs will design and manage their business models and supply chains accordingly. For example, the focal firm might contract *ex ante* (or implement *ex post*) special clauses (i.e., on the partner's compensation policies, retention/loyalty incentives, and non-compete agreements for key talent) to reduce the probability of HCR depletion during the contract. This is especially true if the relation is long term and the contract includes performance-improvement programs, partner-development programs, and gain-sharing agreements (Camuffo, 2018).

Similarly, the acquiring firm might be more willing to absorb at least some of the partner's business risk, allowing *ex post* for unforeseen events not in the contract to preserve the HCR combinations embodied in the partner (Camuffo et al., 2007). If the partner is hard to substitute and the emergence process is long and costly, the focal firm could offer its partner some sort of "insurance" against unexpected variations of production costs or volumes (e.g., in the form of minimum profit levels) in exchange for the advantages associated with the "relational rents" deriving from the access to the HCRs embodied in the partner.

Overall, using the construct of HCRs to explain these interorganizational relationships extends our understanding of how decisions on the firm's strategic direction, business model configuration, organizational boundaries, and vertical integration impact the structure of the firm-level human capital resource (Nyberg et al., 2014). Similarly, it also unveils how HRM systems might have functional equivalents in building a firm's strategic HCRs, and how they might support other HCR-sourcing strategies.

Acqui-hiring: corporate acquisitions for strategic HCRs acquisition

Coff (2002) observes that HCRs often cannot be acquired in efficient labor markets because of demand-side and/or supply-side imperfections (Campbell et al., 2012). Therefore, it is not surprising that many acquisitions are driven by the need to access or build specific HCR combinations when the labor market is inefficient, and that they often occur in human capital-intensive industries.

The early years of Cisco Systems well illustrate how an external growth strategy based on acquisitions also represents a way to get access to strategic HCRs. During the 1990s Cisco developed a reputation for its extremely aggressive growth strategy based on acquisitions. From 1993 through 2000, Cisco completed more than 70 acquisitions and spent more than $18 billion acquiring nine companies in 1998 and 14 in 1999, an average of more than one acquisition per quarter over a five-year period (Chatman et al., 2005). At that time, Cisco's top management clearly eyed the acquisition strategy as a strategic HCR acquisition strategy.

O'Reilly and Pfeffer (2000) highlighted that Cisco's acquisitions were not just to acquire customers, branches, or plants; rather, they were specifically designed to acquire technology and know-how embodied in people, frequently including the founders of the acquired companies. Cisco's then CEO, John Chambers, made explicit that one of the primary purposes of acquisitions was for the engineering talent. Each acquisition entailed not only acquiring its current products, but also the next generation of products through its people.

Cisco's growth strategy through acquisitions in the 1990s can be considered a strategy to acquire strategic HCRs for three major reasons. First, Cisco conceived the acquisition of technology as the acquisition of people and of the combination of KSAOs embodied in individuals. Second, in deciding which companies to target, Cisco adopted a philosophy of breaking up markets into segments and matching them to its business units. This practice allowed Cisco to clarify, at least implicitly, what type of HCR combinations (KSAOs) were necessary and what type of HCR combinations the target firm could offer. Third, Cisco took action to mitigate the risk of departure of key individuals in the post-acquisition phase. Interestingly, this approach suggests a certain level of awareness about the HCR-emergence process (Ployhart and Moliterno, 2011): Cisco actively tried to preserve the stock and the value of HCRs embodied in the target firms through several pre- and post-acquisition HR initiatives.

Cisco is only one of the examples that make the technology industry an ideal setting to observe corporate acquisitions for strategic HCR acquisition. Building on the evidence that large firms often acquire small technology startups to access technologies and capabilities (Arora and Gambardella, 2010; Coff, 1999; Ranft and Lord, 2000, 2002), Chatterji and Patro (2014) analyzed the phenomenon of "acqui-hiring" in the tech sector by describing the acqui-hiring practices of Google and Facebook. According to Chatterji and Patro, acqui-hiring is the acquisition, by large tech companies, of small startup firms, particularly in the pre-commercial stages, with the express purpose of acquiring human capital as opposed to the products, customers, or revenues of the acquired organization.

Although the authors frame their study in terms of dynamic capabilities, we believe that the HCR lens also provides a powerful tool to interpret this phenomenon. For example, when the acquiring firm offers a prominent role in the top management team to the founder of the target firm, it is not only trying to reconfigure the company's capabilities (Chatterji and Patro, 2014). It is also strategically gaining access to the HCRs of the target firm to recombine and integrate them in the firm-level HCRs (Ployhart et al., 2014: 388). Similarly, when acqui-hiring is geared towards the improvement of existing products, Chatterji and Patro clearly refer to a process of recombination of the HCRs in the existing product management units. Finally, when they posit that acqui-hiring might be aimed at developing innovative products under aggressive deadlines, they clearly refer to a hybrid, within-level HCR recombination taking place post-acquisition in the new product development teams.

Firms that intentionally/deliberately acqui-hire, will design and manage the acquisition process accordingly. Therefore, the expectations about post-acquisition turnover by the employee of the acquired firm might affect whether and how much the focal firm bids for the target one (Younge et al., 2015). Firms might design specific HR policies to reduce the likelihood of post-acquisition turnover and negotiate them *ex ante*. Similarly, they might implement post-merger integration activities to reduce the likelihood of post-merger turnover and the resulting depletion of the HCRs of the acqui-hired firm (Zollo and Singh, 2004). For example, "softer" HR integration and less aggressive post-merger reorganization and workforce rightsizing might be instrumental to preserve the HCR combinations embodied in the partner, especially if there are time compression diseconomies in the relevant emerging process.

Come what may, using the HCR concept allows us to view strategic decisions concerning M&As as decisions critically driven by and structurally impacting the firm's human capital resource. Similarly, it provides additional support to the arguments that HRM systems might have functional equivalents and that they might complement other strategies of acquiring and building the firm's strategic HCRs.

Markets for "Problems and Solutions"

The phenomenon of open innovation (Chesbrough, 2006; Enkel et al., 2009) and the use of innovation contests (Terwiesch and Xu, 2008; Boudreau et al., 2011) embedded in platforms like InnoCentive provide another example of an alternative way in which firms can strategically acquire and build HCRs.

The open innovation literature has prevalently emphasized the technological side of this phenomenon and its implications for innovation strategies. With the notable exception of Belenzon and Schankerman (2015), who explicitly study how business models can be designed to tap into open innovation labor markets with heterogeneously motivated workers, there are basically no studies about open innovation platforms as a way to acquire human capital.

We believe this lack of attention derives from the challenge of identifying the causal linkages between the KSAOs of large populations of diverse and geographically dispersed potential contributors on one side of the platforms with the outcomes: the solutions to the problems that firms post and for which they are seeking solutions on the other side of the platform. How do the ideas/solutions offered by contributors (their KSAOs) not only match and solve the problems posted on the platform but eventually also fit the company's business model and strategy? We believe that the HCR concept allows us to uncover and appreciate the human capital sourcing side of this phenomenon, as well as of other, similar phenomena, like external hackathons and jams.

Our point is that when firms strategically frame and decompose problems, organize their solution into a contest with significant incentives, post the problems, and embed this process into a technological platform managed by an intermediary, they also deliberately or inadvertently design an HCR-acquisition strategy. This strategy allows them to "crowdsource," through the problem-solving dyad, HCR combinations, subcombinations, or KSAOs (Felin and Zenger, 2014).

The case of NASA and InnoCentive (Lifshitz-Assaf, 2018) as well as of Procter & Gamble (Dodgson et al., 2006), Lego, and Apple (Lakhani et al., 2013) well illustrate how open innovation, crowdsourcing, hackathons, and jams can be conceptualized as HCR-acquisition strategies. First, the solutions to the problems/challenges posted on the intermediary platform, or the ideas generated in a hackathon or jam, clearly reflect the KSAOs of the individual problem solvers. Second, in some cases (hackathons) these ideas are the results of the interaction between individuals and of the combination of their KSAOs within teams. Third, solutions/ideas emerge from interactions and complementarities during the innovation contest, hackathon, or jam, contingent upon factors like the structure of the process, its duration, and the associated incentives. Fourth, the emergence of such HCRs is clearly grounded on the decomposition of integrated strategic problems into smaller ones which can be put out to the rest of the world for solving. This decomposition process is a key enabler to the acquisition/building of HCRs in this case. It entails the ability to conceptualize the architecture of a strategy or business model as a set of sub-problems that can be articulated, codified (at least to some extent), and posted for solution.

This is in line with the recent conceptualization of strategies as theories about a business problem (Felin and Zenger, 2009). The capability of entrepreneurs and managers is to structure the problem and to recognize its architectural properties, for example if and to what extent it can be decomposed into modular sub-problems that can be solved by different problem solvers (Cabigiosu and Camuffo, 2012; Nickerson and Zenger, 2004). NASA's interaction with InnoCentive is an exemplary case of this process of problem decomposition. NASA's experience shows not only how an organization can build a generalized capability of decomposing tasks and use external innovation communities as a routine part of its research and development efforts (Lakhani et al., 2013), but also an alternative strategy to acquire and build a HCR otherwise difficult to access.

Firms that intentionally/deliberately crowdsource problem solving on platforms, or use hackathons and jams to access KSAOs, build structures and processes and use technologies that allow them to combine the KSAOs of diverse and geographically dispersed individuals in an original way. The emergence process of the HCR combinations in these firms will then depend on the granularity of problem decomposition, the type of intermediary, technology and community, and the incentives provided for the contest, hackathon, or jam. Moreover, the KSAOs of those who take part in the problem decomposition and of the intermediaries involved in the process, such as idea scouts and idea connectors, contribute to this process of emergence (Whelan et al., 2011).

Firms adopting this HCR-acquisition strategy should wisely address the interdependencies and potential conflicts built into this process through appropriate HR policies and practices. For example, failing to assess and address the changes required in the KSAOs and identity of R&D professionals might slow or hinder the HCR-emergence process (Lifshitz-Assaf, 2018).

An exemplary extension of this case is the diffusion, across industries, of business models based on technological platforms and two-side markets. In cases like Uber or Airbnb, and more generally in the "gig economy," HCRs are complex, within- and cross-level multiple combinations where a relatively small number of workers employed by the platform (the "internal HCR") combines with a large number of individuals (and/or units, like in the Airbnb case) "hired" with short-term arrangements to perform specific tasks (Friedman, 2014: 171). These workers have a transactional relationship with the firm and differ from direct employees, temporary workers, and other contractors in their commitment and in their incentives (Kuhn and Maleki, 2017). In this case, the acquisition of HCRs is shaped by the online employment platforms that control how information and human capital flow between the supply and the demand sides of the market (Agrawal et al., 2015).

Overall, using the HCR concept allows us to view strategic decisions concerning open innovation and crowdsourcing as decisions critically driven and structurally impacting a firm's human capital. Similarly, it also further shows how HRM systems might be redesigned to enable the process of emergence of HCRs acquired through a different strategy.

IMPLICATIONS AND RESEARCH AVENUES

In this chapter we have used the construct of HCRs to analyze the different ways in which organizations get access to human capital. We used the typologies by Ployhart et al. (2014) and by Nyberg et al. (2014) to map the different dimensions of the acquisition decisions that firms make when building their HCRs. We then analyzed the characteristics of alternative acquisition channels and of the markets associated with them. We argued that existing frameworks of how organizations acquire unit-level HCRs mainly focus on individual-level hiring (Ployhart et al., 2011). We suggested a broader theoretical perspective that integrates the concept of HCRs from the strategic human capital and human resource management literature (Ployhart and Moliterno, 2011) with the existing theoretical frameworks on alternative acquisition channels, such as supplier–buyer relationships, corporate acquisition, and open innovation. Finally, we conclude that this integrated approach calls for redefining the role of the HR function in the acquisition and development of HCRs.

Table 17.1 summarizes the key characteristics of the different HCRs' acquisition strategies, highlighting their differences in terms of relevant sourcing market, prevalent HCR level, type of HCR combination, locus of HCR emergence, and HCR-acquisition interface. As illustrated by the examples provided in the chapter, firms might concurrently adopt one or more of the three acquisition strategies stylized in this simplified framework, or even combine them in hybrid strategies. For example, NASA contracted InnoCentive to crowdsource problem solving, thus accessing InnoCentive HCRs embodied in the platform. At the same time, problem solvers contributing solutions to the InnoCentive platform are not only individuals, but also teams and even firms, so that, eventually, NASA indirectly accessed the HCRs embodied in these units/firms.

This chapter outlines four major areas for future research on how firms acquire HCRs and transform them into strategic resources that they can use to achieve competitive advantage (Ployhart and Moliterno, 2011). First, future research could explore how the emergence of different types and levels of HCRs vary across alternative acquisition channels. Studies that map and compare these processes of emergence would contribute to our understanding of how firms combine and aggregate HCRs and how these combinations relate to performance (Ployhart et al., 2014). Moreover, research in this area would inform the literatures that traditionally focused on how human capital flows through supply chains, corporate acquisitions, and technological platforms by differentiating between the different components and levels of HCRs. Second, future research might explore how the firm's incentives to select one channel over another vary across these components and levels. This research avenue would provide a more nuanced framework to interpret the firm's make or buy decisions on human capital (Bidwell, 2012). Third, how firms can extend the boundaries of the HR function, promote cross-functional integration, and redefine the organizational boundaries to improve the acquisition of HCRs remain open questions with dramatic managerial relevance. Fourth, future research could analyze the comparative efficiency of the HCR strategic factor markets (Barney, 1986), their imperfections (small numbers, differences in firms' expectations and complementary assets, etc.) and how firms' strategies might try to create them or overcome them in order to acquire individual or unit-level capacities based on individual KSAOs that are accessible for unit-relevant purposes (Nyberg et al., 2014: 376).

CHAPTER SUMMARY

BOX 17.1 KEY TAKEAWAYS

1. The adoption of a human capital resource (HCR) perspective challenges the assumption that firms can build a competitive advantage exclusively by hiring individuals and then developing or combining the human capital embedded in them. Human capital resources are collective, have a structure, and combine diverse elements (KSAOs) at different levels so that there are multiple potential ways to get access to them.
2. Strategic decisions about organizational boundaries, supply chain design and management, external growth, business model design, and ecosystem configuration can be viewed and analyzed as decisions about acquiring, building, and retaining HCRs. All business transactions that embody HCRs can be considered potential HCR acquisition channels so that, beside labor markets, other markets could be considered as potential HCRs sources – including upstream and downstream markets in supply chains, markets for technologies, platforms for crowd-sourced problem solving, and financial markets (for control/ownership).
3. The adoption of an HCR perspective weakens the exclusive logical association between human capital/individuals/hiring/HR and questions whether firms should allocate the responsibility to build HCRs primarily to the HR function, calling for a stronger cross-functional integration to access relevant strategic factor markets for these resources as well as a fundamental rethinking of the role of the HR function.

BOX 17.2 DIRECTIONS FOR FUTURE RESEARCH

1. Strategic human capital and human resource management scholars should think of labor markets, supply chains, platforms/ecosystems, and financial markets as potentially functional equivalent sources of HCRs (strategic factor markets) characterized, under different conditions, by different comparative static and dynamic efficiency. These structural and dynamic properties represent underinvestigated areas and potential research avenues.
2. Firms using a multiple strategic factor market approach to getting access to HCRs should reallocate the responsibilities within the organization and fundamentally rethink of the role of the HR function. How the HR function will evolve and how other functions will take on HCR responsibilities is a brand new area of investigation.
3. The dimensions of the human capital resource (levels, types, functions, combinations, context, antecedents) are likely to affect how firms strategize to get access to HCRs, shaping the comparative effectiveness and efficiency of such strategies in combination with the competitive dynamics in the relevant strategic factor markets. In-depth analysis of how the HCR dimensions shape these strategies is a promising and needed research stream.

NOTES

* The authors would like to thank Anthony Nyberg and Thomas Moliterno for comments and suggestions at various stages of the research on which this chapter is based. Participants in the *Handbook of Research on Strategic Human Capital Resources* also contributed to the development of the chapter. Rajshree Agarwal, Matthew Bidwell, Rhett Brymer, Clint Chadwick, Russ Coff, John Delery, Rebecca Kehoe, and Chris Rider provided feedback on earlier drafts.

1. For example, Bruno Strigini, CEO of Novartis Oncology, retired for personal reasons at the end of 2017.

This was a significant human capital loss as he had navigated the business unit through the Gleevec® patent expiration, and had led the successful integration of the GSK Oncology Product Portfolio acquired in 2015.

2. The content of a recent interview to the Chairman of Novartis, Daniel Vasella, seems to point clearly to the concept of HCRs and their emergence: "the *human resource* is still our most critical ingredient for success. You have to have technology, and you have to invest in it. And, of course, we have to focus on science, because science is the foundation of innovation. But we also have to understand what our customers need. Patients can articulate needs, but seldom solutions. So, in highly technical fields, the people doing the most complicated scientific work sometimes don't know enough about the patient's reality. It is therefore important to bring scientists together with the needs and realities of the patient. We have to make it possible for our scientists, through empathy and imagination, to understand what's going on with patients. And then, thanks to our scientists' knowledge, they can embark on finding potential solutions. That's what I mean by the human resource. Now, this is a very important point. Scientists have to understand fully what the patient needs. But understand is not the right word exactly. Scientists have to have an emotional, intellectual, scientific and human understanding of the patient's needs. They need to understand the impact they have on patients' lives – on individuals. This is true for all our employees and as we rationally and emotionally understand this, our intrinsic motivations become much stronger to do an excellent job. We identify ourselves with common goals that drive the overall corporation" (https://www.kornferry.com/institute/download/download/id/16960/aid/67).
3. Interestingly, these capabilities are of different type. First of all (and this is common to many leadership or competency models), it is not completely clear if they refer to individuals or to the organization. Second, some of them seem to be traceable to knowledge, others to skills, others to abilities.

REFERENCES

Agrawal, A., Horton, J., Lacetera, N., and Lyons, E. (2015). Digitization and the contract labor market: A research agenda. In A. Goldfarb, S. M. Greenstein, and C. E. Tucker (eds), *Economic Analysis of the Digital Economy* (pp. 219–50). Chicago: University of Chicago Press.

Arora, A., and Gambardella, A. (2010). Ideas for rent: An overview of markets for technology. *Industrial and Corporate Change*, *19*(3), 775–803.

Baldwin, C. Y., and Woodard, C. J. (2009). The architecture of platforms: A unified view. In A. Gawer (ed.), *Platforms, Markets and Innovation* (pp. 19–44). Cheltenham, UK and Northampton, MA, USA: Edward Elgar Publishing.

Barney, J., and Felin, T. (2013). What are microfoundations? *Academy of Management Perspectives*, *27*(2), 138–55.

Barney, J. B. (1986). Strategic factor markets: Expectations, luck, and business strategy. *Management Science*, *32*(10), 1231–41.

Barney, J. B., and Wright, P. M. (1998). On becoming a strategic partner: The role of human resources in gaining competitive advantage. *Human Resource Management*, *37*(1), 31–46.

Becker, B., and Gerhart, B. (1996). The impact of human resource management on organizational performance: Progress and prospects. *Academy of Management Journal*, *39*(4), 779–801.

Belenzon, S., and Schankerman, M. (2015). Motivation and sorting of human capital in open innovation. *Strategic Management Journal*, *36*(6), 795–820.

Bidwell, M. (2009). Do peripheral workers do peripheral work? Comparing the use of highly skilled contractors and regular employees. *ILR Review*, *62*(2), 200–225.

Bidwell, M. (2011). Paying more to get less: The effects of external hiring versus internal mobility. *Administrative Science Quarterly*, *56*(3), 369–407.

Bidwell, M. J. (2012). Politics and firm boundaries: How organizational structure, group interests, and resources affect outsourcing. *Organization Science*, *23*(6), 1622–42.

Bidwell, M., and Briscoe, F. (2010). The dynamics of interorganizational careers. *Organization Science*, *21*(5), 1034–53.

Bidwell, M., and Mollick, E. (2015). Shifts and ladders: Comparing the role of internal and external mobility in managerial careers. *Organization Science*, *26*(6), 1629–45.

Bonet, R., Cappelli, P., and Hamori, M. (2013). Labor market intermediaries and the new paradigm for human resources. *Academy of Management Annals*, *7*(1), 341–92.

Boudreau, K. J., Lacetera, N., and Lakhani, K. R. (2011). Incentives and problem uncertainty in innovation contests: An empirical analysis. *Management Science*, *57*(5), 843–63.

Brun, A., Caniato, F., Caridi, M., Castelli, C., Miragliotta, G., Ronchi, S., Sianesi, A., and Spina, G. (2008). Logistics and supply chain management in luxury fashion retail: Empirical investigation of Italian firms. *International Journal of Production Economics*, *114*(2), 554–70.

Brymer, R. A., Chadwick, C., Hill, A., and Molloy, J. (2019). Pipelines and their portfolios: A more holistic view of human capital heterogeneity via firm-wide employee sourcing. *Academy of Management Perspectives*, *33*(2), 207–33.
Cabigiosu, A., and Camuffo, A. (2012), Beyond the "mirroring" hypothesis: Product modularity and interorganizational relations in the air conditioning industry, *Organization Science*, *23*(3), 686–703.
Campbell, B. A., Coff, R., and Kryscynski, D. (2012). Rethinking sustained competitive advantage from human capital. *Academy of Management Review*, *37*(3), 376–95.
Campion, M. A., Fink, A. A., Ruggeberg, B. J., Carr, L., Phillips, G. M., and Odman, R. B. (2011). Doing competencies well: Best practices in competency modeling. *Personnel Psychology*, *64*(1), 225–62.
Camuffo A. (2018), Risk allocation, supplier development and product innovation in automotive supply chains: A study of Nissan Europe. In A. C. Moreira et al. (eds), *Innovation and Supply Chain Management: Relationship, Collaboration and Strategies* (pp. 213–36). Cham: Springer.
Camuffo, A., and Costa, G. (1993). Strategic human resource management – Italian style. *Sloan Management Review*, *34*(2), 59.
Camuffo, A., and De Stefano, F. (2016). Work as commons: Internal labor markets, blended workforces and management. In L. E. Cohen, M. D. Burton, and M. Lounsbury (eds), *The Structuring of Work in Organizations* (pp. 363–82). Bingley, UK: Emerald.
Camuffo, A., and Gerli, F. (2007). Competent production supervisors. *Industrial Relations: A Journal of Economy and Society*, *46*(4), 728–37.
Camuffo, A., and Grandinetti, R. (2011). Italian industrial districts as cognitive systems: Are they still reproducible? *Entrepreneurship and Regional Development*, *23*(9–10), 815–52.
Camuffo, A., Furlan, A., and Rettore, E. (2007). Risk sharing in supplier relations: An agency model for the Italian air-conditioning industry. *Strategic Management Journal*, *28*(12), 1257–66.
Camuffo, A., Gerli, F., Borgo, S., and Somià, T. (2009). The effects of management education on careers and compensation: A competency-based study of an Italian MBA programme. *Journal of Management Development*, *28*(9), 839–58.
Cappelli, P., and Keller, J. R. (2013). Classifying work in the new economy. *Academy of Management Review*, *38*(4), 575–96.
Capron, L., and Guillén, M. (2009). National corporate governance institutions and post-acquisition target reorganization. *Strategic Management Journal*, *30*(8), 803–33.
Chadwick, C. (2017). Toward a more comprehensive model of firms' human capital rents. *Academy of Management Review*, *42*(3), 499–519.
Chatman, J., O'Reilly, C., and Chang, V. (2005). Cisco Systems: Developing a human capital strategy. *California Management Review*, *47*(2), 137–67.
Chatterji, A., and Patro, A. (2014). Dynamic capabilities and managing human capital. *Academy of Management Perspectives*, *28*(4), 395–408.
Chesbrough, H. (2006). *Open Business Models: How to Thrive in the New Innovation Landscape*. Boston: Harvard Business School Press.
Coff, R. W. (1997). Human assets and management dilemmas: Coping with hazards on the road to resource-based theory. *Academy of Management Review*, *22*(2), 374–402.
Coff, R. W. (1999). How buyers cope with uncertainty when acquiring firms in knowledge-intensive industries: Caveat emptor. *Organization Science*, *10*(2), 144–61.
Coff, R. W. (2002). Human capital, shared expertise, and the likelihood of impasse in corporate acquisitions. *Journal of Management*, *28*(1), 107–28.
Crook, T. R., Todd, S. Y., Combs, J. G., Woehr, D. J., and Ketchen Jr, D. J. (2011). Does human capital matter? A meta-analysis of the relationship between human capital and firm performance. *Journal of Applied Psychology*, *96*(3), 443–56.
De Stefano, F., Bagdadli, S., and Camuffo, A. (2018). The HR role in corporate social responsibility and sustainability: A boundary-shifting literature review. *Human Resource Management*, *57*(2), 549–66.
Djelic, M. L., and Ainamo, A. (1999). The coevolution of new organizational forms in the fashion industry: A historical and comparative study of France, Italy, and the United States. *Organization Science*, *10*(5), 622–37.
Dodgson, M., Gann, D., and Salter, A. (2006). The role of technology in the shift towards open innovation: The case of Procter & Gamble. *R&D Management*, *36*(3), 333–46.
Doeringer, P. B., and Piore, M. J. (1985). *Internal Labor Markets and Manpower Analysis*. Armonk, NY: Sharpe.
Eckardt, R., Skaggs, B. C., and Lepak, D. P. (2018). An examination of the firm-level performance impact of cluster hiring in knowledge-intensive firms. *Academy of Management Journal*, *61*(3), 919–44.
Enkel, E., Gassmann, O., and Chesbrough, H. (2009). Open R&D and open innovation: Exploring the phenomenon. *R&D Management*, *39*(4), 311–16.
Felin, T., and Zenger, T. R. (2009). Entrepreneurs as theorists: On the origins of collective beliefs and novel strategies. *Strategic Entrepreneurship Journal*, *3*(2), 127–46.

Felin, T., and Zenger, T. R. (2014). Closed or open innovation? Problem solving and the governance choice. *Research Policy*, *43*(5), 914–25.
Freeman, R. B. (2007). *Labor Market Institutions Around the World*. Cambridge, MA: National Bureau of Economic Research.
Friedman, G. (2014). Workers without employers: Shadow corporations and the rise of the gig economy. *Review of Keynesian Economics*, *2*(2), 171–88.
Grant, R. M. (1996). Toward a knowledge-based theory of the firm. *Strategic Management Journal*, *17*(S2), 109–22.
Groysberg, B., and Lee, L. E. (2009). Hiring stars and their colleagues: Exploration and exploitation in professional service firms. *Organization Science*, *20*(4), 740–58.
Groysberg, B., Lee, L. E., and Nanda, A. (2008). Can they take it with them? The portability of star knowledge workers' performance. *Management Science*, *54*(7), 1213–30.
Hamori, M., Bonet, R., and Cappelli, P. (2011). How organizations obtain the human capital they need. In A. Burton-Jones and J.-C. Spender (eds), *The Oxford Handbook of Human Capital* (pp. 309–32). Oxford: Oxford University Press.
Hunter, L., Beaumont, P., and Sinclair, D. (1996). A "partnership" route to human resource management? *Journal of Management Studies*, *33*(2), 235–57.
Jacobides, M. G., MacDuffie, J. P., and Tae, C. J. (2016). Agency, structure, and the dominance of OEMs: Change and stability in the automotive sector. *Strategic Management Journal*, *37*(9), 1942–67.
Jiang, K., Lepak, D. P., Hu, J., and Baer, J. C. (2012). How does human resource management influence organizational outcomes? A meta-analytic investigation of mediating mechanisms. *Academy of Management Journal*, *55*(6), 1264–94.
Kalleberg, A. L. (2000). Nonstandard employment relations: Part-time, temporary and contract work. *Annual Review of Sociology*, *26*(1), 341–65.
Kochanski, J. T., and Ruse, D. H. (1996). Designing a competency-based human resources organization. *Human Resource Management*, *35*(1), 19–33.
Koulikoff-Souviron, M., and Harrison, A. (2008). Interdependent supply relationships as institutions: The role of HR practices. *International Journal of Operations and Production Management*, *28*(5), 412–32.
Kuhn, K. M., and Maleki, A. (2017). Micro-entrepreneurs, dependent contractors, and instaserfs: Understanding online labor platform workforces. *Academy of Management Perspectives*, *31*(3), 183–200.
Lakhani, K. R., Lifshitz-Assaf, H., and Tushman, M. (2013). Open innovation and organizational boundaries: Task decomposition, knowledge distribution and the locus of innovation. In A. Grandori (ed.), *Handbook of Economic Organization: Integrating Economic and Organizational Theory* (pp. 355–82). Cheltenham, UK and Northampton, MA, USA: Edward Elgar Publishing.
Lengnick-Hall, M. L., and Lengnick-Hall, C. A. (1999). Expanding customer orientation in the HR function. *Human Resource Management*, *38*(3), 201–14.
Lengnick-Hall, M. L., Lengnick-Hall, C. A., and Rigsbee, C. M. (2013). Strategic human resource management and supply chain orientation. *Human Resource Management Review*, *23*(4), 366–77.
Lepak, D. P., and Snell, S. A. (1999). The human resource architecture: Toward a theory of human capital allocation and development. *Academy of Management Review*, *24*(1), 31–48.
Lepak, D. P., Liao, H., Chung, Y., and Harden, E. E. (2006). A conceptual review of human resource management systems in strategic human resource management research. In J. J. Martocchio (ed.), Research in personnel and human resources management, vol. 25 (pp. 217–71). Burlington, VT: Emerald.
Lievens, F., Sanchez, J. I., and De Corte, W. (2004). Easing the inferential leap in competency modelling: The effects of task-related information and subject matter expertise. *Personnel Psychology*, *57*(4), 881–904.
Lifshitz-Assaf, H. (2018). Dismantling knowledge boundaries at NASA: The critical role of professional identity in open innovation. *Administrative Science Quarterly*, *63*(4), 746–82.
Mahapatra, S. K., Narasimhan, R., and Barbieri, P. (2010). Strategic interdependence, governance effectiveness and supplier performance: A dyadic case study investigation and theory development. *Journal of Operations Management*, *28*(6), 537–52.
Marx, M. (2011). The firm strikes back: Non-compete agreements and the mobility of technical professionals. *American Sociological Review*, *76*(5), 695–712.
Marx, M., Strumsky, D., and Fleming, L. (2009). Mobility, skills, and the Michigan non-compete experiment. *Management Science*, *55*(6), 875–89.
Mawdsley, J. K., and Somaya, D. (2016). Employee mobility and organizational outcomes: An integrative conceptual framework and research agenda. *Journal of Management*, *42*(1), 85–113.
Narasimhan, R., Nair, A., Griffith, D. A., Arlbjørn, J. S., and Bendoly, E. (2009). Lock-in situations in supply chains: A social exchange theoretic study of sourcing arrangements in buyer–supplier relationships. *Journal of Operations Management*, *27*(5), 374–89.
Nickerson, J. A., and Zenger, T. R. (2004). A knowledge-based theory of the firm: The problem-solving perspective. *Organization Science*, *15*(6), 617–32.

Nyberg, A. J., and Ployhart, R. E. (2013). Context-emergent turnover (CET) theory: A theory of collective turnover. *Academy of Management Review*, *38*(1), 109–31.
Nyberg, A. J., Moliterno, T. P., Hale Jr, D., and Lepak, D. P. (2014). Resource-based perspectives on unit-level human capital: A review and integration. *Journal of Management*, *40*(1), 316–46.
O'Reilly III, C. A., and Pfeffer, J. (2000). Cisco Systems: Acquiring and retaining talent in hypercompetitive markets. *People and Strategy*, *23*(3), 38–53.
Oettl, A. (2012). Reconceptualizing stars: Scientist helpfulness and peer performance. *Management Science*, *58*(6), 1122–40.
Othman, R., and Abdul Ghani, R. (2008). Supply chain management and suppliers' HRM practice. *Supply Chain Management: An International Journal*, *13*(4), 259–62.
Peteraf, M. A., and Barney, J. B. (2003). Unraveling the resource-based tangle. *Managerial and Decision Economics*, *24*(4), 309–23.
Ployhart, R. E., and Moliterno, T. P. (2011). Emergence of the human capital resource: A multilevel model. *Academy of Management Review*, *36*(1), 127–50.
Ployhart, R. E., Nyberg, A. J., Reilly, G., and Maltarich, M. A. (2014). Human capital is dead; long live human capital resources! *Journal of Management*, *40*(2), 371–98.
Ployhart, R. E., Van Iddekinge, C. H., and MacKenzie, W. I. (2011). Acquiring and developing human capital in service contexts: The interconnectedness of human capital resources. *Academy of Management Journal*, *54*(2), 353–68.
Ranft, A., and Lord, M. (2000). Acquiring new knowledge: The role of retaining human capital in acquisitions of high-tech firms. *Journal of High Technology Management Research*, *11*(2), 295–319.
Ranft, A., and Lord, M. (2002). Acquiring new technologies and capabilities: A grounded model of acquisition implementation. *Organization Science*, *13*(4), 420–41.
Reilly, G., Nyberg, A. J., Maltarich, M., and Weller, I. (2014). Human capital flows: Using context-emergent turnover (CET) theory to explore the process by which turnover, hiring, and job demands affect patient satisfaction. *Academy of Management Journal*, *57*(3), 766–90.
Royal, C., and Althauser, R. P. (2003). The labor markets of knowledge workers: Investment bankers' careers in the wake of corporate restructuring. *Work and Occupations*, *30*(2), 214–33.
Scarbrough, H. (2000). The HR implications of supply chain relationships. *Human Resource Management Journal*, *10*(1), 5–17.
Shippmann, J. S., Ash, R. A., Batjtsta, M., Carr, L., Eyde, L. D., Hesketh, B., Kehoe, J., Pearlman, K., Prien, E. P., and Sanchez, J. I. (2000). The practice of competency modeling. *Personnel Psychology*, *53*(3), 703–40.
Terwiesch, C., and Xu, Y. (2008). Innovation contests, open innovation, and multiagent problem solving. *Management Science*, *54*(9), 1529–43.
Trevor, C. O., and Nyberg, A. J. (2008). Keeping your headcount when all about you are losing theirs: Downsizing, voluntary turnover rates, and the moderating role of HR practices. *Academy of Management Journal*, *51*(2), 259–76.
Waldman, M. (2013), Theory and evidence in internal labor markets. In R. Gibbons and J. Roberts (eds), *The Handbook of Organizational Economics* (pp. 520–71). Princeton: Princeton University Press.
Whelan, E., Parise, S. De Valk, J., and Aalbers, R. (2011), Creating employee networks that deliver open innovation. *MIT Sloan Management Review*, *53*(1), 37–44.
Wright, P. M., and Snell, S. A. (1998). Toward a unifying framework for exploring fit and flexibility in strategic human resource management. *Academy of Management Review*, *23*(4), 756–72.
Wuyts, S., and Geyskens, I. (2005). The formation of buyer–supplier relationships: Detailed contract drafting and close partner selection. *Journal of Marketing*, *69*(4), 103–17.
Younge, K. A., Tong, T. W., and Fleming, L. (2015). How anticipated employee mobility affects acquisition likelihood: Evidence from a natural experiment. *Strategic Management Journal*, *36*(5), 686–708.
Zollo, M., and Singh, H. (2004). Deliberate learning in corporate acquisitions: Post-acquisition strategies and integration capability in US bank mergers. *Strategic Management Journal*, *25*(13), 1233–56.

18. Towards a human-capital resource-based theory of the firm

Alison Mackey and Jay B. Barney

Camuffo and De Stefano's central assertion in Chapter 17 is correct: Firms can access human capital resources (HCRs) both directly, through labor markets, and indirectly, through a variety of other business relationships. If strategic human capital researchers focus only on accessing HCRs through labor markets, they run the risk of failing to appreciate the competitive consequences of these resources accessed in alternative ways. It also follows from these observations that building advantage from HCRs is of concern to the entire firm and not just the HR function. Without a truly cross-functional effort within the firm, important sources of strategic human capital resources (SHCRs) beyond the labor market could be overlooked.

This relates to Kehoe and Bentley's work in this volume (Chapter 16) in that *what* array of human capital (HC) attributes a firm needs for building their ideal human capital pool directly influences *how* firms will attempt to access and build human capital resources. Sometimes firms need HCRs that complement or build on the existing resource base of the firm; but other times firms need such resources that are quite different from what they currently have within the firm. And, when a firm needs HCRs different from what they currently have, they will be unlikely to access these resources from inside the firm or even through traditional means. Rather, the firm will need to go outside the firm and perhaps tap into alternative ways of accessing HCRs – that is, through means such as alliances, mergers or acquisitions, or even crowdsourcing. Such alternative methods of accessing these resources can dramatically alter the composition of the human capital pool for the firm, and in turn alter the SHRCs the firm can build and then exploit. Thus, considerations of what the ideal human capital pool is for a firm (i.e., Kehoe and Bentley's chapter) cannot be separated from the means by which firms access and build HCRs (i.e., Camuffo and De Stefano's chapter).

VIEWPOINTS FROM RELATED LITERATURES

Of course, there are already well-developed literatures on how these other kinds of business relationships can help a firm access various types of potentially SHCRs and thereby gain a competitive advantage. These include the alliance, mergers and acquisitions (M&As), and crowdsourcing literatures. Moreover, some of these literatures focus at least partly on human capital attributes and the assessing and building of SHCRs.

For example, within the work on strategic alliances, scholars have found that alliances are often pursued due to a mutual desire for firms to access or acquire knowledge, skills, or capabilities from one another (Grant and Baden-Fuller, 2004) – particularly attributes not already in the firm's human capital pool. Strategic alliances can be critical for combining complementary assets, particularly in knowledge- and technology-intensive industries such as pharmaceuticals (Hess and Rothaermel, 2011). Social capital and trust can significantly impact the extent to which firms engage in exchange of resources in alliances, which ultimately impacts the innovation that results from such strategies (Tsai and Ghoshal, 1998). How these human and social capital resources are managed is critical to alliance success (Hitt and Ireland, 2002).

Similarly, work in the mergers and acquisitions literature finds that cultural differences in the management of the combining firms can compromise efforts at employee retention, integration of systems, and transfer of capabilities in the implementation phase, and can therefore have an adverse impact on accessing human capital resources through M&As (Buono and Bowditch, 2003; Cartwright and Cooper, 1993; Chatterjee et al., 1992; Marks and Mirvis, 2011). Such differences are amplified for cross-border mergers and acquisitions – an important mode of growth in a complex and global business economy – impacting the transfer of capabilities across firms (Aguilera and Dencker, 2004; Björkman et al., 2007). As Kehoe and Bentley note, firms will need to explicitly assess the fit of human capital attributes they hope to access and develop into HCRs through mergers and acquisitions to the existing resource base of the firm.

Despite these difficulties, we know that many acquisitions are in fact motivated by the desire to acquire HCRs (e.g., technological capabilities). Such capabilities tend to be embedded within both tacit and socially complex knowledge of the targeted firm's existing human capital resources, creating a problem for the would-be acquirers as human assets cannot be purchased or owned, and can leave the firm at any time. Research suggests that retention is critical in post-acquisition implementation for knowledge-intensive firms (Ranft and Lord, 2000).

Lastly, the crowdsourcing literature is also deeply concerned with human capital issues – particularly understanding what the collective human capital attributes are of crowds, how firms can develop HCRs from these attributes, and why people would even engage in this behavior. Harnessing the collective intelligence of crowds seems to rely on both intrinsic and extrinsic motivators such as community-based explanations (i.e., community identification, social contact), employment-based explanations (i.e., skill/task variety, task autonomy, direct feedback from job), and both immediate and delayed payments (i.e. signaling, human capital investment) (see Kaufmann et al., 2011; Lakhani and Wolf, 2005; Leimeister et al., 2009; Organisciak, 2008; Roberts et al., 2006; Schroer and Hertel, 2009). One advantage of crowdsourcing for expanding the human capital pool of the firm is that the human capital can be developed into HCRs without having to be explicitly integrated into the resource base of the firm, and thus issues of fit are less important.

It is likely that strategic human capital scholars interested in how firms can gain access to human capital through business relationships will find this prior work informative. As important, by positioning the question of what and how to access HCRs in these indirect ways, HR managers will be able to become more involved in the central strategic questions facing a firm, including questions about alliances, mergers and acquisitions, and crowdsourcing.

THEORY OF THE FIRM PERSPECTIVES ON ACCESSING HUMAN CAPITAL

However, the main purpose of this chapter is to reframe the question about direct and indirect access to HCRs by examining it in the context of the theory of the firm literature. The theory of the firm literature asks the question: When should assets used by a firm to create and implement its strategies be brought within the boundary of the firm, and when should these assets be kept outside the firm's boundary? Since HCRs are an example of assets that can be important for a firm creating and implementing its strategies, it seems natural to ask this question about potentially strategic HCRs.

In this sense, the decision to access HCRs through labor markets is equivalent to deciding to bring this asset within the boundaries of a firm. The decision to access HCRs indirectly, through other business relationships, is equivalent to deciding to keep this asset outside the boundaries of the firm. Firms that bring the wrong HCRs into their boundaries – through labor markets – could face losing strategic focus and diseconomies of scale. On the other hand, firms that fail to bring the right resources into their boundaries – by accessing this capital indirectly through other business relationships – may risk losing competitive advantage and associated financial performance.

Transactions cost economics (TCE) and resource-based theory (RBT) are the two main theories guiding management scholars in explaining these kinds of boundary decisions. It makes sense to apply these two theories in determining whether HCRs should be accessed directly, through labor markets, or indirectly, through other business relationships. This is done in the next two sections.

Transactions Cost Economics and Access to Human Capital Resources

According to transactions cost economics, firms govern economic exchanges through either market or hierarchical governance with intermediate forms of governance (e.g. complex contracts, strategic alliances, joint ventures) falling somewhere in between those pure forms. Firms seek to minimize transaction costs in choosing the form of governance they use. All else equal, the more elaborate the governance mechanism, the costlier the governance. Thus, market governance should be the least costly form of governance for managing an exchange, and hierarchical governance should be the most costly.

However, cost is not the only consideration as firms must also consider the threat of opportunism in the exchange. Opportunism tends to increase when one party to an exchange has made a large transaction-specific investment in the exchange – something very likely when the resources involved are strategic human capital resources. Exchanges characterized by high levels of transaction-specific investment are difficult to monitor through contractual governance and tend to be brought inside the boundaries of the firm.

What are the implications of transactions cost logic for the decision about accessing HCRs directly, through the labor market, or indirectly, through other business relationships? TCE logic suggests, first, that individuals with high levels of firm-specific human capital will typically be employed by a firm. This is because market contracts are not likely to protect individuals from a firm's opportunistic behaviors once these individuals have made firm-specific investments (Wang and Barney, 2006). So, if a firm wants to build firm-specific human capital resources, it will need to gain access to these resources directly, by hiring individuals in a labor market.

On the other hand, individuals with high levels of general human capital will typically not be employed by a firm. This is because the resources built from these individuals' general human capital can be sold to many possible firms, and market competition for access to this type of HCR protects individuals from the opportunistic actions of firms. Thus, if a firm wants access to general human capital resources it will need to gain access to individuals with this type of human capital indirectly, through business relations with other firms.

This analysis explains, for example, the relationship between operating firms and consulting firms. Operating firms have employees with high levels of firm-specific human capital. This is appropriate for most of this kind of firm's operating decisions. However, when these firms confront issues outside their normal operations – as when they contemplate changing strategies – they need access to general human capital. They gain access and build associated resources based on that human capital, indirectly, by contracting with a strategic consulting firm.

This logic may also apply to the Novartis example described in Chapter 17. Novartis employees may have relatively high levels of firm-specific human capital (e.g., knowledge of how a particular product is related to other Novartis products). But, in the kinds of research Novartis is currently conducting, general human capital (e.g., information about the science and technology associated with the current research, more broadly) may be more important in building SHCRs for Novartis. To retain the advantages of its specific HCRs, while still gaining access to general HCRs, Novartis participates in a research consortium. Notice that Novartis makes this decision even though the transaction-specific investments it makes in this consortium may subject it to threats of opportunism going forward.

Resource-Based Theory and Access to Human Capital Resources

Resource-based theory adds to the theory of the firm literature the important caveat that capabilities matter in boundary decisions (Barney, 1999). This is because gaining access to these capabilities through internal development – a form of hierarchical governance – can be quite costly. Also, gaining access to capabilities through an acquisition may be difficult since, in some settings, acquiring access to a capability destroys the value of that capability. In this setting – when internal development and acquisition are problematic – firms may have to gain access to a capability indirectly, by cooperating with another firm in a business relationship. This may be the case even if there is a threat of opportunism in that exchange.

What are the implications of resource-based logic for the decision about accessing HCRs directly, through the labor market, or indirectly, through other business relationships? Accessing and building HCRs through internal development can be quite costly when human capital is highly inimitable – that is, when its development depends on unique historical conditions that no longer exist, is path-dependent, socially complex, or causally ambiguous (the actions that a firm would need to take to create the capability are not fully known) in nature. In this setting, internal development of HCRs may not be possible.

Faced with this constraint, firms might opt to acquire another company, and to gain access to HCRs that way. But, as mentioned before, sometimes the act of acquiring access to HCRs can destroy the value of those resources. For example, suppose a firm acquires another firm because of this second firm's cooperative culture, which has enabled scientists to develop deep new technological insights. However, if the acquiring firm has a strong non-cooperative culture, it may destroy the cooperative culture that was the cause of the deep technological insights it was seeking in the first place. Moreover, scientists working in the acquired firm may simply leave their new firm to find a place to work that is more consistent with the cooperative approach in their old firm.

Since, in these settings, firms cannot develop their own HCRs internally (thus, not directly) or through an acquisition (another form of directly acquiring HCRs), they may have to gain access to these resources indirectly, through business relationships with business partners of various kinds. Resource-based theory identifies the conditions under which direct and indirect access to human capital resources may be more effective.

CONCLUSION

Clearly, the observation that firms can gain access to and build HCRs directly, through labor markets, or indirectly, through other business relationships, is important. Additionally, the connection between *what* human capital attributes a firm can access and the means of procuring it are important to make explicit. Prior work on alliances, mergers and acquisitions, and crowdsourcing can all provide insights about how access to HCRs can be accomplished indirectly, and the performance implications of this indirect access. However, from a broader perspective, how firms can access HCRs directly and indirectly can be seen as a special case of the theory of the firm. In this context, theories of the firm – including transactions cost economics and resource-based theory, may be relevant. Application of these theories in this human capital context not only helps solidify the importance of recognizing that potentially strategic human capital resources can be accessed either directly or indirectly, but can also be used to explain when these alternatives will be more or less beneficial to a firm's performance.

CHAPTER SUMMARY

BOX 18.1 KEY TAKEAWAYS

1. What array of human capital attributes a firm needs to build their ideal human capital pool directly influences how firms will attempt to access and build human capital resources. Considerations of what the ideal human capital pool is for a firm cannot be separated from the means by which firms access and build HCRs.
2. Firms that bring the wrong HCRs into their boundaries – through labor markets – could face losing strategic focus and diseconomies of scale. Firms that fail to bring the right resources into their boundaries – by accessing this capital indirectly through other business relationships – may risk losing competitive advantage and associated financial performance.
3. If a firm wants build to firm-specific human capital resources, it will need to gain access to these resources directly, by hiring individuals in a labor market. If a firm wants access to general human capital resources, it will need to gain access to individuals with this type of human capital indirectly, through business relations with other firms.

BOX 18.2 DIRECTIONS FOR FUTURE RESEARCH

1. Micro-level research exploring what attributes firms need in their human capital pools should be combined with macro-level research exploring how firms should access and build human capital resources (through traditional labor markets or alternative means).
2. Theory concerning accessing and building human capital resources should be further developed within a theory of the firm context – that is, when should HCRs be brought inside the boundaries of the firm and when should these resources be kept outside?
3. Theories of the firm – including transactions cost economics and resource-based – theory should be integrated within the strategic human capital context to further explain when alternative means of accessing HCRs will be more or less beneficial to a firm's performance.

REFERENCES

Aguilera, R. V., and Dencker, J. C. (2004). The role of human resource management in cross-border mergers and acquisitions. *International Journal of Human Resource Management*, *15*(8), 1355–70.

Barney, J. B. (1999). How a firm's capabilities affect boundary decisions. *MIT Sloan Management Review*, *40*(3), 137.

Björkman, I., Stahl, G. K., and Vaara, E. (2007). Cultural differences and capability transfer in cross-border acquisitions: The mediating roles of capability complementarity, absorptive capacity, and social integration. *Journal of International Business Studies*, *38*(4), 658–72.

Buono, A. F., and Bowditch, J. L. (2003). *The Human Side of Mergers and Acquisitions: Managing Collisions Between People, Cultures, and Organizations*. Washington, DC: BeardBooks.

Cartwright, S., and Cooper, C. L. (1993). The role of culture compatibility in successful organizational marriage. *Academy of Management Perspectives*, *7*(2), 57–70.

Chatterjee, S., Lubatkin, M. H., Schweiger, D. M., and Weber, Y. (1992). Cultural differences and shareholder value in related mergers: Linking equity and human capital. *Strategic Management Journal*, *13*(5), 319–34.

Grant, R. M., and Baden-Fuller, C. (2004). A knowledge accessing theory of strategic alliances. *Journal of Management Studies*, *41*(1), 61–84.

Hess, A. M., and Rothaermel, F. T. (2011). When are assets complementary? Star scientists, strategic alliances, and innovation in the pharmaceutical industry. *Strategic Management Journal*, *32*(8), 895–909.

Hitt, M. A., and Ireland, D. R. (2002). The essence of strategic leadership: Managing human and social capital. *Journal of Leadership and Organizational Studies*, *9*(1), 3–14.

Kaufmann, N., Schulze, T., and Veit, D. (2011). More than fun and money: Worker motivation in crowdsourcing – a study on Mechanical Turk. *AMCIS Proceedings –All Submissions*, *11*, 1–11. http://aisel.aisnet.org/amcis2011_submissions/340.

Lakhani, K. R., and Wolf, R. G. (2005). Why hackers do what they do: Understanding motivation and effort in free/open source software projects, In J. Feller, B. Fitzgerald, S. A. Hissam, and K. R. Lakhani (eds), *Perspectives on Free and Open Source Software*. Cambridge, MA: MIT Press.

Leimeister, J., Huber, M., Bretschneider, U., and Krcmar, H. (2009) Leveraging crowdsourcing: Activation-supporting components for IT-based ideas competition. *Journal of Management Information Systems*, *26*, 197–224.

Marks, M. L., and Mirvis, P. H. (2011). A framework for the human resources role in managing culture in mergers and acquisitions. *Human Resource Management*, *50*(6), 859–77.

Organisciak, P. (2008). Motivation of crowds: The incentives that make crowdsourcing work. Crowdstorming. https://crowdstorming.wordpress.com/2008/01/31/motivation-of-crowds-the-incentives-that-make-crowdsourcing-work/.

Ranft, A. L., and Lord, M. D. (2000). Acquiring new knowledge: The role of retaining human capital in acquisitions of high-tech firms. *Journal of High Technology Management Research*, *11*(2), 295–319.

Roberts, J. A., Hann, I., and Slaughter, S. A. (2006) Understanding the motivations, participation, and performance of open source software developers: A longitudinal study of the Apache Projects. *Management Science*, *52*(7), 984–99.

Schroer, J., and Hertel, G. (2009) Voluntary engagement in an open web-based encyclopedia: Wikipedians and why they do it. *Media Psychology*, *12*(1), 96–120.

Tsai, W., and Ghoshal, S. (1998). Social capital and value creation: The role of intrafirm networks. *Academy of Management Journal*, *41*(4), 464–76.
Wang, H. C., and Barney, J. B. (2006). Employee incentives to make firm-specific investments: Implications for resource-based theories of corporate diversification. *Academy of Management Review*, *31*(2), 466–76.

PART VI

MOBILIZING STRATEGIC HUMAN CAPITAL RESOURCES: TEAMS

19. Team motivation and goal (mis)alignment: the missing link in human capital resources research*

Christopher O. L. H. Porter, Brittney Amber, and Ernie Wang

INTRODUCTION

Twenty-five years ago, an insightful popular press article declared the end of jobs as we knew them (Bridges, 1994). The author noted that in the vast majority of organizations, work was no longer being structured around jobs, but instead around sets of tasks that need to be completed. Around the same time, organizational scholars noted a similar phenomenon—that work roles were no longer static, structured, and based on prescribed roles, but rather were social, unstructured, and emergent (Ilgen and Hollenbeck, 1991; Murphy and Jackson, 1999).

What scholars and practitioners at the time were independently identifying was a fundamental shift across a broad range of firms from individual-based jobs to team-based work structures. In essence, teams were rapidly becoming the norm rather than the exception (Applebaum and Batt, 1994; Cohen and Bailey, 1997; Gordon, 1992) in an effort to be more competitive via increased adaptability, diversity, and decision-making (Devine et al., 1999). Over two decades later, this trend shows no signs of slowing (Martin and Bal, 2012). Teams are here to stay, as are firms' efforts to place people in teams to reap collective, unit-level performance superior to what those people could have accomplished individually.

As a starting point for this chapter, we begin by defining teams. We borrow from Kozlowski and Ilgen, who offered a definition that, although far from succinct, captures widely accepted, central features of teams and helps distinguish them from other forms of groups in work organizations. Teams are:

> (a) two or more individuals who (b) socially interact (face-to-face, or increasingly, virtually); (c) possess one or more common goals; (d) are brought together to perform organizationally relevant tasks; (e) exhibit interdependencies with respect to work, goals, and outcomes; (f) have different roles and responsibilities; and (g) are, together, embedded in an encompassing organizational system, with boundaries and linkages to the broader system context and task environment. (Kozlowski and Ilgen, 2006, p. 79)

Teams lie at the core of most firms and work organizations generally as they are inherently socially constructed systems (Kozlowski, 2012; Kozlowski and Klein, 2000). Put another way, organizations are multilevel systems composed of people who engage in activities for strategic purposes, often via work structured around teams.

Why are teams relevant to strategic human capital resources (HCRs) scholarship? Although rarely acknowledged, the multilevel, social nature of work is a centerpiece of work following the human capital resources tradition. Teams are the vehicle through which human capital translates into important outcomes. Moreover, recent theorizing makes levels and teams issues more explicit. For example, recognizing the "inseparability" of individuals and collectives in conceptualizations of human capital resources, Ployhart et al. (2014) revisited a prior conceptualization of HCR as a unit-level resource (i.e., Ployhart and Moliterno, 2011) to define HCR as individual or unit-level capacities based on individual knowledge, skills, abilities, and other characteristics (KSAOs) established for unit-relevant purposes. Definitions such as this make clear that whether intended to realize greater levels of performance at lower organizational levels (i.e., HCR and its effects on non-strategic performance, or competitive parity) or performance at higher unit levels (i.e., strategic human capital resources, or SHCR, and its effects on competitive advantage), the study of HCR and SHCR is, at its core, the study of teams.

To date, HCR and SHCR theory and research has been useful, helping us understand what knowledge, skills, abilities, and other characteristics can represent critical unit-level resources. This work presumes that unit-level HCRs are derived from individuals' KSAOs, consistent with Ployhart and colleagues' suggestion that HCR simultaneously consists of *individual or unit-level capacities*. However, scholars have just scratched the surface as it concerns understanding how these unit-level capabilities emerge.

In their model, Ployhart and Moliterno proposed a process by which individual human assets (i.e., KSAOs) combine and transform into unit-level HCRs. According to the authors, HCRs originate at the individual level. Individual KSAOs are transformed and amplified to the collective (or unit) level via an "emergence enabling process." In this process, the *complexity of the unit's task environment* (i.e., the degree of interdependence it requires) and *emergence enabling states* – representing members' collective behavioral, cognitive, and affective experiences – interact to influence the emergence of unit-level resources. In short, the complexity of the unit's task environment determines which individual KSAOs have the opportunity to emerge, while the behavioral, cognitive, and affective states facilitate or undermine the emergence of those individual KSAOs to the unit level.

In theoretically explicating how individual-level KSAOs become a unit-level resource, Ployhart and Moliterno's work highlighted the critical role of team processes in the emergence of unit-level capabilities. We extend this work and argue that *team motivation*, which has both state and process components, is perhaps the most critical aspect of the emergence enabling process because of the important influence team motivation has on how members act, think, and feel. We argue that these motivation-related experiences will largely determine whether individual capabilities ultimately emerge into unit-level capabilities (Figure 19.1).

Motivation represents the force that directs, energizes, and sustains behavior over time and across changing circumstances (Diefendorff and Chandler, 2011; Kanfer, 1990). It is the process by which individuals and teams formulate and execute established goals (Kanfer, 2012). As such, team motivation is critical to understanding the emergence of HCRs and SHCRs because, simply put, if people are not motivated to work towards goals that are at least partially aligned, no combination of individual capabilities can result in unit-level capabilities.

Further, we demonstrate the folly in assuming that people in teams are motivated to work together, which is often the case in HCR and SHCR theory and research. Teams are complex because they are composed of people who are complex. Yet, an important

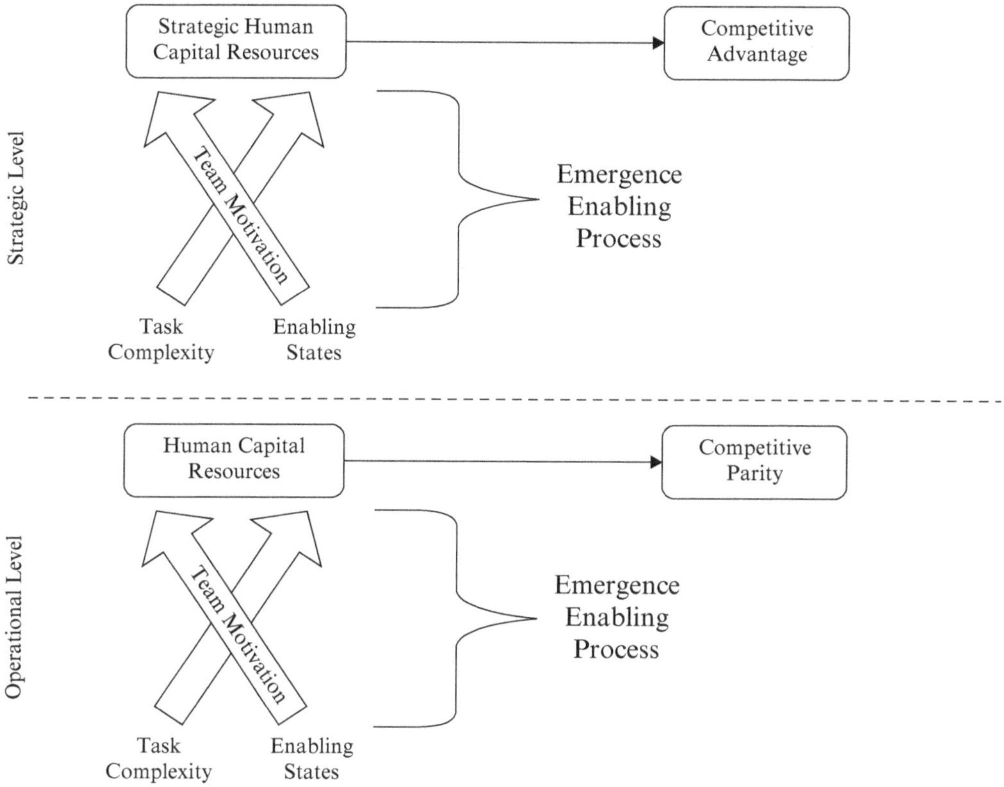

Figure 19.1 The role of team motivation in the emergence enabling process across levels

and, until relatively recently, overlooked aspect of that complexity is that people and teams often have multiple goals that vary in their alignment. In fact, a shared goal among members is a defining feature of a team. In this chapter, we challenge this idea suggesting that in team contexts, where people and teams have multiple goals, those goals may vary in the extent to which they are shared or aligned. We highlight the implications for goal (mis)alignment for team motivation (and by extension the emergence of unit-level capabilities), and we offer a framework useful for thinking about and testing ideas about team motivation, which have largely been taken for granted by HCR, SHCR, and team scholars generally.

Nyberg and colleagues (2014) recently observed that the "what" in HCR models often goes unspecified. Our goal is to highlight team motivation as the critical "what" in the emergence enabling process by which individual KSAOs transform into something meaningful and valuable at the unit level. To be fair, the failure to explicitly model motivation in theory and research is not unique to scholarship on human capital and teams. Indeed, a number of authors have identified motivation as an often inferred "invisible construct" (e.g., Ambrose and Kulik, 1999; Diefendorff and Chandler, 2011; Kanfer et al., 2008). We hope that by shedding light on its importance and by offering a framework that highlights the challenges and opportunities for future theory and research on team motivation, we encourage its more explicit inclusion in HCR and SHCR models. Notably, the importance of team motivation is not dependent on hierarchical level (see again Figure 19.1). As such, the framework we develop is one that assumes isomorphism across organizational levels, and our framework and the processes we describe are relevant broadly to work teams, including higher-level (i.e., strategic) teams and lower-level (i.e., operational) teams. As such, we adopt the term (S)HCR. Where we need to distinguish between the two, we refer to HCR separate from SHCR.

MOTIVATION MATTERS

Motivation is "a psychological process that influences how personal effort and resources are allocated to actions pertaining to work, including the direction, intensity, and persistence of those actions" (Kanfer et al., 2008, p. 5; see also Kanfer, 2011 and Pinder, 1998). However, motivation is also a process enacted by teams and team members over time (Ilgen, 2014). In team settings, motivation becomes significantly more complex. Members can direct their individual efforts towards their own goals and towards team goals. Subunits within teams and teams as entire units can direct their collective efforts towards their own goals and towards the goals of individual members. And, as noted by Chen and Gogus (2008), motivation occurs both in and across teams in organizational contexts, or what they refer to as motivation *in* and *of* teams, respectively.

Over the last decade, we have witnessed a significant increase in the amount of attention devoted specifically to team motivation. Ilgen provided a useful definition of team motivation—one that serves as an appropriate starting point for the discussion that follows. He defined team motivation as "goal generation and striving behaviors among team members in which team and member motivated states interact dynamically and interdependently to influence the direction, intensity, and persistence of member actions relevant to team goals" (Ilgen, 2014, p. 55). The review below summarizes the theory and frameworks that have largely guided our understanding of team motivation, to date. It also indicates several gaps in our understanding, and suggests that our thinking about "team goals" may be oversimplified.

Although not a team motivation model, per se, Marks et al.'s (2001) temporal taxonomy of team processes provided insight into team motivation by distinguishing team processes from team emergent states and by emphasizing the important role of team-emergent states on team functioning. They defined team processes as those involving "members' interact[ion] with other members and their task environment." Team processes are the means by which "members work interdependently to utilize their various resources . . . to yield meaningful outcomes" (p. 357). They go on to identify three superordinate processes: transition, action, and interpersonal processes – all of which are especially relevant to team motivation. First are transitional processes, which occur when teams focus primarily on evaluating and planning team activities for goal accomplishment and include activities such as goal specification and strategy formulation. Second are action processes, which occur when teams focus primarily on goal accomplishment and include monitoring progress toward goals, team monitoring and backup behavior, and coordinating individual activities. According to the authors, interpersonal processes—the third broad, superordinate set of team processes—occur during both transition and action processes providing a foundation for effective transition and action processes. Interpersonal processes include conflict management, motivation and confidence building, and affect management.

While often referenced for its efforts to integrate and propose a temporal perspective as it concerns what teams do (teams engage in transition processes prior to action processes, although both processes can be cyclical), Marks et al.'s model is particularly relevant for team motivation researchers because it situates several motivational constructs into team processes over time (e.g., goal specification as a transition process, collective efficacy as an interpersonal process). Those interested in how individual KSAOs ultimately manifest as (S)HCRs can draw on this framework to better understand the motivational processes that, although often incorrectly assumed to occur, are critical for the emergence of (S)HCRs.

In addition, Marks et al.'s work sheds additional light on team motivation by distinguishing emergent states from processes, and by suggesting that some important aspects of team motivation represent emergent states rather than processes. According to the authors, team emergent states do not represent or capture team interactions, but rather team experiences which can become their own inputs. Thus, for example, while interactions among team members in which they set goals for their team represent a form of team process (i.e., goal specification), it is unique from members' collective beliefs about their ability to accomplish those goals. The latter represents an emergent state that must also be considered if we are to most fully understand how what people bring to their teams yields higher, unit-level inputs that in turn influence performance. This distinction is also important because it provides additional clarity for (S)HCR scholars and team motivation scholars, generally, as it explicitly recognizes that some aspects of team motivation can be considered inputs, processes, and outcomes. It is worth noting that meta-analyses (e.g., DeChurch and Mesmer-Magnus, 2010; Gully et al., 2002; LePine et al., 2008) have provided support for Marks et al.'s notions regarding the importance, and predictive validity, of motivational emergent states and processes on team performance.

Finally, beyond its highlighting the motivational states experienced and motivational behaviors enacted by teams, Marks et al.'s framework is also noteworthy because it acknowledges that teams often simultaneously pursue multiple goals. However, their framework's specific focus on team-level processes largely ignores goals at the individual and subgroup levels and the potential interaction among goals across levels.

DeShon and his colleagues (2004) developed and tested a multiple goal, multilevel model of individual and team processes that focused specifically at the role feedback plays in team- and individual-level self-regulatory (e.g., Carver and Scheier, 1982, 1998) and resource allocation (Kanfer and Ackerman, 1989) processes—processes that largely dominate current thinking about work motivation (Kanfer, 2012). Central to their model is notion that in team contexts, both individuals and teams—their collective counterpart—have goals they seek to accomplish. In addition, the notion that individuals and teams have limited resources to devote to goals at either level, and that they must make decisions about where to allocate those limited resources (e.g., which goals to pursue), is also important to understanding the utility of their work. It is also noteworthy that DeShon et al.'s model is one that articulates parallel, or functionally equivalent, processes at the individual and team levels. They found evidence supporting their hypothesis that the process is largely isomorphic processes, and did so again in subsequent tests (e.g., Chen et al., 2009).

Work by DeShon and his colleagues (2004) moved the team motivation literature forward by demonstrating the utility of developing and testing more complex conceptualizations of motivation in team settings (see also Chen et al., 2009). Moreover, by recognizing goals and goal processes at multiple levels, their work better captured the complex reality of teams. However, an important limitation was their focus on a single goal at each level. Put another way, their ideas are somewhat restrictive in that the focus is on, and their work is best suited for understanding, how people regulate goal-directed behavior when there are a very limited number of goals (i.e., one at each level).

In proposing motivated action theory (MAT), DeShon and Gillespie (2005) offered a dynamic, self-regulatory model that more explicitly acknowledges that people can simultaneously hold multiple, hierarchically ordered goals and that their actions are directed toward the attainment of those goals. Although MAT is not a team motivation model, its tenets have important implications for the study of team motivation.

Central to MAT are four types of goal that exist at four hierarchical levels, ranging from broad, higher-order, fundamental goals to specific, lower-order, more concrete goals that lead to action. Self-goals are at the highest level of the hierarchy and are fundamental outcomes that all people must achieve to "lead normal, healthy, fulfilling lives" (DeShon and Gillepsie, 2005, p. 1105). Higher-order goals include those such as esteem, affiliation, and agency. (Readers might note the similarity to the familiar higher-order needs identified by Maslow, 1943.) Failure to obtain these goals undermines well-being (e.g., psychological and physical health). Self-goals are outcomes in and of themselves, and are disconnected from the means of their achievement. Thus, people must find actions at lower levels of the goal hierarchy. One step below self-goals are principle goals, which are goals that derive from principles that are important to the person and can map well onto personality characteristics or moral foundations (e.g., hardworking, friendly, and fair). Achievement goals are at the next lowest level, and include people's goal orientation or general action patterns which guide goal pursuit is activated. Here, goals become increasingly closer to action and behavior. Finally, at the lowest, most concrete level are action plan goals, which are strategies or pathways for achieving goals, such as seeking feedback, managing impressions, allocating resources, or exploring problems. These action plan goals set behavior into action.

One of the primary goals of the theory is articulating connections between goals across hierarchical levels. Another is developing a framework for organizing and solidifying what the authors considered a rather scattered goal orientation and achievement goal literature (MAT emphasizes goals at this level given the increased reliance on achievement goals to explain motivation—a practice we are also observing as it concerns team motivation). The theory draws on resource allocation models (Kanfer and Ackerman, 1989) to suggest that goals at multiple levels vie for limited attention and resources which, in turn, leads to repeated decisions about how to allocate efforts. Thus, DeShon and Gillespie's work suggests the potential for internal, within person, conflicts. For example, a person's behavior, or actions, targeted toward one goal may complement (i.e., increase the likelihood) other actions or compete with (i.e., decrease the likelihood) other actions.

As it concerns teams, MAT, its goal hierarchy, and the salience of achievement goals also highlight a number of issues relevant to team motivation. For example, MAT suggests people can hold many goals at any given point in time. This can quickly enlarge the number of goals under consideration in a team setting given that teams are composed of multiple people. Obviously, as the number of goals increases, it seems likely that some goals may be shared while others may not, leading to potential external, between-person conflicts. And, extending MAT to higher levels (which, based on prior theory and research suggesting motivation is largely isomorphism across levels, seems appropriate), it stands to reason that in teams members face and must reconcile multiple goals at multiple levels. Whether one agrees with MAT's notion that only single goals are pursued at one time—we do not in light of theory and research at both the individual and team levels suggesting multiple goals can be balanced—the theory offers an interesting lens through which one might better view the topic of team motivation.

In their effort to address the lack of well-developed team motivation theories (Kozlowski and Bell, 2003), Chen and Kanfer (2006) challenged but ultimately proposed that "motivation processes are functionally similar at the individual and team levels of analysis" (p. 233). Specifically, they identified motivational states, goal generation (also called goal choice), and goal striving as key processes that occur at the individual *and* the team level. Importantly however, they highlighted the interplay between levels, suggesting contextual bottom-up and top-down influences. In doing so, Chen and Kanfer offered one of the most extensive theoretical models of team motivation. For example, through bottom-up effects, they proposed that individual goal generation and goal striving affect team goal generation and goal striving, respectively. They proposed that these effects are reciprocal, such that team goal generation and goal striving also affect individual goal generation and goal striving.

However, Chen and Kanfer's model does much more than articulate the similarities between individual and team-level motivational processes; it suggests they are inseparably intertwined. Unfortunately, an important challenge remains to the extent that scholars are just beginning to explore the relationships that result from these connections, and have few guiding frameworks for doing so. In addition, despite how elaborate it is, the Chen and Kanfer model could be further expanded to better accommodate the existence of multiple goals at each level.

A final model worth mentioning was offered by Park et al. (2013), who sought to develop a theory that incorporated several major team motivation theories—a theory they labelled interdependent regulatory dynamics theory. As its name suggests, the theory emphasizes the interdependent and dynamic nature of team motivation, depicting the processes through which team members decide how to allocate effort and resources between individual goals and team goals over time. In contrast to much previous work, the authors questioned the extent to which individual motivation and team motivation are functionally similar. In addition, the theory maintains that, in teams, there are multiple individual feedback loops (one for each team member) as well as shared team feedback loops, and that members' individual feedback loops can converge over time. As this happens, team feedback loops, which reference the team goal, are expected to increase in salience exerting increasing influence on members. This, in turn, is proposed to ensure shared goals.

As we take inventory of just how far the team motivation literature has come and its potential to inform future (S)HCR theory and research, we are certainly encouraged. There is a fair amount of agreement that individual and team motivational states (e.g., efficacy) and processes—i.e., goal choice and goal striving (Chen and Kanfer, 2006; Kanfer, 2012)—are functionally similar, although there remains debate about the boundaries of their similarities. Related, theories that provide the foundation for our understanding of motivation at the individual level (e.g., self-regulatory and resource allocation processes) have proved quite useful for understanding team motivation, and scholars continue to develop ideas about team motivation drawing on these models.

While, by definition, team motivation models embrace and incorporate the notion of a shared team goal, they vary widely in the extent to which they recognize goals at the individual and other levels. Just as important, they also vary in the extent to which they acknowledge that within levels, multiple goals exist. This has clearly impacted research. Park et al. (2013) noted that most studies on team motivation continue to look at situations in which teams are working toward a single goal, leaving a "dearth of research on teams working on multiple goals" (p. 1358). Chen and Kanfer (2006) similarly observed that the teams literature is struggling to capture and understand the complex interdependencies between the team and individual team members regarding motivational processes and goals.

To this end, in the next section we offer a framework that not only highlights the several ways in which multiple goals manifest in team settings, but also, just as important, demonstrates how those goals may or may not align—an issue that has largely been assumed away. Most frameworks do not consider the issue of goal alignment, which is critical for team motivational states and processes as a part of the enabling emergent process. To be clear, our perspective rejects the idea that people in team settings commonly choose and devote effort toward a single individual goal or team goal. That is, we reject the notion that people pursue single goals in isolation—a notion Diefendorff and Chandler (2011) claim characterizes the "vast majority of research on work motivation." When multiple people are thrust together in a team, we suspect that goal misalignment is common. Team scholars have begun to embrace goal (mis)alignment in teams, and those interested in (S)HCR must as well if they are to understand the emergence of unit-level capabilities from individual-level capabilities.

GOAL (MIS)ALIGNMENT WITHIN AND ACROSS TEAMS

As evidenced by the prior discussion, one cannot discuss motivation without explicitly discussing goals. Goals help us understand the "motivation for what" question (Dalal and Hulin, 2008; Ilgen, 2014) because they are cognitive representations of desired end-states. They are the guiding principles that people consciously and intentionally set and that steer their actions and behavior (Austin and Vancouver, 1996). As we noted at the outset, we often assume at least some degree of goal congruence or alignment when we think of teams. Kozlowski and Ilgen's definition explicitly specifies that members in teams have one or more *common* goals. While we do not disagree that members should share at least one goal (otherwise why organize into a team-based structure in the first place?), it is vital for future (S)HCR theory and research—and any efforts to understand team motivation—to readily acknowledge the existence of multiple goals at multiple levels in teams and their potential for (mis)alignment. By understanding how multiple goals operate at the unit level—both within and across units—(S)HCR theory and research can be better equipped to address the important yet overlooked interconnectedness between individuals and teams (Chen and Kanfer, 2006), which in turn will help us understand why and how members' KSAOs (i.e., member inputs) translate into relevant outputs.

Before introducing our framework, a couple of points are worth noting. Following DeShon et al. (2004), Chen and Kanfer suggested that teams are most effective when there is congruence (or alignment) among members' goals, both horizontally (between members' goals) and vertically (between members' goals and teams' goals). Our framework extends this idea in several ways, utilizing the vertical and horizontal distinction. However, our framework does not speak to the value, per se, of goal alignment. In fact, we can envision, and some research has provided evidence indicating, that there are situations in which (mis)alignment is beneficial.

Our framework also recognizes that multiple types of teams exist in firms, and that those teams can be distinguished based on hierarchical level. At the lowest firm levels, there are operational teams (e.g., production teams). These teams conduct the day-to-day business of the firm. At the highest firm levels are strategic teams. They are largely decision-making teams that set direction for the firm as a whole (e.g., top management teams, governance boards, etc.). We remind readers that we assume a high degree of functional similarity across these levels as it concerns team motivation and, by extension, goal (mis)alignment.

Related, our framework is unique in that it connects teams at various hierarchical levels within firms. Decisions made by a strategic leadership team inevitably influence operational teams. For example, in a manufacturing context, the decision by a team of executives to embrace or abandon a product or service influences the goals and behaviors of production teams, either directly in terms of what is accomplished or indirectly by changing resources available to those teams. Further, our framework is unique in that it allows for both bottom-up and top-down influences. Few, if any, team motivation models consider the former; yet the goals and goal achievements by lower-level teams influence the goals and goal achievements by higher-level teams. For example, production teams that fail to identify faulty products and services, ignore safety, hurt end users, or whose work undermines or diminishes customers' trust create situations that must ultimately be managed by strategic teams, via strategic goals and efforts.

Finally, by explicating a team motivation process that links teams across levels, our framework not only offers an approach that highlights the centrality of goals and goal (mis)alignment within organizations as systems but, just as important, also uniquely addresses the need to better understand motivation in and of teams (cf., Chen and Kanfer, 2006). Hence, the approach we take is a multilevel one consistent with recent perspectives on (S)HCRs (cf., Ployhart et al., 2014).

Table 19.1 presents eight types of goal alignment central to our framework. The framework categorizes goals using two dimensions—level and direction. Direction describes the type of alignment, vertical or horizontal. Distinctions between vertical and horizontal alignment have been made previously (e.g., Chen and Kanfer, 2006), and we extend the use of this framework beyond alignment at a single team level. Turning to level, we propose that to be useful for (S)HCR scholars, horizontal and vertical alignment needs to be applied to four distinct levels. These levels—intrapersonal, interpersonal, intra-team, and inter-team—capture goal (mis)alignment within team members, between team members, within teams, and between teams, respectively. In combining these two dimensions, level and direction, we distinguish eight types of goal (mis)alignment, which we describe in detail below. Our framework challenges the assumption of goal alignment, but also suggests an important avenue for future work seeking to explain the extent to which and the conditions under which members' KSAOs translate into team effectiveness.

Table 19.1 Multilevel goal (mis)alignment in teams

Level	Alignment Type	
	Horizontal	Vertical
Within Firm/ Between Team	*Inter-team horizontal (mis)alignment* The extent to which the goals of teams at the same organizational level are aligned	*Inter-team vertical (mis)alignment* The extent to which the goals of teams at different organizational levels are aligned
Within Firm/ Within Team	*Intra-team horizontal (mis)alignment* The extent to which the goals of the team are aligned	*Intra-team vertical (mis)alignment* The extent to which the lower-level goals of the team are aligned with the higher-level goals of the team
Within Team/ Between Person	*Interpersonal horizontal (mis)alignment* The extent to which the personal (self) goals of members of the same team are aligned	*Interpersonal vertical (mis)alignment* The extent to which the personal goals of members are aligned with team goals
Within Team/ Within Person	*Intrapersonal horizontal (mis)alignment* The extent to which members' own self-goals are aligned	*Intrapersonal vertical (mis)alignment* The extent to which members' own lower-level goals are aligned with their higher-level goals

Within Team/Within Person (Intrapersonal) Goal (Mis)alignment

Intrapersonal vertical (mis)alignment represents the extent to which a person's goals—which, as DeShon and Gillespie (2005) highlight, are hierarchically structured—are consistent and overlap. Intrapersonal goals are vertically aligned when there is a high degree of consistency between lower-level goals (i.e., sub-goals and lower-level actions such as behavioral routines) and the higher-level goals they are engaged to meet. As DeShon and Gillespie suggested, most motivation theories assume some degree of intrapersonal vertical alignment; however, there is no shortage of research indicating this is not always the case. As an example, a team member might have an affiliation goal, yet have moments when they decide to and act on a desire to distance themselves from their team and team activities, perhaps to satisfy some competing goal or goals.

Intrapersonal goals are horizontally aligned when a member's various goals are consistent with one another. Take, for instance, a tenure-track faculty member (Member A) working on a team charged with redesigning an MBA curriculum. Let's assume this faculty member has three personals goals, all of which are related in some way to the shared team goal of a successful MBA curriculum redesign: 1) expediting the conclusion of the teams' work, 2) minimizing the amount of work for which she herself is personally responsible, while at the same time, 3) demonstrating her competence and ability to head the MBA program at some time in the future. It might be the case that the first goal (expediting the conclusion of the teams' work) overlaps, or aligns, with the third goal (demonstrating competence and ability), although this is not necessarily the case. However, the second goal of minimizing her work is likely to conflict with the third goal of demonstrating competence and ability. Intrapersonal horizontal (mis)alignment captures the extent to which these three goals align, although we recognize the principle of multifinality (McDougal, 1923) and equifinality (Broadbent, 1985)—single lower-level actions can meet multiple higher-level goals simultaneously, and different actions can meet higher level goals, respectively.

Of course, this situation quickly becomes more complex when we take into account that this faculty member is likely to have other personal goals—ones that most models of team motivation fail to consider. For example, as a tenure-track faculty member, she likely also holds a personal goal of research excellence, which, for the sake of simplifying our example, let's say, includes completing two papers she intends to submit to top-tiered journals and completing a book chapter during the same time that the team is working on its task. There may be considerable alignment between her personal goal of minimizing her work on the MBA curriculum and her goal of focusing on her research. In fact, efforts towards the former may help her accomplish the latter (i.e., multifinality). However, her efforts to focus on or prioritize her research may undermine her ability to demonstrate her potential to someday head the MBA program. This might be particularly true if other team members perceive her to be less committed to the team goal than she is to her research goals.

Within Team/Between Person (Interpersonal) Goal (Mis)alignment

Interpersonal goals are horizontally aligned when members' personal goals overlap with each other. Going back to our example, our tenure-track faculty member only represents a single member of the MBA curriculum team. Perhaps there is another member of the team (let's call him Member B) for whom being on the team in and of itself is a source of pride and satisfaction. In fact, team membership itself might help satisfy this member's affiliation goal if he has a strong need to satisfy that goal and sees at least some subset of other members of the team as people with whom he would like to be affiliated. Taking this one step further, while sharing the team goal of successfully redesigning the MBA curriculum, he might want to extend the amount of time the team is intact, which directly conflicts or misaligns with Member A's goal of expediting the completion of the team's task. And, did we mention that our two faculty members do not get along with one another? They do not; and it turns out that Member B holds a personal goal (i.e., self-goal) of undermining Member A whenever the opportunity presents itself. Although our example is a simple one (and we hope such an example is difficult for readers to imagine in their own departments and schools), it represents just the sort of additional complexity that occurs when people work interdependently.

Interpersonal goals are vertically aligned when members' personal goals overlap with team goals. As our running MBA example highlights, members can hold goals that have little if anything to do with team goals. Moreover, members may have personal goals that compete with team goals. Member A's personal goal of wanting the team's task to wrap up quickly might be inconsistent with the team goal of a successful curriculum redesign. Member B, who may go out of his way to challenge or dismiss any suggestion from Member A—even when her suggestions have the potential to improve the MBA curriculum—might actually hinder progress toward the shared team goal in an effort to satisfy his personal goal of antagonizing Member A and making her look incompetent.

CEOs whose primary goals are maintaining their celebrity status while the rest of their executive team shares a primary focus on more tangible, arguably more important, aspects of firm performance might represent yet another example of interpersonal vertical misalignment (see Bermiss and Darnell, Chapter 20 this volume).

Within Firm/Within Team (Intra-Team) Goal (Mis)alignment

Intra-tcam goals are horizontally aligned when the team's various goals are complementary or consistent. While some teams may have overlapping goals that provide easy transitions for team members when pursuing those goals or when switching their focus across goals, this is certainly not always the case. Indeed, some teams have scattered, seemingly disjointed goals, requiring team members to act far more strategically when allocating resources (e.g., effort). In some cases, team goals may be so misaligned that trade-offs must be made by the team. Speed and accuracy goals represent potentially competing goals that a number of work teams are routinely forced to reconcile. In our MBA curriculum redesign team example, these competing goals might manifest as balancing efforts to submit a curriculum the team believes is the best it can develop (with courses sure to attract faculty and students and be superior over their competitors' curriculums) versus satisficing to meet school or university submission deadlines.

Intra-team goals are vertically aligned when hierarchically structured team goals are consistent and overlap. There is a greater degree of vertical alignment when there is consistency between lower-level goals (i.e., sub-goals and lower-level actions such as team-level behavioral routines) and higher-level team goals. Examples of higher-level team goals include team values and norms that guide the team—such as integrity, valuing diversity, creativity, and innovation (Note that team values and norms can be independent of firm values and norms.) For example, when initially forming their team, members may decide to set standards of mutual respect and helping. In this case, intra-team vertical alignment exists to the extent that lower-level sub-goals, actions, and behavioral routines by the team are consistent with these standards (e.g., members avoid chastising other members, members demonstrate a willingness to help other members who need help accomplishing their tasks).

Within Firm/Between Team (Inter-Team) Goal (Mis)alignment

Given our specific interest in (S)HCR, at the highest level, our framework highlights two types of (mis)alignment that occur within firms, albeit between teams—inter-team horizontal (mis)alignment and inter-team vertical (mis)alignment. Inter-team goals are horizontally aligned when teams at the same level within a firm hold goals that either overlap or are consistent with each other. For example, although distinct from our MBA curriculum redesign team, other teams might exist within the school (MBA admissions team, the MBA program leadership team) that share the curriculum redesign team's secondary goal of seeing the MBA program remain a top-ranked program. The program leadership team may engage in activities that directly support the goal, perhaps by providing support (e.g., benchmarking data, facilitating access to students and other program faculty, etc.) seemingly enacting sub-goals and routines clearly indicative of a high degree of alignment with the goals of the curriculum redesign team. By selectively admitting students into the program, the admissions team, on the other hand, may be meeting a team goal unique to the admissions teams that is nevertheless consistent with that of the curriculum redesign team's secondary goal of keeping the program ranked highly. The aforementioned examples represent common interactions between teams, and may be even more likely to occur to the extent that team members belong to more than one team. They also highlight the reality of multiple goals at the team level akin to the existence of multiple goals at the individual, member level.

Finally, inter-team goals are vertically aligned when teams at different levels within a firm hold goals that overlap and are consistent with each other. We extend our MBA program example one more time as advisory councils and committees of deans and associate deans are typically seen as, and represent, strategic units in business schools, and operate at a higher hierarchical level than our operational, curriculum redesign team. An advisory council composed of members resistant to curriculum changes would clearly represent a case of inter-team vertical misalignment. Importantly, our framework does not dictate the primacy of goals at one level over goals at another. Thus, if the curriculum redesign team had an additional goal of rolling out their redesigned curriculum two years after its approval (perhaps it will take that long to hire needed faculty or to appropriately market the new curriculum) but the advisory council wants the roll-out immediately, neither goal is necessarily better than other. Instead, they are just misaligned.

Moving away from our MBA program example to a business one, firms with top management teams focused on innovation may hold goals difficult to align with operational teams and the business unit teams who, for example, may be focused on cost cutting.[1] Disputes between management and labor also represent examples of inter-team vertical misalignment.

Team Goal Multiverse Model

Figure 19.2 provides an illustrative example of how goal (mis)alignment can present itself in teams, and highlights the importance of motivation in (S)HCR models. We refer

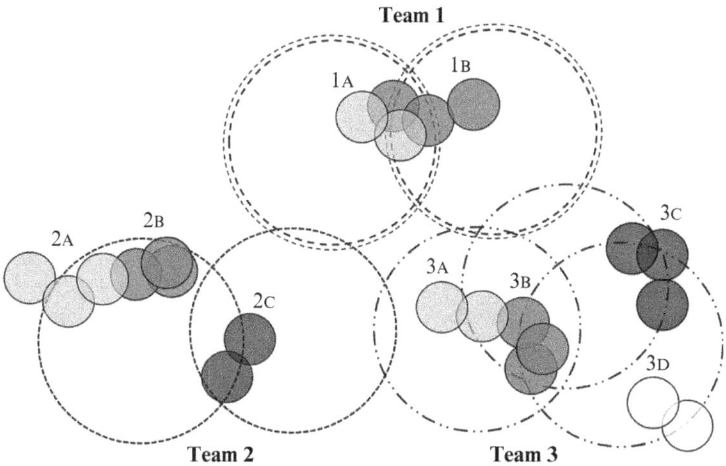

Figure 19.2 Team Goal Multiverse (TGM) model

to this model as the Team Goal Multiverse (TGM) model given how reminiscent it is of illustrations depicting the multiverse, in which multiple parallel universes exist in space, yet they exist in their own bubble.[2] This model depicts varying ways in which team and team member goals may be (mis)aligned—within and across teams, team members, and organization level. In our example, we present three teams with varying numbers of team members. Team 1 is a strategic management team with two members. Teams 2 and 3 are operational teams with three and four members, respectively. In this visual example, the larger circles represent team goals, while the smaller circles represent team members' goals.

In Team 2, the team members (2A, 2B, and 2C) are largely united. The team has two team goals, one of which is shared by all of the members. At the within-person level, team members 2A and 2B each have three personal goals and team member 2C has two personal goals; the members vary in the extent to which their goals overlap, as indicated by the small Venn diagrams. Team 3, which is another team at the same level within the firm, has three team goals. At the within-person level, team members 3A and 3D each have two personal goals and team members 3B and 3C have three personal goals. Again, the members vary in the extent to which their goals overlap, as indicated by the small Venn diagrams for each team member. Finally, Team 1, which is higher in the firm's hierarchy compared to the other teams, has two team goals and two team members, 1A and 1B, each of whom has two and three personal goals, respectively. Each team also varies in the extent to which their team goals overlap or align. Team 3, for example, has rather strong alignment of its team goals compared to Teams 1 and 2. The overlapping in goals depicts both alignment and misalignment.

By modeling the teams in this way, we can visually represent the previous eight types of goal (mis)alignment we have discussed (see Table 19.1). Intrapersonal horizontal goal alignment can be seen in the overlaps of individuals' personal goals. For example, in Team 2, member 2B has a strong degree of overlap between their three goals compared to members 2A or 2C, whose goals only slightly overlap with each other. In fact, each team member represented has a varying degree to which their own goals overlap or are consistent, showing that team members may be working towards multiple personal goals which may themselves be misaligned. Intrapersonal vertical alignment is largely assumed (i.e., that individuals' higher-level goals will inform their lower-level goals) and therefore not depicted visually, as any of the team members' personal goals may exist within the goal hierarchy.

Interpersonal horizontal (mis)alignment can be seen by the overlap, or more aptly the lack thereof, between team members. Team 1 shows more overlap between its members' personal goals, indicating a stronger degree of horizontal alignment, compared to Team 3, in which there is only one small area of overlap between member 3A's and member 3B's goals. The members in Team 1 are working towards a couple of similar goals, while in Team 3 almost all the members are working towards multiple different goals. Interpersonal vertical alignment is represented by the overlap in team goals and team members' personal goals. For example, Team 3 has two members (3A and 3B) with personal goals that are strongly consistent with the team goals, overlapping quite a bit in the center of the Venn diagram. The other two team members (3C and 3D), however, have some personal goals that align with their team goals and other personal goals that do not align as well with their team goals. In fact, the latter personal goals fall outside of their team's goals. In both cases, this indicates vertical (mis)alignment. As another example, team member 2A possesses one goal that is completely misaligned with their team's goals, but possesses two goals that still fall within one of the team goals. This depicts both vertical alignment and misalignment, as a team member may have goals that fall within team goals (vertical alignment) as well as outside team goals (vertical misalignment). Additionally, the strategic team (Team 1) shows strong interpersonal vertical alignment, as each team member's personal goals fall within the team goals and even align with multiple team goals.

Intra-team horizontal alignment is depicted in the overlap of team goals at the center of the Venn diagrams created by teams' multiple goals. Team 3, for instance, shows very strong intra-team horizontal alignment, as their three goals overlap quite a bit. Team 2's goals are comparatively less consistent with each other, only slightly overlapping and indicating less horizontal alignment. As teams likely possess several goals, there may be variance in the extent to which their goals overlap, just like at the intrapersonal level. That means a team may have some goals that have strong intra-team horizontal alignment and other goals that do not overlap at all. Other teams may have multiple goals that have almost no alignment. Intra-team vertical alignment is similar to intrapersonal vertical alignment in that it is largely assumed and difficult to visually present idiosyncratically from horizontal alignment. Recall, team goals may exist anywhere within the goal hierarchy, from very narrow action goals to high-level organizational values.

Finally, at the highest level of goal (mis)alignment, inter-team horizontal alignment is depicted in the model with overlapping of team goals at the same level of an organization's hierarchy. For example, Team 2 and Team 3 each have a goal that overlaps. Specifically, as these teams are both at the same organizational level, any consistency, or overlap, represents horizontal alignment at this level. However, teams can also have goals that do not overlap—goals that may, in fact, not overlap at all. Finally, inter-team vertical alignment is depicted in the overlap of team goals across the organization's hierarchy. Team 1 (the strategic team) has two goals, and each overlaps at least slightly with a Team 2 and Team 3 goal. Team 1, for example, has more inter-team vertical alignment with Team 3 than that it does with Team 2; one of Team 1's goals overlaps with two of Team 3's goals, while that same Team 1 goal overlaps only slightly with one of Team 2's goals.

Our TGM model not only serves as a visual representation of our taxonomy of goal (mis)alignment; it also highlights the many assumptions (S)HCR and other team scholars make about goals and motivation in teams. While teams may, by definition, be interdependent groups of people working towards a shared goal, there are many ways in which teams' and their members' goals may (mis)align. We challenge (S)HCR and other team scholars to rethink these assumptions and explicitly test ideas about each type of (mis)alignment. As we noted at the outset, simply combining individual capabilities does not result in unit-level capabilities. Taking goal (mis)alignment into account can help reveal when individual capabilities will actually be combined to create (S)HCRs.

MOVING FORWARD

As we have argued throughout this chapter, future work on the emergence enabling process that translates individuals' KSAOs into (S)HCRs must address the reality of multiple goals across multiple levels that impact team motivation. Although considerable theory and research on team motivation has laid a foundation for this future work, much of it has significant limits for understanding the complexity presented by goal (mis)alignment. We are not suggesting that the theories (S)HCR and other team scholars have routinely employed are no use for understanding goal (mis)alignment. To the contrary; scholars who have forayed into this complex space have successfully extended and applied a number of widely utilized perspectives, such as self-regulation and resource allocation theories and models, to the team level (e.g., Chen and Kanfer, 2006; DeShon et al., 2004; Porter et al., 2010). However, we believe the time has come for (S)HCR and team scholars to embrace the reality of multiple goals at multiple levels in team contexts and draw from, develop, and continue to build models that include them. Below, we introduce several theoretical frameworks we believe have the potential to offer additional insight to (S)HCR scholars and that provide insight to our TGM model.

Peterson and Behfar (2005) proposed a model that squarely highlights the potential for goal (mis)alignment, suggesting that goal conflicts are inevitable. They further suggest that a central role of leaders is helping their teams regulate the tensions that arise from goal conflicts. Their model is grounded in self-regulation, which they extend to the team level by largely assuming isomorphism. However, consistent with our framework, they note that goal (mis)alignment and the motivational processes that result are significantly more complex in teams because they "consist of multiple individuals with differing perspectives, expectations, goals, needs, wants, and motivations" (p. 149). In addition to recognizing the inherent multilevel nature of goals in teams and other collective work settings, they argued that effective teams are ones that acknowledge and resolve goal tensions, specifically the trade-offs that often need to be made among goals that seemingly compete with one another in an effort to "balance competing motives and interests." It is noteworthy that, despite acknowledging the role of people in team contexts (that teams are composed of members who have their own goals), Peterson and Behfar's ideas regarding team motivational processes are largely, if not entirely, focused on team regulation and team goals.

In a recent study, Porter et al. (2016) drew from and expanded Peterson and Behfar's work to develop predictions about the potential for leaders' influence on compensatory behaviors in teams. They found some evidence that leaders could help teams effectively strike a balance between the pursuit of learning and performance goals. Specifically, leaders who should have focused on learning goals seemingly helped offset the negative effects of their teams' exclusive focus on performance goals. Our TGM framework extends this thinking across levels, and suggests that tensions can exist within and between teams.

While primarily used to highlight that team members simultaneously pursue individual and team goals and to show isomorphic processes at both levels, DeShon et al.'s multiple-goal regulation model and Chen and Kanfer's integrative model—and findings based on initial tests of their common ideas (e.g., Chen et al., 2009)—provide potentially useful insight for incorporating the existence of multiple goals in teams in future research. Consistent with expectations one might derive from resource allocation theory (Kanfer and Ackerman, 1989), DeShon and his colleagues noted that individual and team goals can present a zero-sum situation in that effort devoted towards goals at one level comes at the expense of effort devoted towards goals at another, in particular when goals at each level are not compatible (i.e., are misaligned).

Similar to DeShon and Gillespie's (2005) focus on goal orientations in an effort to provide a unified theory of achievement motivation, Porter (2008), also recognizing the potential utility of goal orientation for shedding light on motivation in team settings, developed a multilevel, multiconceptualization framework of goal orientation in teams. The framework identified three distinct types of goal orientations in teams: members' (including leaders') dispositional goal orientations; composition goal orientations that result from simple but varying aggregations of members' dispositional goal orientations; and collective goal orientations that result from emergent processes and result in "true" team-level manifestations of goal orientation (see also Kozlowski and Klein, 2000).

Most important for our understanding of the complex interplay of multiple goals in teams, however, are the framework's implications for interactions among the various types of goal orientation in teams. The taxonomy Porter developed points to six unique interactions among the various types of goal orientation in teams that can occur and that he urged scholars to explore. Scholars have slowly begun answering this call, but there remain significant opportunities to further examine the interplay of achievement goals and the additional complexity they present in teams.

Westaby's (2012) dynamic network theory (DNT) provides a potentially useful perspective for exploring the (mis)alignment our TGM model identifies. What makes DNT novel relative to a number of the aforementioned team motivation models is its explicit focus on teams as social settings in which members' motivations, including members' own attempts at self-regulation, are influenced by others. DNT also implies that teams can be motivationally diverse, and predicts effects for that diversity on outcomes, including affective outcomes. At the core of the theory is its elaboration on the numerous roles those within a social network play directly and indirectly promoting (motivating) and constraining (resisting) others' goal pursuits. In DNT terms, *goal strivers* and *system supporters* serve motivation roles. Goal strivers directly and willfully pursue specific goals, while system supporters provide support to goal strivers. In contrast, the theory suggests that *goal preventers* and *supportive resistors* serve resistance roles. Goal preventers directly and willfully prevent goal strivers from achieving specific goals, while supportive resistors provide support to goal preventers. Importantly, because of their theoretical independence, goal strivers and system supporters can also prevent and resist goal preventers' and supportive resisters' goals.

By acknowledging the existence of multiple goals in team settings, DNT is obviously well-suited for providing insight regarding interpersonal intra-team horizontal (mis)alignment. However, we believe it also has the potential to help explain both goal generation and goal striving processes across levels. In particular, its network perspective takes into account actors outside of the team, and can include members of other teams and non-work influences (e.g., members' spouses, family, and others within their broader social network who can influence goal-related behavior). Finally, it is worth noting that DNT is similar to some other theoretical perspectives that conceptualize goal generation and, to some extent, goal striving as drawing from limited personal resources.

Fitzsimons et al.'s (2016) recent extension of prior work by Fitzsimons and colleagues (Finkel et al., 2016; Fitzsimons and Finkel, 2015; Fitzsimons et al., 2015) on transactive goal dynamic (TGD) theory from the dyadic to the team level provides another theoretical lens that may be useful for developing testable predictions using constructs from our framework. Initial versions of the theory focused on the effects of relationships between individuals and within dyads or teams on goal setting, goal pursuit, and goal achievement. In their more recent formulation of TGD theory, the authors sought to provide a multilevel model of goals—one that includes cross-level linkages among individuals and teams.

At its core, the theory suggests that members combine and share their mental resources to create a team regulatory system (despite the team context, the authors refer to the system as a self-regulatory system), similar to the way theory and research on transactive memory system argues that members combine and share their knowledge regarding which members know what information (Liang et al., 1995; Hollingshead, 1998; Ellis et al., 2008). Moreover, the theory emphasizes the social (i.e., relational), interdependent nature of regulation in teams, focusing specifically on others' influence on members' goal choice and goal striving in its attempts to provide insight into the role of members' connectedness and reliance on one another in goal pursuits. And, the importance it places on interdependence in terms of the connection among all of the goals in the team regulatory system is consistent with Ployhart and Moliterno's (2011) focus on task complexity.

As it concerns our team goal multiverse framework, TGD similarly holds that, in teams, members simultaneously hold and pursue multiple goals; but TGD differentiates goals based on (1) who holds the goal, (2) who pursues the goal, and (3) whose outcomes are the target of the goal. For example, Fitzsimons and her colleagues (2016) distinguish between one member's goals that are unique to that member (e.g., one member who is striving for individual, personal recognition for himself) and parallel goals that may be shared by multiple members (e.g., several team members who are all striving for individual, personal recognition themselves). From a team-goal multiverse perspective, the latter would represent a form of interpersonal horizontal alignment; but TGD further distinguishes goals by target, hence providing a more complex taxonomy of goals in teams. It remains to be seen if this additional complexity is warranted; however we suspect that the answer to this will largely depend on the research question. If, for instance, a researcher is interested in compensation in top management teams, who gets what bonuses and incentives may matter, especially if compensation varies across members of the team. In this case, the fine-grained distinctions made by TGD might be relevant. What is most important here, however, is that TGD offers a novel, potentially useful framework that suggests ways of capturing the inherent complexity of motivation in teams in which members may or may not be aligned beyond a single, shared team goal.

In sum, we began this chapter by arguing that team motivation is critical to the emergence enabling process because individual KSAOs will not transform into a true unit-level (S)HCR in the absence of team motivation. We then demonstrated that our understanding of team motivation has been hindered by insufficiently complex models of team motivation—models that vary in the extent to which they take into account the existence of multiple goals at multiple levels and the potential for mis(alignment) in these goals. As we have shown, there are a growing number of theoretical frameworks and perspectives available for scholars willing to embrace more complex approaches to studying team goals and motivation. We conclude with some final thoughts, and by discussing some implications of our TGM framework for future theory and research on (S)HCR and team motivation, more broadly.

CONCLUDING THOUGHTS

While certainly not unique to it, the (S)HCR literature is nevertheless plagued with a black box problem (Nyberg et al., 2014). Our goal in writing this chapter was to ensure that efforts to open the black box regarding how individual resources (i.e., member KSAOs) ultimately manifest as unit-level capabilities recognize the important and implied role of team motivation. Further, we hoped to ensure that future theory building and research efforts by (S)HCR and team scholars would better address the issue of goal (mis)alignment by challenging the assumption that teams and members focus on a small subset of goals that are inevitably shared. The literature we highlighted and the framework we offered suggest a number of important implications for future work, but there are a few we would be remiss if we did not mention.

Our focus on team motivation clearly indicates that our primary interests concern team states and processes. Having said that, because team motivation is part of the emergence enabling process, we obviously encourage research on team inputs. Indeed, what we offered here has important implications for the study of team inputs. For example, we hope our efforts to draw attention to goal (mis)alignment in team settings encourages (S)HCR and team scholars to significantly broaden the inputs they investigate. To date, both sets of scholars have explored a relatively limited set of KSAOs believed linked to team effectiveness. By highlighting the potential for goal (mis)alignment, our framework not only suggests the importance of KSAOs more tightly linked to goal choice and goal striving; it also suggests the importance of KSAOs likely to influence the social processes invoked to resolve goal (mis)alignment (Ilgen, 2014).

Related, although we argued for similar team motivational processes and types of (mis)alignment across hierarchical levels in firms, we would be remiss if we ignored Chen and Gogus (2008), who suggested that motivational inputs may be different depending on the level in which a team resides. For example, they argued that at higher organizational levels, inputs are more likely to reside outside the firm.

As it concerns future empirical research, although Ployhart and Moliterno (2011) urged scholars to avoid proxy measures of human capital and although we generally encourage the use of direct, explicit measures of inputs and processes when and where possible, we suspect that SHCR scholars, in particular, might be uniquely positioned to develop novel ways of capturing motivation-related variables since they often use proxies in their studies. Firm-level investments may represent a reasonable proxy for the intention and efforts of strategic teams. As another example, statements to shareholders and information obtained from earning conference calls may provide insights into the goals set by a management team. With that said, we realize that a balance must be struck between explicit motives—which might be easier to measure, more valid, and more reliable but difficult to obtain depending on the accessibility of the team—and alternative measures (e.g., proxies, implicit measures). (Readers should see Kanfer, 2012, for insight on developments on implicit motive measurement.)

Related to this, despite our optimism about the potential for more research on team motivation, we recognize and appreciate the difficulty measuring it. Kanfer suggested that motivation cannot be directly measured, which may explain why it is so elusive in (S)HCR models and empirical research. Honestly, quite a bit of research squarely centered on the team motivation literature does not actually measure motivation. Instead, performance is typically used as a proxy, often with unanticipated consequences (Diefendorff and Chandler, 2011; Kanfer, 2012). We echo Diefendorff and Chandler, who recommended that choices about how to best operationalize motivation be theoretically driven.

Our work and our framework situate teams in a broader organizational context. In most work settings, teams at the highest levels are strategic while teams at the lowest level are operational. With that said, we realize standalone teams still exist. That is, there continue to be teams (although we would guess that there are not very many) that operate largely in isolation and are not nested in the way that most systems thinking assumes. While our framework may be ideally suited for teams nested within firms, it can nevertheless accommodate teams that face less complexity and have a less nested structure. For example, even in standalone teams, there is the potential for intrapersonal and interpersonal horizontal and vertical (mis)alignment.

Finally, it might be tempting to conclude that we believe goal misalignment is dysfunctional. We caution against such a conclusion. Despite the positive value implicitly attached to goal alignment, and to a large extent assumed and advocated by many team scholars, we do not believe there is sufficient evidence to conclude it is necessarily superior to goal misalignment. In fact, as with many of the topics studied by (S)HCR and team scholars, it is likely the case that goal (mis)alignment might sometimes be advantageous. We hope future work explores this possibility.

CHAPTER SUMMARY

BOX 19.1 KEY TAKEAWAYS

1. Teams are critical to the study of (S)HCRs, as is team motivation because team motivation is perhaps the most important yet often neglected mechanism needed for individual-level KSAOs to emerge into unit-level capabilities.
2. (S)HCR theory and research must fully acknowledge and better incorporate the existence of multiple goals at multiple levels in teams, which highlights the potential for goal misalignment which, in turn, can influence the enabling process needed for (S)HCR emergence.
3. The Team Goal Multiverse (TGM) model was proposed to provide a sound typology of goal (mis)alignments in team settings.

BOX 19.2 DIRECTIONS FOR FUTURE RESEARCH

Topics	Descriptions
Goal (mis)alignment and team motivation	Further develop and test models that explicitly recognize that in teams there are often multiple goals at multiple levels.
Goal (mis)alignment and (S)HCR	Delineate and test the role that goal (mis)alignments play in enabling the integration and emergence of individual-level KSAOs to (S)HCR and goal (mis)alignments relationships with a broader set of team inputs, processes, and outcomes.
Measurement of team motivation in (S)HCR research	Develop and validate theory-driven team motivation measures.

NOTES

* We thank Jake P. Gale for his help with this chapter.
1. For concerned readers, no MBA committee duties were neglecting during the writing of this chapter.
2. Coincidently, our depiction of the TGM model also looks quite a bit like wall art currently hanging about the stairwell in one of our homes, which was not realized until after the figure was largely completed.

REFERENCES

Ambrose, M. L., and Kulik, C. T. (1999). Old friends, new faces: Motivation research in the 1990s. *Journal of Management*, *25*, 231–92.

Applebaum, E., and Batt, R. (1994). *The New American Workplace: Transforming Work Systems in the United States*. Ithaca, NY: ILR Press.

Austin, J. T., and Vancouver, J. B. (1996). Goal constructs in psychology: Structure, process, and content. *Psychological Bulletin*, *120*, 338–75.

Bridges, W. (1994). The end of the job. *Fortune*, *130*, 62–74.

Broadbent, D. B. (1985). Multiple goals and flexible procedures in the design of work. In M. Frese and J. Sabini (eds), *Goal Directed Behavior: The Concept of Action in Psychology* (pp. 285–94). Hillsdale, NJ: Erlbaum.

Carver, C. S., and Scheier, M. F. (1982). Control theory: A useful conceptual framework for personality–social, clinical, and health psychology. *Psychological Bulletin*, *92*, 111–35.

Carver, C. S., and Scheier, M. F. (1998). *On the Self-Regulation of Behavior*. Cambridge: Cambridge University Press.

Chen, G., and Gogus, C. I. (2008). Motivation in and of work teams: A multilevel perspective. In R. Kanfer, G. Chen, and R. D. Pritchard (eds), *Work Motivation: Past, Present, and Future* (pp. 285–317). New York: Routledge.

Chen, G., and Kanfer, R. (2006). Toward a systems theory of motivated behavior in work teams. *Research in Organizational Behavior*, *27*, 223–67.

Chen, G., Kanfer, R., DeShon, R. P., Mathieu, J. E., and Kozlowski, S. W. J. (2009). The motivating potential of teams: Test and extension of Chen and Kanfer's (2006) cross-level motivation model of motivation in teams. *Organizational Behavior and Human Decision Processes*, *110*, 45–55.

Cohen, S. G., and Bailey, D. E. (1997). What makes teams work: Group effectiveness research from the shop floor to the executive suite. *Journal of Management*, *23*, 239–90.

Dalal, R. S., and Hulin, C. L. (2008). Motivation for what? A multivariate dynamic perspective of the criterion. In R. Kanfer, G. Chen, and R. Pritchard (eds), *Work Motivation: Past, Present, and Future* (pp. 63–100). New York: Taylor & Francis.

DeChurch, L. A., and Mesmer-Magnus, J. R. (2010). The cognitive underpinnings of effective teamwork: A meta-analysis. *Journal of Applied Psychology*, *95*, 32–53.

DeShon, R. P., and Gillespie, J. Z. (2005). A motivated action theory account of goal orientation. *Journal of Applied Psychology*, *90*, 1096–127.

DeShon, R. P., Kozlowski, S. W., Schmidt, A. M., Milner, K. R., and Wiechmann, D. (2004). A multiple-goal, multilevel model of feedback effects on the regulation of individual and team performance. *Journal of Applied Psychology*, *89*, 1035–56.

Devine, D. J., Clayton, L. D., Phillips, J. L., Dunford, B. B., and Melner, S. B. (1999). Teams in organizations: Prevalence, characteristics, and effectiveness. *Small Group Research*, *30*, 678–711.

Diefendorff, J. M., and Chandler, M. M. (2011). Motivating employees. In S. Zedeck, H. Aguinis, W. F. Cascio, M. J. Gelfand, K. Leung, S. K. Parker, and J. Zhou (eds), *APA Handbook of Industrial and Organizational Psychology: Maintaining, Expanding, and Contracting the Organization* (Vol. 3, pp. 65–135). Washington, DC: American Psychological Association.

Ellis, A. P. J., Porter, C. O. L. H., and Wolverton, S. A. (2008). Learning to work together: An examination of transactive memory system development in teams. In V. I. Sessa and M. London (eds), *Work Group Learning: Understanding, Improving, and Assessing How Groups Learn in Organizations* (pp. 91–115). New York: Taylor & Francis.

Finkel, E. J., Fitzsimons, G. M. and vanDellen, M. R. (2016). Self-regulation as a transactive process: Reconceptualizing the unit of analysis for goal setting, pursuit, and outcomes. In K. D. Vohs and R. F. Baumeister (eds), *Handbook of Self-Regulation* (pp. 264–82). New York: Guilford.

Fitzsimons, G. M., and Finkel, E. J. (2015). Goal interdependence. *Current Opinion in Psychology*, *1*, 10–13.

Fitzsimons, G. M., Finkel, E. J., and vanDellen, M. R. (2015). Transactive goal dynamics. *Psychological Review*, *122*, 648–73.
Fitzsimons, G. M., Sackett, E., and Finkel, E. J. (2106). Transactive goal dynamics theory: A relational goals perspective on work teams and leadership. *Research in Organizational Behavior*, *36*, 133–55.
Gordon, J. (1992). Work teams: How far have they come? *Training*, *29*, 59–65.
Gully, S. M., Incalcaterra, K. A., Joshi, A., and Beaubien, J. M. (2002). A meta-analysis of team-efficacy, potency, and performance: Interdependence and level of analysis as moderators of observed relationships. *Journal of Applied Psychology*, *87*, 819–32.
Hollingshead, A. B. (1998). Retrieval processes in transactive memory systems. *Journal of Personality and Social Psychology*, *74*, 659–71.
Ilgen, D. R. (2014). Work team motivation: Progress and perils. In J. K. Ford, J. R. Hollenbeck and A. M. Ryan (eds), *The Nature of work: Advances in Psychological Theory, Methods, and Practice* (pp. 51–67). Washington, DC: American Psychological Association.
Ilgen, D. R., and Hollenbeck, J. R. (1991). The structure of work: Job design and roles. In M. D. Dunnette and L. M. Hough (eds), *Handbook of Industrial and Organizational Psychology* (Vol. 2, pp. 165–207). Palo Alto, CA: Consulting Psychologists Press.
Kanfer, R. (1990). Motivation theory and industrial and organizational psychology. In M. D. Dunnette and L. Hough (eds), *Handbook of Industrial and Organizational Psychology* (pp. 75–170). Palo Alto, CA: Consulting Psychologists Press.
Kanfer, R. (2011). Determinants and consequences of subjective cognitive fatigue. In P. L. Ackerman (ed.), *Cognitive Fatigue: Multidisciplinary Perspectives on Current Research and Future Applications* (pp. 189–207). Washington, DC: American Psychological Association.
Kanfer, R. (2012). Work motivation: Theory, practice, and future directions. In S. W. J. Kozlowski (ed.), *The Oxford Handbook of Organizational Psychology* (Vol. 1, pp. 455–95). Oxford: Oxford University Press.
Kanfer, R., and Ackerman, P. L. (1989). Motivation and cognitive abilities: An integrative/aptitude-treatment interaction approach to skill acquisition. *Journal of Applied Psychology*, *74*, 657–90.
Kanfer, R., Chen, G., and Pritchard, R. D. (2008). The three C's of work motivation: Content, context, and change. In R. Kanfer and G. Chen (eds), *Work Motivation: Past, Present, and Future* (pp. 1–16). New York: Routledge.
Kozlowski, S. W. J. (2012). Groups and teams in organizations: Studying the multilevel dynamics of emergence. In A. B. Hollingshead and M. S. Poole (eds), *Methods for Studying Small Groups: A Behind-the-Scenes Guide* (pp. 260–80). New York: Routledge.
Kozlowski, S. W. J., and Bell, B. S. (2003). Work groups and teams in organizations. In W. C. Borman, D. R. Ilgen, and R. J. Klimoski (eds), *Handbook of Psychology: Industrial and Organizational Psychology* (Vol. 12, pp. 333–75). London: Wiley.
Kozlowski, S. W., and Ilgen, D. R. (2006). Enhancing the effectiveness of work groups and teams. *Psychological Science in the Public Interest*, *7*, 77–124.
Kozlowski, S. W. J., and Klein, K. J. (2000). A multilevel approach to theory and research in organizations: Contextual, temporal, and emergent processes. In K. J. Klein and S. W. J. Kozlowski (eds), *Multilevel Theory, Research, and Methods in Organizations: Foundations, Extensions, and New Directions* (pp. 3–90). San Francisco: Jossey-Bass.
LePine, J. A., Piccolo, R. F., Jackson, C. L., Mathieu, J. E., and Saul, J. R. (2008). A meta-analysis of teamwork processes: Tests of a multidimensional model and relationships with team effectiveness criteria. *Personnel Psychology*, *61*, 273–307.
Liang, D. W., Moreland, R., and Argote, L. (1995). Group versus individual training and group performance: The mediating role of transactive memory. *Personality and Social Psychology Bulletin*, *21*, 384–93.
Marks, M. A., Mathieu, J. E., and Zaccaro, S. J. (2001). A temporally based framework and taxonomy of team processes. *Academy of Management Review*, *26*, 356–76.
Martin, A., and Bal, V. (2012). *The State of Teams: A CCL Research Report*. Greensboro, NC: Center for Creative Leadership.
Maslow, A. H. (1943). A theory of human motivation. *Psychological Review*, *50*, 370–96.
McDougal, T. H. (1923). *Outline of Psychology*. New York: Scribner's.
Murphy, P. R., and Jackson, S. E. (1999). Managing work role performance: Challenges for twenty-first-century organizations and their employees. In D. R. Ilgen and E. D. Pulakos (eds), *The Changing Nature of Performance: Implications for Staffing, Motivation, and Development* (pp. 325–65). San Francisco: Jossey-Bass.
Nyberg, A. J., Moliterno, T. P., Hale Jr, D., and Lepak, D. P. (2014). Resource-based perspectives on unit-level human capital: A review and integration. *Journal of Management*, *40*, 316–46.
Park, G., Spitzmuller, M., and DeShon, R. P. (2013). Advancing our understanding of team motivation: Integrating conceptual approaches and content areas. *Journal of Management*, *39*, 1339–79.
Peterson, R. S., and Behfar, K. J. (2005). Leadership as group regulation. In D. M. Messick and R. M. Kramer (eds), *The Psychology of Leadership: New Perspectives and Research* (pp. 143–62). Mahwah, NJ: Erlbaum.

Pinder, C. C. (1998). *Work Motivation in Organizational Behavior*. Upper Saddle River, NJ: Prentice Hall.
Ployhart, R. E., and Moliterno, T. P. (2011). Emergence of the human capital resource: A multilevel model. *Academy of Management Review*, *36*, 127–50.
Ployhart, R. E., Nyberg, A. J., Reilly, G., and Maltarich, M. A. (2014). Human capital is dead; long live human capital resources! *Journal of Management*, *40*(2), 371–98.
Porter, C. O. L. H. (2008). A multilevel, multiconceptualization perspective of goal orientation in teams. In V. I. Sessa and M. London (eds), *Work Group Learning: Understanding, Improving and Assessing How Groups Learn in Organizations* (pp. 149–74). New York: Erlbaum.
Porter, C. O. L. H., Webb, J. W., and Gogus, C. I. (2010). When goal orientations collide: Effects of learning and performance orientation on team adaptability in response to workload imbalance. *Journal of Applied Psychology*, *95*(5), 935–43.
Porter, C. O. L. H., Franklin, D. A., Swider, B. W., and Yu, R. C. F. (2016). An exploration of the interactive effects of leader trait goal orientation and goal content in teams. *Leadership Quarterly*, *27*, 34–50.
Westaby, J. D. (2012). *Dynamic Network Theory: How Social Networks Influence Goal Pursuit*. Washington, DC: American Psychological Association.

20. Mobilizing human capital to manage negative events

Y. Sekou Bermiss and Samantha Darnell

In 2015, United Airlines CEO Jeff Smisek, EVP of Communications and Government Affairs Nene Foxhall, and SVP of Corporate and Government Affairs Mark Anderson resigned after allegations of a corruption scandal surfaced involving the Port Authorities of New York and New Jersey (Harwell and Zezima, 2015). Even though the evidence demonstrated the executives' culpability in the scandal which resulted in a total of about \$4.6M in fines from the U.S. Securities and Exchange Commission (SEC) and the Justice Department, they were allowed to resign with substantial severance packages, which drove a pension fund to sue United's directors. The investors claimed they were harmed by the severance payments as well as the board's refusal to demand Smisek return the severance payments (Feeley, 2017). Oscar Munoz joined United as CEO to replace Smisek. The first several months of Munoz's tenure were greeted positively as he received credit for a string of successes. But a few months after receiving a 'Communicator of the Year' Award, Munoz was under attack for a series of inadequate responses to scandals. United's stock price dropped, a boycott United campaign was launched, and Munoz lost his future appointment as chairman of the board (Wattles and Ostrower, 2017).

There is an old adage which states that a leader's true colors are only revealed during times of difficulty. For many executives, their most difficult periods are precipitated by an unforeseen negative event, which we define as events that attract negative attention due to organizational wrongdoing, negligence, or errors in judgement (Zavyalova et al., 2016). Negative events include scandals, which occur when the transgressions of a firm are publicized through the media (Graffin et al., 2013; Sims, 2009), and crises, which occur when a negative event threatens the survival of the entire organization (Bundy and Pfarrer, 2015; Mishra, 1996). Negative events have been investigated using a myriad of proxy measures, including downsizing (Love and Kraatz, 2009), unexpected negative earnings (Pfarrer et al., 2010), and product recalls (Rhee and Haunschild, 2006). Despite the numerous anecdotal examples of how firm outcomes are driven by the behavior of their top managers after a negative event, the research on how organizations manage negative events has focused primarily on firm-level resources such as a reputation (Godfrey et al., 2009) and stakeholder identification (Zavyalova et al., 2016). This research, while informative, has largely ignored the role of strategic human capital resources in explaining how effectively firms are able to maintain competitive advantage in light of negative events. In this chapter, we tackle this gap and specifically outline the strategic actions that firms take to maintain competitive advantage when faced with negative events, and highlight how the firm's strategic human capital resources are mobilized to execute these actions.

MOBILIZING HUMAN CAPITAL RESOURCES IN RESPONSE TO NEGATIVE EVENTS

We define strategic human capital resources as individual or unit-level capacities that are based on individual-level knowledge, skills, abilities, and other characteristics (KSAOs) but provide a competitive advantage to the firm within markets (Ployhart and Moliterno, 2011; Ployhart et al., 2014). Top managers are the individuals whose KSAOs most directly impact a firm's performance (Carpenter et al., 2004; Mackey, 2008). Top managers, including the chief executive officer (CEO) and other members of the top management team (TMT), impact firm performance because they are responsible for formulating and executing the firm's strategy (Hambrick and Mason, 1984) as well as any subsequent changes to that strategy (Wiersema and Bantel, 1992). Moreover, the KSAOs of top managers are predictive of the actions that firms take when confronted with environmental uncertainty (Cho and Hambrick, 2006; Hambrick et al., 1996; Henderson et al., 2006). In addition, firm performance is significantly explained by individual characteristics of top managers such as personality (Chatterjee and Hambrick, 2007; Peterson et al., 2003), functional knowledge (Bermiss and Murmann, 2015; Waller et al., 1995), and interests and values (Briscoe et al., 2014; Christensen et al., 2015).

For firms confronted with a negative event, one of the most immediate concerns by executives is to salvage the firm's reputation. A negative event, such as product recall, can become particularly detrimental to a firm's competitive advantage if the event causes the loss of social approval from critical stakeholders such as employees, customers, and shareholders (Bundy and Pfarrer, 2015). Avoiding this fate requires firms to repair the trust with critical stakeholders after experiencing a negative event (Mishra, 1996); however the responses of a firm after a negative event require executives to balance their own (potentially) biased perspective of the negative event (Staw et al., 1981) with the external perceptions of the negative event from the firm's stakeholders (King and Soule, 2007; Zavyalova et al., 2016). In the next section we identify the research on strategic responses to negative events that are centrally driven by the mobilization of strategic human capital within the firm. We categorize the strategic actions as either being preventative mobilization, which are actions that must take place before a negative event occurs, or reactive mobilization, which are actions that take place after the firm has experienced a negative event. In addition, we distinguish between mobilization actions that are directed internally within the firm (i.e., employees, policies) and actions that are directed externally to the firm (i.e., externally held perceptions of the firm).

PREVENTATIVE MOBILIZATION

Executives rarely know the timing or the type of a negative event that may impact their firm, thus making preparation efforts a challenge. Previous research has identified resources that provide a firm with performative advantages when preventing or managing a negative event. In order to attain these benefits, however, firms often need to develop these resources before a negative event occurs. In this section, we highlight the strategic human capital resources that allow firms to develop preventative resources to either prevent or mitigate damage from a negative event.

Directed Internally to the Firm

CEO characteristics

The chief executive officer of a firm is one of the most prominent examples of a strategic human capital resource. CEOs are appointed because their human capital is believed to be accessible and relevant for the competitive advantage of the firm (Finkelstein et al., 2008). The CEO is also the most publicly visible member of the top management, and wields strong influence on the characteristics and outputs of a firm's top management team (Hambrick, 1994). As such, a firm's CEO is a critical strategic human capital resource for preventing or managing a negative event. Two CEO characteristics, celebrity and overconfidence, are of primary relevance for firms dealing with negative events.

Due to the increasingly public facing nature of the modern CEO, the frequency and tenor of CEO media coverage is a major influence on stakeholder evaluations of firms (Rindova et al., 2005). When a CEO's actions are distinctive and consistent over time and across situations, media accounts are more likely to make dispositional rather than situational attributions about the outcomes of their firms (Hayward et al., 2004). When journalists ascribe a firm's positive performance to the CEO it creates an inflated interpretation of the CEO's performance which becomes an anchor for future explanations of firm performance. This is a powerful fundamental attribution error because of a "combination of cognitive constraints and self-interested motivation" that makes journalists prone to using dispositional attributions of a CEO to explain firms' actions and performance. It is the outsized credit for a firm's performance to its CEO that has created the modern celebrity CEO (Hayward et al., 2004: 643).

Celebrity CEOs can be a critical resource to a firm during times of distress. Media depictions of a firm after a negative event influence stakeholders' understanding of what happened, the firm's culpability, and the scandal's impact on short- and long-term firm performance. Just as celebrity firms are penalized less than non-celebrity firms for poor performance (Pfarrer et al., 2010), it is likely that celebrity CEOs will be penalized less than non-celebrity CEOs for their firm's involvement in a negative event. Just as journalists rely on prior characterizations of CEOs when analyzing positive firm performance, journalists might also rely on their established attributions about celebrity CEOs when covering negative events that could buffer the accused parties from more negative media attention (Weber and Wiersema, 2017). In other words, for similar misconduct, firms with celebrity CEOs are likely to be treated more favorably by the media than firms with non-celebrity CEOs. The strong media reputation that results from a celebrity CEO can provide a firm with significant competitive advantage (Deephouse, 2000).

CEO overconfidence, defined as "the extent to which individuals tend to overestimate the accuracy of their knowledge and judgments" (Chen et al., 2015), is another characteristic that can impact how well a firm can quickly rebound from a negative event. Overconfident CEOs are more likely to perceive their own evaluation or analysis as accurate, and be less likely to "hear" conflicting feedback from other TMT members. Additionally, overconfident CEOs make riskier decisions (Malmendier and Tate, 2008; Simon and Houghton, 2003) such as overlooking stakeholder concerns which may stoke a scandal or crisis and exacerbate the damage from a negative event.

Stakeholder relationship management

Negative events can originate from a variety of stakeholder groups. In today's age of greater information transparency, quickly disseminated news, and open communication platforms, disconnected stakeholder groups can generate independent campaigns against a firm with little or no inter-group coordination. Because of the dispersion of a firm's stakeholder groups and the groups' potential to inflict significant reputational and/or financial harm on a firm, it is necessary for executives to understand who their stakeholders are as well as which issues are most important to them. Stakeholder theory suggests that firms that actively identify and engage with their stakeholders experience numerous types of economic and policy benefits (Freeman, 1984; Henisz et al., 2014). Conversely, because stakeholders can create negative impact, identifying stakeholder groups is a necessary first step for top managers seeking to build relationships and prevent scandals or crises. Firms with the strongest stakeholder engagement are the most protected against decreases in performance after a negative event (Henisz et al., 2014).

Identifying all potentially important stakeholder groups can be particularly complex for managers as firms evolve into new lines of business, expand into new market areas, or adapt to changes in their regulatory environments. Given that stakeholder attributes – specifically power, legitimacy, and urgency – are variable and socially constructed, the individuals and groups that constitute a firm's stakeholders, as well as the issues of importance to them, will evolve over time. To be in a position to quickly and adequately respond to stakeholders' concerns to either prevent or respond to a scandal, executives must regularly: 1) refine the firm's evolving list of stakeholders; 2) understand how a firm's actions could impact distinct stakeholders; and 3) be attuned to stakeholders' power in the current environment (Mitchell et al., 1997). For these reasons, a top management team that can closely monitor and manage stakeholder relationships constitutes a strategic human capital resource for firms in the event that they experience a negative event.

Previous research suggests that a diverse top management team should provide a more valuable resource to their firm than a homogenous top management team. A diverse collection of executives will be associated with diverse groups in their professional and personal lives, and formally or informally maintain ties to those groups while occupying their executive positions. Some examples include diversity of functional experiences (e.g., job functions, compensation structures, organizations, or industry) and diversity of demographics (e.g., gender, race, and religion). A diversity of experiences should improve a TMT's ability to recognize, evaluate, and build relationships with their firm's array of stakeholder groups. For example, if an individual represents a historically marginalized group and/or has experienced discrimination themselves, they could more quickly recognize the potential effects of an action on marginalized groups, understand the groups' concerns, and engage with them to proactively assuage their concerns. By representing a diversity of backgrounds and experiences, a TMT could be better positioned to identify relevant stakeholder groups, anticipate their concerns, and begin a dialogue with groups to prevent issues from becoming negative events.

The diversity of professional experiences could also become increasingly important as firms face new risks and threats from the environment. An executive with the capabilities needed to identify, protect, and manage, for example, a cybersecurity breach affecting millions of clients' data may not match the profile of the executives who are generally recruited and promoted to fill a top manager position. Similarly, an individual able to navigate the economic, social, and ethical implications of artificial intelligence might have a functional background that is foreign to a firm's board of directors and TMT, but would contribute the informed perspective the firm might be lacking at the top. Firms that prioritize identifying potential members of the TMT by recognizing and anticipating where their firms are vulnerable to new threats driven by technological advances and social changes could be better positioned to prevent, prepare for, and address these events in the future.

Directed Externally to the Firm

External reputation

A firm's media coverage can influence external evaluations of a firm before or after a negative event. While investors, for example, use a variety of information sources to evaluate firms (Barber and Odean, 2000; Drake et al., 2012), mass media coverage of executives and firms supplies timely and easily accessible firm news and analysis. Depending on the frequency and tenor of a firm's coverage in the media, investors and other stakeholders can positively or negatively alter their perceptions and evaluations of a firm. For example, firms with more prior media attention are partially protected from negative abnormal returns after being the target of a protest (King and Soule, 2007). Since investors have already developed perceptions of firms that are regularly covered in the media, news of a protest does not significantly impact investors' evaluations of firms. The valence of the media coverage is also an important component in determining a firm's reputation. Firms with more positive affect in their media coverage have been shown to experience smaller market penalties for negative earnings surprises than firms with less positive affect in their coverage (Pfarrer et al., 2010).

While firms are not able to dictate their media coverage, the internet has decreased the perceived distance between TMTs, the media, and the public. Digital and social media technologies have increased executives' ability and the public's expectations of them to actively participate in media. Executives have long acted as conduits between the firm and capital markets, and a small percentage of CEOs have become celebrity-like figures; but the extent to which non-CEO executives and board members have become public figures has increased significantly in recent years. Journalists and commentators exploit social media platforms and digital media to make their evaluations of firms and executives available to the public in real time, and as a result have thrust executives and board members farther into the limelight.

Since most executives are not digital natives, a lack of understanding of more modern forms of communication or overall tech illiteracy could increase an executive's risk of committing a consequential faux pas. In addition, a TMT's collective ability to anticipate how a message could be received or used online could prevent them from occurring. In this regard, an executive's understanding of modern communication tools could be a relevant human capital resource with the potential to prevent or curtail a negative event. If United Airline's executive team had appreciated the visual power of the video of the passenger re-accommodation scandal that quickly went viral, for example, perhaps they could have identified the need for a stronger immediate response and reduced the strength of the public outrage (Wattles and Ostrower, 2017).

REACTIVE MOBILIZATION

Directed Internally to the Firm

Single-loop vs. double-loop redressive actions

Once a negative event has occurred, organizations are forced into a reactive position and can employ a variety of strategies to manage the potentially damaging effects of the event. Following a negative event, firms can choose to execute single-loop redressive actions which are short-term and routine in nature, or double-loop actions which are more long-term (Sims, 2009). Some examples of single-loop redressive actions are: denials, referential accounts in which the organization takes responsibility but reframes the discussion to improve firm perceptions; reactive decoupling, in which the organization separates from the individuals that committed the wrongful act; and ideological justifications. Double-loop redressive actions include fixing the outcome by setting specific goals that address the root problems, rewarding positive behaviors that will gain positive media attention; employee training; proactive decoupling, where the firm separates from the responsible actor; and the implementation of new policies. In this section, we'll discuss examples of single- and double-loop redressive actions and the strategic human capital resources that can be mobilized to pursue post-negative event strategies that provide organizations with a competitive advantage.

Technical vs. ceremonial organizational changes

Research has shown that organizations that announce technical changes after wrongdoing receive less negative media coverage than organizations that announce ceremonial changes (Zavyalova et al., 2012). Technical changes signal that the organization recognizes the need for change and is implementing procedural or personnel changes, whereas ceremonial changes are perceived as an organization trying to deflect attention from the wrongdoing while not addressing the actual issue and increase the effect of wrongdoing on the tenor of media attention (Zavyalova et al., 2012). Some types of technical organizational changes that can signal an organization's willingness to change include employee performance metrics adjustments, changes to internal processes and procedures, and employee departures.

Performance metrics adjustments

If an organization or stakeholders identify an issue that resulted from incentive structures that rewarded inappropriate behavior, an organization can pursue redressive actions that correct employee performance evaluation metrics or compensation structures to promote employee actions that align with stakeholders' interests (Sims, 2009). Changing how employees are evaluated or compensated can be a tangible signal that the previous processes did not effectively incentivize proper employee behavior. For example, in response to the fake account scandal, Wells Fargo eliminated sales goals in retail banking, acknowledging the role its aggressive sales expectations played in incentivizing unethical behavior among its employees (Messick and Folk, 2016). As part of several internal changes at Citibank after the 2004 illegal European bond trading and Japanese private banking scandals, standards for annual reviews and compensation were changed (Der Hovanesian, 2006). While these examples demonstrate internal efforts to align desired employee behaviors to performance evaluations, communicating such changes externally also signals to stakeholders evaluating the organization's post-negative event corrective actions that the organization is making long-term changes (Sims, 2009; Zavyalova et al., 2012).

Internal process changes

Another type of tangible organization change that can comprise part of a post-negative event strategy is a change to internal processes. Such double-loop redressive actions communicate a commitment to long-term change by acknowledging the ineffectiveness or gap in the previous process. For example, following the scandal that erupted after the viral video of a passenger being forcibly removed from a flight, United Airlines changed the employee booking policy to reduce the future need to bump passengers (Reuters, 2017). In reaction to a major recall of children's toys in 2007, Mattel adopted a new testing procedure and increased oversight at contract manufacturers' factories to prevent the manufacture and shipment of unsafe products (Grant, 2007). Process changes address "the causes of wrongdoing" (Zavyalova et al., 2012: 1094) and can be part of an effective set of redressive actions.

Characteristics that Can Influence an Organization's Pursuit of Technical Changes

The characteristics of a firm's top management team will impact its decision to enact technical changes after a negative event. A KSAO that could be relevant to an executive's position on implementing technical changes is their openness to change. To effectively signal to external stakeholders that an organization recognizes that previous processes or policies enabled the negative event, and therefore changes to their organization are warranted, the TMT must be willing to propose and enact changes. A TMT heavily weighted by executives with either high or low openness to change could result in a TMT with an excessive or limited openness to change.

As discussed in the previous section on characteristics that could enhance an organization's ability to prevent negative events, a diverse TMT could enable organizations to maintain a wider array of stakeholder relationships. Diversity among executives could also improve an organization's ability to understand the types of changes that will resonate with external stakeholders and, therefore, better predict how the changes will be received. If a technical change is not perceived outside the firm to adequately address an underlying issue, stakeholders could interpret the organization's efforts as insincere, rendering the change ineffective in the effort to manage external perceptions post-negative event. In these ways, a TMT's openness to change and diverse set of stakeholder relationships are strategic human capital resources that can be mobilized to reduce the negative impact of a scandal or crisis and better maintain their competitive advantage.

Executive departure

The voluntary or involuntary departure of executives following a scandal is a common reactive strategy as it is a clear attempt to signal the organization acknowledges the need for change (Pfarrer et al., 2008; Sims, 2009). For example, after a string of scandals during 2017 resulted in stakeholders calling for widespread changes within the company, the board of directors of Uber removed the founder as CEO (Kolhatkar, 2018). During the investigation of the Wells Fargo fake account scandal beginning in 2016, several executives and board members were fired due to their direct or indirect involvement in the fraudulent actions (Egan, 2016; Freed, 2017).

The upper echelons perspective suggests that a firm's strategic decisions are directly shaped by the characteristics, experiences, and composition of the firm's top management team (Hambrick and Mason, 1984). Given the responsibility executives have in directing a firm's strategy, it follows that one or more executives are routinely held responsible for major negative events, as evident by their departure. Since a change in the makeup of a team can alter the content of the KSAOs present within that team (Ployhart et al., 2014), an executive departure could change the relevant KSAOs present within a firm's TMT. If the departing executive lacked a KSAO that could have prevented the negative event from occurring (or possessed a KSAO that was improperly directed and contributed to the event), a departure could be more than a signal to stakeholders that an organization has identified the responsible party and is committed to change; it could be also an opportunity to add an executive to the TMT who possesses KSAOs that were previously lacking that can be mobilized in the future to prevent or manage a similar negative event. This is a fruitful direction for future research as very little research has simultaneously studied human capital resources and turnover (Hausknecht, Chapter 27 this volume).

Returning to the discussion of CEO celebrity, this characteristic might influence a board's ability to pursue the most effective strategy post-scandal. The media reaction received by a celebrity CEO in the wake of misconduct allegations or during the response to a scandal could taint the board of directors' decision-making process regarding a CEO's future position with the firm. Previous research has shown that more powerful CEOs are less likely to be dismissed and members of the TMT are more likely to be scapegoated for poor performance (Boeker, 1992). In this regard, celebrity could protect a CEO from a forced exit if the board decides the responsibility lies elsewhere and does not implicate the CEO. Celebrity status could also protect a CEO from immediate firing after the first scandal that occurs under his/her leadership. It is possible that the celebrity feedback loop that involves executives, directors, the media, analysts and others delays a CEO's exit if more than one scandal occurs during the CEO's tenure. In addition, celebrity CEO departures are seen by directors as riskier than non-celebrity CEO departures (Graffin et al., 2011), and a board might not be inclined to pursue a riskier strategy during an already turbulent period for the firm. Lastly, directors could allow a celebrity CEO to escalate commitment to a failing strategy further than a non-celebrity CEO in an effort to save face and his/her celebrity status (Sinha et al., 2012). By permitting a celebrity CEO to remain in the top leadership position too long, a firm risks damaging its other post-negative event strategies and maintaining competitive advantage.

In these ways, a celebrity CEO could impede organizational efforts to manage negative events. If an organization's directors allow the celebrity feedback loop to interfere with their evaluation of the best strategy for the organization, they risk keeping a celebrity CEO too long and hurting firm performance. By diversifying the directors' relationships with the celebrity CEO, a balance of independent and inside directors could improve a board's ability to objectively evaluate a CEO's culpability in a scandal and the effects of removing or retaining the CEO. As an executive departure can be a key element of a strategy to manage the damaging effects of a negative event, a board with more diverse ties within and outside the firm could improve the board's ability to objectively consider the need for executive departures which could allow a firm to maintain or regain its competitive advantage.

Reputation (crisis) management capabilities

The tangible organization changes discussed above can be pursued as part of an organization's broader post-negative event response strategy. Heugens and colleagues outlined four strategies organizations follow to direct their organizational actions. The strategies (dialogue, corporate silence, advocacy, and crisis communication), or "reputation management capabilities," are "sets of decision rules that allow an organization to protect or improve upon its relative standing amongst its peers as perceived by its stakeholders" (Heugens et al., 2004: 1350). Decision rules can also be interpreted as process and communication channels that direct where an individual focuses their attention by dictating the "spatial, temporal, and procedural" dimensions that shape their organizational contexts by increasing the availability and salience of specific issues and answers (Ocasio, 1997: 195). In this reputation-management context, decision rules guide which capabilities an organization taps as well as individuals' actions by directing attention to specific actions, issues, and stakeholder groups. To enact any of the four capabilities, organizations follow sets of decision rules that link individual actions in such a way that leads to the organizational outcome.

Corporate silence and crisis communication are reactive and internal strategies that can represent, among other things, different approaches to stakeholder engagement. Corporate silence attempts to minimize the organization's association with the reputational threat, and stipulates that any communication that is required is centralized to one or a small group of trained individuals. Crisis communication capabilities allow for organizations to effectively exchange "information with interested outside constituencies during immediate reputational threats" (Heugens et al., 2004: 1366).

Since different negative events require different reactive strategies, depending on the organization and situation, possessing a variety of capabilities could be a valuable resource for an organization so that it may access the necessary capability if the situation changes. An organization's capacity to enact any of the four capabilities and its choice of strategy following a negative event can represent differences in organizational attention to stakeholder groups and external threats. These differences could be represented by a firm's enterprise logic, defined as managers' conceptualization of the firm's relationship with society which helps explain the scope of corporate attention to stakeholders (Crilly and Sloan, 2012). Firms with a more rigid, constrained, dominant logic, referred to as a firm-centric enterprise logic, view stakeholder relations as contractual transactions and emphasize threat reduction in stakeholder engagements. Firms with an extended enterprise logic recognize "the interdependence of stakeholder interests and the sustainability of the firm" (Crilly and Sloan, 2012: 1175); the extended enterprise logic is associated with broader scopes of attention, resulting in more stakeholders achieving salience from the managers' perspectives and thus more effective stakeholder management.

Although specific actions that make up any of the reputation management capabilities could be executed by non-executive members of an organization, the TMT's ability to direct an organization's strategy (Hambrick and Mason, 1984) suggests their collective enterprise logic could influence the identification of and attitude towards engagement with stakeholders, and ultimately influence the development and revision of negative event management strategies. Accordingly, if the TMT's enterprise logic enables effective stakeholder engagement when reacting to a negative event, the enterprise logic could be a valuable human capital resource that can be mobilized when the situation arises.

Additional executive characteristics could also influence a TMT's choice of reputation-management strategies. For example, discomfort with uncertainty and threat sensitivity could influence an executive's willingness to pursue a novel strategy. Executives less comfortable with uncertainty and more sensitive to external threats might be more likely to recommend previously used reputation management capabilities than executives with greater comfort with uncertainty and less external threat sensitivity. For instance, firms will reuse strategies to bolster their tarnished reputation, and have been shown to double down on previously used strategies as the reputation threat increases (McDonnell and King, 2013). If the threats to a firm are similar to those executives have experienced in the past, using tried and true strategies more comfortable to individuals with greater discomfort with uncertainty could be effective. However, since stakeholder groups and the environment in which the firm is operating are continuously variable (Mitchell et al., 1997), the firm could be threatened in ways the firm or industry has not previously experienced. In the face of new threats such as automation, globalization, and data security, an embrace of flexibility and willingness to try something new might be necessary. When facing new types of threats, a TMT's willingness to pursue a new negative event management strategy more appropriate for the specific situation could increase a firm's ability to maintain competitive advantage.

External to the Firm

Matching firm's response to stakeholder expectations

If organizations take actions, whether single- or double-loop, that do not match their stated values post-scandal, stakeholders will notice. Bundy and Pfarrer (2015) theorize that the degree of the stakeholders' perception of organizational responsibility and the organization's response strategy must be matched to reduce social approval loss, while a mismatched strategy could cause evaluators to reconsider their approval of an organization, resulting in less predictable levels of social approval loss. For example, in the United Airlines corruption scandal previously mentioned, three executives were forced to resign but received substantial severance packages, which serves as a lukewarm example of reactive decoupling. The responsible executives' dismissal sends a message to stakeholders that the organization recognizes their role in the scandal and signals they do not represent the organization's values. But, by awarding the departing executives handsome financial rewards after clearly unethical conduct, the organization muddied the waters and sent inconsistent signals that resulted in a lawsuit brought by institutional investors (Feeley, 2017).

An organization's social approval is most salient to evaluators at higher and lower levels (such as Amazon and Goldman Sachs, respectively), rather than at mixed levels (such as Walmart), when the majority of evaluators have reached concurrence regarding an organization's social approval (Bundy and Pfarrer, 2015). In this way, high social approval could act similarly to celebrity as a buffer or a burden. Just as celebrity encourages the media to not reevaluate their judgements about a CEO or firm once established (Hayward et al., 2004), evaluators that have reached concurrence about an organization want to maintain their previously crafted judgements about an organization's level of social approval at the onset of a crisis (Bundy and Pfarrer, 2015).

Publicly accepting responsibility for a negative event can come in many different forms. For example, after the 2007 children's toy recall, Mattel launched an advertising campaign reiterating their commitment to toy safety (Story and Barboza, 2007). Following a scandal-ridden year during which the company received substantial negative media coverage, the new Uber CEO issued multiple public apologies, one to the city of London after a contentious regulatory battle and another to users after not disclosing a data breach (Kolhatkar, 2018). These advertising and public relations activities are examples of advocacy capabilities that are aimed at improving the organization's image in the public eye (Heugens et al., 2004).

Although celebrity could buffer an organization against more severe effects of a negative event, CEO celebrity and overconfidence could potentially negatively influence an organization's willingness to accept responsibility for an issue. The forces that help create a CEO's celebrity could also lead to overconfidence or even hubris if problematic decisions are made (Hayward et al., 2004). Overconfident CEOs have been shown to make riskier decisions (Malmendier and Tate, 2008; Simon and Houghton, 2003). In the context of matching an organization's response to stakeholder expectations, the higher risk option could be to deflect responsibility if stakeholders are expecting acceptance, and vice versa. By recognizing this potential effect of CEO celebrity, an organization can then develop the appropriate decision rules or capabilities that can mobilize the TMT's capabilities to pursue a strategy that more closely aligns with stakeholder expectations and improves an organization's chances of maintaining competitive advantage. Other members of the TMT can tap into unit-relevant KSAOs previously discussed such as their broad enterprise logic and diverse network of stakeholder relationships to better understand how various actions would be perceived and either support or challenge an overconfident CEO's position.

Meetings with key stakeholders

During the post-crisis period, stakeholders' demands and salience evolve, and organizations must take the appropriate actions throughout the process to achieve reintegration with stakeholders (Pfarrer et al., 2008). A TMT's evaluation of the salience of stakeholders at different times during the post-crisis period could impact the effectiveness of their chosen strategies. For example, Uber's CEO met with Uber drivers in India after they organized a strike over declining wages (Kolhatkar, 2018). Given Uber's operational dependence on having a critical mass of active drivers, the CEO acknowledged the need to engage in a dialogue with this key stakeholder group.

A TMT's collective enterprise logic can influence their dialogue capability by narrowing or widening the scope of stakeholders to which they devote attention; the enterprise logic also encourages or discourages them from engaging with stakeholders collaboratively depending on the threat level they associate with collaboration. Threat sensitivity could also influence an executive's perception of the threat level associated with collaborations with stakeholders, a component of enterprise logic (Crilly and Sloan, 2012). While the dialogue capability is primarily discussed by Heugens and colleagues (2004) as a proactive capability, collaborations with stakeholders can also be a part of an organization's reactive strategy.

As discussed in the section on preventative measures, the diversity of a TMT could influence an organization's ability to engage effectively with key stakeholders. KSAOs relevant to an executive's capacity to identify or collaborate with stakeholders could include internal and external networks, professional and personal backgrounds, and identities. Social weighting, a type of rationalization described as how much attention one gives to the values and beliefs of another (Ashforth and Anand, 2003), could be influenced by aspects of an individual's attention or enterprise logic. If a TMT rationalizes the use of a certain scandal or crisis response strategy since they undervalue the values and beliefs of a stakeholder group, they could inaccurately forecast the impact of a strategy and risk losing competitive advantage.

In general, if a situation changes, "some individual level KSAOs [can become] more unit relevant than others," resulting in a different content of human capital even with consistent individual members (Ployhart et al., 2014: 388). A negative event signifies that a situation has changed and could alter the relevance of some KSAOs. If members of a TMT have similar individual-level KSAOs, the relevance of the TMT's human capital resource content could change after a negative event but is limited by the lack of diversity of the TMT. If a TMT has redundant relationships with one stakeholder group and no relationships with several others, the executives' ability to effectively interface with stakeholders more broadly after a negative event is stunted. The strategic potential of the human capital resource of the relationship with the one stakeholder group could be accessed and used in a way that is economically relevant to the unit, but the same cannot be said for the other stakeholder groups. Just as non-redundant network ties can increase the information flow to a group (Miller and del Carmen Triana, 2009), a diversity of stakeholder relationships would maximize this SHCR in a multitude of contexts since executives would have a broader, and therefore a greater, capacity to reactively engage with groups to manage a threat.

CONCLUSION

In this chapter, we examined the strategies that firms can use to effectively manage a negative event. Drawing from research on organization-level attributes that affect an organization's response to negative events, we highlighted human capital resources that are derived from individual-level KSAOs that influence a top management team's capacity to either prevent negative events through proactive stakeholder relationships or to react to negative events through effective, situation-appropriate reputation-management strategies. Specifically, we suggest that CEO celebrity, TMT functional diversity, and ability to navigate the modern media environment are characteristics that will influence an organization's ability to prevent a negative event, an outcome with potentially significant competitive advantages. Openness to change, non-redundant ties to stakeholder groups, a broad enterprise logic, threat sensitivity, and comfort with uncertainty are characteristics that can be mobilized post-negative event to minimize the damage to the firm.

CHAPTER SUMMARY

BOX 20.1 KEY TAKEAWAYS: CATEGORIZATION OF SHCRS FOR MANAGING NEGATIVE EVENTS

Primary focus of action	Preventative SHCRs	Reactive SHCRs
More internally focused	• CEO with celebrity but not overconfidence • Diverse TMT with abilities to develop positive relationships with wide range of stakeholders	• TMT with values that prefer double-loop (vs. single-loop) redressive actions • TMT with knowledge of reputation-management decision rules
More externally focused	• TMT with abilities to build and maintain positive media reputation	• TMT with cognitive abilities to match firm's response to stakeholder expectations • TMT with skills and personality to meet and appease stakeholders

BOX 20.2 DIRECTIONS FOR FUTURE RESEARCH

1. The increased scrutiny of executives and decreased perceived distance between TMTs and stakeholders resulting from digital and social media will likely continue and provide opportunities to further study the impacts of the digital media landscape on executive and firm performance.
2. As TMTs, hopefully, continue to diversify, there will be opportunities to study whether those more diverse teams are better able to engage proactively with stakeholders to prevent negative events and collaborate reactively to address issues after they have come to a head. This scenario could provide a fruitful area for future research focused on the effectiveness of stakeholder engagement by heterogeneous versus homogeneous TMTs.
3. Several of the characteristics we highlighted as potential determinants of a TMT's ability to pursue specific actions can be viewed as elements of an individual's political ideology. Openness to change, threat sensitivity, and comfort with uncertainty have been studied as characteristics of political ideology. Given the growth of interest in the effects of political ideology on organizational behavior among management scholars and the potential connection between an individual's ideology and their attitude towards stakeholder relationships, further research exploring the potential links between individual (executive) and unit-level (TMT or organizational) political ideologies and how organizations manage negative events is warranted.

REFERENCES

Ashforth, B. E. and Anand, V. (2003). The normalization of corruption in organizations. *Research in Organizational Behavior*, *25*, 1–52.

Barber, B. M. and Odean, T. (2000). Trading is hazardous to your wealth: The common stock investment performance of individual investors. *Journal of Finance*, *55*(2), 773–806.
Bermiss, Y. S. and Murmann, J. P. (2015). Who matters more? The impact of functional background and top executive mobility on firm survival. *Strategic Management Journal*, *36*(11), 1697–716.
Boeker, W. (1992). Power and managerial dismissal: Scapegoating at the top. *Administrative Science Quarterly*, *37*(3), 400–421.
Briscoe, F., Chin, M. K., and Hambrick, D. C. (2014). CEO Ideology as an element of the corporate opportunity structure for social activists. *Academy of Management Journal*, *57*(6), 1786–809.
Bundy, J. and Pfarrer, M. D. (2015). A burden of responsibility: The role of social approval at the onset of a crisis. *Academy of Management Review*, *40*(3), 345–69.
Carpenter, M. A., Geletkanycz, M. A., and Sanders, W. G. (2004). Upper echelons research revisited: Antecedents, elements, and consequences of top management team composition. *Journal of Management*, *30*(6), 749–78.
Chatterjee, A. and Hambrick, D. C. (2007). It's all about me: Narcissistic chief executive officers and their effects on company strategy and performance. *Administrative Science Quarterly*, *52*(3), 351–86.
Chen, G., Crossland, C., and Luo, S. (2015). Making the same mistake all over again: CEO overconfidence and corporate resistance to corrective feedback. *Strategic Management Journal*, *36*(10), 1513–35.
Cho, T. S. and Hambrick, D. C. (2006). Attention as the mediator between top management team characteristics and strategic change: The case of airline deregulation. *Organization Science*, *17*(4), 453–69.
Christensen, D. M., Dhaliwal, D. S., Boivie, S., and Graffin, S. D. (2015). Top management conservatism and corporate risk strategies: Evidence from managers' personal political orientation and corporate tax avoidance. *Strategic Management Journal*, *36*(12), 1918–38.
Crilly, D. and Sloan, P. (2012). Enterprise logic: explaining corporate attention to stakeholders from the "inside-out." *Strategic Management Journal*, *33*(10), 1174–93.
Deephouse, D. (2000). Media reputation as a strategic resource: An integration of mass communication and resource-based theories. *Journal of Management*, *26*(6), 1091–12.
Der Hovanesian, M. (2006). Rewiring Chuck Prince, Bloomberg.com. Retrieved from www.bloomberg.com/news/articles/2006-02-19/rewiring-chuck-prince.
Drake, M. S., Roulstone, D. T., and Thornock, J. R. (2012). Investor information demand: Evidence from Google searches around earnings announcements. *Journal of Accounting Research*, *50*(4), 1001–40.
Egan, M. (2016). 5,300 Wells Fargo employees fired over 2 million phony accounts, CNNMoney. Retrieved from money.cnn.com/2016/09/08/investing/wells-fargo-created-phony-accounts-bank-fees/index.html.
Feeley, J. (2017). United directors sued over ousted CEO's severance package, Bloomberg.com. Retrieved from www.bloomberg.com/news/articles/2017-05-10/united-directors-sued-over-ousted-ceo-s-severance-package.
Finkelstein, S., Hambrick, D., and Cannella, A. (2008). *Strategic Leadership: Theory and Research on Executives, Top Management Teams, and Boards*. New York: Oxford University Press.
Freed, D. (2017). Wells Fargo changes board, names Duke chair in response to scandal, Reuters. Retrieved from www.reuters.com/article/us-wells-fargo-moves-idUSKCN1AV2BC.
Freeman, R. E. (1984). *Strategic Management: A Stakeholder Approach*. Boston: Pitman.
Godfrey, P. C., Merrill, C. B., and Hansen, J. M. (2009). The relationship between corporate social responsibility and shareholder value: An empirical test of the risk management hypothesis. *Strategic Management Journal*, *30*(4), 425–45.
Graffin, S. D., Carpenter, M. A., and Boivie, S. (2011). What's all that (strategic) noise? Anticipatory impression management in CEO succession. *Strategic Management Journal*, *32*(7), 748–70.
Graffin, S. D., Bundy, J., Porac, J. F., Wade, J. B., and Quinn, D. P. (2013). Falls from grace and the hazards of high status: The 2009 British MP expense scandal and its impact on parliamentary elites. *Administrative Science Quarterly*, *58*(3), 313–45.
Grant, J. (2007). Mattel scrutinizing suppliers after recalls, Reuters. Retrieved from www.reuters.com/article/us-mattel-manufacturing-recall/mattel-scrutinizing-suppliers-after-recalls-idUSN1445090120070814.
Hambrick, D. C. (1994). Top management groups: A conceptual integration and reconsideration of the "team" label. In B. M. Staw and L. L. Cummings (eds), *Research in Organizational Behavior*, *16*, 171–214. Greenwich, CT: JAI Press.
Hambrick, D. C. and Mason, P. A. (1984). Upper echelons: The organization as a reflection of its top managers. *Academy of Management Review*, *9*(2), 193–206.
Hambrick, D. C., Cho, T. S., and Chen, M.-J. (1996). The influence of top management team heterogeneity on firms' competitive moves. *Administrative Science Quarterly*, *41*(4), 659–84.
Harwell, D. and Zezima, K. (2015). United Airlines chief steps down amid federal investigation, *Washington Post*. Retrieved from www.washingtonpost.com/business/economy/united-airlines-chief-to-step-down-amid-federal-investigation/2015/09/08/de44c496-566c-11e5-abe9-27d53f250b11_story.html?noredirect=onandutm_term=.c40759ad2046.
Hayward, M. L. A., Rindova, V. P., and Pollock, T. G. (2004). Believing one's own press: The causes and consequences of CEO celebrity. *Strategic Management Journal*, *25*(7), 637–53.

Henderson, A. D., Miller, D., and Hambrick, D. C. (2006). How quickly do CEOs become obsolete? Industry dynamism, CEO tenure, and company performance. *Strategic Management Journal*, *27*(5), 447–60.
Henisz, W. J., Dorobantu, S., and Nartey, L. J. (2014). Spinning gold: The financial returns to stakeholder engagement. *Strategic Management Journal*, *35*(12), 1727–48.
Heugens, P. P., Van Riel, C., and Van Den Bosch, F. A. (2004). Reputation management capabilities as decision rules. *Journal of Management Studies*, *41*(8), 1349–77.
King, B. and Soule, S. (2007). Social movements as extra-institutional entrepreneurs: The effect of protests on stock price returns. *Administrative Science Quarterly*, *52*(3), 413–42.
Kolhatkar, S. (2018). At Uber, a new C.E.O. shifts gears, *The New Yorker*. Retrieved from www.newyorker.com/magazine/2018/04/09/at-uber-a-new-ceo-shifts-gears.
Love, E. G. and Kraatz, M. (2009). Character, conformity, or the bottom line? How and why downsizing affected corporate reputation. *Academy of Management Journal*, *52*(2), 314–35.
Mackey, A. (2008). The effect of CEOs on firm performance. *Strategic Management Journal*, *29*(12), 1357–67.
Malmendier, U. and Tate, G. (2008). Who makes acquisitions? CEO overconfidence and the market's reaction. *Journal of Financial Economics*, *89*(1), 20–43.
McDonnell, M. H. and King, B. (2013). Keeping up appearances: Reputational threat and impression management after social movement boycotts. *Administrative Science Quarterly*, *58*(3), 387–419.
Messick, R. and Folk, M. (2016). Wells Fargo to eliminate product sales goals for retail bankers. Wells Fargo News Releases. September 13.
Miller, T. and del Carmen Triana, M. (2009). Demographic diversity in the boardroom: Mediators of the board diversity–firm performance relationship. *Journal of Management Studies*, *46*(5), 755–86.
Mishra, A. K. (1996). Organizational responses to crisis. In R. M. Kramer and T. R. Tyler (eds), *Trust in Organizations: Frontiers of Theory and Research*, 261–87. Newbury Park, CA: Sage.
Mitchell, R. K., Agle, B. R., and Wood, D. J. (1997). Toward a theory of stakeholder identification and salience: Defining the principle of who and what really counts. *Academy of Management Review*, *22*(4), 853–86.
Ocasio, W. (1997). Towards an attention-based view of the firm. *Strategic Management Journal*, *18*(S1), 187–206.
Peterson, R. S., Martorana, P., and Owens, P. D. (2003). The impact of CEO personality on TMT dynamics: One mechanism by which leadership affects organizational performance. *Journal of Applied Psychology*, *88*, 795–808.
Pfarrer, M., Pollock, T., and Rindova, V. (2010). A tale of two assets: The effects of firm reputation and celebrity on earnings surprises and investors' reactions. *Academy of Management Journal*, *53*(5), 1131–52.
Pfarrer, M. D., Decelles, K. A., Smith, K. G., and Taylor, M. S. (2008). After the fall: Reintegrating the corrupt organization. *Academy of Management Review*, *33*(3), 730–49.
Ployhart, R. E. and Moliterno, T. P. (2011). Emergence of the human capital resource: A multilevel model. *Academy of Management Review*, *36*(1), 127–50.
Ployhart, R. E., Nyberg, A. J., Reilly, G., and Maltarich, M. A. (2014). Human capital is dead; long live human capital resources! *Journal of Management*, *40*(2), 371–98.
Reuters. (2017). United changes crew booking policy after passenger dragged off plane, Reuters. Retrieved from www.reuters.com/article/us-ual-crew/united-changes-crew-booking-policy-after-passenger-dragged-off-plane-idUSKBN17H00M.
Rhee, M. and Haunschild, P. R. (2006). The liability of good reputation: A study of product recalls in the U.S. automobile industry. *Organization Science*, *17*(1), 101–17.
Rindova, V. P., Williamson, I. O., Petkova, A. P., and Sever, J. M. (2005). Being good or being known: An empirical examination of the dimensions, antecedents, and consequences of organizational reputation. *Academy of Management Journal*, *48*(6), 1033–49.
Simon, M. and Houghton, S. M. (2003). The relationship between overconfidence and the introduction of risky products: Evidence from a field study. *Academy of Management Journal*, *46*(2), 139–49.
Sims, R. (2009). Toward a better understanding of organizational efforts to rebuild reputation following an ethical scandal. *Journal of Business Ethics*, *90*(4), 453–72.
Sinha, P. N., Inkson, K., and Barker, J. R. (2012). Committed to a failing strategy: Celebrity CEO, intermediaries, media and stakeholders in a co-created drama. *Organization Studies*, *33*(2), 223–45.
Staw, B. M., Sandelands, L. E., and Dutton, J. E. (1981). Threat rigidity effects in organizational behavior: A multilevel analysis. *Administrative Science Quarterly*, *26*(4), 501–24.
Story, L. and Barboza, D. (2007). Mattel recalls 19 million toys sent from China, *New York Times*. Retrieved from www.nytimes.com/2007/08/15/business/worldbusiness/15imports.html.
Waller, M. J., Huber, G. P., and Glick, W. H. (1995). Functional background as a determinant of executives' selective perception. *Academy of Management Journal*, *38*(4), 943–74.
Wattles, J. and Ostrower, J. (2017). United Airlines CEO Oscar Munoz won't be promoted to chairman, CNNMoney. Retrieved from https://money.cnn.com/2017/04/21/news/companies/united-airlines-oscar-munoz-chairman-board/index.html.
Weber, L. and Wiersema, M. (2017). Dismissing a tarnished CEO? Psychological mechanisms and unconscious biases in the board's evaluation. *California Management Review*, *59*(3), 22–41.

Wiersema, M. F. and Bantel, K. A. (1992). Top management team demography and corporate strategic change. *Academy of Management Journal*, *35*(1), 91–121.
Zavyalova, A., Pfarrer, M. D., Reger, R. K., and Hubbard, T. D. (2016). Reputation as a benefit and a burden? How stakeholders' organizational identification affects the role of reputation following a negative event. *Academy of Management Journal*, *59*(1), 253–76.
Zavyalova, A., Pfarrer, M. D., Reger, R. K., and Shapiro, D. L. (2012). Managing the message: The effects of firm actions and industry spillovers on media coverage following wrongdoing. *Academy of Management Journal*, *55*(5), 1079–101.

21. The vital role of teams in the mobilization of strategic human capital resources

Robert E. Ployhart and Gilad Chen

The mobilization and deployment of strategic human capital resources is a topic that is widely recognized as important, but remains poorly understood (Penrose, 1959; Sirmon et al., 2007). It is fair to say that most work focused on understanding the mobilization and deployment of strategic human capital resources has emphasized the role of capabilities (e.g., managerial, dynamic, Eisenhardt and Martin, 2000; Moliterno and Wiersema, 2007; Teece et al., 1997). Research on capabilities is often (appropriately) focused primarily on the characteristics, actions, and processes of key managers and teams charged with making strategic choices about human capital resources (e.g., Castanias and Helfat, 1991). However, the question that is not often deeply examined in this literature is the very nature of the human capital resources that are supposedly strategic and that need to be mobilized and deployed; that is, what are the core processes through which individual-level capabilities emerge to form firm-level competitive advantage (Ployhart and Moliterno, 2011)?

In this chapter we argue that it is time for the field of strategic human capital resources to recognize and embrace the vital importance of teams. We argue that most of the action that takes place in the mobilization and deployment of human capital resources exists at the "meso level" of organizational scholarship, which contains research on groups, teams, and collective constructs and processes. This meso level sits between individuals and the firm—i.e., the domains of organizational behavior (OB) and microfoundations. The reason we focus on groups and teams is less academic than practical: groups and teams are the basic building blocks of the modern organization (Mathieu et al., 2017). Thus, to understand the mobilization and deployment of human capital resources requires understanding the structure and function of small groups and teams.

However, the focus on groups and teams has not historically been the emphasis in strategic human capital research. Strategic human capital resources are "individual or unit-level capacities based on individual KSAOs that are accessible for unit-relevant competitive advantage" (Ployhart et al., 2014: 376). Whether human capital resources are strategic (or not) is dependent on whether the performance outcome is relevant for performance parity (staying in the game) versus competitive advantage (disrupting the game). As a field, most human capital resource scholarship has existed at one of two levels. On the macro side, early research by economists Mincer, Schultz, and Becker came to define human capital from an economic perspective (culminating in Becker, 1964). This work was then extended and adapted into strategic management, where the focus came to emphasize human capital as a resource to be leveraged for competitive advantage (Wernerfelt, 1984; Barney, 1991). On the micro side, an attempt to understand the linkages between individual knowledge, skills, abilities, and other characteristics (KSAOs) predated the economic approach and used different language, but was nevertheless focused on understanding the performance and financial consequences of people (Hall et al., 1917).

Both micro and macro domains have sought to understand the effects of people on organizational outcomes. The two domains differ only with respect to; (a) the level of theory and analysis; (b) the nature of the outcomes; (c) the extent to which they focus on KSAOs; and (d) the extent to which they recognize factor markets and competitive contexts. Note that factor markets represent how and where organizational resources are acquired or exchanged. The factor market for human capital resources is the labor market, but also may include the market for acquiring or divesting of firms and business units (Barney, 1986; Denrell et al., 2003; Moliterno and Wiersema, 2007). Micro research has been primarily individual level, focused on linking KSAOs and job performance without consideration of factor markets (Cappelli and Sherer, 1991). Macro research has been primarily firm (or higher) level, focused on understanding heterogeneity in firm-level outcomes due to human capital resources, but without much explicit consideration of the KSAO origins of those resources. Similarities and differences between micro and macro human capital research have been discussed extensively (Molloy et al., 2011; Wright and Boswell, 2002; Wright et al., 2014).

Both micro and macro traditions have generated innumerable insights and greatly enhanced our understanding of how people, individually *or* collectively, influence performance, individually *or* organizationally. Yet even with there being greater integration across scholarly levels and disciplines, pervasive divisions between micro and macro remain (Nyberg et al., 2014; Wright et al., 2014). It is particularly curious and unfortunate that the meso level, which connects both literatures, has to date been scarcely recognized as informing our understanding of strategic human capital resources (see Ployhart, 2015). There are of course some exceptions, including the work on top management teams (TMTs) (Hambrick and Mason, 1984) and human capital resource emergence (Ployhart and Moliterno, 2011), but these remain exceptions.

As we have argued before (Felin et al., 2015; Ployhart, 2015; Ployhart and Hale, 2014), we believe that a full integration of meso-level scholarship is needed to fully understand the nature, antecedents, and consequences of human capital resources. Human capital resources originate in the KSAOs of individuals, but come to form collective (firm- or unit-level) resources due to an emergence enabling process that resides at the meso level (Ployhart and Moliterno, 2011). It has become reasonably well accepted that human capital resources only emerge from individual KSAOs via meso constructs and processes (e.g., in particular, through groups and teams). However, it appears that researchers are not fully embracing the consequences of this fact. That is, research has been too willing to infer and assume that meso-level processes are occurring, to avoid digging into the messy task of explicating the precise nature of these processes and how they shape the transition from KSAO to strategic resource.

We take a simple position: *significant and potentially disruptive advancements will occur to the field of strategic human capital resources by integrating research with meso-level theorizing on groups and teams*. We further propose that such theoretical advancements will simultaneously increase the practical relevance and actionable implications of strategic human capital resources scholarship—a concern that has been growing (e.g., Kaufmann, 2015; Kryscynski and Ulrich, 2015). We will develop these arguments across the remainder of this chapter; but for now it is sufficient to note that denying the role of meso-level theory in human capital resources is to deny the social reality we all know and personally experience.

There are two important caveats we want to ensure readers recognize at the outset. First, nothing in our arguments denigrates past, present, or future strategic human capital resources research. We are not arguing that all research has to change in our intended direction, and important insights will surely be gained with research proceeding in its current trajectory. We could not be critical of strategic human capital resource research if there was not already a solid body of research to evaluate. We are instead arguing that perhaps the most valuable insights will not be tackled. Second, we do not believe our approach is simply to apply OB, meso-level theory to strategic human capital resources. We do not believe OB has the answers and that strategic human capital scholars must only be aware of them. No, our approach is based on an assumption that both strategic human capital resources research and meso-level OB research must change in significant and fundamental ways. This is good for both disciplines because both literatures stand to gain. For example, outside of TMTs, very few (if any) OB-focused articles on teams have examined the *strategic, firm-level* impact of team-related phenomena. Similarly, there are few articles framed in OB that link meso-level theory and constructs to firm-level profit, growth, or innovation. Thus, we do not criticize the research that has been done, but we are critical of the direction the field is going. Explicit recognition of groups and teams will do nothing less than redirect the field.

CHAPTER STRUCTURE AND DEFINITIONS

We begin by laying out the structure for this chapter and providing definitions for key constructs and terms. This is important, given that research on strategic human capital resources is multidisciplinary (spanning economics, sociology, and psychology) and multilevel (spanning competitive environment, firm, unit, and individual levels). Scholars will necessarily view any human capital topic from their own theoretical and disciplinary lens, and as such the same concepts may have different terms and/or meaning in different literatures. Clarifying these terms is thus vital for making our arguments accessible to multiple audiences.

We then shift to briefly review two chapters in this volume intended to understand the role of teams in the mobilization of strategic human capital resources: Bermiss and Darnell, "Mobilizing human capital to manage negative events"; and Porter et al., "Team motivation and goal (mis)alignment." The two chapters then are used to illustrate many of our points relating to the inclusion of meso-level theory in understanding strategic human capital resources. The chapters are not used as foils to criticize the field, but they do illustrate the strengths and opportunities of advancing a meso-level understanding of strategic human capital resources. We then turn to addressing five questions relating to meso-level theorizing and strategic human capital resources:

1. What answers do we know (big or small)?
2. Where is the field overall deficient?
3. What research paths/debates should be retired?
4. Where can we draw interesting lessons?
5. Where are opportunities to advance the field?

Definitions

In terms of levels, the meso level is primarily in the space between individuals and strategic business units (SBUs). The meso level contains the scholarship on groups and teams, and it is traditionally within-firm (although it doesn't have to be). The macro level is the level of SBUs, firms, and even higher levels (e.g., industry, economies, markets, etc.). The micro level is the level of individuals (and intraindividual KSAO constructs).

As noted, we adopt the framework and definitions used in Ployhart et al. (2014: 376): strategic human capital resources are "individual or unit-level capacities based on individual KSAOs." Human capital resources become strategic when they influence competitive advantage. Human capital is "the subset of KSAOs that are relevant for achieving economic outcomes" (Ployhart et al., 2014: 376). Thus, resources are in this chapter those forms of human capital that exist at the collective or unit level. This latter condition is slightly different than the framework proposed by Ployhart et al., but it helps clarify arguments in this chapter with no loss of meaning.

Performance exists at different levels, and includes job performance (task and citizenship behaviors; Campbell and Wiernik, 2015), team performance (collective goal accomplishments, team viability, and member attitudes; Kozlowski and Bell, 2013; Mathieu et al., 2017), and firm performance (including productivity; or market, financial, or accounting performance; Richard et al., 2009). In addition to performance, another important outcome in the strategic human capital management literature is the concept of competitive advantage. Competitive advantage occurs when a firm earns more than its marginal breakeven competitor (Peteraf and Barney, 2003) or, more simply, when a firm generates above-normal returns. Competitive advantage and performance are related but not interchangeable. Performance tends to follow a "more is better" approach (e.g., higher-quality human capital leads to higher performance). Competitive advantage tends to follow a "differentiation" approach – e.g., how does human capital differentiate the firm from competitors? (Ployhart and Hale, 2014). Both types of criteria are relevant, but competitive advantage primarily exists at the macro (firm) level and is partly determined based on competitive environment and factor markets.

THOUGHTS ON MOBILIZING STRATEGIC HUMAN CAPITAL RESOURCES

This part of the book is titled "Mobilizing Strategic Human Capital Resources: Teams," and the chapters in this section are to emphasize how firms mobilize and deploy groups and teams to enhance firm performance and competitive advantage. The two chapters that address this topic do so from meso and macro perspectives. Here we review these two chapters, not so much critiquing them independently but rather focusing on how they may contribute to understanding the deployment and mobilization of strategic human capital resources.

At the macro level, Bermiss and Darnell consider the mobilization of human capital resources to address negative events. Importantly, they recognize that mobilization of these resources may be done proactively or reactively. Most of their chapter focuses on the role of the CEO, which is obviously important and appropriate given their theoretical focus. In terms of human capital (and human capital resources), they review research suggesting that the KSAOs and related characteristics of CEOs contribute to firm-level outcomes. They also consider the role of TMTs. As is typical in the macro literature, Bermiss and Darnell emphasize firm-level outcomes and recognize the importance of the broader competitive environment. They do not give much systematic attention to the underlying nature of strategic human capital resources.

At the meso level, Porter et al. introduce a team goal multiverse model to understand the nature of goal alignment and misalignment in teams. Their model recognizes that teams exist at lower (operational) and higher (strategic) levels. Importantly, they argue that motivation (and specifically team motivation) lies at the heart of human capital resource emergence. And yet, they note there is little strategic human capital resource research that recognizes the central role of motivation as a determinant of human behavior—individually or collectively. As is typical in the meso literature, Porter et al. emphasize team-level processes and cross-level linkages between individuals and teams. They do not give much systematic attention to the broader competitive environment or how teams may connect to firm-level outcomes or competitive advantage.

Both chapters raise a number of interesting and important ideas within their respective areas. Both chapters are likely to stimulate new research on their respective topics, as they are both well-embedded within their respective literatures. However, both chapters are illustrative of the challenges with conducting research on strategic human capital resources. Despite being in macro and meso disciplines, they share the *same challenges* when it comes to informing questions about human capital resources. These challenges do not reflect limitations of the chapters, but rather highlight the difficulties of connecting team and meso-level research to human capital resources. We detail these challenges below.

Defining Human Capital Resources

Both chapters provide concise summaries of human capital resources that are consistent with recent research. While such citations are helpful and necessary when a construct exists in multiple disciplines, the definitions do not fit neatly into the frameworks proposed in both chapters. This, in turn, can make it difficult for the chapters to have the impact on strategic human capital scholarship that they should. For example, we agree with Porter et al. that motivation has trait-like stable elements and is important for group functioning. However, motivation (and goal choice and persistence) has not historically been a formal part of human capital resource research, and hence it may be difficult for human capital scholars to appreciate the insights offered by Porter et al. Bermiss and Darnell face the same challenges. They introduce human capital resources and KSAOs, but the real focus of their research is constructs such as confidence that are not historically considered human capital resources. We agree with Bermiss and Darnell that factors such as overconfidence are important; but we suspect human capital scholars will not immediately recognize the implications of their framework because it is different from the way human capital resources have traditionally been conceptualized. Thus, the many important insights offered by both chapters for the field of strategic human capital resources will likely not be fully appreciated simply because the focal constructs do not fit neatly into existing definitions and frameworks.

To realize the insights offered in both chapters will require scholars to explicate how/where/why/when the constructs of their focus map onto human capital and when they do not. This would clarify the "inputs" considered in both chapters, and makes it easier to identify their implications. But, more important, such an effort offers new insights for understanding human capital resources. Clarifying how human capital resources relate to goals, goal alignment, and motivation more generally could be a major contribution. Clarifying how CEO and executive human capital is related to, but distinct from, human capital resources and KSAOs could lead to new insights into how human capital leads to confidence and stakeholder relationship behaviors. Answering these questions would contribute to something very new and different from what is found in the existing literature.

Within-Level Focus

Both chapters also stay closely within their respective levels (group or firm). This is understandable and appropriate given the focus of the chapters. The challenge now becomes understanding how the chapters enhance our understanding of the deployment of strategic human capital resources. Porter et al. are suggestive of this process in their Figure 19.1, proposing that team motivation is an enabling state leading what shapes resource emergence. This is an important start, and digging further into how motivation shapes human capital resource emergence could be a great contribution and prompt a number of new questions. For example, how and why does goal alignment influence human capital resource emergence? Is motivation itself a collective resource, and how might motivation interact with other resources to form complementarities? The strategic human resource (HR) literature has adopted an ability–motivation–opportunity (AMO) framework for decades; Porter et al. could advance this literature by explaining how ability and motivation interrelate.

Bermiss and Darnell focus on the firm level, as they should, given their chapter's aim. Consequently, some interesting questions regarding the human capital side of the equation become salient after reading their chapter. For example, are the KSAOs of a CEO simply KSAOs, are they human capital, are they human capital resources, etc.? Similarly, at the executive level, the distinction between performance parity and competitive advantage may be invisible; so what are the ramifications for theory (e.g., are all human capital resources strategic at executive levels?). There is plenty of theory and empirical evidence suggesting executive KSAOs (e.g., personality, intelligence) and TMT characteristics have firm- and even market-level consequences. But what do we really know about these characteristics when viewed from the field of strategic human capital resources? At executive levels, do the distinctions that have come to define the field even matter? Do classic generic and specific human capital distinctions matter at this level? And, if such distinctions do not exist, it would be very interesting to then develop theory why the distinctions disappear and at which levels the distinctions lose meaning (Porter et al. hint at this, noting distinctions between operational and strategic).

We fully realize questions such as these may not have been the core purpose of the chapters' authors, and hence we do not raise these questions as criticisms of their work. Both chapters are well done and clearly have implications for understanding the mobilization of strategic human capital resources. Rather, we raise these questions with the purpose of noting that the cross-level nature and composition of human capital resources is the most challenging aspect of the theorizing. Addressing these cross-level questions provides many opportunities, and can start from existing within-level research such as that contained in Chapters 19 and 20.

One Study's Assumption is Another Study's Focus

This critique is a classic in the literature, as different disciplines must make assumptions about theoretically irrelevant variance to focus on the theoretically relevant variance (Wright and Boswell, 2002). Thus, one's theory and discipline define what variance is relevant and irrelevant—but both types of variance always exist. This is especially true with research on collective human capital resources at the firm level. At this level, competitive environments, industry effects, and strategic factor markets all shape the nature and consequences of human capital resources (strategic or not). Bermiss and Darnell recognize this broader context explicitly and in the tradition of strategic management. On the other hand, Porter et al. do not consider the role of these broader contextual factors as shaping the processes they seek to understand—in the tradition of most organizational behavior research. The consequence is that it is harder to determine how team motivation and the processes so carefully developed in Porter et al. contribute to firm performance and competitive advantage—which is one of the main objectives of research on strategic human capital resources. At the same time, the rich development of human capital resource processes found in Porter et al. is "assumed" or left unaddressed in Bermiss and Darnell.

No study or article can or should try to account for all sources of variance. This requires researchers to be explicit about the conceptual content their study will privilege and the content it will assume or ignore. But even more important is the recognition that a focus on strategic outcomes, like competitive advantage, simply cannot be understood without explicit attention to the broader competitive environment. And, by incorporating the broader context, the limits and opportunities of micro and meso research become clearer. For example, in what competitive environments is team alignment more likely to exist? In what competitive environments is team alignment likely to matter more?

Conclusion

We wish to reiterate that our critique of Chapters 19 and 20 is not a critique of the authors or what is in the chapters—they are interesting and offer unique insights that should stimulate future research. Yet even these well-developed contributions illustrate the challenges of conducting multidisciplinary work on human capital resources because such work requires *developing new theories and frameworks* to account for different foci, levels, and contexts. Thus, the chapters provide perfect illustrations of the many exciting and interesting ideas that could inform strategic human capital resource research. There is an enormous literature across micro, meso, and macro domains that could have implications for understanding human capital resources; whether this literature does have implications is another question entirely, and one that has scarcely been addressed. Hence, the remainder of this chapter is intended to take stock of the field and push toward a more holistic understanding of human capital resources.

WHAT ANSWERS DO WE KNOW (BIG OR SMALL)?

What we know about the mobilization and deployment of strategic human capital resources exists primarily in the study of dynamic capabilities and resource-based theory (RBT). There are a number of insightful studies that examine how executives conceptualize their firm's resources, bundle and deploy them for competitive advantage, or reconfigure them for new purposes (Adegbesan, 2009; Moliterno and Wiersema, 2007; Sirmon et al., 2007; Teece et al., 1997). The chapter by Bermiss and Darnell does a nice job of summarizing some of this literature and illustrating one approach for understanding resource mobilization and deployment. Based on this body of work, we know at a minimum that managerial actions shape the acquisition, development, and deployment of strategic human capital resources. This is possibly stating the obvious, but it is not always obvious in practice. For example, the endless debate about whether top managers are worth their compensation is highly dependent on knowing that managerial actions can significantly shape a firm's fate.

We also know a lot about the internal functioning of top management teams (for review, see Bromiley and Rau, 2016). Seminal work by Hambrick and Mason (1984) has argued that internal collective processes involving members of top management teams can affect important team and organizational outcomes. Subsequent empirical work has provided support for these assertions. For example, a study by Barrick and colleagues (2007) found that top management teams' cohesion and communication positively related to indices of both team and organizational effectiveness, especially when top management teams arranged their work such that there was greater interdependence among members. The chapter by Porter et al. summarizes some of this literature as well, and even though their focus is not directly on TMTs, the processes they invoke are certainly relevant to such teams.

Finally, we know that there are multiple types of human capital resources; these resources exist at multiple levels, yet all collective resources originate from individual KSAOs that are transformed through an emergence enabling process (Nyberg et al., 2014; Ployhart and Moliterno, 2011; Ployhart et al., 2014). Some human capital resources are more strategically important than others. We also know that the value or strategic impact of human capital resources is affected (moderated) by the broader environment and context, that the value or relevance of a human capital resource is dependent on the outcome, and that the value or impact of human capital resources may change over time (Sirmon et al., 2007; Ployhart and Hale, 2014). Thus, there is sufficient research to support an inference that meso-level constructs and processes—particularly groups and teams—are central to the *nature* of human capital resources, and the *management* of human capital resources. If correct, then the corollary is that one cannot understand human capital resources without understanding groups and teams.

WHERE IS THE FIELD OVERALL DEFICIENT?

Ployhart (2015) referred to meso-level constructs and processes as the equivalent of "dark energy and matter" in strategic human capital research. The analogy is appropriate because meso-level constructs and processes are critical but not easily observed, and hence they do not get theorized or measured in most human capital research. This can be illustrated in the Bermiss and Darnell chapter, where meso-level research is cited but not a major, formal emphasis of the chapter. The challenge is also illustrated in Porter et al., who give great attention to team processes but little attention to strategic, firm-level outcomes (or factor markets). These two chapters illustrate different sides of what is essentially a challenge in conducting cross-level research. Both studies are strong within their respective levels and provide a good starting point for understanding how groups and teams are mobilized and deployed to drive firm-level performance outcomes (i.e., across levels). The next step is to address the cross-level implications.

The field needs to adopt an explicit focus on meso-level constructs and processes linked to firm-level or strategic outcomes (Ployhart, 2015). The chapters by Porter et al. and Bermiss and Darnell contribute to an understanding of this issue; but the next evolution of this research will require focusing on the central question of how group and team processes contribute to firm outcomes. The microfoundations movement in strategic management is one response to this neglect (Coff and Kryscynski, 2011; Barney and Felin, 2013; Felin et al., 2015), as is OB-focused research seeking to connect to firm-level outcomes (Barrick et al., 2007; Barrick et al., 2015). But both areas do not yet seem to be fully embraced or integrated into the mainstream human capital literature. Thus, one major area of deficiency is understanding how team-level collective processes contribute to firm outcomes and competitive advantage.

A second deficiency is identifying when human capital resources do not contribute to firm outcomes, or even contribute negatively. If it is correct that the value or impact of human capital resources is dependent on the nature of the outcome, and value may change over time, then it is certainly reasonable to expect weak or even negative relationships between human capital resources and firm outcomes. And yet a meta-analysis on human capital and unit outcomes found only four out of 66 studies with an effect size that was negative (Crook et al., 2011). These negative effect sizes also tended to be small, with the largest being only −.13. The emphasis on finding positive effects is one pervasive in management and the social sciences more generally, and it is sensible to focus on what makes a difference (versus what does not). But, as a community of scholars seeking to understand human capital resources, it is incumbent on us all to understand both ends of the distribution. Just as the surrounding silence defines a note in music, knowing where human capital resource effects are absent or negative helps better define where such resources do matter.

WHAT RESEARCH PATHS/DEBATES SHOULD BE RETIRED?

There is not much research linking groups and teams to strategic outcomes, and hence there is not much to be debated. But there are some issues that surround this topic that are debated, and we comment on each as it relates to the focus of this chapter.

First, like others (Coff and Raffiee, 2015; Kryscynski and Ulrich, 2015; Nyberg et al., 2018), we believe it's time to move past the distinction between generic and specific forms of human capital. The generic–specific human capital distinction comes out of the early work by economists such as Becker (1964), and for their purposes the distinction made sense. Generic human capital resources are those relevant for many different firms, while specific human capital resources are relevant only for a particular firm. Such a distinction seemingly fits nicely with RBT arguments about resource differentiation and protecting resources from competitors (e.g., inimitability arguments; Barney, 1991). However, when viewing human capital resources from a more psychological (meso) lens, the distinction does not work well. Any collective human capital resource will necessarily be specific to a firm because of emergence processes, the nature of the performance outcomes, and the firm's strategy (Kryscynski and Ulrich, 2015; Ployhart et al., 2014). As Ployhart (2015) argued, the socially constructed nature of most meso-level constructs (particularly group and team processes) ensures that those resources are specific to a firm.

Second, debates in the macro literature about how much there is to be learned about firm strategy by examining employees *within* the firm (e.g., microfoundations) is unproductive. Microfoundations scholars (e.g., Barney and Felin, 2013; Felin and Hesterly, 2007; Foss, 2011) develop arguments that respond to criticisms about the value of studying microfoundations. These arguments tend to question whether there is much insight to be gained about between-firm performance and competitive advantage, by taking a deep look into the within-firm, lower-level nature of employees. We have noted that there is evidence to suggest people matter for firm-level outcomes. Thus, questions that relate to "do people matter?" are perhaps theoretically interesting but they distract from the far more important practical question of how, when, and why meso-level processes transform individual-level human capital towards positive contributions to firm outcomes.

Finally, if human capital resources originate from the KSAOs of individuals via an emergence enabling process, then there is no point in worrying about "infinite regress" (Felin et al., 2015) or if there is one versus many types of human capital resources (Ployhart et al., 2014). For example, a team of just four people may operate very differently under different task contexts and at different times (Hollenbeck et al., 2012; Mathieu et al., 2017) because each person has KSAOs that can (and often are) expressed differently in different situations. Indeed, there are 9,999 unique combinations of a four-digit lock (the 10,000th can't exist since the lock would already be open). It is difficult to accept there should exist only one type of human capital resource; such an expectation flies in the face of a century of individual-level and meso-level research (Mathieu et al., 2017; Sackett et al., 2017).

Thus, focusing on these "debates" or questions distracts attention from what we really need to know: how meso-level constructs and processes, particularly relating to groups and teams, influence firm outcomes. Such understanding is needed to know how to mobilize and deploy human capital resources for competitive advantage.

WHERE CAN WE DRAW INTERESTING LESSONS?

When trying to solve a new problem, it's helpful to first see if someone else has already solved it. The field of strategic human capital resources does not need to reinvent the wheel, and it does not need to learn painful lessons already learned in other areas. The focal question of how groups and teams contribute to firm outcomes is essentially a question of how lower-level (team-level) resources combine and are deployed to influence higher-level (firm-level) outcomes. This is a "bottom-up" process, and the nature of this cross-level relationship is likely to be affected by context, time, and the nature of the outcome (cf. Kozlowski and Klein, 2000). Of course, these challenges are similar to those that have been worked through in the groups and teams literature, except that the focus is on understanding how individuals combine to influence team-level outcomes, moderated by context, time, and the nature of the team outcome. Although the content and levels may differ, the basic questions may essentially be the same. And, therefore, one can observe the progression and lessons learned in the groups and teams literature as a means to guide strategic human capital resource research. We do not assert groups and teams are the same as organizations; only that the questions and challenges are highly similar.

In two recent articles, Mathieu and his colleagues (2017, 2018) have traced the evolution of team research in organizational settings. They have organized the literature around three major themes. First, in early research, triggered by Kurt Lewin (1936), researchers focused primarily on individual attitudes and behaviors in the context of groups – and specifically as influenced by the social or task environments of groups. Later on, researchers moved on to studying teams as important collectives in their own right, focusing on such issues as pattern of interactions and communication in teams (e.g., Bales, 1950) and patterns of team tasks (e.g., Steiner, 1972). Finally, from the latter part of the 20th century until today, more and more research has focused on teams as complex open systems – for example, how teams are affected by the broader organizational context or even the context outside the organization, and how teams serve as important contexts within which individuals can impact the organization. This latter phase in the evolution of studying teams clearly has much to offer the field of strategic human capital resources; and yet, to date we have not seen sufficient integration between the teams and the strategic human capital resources.

WHERE ARE OPPORTUNITIES TO ADVANCE THE FIELD?

To this point we see that much of the core needed to understand human capital resources exists at the meso level, while understanding the consequences of human capital resources exists at the macro level. Given that groups and teams are the dominant way of structuring human capital resources in firms, groups and teams must therefore be present to have a basic understanding of how to mobilize and deploy human capital resources. There exists an opportunity to significantly redirect and disrupt the field of strategic human capital resources by integrating research on groups and teams with research on strategic human capital resources and competitive advantage. We outline a broad agenda to accomplish such a lofty goal.

Understand Teams as the Locus of Human Capital Resources

As noted above, strategic human capital research has either been macro or micro. One of the more novel insights from microfoundations research has been to put the locus of human capital resources at the level of interpersonal interactions—that is, the meso level. Future research should build from the microfoundations movement to more strongly incorporate the theory and research from organizational behavior and organizational psychology (e.g., Felin et al., 2015; Foss, 2011). To this end, treating the group or team as the locus of human capital resources, rather than as simply a throughput or by-product of emergence, could prove to be very interesting.

There are at least two important ways in which teams can help explain the processes through which individual-level KSAOs emerge to impact organizational-level outcomes (as well as becoming a source for competitive advantage). First, teams serve as a critical and immediate context in which individual-level behaviors can impact organizational outcomes. For example, employees can translate their talents into positive organizational outcomes through such behaviors as customer service, creativity and innovativeness, or whistle-blowing – and such behaviors often occur in team contexts. Of course, individuals can also engage in counter-productive behaviors in teams, such as engaging in unethical conduct that could harm organizations. Second, almost all modern organizations organize their work around team-based structures. To better leverage their employees' talents, more and more organizations now assign their employees to work on multiple teams simultaneously (O'Leary et al., 2011). Organizations using multiple team membership design hope for more efficient leveraging of employee talent, so that employees can enhance coordination and learning across teams through engagement in such behaviors as proactivity (Chen et al., 2019).

If one adopts this perspective, then a number of new questions are raised that currently have not been considered. For example, how do teams with different functions, and based on different compositions, contribute to different types of human capital resources? Do firms that use temporary teams contribute to different firm-level resources or outcomes than firms that rely on intact teams? How does membership in multiple teams lead to different goals and motivations, and what does this do for emergence and firm outcomes (see Chapter 19). We know that combining different types of people into different types of teams will create different types of team-level human capital resources. Now, how does combining teams in different ways lead to different types of human capital resources and different consequences at the firm level?

Team-Level Origins of Competitive Advantage

A closely related set of questions stems from conceptualizing teams as the origin of competitive advantage. Classic RBT argues that resources may contribute to a competitive advantage when they are valuable and rare, and sustainable competitive advantage when the resource is also difficult (or costly) to imitate and difficult to substitute (Barney, 1991; Dierickx and Cool, 1989). Based on this logic, strategic management research has argued that only specific human capital resources may contribute to competitive advantage (because they cannot be easily copied). Yet, as Ployhart (2015) argued, the processes that give rise to teams are likely to be among the most socially complex, causally ambiguous, and path-dependent, and thus it is meso-level team processes that are likely to be most important for competitive advantage. The question is whether this is true. Do firms that rely more on (or on different types of) team-based structures perform better? Do team-structured organizations better develop and maintain competitive advantage? Research suggests that star employees who switch firms often fail to perform as well at the new firm (e.g., Groysberg et al., 2008). Such a finding is usually interpreted as support for specific human capital; it could just as easily support the interpretation that the locus of the star's performance was not the star but the star's team.

Identify Which Elements of Group and Team Systems are the Same as the Firm Level (and Which are Different)

It is inappropriate and a cross-level fallacy to assert group- and team-level processing to the organization level (Rousseau, 1985). Firms are obviously larger, more entwined with the broader context, and consist of more subsystems (e.g., Felin et al., 2009; Zenger, 1994). However, we also argued above that there are lessons to be learned from research on groups and teams. A fruitful area of theory and empirical research will be to explore and identify the elements where firm levels and team levels have identical elements. Interestingly, this was the goal of General Systems Theory (von Bertalanffy, 1968). It is possible that there are no overlapping elements. But if there are at least some that overlap, then recognizing these elements will speed up our understanding of firm-level human capital resources.

At the same, it is instructive to know which elements are different and why. Such differences point to the possibility of different phenomena that exist at higher levels, either because they are truly unique or because of emergence processes that create partial isomorphism. This leads to many questions. For example, are the laws that govern small groups and teams similar, identical, or different from those that govern firms? Is the small group or team a good metaphor for understanding organizations? Are there characteristics of firms that cause one to reconsider the nature of teams in different ways?

Note that all of these questions are posed to consider the levels that exist between teams and organizations. This intermediate meso–macro terrain is one that has not been fully considered in terms of theory. Units in this space include strategic business units, divisions, lines of business, stores, restaurants, and so on. There is considerable research that examines units at this level, but not much theory that poses there are unique processes or phenomena that exist at this level. Hence, the connection between teams to organizational-level outcomes is very much unknown. Addressing this neglect will require developing new theory and employing a variety of methodologies. We anticipate this is an area where computational models should be embraced and employed on a grand scale because the data needed to study phenomena at this level are difficult to obtain.

Understand How Groups and Teams May be Leveraged to Mobilize and Deploy Human Capital Resources

The final direction we encourage for research goes back to the questions posed at the start of this chapter: how does a firm mobilize and deploy its human capital, given that groups and teams are the way that human capital resources are structured in organizations? For firms that choose to make strategic changes, or struggle with dynamic or changing environments, how can groups and teams be leveraged to successfully implement such changes? For example, consider a firm that pursues an innovation strategy to capitalize on a new market opportunity. How can such a firm use groups and teams as a way to acquire, develop, and then mobilize and deploy the new human capital resources? How does one coordinate or revise existing teams to make this transformation? Should individuals be assigned to multiple teams so that they gain greater tacit knowledge of the firm and its processes? How might team members be reassigned to build new compositions of team-level human capital resources? How might the teams be restructured in a new multi-team system to most quickly spread innovation and diffusion throughout the firm?

In all of these questions, the *team* is the lowest level of interest. In our experience as researchers and practitioners, we have rarely seen explicit emphasis on the team as the focus for such strategic, firm-level interventions (TMT notwithstanding). It is far more common to focus on individuals (e.g., what new skills must they learn) or on HR practices intended to influence individuals, then to consider how one develops teams or creates HR practices to shape team characteristics. Here lies an amazing opportunity for scholars to develop theory that may profoundly influence our understanding of strategic human capital resources.

CONCLUSION

Teams—not individuals—are the building blocks of modern organizations. Any theory of strategic human capital that does not explicitly recognize this fact is not sufficiently explaining the nature of modern work. Research that seeks to understand the role of groups and teams in the mobilization of human capital resources will require new theories and ways of conceptualizing human capital resources. Existing approaches remain stubbornly single level; understanding the role of teams in the mobilization of strategic human capital resources will require cross-level theorizing that starts with teams and ends with firms. Such research will be challenging but has the potential to significantly disrupt the field of management in a positive manner.

CHAPTER SUMMARY

BOX 21.1 KEY TAKEAWAYS

1. Teams are the building blocks that comprise the human capital architecture of modern organizations.
2. The deployment of human capital resources is really the deployment of teams.
3. Significant advancements will occur to the field of strategic human capital resources by integrating research with meso-level theorizing on groups and teams.

BOX 21.2 DIRECTIONS FOR FUTURE RESEARCH

1. Cross-level and multidisciplinary research is needed to examine whether teams are the locus of human capital resources.
2. Research must link meso-level, team processes to firm-level outcomes to determine whether and how teams may contribute to firm performance and competitive advantage.
3. Research needs to understand how groups and teams may be leveraged to mobilize and deploy human capital resources.

REFERENCES

Adegbesan, J. A. (2009). On the origins of competitive advantage: Strategic factor markets and heterogeneous resource complementarity. *Academy of Management Review*, *34*, 463–75.

Bales, R. F. (1950). *Interaction Process Analysis: A Method for the Study of Small Groups*. Cambridge, MA: Addison-Wesley.

Barney, J. B. (1986). Strategic factor markets: Expectations, luck, and business strategy. *Management Science*, *32*, 1231–41.

Barney, J. B. (1991). Firm resources and sustained competitive advantage. *Journal of Management*, *17*, 99–120.

Barney, J. and Felin, T. (2013). What are microfoundations? *Academy of Management Perspectives*, *27*, 120–37.

Barrick, M. R., Bradley, B. H., Kristof-Brown, A. L., and Colbert, A. E. (2007). The moderating role of top management team interdependence: Implications for real teams and working groups. *Academy of Management Journal*, *50*, 544–57.

Barrick, M. R., Thurgood, G. R., Smith, T. A., and Courtright, S. H. (2015). Collective organizational engagement: Linking motivational antecedents, strategic implementation, and firm performance. *Academy of Management Journal*, *58*, 111–35.

Becker, G. S. (1964). *Human Capital*. NewYork: Columbia University Press.

Bromiley, P., and Rau, D. (2016). Social, behavioral, and cognitive influences on upper echelons during strategy process: A literature review. *Journal of Management*, *42*, 174–202.

Campbell, J. P., and Wiernik, B. M. (2015). The modeling and assessment of work performance. *Annual Review of Organizational Psychology and Organizational Behavior*, *2*, 47–74.

Cappelli, P., and Sherer, P. D. (1991). The missing role of context in OB: The need for a meso-level approach. *Research in Organizational Behavior*, *13*, 55–111.

Castanias, R. P., and Helfat, C. E. (1991). Managerial resources and rents. *Journal of Management*, *17*, 155–71.

Chen, G., Smith, T. A., Kirkman, B. L., Zhang, P., Lemoine, G. J., and Farh, J. L. (2019). Multiple team membership and empowerment spillover effects: Can empowerment processes cross team boundaries? *Journal of Applied Psychology*, *104*, 321–40.

Coff, R. W., and Kryscynski, D. (2011). Drilling for micro-foundations of human capital-based competitive advantages. *Journal of Management*, *37*, 1429–43.

Coff, R., and Raffiee, J. (2015). Towards a theory of perceived firm-specific human capital. *Academy of Management perspectives*, *29*, 326–41.

Crook, T. R., Todd, S. Y., Combs, J. G., Woehr, D. J., and Ketchen, Jr, D. J. (2011). Does human capital matter? A meta-analysis of the relationship between human capital and firm performance. *Journal of Applied Psychology*, *96*, 443–56.

Denrell, J., Fang, C., and Winter, S. G. (2003). The economics of strategic opportunity. *Strategic Management Journal*, *24*, 977–90.

Dierickx, I., and Cool, K. (1989). Asset stock accumulation and sustainability of competitive advantage. *Management Science*, *35*, 1504–11.

Eisenhardt, K. M., and Martin, J. A. (2000). Dynamic capabilities: what are they? *Strategic Management Journal*, *21*, 1105–21.

Felin, T. and Hesterly, W. S. (2007). The knowledge-based view, nested heterogeneity, and new value creation: Philosophical considerations on the locus of knowledge. *Academy of Management Review*, *32*, 195–218.

Felin, T., Foss, N., and Ployhart, R. E. (2015). The microfoundations movement in strategy and organization theory. *Academy of Management Annals*, *9*, 575–632.

Felin, T., Zenger, T. R., and Tomsik, J. (2009). The knowledge economy: Emerging organizational forms, missing microfoundations, and key considerations for managing human capital. *Human Resource Management*, *48*, 555–70.

Foss, N. J. (2011). Why micro-foundations for resource-based theory are needed and what they may look like. *Journal of Management*, *37*, 1413–28.

Groysberg, B., Lee, L. E., and Nanda, A. (2008). Can they take it with them? The portability of star knowledge workers' performance. *Management Science*, *54*, 1213–30.

Hall, G. S., Baird, J. W., and Geissler, L. R. (1917). Foreword. *Journal of Applied Psychology*, *1*, 5–7.

Hambrick, D. C., and Mason, P. A. (1984). Upper echelons: The organization as a reflection of its top managers. *Academy of Management Review*, *9*, 193–206.

Hollenbeck, J. R., Beersma, B., and Schouten, M. E. (2012). Beyond team types and taxonomies: A dimensional scaling conceptualization for team description. *Academy of Management Review*, *37*, 82–106.

Kaufman, B. E. (2015). The RBV theory foundation of strategic HRM: Critical flaws, problems for research and practice, and an alternative economics paradigm. *Human Resource Management Journal*, *25*, 516–40.

Kozlowski, S. W. J., and Bell, B. S. (2013). Work groups and teams in organizations. In N. Schmitt and S. Highhouse (eds), *Handbook of Psychology: Vol. 12. Industrial and Organizational Psychology*, 412–69. London: Wiley.

Kozlowski, S. W. J. and Klein, K.J. (2000). A multilevel approach to theory and research in organizations: Contextual, temporal, and emergent processes. In K. J. Klein and S. W. J. Kozlowski (eds), *Multilevel Theory, Research, and Methods in Organizations: Foundations, Extensions, and New Directions*, 3–90. San Francisco: Jossey-Bass.

Kryscynski, D., and Ulrich, D. (2015). Making strategic human capital relevant: A time sensitive opportunity. *Academy of Management Perspectives*, *29*, 357–69.

Lewin, K, (1936). *Principles of Topological Psychology*. New York: McGraw-Hill.

Mathieu, J. E., Wolfson, M. A., and Park, S. (2018). The evolution of work team research since Hawthorne. *American Psychologist*, *73*, 308–21.

Mathieu, J. E., Hollenbeck, J. R., van Knippenberg, D., and Ilgen, D. R. (2017). A century of work teams in the *Journal of Applied Psychology*. *Journal of Applied Psychology*, *102*, 452–67.

Moliterno, T. P., and Wiersema, M. F. (2007). Firm performance, rent appropriation, and the strategic resource divestment capability. *Strategic Management Journal*, *28*, 1065–87.

Molloy, J. C., Ployhart, R. E., and Wright, P. M. (2011). The myth of "the" micro–macro divide: Bridging system-level and disciplinary divides. *Journal of Management*, *37*, 581–609.

Nyberg, A. J., Moliterno, T. P., Hale, D., and Lepak, D. P. (2014). Resource-based perspectives on unit-level human capital: A review and integration. *Journal of Management*, *40*, 316–46.

Nyberg, A., Reilly, G., Essman, S., and Rodrigues, J. (2018). Human capital resources: A call to retire settled debates and to start a few new debates. *International Journal of Human Resource Management*, *29*(1), 68–86.

O'Leary, M. B., Mortensen, M., and Woolley, A. W. (2011). Multiple team membership: A theoretical model of its effects on productivity and learning for individuals and teams. *Academy of Management Review*, *36*, 461–78.

Penrose, E. T. (1959). *The Theory of the Growth of the Firm*. New York: Wiley.

Peteraf, M. A., and Barney, J. B. (2003). Unraveling the resource-based tangle. *Managerial and Decision Economics*, *24*, 309–23.

Ployhart, R. E. (2015). Strategic organizational behavior (STROBE): The missing voice in the strategic human capital conversation. *Academy of Management Perspectives*, *29*, 342–56.

Ployhart, R. E., and Hale, D. (2014). The fascinating psychological microfoundations of strategy and competitive advantage. *Annual Review of Organizational Psychology and Organizational Behavior*, *1*, 145–72.

Ployhart, R. E., and Moliterno, T. P. (2011). Emergence of the human capital resource: A multilevel model. *Academy of Management Review*, *36*, 127–50.

Ployhart, R. E., Nyberg, A. J., Reilly, G., and Maltarich, M. A. (2014). Human capital is dead; long live human capital resources! *Journal of Management*, *40*, 371–98.

Richard, P. J., Devinney, T. M., Yip, G. S., and Johnson, G. 2009. Measuring organizational performance: Toward methodological best practice. *Journal of Management*, *35*, 718–804.

Rousseau, D. (1985). Issues of level in organizational research: Multilevel and cross-level perspectives. In L. L. Cummings and B. M. Staw (eds), *Research in Organizational Behavior*, vol. 7: 1–37. Greenwich, CT: JAI Press.

Sackett, P. R., Lievens, F., Van Iddekinge, C. H., and Kuncel, N. R. (2017). Individual differences and their measurement: A review of 100 years of research. *Journal of Applied Psychology*, *102*, 254–73.

Sirmon, D. G., Hitt, M. A., and Ireland, R. D. (2007). Managing firm resources in dynamic environments to create value: Looking inside the black box. *Academy of Management Review*, *32*, 273–92.

Steiner, I. D. (1972). *Group Processes and Group Productivity*. New York: Academic Press.

Teece, D. J., Pisano, G., and Shuen, A. (1997). Dynamic capabilities and strategic management. *Strategic Management Journal*, *18*, 509–33.

von Bertalanffy, L. (1968). *General Systems Theory*. New York: Braziller.

Wernerfelt, B. (1984). A resource-based view of the firm. *Strategic Management Journal*, *5*, 171–80.

Wright, P. M., and Boswell W. R. (2002). Desegregating HRM: A review and synthesis of micro and macro human resource management research. *Journal of Management*, *28*, 247–76.

Wright, P. M., Coff, R., and Moliterno, T. P. (2014). Strategic human capital: Crossing the divide. *Journal of Management*, *40*, 353–70.

Zenger, T. R. (1994). Explaining organizational diseconomies of scale in R&D: Agency problems and the allocation of engineering talent, ideas, and effort by firm size. *Management Science*, *40*, 708–29.

22. Organizational crisis: the need for transformative boards and top management teams

Margarethe Wiersema

COMMENTARY ON BERMISS AND DARNELL

In their chapter "Mobilizing human capital to manage negative events" Bermiss and Darnell adopt the perspective of human capital as a resource that can be utilized to both prevent and manage unforeseen negative events such as a scandal and crisis. These events can stem from corporate malfeasance such as environmental pollution, product malfunction, customer mistreatment, employee wage and work conditions, gender and race bias, and financial fraud. They can also be due to personal misconduct, such as Uber's CEO Travis Kalanick yelling at a driver. Adverse incidents, however, are not always the result of misconduct or negligence, but can also be due to errors of judgment that lead to unintended consequences such as data systems and policies that subject the firm to undue risk (e.g., cyber-attacks). Organizational crisis can also emerge when activist investors come knocking on the door and lobby for change to enhance shareholder value. The antecedents of an organizational crisis can thus stem from endogenous factors as well as from external forces that are difficult to predict or anticipate.

Given that organizations operate in an era of more intense accountability (i.e., thanks to the rise of social media), corporate malfeasance or errors in judgment can quickly escalate and become public relations disasters for firms. Through a human capital perspective, Bermiss and Darnell provide insights into how companies can avoid these occurrences as well as diminish their potential negative consequences. They specifically focus on the actions that can be taken to enhance the firm's strategic human capital at the top of the organization to manage negative events. In discussing the role of the firm's strategic human capital resources, the authors do an excellent job of identifying characteristics of the CEO and top management team (TMT) that are likely to provide the firm with the requisite human capital resources that may prevent or mitigate negative events. The authors draw attention to the importance of the abilities of members of the TMT to engage with a wide range of stakeholders and to build and maintain a positive media reputation. In addition, they draw attention to the role of CEO celebrity in dealing with organizational crisis. They posit that future research should address how turnover within the TMT that increases the diversity of its composition may become an important way to enhance the firm's strategic human capital resources to deal with wrongdoing or negligence. Thus, they address the dynamic nature of human capital in the context of organizational crisis and scandal, and how it constitutes an important strategic resource that enables firms to prevent as well as improve their handling of negative events.

In the rest of this chapter, I seek to further motivate scholarly research on the role, composition, and dynamics of strategic human capital resources to prevent and manage unforeseen negative events. I first give some context by discussing the social, technological, and competitive market factors contributing to the increased occurrence of negative events so that we can better understand the broader sources of shortcomings in the firm's strategic human capital resources. I then focus on discussing how the processes and practices by which the firm's executive and board directors are appointed determine the firm's strategic human capital resources, and thus have a direct bearing on the ability of the firm to prevent and manage these incidences. While research on "upper echelons" has recognized that executive and director appointments are highly influential in determining the strategic direction and performance of firms, there has been little consideration as to the recruitment processes and practices that determine who is appointed. I argue that these practices have not enabled companies to be dynamic in renewing their strategic human capital resources, but instead have led to homogeneity in the skills, experiences, and knowledge that reside within the firm's leadership. In light of a contextual environment of increased scrutiny and accountability, as well as technology and competitive developments that require companies to adapt in order to stay competitive, we need to examine how companies can enhance their recruitment processes and practices so that they have the requisite strategic human capital resources at the top to prevent or mitigate the effects of negative events.

ORGANIZATIONAL CRISIS

Organizational crises have been defined as "specific, unexpected, and non-routine events" that threaten to harm the organization (Seeger et al., 2003). In understanding what precipitates organizational crises, such as corporate malfeasance, many have pointed to unethical conduct stemming from the organization's culture or climate (Trevino, 1986; Victor and Cullen, 1988). Others have pointed to the role of underlying incentives for misconduct and lack of compliance (Ferrell et al., 1998; Harris and Bromiley, 2007). Scholars have also drawn attention to the importance of the firm's leadership in determining ethical behavior (Brown, Trevino, and Harrison, 2005). In addition to wrongdoing or negligence, companies are also prone to errors of judgment that can lead to an organizational crisis. These do not stem from unethical behavior, but can be the result of erroneous assumptions about technology or the processes that the organization has in place to safeguard against undue risks. For example, companies that operate in industries that are prone to catastrophic failure due to technological complexity and tight coupling will inevitably encounter such events (Perrow, 1984). As companies increasingly rely on complex technologies, they become subject to risks that may not be thoroughly understood or anticipated. Cyber-attacks (e.g., Equifax exposing the personal information of 143 million people) and data scandals where private information is shared without the user's consent (e.g., Facebook providing user data to Cambridge Analytica) represent organizational crises that stem from inappropriate data oversight and privacy policies. Despite our collective wisdom and knowledge of their antecedents, the incidence of these negative events has not diminished; and many scholars would argue that, because of the increasing complexity of organizations and their environments as well as greater technological sophistication, they will continue to increase (Jurkiewicz and Grossman, 2012; Perrow, 1984).

In addition to organizational factors that lead to a crisis, there are contextual factors that have led to increased attention on these negative events. Heightened attention is due to the context in which companies operate today. Corporate wrongdoing or errors of misjudgment are increasingly prone to come to light as the result of endless news cycle and social media scrutiny that can blow up even a trivial and isolated incident into a corporate scandal. As social media becomes even more important as a communication medium, it will increasingly draw attention to and shape how events are perceived by the public. Finally, the capital market, by drawing attention to the firm's financial performance, can also create an organizational crisis. In particular, with more than $62 billion deployed and more than 600 campaigns globally in 2017, activist hedge funds represent the "new sheriffs of the boardroom" (Murray, 2005).[1] Regardless of industry, size, or firm performance, no public company is considered to be safe from being targeted by activists. By aggressively criticizing a company's governance and management, and by utilizing the media to push their agenda, activist hedge funds can create an organizational crisis for a company. Companies thus face an era of heightened scrutiny and accountability, in which technological and market forces have further intensified the need to adapt in order to avoid an organizational crisis.

ROLE OF THE FIRM'S LEADERSHIP IN PREVENTING OR MITIGATING ORGANIZATIONAL CRISIS

What precipitates these organizational crises and how best to address them represent important managerial issues. An organizational crisis can significantly harm the company's reputation and image with its various constituents. Ultimately it is the firm's leadership that must provide the proper oversight and governance so that decision-making takes into account technological complexity and the changing competitive/social context in which companies operate, as well as providing an organizational climate and culture that assures ethical behavior. The strategic human capital resources that reside within the board and top management thus represent an important and dynamic resource in preventing and addressing an organizational crisis. As Ployhart and Moliterno (2011: 127) point out, human capital resources are comprised of individuals that "possess a stock of skills, knowledge, and experiences." It is also a dynamic concept in that, due to individual level differences in knowledge, skills and abilities, additions to and departures of individuals will reconstitute the firm's human capital resources (Nyberg et al., 2014). The processes by which executives and board directors are selected thus represent important factors that influence the composition of the firm's strategic human capital resources. Critically examining these processes and how they influence the "stock of skills, knowledge, and experiences" can shed light as to how the firm's strategic human capital resources can prevent and manage an organizational crisis.

An investigation into board and executive selection and promotion reveals that these processes are defined largely by past practices. Executive career paths are typically defined by the historical key success factors of the business so that managers acquire the requisite work experiences and knowledge. This ensures continuity in the skills and knowledge that are needed at the top of the organization. Over time, as the firm's business and social environment changes, however, there will be a disconnect between the firm's strategic human capital resources and what is needed to manage in the new environment. As an example, Mark Fields moved up the ranks within Ford, first running Ford's Argentina operations, then managing Mazda Motor (a subsidiary of Ford), then serving as head of Ford's Premier Automotive Group and Ford of Europe, and finally taking the role of chief of the Americas division before being appointed COO in 2012 and then CEO in 2014. His career path characterized by managing Ford's different car brands and geographic regions reinforces a traditional perspective of the industry. However, the disruption of the auto industry due to digital technology and autonomous cars resulted in a severe gap between the knowledge and skill set that is essential but no longer sufficient to manage the future. CEO Fields' lack of vision to move Ford into the digital age led to his firing in 2015. Ford is not alone in having to manage digital disruption, as many auto firms found themselves ill-equipped to deal with the digital technology disruption occurring in the auto industry.

Deficiencies in a firm's strategic human capital resources can occur along many dimensions and are sometimes recognized, but not necessarily addressed. For example, the importance of artificial intelligence (AI) is not disputed; but, lacking an in-depth knowledge of its capabilities, the firm's executives may not fully understand the impact that the technology will have on their business model. Technological skills and knowledge can also reside at lower levels of the organization, but then fail to get the attention of the firm's leadership because management doesn't seem to care or understand. When the firm's leadership fails to recognize the implications of such a knowledge gap, the potential for an organizational crisis emerges.

Similar to the firm's executives, the strategic human capital resources residing in the firm's board are also defined by the processes and practices by which directors are appointed. The means by which directors are identified and appointed used to be a quite informal and closed process, where the Nomination Committee or the Chair or CEO would rely on "who they knew" to identify potential candidates. Private interviews of potential candidates with the board and CEO would follow and, through the process of vetting, an individual is identified to be nominated to the board. More recently, it has become a more formalized and professional search process as firms increasingly rely on executive search firms, especially in Europe where board gender diversity quotas need to be met. In the UK for example, governance regulations required that board selection is a formal search process, using an executive search firm.

Even when firms rely on executive search firms for the appointment of executives and board members, however, there is still a vetting process whereby the final candidate is chosen. In terms of background, the board and CEO are typically looking for someone they can relate to with a similar executive background to themselves and an individual who they feel comfortable with – by either knowing him/her directly or indirectly through business contacts. The screening and vetting process is subject to contextual influences and cognitive biases, which leads to the selection of candidates that are highly similar to existing board members and/or the CEO. Similarity-attraction theory suggests that individuals perceive individuals that are similar to themselves more positively (Montoya and Horton, 2004). Mutually shared experience or qualities, through homophily (i.e., an affinity for similar others), facilitate interactions and thereby foster personal connections. Whether it is conscious or not, individuals enjoy an easier mutual understanding and are more comfortable with others who share similar characteristics and experiences (Marsden, 1987; McPherson et al., 2001). The more positive perception results in a bias in the evaluation of individuals, leading to the appointment of individuals that are similar (Pulakos and Wexley, 1983; Tsui and O'Reilly, 1989; Wexley and Nemeroff, 1973). This has been shown to influence the selection of both the CEO and board directors (Westphal and Zajac, 1995; Wiersema et al., 2018; Zajac and Westphal, 1996). When individuals are attracted to others highly similar to themselves, it leads to promotion and appointment processes and practices that result in greater homogeneity in background and experiences as well as cognitive perspectives, resulting in a lack of dynamism to the firm's strategic human capital resources.

At the board level, social network biases also come into play since they not only influence the identification of prospective board candidates, but also operate in vetting those considered for appointment (Withers et al., 2012). Not surprisingly, boards are highly homogeneous on demographic characteristics (e.g., gender, age), and in their executive experience, knowledge, and skill sets – leading to similarity in cognitive perspectives and mindsets. While the composition of such a board may excel at providing advice in a world that is static, they may be ill-suited for being sensitive to or aware of issues that may lead to an organizational crisis or responding to negative events when they occur.

Lack of accountability and transparency in organizations also can arise from social processes in the firm's leadership, which can in turn lead to an organizational crisis. Corporate misconduct, poor performance, and errors of judgment may constitute behaviors that are ignored or never addressed due to psychological processes that affect social judgment such as ingroup–outgroup biases (Bettencourt et al., 1997). According to this theory, perception of actions and behaviors is influenced by whether the individual is an "ingroup" or "outgroup" member. When one is perceived as an ingroup member, the rest of the group (e.g., the board) will have a more positive perception, and thus will be less likely to blame the individual and hold the person accountable. From the perspective of corporate malfeasance, by being part of an exclusive "insider" club, such as the firm's TMT or board, individuals are reluctant to call out bad behavior on someone that is also a member of the club. The degree of awareness of sexual assault and harassment, for example, was very low until the allegations of sexual abuse by Harvey Weinstein created the #MeToo movement, which placed it front and center. What was clearly evident is that the misconduct was well known among leaders in the media and entertainment industry, yet no one was willing to call out the behavior. Instead, the parties that knew turned away and closed ranks to protect themselves rather than questioning and bringing attention and accountability to the sexual abuse.

These psychological processes hold especially true for boards, where social pressures to conform and the status and pecuniary rewards of membership to an exclusive group lead to group behavior in which no one wants to be "the skunk" at the picnic. As one director stated in regards to joining a board: "You are now a member of the most elite club in corporate America. You are afraid to do or say anything that gets you kicked off the island."

In summary, the composition of the firm's leadership in terms of their past experiences, knowledge, and skills is an important component of the firm's strategic human capital resources. The selection and appointment processes and practices at the board and executive level influence the stock of this resource. Not only does this resource represent a key component of the firm's dynamic managerial capability (Adner and Helfat, 2003), but, as I have argued, it also provides the firm with the capability by which to prevent and manage an organizational crisis. When a firm's leadership is highly homogeneous in terms of their experiences, background, and knowledge, it is likely to lead to cognitive perspectives that fail to recognize changes occurring within the firm's social and competitive environment, as well as a lack of awareness or sensitivity to the firm's various constituents. This knowledge gap means that the firm will not necessarily be aware of or sensitive to corporate misconduct or technological/competitive developments that could impair the firm's ability to compete. Given the social, technological, and competitive changes that firms must continually be aware of and stay abreast of, boards and top management teams must have the requisite strategic human capital resources to provide firms with the oversight and leadership needed.

NEED FOR TRANSFORMATIVE BOARDS AND TMTS

Companies must learn to navigate this changed world of increased scrutiny and accountability. Since the firm's leadership is command central when negative events occur, they must be better equipped to handle the challenges posed by an organizational crisis. With regard to corporate malfeasance, the board and executives of the firm are instrumental in setting the tone, as well as providing the incentive structure and creating an organizational climate that discourages unethical behavior as well as deciding how to respond to such events. Board and managerial oversight also determines the awareness and sensitivity to factors such as technological developments or investor expectations that can precipitate a potential organizational crisis. The upper echelon literature recognizes that executive and director appointments are highly important and influential in determining the strategic direction, corporate governance, and performance of the firm (Finkelstein et al., 2009). However, there has been little consideration as to the recruitment and promotion processes and practices, as well as the policies or actions that result in executive/director departure that determines the composition or stock of human capital resources available to the firm. We need to examine how these processes can be enhanced to arrive at strategic human capital resources that enable firms to better prevent and manage an organizational crisis.

An important component of the firm's strategic human capital resources is the skills, knowledge, and experiences that reside within its leadership. Earlier I suggested that recruitment and promotion practices have not enabled companies to be dynamic in renewing their stock of human capital resources, but instead lead to homogeneity in the skills, experiences, and knowledge that reside with the firm's leadership. This results in a shortfall in the strategic human capital resources residing within the firm's leadership in terms of its ability to manage in an environment where competitive, technological, and social factors have disrupted conventional thinking and norms. For the firm's strategic human capital resources to be more dynamic necessitates conducting a skill audit to identify the changes and developments in the firm's competitive marketplace and social context, as well as advancements in technologies that could have an impact on the firm. While this seems intuitively obvious and would lead to better-equipped management teams and boards, few organizations conduct such audits when it comes to their leadership team. Instead, as previously alluded to, the reliance on social networks and traditional practices in conjunction with psychological biases results in a tendency to appoint more of the same – e.g., individuals highly similar in terms of career experiences, backgrounds, and knowledge. A skill audit is difficult to conduct among a body of individuals that may not be sensitive to what is missing in terms of skills and knowledge. As one board member reflected, "after a while you become part of the furniture, it becomes difficult to get new thinking in there." From talking to board directors, it is usually not until a fresh face appears on the board with a different perspective that the board realizes what they are missing in terms of key skills and expertise. Thus, boards need to conduct self-evaluations and assess the firm's environment to identify the critical issues that the company faces and how well prepared they are to handle these. Consideration should be taken as to whether there is adequate awareness and sensitivity to the firm's various constituents and how they perceive the firm. A critical examination of the issues the firm's leadership needs to be attuned to can help identify the skills, knowledge, experiences, and/or perspectives that are missing. A continual self-evaluation of what is needed that takes into account the changing competitive, technological, and social context in which the firm operates should lead to a more dynamic board and management team that is better versed in dealing with organizational crises.

In addition to more proactively thinking about who is being recruited, managing the firm's strategic human capital resources so that the firm is better equipped to handle an organizational crisis also involves actively thinking about who departs the firm. While there may be some degree of formality in terms of processes and practices by which firms recruit and promote their executives and appoint board directors, there is typically little in the way of process or transparency as to what leads to departure within the executive and board ranks. A firm's executives can voluntarily depart the firm – either through retirement or being hired away – or they are dismissed.[2] It is the board that monitors and thus holds the firm's executives accountable. Prior research on CEO turnover has shown that the board is influenced by both the firm's performance and by external constituents, such as financial analysts, in dismissing the CEO (Denis and Serrano, 1996; Shen and Cannella, 2002; Wiersema and Zhang, 2011; Zhang, 2006). In addition, activist hedge funds, by drawing attention to poor performance and governance, have had a significant influence on CEO and board turnover (Brav et al., 2008). Corporate malfeasance also leads to involuntary turnover within the top management team (Arthaud-Day et al., 2006; Desai et al., 2006). The empirical evidence indicates that executive dismissal is a reactive response on the part of the board to restore the firm's legitimacy with its constituents (Suchman, 1995).

With regard to the board, once directors are appointed, they rarely leave of their own accord. While some firms have age limits for board directors, within the US and most of the world (the UK being the exception) there are no term limits to board directorships. Within the S&P 1500, average board director tenure is 8.7 years, with 20.4 percent of all board seats held by individuals 70 years of age or older (ISS, 2016). Technically, a board director needs to be voted on and approved by the firm's shareholders on a regular basis. However, given that they generally run unopposed, directors continue to serve until they are no longer nominated, resulting in little board refreshment. In addition, group dynamics within the board make it difficult for the board to have a conversation on non-renewing a particular director to the board. Only when a board member steps off the board is there an opportunity to appoint a new director. As a result, the process of board renewal is often too slow, resulting in stagnant boards composed of directors who are less likely to be current with changes in technological, competitive, or social factors that may precipitate an organizational crisis. Not surprisingly, in a recent survey two-thirds of institutional investors identified directors with long tenure as a cause for concern.

Activist hedge funds have brought attention to the problem of stale boards as their number one demand is to obtain board representation. They seek to appoint directors who possess industry knowledge and expertise to provide the requisite oversight which they find lacking in the firms they target. Their objective is that, by equipping the board with directors that are highly knowledgeable and not wedded to the past, they can influence the board to take actions to enhance firm value. With more than 100 activist-supported board director appointments in 2017 alone (Lazard Shareholder Advisory Group, 2018), they have had a significant influence on board composition.

The use of skill audits and imposing board term limits are two ways in which companies can generate executive and board renewal that can lead to strategic human capital resources that are better equipped to deal with an organizational crisis. Analyzing the technological, competitive, and social developments that are having an impact on the businesses of the firm will help with identifying the skills, knowledge, and experience that are needed at the top. Such an analysis should also include the broader social environment in which companies operate, and the various constituents of the firm and their concerns. Looking outside the organization to examine what is happening across other industries will enable a better understanding of how these developments are likely to have an impact on the firm. As an example, the impact of digital technologies, which is disrupting the automotive and entertainment industries, needs to be considered since it will likely affect every industry in a significant way. Failure to take into consideration how digital technologies are likely to impact one's industry can lead to a crisis precipitated by digital disruption to the company's business model. To prevent such a crisis requires executives and board members that think more broadly and are not constrained by conventional thinking. Similarly, activist hedge funds have altered the firm's relationship with its investor base, such that executives and boards now must be more attuned to their institutional investors.

The analysis underlying a skill audit should drive the processes and practices that determine who is appointed and/or promoted, as well as the career paths for executives, so that the requisite skills are acquired and developed. An understanding of the skills gap should also be used proactively to prune the firm's leadership so that renewal can occur. Companies should adopt term limits on board directorships and actively promote a healthy level of turnover within the board. For the executive ranks, critical evaluations of the entire top management team should be conducted by the board regularly to examine whether the firm's leadership has the requisite skills and what steps need to be taken to address any shortcomings. Actively managing both appointment and turnover within the board and top management should lead to greater renewal and improve the firm's stock of strategic human capital resources so that there is greater awareness of and sensitivity to issues that may lead to an organizational crisis.

Aside from regarding the firm's strategic human capital resources as something that needs to be actively managed, there is also the issue of what occurs within the board room and executive ranks. Even with a diverse leadership team, a firm can be plagued by behaviors and actions that put the firm at risk. Group norms and dynamics can lead to a failure to recognize and call out behaviors that are not acceptable, as well as a reluctance to ask hard questions or to raise awareness of issues that could potentially lead to an organizational crisis. Creating an atmosphere where thoughtful disagreement can occur is important in order to allow for a wider set of perspectives and greater transparency to highlight questionable behaviors or actions. To bring the needed change in dynamics, executive and board meetings should be more interactive to allow for such discussions to take place.

CONCLUSION

While strategy scholars are paying increasing attention to strategic human capital resources as a source of competitive advantage and as an important component of the firm's dynamic managerial capabilities (Adner and Helfat, 2003), our understanding of what determines the firm's strategic human capital resources is still little understood. In their review of the human capital literature, Nyberg et al. (2014) point out that too little attention is paid to the organizational processes that determine the firm's human capital resources. The deficiency in our understanding of the processes and practices that lead to executive selection, according to Berns and Klarner (2017), is due to our "event-based" orientation on executive succession. That is, extant research has predominantly focused on the determinants of executive succession and how firm performance (Boeker and Goodstein, 1993), governance (Shen and Cannella, 2002; Zajac and Westphal, 1996), and the nature of succession (e.g., routine versus non-routine) (Parrino, 1997) may drive the appointment decision. Far less attention has been paid to the processes by which executives are appointed, despite evidence that boards are not adept at executive selection (Wiersema, 2002). Similarly, scholarly research has not fully accounted for the socio-cognitive processes that influence the selection of board members (Withers et al., 2012). As a result, while executive selection and board appointments represent some of the most important decisions made by the board and are an important determinant of the firm's strategic human capital resources, little is known about the process and practices used to make these appointments.

Our lack of knowledge on the processes and practices underlying executive and board appointments means that not only do we not fully understand what determines an important component of the firm's strategic human capital resources, but we also lack an understanding of what leads to changes in the composition of this resource. Strategic human capital resources, like the firm's other resources, are dynamic in that firms have the capability to create, extend, or modify them. Since the firm's strategic human capital resources are determined by its "individual-level human resources" (Nyberg et al., 2014: 318), firms need the capability to enhance and renew the stock of their strategic human capital resources to adapt to changes in their environment.

In the discussion in this chapter, as in Chapter 20 by Bermiss and Darnell, we have sought to highlight the importance of the firm's strategic human capital resources to prevent and manage an organizational crisis. However, for firms to be better equipped at handling such negative events, they must enhance and renew the skills, knowledge, and experiences residing in their leadership. In analyzing the firm's stock of human capital resources at the leadership level, Kor and Mesko (2013) identify both team composition and team interactions as important components. Upper echelon research has predominantly focused on demographic characteristics such as age, education, and organizational tenure as determinants of team composition that can influence decision-making. But there are other drivers influencing both team composition and interaction. Socialization theory, for example, suggests that individuals learn the norms, customs, and values within the organization as well as the behaviors and perspectives that are customary (Van Maanen and Schein, 1979). These socialization pressures can lead to conformity in behavior and thinking. The implication of socialization is more profound for executives since it is likely to affect the entire organization. Thus, organizational socialization processes may contribute to the adoption of behaviors that may or may not be desirable. Recently, as a result of internal survey, women at Nike accused the company of workplace misconduct and discrimination. The *New York Times* revealed that the company has "a toxic work environment for women, with a boys' club culture that excluded them from promotions and leadership opportunities" (Creswell et al., 2018). After an internal investigation, CEO Mark Parker took actions to improve the company's culture by dismissing several senior managers amid allegations of harassment and discrimination, and addressing gender pay discrepancies.

Thus, the ability to prevent and manage an organizational crisis stems not only from individual-level differences within the firm's leadership due to background and experiences; it is also due to organizational socialization, which influences the perspective, values, and modes of behavior and thinking within the team. Companies and their executives and boards operate in an environment where it is all too easy to violate expectations of behavior. Yet, we know little about what determines the ability of the firm's strategic human capital resources to manage in such an environment. Instead, extant research has predominantly focused on trait characteristics as a determinant of organizational outcomes. The lack of attention to the determination of the firm's strategic human capital resources can be attributed in part to the difficulty of conducting such research. By drawing attention to the importance of the firm's strategic human capital resources, I hope to motivate research inquiry into the topic. For management scholars this represents a rich avenue for research that more fully examines the organizational processes that shape and mold behavior within the executive ranks. Similarly, research that seeks to better understand the process by which boards appoint directors and executives would provide much-needed insight into the "black box" that determines an important component of the firm's strategic human capital resources. While there are significant difficulties with assessing such information, an exploratory approach using field interviews would add considerably more insight than further empirical analysis of readily available data such as demographic traits.

The issue of understanding how organizational processes and practices influence the capability of the firm's strategic human capital resources is also a pressing issue for practitioners. To manage the firm's strategic human capital resources effectively, the firm's leaders need to have greater strategic oversight of the processes and practices that determine the composition of these resources. All too often firms caught in an organizational crisis are under intense pressure to manage the event. Not surprisingly, many respond in a ceremonial fashion by taking actions to indicate that they have done so (e.g., firing the executive responsible), without actually addressing the underlying processes that may be key causal factors. In light of an environment of increased scrutiny and accountability, and as a result of changes in technological and market forces, the likelihood that companies will encounter an organizational crisis as a result of malfeasance, personal misconduct, or errors of judgment is not set to diminish. Yet, many companies have processes and practices that are clearly not ideal for providing the requisite human capital resources to avoid such events. Boards need to be better equipped to guide the processes that determine the firm's strategic human capital resources at the top. In doing so, companies can become more adept at preventing the occurrence of an organizational crisis and in providing leadership to mitigate the effects of such events when they do occur.

CHAPTER SUMMARY

BOX 22.1 KEY TAKEAWAYS

1. The firm's strategic human capital resources that reside within the board and top management are key to preventing and managing an organizational crisis. However, recruitment and promotion practices can inhibit companies from renewing their strategic human capital resources in order to adapt to changes in their competitive, social, and technological context.
2. The processes and practices that lead to board of director appointments are particularly problematic in that they rely too much on "who you know." This has resulted in stagnant boards composed of directors who are less likely to be current with changes in technological, competitive, or social factors that may precipitate an organizational crisis.
3. Boards need to conduct skill audits to identify the changes and developments in the firm's competitive marketplace and social context as well as advancements in technology, and use these audits to identify the skills, knowledge, experiences, and perspectives that are needed within the top management team and within the board.

BOX 22.2 DIRECTIONS FOR FUTURE RESEARCH

1. Exploratory research is needed so that we can better understand the processes and practices that lead to executive and board appointments and how they can be improved. Rather than relying on secondary data, greater insight could be gained from interviewing the individuals (e.g., the board) making these appointments to understand the factors that determine the firm's strategic human capital resources.
2. Companies operate in an era of heightened attention due to the endless news cycle, social media, and activists in the capital market that highlight poor performance and deficient corporate oversight. Research addressing these changes in the firm's external context may shed light as to the role that these factors play in driving executive decision-making.
3. Organizational crises can stem from a variety of unforeseen events – from financial fraud, employee mistreatment, to personal misconduct. At the root of many of these events are the values and modes of behavior and thinking that reside within the organization. Research is needed to better understand how companies can manage their strategic human capital resources to minimize the underlying factors that lead to an organizational crisis.

NOTES

1. Activist hedge funds are private investment vehicles that acquire stakes in public companies in order to influence change in the companies they target. They are not subject to federal oversight, and have a compensation structure whereby they collect not only a 1–2 percent fee based on assets under management, but also earn 20 percent of the gain in value of the investment portfolio, which propels their desire to seek changes in the companies they target.

2. It should be noted that rarely do companies state that an executive or board member is dismissed, but instead announcements usually indicate the individual has resigned. Research on executive turnover has identified that many of these so-called "resignations" are in fact dismissals (Wiersema and Zhang, 2011), as evidenced by the absence of announcing the executive's replacement as well as by the fact that the departure was unexpected, resulting in a stock market reaction to the news.

REFERENCES

Adner, R., and Helfat, C. E. (2003). Corporate effects and dynamic managerial capabilities. *Strategic Management Journal*, *24*(10), 1011–25.

Arthaud-Day, M. L., Certo, S. T., Dalton, C. M., and Dalton, D. R. (2006). A changing of the guard: Executive and director turnover following corporate financial restatements. *Academy of Management Journal*, *49*, 1119–36.

Berns K. V., and Klarner P. (2017). A review of the CEO succession literature and a future research program. *Academy of Management Perspectives*, *31*(2), 83–108.

Bettencourt, B. A., Dill, K. E., Greathouse, S. A., Charlton, K., and Mulholland, A. (1997). Evaluations of ingroup and outgroup members: The role of category-based expectancy violation. *Journal of Experimental Social Psychology*, *33*(3), 244–75.

Boeker, W., and Goodstein J. (1993). Performance and successor choice: The moderating effects of governance and ownership. *Academy of Management Journal*, *36*(1), 172–86.

Brav, A., Wei, J., Partnoy, F., and Thomas, R. (2008). Hedge fund activism, corporate governance, and firm performance. *Journal of Finance*, *63*(4), 1729–75.

Brown, M. E., Treviño, L. K., and Harrison, D. A. (2005). Ethical leadership: A social learning perspective for construct development and testing. *Organizational Behavior & Human Decision Processes*, *97*(2), 117–34.

Creswell, J., Draper, K., and Abrams, R. (2018). At Nike, revolt led by women leads to exodus of male executives. *New York Times*, 28 April: A1. Retrieved from https://www.nytimes.com/2018/04/28/business/nike-women.html.

Denis, D. J., and Serrano, J. M. (1996). Active investors and management turnover following unsuccessful control contests. *Journal of Financial Economics*, *40*(2), 239–66.

Desai, H., Hogan, C. E., and Wilkins, M. S. (2006). The reputational penalty for aggressive accounting: Earnings restatements and management turnover. *Accounting Review*, *81*(1), 83–112.

Ferrell, O. C., LeClair, D. T., and Ferrell, L. (1998). The federal sentencing guidelines for organizations: A framework for ethical compliance. *Journal of Business Ethics*, *17*(4), 353–63.

Finkelstein, S., Hambrick, D. C., and Cannella, A. A. (2009). *Strategic Leadership: Theory and Research on Executives, Top Management Teams, and Boards*. Oxford: Oxford University Press.

Harris, J., and Bromiley, P. (2007). Incentives to cheat: The influence of executive compensation and firm performance on financial misrepresentation. *Organization Science*, *18*(3), 350–67.

ISS (2016). ISS 2016–2017 global policy survey. Institutional Shareholder Services. September 29.

Jurkiewicz, C. L., and Grossman, D. (2012). Evil at work. In Jurkiewicz, C. L. (ed.). *The Foundations of Organizational Evil*, Armonk, NY: Sharpe.

Kor, Y. Y., and Mesko, A. (2013). Dynamic managerial capabilities: Configuration and orchestration of top executives' capabilities and the firm's dominant logic. *Strategic Management Journal*, *34*(2), 233–44.

Lazard Shareholder Advisory Group (2018). Lazard's 2017 activism year in review. Retrieved from https://www.lazard.com/media/450414/lazards-review-of-shareholder-activism-q4-2017pdf.pdf.

Marsden, P. V. (1987). Core discussion networks of Americans. *American Sociological Review*, *52*(1), 122–31.

McPherson, M., Smith-Lovin, L., and Cook, J. M. (2001). Birds of a feather: Homophily in social networks. *Annual Review of Sociology*, *27*(1), 415–44.

Montoya, R. M., and Horton, R. S. (2004). On the importance of cognitive evaluation as a determinant of interpersonal attraction. *Journal of Personality and Social Psychology*, *86*(5), 696–712.

Murray, A. (2005). Hedge funds are new sheriffs of boardroom. *Wall Street Journal*, December 14.

Nyberg, A. J., Moliterno, T. P., Hale Jr, D., and Lepak, D. P. (2014). Resource-based perspectives on unit-level human capital: A review and integration. *Journal of Management*, *40*(1), 316–46.

Parrino, R. (1997). CEO turnover and outside succession a cross-sectional analysis. *Journal of Financial Economics*, *46*(2), 165–97.

Perrow, C. (1984). *Normal Accidents: Living with High-Risk Technologies*. New York: Basic Books.

Ployhart, R. E., and Moliterno, T. P. (2011). Emergence of the human capital resource: A multilevel model. *Academy of Management Review*, *36*(1), 127–50.

Pulakos, E. D., and Wexley, K. N. (1983). The relationship among perceptual similarity, sex, and performance ratings in manager-subordinate dyads. *Academy of Management Journal*, *26*(1), 129–39.

Seeger, M., Sellnow, T., and Ulmer, R. (2003). *Communications and Organizational Crisis*. Westport, CT: Praeger.
Shen, W., and Cannella, A. (2002). Power dynamics within top management and their impacts on CEO dismissal followed by inside succession. *Academy of Management Journal*, *45*(6), 1195–206.
Suchman, M. C. (1995). Managing legitimacy: Strategic and institutional approaches. *Academy of Management Review*, *20*(3), 571–610.
Trevino, L. K. (1986). Ethical decision making in organizations: A person-situation interactionist model. *Academy of Management Review*, *11*(3), 601–17.
Tsui, A. S., and O'Reilly III, C. A. (1989). Beyond simple demographic effects: The importance of relational demography in superior-subordinate dyads. *Academy of Management Journal*, *32*(2), 402–23.
Van Maanen, J., and Schein E. H. (1979). Toward of theory of organizational socialization. *Research in Organizational Behavior*, *1*, 209–64.
Victor, B., and Cullen, J. B. (1988). The organizational bases of ethical work climates. *Administrative Science Quarterly*, *33*(1), 101–25.
Westphal, J. D., and Zajac, E. J. (1995). Who shall govern? CEO/board power, demographic similarity, and new director selection. *Administrative Science Quarterly*, *40*(1), 60–83.
Wexley, K. N., and Nemeroff, W. F. (1973). The effects of racial prejudice, race of applicant, and biographical similarity on interviewer evaluations of job applicants. *Proceedings of the Annual Convention of the American Psychological Association*, 593–4. Retrieved from http://psycnet.apa.org.
Wiersema, M. F. (2002). Holes at the top: Why CEO firings backfire. *Harvard Business Review*, *80*(12), 70–77.
Wiersema, M. F., and Zhang, Y. (2011). CEO dismissal: The role of investment analysts. *Strategic Management Journal*, *32*(11), 1161–82.
Wiersema, M. F., Nishimura, Y., and Suzuki, K. (2018). Executive succession: The importance of social capital in CEO appointments. *Strategic Management Journal*, *39*(5), 1473–95.
Withers, M. C., Hillman, A. J., and Cannella Jr, A. A. (2012). A multidisciplinary review of the director selection literature. *Journal of Management*, *38*(1), 243–77.
Zajac, E. J., and Westphal, J. D. (1996). Who shall succeed? How CEO/board preferences and power affect the choice of new CEOs. *Academy of Management Journal*, *39*(1), 64–90.
Zhang, Y. (2006). The presence of a separate COO/president and its impact on strategic change and CEO dismissal. *Strategic Management Journal*, *27*(3), 283–300.

PART VII

COMPENSATING STRATEGIC HUMAN CAPITAL RESOURCES: INCENTIVES

23. A pay system model for turning human capital resources into action

Anthony J. Nyberg and Greg Reilly

Human capital resources (HCRs) are essential for firm success (Call et al., 2015; Nyberg et al., 2014; Ployhart et al., 2011; Reilly et al., 2014; Shaw et al., 1998; Wright et al., 1994). HCRs differ from other firm resources in that employees must be continually motivated and incentivized to stay and perform well (Coff, 1997). Pay is an especially important managerial lever affecting HCR make-up, motivation, and behaviors (Nyberg et al., 2018a). However, we lack clarity about how pay – the most common tool for affecting the sorting, motivation, and behavior of employees – ultimately drives unit performance (Gupta and Shaw, 2014; Larkin et al., 2012).

In this chapter, we focus on the mechanisms that link pay with HCRs and, ultimately, unit performance. To develop insights about pay, HCRs, and unit performance, we use HCRs as a conceptual bridge uniting two developed relationships – the links between pay and individual behaviors and between unit resources and performance.

HCRs are conceptualized (Ployhart and Moliterno, 2011) as "individual or unit-level capacities based on individual knowledge, skills, abilities, and other characteristics (KSAOs) that are accessible for unit-relevant purposes" (Ployhart et al., 2014: 374). This is based on the idea that the relevant KSAOs for achieving economic outcomes make up an employee's human capital (Becker, 1964). In a conceptual shift from the previous focus on individual human capital, however, researchers have turned attention to unit HCRs (Campbell et al., 2012), and this shift requires a parallel shift regarding the role of pay.

Pay, which includes "all forms of financial returns and tangible services and benefits employees receive as part of an employment relationship" (Newman et al., 2017: 677), is ubiquitous and consequential (Gerhart and Rynes, 2003). Although pay is well known to sort and motivate individual employees (e.g., Gupta and Shaw, 2014; Larkin and Leider, 2012; Lazear, 2000), we know substantially less about pay effects on an overall HCR (Nyberg et al., 2018a). Most research into pay as a motivator relies on individual-based theories (e.g., expectancy), assuming that individual performance outcomes aggregate to influence unit outcomes (Larkin et al., 2012; Nyberg et al., 2016). However, this simplified view of pay as it relates to unit performance fails to answer three fundamental questions: 1) How do salary levels affect HCRs and unit outcomes? 2) How does the proportion of pay for performance (PFP) affect HCRs and unit outcomes? 3) How does the organizational level of PFP targets affect HCRs and unit outcomes (e.g., paying employees for reaching individual goals versus paying them for reaching unit goals)?

To explain how pay decisions affect composition, quality, and effectiveness of HCRs, we use components of the multidimensional HCR construct (Ployhart et al., 2014) to provide a pay system framework. We show how three key pay practice decisions enhance HCR utilization via sorting and incentivizing employees. This lens provides insights for building on prior pay research.

CURRENT PAY AND UNIT PERFORMANCE CONVERSATION

Most pay research continues to focus on the individual (Gerhart, 2017; Gerhart et al., 2009), but scholars recognize that pay is related to unit performance (e.g., Gerhart and Milkovich, 1990; Gerhart et al., 1992; Nyberg et al., 2018a). Extant research shows why a new model is needed for examining how pay systems affect employees and units.

Pay Systems and Pay Practice Decisions

In designing pay systems, firms must determine the strategic value of their employees (Lepak and Snell, 1999), the amount they should pay given their expectations, and the bases used to measure performance (that pay is contingent on), such as individual behavior or unit performance. They also must weigh market factors such as demand for skills, strategic factors for those skills, and social factors such as how employees and other stakeholders view pay levels. To consider how pay systems affect HCRs, we review three key pay practice decisions.

Salary level

Organizations generally make pay level decisions relative to the market. Their decisions affect how they attract applicants and retain employees (Gerhart and Trevor, 1996). If pay appears to be equitable in comparison with referent others, people will be attracted to the firm and employees will be more likely to be satisfied with their pay (Adams, 1963; Trevor and Wazeter, 2006). Additionally, efficiency wage theory suggests that paying above market attracts employees who will be motivated to work harder to retain their high pay (Akerlof, 1984), leading to high-quality talent pools, higher individual potential, lower turnover (Akerlof and Yellen, 1986) and, consequentially, higher unit performance.

In contrast, organizations may perform better by offering below-market pay, especially when employees lack movement opportunities or knowledge about mobility options, or when an abundant labor supply makes it relatively inexpensive to replace departing employees (Cascio, 2000). It may also be possible for companies to pay above-market salaries for some jobs and below-market salaries for others (Gerhart, 2000).

PFP proportions

Academic researchers (e.g., Ariely et al., 2009; Deci and Ryan, 1980; Deming, 1986; Lawler, 2000; Ockenfels et al., 2014; Pfeffer, 1998) and the popular business press (e.g., Green, 2010; Kohn, 1993; Pink, 2009) have questioned the effectiveness of PFP. However, it is clear that PFP affects individual performance outcomes (e.g., Gerhart et al., 2009; Jenkins et al., 1998). The discrepancy in perspectives may indicate that contextual factors associated with implementation, research design, and reward salience can lead to discrepant conclusions (e.g., Gerhart and Rynes, 2003; Lawler and Jenkins, 1992; Mitra et al., 1997; Nyberg et al., 2016).

Empirical evidence shows that PFP is associated with higher individual performance in the rewarded dimensions (Fang and Gerhart, 2012; Gerhart, 2017; Gerhart and Fang, 2014, 2015; Shaw, 2015). There is also evidence that collective PFP (or pay that is contingent on collective outcomes) leads to higher collective performance (Alchian and Demsetz, 1972; Conroy et al., 2014; Dumaine, 1994; Nyberg et al., 2018a) as PFP enhances quality of talent, the pursuit of common goals, and competitive parity (Gerhart and Fang, 2014; Gerhart and Rynes, 2003; Nyberg, 2018a; Shaw, 2015).

In contrast with the processes that drive individual PFP (Gerhart et al., 2009), complex social processes are involved in influencing collective outcomes (Beersma et al., 2003). Hence, to understand how PFP proportions affect HCRs, we must consider the sorting and incentive effects (Gerhart and Rynes, 2003; Lazear, 1986). Further heightening the challenge is that the literature has generally relied on individual theory to explain collective outcomes, and has thus failed to consider the social complexity involved when groups work together to pursue common goals.

Organizational level of PFP targets

Another critical pay practice decision involves determining whether PFP will be targeted at individual- or unit-level. PFP can motivate specific behaviors (Gerhart et al., 2009), partly because pay is an instrumental exchange medium (Locke et al., 1980) for directing employee action (Jenkins et al., 1998; Shaw and Gupta, 2007) and attitudes (Shaw et al., 2003) by increasing attention, focus, time, and effort on the specified goals (Chang and Wang, 2019; Gerhart and Rynes, 2003). However, a focus on the paid individual targets may have unintended consequences at other levels of the organization (Lawler, 2001), like failing to perform other behaviors important to the organization (Pfeffer, 1998). For example, PFP that rewards individual sales performance may damage unit performance by inhibiting cooperation and helping behaviors (Barnes et al., 2011). PFP targets can conflict both within and across levels. For example, customer service suffers when PFP is designed to both motivate sales and customer service (Sharma and Sarel, 1995). Similarly, pay for reducing unit inventory is likely to divert attention from the need for low-cost purchasing and cause overall decline in timely delivery. Consequently, organizations must carefully determine which organization level of PFP targets will drive optimal performance.

To offset individualistic behaviors created by PFP focused on individual targets, organizations often attach pay outcomes to higher organizational level targets, for example by awarding stock options for overall organizational performance. By offering unit-level PFP along with individual-level PFP, it may be the case that mixed messages of two different PFP practices could weaken the effect of either single pay practice. We can reasonably expect that the organizational level of PFP focused on the individual targets or unit targets will alter the relationship among individuals and change behaviors, thus affecting employee coordination and communication. For example, adding unit-level pay can encourage group cohesion and teamwork (Bamberger and Levi, 2009; Barnes et al., 2011; Conroy and Gupta, 2015).

Pay System Mechanisms

The extant research focuses on two primary mechanisms by which pay systems influence unit performance outcomes (Gerhart and Milkovich, 1990; Lazear, 1986, 1999). Pay has a *sorting effect* as it influences the composition of the workforce (via attraction, selection, and attrition; Schneider, 1987). Pay also has an *incentive effect* when it influences the motivation, attitudes, attention, effort, and behavior of current employees.[1]

Sorting effects

Sorting is the degree to which employees select organizations based on the pay type provided by the organization. Sorting works through both employee attraction and attrition. The HCR composition depends on competitive pay that attracts applicants and retains employees (Nyberg et al., 2014), thus affecting the skills and abilities contained in the talent pool (Gerhart et al., 2009). Salary levels (and fixed benefits) are known to affect employee quality (Akerlof, 1984; Cappelli and Chauvin, 1991), but the sorting literature has primarily examined how different types of pay attract different types of employee (Gerhart and Rynes, 2003). For instance, one organization switched from a system that paid employees a fixed amount regardless of output to a piece rate system, and found that employees who favored a piece rate system quickly replaced workers who preferred a fixed rate (Lazear, 2000). An experiment also showed that higher performers were more likely to prefer pay based on output (Cadsby et al., 2007).

Similarly, pay preferences were shown to affect individual choices about where to work (Cable and Judge, 1994). Furthermore, applicants can see pay systems as signaling job attractiveness by providing information about ambiguous organizational attributes (Gerhart et al., 1992; Rynes and Miller, 1983). Over time, the higher the percentage of individual PFP, the greater likelihood of attracting good performers who have higher risk tolerance and tend to be confident about their skills (Dohmen and Falk, 2011; Larkin and Leider, 2012). However, it is unclear how the organizational level at which pay is targeted enhances or undermines sorting effects. Sorting mechanisms may work exactly the same under individual PFP or unit-level PFP targets (e.g., team, department). Alternatively, higher performers may eschew high levels of PFP when that PFP targets unit-level outcomes because of concerns about free riding. Pay for performance may also be context-dependent. For instance, in some contexts, high performers appear to prefer team PFP over individual PFP, despite the threat of free riding or concerns about being paid inadequately for individual productivity (Hamilton et al., 2003).

Sorting also affects employee attrition as employees learn how the organization functions. For example, if PFP is based on team-level targets, do all employees pull their weight or do some free ride? According to meta-analyses (e.g., Hoffman and Woehr, 2006; Kristof-Brown et al., 2005; Verquer et al., 2003), when individuals fit their workplace (and rewards can be a dimension of organizational fit), they tend to stay longer and have lower turnover intentions. In contrast, workers are often pushed out for low performance or voluntarily leave because of low job satisfaction; but pay systems can directly or indirectly increase both performance and job satisfaction, decreasing the likelihood of leaving (Nyberg, 2010; Trevor, 2001; Trevor et al., 1997).

Consequently, changes to PFP proportions are likely to focus employee attention on outcomes related to PFP. Hence, higher PFP proportions based on common outcomes will also attract employees of similar quality and characteristics because potential employees perceive that the organization desires and rewards common employee attributes. Thus the mechanisms of sorting and attraction–selection–attrition (ASA; Schneider, 1987) lead to a more homogenous workforce.

Incentive effects

Motivation is directly tied to pay (Jenkins et al., 1998; Locke et al., 1980; Rynes et al., 2004). Motivated employees work toward outcomes that are relevant to the attainment of tangible and intangible rewards (Gagné and Deci, 2005; Vroom, 1964). Collective group incentives will create common goals, generating aggregate, common group effort to achieve the same rewarded outcomes (Kerr and Tindale, 2004; Robbins, 2001). Motivation is reinforced when individuals see others acting toward the same goal (Aarts et al., 2004). Common motivations promote shared norms, so that each member adjusts expectations regarding effort and performance accordingly (Hackman and Morris, 1975). Thus, higher PFP proportions directed to the workforce as a whole should generate a group focus on similar goals, which may not align with organizational desires.

Pay is more motivational when clearly connected to performance and when individuals feel that their specific inputs have a positive influence, often called "line of sight" (Gerhart and Rynes, 2003; Lawler, 1971). However, organizations often fail to tie pay to desired actions. To overcome this, they should make extraordinary efforts to ensure that annual performance reviews tie pay to the desired outcomes and accurately reflect individual input to avoid causing workers to perceive that pay is unrelated to performance (Rynes et al., 2005). Thus, effective feedback motivates employees by showing that pay is strongly related to performance (Locke et al., 1980). Additionally, frequent, quality feedback is associated with development (Kahneman, 2011) and individual performance. That is, "Consistent with previous theorizing in both economics (Milgrom and Roberts, 1992) and psychology (Vroom, 1964), we tentatively propose that (a) pay differentiations will be more motivational to the extent that differences in performance are clearly detectable and measureable and (b) observed pay differentiations are correlated with those differences" (Gerhart and Rynes, 2003: 260).

Shortcomings of Extant Frameworks

Understanding the relation between pay and unit performance faces two main challenges. First, individual pay-driven behaviors have been weakly connected, conceptually and empirically, with the desired collective outcomes, indicating that we fail to fully understand how pay systems influence unit outcomes and lack fundamental understanding of the most common and important mechanisms that convert individual resources into more complex collective-level HCRs (Nyberg et al., 2018a). To address this first weakness, we show how pay helps to build HCR capacities and ensure that they are reliably enacted over time.

Second, researchers have inadequately explored the connections between pay practice decisions and the two pay system mechanisms in terms of their interactions in the creation and enactment of HCRs. Economists note that productivity requires that employees are matched to incentive systems (Milgrom and Roberts, 1992). When pay is matched well to HCRs, performance should be higher than when it is poorly matched (Weller et al., 2019). Hence, our model explains how pay systems influence behaviors across contexts. Failure to understand how and why pay system mechanisms coexist can lead to simplified expectations, and obscure an examination of how pay systems affect overall HCRs. To address this issue, we explore how each pay decision combines with the other two pay decisions to affect HCR.

USING AN HCR LENS TO BETTER UNDERSTAND UNIT-LEVEL PAY EFFECTS

One key shortcoming of pay research is a failure to understand the link between pay systems and unit outcomes or to understand how pay practices and systems turn into performance, sometimes referred to as the "black box." The linkage is more understandable when we apply an HCR lens (Nyberg et al., 2018b) to devise pay systems that more effectively achieve specific and often dynamic objectives.

Researchers from diverse fields such as design, operations, and strategic management have long argued that unit performance is superior when business processes are designed to achieve specified aims (Nyberg et al., 2016). Furthermore, the resource-based view (RBV) suggests that business process designs will yield higher performance outcomes when resources are aligned and complementary, waste is reduced, and effort is focused. Although this theorizing has long included human resources, we deepen that work by concentrating on its implications for HCR and the pay practices meant to influence them.

Organizations enhance unit performance by hiring employees who have KSAOs that will strengthen the combination of KSAOs prevalent in the firm (Barney, 1991; Ployhart et al., 2014). The KSAOs of a new hire or newly promoted member of the unit must combine with the KSAOs of current members. Individual selection can also generate collective-level resources (Ployhart et al., 2014; Ployhart and Moliterno, 2011). The resource-based view predicts that valuable resources can influence unit performance by enabling strategy enactment (Barney, 1991). A critical mass of valuable human capital is essential if HCRs are to influence unit performance (Dierickx and Cool, 1989), even when high-quality human capital is available. For example, many retail units value customer service orientation; but when a store has too few employees, they cannot provide adequate customer service even if they are highly service oriented (Ployhart et al., 2009). The precise critical mass threshold likely differs according to many factors such as industry, environmental complexity, and competitive environment. More important, the relationship between a valuable HCR and unit performance is affected by incentives, unit pay, and the stock of KSAOs within the unit (Hausknecht and Holwerda, 2013; Hausknecht and Trevor, 2011; Nyberg and Ployhart, 2013).

We suggest that an HCR-based view, which connects people with unit outcomes, means that higher unit performance is associated with greater fit among HCRs, better alignment between HCRs and other resources, and better fit between HCRs and the strategies for achieving performance objectives. The thinking mirrors predictions that resources are generally related to unit performance. It also aligns with practitioner advice in human resource management (Barriere et al., 2018), suggesting the need to first identify firm strategy, process capabilities, and the skills needed before considering *who* is right for a role.

HCR-based view thinking implies that firms could define a wide range of specific HCRs according to process and resource designs aimed at achieving performance outcomes. Although firms hire employees to join their team, managers using HCR-based view thinking are likely to assess potential hires according to whether they meet specific HCR needs to move business processes closer to desired levels. Pay system designers will focus on assigning pay levels that will persuade employees with particular HCRs to select into or out of firms.

HCRs can function at both individual and collective levels (Ployhart et al., 2014), which highlights a complex, additional insight about the pay–unit performance relationship. Specifically, pay should attract, retain, and motivate employees who have individual HCRs such as knowledge and skills and also contribute to creating a collective-level HCR through influencing the emergent processes, such as transactive memory systems, in which they are one of many employees vital to the usefulness of the resource.

HCR Capacity versus HCR Enactment

One aspect of HCRs is that they describe potential rather than realized *capacities* for performance from individuals or groups (Ployhart et al., 2014). Consequently, we can distinguish between HCR capacity and the enactment of the HCR capacity, defined as the realized usage of specific HCRs at a given performance level at a given time. For example, a creative team acts as an advertising agency applying HC and collective HCR to identify what sells and to translate those ideas into a finished product. Capacity is not a discrete have/have not proposition. Rather, for each type of HCR noted above, a *level of capacity* is implied (Nyberg et al., 2014). Just as an industrial machine's capacity is defined as the maximum level of output it produces, the advertising team would have a maximum possible capacity for each of its HCRs. Furthermore, an industrial machine is likely to produce an actual output that is less than its capacity. Similarly, employees perform below their full capacity at various times. This distinction between HCR capacity and enactment has important implications for how pay can influence unit performance via HCRs because we must also consider that pay plays a role in enacting the HCR capacity. At times, realized output can come close to the defined capacity of a HCR. However, one key unique aspect of HCRs is that realized output will often be far below capacity because of the complexities of employee motivation and behavior. Although an industrial machine or automated conveyor can be expected to generate output at consistent levels, people are more complex. These insights provide another understanding of how pay influences HCR effects on unit outcomes by determining which HCRs are more or less likely to be available and enacted near capacity.

Pay impact on HCR capacity

When pay system designers consider organizational needs, their understanding of which HCRs are desirable is valuable, but only as a starting point. Instead, the distinction between the make-up of HCRs within the workforce and the need to motivate the workers who possess those HCRs suggests a wide array of targets. Although pay systems usually focus on individual behaviors, an HCR lens encourages targeting the collective of employees that makes up the HCR for pay-based rewards. Decision makers should start by considering the end goal of unit performance.

HCRs can be measured in different ways. Most scholars consider average KSAO level, but an HCR-based view shows that minimum, maximum, or variance of HCRs may better reflect the construct to explain unit performance. We suggest that the ideal choice of HCR measurement is context-dependent. For example, to ensure adherence to regulation, units need minimum regulatory knowledge. No further unit performance benefits accrue when additional people possess the same knowledge.

Pay impact on HCR enactment

The benefits of HCR-based view thinking we have discussed have focused on the potential for pay to affect HCR capacities in ways that are most beneficial for unit performance. We must also consider how pay can influence those HCRs to be enacted into desired behaviors over time. Rather than focusing on individual behaviors, pay system designers might analyze the variance between unit capacities for specific individuals or group behaviors and the actual performance of people and groups over time. In some situations, PFP could be effective when pay targets HCRs with high variance between capacity and enactment rather than simply targeting the most valuable HCRs.

Firms can also identify why some HCR enactment is below the HCR capacity. For instance, a programmer might rely heavily on creativity for yielding rapid, innovative, and effective solutions, and the programmer's capacity would likely reflect the results. However, creativity by nature is difficult to apply effectively and consistently, so the programmer might enact creative skills at lower levels in some circumstances. We might also expect enactment to be lower than capacity for utilization of HCRs where incentives are highly important. In some cases, people may enact certain HCR capacities only if the right incentives are applied. Therefore, pay designers should understand which HCRs are most and least likely to be enacted and further developed with different pay decisions.

A PAY SYSTEM PERSPECTIVE

Researchers and practitioners often ignore considering pay system complexity despite it being necessary to understand how the pay system influences the HCR capacity and enactment. Some of the research challenge involves the number of moving parts and the naturally recursive nature of each aspect of the system on most other aspects of the system. Our version is also simplified, but it is a beginning for considering how three key pay practice decisions combine to work through two key mechanisms to influence the capacity and enactment of the HCR.

Sorting Effects

Current HCR descriptions tend to focus on the emergent qualities that lead to HCR formation once employees are within the unit (Wright et al., 2014), ignoring how employees with desirable HCRs are attracted to the unit. To understand how to maximize the formation of HCRs, particularly when individuals within the HCR have potentially competing interests (Cerasoli et al., 2014; Garbers and Konradt, 2014; Jenkins et al., 1998), we must consider the effects of pay practice decisions, the organizational tools designed to attract employees and affect their attitudes and behaviors (Conroy et al., 2014; Gupta and Shaw, 2014; Shaw, 2014; Trevor et al., 2012).

Sorting effects of salary level

As discussed by Conroy in Chapter 1, salary level matters as it affects pay satisfaction and sorting (Gerhart and Rynes, 2003), both for attracting and retaining HCRs. Firms that offer high salary levels signal the market that they are high-quality employers, leading to higher applicant interest and overcoming the information asymmetry common in hiring

(Chadwick, 2017). Higher salary levels can also increase HCR capacity by decreasing HCR turnover. Thus, salary levels affect the stock and flow of HCR capacity or the quality of HCR and its leavers, as Hausknecht describes (see Chapter 27). Salary level affects HCRs by influencing individuals to self-select into and out of the firm. If a firm pursues an above-market pay level strategy, it should attract more talented employees than its competitors. Firms that pursue below-market pay level strategies will attract applicants who have relatively lower individual human capital in domains that are highly sought after by talent market competitors. In this case, a potentially viable talent strategy is to build a differentiated production function and complementary resource structure that favors less-demanded human capital characteristics rather than the most popular human capital capabilities. Similarly, a company can purposely structure its HCR and other resources to benefit from HC that is otherwise undervalued in the marketplace.

Sorting effects of salary level and PFP proportions

When we consider salary levels with PFP proportions rather than either alone, different insights occur. For instance, salary levels are likely to influence HCR capacity through sorting effects, but so will PFP proportions (Larkin et al., 2012; Lazear, 2000). However, it is unclear how salary level and PFP proportions interact to affect sorting and HCR make-up. According to our understanding, higher salary levels should reduce employee concerns about pay risks. Thus, high salary levels may induce risk-averse employees to apply for positions that pay contingent on performance, which they might avoid otherwise. Additionally, low salary levels may cause pay dissatisfaction, and thus make recruiting and retaining employees more difficult. However, combined with high PFP proportions, relatively low salary levels can attract employees who believe they can achieve higher total pay through greater performance.

Sorting effects of salary level, PFP proportions, and organizational level of PFP targets

Pay research primarily focuses on the individual (Gerhart et al., 2009). Although a rich history of pay research has examined collectives such as teams (Guthrie and Hollensbe, 2004), departments (Rynes et al., 2005), and upper echelons (Sesil and Lin, 2011), most of the work examined how individual or collective pay can enhance total group output, but has rarely examined *how* pay helps develop individual talent into a cohesive functioning HCR capacity (Nyberg et al., 2018a). Evidence is clear that both salary level and PFP proportions can affect who joins and who leaves the firm (Gerhart and Rynes, 2003), although the two constructs are rarely examined together in the context of sorting (Kuvaas et al., 2017). In addition to the two pay practice decisions, organizations must also determine the organizational level at which to target PFP. Even pay theories that do talk about how to achieve more effective employee performance geared toward collective outcomes do not adequately consider the full effect of pay systems (Nyberg et al., 2018a). For instance, an agency theory perspective suggests aligning the interests of agents with principles to entice agents to behave according to principles, but it fails to explain sorting effects resulting from focusing PFP on collective outcomes.

For example, as discussed, salary levels lead to higher attraction and reduced attrition, which are also influenced by the relative presence and proportion of PFP. However, we do not know how the two pay decisions interact with concerns about the organizational level at which PFP is focused, or how salary levels may combine with PFP proportions when PFP is targeted at different organizational levels to overcome or exacerbate potential challenges of pay based on collective outcomes. For instance, high PFP proportions based on team-level PFP targets could attract employees who prefer being on teams, and thus influence HCR capacity. In contrast, teams literature often assumes that collective-level PFP targets could lead higher performers to eschew such situations to avoid carrying the load for others. Alternatively, it may depend on position in the company relative to the level at which pay is focused (e.g., line of sight). Thus, for instance, stock options may be useful for attracting talented members of the top management team (TMT), but less so for employees at lower levels of the organization.

Incentive Effects

The challenge in understanding the role of pay in effecting the motivation and behavior of the HCR must also be considered from both individual and collective perspectives. Nevertheless, most pay research is rooted exclusively in economic (e.g., agency theory) or psychological theories (e.g., expectancy theory) without much consideration for the other perspective (Larkin et al., 2012; Nyberg et al., 2016). Research involving individual responses to pay strongly relies on psychological theories such as expectancy theory (Vroom, 1964), whereas the attempts to understand pay influence on organizations have been traditionally focused within an economics framework (Jensen and Meckling, 1976). Compounding these challenges is that psychology and economics researchers rarely exchange lessons (Gupta and Shaw, 2014; Shaw, 2014). Interest in bridging conversations is increasing (e.g., Larkin et al., 2012; Nyberg et al., 2016), but the lack of clearly defined HCR-relevant pay research (Gupta and Shaw, 2014; Shaw, 2014, 2015) prevents us understanding how pay affects HCR formulation and motivation.

Incentive effects of salary level

Although pay levels clearly influence HCR capacity through sorting, we are less clear about the incentive effects of salary level. Intuitively, higher salary should motivate higher performance; but we lack empirical clarity as to how or why, particularly if increased performance is not tied directly to pay. Efficiency wage theory explains that a higher salary level attracts higher performers and motivates sufficient performance to keep the position (Akerlof, 1984). However, beyond understanding that high salary levels attract higher performers (sorting) and motivates enough performance to avoid being fired, how salary level motivates and shapes the behavior of employees is indeterminate, potentially meaning that salary level predicts sorting but not incentive effects.

Incentive effects of salary level and PFP proportions

Several meta-analyses and reviews have shown that the incentive effects of PFP affect performance (e.g. Gerhart et al., 2009; Gerhart and Rynes, 2003; Guzzo et al., 1985; Jenkins et al., 1998; Locke et al., 1980). Furthermore, employees tend to focus on job aspects that are tied to PFP (Locke et al., 1980). Although salary level may not necessarily directly affect HCR motivation, it may do so when considered in combination with PFP. The challenge of understanding the influence of PFP proportions on these outcomes is further complicated by the potentially different outcomes based on each individual's PFP proportion versus salary level within a team or work group. For instance, if salary level is relatively low compared to the PFP proportions, employees may focus even more on aspects that will be rewarded through PFP. In contrast, under relatively high levels of secure pay compared to the PFP proportion, employees may be less motivated by PFP. It is unclear how salary level and PFP proportions interact, but it is likely that they could mutually enhance or suppress effects.

Incentive effects of salary level, PFP proportions, and organizational level of PFP targets

How salary levels combine with PFP to overcome or exacerbate challenges associated with that level at which PFP is targeted is also unclear. Challenging the alignment of these interests is the lack of clarity about how to incentivize employees to exert maximum effort while delivering unit outcomes (DeMatteo et al., 1998). Paying employees based on unit outcomes can help align individual incentives with unit outcomes; but individual incentives can undermine team performance, and collective-based incentives can undermine individual performance by encouraging social loafing (Karau and Williams, 1993; Pearsall et al., 2010) and discouraging cooperation (Bamberger and Levi, 2009).

Through thinking about all three pay practice decisions, organizations might be able to leverage one to offset challenges of the others. For instance, firms might overcome the challenges of targeting PFP to organizational levels other than the individual (e.g., shirking) by offering PFP proportions high enough to engender focus and effort. Similarly, examining the role of unit pay outside the lab may indicate that salary level makes a meaningful difference in overcoming shirking concerns. For example, when salary level or PFP proportions are sufficiently high, the threat or fear of losing that position may be so great that it overcomes shirking concerns. In contrast, relatively low salary levels and/or small PFP proportions could heighten the sense that others could carry the load, thus increasing shirking potential and reducing incentive effects.

In situations with a high proportion of PFP and where PFP targets are focused on unit-level outcomes – such as when a high proportion of PFP is tied to team-level performance (e.g., team sports, scientists, or entrepreneurs) – we would expect the focus would be on unit outcomes. In such situations, employees would be motivated to take risks to achieve unit outcomes. For example, in start-up firms where the entrepreneurial team is heavily incentivized by stock if the value rises, they would want to see the firm do well and embrace risk taking because stock options motivate risk taking. The sorting effect would likely result in more risk-taking employees seeking a risk-seeking team-like environment. This fits particularly well in small start-up firms where roles are often more ambiguous and require mutual help and extra-role behaviors. Such a model could create a climate for risk taking and teamwork.

Alternatively, when the PFP proportion is low relative to total pay or salary, and most of the PFP targets are at the individual level, the situation may provide little incentive for risk taking or assisting others, attracting less ambitious, individually focused employees who are also risk averse. In contrast, under high relative proportion levels of PFP incorporating individual targets, we could expect highly confident, high performers who seek risks (Larkin and Leider, 2012) but potentially fail to generate supportive behaviors. High PFP proportions incorporating individual-level targets are often found in stagnant situations where tasks are more independent and in sales jobs where companies focus on specific individual goals to induce individual effort and focus.

IMPLICATIONS AND AVENUES FOR FUTURE RESEARCH

The shift from examining human capital at the individual level to the HCR level (e.g., Nyberg et al., 2014; Ployhart et al., 2014) creates new strategic thinking about how employees are motivated to help organizations compete (Wright et al., 2014). Investigations necessarily combine what we know from micro- and macro-level research to explain how various actors are motivated and can collectively achieve higher-order outcomes (Coff and Raffiee, 2015; Hollenbeck and Jamieson, 2015; Kryscynski and Ulrich, 2015; Nyberg and Wright, 2015; Ployhart, 2015). However, conversations about HCRs should examine the role of pay as the primary lever organizations use to influence the make-up and motivations of HCRs.

Directions for Further Research

Pay and leaders

Leaders must carefully establish and communicate pay information, cognizant of the expected and the unintended collective outcomes that may occur in dynamic systems. For example, group leaders might set pay objectives that inform workers about expected behaviors; but if other pay decisions conflict with or fail to support the intended behaviors, the pay objectives will probably fail to evoke the expected outcomes. When leaders share objectives with lower levels (e.g., a CEO announces new product development plans), the objectives will be motivational depending on whether the related objectives are communicated throughout the organization and remain consistent. Pay affects leaders' behavior too, so the pay factor will affect employees across organizational levels.

Furthermore, leaders must stay vigilant because system efficacy can change even without clear disrupters. Shifts in complexity, employees, referent others (even outside the system), and pay objectives all affect pay system outcomes. If a leader emphasizes specific objectives, employees are likely to alter their attention to focus on those objectives, even if the pay system remains the same. Adding a new objective or emphasizing a current objective can reduce effort and attention to other areas. Leaders must then anticipate diminished productivity elsewhere, even in previously strong areas. Similar effects are likely at the group level. Future research would benefit from examining the role of leaders in communicating pay systems.

Strategic HR management

Strategic HR management research (e.g., Wright et al., 2001; Wright and McMahan, 1992) often addresses HR practice–unit performance relationships by assuming an aggregate level of human capital (Wright and McMahan, 2011), believing in the importance of aligning HR practices (Becker and Gerhart, 1996). Researchers have long sought to explain the black box of mechanisms that allow HR policies and practices to influence collective outcomes and ultimately affect organizational performance (Bowen and Ostroff, 2004; Cappelli and Sherer, 1991; Gerhart, 2005). For example, Liao et al. (2009) examined high-performance work practices from aggregate employee perspectives and related them to service performance. Strategic HR management scholars focus less on the nature of HCR and more on how to influence HCR to drive performance, such as how HR practices relate to unit performance through the mediating effects of HCR (Nyberg et al., 2018b).

Additional mechanisms should be considered when considering how work practices can optimize the coordination, communication, and motivation of employees to maximize organizational performance by aligning pay practices across a collective pay system.

In addition, considering pay as a system suggests new thinking about HR practices. Aligning HR practices is commonly believed important for achieving organizational outcomes (Becker and Gerhart, 1996; Delery and Doty, 1996), but thinking about pay as a system reveals that the assumption might fail under specific circumstances. Pay is likely a unique HR function, for which weak alignment can offer benefits. This argument reveals multiple opportunities for exploring how pay systems can best operate with other HR practices, organizational strategy, and the external environment.

Microfoundations

Strategic management literature is increasingly interested in microfoundations (Felin and Foss, 2005; Felin and Hesterly, 2007; Foss, 2011) – often articulated as a need to understand individual-level constructs in the context of firm-level theorizing – with a desire to understand emergent human capital processes (Coff and Kryscynski, 2011). These ideas have been advanced by contrasting individual- and collective-level explanations (Felin et al., 2015). PFP in HCR informs this research by providing means to identify how pay practices emerge to become collective-level explanations of organizational actions. Thinking of pay as a system suggests new thinking about the strategic value of compensation, but more research is required to identify how to use pay to compete strategically.

Additional questions

Rigorous empirical testing is also needed to confirm the relationships posited here. For example, what is the best mechanism for determining HCR pay effectiveness? How and when does the relative importance of different pay practices change over time or by context? Which measures capture the configuration of elements in the HCR pay system? Researchers could examine the role of context too; for example, how do culture and environmental complexity buffer or magnify total effects in a pay system?

An immediate, potentially far-reaching implication might also stem from studying the effects of how pay practices work in concert to affect sorting, motivation, and behavior of the current employees, including how pay practices emerge in a HCR pay system and the decision-making processes involved. Studying sorting effects also would be worthwhile. Extant research notes how individual pay practices influence sorting (Gerhart and Rynes, 2003), but many questions remain about how employees view collective pay systems and what they consider when they join an organization. Do new hires note only immediate pay practices, look forward to potential future pay practices, or anticipate some combination? Do they prefer practices that reward behaviors within their control or contributions to higher outcomes? It is worth investigating the precise role that pay systems have on shaping organizational culture, as well as how pay systems and culture interact to influence employee sorting, attitudes, and behaviors.

Research should also explore differences across levels. Pay practices may feature different characteristics at team versus department levels. Bundling multiple levels or jobs in investigations of pay could lead to erroneous conclusions about the effects of pay on specific employees. Researchers should consider jobs of similar complexity when conducting pay practice research because complexity may drive the consequences of pay such that combining jobs or levels of different complexities would mask these consequences. Alternatively, failing to consider the full complexity of the pay system can also lead to erroneous conclusions about the total effect of pay on unit performance.

The logic presented implies that pay practices implemented at one level can substitute for those at another level. With sufficient organizational power, leaders might reconcile competing individual goals and strike a balance that benefits unit performance. For example, pay systems could encourage and facilitate cooperation and focus on team outcomes, even if pay is based on individual achievement. Two sales employees working solely on commission likely compete for customers, at the expense of total sales. Team leaders compensated according to higher-level outcomes have incentives to dissuade the extreme pursuit of individual motivations, and, in combination and context, this pay system could optimize individual and collective performance.

Finally, research should consider the duration of pay practice effects and the effectiveness of various pay practice combinations in an HCR development cycle. For example, researchers could investigate how pay practice timing effects depend on contextual complexity.

CONCLUSION

We have described a pay system that focuses on three pay practice decisions intended to influence the make-up, motivation, and behavior of HCRs: salary level, PFP proportion, and the organizational level at which PFP targets. Sorting and incentive effects are the primary means by which pay practice decisions exert influence on the HCR capacity. HCR enactment, through individual and coordinative performance, reflects how well the unit utilizes the available HCR capacities, with unit performance as the end product; and this too is influenced by the three pay practice decisions discussed.

Despite pay system ramifications, most pay research focuses on studying single pay practice decisions on individual-level outcomes, limiting our understanding of unit-level effects of pay, mainly due to the lack of theory (Nyberg et al., 2018a; Shaw, 2014), and how different pay decisions work together in a system. To address these issues, we propose a pay system framework grounded in psychology and economics theories. Thus, we emphasize the emergent and dynamic nature of strategic pay systems and their reciprocal relationship with HCR over time. This holistic perspective expands the exploration of pay consequences across groups and levels. Rather than studying either individual or unit outcomes, research should expand the view to observe combined pay practices and interactions that affect HCR capacities and enactment.

CHAPTER SUMMARY

BOX 23.1 KEY TAKEAWAYS

Ideas	Explanation
1. Pay systems	To understand how pay influences HCR through both sorting and incentive effects, pay decisions should be considered simultaneously as part of the entire pay system influencing both the capacity and enactment of HCRs.

2. Salary level and PFP percentage	Salary level influences sorting rather than incentive effects, but sorting and incentive effects are both influenced when salary level is considered with PFP proportions and organization level of PFP targets.
3. Pay systems and HCR	Pay systems influence HCR capacity and ability to enact its capacity, thus showing pay systems as both antecedents of HCR and triggers that enact the HCR capacity.

BOX 23.2 DIRECTIONS FOR FUTURE RESEARCH

Ideas	Explanation
1. Examine pay practice combination effects	Future research should examine the effects of different pay practice combinations on HCR capacity and HCR enactment.
2. Examine the combined influence of organizational pay target level and salary	To examine how pay at different levels can influence individual and unit performance, future research should examine the effects of targeting PFP to unit-level outcomes in combination with different salary levels and different relative levels of PFP to salary level.
3. Examine the role of pay systems on climate	Future research should examine the role of pay systems on organizational climate and subsequent climate influences on HCR.

NOTE

1. Incentive effects can have a technical meaning. However, following Gerhart (2017), we broadly define incentive as an "inducement offered in advance to influence future performance" (Newmanand et al., 2017: 709).

REFERENCES

Aarts, H., Gollwitzer, P. M., and Hassin, R. R. (2004). Goal contagion: Perceiving is for pursuing. *Journal of Personality and Social Psychology*, *87*, 23–37.

Adams, J. S. (1963). Toward an understanding of inequity. *Journal of Abnormal and Social Psychology*, *67*, 422–36.

Akerlof, G. A. (1984). Gift exchange and efficiency-wage theory: Four views. *American Economic Review*, *74*, 79–83.

Akerlof, G. A., and Yellen, J. L, (1986). *Efficiency Wage Models of the Labor Market*. Cambridge: Cambridge University Press.

Alchian, A. A., and Demsetz, H. (1972). Production, information costs, and economic organization. *American Economic Review*, *62*, 777–95.

Ariely, D., Gneezy, U., Loewenstein, G., and Mazar, N. (2009). Large stakes and big mistakes. *Review of Economic Studies*, *76*, 451–69.

Bamberger, P., and Levi, R. (2009). Team-based reward allocation structures and the helping behaviors of outcome-interdependent team members. *Journal of Managerial Psychology*, *24*, 300–327.

Barnes, C. M., Hollenbeck, J. R., Jundt, D. K., DeRue, D. S., and Harmon, S. J. (2011). Mixing individual incentives and group incentives: Best of both worlds or social dilemma? *Journal of Management*, *37*, 1611–35.

Barney, J. B. (1991). Firm resources and sustained competitive advantage. *Journal of Management*, *17*, 99–120.

Barriere, M., Owens, M. and Pobereskin, S. (2018). Linking talent to value. *McKinsey Quarterly*, April.

Becker, B. E., and Gerhart, B. (1996). The impact of human resource management on organizational performance: Progress and prospects. *Academy of Management Journal, 39*, 779–801.

Becker, G. S. (1964). *Human Capital*. New York: Columbia University Press.

Beersma, B., Hollenbeck, J. R., Humphrey, S. E., Moon, H., Conlon, D. E., and Ilgen, D. R. (2003). Cooperation, competition, and team performance: Toward a contingency approach. *Academy of Management Journal, 46*, 572–90.

Bowen, D. E., and Ostroff, C. (2004). Understanding HRM-firm performance linkages: The role of the strength of the HRM system. *Academy of Management Review, 29*, 203–21.

Cable, D. M., and Judge, T. A. (1994). Pay preferences and job search decisions: A person-organization fit perspective. *Personnel Psychology, 47*, 317–48.

Cadsby, B. C., Song, F., and Tapon, F. (2007). Sorting and incentive effects of pay for performance: An experimental investigation. *Academy of Management Journal, 50*, 387–405.

Call, M.L., Nyberg, A.J., Ployhart, R.E., and Weekley, J. (2015). The dynamic nature of collective turnover and unit performance: The impact of time, quality, and replacements. *Academy of Management Journal, 58*, 1208–32.

Campbell, B. A., Coff, R., and Kryscynski, D. (2012). Rethinking sustained competitive advantage from human capital. *Academy of Management Review, 37*, 376–95.

Cappelli, P. and Chauvin, K. (1991). An interplant test of the efficiency wage hypothesis. *Quarterly Journal of Economics, 106*, 769–87.

Cappelli, P., and Sherer, P. D. (1991). The missing role of context in OB. *Research in Organizational Behavior, 13*, 55–110.

Cascio, W. F. (2000). *Costing Human Resources: The Financial Impact of Behavior in Organizations* (4th edn). Boston, MA: Kent.

Cerasoli, C. P., Nicklin, J. M., and Ford, M. T. (2014). Intrinsic motivation and extrinsic incentives jointly predict performance: A 40-year meta-analysis. *Psychological Bulletin, 140*, 980–1008.

Chadwick, C. (2017). Towards a more comprehensive model of firms' human capital rents. *Academy of Management Review, 42*, 499–515.

Chang, H.-C., Wang, C.-Y., and Hawamdeh, S. (2019). Emerging trends in data analytics and knowledge management job market: Extending KSA framework. *Journal of Knowledge Management, 23*(4), 664–86.

Coff, R. W. (1997). Human assets and management dilemmas: Coping with hazards on the road to resource-based theory. *Academy of Management Review, 22*, 374–402.

Coff, R. W., and Kryscynski, D. (2011). Drilling for micro-foundations of human capital based competitive advantages. *Journal of Management, 37*, 1429–48.

Coff, R., and Raffiee, J. (2015). Toward a theory of perceived firm-specific human capital. *Academy of Management Perspectives, 29*, 326–41.

Conroy, S. A., and Gupta, N. (2015). Team pay-for-performance: The devil is in the details. *Group and Organization Management, 41*, 32–65.

Conroy, S. A., Gupta, N., Shaw, J. D., and Park, T. Y. (2014). A multi-level approach to the effects of pay variation. *Research in Personnel and Human Resources Management, 32*, 1–64.

Deci, E. L., and Ryan, R. M. (1980). The empirical exploration of intrinsic motivational processes. *Advances in Experimental and Social Psychology, 13*, 39–80.

Delery, J. E., and Doty, D. H. (1996). Modes of theorizing in strategic human resource management: Tests of universalistic, contingency, and configurational performance predictions. *Academy of Management Journal, 39*, 802–35.

DeMatteo, J. S., Eby, L. T., and Sundstrom, E. (1998). Team-based rewards: Current empirical evidence and directions for future research. In G. R. Ferris (ed.). *Research in Organizational Behavior*, 141–83. Oxford: Elsevier Science.

Deming, W. E. (1986). *Out of the Crisis*. Cambridge, MA: MIT Press.

Dierickx, I., and Cool, K. (1989). Asset stock accumulation and sustainability of competitive advantage. *Management Science, 35*, 1504–11.

Dohmen, T., and Falk, A. (2011). Performance pay and multidimensional sorting: Productivity, preferences, and gender. *American Economic Review, 101*, 556–90.

Dumaine, B. (1994). The trouble with teams. *Fortune, 130*, 86–88.

Fang, M., and Gerhart, B. (2012). Does pay for performance diminish intrinsic interest? *International Journal of Human Resource Management, 23*, 1176–96.

Felin, T., and Foss, N. J. (2005). Strategic organization: A field in search of micro-foundations. *Strategic Organization, 3*, 441–55.

Felin, T., and Hesterly, W. S. (2007). The knowledge-based view, nested heterogeneity, and new value creation: Philosophical considerations on the locus of knowledge. *Academy of Management Review, 32*, 195–218.

Felin, T., Foss, N. J., and Ployhart, R. E. (2015). The microfoundations movement in strategy and organization theory. *Academy of Management Annals, 9*, 575–632.

Foss, N. J. (2011). Micro-foundations for the resource-based view? *Journal of Management*, *37*, 1413–28.
Gagné, M., and Deci, E. L. (2005). Self-determination theory and work motivation. *Journal of Organizational Behavior*, *26*, 331–62.
Garbers, Y., and Konradt, U. (2014). The effect of financial incentives on performance: A quantitative review of individual and team-based financial incentives. *Journal of Occupational and Organizational Psychology*, *87*, 102–37.
Gerhart, B. (2000). Compensation strategy and organizational performance. In S. L. Rynes and B. Gerhart (eds), *Compensation in Organizations*, 151–94. San Francisco: Jossey-Bass.
Gerhart, B. (2005). Human resources and business performance: Findings, unanswered questions, and an alternative approach. *Management Revue*, *16*, 174–85.
Gerhart, B. (2017). Incentives and pay for performance in the workplace. *Advances in Motivation Science*, *4*, 91–140.
Gerhart, B., and Fang, M. (2014). Pay for (individual) performance: Issues, claims, evidence and the role of sorting effects. *Human Resource Management Review*, *24*, 41–52.
Gerhart, B., and Fang, M. (2015). Pay, intrinsic motivation, extrinsic motivation, performance, and creativity in the workplace: Revisiting long-held beliefs. *Annual Review of Organizational Psychology and Organizational Behavior*, *2*, 489–521.
Gerhart, B., and Milkovich, G. T. (1990). Organizational differences in managerial compensation and financial performance. *Academy of Management Journal*, *33*, 663–91.
Gerhart, B., and Rynes, S. L. (2003). *Compensation: Theory, Evidence, and Strategic Implications*. Thousand Oaks, CA: Sage.
Gerhart, B., and Trevor, C. O. (1996). Employment variability under different managerial compensation systems. *Academy of Management Journal*, *39*, 1692–712.
Gerhart, B., Milkovich, G., and Murray, B. (1992). Pay, performance and participation. In D. Lewin, O. Mitchell, and P. Sherer (eds), *Research Frontiers in Industrial Relations and Human Resources*. Madison, WI: IRRA.
Gerhart, B., Rynes, S. L., and Fulmer, I. S. (2009). Pay and performance: Individuals, groups, and executives. *Academy of Management Annals*, *3*, 251–315.
Green, F. (2010). Well-being, job satisfaction and labour mobility. *Labour Economics*, *17*, 897–903.
Gupta, N., and Shaw, J. D. (2014). Employee compensation: The neglected area of HRM research. *Human Resource Management Review*, *24*, 1–4.
Guzzo, R.A., Jette, R.D. and Katzell, R.A. (1985). The effects of psychologically based intervention programs on worker productivity: A meta-analysis. *Personnel Psychology*, *38*, 275–91.
Hackman, J. R., and Morris, G. G. (1975). Group tasks, group interaction process, and group performance effectiveness. In L. Berkowitz (ed.), *Advances in Experimental Social Psychology*, vol. 7, 47–99. New York: Academic Press.
Hamilton, B. H., Nickerson, J. A. and Owan, H. (2003). Team incentives and worker heterogeneity: An empirical analysis of the impact of teams on productivity and participation. *Journal of Political Economy*, *111*, 465–97.
Hausknecht, J. P., and Holwerda, J. A. (2013). When does employee turnover matter? Dynamic member configurations, productive capacity, and collective performance. *Organization Science*, *24*, 210–25.
Hausknecht, J. P., and Trevor, C. O. (2011). Collective turnover at the group, unit, and organizational levels: Evidence, issues, and implications. *Journal of Management*, *37*, 352–88.
Hoffman, B. J., and Woehr, D. J. (2006). A quantitative review of the relationship between person–organization fit and behavioral outcomes. *Journal of Vocational Behavior*, *68*, 389–99.
Hollenbeck, J. R., and Jamieson, B. B. (2015). Human capital, social capital, and social network analysis: Implications for strategic human resource management. *Academy of Management Perspectives*, *29*, 370–85.
Jenkins Jr, G. D., Mitra, A., Gupta, N., and Shaw, J. D. (1998). Are financial incentives related to performance? A meta-analytic review of empirical research. *Journal of Applied Psychology*, *83*, 777–87.
Jensen, M. C., and Meckling, W. H. (1976). Theory of the firm: Managerial behavior, agency costs and ownership structure. *Journal of Financial Economics*, *3*, 305–60.
Kahneman, D. (2011). *Thinking, Fast and Slow*. New York: Macmillan.
Karau, S. J., and Williams, K. D. (1993). Social loafing: A meta-analytic review and theoretical integration. *Journal of Personality and Social Psychology*, *65*, 681–706.
Kerr, N. L., and Tindale, R. S. (2004). Group performance and decision making. *Annual Review of Psychology*, *55*, 623–55.
Kohn, A. (199)3. Why incentive plans cannot work. *Harvard Business Review*, *71*, 54–63.
Kristof-Brown, A. L., Zimmerman, R. D., and Johnson, E. C. (2005). Consequences of individual's fit at work: A meta-analysis of person-job, person-organization, person-group, and person-supervisor fit. *Personnel Psychology*, *58*, 281–342.
Kryscynski, D., and Ulrich, D. (2015). Making strategic human capital relevant: A time-sensitive opportunity. *Academy of Management Perspectives*, *29*, 357–69.
Larkin, I., and Leider, S. (2012). Incentive schemes, sorting, and behavioral biases of employees: Experimental evidence. *American Economic Journal: Microeconomics*, *4*, 184–214.

Larkin, I., Pierce, L., and Gino, F. (2012). The psychological costs of pay-for-performance: Implications for the strategic compensation of employees. *Strategic Management Journal*, *33*, 1194–214.
Lawler, E. E. (1971). *Pay and Organizational Effectiveness: A Psychological View*. New York: McGraw-Hill.
Lawler, E. E., and Jenkins Jr, G. D. (1992). Strategic reward systems. In M. D. Dunnette, and L. M. Hough (eds), *Handbook of Industrial and Organizational Psychology* (2nd edn), vol. 3: 1009–55. Palo Alto, CA: Consulting Psychologists Press.
Lawler, E. J. (2001). An affect theory of social exchange. *American Journal of Sociology*, *107*, 321–52.
Lazear, E. P. (1986). Salaries and piece rates. *Journal of Business*, *59*, 405–31.
Lazear, E. P. (1999). Personnel economics: Past lessons and future directions: Presidential address to the Society of Labor Economists, San Francisco, May 1, 1998. *Journal of Labor Economics*, *17*(2), 199–236.
Lazear, E. P. (2000). Performance pay and productivity. *American Economic Review*, *90*, 1341–61.
Lepak, D. P., and Snell, S. A. (1999). The human resource architecture: Toward a theory of human capital allocation and development. *Academy of Management Review*, *24*, 31–48.
Liao, H., Toya, K., Lepak, D. P., and Hong, Y. (2009). Do they see eye to eye? Management and employee perspectives of high-performance work systems and influence processes on service quality. *Journal of Applied Psychology*, *94*, 371–91.
Locke, E. A., Feren, D. B., McCaleb, V. M., Shaw, K. N., and Denny, A. T. (1980). The relative effectiveness of four methods of motivating employee performance. In K. D. Duncan, M. M. Gruenberg, and D. Wallis (eds), *Changes in Working Life*, 363–88. Chichester: Wiley.
Milgrom, P., and Roberts, J. (1992). *Economics, Organizations and Management*. Englewood Cliffs, NJ: Prentice Hall.
Mitra, A., Gupta, N., and Jenkins Jr, G. D. (1997). A drop in the bucket: When is a pay raise a pay raise? *Journal of Organizational Behavior*, *18*, 117–37.
Newman, J. M., Gerhart, B., and Milkovich, G. T. (2017). *Compensation* (12th edn). New York: McGraw-Hill.
Nyberg, A. J. (2010). Retaining your high performers: Moderators of the performance–job satisfaction–voluntary turnover relationship. *Journal of Applied Psychology*, *95*, 440–43.
Nyberg, A. J. and Ployhart, R. E. (2013). Context-emergent turnover (CET) theory: A theory of collective turnover. *Academy of Management Review*, *38*, 109–31.
Nyberg, A. J. and Wright, P. M. (2015). 50 years of human capital research: Assessing what we know; exploring where we go. *Academy of Management Perspectives*, *29*, 287–95.
Nyberg, A. J., Pieper, J. R., and Trevor, C. O. (2016). Pay-for-performance's effect on future employee performance: Integrating psychological and economic principles toward a contingency perspective. *Journal of Management*, *42*, 1753–83.
Nyberg, A. J., Moliterno, T. P., Hale, D., and Lepak, D. P. (2014). Resource-based perspectives on unit-level human capital: A review and integration. *Journal of Management*, *40*, 316–46.
Nyberg, A. J., Maltarich, M. A., Abdulsalam, D., Essman, S. M., and Cragun, O. (2018a). Collective pay for performance: A cross-disciplinary review and meta-analysis. *Journal of Management*, *44*(6), 2433–72.
Nyberg, A. J., Reilly, G., Essman, S., and Rodrigues, J. (2018b). Human capital resources: A call to retire settled debates and to start a few new debates. *International Journal of Human Resource Management*, *29*, 68–86.
Ockenfels, A., Sliwka, D., and Werner, P. (2014). Bonus payments and reference point violations. *Management Science*, *61*, 1496–513.
Pearsall, M. J., Christian, M. S. and Ellis, A. P. (2010). Motivating interdependent teams: Individual rewards, shared rewards, or something in between? *Journal of Applied Psychology*, *95*, 183–91.
Pfeffer, J. (1998). *The Human Equation: Building Profits by Putting People First*. Boston, MA: Harvard Business School Press.
Pink, D. (2009). *Drive: The Surprising Truth About What Motivates Us*. New York: Riverhead.
Ployhart, R. E. (2015). Strategic organizational behavior (STROBE): The missing voice in the strategic human capital conversation. *Academy of Management Perspectives*, *29*, 342–56.
Ployhart, R. E., and Moliterno, T. P. (2011). Emergence of the human capital resource: A multilevel model. *Academy of Management Review*, *36*, 127–50.
Ployhart, R. E., Van Iddekinge, C. H., and MacKenzie Jr, W. I. (2011). Acquiring and developing human capital in service contexts: The interconnectedness of human capital resources. *Academy of Management Journal*, *54*, 353–68.
Ployhart, R. E., Weekley, J. A., and Ramsey, J. (2009). The consequences of human resource stocks and flows: A longitudinal examination of unit service orientation and unit effectiveness. *Academy of Management Journal*, *52*, 996–1015.
Ployhart, R. E., Nyberg, A. J., Reilly, G., and Maltarich, M. A. (2014). Human capital is dead; long live human capital resources! *Journal of Management*, *40*, 371–98.
Reilly, G., Nyberg, A. J., Maltarich, M., and Weller, I. (2014). Human capital flows: Using context-emergent turnover (CET) theory to explore the process by which turnover, hiring, and job demands affect patient satisfaction. *Academy of Management Journal*, *57*, 766–90.

Robbins, S. (2001). *Organizational Behavior* (9th edn). Englewood Cliffs, NJ: Prentice Hall.
Rynes, S. L., and Miller, H. E. (1983). Recruiter and job influences on candidates for employment. *Journal of Applied Psychology*, *68*, 147–54.
Rynes, S. L., Gerhart, B., and Minette, K. A. (2004). The importance of pay in employee motivation: Discrepancies between what people say and what they do. *Human Resource Management*, *43*, 381–94.
Rynes, S. L., Gerhart, B., and Parks, L. (2005). Personnel psychology: Performance evaluation and pay for performance. *Annual Review of Psychology*, *56*, 571–600.
Schneider, B. (1987). The people make the place. *Personnel Psychology*, *40*, 437–53.
Sesil, J. C., and Lin, Y. P. (2011). The impact of employee stock option adoption and incidence on productivity: Evidence from US panel data. *Industrial Relations: A Journal of Economy and Society*, *50*(3), 514–34.
Sharma, A., and Sarel, D. (1995). The impact of customer satisfaction based incentive systems on salespeople's customer service response: An empirical study. *Journal of Personal Selling and Sales Management*, *15*, 17–29.
Shaw, J. D. (2014). Pay dispersion. *Annual Review of Organizational Psychology and Organizational Behavior*, *1*, 521–44.
Shaw, J. D. (2015). Pay dispersion, sorting, and organizational performance. *Academy of Management Discoveries*, *1*, 165–79.
Shaw, J. D., and Gupta, N. (2007). Pay system characteristics and quit patterns of good, average, and poor performers. *Personnel Psychology*, *60*, 903–28.
Shaw, J. D., Delery, J. E., Jenkins Jr, G. D., and Gupta, N. (1998). An organization-level analysis of voluntary and involuntary turnover. *Academy of Management Journal*, *41*, 511–25.
Shaw, J. D., Duffy, M. K., Mitra, A., Lockhart, D. E., and Bowler, M. (2003). Reactions to merit pay increases: A longitudinal test of a signal sensitivity perspective. *Journal of Applied Psychology*, *88*, 538–44.
Trevor, C. O. (2001). Interactions among actual ease-of-movement determinants and job satisfaction in the prediction of voluntary turnover. *Academy of Management Journal*, *44*(4), 621–38.
Trevor, C. O., and Wazeter. (2006). A contingent view of reactions to objective pay conditions: Interdependence among pay structure characteristics and pay relative to internal and external referents. *Journal of Applied Psychology*, *91*, 1260–75.
Trevor, C. O., Gerhart, B., and Boudreau, J. W. (1997). Voluntary turnover and job performance: Curvilinearity and the moderating influences of salary growth and promotions. *Journal of Applied Psychology*, *82*, 44–61.
Trevor, C. O., Reilly, G., and Gerhart, B. (2012). Reconsidering pay dispersion's effect on the performance of interdependent work: Reconciling sorting and pay inequality. *Academy of Management Journal*, *55*, 585–610.
Verquer, M. L., Beehr, T. A., and Wagner, S. H. (2003). A meta-analysis of relations between person–organization fit and work attitudes. *Journal of Vocational Behavior*, *63*, 473–89.
Vroom, V. H. (1964). *Work and Motivation*. New York: Wiley.
Weller, I., Hymer, C., Nyberg, A. J., and Ebert, J. (2019). How matching creates value: Cogs and wheels for human capital resources research. *Academy of Management Annals*, *13*(1), 188–214.
Wright, P. M., and McMahan, G. C. (1992). Theoretical perspectives for strategic human resource management. *Journal of Management*, *18*, 295–20.
Wright, P. M., and McMahan, G. C. (2011). Exploring human capital: Putting human back into strategic human resource management. *Human Resource Management Journal*, *21*, 93–104.
Wright, P. M., Coff, R., and Moliterno, T. P. (2014). Strategic human capital: Crossing the great divide. *Journal of Management*, *40*, 353–70.
Wright, P. M., Dunford, B. B., and Snell, S. A. (2001). Human resources and the resource based view of the firm. *Journal of Management*, *27*, 701–21.
Wright, P. M., McMahan, G. C., and McWilliams, A. (1994). Human resources and sustained competitive advantage: A resource-based perspective. *International Journal of Human Resource Management*, *5*, 301–26.

24. Strategic compensation: a critique and research agenda

Ian Larkin

INTRODUCTION

Research in the strategy field on the topic of compensation continues to grow. Between 2004 and 2009, five leading journals in strategy (*Strategic Management Journal*, *Organization Science*, *Management Science*, *Academy of Management Journal*, and *Academy of Management Review*) published 152 papers that listed "compensation" in the topic field in the Social Sciences Citation Index. Between 2011 and 2016, this number grew to 227. In 2010, the Strategic Management Society (SMS) formed two new interest groups, on Strategic Human Capital and Behavioral Strategy (Coff, 2010); and in 2017 over 10 percent of papers presented at the SMS Special Conference on the Microfoundations for Strategic Management Research dealt in some way with compensation (Foss and Pedersen, 2014).

Practitioners, too, increasingly see compensation as a critical lever. Of the 20 top *Harvard Business Review* articles in 2015 as voted by readers, five spent a considerable amount of time discussing compensation: "Reinventing Performance Management" by Buckingham and Goodall; "What I Learned from a Year of Job Rejections" by Mufleh; "How to Overcome Burnout and Stay Motivated" by Knight; "5 Signs it's Time for a New Job" by Chamorro-Premuzic; and "Setting the Record Straight on Switching Jobs" by Gallo (Bell, 2015). Amazingly, none of the top 20 *HBR* articles in 2000 had the word "compensation" anywhere in them. The 2009 book *Drive* by former *New York Times* journalist Dan Pink, a 40-week *Times* best-seller, explicitly argued that the traditional method of compensating employees was detrimental (one edition's blurb summarized the book as "Carrots & Sticks are so Last Century"). Pink's TED Talk on the book has been viewed over 7 million times, and a clever cartoon sketch of a synopsis of the book that Pink gave to the Royal Society of Arts in the UK has been viewed over 17 million times (RSA Animate, 2010) – I personally have been emailed a link to this talk by former students or executives over 1,000 times in the nine years since it launched. *Forbes* named Pink one of the top ten Most Influential Business Thinkers in 2017, just four spots below Michael Porter and ahead of leading strategy thinkers such as Pankaj Ghemawat, Amy Edmondson, and Jim Collins (Kauflin, 2017).

There is evidence that this interest in compensation mirrors the increasing importance firms place on designing optimal incentive plans. Firms like Google, Facebook, and Amazon are widely believed to use novel incentive plans to attract and retain employees (Martocchio, 2016); even more tellingly, many top Ph.D. students and even faculty in strategy, economics, organizational behavior and related fields have left academia to work in the "People Departments" of these firms (Lohr, 2016), presumably helping to use science to craft better incentive plans. Just in my personal network, I count over 20 such experts, all of whom have a Ph.D. and could work in academia should they choose. Indeed, at least 10 percent of the 227 compensation articles in leading strategy journals, and many more papers in top journals in economics, human resource management and organizational behavior, involve field experiments undertaken by actual companies. A 2015 *Economist Intelligence Unit* survey reported that the top issue CEOs felt their companies would face in the next 5–10 years was related to "people management" – well ahead of slowing growth, the need to innovate, increased competition, globalization, or government regulation (Humphreys and Hoffman, 2015).

Academics and practitioners alike clearly see an increasing overlap between strategy and incentive systems. However, I argue in this chapter that the "strategic compensation" literature has thus far failed to show a link between these two words, and that we do not actually know whether, and if so exactly how, compensation can be "strategic." By "strategic" I use the classic definition from Porter (1985) – that the resource or factor, in this case the compensation system, contributes to an organization's ability to outperform competitors without this performance edge being competed away over time via imitation. We have learned an incredible amount about the performance implications of compensation in the last 10–20 years, but I argue that whether and how compensation allows strategic *out*performance is not a topic we know much about.

My goal for this chapter is to lay out why we do not know if compensation is truly strategic, discuss high-level models of what a theory of strategic compensation would look like, and discuss how our research paradigm needs to shift should compensation scholars want to address whether and how a compensation system can be strategic. The chapter does not attempt a systemic review of all that scholars have learned about compensation in the explosion of compensation research in the last ten years. There are several very careful, comprehensive reviews of recent advancements in the compensation literature (Gerhart et al., 2009).

I organize the chapter in three parts. First, I present an overview of the classic question, "What is strategy?" through a compensation lens to lay out plausible ways that compensation could actually be a strategic lever. I also attempt to demonstrate in this section that there are a number of inconsistencies and logical fallacies in the emerging conventional wisdom about how compensation could plausibly be strategic. Second, I critique the research approach compensation scholars – including myself – often take, and argue that this approach only exacerbates our inability to identify whether and how compensation can contribute to strategic advantage. Finally, I end with thoughts about a new research approach that I believe could help overcome this gap.

STRATEGY, COMPENSATION, AND STRATEGIC COMPENSATION

What is "Strategic"? A Brief Primer

At its core, the field of strategy attempts to explain how some firms are able to achieve higher levels of performance than competitors over a sustained period of time. In theory, a competitor with lower performance than another competitor should ascertain the sources of the better-performing firm's enhanced performance, and copy those sources.

Simply showing a performance difference due to an activity taken by the firm is not enough to call that activity "strategic"; to qualify as strategic there must be some barrier that renders competitors unable to imitate the activity (Porter, 1996).

Researchers in strategy stress that operational efficiency and strategic outperformance are two separate concepts (Porter, 1996). An inefficient firm is defined as one that is not performing as well as it could because it could reduce its costs without harming its product quality, as measured by its customers' willingness to pay for its products. A firm can improve its performance by becoming efficient – reducing unneeded costs but maintaining the same overall willingness to pay. An inefficient competitor will perform worse than an efficient one; but to a strategist this is the realm of operations, not strategy. A strategic firm takes steps to improve performance that even an operationally efficient is unable to imitate.

Of course, the average firm is operationally inefficient, and can therefore improve performance by identifying and ridding the source of inefficiency. Empirically it can be difficult to distinguish an inefficient firm that is improving its efficiency from an efficient firm taking steps that allow it to perform even better than other efficient firms. Much of the theoretical development in the strategy literature specifically identifies activities that both improve performance and are difficult to imitate, and empirical researchers then set out to find evidence that corroborates both criteria (Newbert, 2007).

Compensation and Performance: Efficiency or Strategy?

Studies that demonstrate the link between employee compensation and employee and firm performance have been around for decades, but have taken on added prominence in the last decade or so. The compensation field has traditionally concentrated on the effects of employee compensation on other variables, such as job satisfaction and employee turnover (Coughlan and Schmidt, 1985; Igalens and Roussel, 1999).

This focus on the link between compensation and employee and firm performance is undoubtedly a positive development for the compensation field. However, it begs an important question: if a positive link between a given compensation policy and a firm's overall performance is persuasively demonstrated, is this link simply about increasing efficiency of the firm's compensation plan? Or does it demonstrate a link between compensation and strategic advantage? Put another way: was the firm's compensation plan without the policy in place simply inefficient?

My read on the empirical literature on compensation and performance is that the literature is essentially completely silent on this distinction. In fact, I do not believe that this distinction is commonly made in the empirical literature in Strategic Human Resource Management (SHRM); one widely cited introduction to SHRM defined the field as "the link between human resource practices and firm performance" (Collins and Clark, 2003). No distinction is made between improving previously inefficient practices and generating sustainable paths by which firms can outperform competitors.

The distinction between efficiency and strategy is important for a number of reasons, and the final section of this chapter discusses these in more detail. The academic field of strategy argues that choices around a firm's strategy are what determine its long-term success as a company, and should be the key focus of the top executives in a firm. Efficiency, on the other hand, is a lower-level problem best addressed by middle-level managers

(Kaplan and Norton, 2008). Highly successful firms will have both a well-defined strategy and a focus on efficiency, but the average company is underperforming and should likely focus on efficiency before thinking about strategy.

Determining that compensation is primarily about efficiency would by no means belittle the importance of compensation within firms. Being efficient at automobile manufacturing or retail logistics or countless other complex, highly interrelated processes is extremely difficult. One prominent theme developed later in this chapter is that compensation must be thought of not as a simple salary number, but as a system that rewards employees for performance on assigned tasks. This broader view of compensation means that the task of compensating employees is at least of a similar magnitude of complexity as manufacturing a car. That many firms get aspects of this complex process wrong is unsurprising, and there still would be significant scope for scholars of compensation to help craft more efficient compensation schemes. Also, as discussed below, it could be the case that compensation plays a critical but ultimately supporting role to a strategy based on human resources, but where the strategic advantage does not ultimately stem from compensation itself. Understanding the role of compensation in any truly strategic human resource-led strategy is inarguably important.

However, I think it is worth examining the potential models by which compensation might be strategic. For one, as noted above, CEOs across many industries state that compensation, as well as closely related problems like attracting and retaining the right people, is one of the top issues they face, and they expect it only to rise in importance in the coming decade. My relatively strong prior is that many if not most senior executives would state that their compensation plan, broadly defined, is a key part of their company's strategy. For academic researchers, developing specific models of how compensation might actually contribute to sustainable strategic advantage is critical to inform the design of empirical work that can help distinguish between the efficiency and strategic role of compensation within organizations.

Potential Models of Strategic Compensation

Some inconvenient truths to be addressed by strategic compensation theory

To build a coherent theory of strategic compensation, scholars will need to build a theoretical scaffolding that logically explains how compensation can be used by a company to sustainably outperform competitors over time. The idea that compensation can lead to outperformance has several immediate implications which are not shared by all scholars of compensation. Before turning to the specifics of what a model of strategic compensation might look like, I first discuss these inconsistencies.

Argument 1: A theory of strategic compensation must take seriously the notion that "pay-for-performance" (PFP) works.

Some 20 years before the publication of Dan Pink's *Drive*, micro-organizational behavior (OB) scholars such as Jeffrey Pfeffer (1998b) argued that making employee pay contingent on their individual performance was dangerous and ultimately detrimental to organizational performance. Pfeffer's case (1998a), "SAS Institute: A Different Approach to Incentives and People Management Practices in the Software Industry," which documents a successful enterprise software company that does not use pay-for-performance to compensate any employee, is to this day a mainstay of core organizational behavior classes and is taught to tens of thousands of MBA students every year. Pink's book painstakingly cites dozens of laboratory experiments and field studies that demonstrate costs of pay-for-performance schemes, and that these costs can be avoided by using alternative schemes.

Of course, many scholars in a diverse set of fields argue that the weight of empirical evidence suggests the opposite: that pay-for-performance causes employees to perform better (Lazear, 2000). In the next section of this chapter, I argue that continuing this decades-old debate is detrimental to continued progress on understanding the role of compensation in firm performance, be it for strategic or efficiency reasons. Here, though, it is important to point out that, for compensation to be a strategic lever, pay-for-performance logically must be part of the equation. This is exactly because strategy is about understanding superior firm performance. *Any* factor that is core to a firm's strategy by definition must contribute positively to its performance. While separating causality is likely impossible, it is both empirically well-established and logically appealing that firm performance is very highly correlated with employee performance. It is therefore essentially a tautology to argue that a strategic compensation plan must reward employee performance; if it did not do so, then it is difficult to see how compensation could lead to higher employee and ultimately firm performance. Thus, I believe that Pfeffer and other non-believers of the efficacy of pay-for-performance inherently argue that a compensation plan can *not* be strategic. This may be a defensible view, but I believe that some scholars of compensation – although not necessarily Pfeffer himself – argue that compensation is strategic, and that pay-for-performance does not work. I do not see logically how these two arguments can both be true.

This is not to argue that the economists have won and we should revert to the conclusion that piece rates and merit bonuses are the best compensation plans. (When I first presented the idea for this chapter to a group of SHRM scholars, I was accused by one leading scholar of doing just that!) Indeed, as argued below, I actually believe that a strategic view of compensation may likely have a smaller role for individual bonus plans than the typical economist might think. However, from a logical perspective, core to the notion of any theory of strategic compensation must be that employees are rewarded for performance. A theory of strategic compensation by definition must define exactly what these rewards are, how they are determined, and how and why these rewards will cause employees to perform better. Ultimately, a theory of strategic compensation exactly *is* a theory of pay-for-performance, by definition.

I do concede that some may consider this argument to be didactic, and that I am simply extending the notion of "pay" to "rewards." The argument might be that monetary pay-for-performance does not work, but non-monetary rewards for performance do work. To this critique I have two responses. First, I think explicitly making this argument is critical if we are to unpack whether and how compensation can be strategic, and I do not think this distinction is nearly as clear in the existing literature as it needs to be. Second, and more importantly, I would argue that even with an extended notion of "rewards," my critiques below about the failure of scholars to link compensation to strategy still hold.

Argument 2: A theory of strategic compensation must recognize that a dollar in increased pay is a dollar in increased costs.

One of the key insights from the strategy literature is that firms only capture a portion – sometimes a very small portion – of the value they create through their products and services (Lepak et al., 2007). For example, competition may drive down prices, giving consumers a large share of value created via consumer surplus and lowering a firm's value capture. Indeed, the whole notion of strategic sustainability and barriers to imitation is about the ability to avoid price competition and drive a wedge between price charged and costs incurred (Chen, 1996).

Like any factor input used in a firm's value chain, the cost expended for human capital, i.e., compensation, directly reduces the amount of value captured by a firm. As a firm pays more for the same amount and quality of human capital, its performance goes down by a corresponding amount. If pay is in monetary dollars only, then a dollar spent in pay directly substitutes for a dollar of performance. When scholars evaluate the strategic benefit of other types of assets, this identity is not a difficult one; indeed, the core insight of the strategy field is that a firm must either be able to generate similar value via a mix of activities via a lower cost or generate higher value to consumers of their product or service via a mix of assets at a similar cost (Porter, 1996). But with human assets this basic math is often neglected. As discussed below, coming up with a theory of strategic compensation requires that we take this identity seriously. Pay is a *cost*, and for a given level of product or service quality, a strategic firm by definition wants to minimize it. Importantly, even if "pay" is given to employees in non-pecuniary ways, managing the system that generates this "pay" is by definition costly. Firms simply cannot generate value via any factor such as compensation without paying for it.

Argument 3: A theory of strategic compensation must consider not just pay levels, but the *system* used to reward employees.

It is common to treat the words "compensation" and "pay" as synonyms (Milkovich and Newman, 1984), but effectively researching the impact of compensation on performance requires a broader unit of analysis. If we accept the argument that a theory of strategic compensation must ultimately involve pay-for-performance, then the theory must cover not just pay levels, but employee performance levels too. (In fact, even if one rejects the notion that strategic compensation requires paying for performance, one still must measure employee performance in order to know whether a given pay system improved said performance and thereby made the firm more efficient.) Taking the next logical step, measuring employee performance, requires a definition of the tasks assigned to employees. It is therefore impossible to consider the effects of a pay-for-performance system without thinking through each of these three steps: 1) what tasks are delegated to employees; 2) how performance on these tasks is measured; and 3) the rewards that are given depending on the measured performance (Baker et al., 1988).

This insight is not new and certainly is not mine; the "three-legged stool" of incentive system design was first proposed by the organizational economist Michael Jensen, the same researcher who (with William Meckling) wrote the first paper explaining the concept of agency theory in economics (Jensen and Meckling, 1976). I propose that the three-legged stool framework for defining compensation is useful as a starting place to build a theory of strategic compensation because it so neatly links the unit of performance measurement – the tasks delegated to employees – to the rewards given to employees for that performance. It also matches firm and employee practice; in pay-for-performance systems, employees are typically reminded of the tasks delegated to them, shown their performance on their tasks, and then told their pay.

This unit of analysis – the assigned task/performance measurement/rewards triplet – is arguably narrow enough to allow detailed, specific theory building, and also to distinguish theories of strategic compensation from theories of other critical pieces of HR systems. But it is broad enough that it encapsulates one of the core HR systems used by all firms. This definition has one other benefit – many scholars are increasingly arguing that job design and delegation are in and of themselves ways to reward employees (Orth and Volmer, 2017), and that performance measurement, particularly when done relative to peers, can also be motivating or demotivating (Blanes i Vidal and Nossol, 2011; Barankay, 2012). This broader definition recognizes that rewards encompass more than just pay. It also clarifies that, because compensation is such a complex system, running and managing the system even if it doesn't involve monetary pay-for-performance is ultimately costly for firms.

What a Theory or Theories of Strategic Compensation Might Look Like

A meaningful theory of strategic compensation must explain how a firm's compensation system can cause it to outperform competitors over a sustained period of time. How might a compensation system do this? This section does *not* attempt to build theories of strategic compensation, but does lay out two high-level models of what theories of strategic compensation might look like.

I use the two Porterian "Generic Strategies" of product differentiation and cost leadership as the building blocks for the models (Porter, 1979). According to Porter, the two canonical strategic models of cost and differentiation pursue the same objective – greater value creation allowing greater value capture – via opposite but analogous strategies. In a differentiation strategy, firms pursue activities that increase the value of their products even though they also face higher costs by pursuing these activities; successful differentiators have higher willingness to pay, and therefore prices that more than make up for their higher costs compared to competitors. In a cost strategy, firms perform activities at a lower cost than competitors (perhaps by avoiding some costly activities altogether), and their reduced costs more than make up for the reduced willingness to pay, and therefore prices for their products. These two models, while certainly far from comprehensive or complete, are a useful starting point to think about strategic models that use any activity or capability of a firm.

It is important to note that these two theories are not mutually exclusive within an industry (Dess and Davis, 1984) and, as discussed in the final section of the chapter, may actually be complementary. Within a given industry, different firms can and do succeed in taking opposite strategies from other successful companies. Indeed, a strategy scholar would find it comforting if both of the models below proved workable, since a core lesson in strategy is there are multiple ways for firms to be strategically successful even within the same industry.

A differentiation or "synergy" theory of strategic compensation

One model of strategic compensation would hold that a firm used compensation to make its end products more valuable, allowing it to capture more value despite the fact that it paid more for its human resources in the first place. Of course, it is easier to lay out this high-level idea than it is to actually theorize about what the causal links between the compensation plan and product value are.

However, we can logically refute certain models that at first glance appear to be a differentiation theory of strategic compensation. The first is that higher compensation simply allows a firm to attract more high-quality workers, which then drives higher-quality end products. Even if this very logical explanation were true (and I believe it likely is), competition for top talent would drive the price of this talent to the incremental value it creates (Dyl, 1988). This would mean that the factor itself – in this case human capital – would capture all the increased value it brings.

This dynamic is very well researched in the labor economics literature on "compensating differentials," which argues that in competitive labor markets, returns to labor skills will be captured by employees, not employers (Smith, 1979). In fact, efficiency wage theory, also from economics, holds that in many circumstances highly skilled labor will be paid more than the prevailing market wage, for example to reduce turnover costs or to motivate unobservable effort (Katz, 1986). Given Argument 2 above, simply paying more to hire better workers cannot be a source of strategic advantage, given the one-to-one tradeoff between higher monetary pay and lower firm performance.

A more nuanced version of the "pay more to get better employees" model holds that some workers will be more productive working for a given firm than they would for any other firm. Perhaps the firm where the worker has the highest value sees increased overall value from teamwork across certain worker types, has a unique production system that makes these workers more efficient, or has a superior training system that increases a worker's value only if she chooses to work at that firm. Under these circumstances, it makes sense to pay these workers more than they would earn elsewhere in order to unlock the value of their increased productive capability.

There surely are examples of within-firm synergies that cause a given worker to be more productive at one firm than at any other firm. Logically we would expect workers in these situations to earn higher pay, and for employers who realize these synergies to perform better than competitors. After all, if a firm can enjoy synergies from hiring high-value workers that other firms do not enjoy, and does not have to pay the full value of the synergy to the workers themselves (because market rates do not reflect the value of the synergy), then that firm will perform better than competitors, *ceteris paribus*. Notably, though, in each case mentioned above, the source of the synergy is *not* the compensation system; instead it is the teamwork system, the production system, or the training system. In situations like these, workers will end up getting paid more than they would at firms that do not have these synergies; but this is an output of the value-creating synergy that derives from a different source than compensation, not a causal factor for the higher performance in the first place. This argument is quite related to the discussion of optimal compensation for firm-specific human capital (FSHC) – investments in improvements that are only realized if an employee remains at a certain firm (Coff, 1997). Compensation models in situations with FSHC argue that companies should not rely on market wages, since employees will have no incentive to invest in FSHC unless they are paid a share of the value created. Again, the source of value creating in a system with FSHC is the strategic element, and the fact that firms must compensate employees at above-market rates to invest in FSHC is a necessary supporting output, not the source of the value creation itself.

Therefore, a differentiation theory of strategic compensation must identify a causal mechanism whereby employees are more productive at a given firm because of the compensation system itself. This seems a tall order, and likely an impossible one if one focuses only on the pay dimension. But when I consider this potential model, I always think of the performance management model used by Jack Welch at General Electric (Welch, 2001), where managers were assigned challenging job assignments that required skills and industry expertise they had not yet developed (a delegation choice); given in-depth annual reviews where they were measured for both financial performance of their assigned business unit and for their demonstrated potential for growth; and where they were force-ranked against all peers (a performance measurement choice); and where they were rewarded primarily not by higher immediate salary but via promotions within GE and/or by being highly attractive to other companies (a rewards choice). Finally, the bottom 10 percent of managers at every level were fired on an annual basis (also a rewards choice, since punishment is simply a negative reward – an important part of the compensation system that in my view has been far too neglected by compensation researchers).

Of course, Welch's performance management model has fallen completely out of favor, even at GE itself (Gryta and Mann, 2018), and when I raise it as an interesting example of strategic compensation, some of my colleagues in the field tend to react similarly as they do when I say we need to stop denigrating the notion of pay-for-performance. As discussed below, I think we spend too much time arguing about the "right" model for compensation, rather than thinking about the causal drivers that can lead to higher performance via compensation. What the GE model illuminates is not that the GE model itself is superior, but that it is possible to build a theory with specific, testable mechanisms that would explain how a compensation system drives better performance. In GE's case, the story goes like this: the assignment of challenging jobs combined with the detailed and competitive performance measurement, which focused on both short-term performance and long-term potential, gave managers additional motivation and means to achieve stretch goals than would happen under a system with less challenging responsibilities and less emphasis on measurement and communication of performance. While short-term pay at GE was undoubtedly lower than at competitors (Welch, 2001), the system itself was extremely costly, both because senior managers spent a huge amount of time on performance measurement and communication with subordinates and because some employees failed given the constant challenges they faced.

One can start to see the germ of a theory here focused on strategic advantage via the compensation system. An actual theory would more scientifically and specifically lay out the proposed mechanisms, develop hypotheses to test, talk about boundary conditions, and address the question of why competitors could not simply copy GE's system. Interestingly, GE's performance management system was very popular in the late 1980s and 1990s, but most companies had difficulty matching GE's level of success with it. The cynical view of this failure would hold that the system itself was not the driver of GE's extraordinary success under Jack Welch, but a strategist might also consider whether the failure of competitors to successfully adopt GE's system points to some barrier to imitation; if a barrier to imitation existed, it would also exactly explain why only GE was successful with the system. One barrier to imitation mentioned by Porter (1996) is the use of a system so complex, inter-related, and path-dependent that it is virtually impossible for another firm to imitate. GE's system, which took up to 30 percent of senior management time (Welch, 2001), is inarguably extremely complex and inter-related.

Building a true theory of a differentiation- or synergy-based strategic compensation system seems a worthwhile task. Notably, this theory would be more specific to compensation than the existing theories of "Total HR Management." It is undoubtedly true that a strategic compensation system would need to work alongside a broader HR system. Narrowing the theory's focus specifically to the compensation system elements of delegation, performance measurement, and rewards/punishments would in my view help us understand the logic behind whether and how compensation could drive stronger performance, and build specific tests to determine whether the theory is supported by empirical evidence.

A cost-based theory of strategic compensation

Firms following a cost strategy find ways to lower costs by pursuing cheaper sets of activities or avoiding some activities altogether. They create value when the corresponding reduction in product quality is less than the cost savings. Again, the "compensating differentials" argument from labor economics would argue that paying workers less would cause a firm's most productive workers to leave for more lucrative opportunities (Topel, 1984). A firm that could effectively pay some of its workers less than they would make at market rates could have lower costs, and thereby create and capture more value than the competitor.

Because wages are a cost, this theory is in many ways more intuitive than the differentiation story of strategic wages. In my view, it also more closely matches the trajectory of recent research in compensation. For example, recent research suggests some employees are willing to accept lower wages for a company with a socially responsible mission (Burbano, 2016), or for companies who give employees a sense of higher overall purpose beyond simply making profits (Grant, 2007).

However, it is less clear why competitors could not simply imitate a firm's socially responsible mission or higher purpose. While a tobacco company could not argue its mission is more socially responsible than, say, a company investigating advancements in gene therapy, a tobacco company only competes against other tobacco companies. The same can be said about corporate purpose statements. The travel website Travelzoo tells all of its employees that, "If we all traveled, there would be significantly more peace on Earth," while accountant KPMG says, "We can see ourselves as bricklayers or cathedral builders, helping to sustain confidence in the capital markets" (Feintzeig, 2015). But this purpose arguably applies just as much to both companies' competitors. Regardless, employees across firms within industries are highly correlated in the purpose they feel stems from their job; in industries like airlines, fewer than 10 percent of employees connect their job to purpose, while for neurosurgeons nearly 100 percent do so (Wrzesniewski et al., 1997).

Still, the notion that firms can use the compensation system to pay employees in non-monetary ways, and thereby avoid the one-for-one tradeoff between monetary pay and firm profits, is appealing. I do not think we yet have a convincing theory of the exact mechanisms by which this effect happens, and why competitors cannot copy any cost-reducing method designed by a competitor. This certainly seems to be happening with "purpose"; the *Wall Street Journal* reports that: "The words 'mission,' 'higher purpose,' 'change the world' or 'changing the world' were mentioned on earnings calls, in investor meetings and industry conferences 3,243 times in 2014, up from 2,318 five years ago" (Feintzeig, 2015).

A cost-based theory of strategic compensation also very well may require us to reconcile ourselves to one fact with which many compensation scholars may be uncomfortable: firms might strategically minimize wages by exploiting behavioral biases of their employees. This is very similar to the argument that gyms and cell phone plans exploit overconfidence of consumers. For example, research has shown that highly non-linear pay-for-performance plans may attract overconfident employees who mistakenly focus on a part of the pay curve that they are highly unlikely to reach (Larkin and Leider, 2012). In fact, these types of plans are very prevalent in many industries, particularly sales. Strategic marketing scholars are very comfortable with the notion that firms should recognize and tailor their product and marketing design based on consumers' biases. I am not sure whether SHRM scholars are comfortable with the idea that strategic compensation may mean doing the same with the compensation system used for at least some employees. However, I believe some firms do tailor compensation plans in exactly this way, and we should take this notion seriously if we are to understand whether and how compensation can be strategic. I do note the argument can go both ways. Firms may help employees overcome their behavioral biases to be, for example, healthier and thereby more productive, through the use of carefully designed employee wellness programs as part of the compensation system (Gubler et al., 2018).

Distinguishing Differentiation- and Cost-Based Theories

At first glance, the two models laid out above may appear similar. In a differentiation strategy, a firm may design jobs in a way that makes them more exciting or meaningful for employees, meaning they have to pay them less than they would if the job were not as attractive. Could firms both enjoy synergies that lead to higher quality via the compensation system *and* have lower cost compensation than competitors because employees are rewarded in non-monetary ways?

Research in strategy shows that this "bliss strategy" that combines higher quality and lower costs is rarely if ever seen (Porter, 1996), and it is unlikely in compensation strategy as well. First, even the most altruistic employees *do* care about their salary level, and firms that enjoy higher product value due to their compensation system but that *take* salary from employees in the process place their own competitive edge at risk. It is important to remember that competitors will attempt to imitate any source of value capture, so squeezing employee pay if there is a true quality synergy would be foolhardy.

Second, it is important to recognize that *all* firms attempt to minimize costs for a given product value, and analogously maximize product value for a given cost level. For example, Apple clearly pursues a differentiation strategy for its phones, but recently announced it would use lower-quality glass for its handset face because consumers did not value enough the expensive glass it had traditionally used (Yarow, 2014). Conversely, a company following an extreme cost strategy – the European budget airline Ryanair – recently increased its spending on customer service as even price-conscious consumers were deserting the company due to long call waiting times (Topham, 2014). A compensation differentiator will try to have the lowest possible wage bill given its model, and a company following a low-cost compensation model will try to have the most valuable product it can. There are therefore clear empirical predictions that distinguish the two models:

- A differentiator will have higher spending per employee on compensation than competitors; firms using a cost strategy will have lower spending on compensation than competitors.
- A differentiator will have higher product quality and higher market prices than competitors; firms using a cost strategy will be lower than competitors in both dimensions.

BARRIERS TO STRATEGIC COMPENSATION RESEARCH: WHAT OUR CURRENT RESEARCH APPROACH GETS WRONG

Building sound theory in strategy is difficult, and even within HR compensation is not likely to be the lowest-hanging fruit as SHRM scholars attempt to bridge the strategy and HR literatures. Still, I feel that the current research approach to compensation contains a number of elements which are unhelpful to building and testing theories of strategic compensation. In my view these problems contribute to a lack of dialogue among compensation scholars with different disciplinary backgrounds and research tastes, and therefore go beyond the fact that we still lack an integrated theory of strategic compensation. A recognition and discussion of these problems will help our research achieve more as a field, and contribute to greater collaboration with scholars who are not experts in compensation.

Admittedly the critiques below are short on specific examples because it is not good form to criticize colleagues' work in non-peer reviewed work such as this. I therefore limit my examples to those I have made already in other research, or to my own work. However, I hope that all scholars of compensation will think about these critiques.

A Focus on Absolutes

Much of the compensation literature focuses on the ultimate superiority of a given system over another. Pink's book says that all compensation systems need to exclusively reward three factors – autonomy, mastery, and purpose (Pink, 2009). Pfeffer's work argues that individual pay-for-performance is detrimental (Pfeffer, 1998b). Much of the work in economics argues the opposite (Larkin et al., 2012).

Compensation scholars could learn two lessons from our strategy colleagues: 1) there are multiple paths to success even in the same industry or competitive set; and 2) research on performance needs to ask "when" and "how," *not* simply "if," one system is superior to another. Take the SAS Institute case (Pfeffer, 1998a). SAS Institute is an undoubtedly successful company, and Pfeffer's case and other research make a very strong case that the egalitarian compensation plan plays a large role in this success. Other highly successful enterprise software companies such as Oracle take the exact opposite approach to compensation, with a very heavy focus on individual pay-for-performance and a highly skewed compensation system that disproportionately rewards a few employees (Larkin, 2014). In fact, my own MBA case "Arck Systems," loosely based off a competitor to Oracle, argues that the compensation plan used at the company is in large part responsible for its success (Larkin, 2011). One could argue about relative success – the two companies were founded at around the same time, yet Oracle is about ten times larger and is much more profitable, and also has a higher market share in most of its product segments; but that is the exact trap I believe compensation scholars need to avoid.

However, we fall into this trap all the time. GE's competitive up-or-out system is now widely held by both academics and practitioners as an example of a compensation policy that no company should ever use. The same observers hold that annual performance appraisals are things of the past. The new conventional wisdom is that allowing employees to design their own jobs and set their own goals is something that always works. The list goes on and on.

This debate over absolutes can in my mind lead to severely counterproductive debates among compensation scholars. For example, the literature on the positive effects of goal-based compensation systems is arguably one of the most robust in the entire human resource and organizational behavior literatures (Locke and Latham, 2002). However, based on a much smaller set of research (some of which is described below) and numerous compelling (and true) anecdotes, several prominent scholars have recently attacked the literature on goals with a widely cited piece called "Goals Gone Wild" (Ordóñez et al., 2009a). While these scholars made many valid arguments about the potential costs of goals in certain circumstances, I feel that, beyond the unfortunate title (which seems to allude to a distasteful video series), their conclusions are far too sweeping and negative about the efficacy of goals. I agree that the goals literature is also far too focused on the benefits of goals without thinking about costs and boundary conditions, but in my view their critique made the same mistake, but from the other side. This piece unfortunately engendered a strong counter-response from researchers espousing goals (Locke and Latham, 2009), which led to a counter-counter-response (Ordóñez et al., 2009b), with both sides claiming the other had abandoned "good scholarship." To be honest, I find the entire discussion counterproductive. My own belief is that, like any compensation system, goals often work, and often do not work; and, rather than arguing about whether or not they work, we need to define boundary conditions that help us define the circumstances under which goals should be used and when they should be avoided.

This same debate happens with many elements of a compensation plan, not just goals: pay-for-performance is another prominent example, as is disclosure of relative performance rank, the use of corporate awards, or countless other examples. These debates about "whether" a compensation system or element works are to me an exact symptom of the lack of good theory building around compensation, performance, and strategy. Ultimately, good theory helps scholars and practitioners map causes to outcomes, and a good theory will be ambidextrous and help us understand when a given lever will lead to a desirable outcome, and when it will not. Are autonomy, mastery, and purpose the key facets of a compensation plan? Is pay-for-performance detrimental? Does pay-for-performance drive stronger performance? Should employees be force curved against each other? Should we allow employees autonomy to design their own jobs? The answer to *all* of these questions is the same: *sometimes*. If the answer were "always" or "never," then we should see all companies converge towards that practice over time. We simply do not see this convergence, and never have. The role of theory is to explain how and when these practices should be used, *not* to explain that one way is better than another. Again, strategists are ahead of us in understanding this; we are being outperformed, and I do not believe there is a barrier to imitation regarding the best practice of avoiding absolutes and instead focusing our theory building on predicting when and explaining how.

Confusing Marginal Effects for Baseline Effects

Quantitative empirical research largely focuses on identifying the marginal effect of one variable on another. What is the effect of taking a medicine on a health outcome, compared to those who take a sugar pill? Empirical research in compensation largely takes this exact approach. For example, Dan Pink tells a compelling story of the software company Atlassian giving all its engineers one day a quarter without any job assignments, responsibilities, or reporting structures. Employees are told to go work on whatever they want, with whomever they want, and simply report back the results of this work. The result, Pink says in his book (p. 93) and video talk, is that Atlassian generates more new ideas on this day than any other day in the quarter.

The "so what" Pink drives from Atlassian's experience is that firms should "just get out of the way," give autonomy to workers, and stop paying performance bonuses for new ideas. Here Pink makes the fundamental mistake of confusing a marginal effect – the effect of adding *one day* of autonomy to *89 days* without it – with a baseline effect. In its baseline system, Atlassian goes directly against Pink's recommendation and pays its employees for performance. According to the recruiting website Glassdoor (2018), Atlassian pays its software engineers annual performance bonuses of nearly 30 percent of salary, and formally assesses the quality of their innovative output (among other criteria) when assigning bonuses. Adding a small marginal bump in autonomy worked; but Atlassian has not moved to a system of full autonomy with no link between pay and performance – in fact, for the vast majority of a worker's time working, they are not fully autonomous and are paid for performance.

Once this point is made – that marginal effects are dependent on the baseline system against which they are measured – it is extremely obvious. Pink is not an academic, so he can be forgiven for the gigantic, faulty leap of logic he makes with this (and a number of other) policy recommendations; but we academics who study compensation make the same leap all the time as we present the implications of our own work. Our studies identify marginal effects of a compensation policy change, but we usually spend little time talking about the baseline system against which this effect was measured, and we often far overshoot the support against which our variable was measured when we talk about policy implications. I read the discussion and conclusion sections of many papers on compensation, including some of my own, and shake my head at the propensity we have as a field to make sweeping generalizations about baseline systems when all we have identified is a marginal effect. It is simply sloppy reasoning.

Looking for Free Motivation and Costless Nudges

As many researchers in compensation have turned against pay-for-performance, research has naturally turned to alternative ways to motivate employees that do not involve pay. Many studies emphasize the fact that non-pay motivators are "free," and therefore must be cost effective because the return on investment is effectively infinite.

For example, the literature on corporate awards emphasizes the fact that they motivate without apparent cost. This idea is so prominent in the awards literature that it even appears in paper titles; e.g. "Getting More Work for Nothing? Symbolic Awards and Worker Performance" (Kosfeld and Neckerman, 2010). Similarly, recent work on performance feedback suggests that simply showing people their relative ranking on a task is a free motivator; one paper's abstract says, "We find that merely providing this information leads to a large and long-lasting increase in productivity that is *costless* to the firm" (Blanes i Vidal and Nossol, 2011, emphasis in the original). The increased emphasis on "free" motivation matches the many studies on the impact of "nudges" on consumer and employee decision making.

There are several problems with "nudges" in compensation settings. For one, in at least some circumstances they are costlier than recognized by their supporters. Both corporate awards (Gubler et al., 2016) and disclosure of relative performance have been shown to be highly demotivating to some employees in certain circumstances (Barankay, 2012; Edelman and Larkin, 2015), and we do not have strong theory about when to use them and when not to. Second, most research on nudges are either experimental or look at a relatively short time period (Goodwin, 2012). The effects of many compensation-based nudges, such as "gamification in the workplace," have been shown to wear off in as little as two weeks (Larkin and Ramirez, 2018). Most importantly, it is hard to envision a scenario whereby designing nudges to bring "free" motivation is a driver of significant differences in employee performance. Nudges may work for decisions people make quickly based on heuristics or rules-of-thumb, but decades of HR research suggests actions taken on the job – especially those that are intimately tied to performance – are much more deliberate than those affected by nudges (Becker and Gerhart, 1996). Again, strategists are ahead of the game here; one of the key lessons in strategy is, "It's all about tradeoffs, and you never get something for nothing." The fact that we are focused on "free motivators" is in my view a mistake.

Difficulty with Two Types of Employee Heterogeneity

No HR scholar is surprised by the notion that employees are heterogeneous in their motivators, abilities, and countless other factors. Robust research showing the effects of different compensation system elements on *average* employee performance is still relatively new, and demonstrating heterogeneous treatment effects in a meaningful way is very difficult. Much existing research simply focuses on observables such as gender, age, and tenure within a company; these factors represent a good starting place, but motivation and performance are at best weakly correlated with these explanatory variables. There surely exist stronger differences in motivators that are harder to measure.

There is a second source of heterogeneity that is largely missing from current research: the fact that an individual employee will have different sources of motivation that can be activated in different levels depending on the stimulus. Recent research on corporate purpose, for example, finds that most of the approximately one-third of employees who respond to meaningful corporate purpose with increased effort also respond to increased extrinsic rewards such as pay and recognition (Berg et al., 2013). We know virtually nothing about how different compensation policies affect the same person differently, much less how to best craft a compensation system that takes advantage of an individual's full set of motivators.

Indeed, it is worth emphasizing (almost as its own sub-section) that continued arguing by those who ascribe to a self-interested, rational employee like that modeled in agency theory and those who believe that psychology, not money, is the largest driver of employee motivation is detrimental. Both camps are right, and both are wrong. We need to stop believing that employees who care about their company's purpose or that value autonomy or that will sacrifice salary for recognition (as I show in my 2011 paper about sales awards in enterprise software) do not care about their pay levels. The average employee is motivated *both* by money *and* by non-pecuniary factors (Larkin et al., 2012). We need research that combines the insight of both lines of thought.

An Overemphasis on CEO Pay

In the last decade, approximately 70 percent of the empirical research on compensation has focused on the pay of top management team (TMT) members such as CEOs (Larkin et al., 2012). A cynic might argue that this focus stems from data availability, since public companies are required to disclose the salary of their five most highly compensated executives. It is much more difficult to obtain data on pay of non-executive employees, especially across many firms.

The CEO pay literature is obviously extremely valuable, but I feel it plays a limited role in our understanding of strategic compensation. For one, the available evidence strongly suggests that higher firm performance drives higher CEO pay, and not vice versa, and that firm size and length of employment, not CEO-specific factors, are the primary drivers of CEO pay differentials. Furthermore, CEO compensation contracts across public companies may differ in pay levels, but the form pay contracts take is actually quite homogenous. This is in contrast to the form of compensation across workers even in the same industry or company, which tends to be highly variable – especially considering an expanded definition of "compensation" that includes job design and performance measurement.

Data and research on CEO pay is inarguably valuable, but it has proved largely unhelpful in building an understanding of how pay systems affect individual or firm performance. To unpack this question we need more and better research on non-executive pay.

RESEARCHING STRATEGIC COMPENSATION: WHAT WILL IT TAKE?

Building Theories of Strategic Compensation

A theory of strategic compensation will explain how a firm's compensation system can lead to higher employee performance for that firm's employees, and why competitors are either unable to imitate that system, or why imitation of that system will not lead to the same level of employee performance. While strategy is ultimately about firm- and not employee-level performance, I believe the link between employee and firm performance is well enough established that it could be left out of a theory. Additionally, good theory must choose where to draw boundaries, and the boundary between employee and firm performance seems like a logical one.

The arguments developed above, along with longstanding existing compensation theory, strongly suggest that a theory that rests on pay levels alone is unlikely to logically predict performance that is sustainably better than competitors. In addition, defining compensation as a system rather than a pay level reflects that pay-for-performance links the tasks assigned employees to their rewards, which requires a method of measuring performance. Notably, all three elements of this simplified compensation system are known to affect employee motivation.

Describing the channels by which employee performance is affected by these three elements will be difficult because there are a wide variety of pecuniary and psychological factors by which compensation systems affect performance. Indeed, it is unclear *ex ante* which intermediate variables affect performance – motivation/effort? Decision quality? Task alignment? Teamwork? Risk tolerance? The empirical literature suggests all of these variables can be affected by various compensation structures. Serious thinking will need to be done about which of these variables can viably lead to sustainable performance improvements via compensation. Reflecting my bias as a scholar, I feel that focusing on motivation and effort will likely bear the most fruit, but I am not confident in this prediction. I am confident that any good theory will need to focus on one or two of these channels, rather than attempt to cover them all.

It is also *ex ante* unclear whether a theory of strategic compensation will primarily rely on arguments around employee improvement, or employee sorting – meaning the attraction and retention of a certain group of employees (Booth and Frank, 1999). I suspect that the majority of compensation scholars 15 years ago would have said that sorting is the more important variable, but that the majority today would say the opposite. Conceptually a sorting argument seems more difficult to make, since it is arguably easier to hire highly skilled employees than it is to perfectly motivate them.

The most challenging part of the theory building will be to persuasively describe the mechanisms that lead to stronger employee performance due to compensation system elements. Again, the well from which researchers can draw is vast, and encompasses a wide range of theories from social psychology, judgment and decision making, sociology, and economics. In combination across these fields, our knowledge of factors that contribute to employee performance is gigantic. But sifting among this knowledge base to key in on mechanisms that lead to sustainable improvements in performance will require a lot of thought.

Empirically Testing Theories of Strategic Compensation

If the requirements to build a real theory of strategic compensation seemed daunting, empirically testing these theories is even more difficult. Data on employee compensation is difficult to acquire, and although companies are increasingly willing to share data with academic researchers, robust statistical identification with observational data is nearly impossible. As Michael Jensen (1983) famously quipped, "In organizations, everything is endogenous," so merely acquiring a database of a firm's compensation plan – job allocation, performance measurement, and pay – is unlikely to allow direct testing of a theory.

There is a related problem – often the positive and negative effects of certain compensation policies run in the same way (Larkin and Pierce, 2016; Singh and Larkin, 2015).

Pay-for-performance in my view almost surely motivates higher effort in many cases; but it also motivates detrimental, costly behavior such as cheating in many cases. If we collect data only on employee performance, and do not or cannot collect data on negative outcomes, we will overestimate the benefit of a given system. The exact opposite is true of studies that only focus on costs such as cheating – they overestimate the costs of a system.

As noted previously, firms are increasingly open to running experiments, but these tend to be about relatively minor parts of the compensation plan, for obvious reasons. As a rule, firms do not experiment with compensation plan elements that are thought to be strategic, such as core tasks assigned to skilled employees or whether to fire a certain percentage of low performers every year. Laboratory experiments and field experiments with online labor marketplaces such as Upwork will continue to yield insight, but abstract away from many of the long-term considerations of incentive systems such as careers, promotions, and organizational culture.

Much more attention needs to be paid to analyzing compensation at the system level, meaning the interaction of job design, performance measurement, and compensation. There is a real role for experiments here, but it likely means changing standard experimental design. In many OB and HR journals, for example, a hypothesized marginal effect is tested via a number of studies in separate task domains and participant settings in order to demonstrate generalizability and that the effect is not specific to one task. This approach has obvious strengths, but leaves little room to examine systems – how combinations of factors and their variation interact to affect performance. To take another example from the goals literature, one prominent paper using a laboratory experiment on goals and cheating argues that goals cause cheating, but varied both the setting of a goal and the communication of a social comparison when making a goal (Schweitzer et al., 2004). Later research found that by carefully unpacking these two systemic elements, goals did not cause increased cheating, and the effect was due to social comparisons and to different pay levels commonly used in goal-based systems (Chao and Larkin, 2017). We need more careful research at the compensation systems level, not the compensation element level. Experiments in operations research, where systems design has played a more central role, can be informative as compensation scholars begin to truly understand compensation at the systems level.

There is also a role for detailed, careful qualitative research, as this research is in many ways best suited to analyze nuanced systems-level effects. One great example of compensation research of this type is the research stream on compensation for highly creative tasks (Amabile, 1998). In general I am not persuaded by the laboratory experiments on motivational crowding out, which show that adding and then removing monetary pay for a task causes post-removal performance to plummet below the level before pay was introduced at all. These experiments arguably stem from participant anger that a monetary incentive was removed rather than any change in intrinsic motivation; indeed, a number of large-scale, careful field experiments in firms fail to show a crowding-out effect (Esteves-Sorenson and Broce, 2016). However, the qualitative work that argues that pay-for-performance is detrimental to creativity is very careful and highly believable. The compensation literature needs more work like this.

The good news is empirical researchers can start to run studies at the systems level even before the theory of strategic compensation has caught up. There are numerous inconsistencies and confounded results that careful systems-level research can help illuminate.

CONCLUSION

Compensation remains a hot topic for both business practitioners and management scholars. We need more and better research linking compensation to firm performance, so the debate about whether and how a firm's compensation system can lead to strategic competitive advantage may seem didactic. However, the distinction between compensation as a strategic vs. efficiency lever for firms is critical for both managers and academics. From the manager point of view, if compensation is simply an efficiency lever, a smart executive will simply hire compensation experts to optimize the system, and spend her time on the firm's key strategic issues. In contrast, if a firm's strategic advantage over rivals critically depends on its compensation system, the executive will want to be intimately familiar with the system used at the firm, and be deeply involved in key decisions around its design and management.

For academics, the case for distinguishing between efficiency and strategy is more nuanced, but just as important. Scholars of operational efficiency spend their time identifying sources of unneeded costs, systemic frictions, and unanticipated blockages. The focus of this research is on steps managers should take to have an efficient system that minimizes these sources of cost. Scholars of strategy look at systems from a fundamentally different approach – one that is not quite the opposite of that held by operations scholars, since strategy considers costs as well, but from a viewpoint that stresses different key factors. In strategy, scholars are focused on value creation and imitability by other firms. A strategic firm must not only be efficient, but must also create value above and beyond its competitors in a way that cannot be imitated.

Indeed, the implicit argument I make in this chapter is that much of the literature on strategic compensation, including much of my own, identifies performance differences due to compensation system changes, and waves its hands and calls this change evidence of "strategic compensation." This simply is not enough. We need to be more nuanced and careful in our thinking, writing, and communication about our research.

As an empirical researcher, I am biased towards unique settings with rich data that allow the measurement of performance differences. But I now believe that without a much more rigorous theory or set of theories about how and why compensation is strategic, empirical evidence alone can only take us so far. We know a lot about the performance effects of different elements of compensation systems. Although empirical research on compensation at the systems level is, as noted above, still greatly needed, I think the next step in more tightly linking the literatures on compensation systems and strategy is to build rigorous, testable theories on exactly how and when compensation can truly be strategic.

CHAPTER SUMMARY

BOX 24.1 KEY TAKEAWAYS

1. The distinction between compensation as a strategic and efficiency lever for firms is critical for both managers and academics.
2. Much of the literature on strategic compensation identifies performance differences due to compensation system changes, and calls such changes evidence of "strategic compensation."

BOX 24.2 DIRECTIONS FOR FUTURE RESEARCH

1. Future research should engage in much more rigorous theory or set of theories about how and why compensation is strategic.
2. More empirical research on compensation at the systems level is needed.
3. Research should more tightly link the literatures on compensation systems and strategy to build rigorous, testable theories on how and when compensation can be strategic.

REFERENCES

Amabile, Theresa (1998). How to Kill Creativity. *Harvard Business Review*. September–October. https://hbr.org/1998/09/how-to-kill-creativity.

Barankay, Iwan (2012). Rank Incentives: Evidence from a Randomized Workplace Experiment. https://faculty.wharton.upenn.edu/wp-content/uploads/2012/07/rankincentives_1.pdf.

Baker, George P., Michael C. Jensen, and Kevin J. Murphy (1988). Compensation and Incentives: Practice vs. Theory. *Journal of Finance 43*(3), Papers and Proceedings of the Forty-Seventh Annual Meeting of the American Finance Association, Chicago, Illinois, December 28–30, 1987 (July 1988), pp. 593–616.

Becker, Brian, and Barry Gerhart (1996). The Impact of Human Resource Management on Organizational Performance: Progress and Prospects. *Academy of Management Journal 39*(4): 779–801.

Bell, Katherine (2015). Your Favorite HBR Articles of 2015. *Harvard Business Review*. December 24. https://hbr.org/2015/12/your-favorite-hbr-articles-of-2015.

Berg, Justin M., Jane E. Dutton, and Amy Wrzesniewski (2013). Job Crafting and Meaningful Work. In Bryan J. Dik, Zinta S. Byrne, and Michael F. Steger (eds), *Purpose and Meaning in the Workplace*. Washington, DC: American Psychological Association: 81–104.

Blanes i Vidal, Jordi, and Mareike Nossol (2011). Tournaments Without Prizes: Evidence from Personnel Records. *Management Science 57*(10): 1721–36.

Booth, Alison L., and Jeff Frank (1999). Earnings, Productivity, and Performance-Related Pay. *Journal of Labor Economics 17*(3): 447–63.

Burbano, Vanessa C. (2016). Social Responsibility Messages and Worker Wage Requirements: Field Experimental Evidence from Online Labor Marketplaces. *Organization Science 27*(4): 1010–28.

Chao, Matthew, and Ian Larkin (2017). Why Do Goal-Based Incentives Cause Cheating? Unpacking the Confounding Effects of Goals, Social Comparisons and Monetary Pay. Working Paper.

Chen, Ming-Jer (1996). Competitor Analysis and Interfirm Rivalry: Toward A Theoretical Integration. *Academy of Management Review 21*(1): 100–134.

Coff, Russell W. (1997). Human Assets and Management Dilemmas: Coping with Hazards on the Road to Resource-Based Theory. *The Academy of Management Review 22*(2): 374–402.

Coff, Russell W. (2010). Strategic Human Capital Newsletter: Inaugural Issue. https://www.strategicmanagement.net/ig-strategic-human-capital/overview.

Collins, Christopher J., and Kevin D. Clark (2003). Strategic Human Resource Practices, Top Management Team Social Networks, and Firm Performance: The Role of Human Resource Practices in Creating Organizational Competitive Advantage. *Academy of Management Journal 46*(6): 740–51.

Coughlan, Anne T. and Ronald M. Schmidt (1985). Executive Compensation, Management Turnover, and Firm Performance: An Empirical Investigation. *Journal of Accounting and Economics* 7(1–3): 43–66.

Dess, Gregory G. and Peter S. Davis (1984). Porter's (1980) Generic Strategies as Determinants of Strategic Group Membership and Organizational Performance. *Academy of Management Journal* 27(3): 467–88.

Dyl, Edward A. (1988). Corporate Control and Management Compensation: Evidence on the Agency Problem. *Managerial and Decision Economics* 9(1): 21–5.

Edelman, Benjamin, and Ian Larkin (2015). Social Comparison and Deception across Workplace Hierarchies: Field and Experimental Evidence. *Organization Science* 26(1): 78–98.

Esteves-Sorenson, Constança, and Robert Broce (2016). Do Monetary Incentives Undermine Performance on Intrinsically Enjoyable Tasks? A Field Test. Working Paper.

Feintzeig, Rachel (2015). I Don't Have a Job. I Have a Higher Calling. *Wall Street Journal*. February 24. https://www.wsj.com/articles/corporate-mission-statements-talk-of-higher-purpose-1424824784.

Foss, Nicolai, and Torben Pedersen (2014). Agenda for SMS Copenhagen Special Conference on Microfoundations for Strategic Management Research. https://copenhagen.strategicmanagement.net/pdf/program-booklet.pdf.

Gerhart Barry, Sara L. Rynes, and Ingrid Smithey Fulmer (2009). Pay and Performance: Individuals, Groups, and Executives. *Academy of Management Annals* 3(1): 251–315.

Glassdoor (2018). Atlassian. https://www.glassdoor.com/Salary/Atlassian-Salaries-E115699.htm. Accessed December 4, 2018.

Goodwin, Tom (2012). Why We Should Reject "Nudge." *Politics* 32(2): 85–92.

Grant, Adam M. (2007). Relational Job Design and the Motivation to Make a Prosocial Difference. *Academy of Management Review* 32(2): 393–417.

Gryta, Thomas, and Ted Mann (2018). GE Powered the American Century – Then It Burned Out. *Wall Street Journal*. December 14. https://www.wsj.com/articles/ge-powered-the-american-centurythen-it-burned-out-11544796010.

Gubler, Timothy, Ian Larkin, and Lamar Pierce (2016). Motivational Spillovers from Awards: Crowding Out in a Multitasking Environment. *Organization Science* 27(2): 286–303.

Gubler, Timothy, Ian Larkin, and Lamar Pierce (2018). Doing Well by Making Well: The Impact of Corporate Wellness Programs on Employee Productivity. *Management Science* 64(11): 4967–87.

Humphreys, David, and Brad Hoffman (2015). The Workforce of the Future: An Assessment of Technology Proficiency. Economist Intelligence Unit. https://eiuperspectives.economist.com/sites/default/files/EIU_ATT_The%20workforce%20of%20the%20future_PDF_0.pdf.

Igalens, Jacques and Patrice Roussel (1999). A Study of the Relationships between Compensation Package, Work Motivation and Job Satisfaction. *Journal of Organizational Behavior* 20(7): 1003–25.

Jensen, Michael C. (1983). Organization Theory and Methodology. *Accounting Review* 58(2): 319–39.

Jensen, Michael C., and William H. Meckling (1976). Theory of the Firm: Managerial Behavior, Agency Costs and Ownership Structure. *Journal of Financial Economics* 3(4): 305–60.

Katz, Lawrence F. (1986). Efficiency Wage Theories: A Partial Evaluation. *NBER Macroeconomics Annual 1*: 235–75.

Kauflin, Jeff (2017). The World's Most Influential Business Thinkers 2017. *Forbes*. November 14. https://www.forbes.com/sites/jeffkauflin/2017/11/14/the-worlds-most-influential-business-thinkers-2017/#7035691b5ec4.

Kaplan, Robert S., and David P. Norton (2008). *The Execution Premium: Linking Strategy to Operations for Competitive Advantage*. Boston, MA: Harvard Business School Press.

Kosfeld, Michael, and Susanne Neckerman (2010). Getting More Work for Nothing? Symbolic Awards and Worker Performance. IZA DP No. 5040.

Larkin, Ian (2011). Arck Systems (A). Harvard Business School Case 911-056.

Larkin, Ian (2014). The Cost of High-Powered Incentives: Employee Gaming in Enterprise Software Sales. *Journal of Labor Economics* 32(2): 1–29.

Larkin, Ian, and Stephen Leider (2012). Incentive Schemes, Sorting and Behavioral Biases of Employees: Experimental Evidence. *American Economic Journal: Microeconomics* 4(2): 184–214.

Larkin, Ian, and Lamar Pierce (2016). Compensation and Employee Misconduct: The Inseparability of Productive and Counterproductive Behavior in Firms. In Donald Palmer, Kristin Smith-Crowe, and Royston Greenwood (eds), *Organizational Wrongdoing: Key Perspectives and New Directions*. Cambridge: Cambridge University Press: 270–95.

Larkin, Ian, and Cristian Ramirez (2018). Gamification and Employee Motivation: Evidence from a Fuel Savings Gamification Program at a Major Trucking Fleet. Working Paper, UCLA.

Larkin, Ian, Lamar Pierce, and Francesca Gino (2012). The Psychological Costs of Pay-for-Performance: Implications for the Strategic Compensation of Employees. *Strategic Management Journal* 33(10): 1194–214.

Lazear, Edward P. (2000). Performance Pay and Productivity. *American Economic Review* 90(5): 1346–61.

Lepak, David P., Ken G. Smith, and M. Susan Taylor (2007). Value Creation and Value Capture: A Multilevel Perspective. *Academy of Management Review* 32(1): 180–94.

Locke, Edwin A., and Gary P. Latham (2002). Building a Practically Useful Theory of Goal Setting and Task Motivation: A 35-Year Odyssey. *American Psychologist* 57(9): 705–17.

Locke, Edwin A., and Gary P. Latham (2009). Has Goal Setting Gone Wild, or Have Its Attackers Abandoned Good Scholarship? *Academy of Management Perspectives 23*(1): 17–23.
Lohr, Steve (2016). Goodbye, Ivory Tower. Hello, Silicon Valley Candy Store. *New York Times*. September 3. https://www.nytimes.com/2016/09/04/technology/goodbye-ivory-tower-hello-silicon-valley-candy-store.html.
Martocchio, Joseph J. (2016). *Strategic Compensation: A Human Resource Management Approach* (9th edn). Boston: Prentice Hall.
Milkovich, George T., and Jerry M. Newman (1984). *Compensation*. Plano, TX: Business Publications.
Newbert, Scott L. (2007). Empirical research on the resource-based view of the firm: an assessment and suggestions for future research. *Strategic Management Journal 28*(2): 121–46.
Ordóñez, Lisa D., Maurice E. Schweitzer, Adam D. Galinsky, and Max H. Bazerman (2009a). Goals Gone Wild: The Systematic Side Effects of Overprescribing Goal Setting. *Academy of Management Perspectives 23*(1): 6–16.
Ordóñez, Lisa D., Maurice E. Schweitzer, Adam D. Galinsky, and Max H. Bazerman (2009b). On Good Scholarship, Goal Setting, and Scholars Gone Wild. *Academy of Management Perspectives 23*(3): 82–7.
Orth, Maximilian, and Judith Volmer (2017). Daily within-person effects of job autonomy and work engagement on innovative behaviour: The cross-level moderating role of creative self-efficacy. *European Journal of Work and Organizational Psychology 26*(4): 601–12.
Pfeffer, Jeff (1998a). SAS Institute: A Different Approach to Incentives and People Management Practices in the Software Industry. Stanford University Case No.HR6A.
Pfeffer, Jeff (1998b). Six Dangerous Myths about Pay. *Harvard Business Review*. May–June. https://hbr.org/1998/05/six-dangerous-myths-about-pay.
Pink, Daniel H. (2009). *Drive: The Surprising Truth About What Motivates Us*. New York: Riverhead.
Porter, Michael E. (1979). How Competitive Forces Shape Strategy. *Harvard Business Review*. March–April. https://hbr.org/1979/03/how-competitive-forces-shape-strategy.
Porter, Michael E. (1985). *Competitive Advantage: Creating and Sustaining Superior Performance*. New York: Simon and Schuster.
Porter, Michael E. (1996). What Is Strategy? *Harvard Business Review*. November–December. https://hbr.org/1996/11/what-is-strategy.
RSA Animate (2010). Drive: The surprising truth about what motivates us. https://www.youtube.com/watch?v=u6XAPnuFjJc.
Schweitzer, Maurice E., Lisa D. Ordóñez, and Bambi Douma (2004). Goal Setting as a Motivator of Unethical Behavior. *Academy of Management Journal 47*(3): 422–32.
Singh, Ravi, and Ian Larkin (2015). Auditor Conservatism, Incentive Compensation, and the Quality of Financial Reporting. *Journal of Law, Economics, and Organization 31*(4): 721–51.
Smith, Robert S. (1979). Compensating Wage Differentials and Public Policy: A Review. *ILR Review 32*(3): 339–52.
Topel, Robert H. (1984). Equilibrium Earnings, Turnover, and Unemployment: New Evidence. *Journal of Labor Economics 2*(4): 500–522.
Topham, Gwyn (2014). Ryanair Puts 32% Jump in Profits Down to Being Nicer. November 3. *The Guardian*. https://www.theguardian.com/business/2014/nov/03/ryanair-raises-profit-surge-winter-bookings.
Welch, Jack, with John A. Byrne (2001). *Jack: Straight from the Gut*. New York: Warner Books.
Wrzesniewski, Amy, Clark McCauley, Paul Rozin, and Barry Schwartz (1997). Jobs, Careers, and Callings: People's Relations to their Work. *Journal of Research in Personality 31*(1): 21–33.
Yarow, Jay (2014). Here's Why Apple Didn't Use an "Unbreakable" Sapphire Screen for the iPhone 6. *Business Insider*. September 23. https://www.businessinsider.com/heres-why-apple-didnt-use-unbreakable-sapphire-glass-for-the-iphone-6-2014-9.

25. Commentary on Larkin and Nyberg and Reilly

Barry Gerhart

I have been asked to comment on two chapters on compensation, one written from a "micro" perspective (Nyberg and Reilly) and the other from a "macro" perspective (Larkin). As part of this, I have been asked to identify commonalities and differences in the perspectives, as well as provide my own thoughts. The overriding goal is to help "push the field forward."

BASIC FACTS ON COMPENSATION IN THE WORKPLACE AND A FEW "REALITY CHECKS"

Let me begin with a few general observations on the study of compensation, including some definitions and basic facts (descriptive data). The descriptive data are important because they (one hopes) provide an anchor in reality (a "reality check"). Research that is meant to inform policy and practice in organizations should perhaps not deviate too far from studying compensation as we observe it in the workplace (unless, of course, it is to develop and study something innovative/new that is not currently part of compensation practice). Compensation can be defined as "any direct or indirect payments to employees, such as wages, bonuses, stock, and benefits" (Gerhart and Milkovich, 1992). For present purposes, I will put aside the (sizeable) indirect component (i.e., benefits, including insurance and retirement, which in the United States are received primarily through employers and account for about 46 cents on top of every dollar of direct pay, or about 32 percent of total combined direct + indirect payments).

The direct component includes base salary, short-term incentives/bonuses, and long-term incentives. Base salary is fixed in the sense that it is very rarely reduced and, in recent years, has increased by about 3 percent per year on average in the United States (not counting increases due to promotion and/or change of employer), with those in the highest of five performance rating categories (about 7 percent of employees) receiving a 4.5 percent base salary increase, with those in the next highest (29 percent) receiving 3.6 percent and those in the middle category (56 percent) receiving 2.6 percent. The remaining two categories account for 8 percent of employees and the mean increase is 0.8 percent (Gerhart et al., 2019, Chapter 10).

The incentive components are also referred to as "variable pay" because in theory (and often in practice) the payouts differ over time depending on performance and/or employer ability to pay (e.g., profitability). Also, variable pay (e.g., a bonus) does not become part of base pay (and is thus not an addition to fixed costs in future years). Variable pay as a percentage of direct compensation is strongly and positively related to job level. For nonexempt workers, short-term incentives average 3–4 percent of variable pay and are primarily determined not by individual performance, but by corporate and/or business unit performance (Gerhart et al., 2019, Chapter 9)[1] For non-executive exempt employees, it rises to about 7 percent of salary, still with corporate and/or business unit performance as the primary determinants. At the executive level, it is about 27 percent, still with corporate/business performance as the primary driver, but which now may provide more line of sight given the potential for workers at this level to influence those performance metrics. Those at the executive level also receive the bulk of long-term incentive opportunity. A chief executive officer (CEO) will typically receive most of his/her direct compensation in the form of variable pay (short-term incentives, often based on profitability plus long-term incentives, based primarily on stock returns).[2]

It is also important to note that if one defines pay for performance (PFP) as "the degree to which, over time, employee pay covaries positively with performance, measured as some combination of individual and/or group/organization measures of performance" (Gerhart, 2017), then the primary mechanism by which pay and performance are related over the course of a career for the vast majority of workers is through the positive effect of performance on the probability of promotions to higher job levels, with each promotion leading to not only a higher base salary but also larger variable pay earnings potential (Gerhart, 2017; Trevor et al., 1997). Over the course of a career, it is promotions, as influenced by performance, which account for the bulk of PFP (as defined above). Within a single organization, the question is: are employees having consistently high performance significantly more likely than those with lower performance to rise to the top of the total compensation distribution? From a worker point of view, the question is: if I have consistently high performance, am I more likely to than those with lower performance to rise to the top of the total compensation distribution, either in my present organization or in a different organization?

By implication, whether the annual pay base pay increase per year (which averages 3 percent across all workers and averages 4.5 percent for a small group of the highest performers) is related to performance is of interest, but misses, at least when focusing on any single year, most of what is PFP, which we have defined in terms of the connection over the course of a career between pay and performance – which is primarily a function of promotion/advancement. That being said, the goal is to include as many components of PFP as possible, which will vary in terms of time frame (quarterly, annual, long-term, career), strength/intensity, performance measure (level – individual, unit, organization; results-based, behavior-based), and whether it is fixed or variable (i.e., becomes part of base pay or not). One trend we have seen is that when it comes to annual pay programs, bonuses (variable pay) have grown over time relative to base pay increases (fixed pay). Some anticipated this shift early on (Schwab and Olson, 1990), and it is important that some recent research has sought to better understand the consequences and mechanisms of these different annual pay programs (Nyberg et al., 2016).

Returning to the "reality check" idea, this means it is difficult to study this central component of PFP (the PFP relationship over the course of a career) in the laboratory or even in a field setting in the absence of longitudinal data. When it comes to variable pay, it might seem at first blush easier to study in the laboratory and/or field settings. However, *the* most typical academic study of variable pay is the study of individual incentives (variable pay based on individual physical output). For example, meta-analytic summaries of PFP effects on performance in the psychology literature typically operationalize PFP as individual incentives (e.g., Byron and Khazanchi, 2012; Jenkins et al. 1998), and these reviews also document that individual incentives have substantial average positive effects on performance. Reviews of PFP that include research on other forms of PFP also generally concludes overall positive effects of PFP (e.g., Gerhart et al., 2009; Gerhart, 2017; Shaw and Gupta, 2015). Other psychological research also operationalizes PFP as individual incentives in studying other dependent variables (e.g., intrinsic motivation, Deci et al., 1999). Reviews of empirical economic research on PFP also focus on individual incentives (e.g., Oyer and Schaefer, 2011). Larkin seems to also define PFP in terms of incentives. Finally, well-known critiques of PFP in the more applied literature (e.g., Pfeffer, 1998; Pink, 2009) largely focus on problems that arise from using individual incentives. (This is likely the basis of Larkin's sense that psychologists do not generally believe that PFP works.)

However, the reality check here is that individual incentive plans are actually quite rare in the workplace, by one estimate covering fewer than 4 percent of U.S. non-sales workers (Gerhart, 2017). An individual incentive is the type of plan that Frederick Taylor implemented at Bethlehem Steel to incentivize workers to manually pick up and move more pieces of pig iron (by paying them a piece rate for each pig moved) in his book *The Principles of Scientific Management*, which was written over 100 years ago (Gerhart, 2017). It is not exactly the PFP plan of broad applicability to "21st-century work." As such, the reality check tells us that PFP research has historically been disconnected and different from the way PFP is actually executed in workplaces of today. (This is contrary to Larkin's discussion on p. 407, which seems to equate PFP with "piece rates and bonuses.")

Instead, as noted, PFP is a function of annual base pay increases, short-term and long-term variable pay plans (which rarely use physical output performance measures), and promotion/advancement to higher job levels (Gerhart and Milkovich, 1992; Gerhart, 2017), which have higher salaries and higher variable pay opportunities. As Nyberg and Reilly point out, most organizations use more than one form of PFP, consistent with earlier observations in the literature. ("In many organizations, employees are covered by multiple plans . . . In fact, if each plan is better at achieving some objectives than others, a mix of plans may make a good deal of sense" [Gerhart and Milkovich, 1992].) See also Gerhart et al., 1996, who talk about organizations using a "diversification" approach to compensation design to improve performance while reducing risk.

Another reality check has to do with the distinction between incentive effects and sorting effects in the workplace (Gerhart and Fang, 2014, 2015; Gerhart and Milkovich, 1992; Gerhart and Rynes, 2003). Nyberg and Reilly explain the importance of these two mechanisms and provide a review of the evidence. The sorting mechanism was basically "missed" by researchers for many years, with an important study by Lazear (2000) playing a major role in directing attention to sorting. However, as Gerhart and Fang (2015) point out, the sorting mechanism (with important exceptions like Cadsby et al., 2007) is, probably unintentionally, "designed out" in almost all experimental research on PFP. By definition, any time that subjects are randomly assigned to conditions in a between-subject design (e.g., incentive versus no incentive), there can be no sorting, which is by definition nonrandom and depends on worker preferences, which in turn likely depend on worker performance (and thus earnings potential under incentive versus no incentive payment schemes). In any case, as Nyberg and Reilly's review and previous reviews (e.g., Gerhart and Fang, 2014) demonstrate, the generally positive effects of PFP occur to an important extent via sorting. (This is contrary to Larkin's claim on p. 419 that most researchers have shifted their view to the belief that sorting does not much matter.)

AREAS OF CONVERGENCE AND DIVERGENCE IN FOCUS BY THE TWO CHAPTERS

Next, I will summarize some key issues from both chapters, including where they converge (not much) and where they diverge (mostly). (By "converge" I mean both chapters addressed a particular topic, not that they agreed or disagreed.) I will also provide some commentary on the authors' arguments.

The main convergence seems to be that both agree that PFP is central to any understanding of compensation. However, there is not much convergence beyond that. Nyberg and Reilly are focused on how PFP affects unit-level outcomes because they observe that such effects may not be the same as those studied and identified at the individual level. They are also interested in intervening mechanisms (opening the proverbial "black box"). Larkin's focus, by contrast, is taking on critics who make statements to the effect that PFP does not work. I agree with Larkin that PFP is better than alternatives. Further, I have a concern here, as noted above, that Larkin (p. 407) seems to equate PFP with "piece rates and merit bonuses." As also noted above, that is too narrow of a definition of PFP.

Another area of convergence is that both chapters agree that compensation is multidimensional. In Larkin's case, that includes reminding readers that compensation is not just about pay level: "must consider not just pay levels, but the system used to reward employees" (p. 408). Again, Nyberg and Reilly are more detailed in their treatment of this issue, making an effort to explain how each of three dimensions of compensation (salary level, PFP proportions, and organizational level of PFP) connect to/operate via two key mechanisms of PFP: incentive and sorting effects, to influence "creation and enactment of HCRs" (p. 388).[3] Although most treatments of compensation in the management literature recognize this multidimensionality (e.g., Gerhart and Milkovich, 1992), with few exceptions (e.g., Brown et al., 2003; Gomez-Mejia and Balkin, 1992), there is not much theory or empirical evidence on the interplay of the multiple dimensions of compensation (Park and Sturman, 2012).

Otherwise, there is little convergence in focus in the chapters. So, if the goal of choosing one "micro" and one "macro" perspective was to get different views, that goal was certainly achieved here. At a broad level, the Larkin chapter comes across as asking big questions and posing tentative answers in some cases, but without delving into an existing literature in multiple disciplines that is relevant. Admittedly, that would be a larger task. Perhaps asking the big questions will be a first step toward more scholars learning about this important literature. Nyberg and Reilly, in comparison, while addressing important questions, take a more focused approach and one that is grounded more firmly in the existing literature. Their aim is to get very specific about how three dimensions of compensation affect performance through two mechanisms, and the degree to which this depends on level of analysis.

Now, let me turn to areas of divergence in focus. Larkin makes the following additional points. First, he distinguishes between efficiency and strategy, and argues that strategy can be a source of competitive advantage but efficiency cannot. Maybe. However, and at the risk of arguing by example (which could be an exception), it took competitors in automobile production decades to come close to the efficiency and quality of Japanese producers, and it is still not clear they have been fully caught; same for Southwest's advantage in the airline industry if both efficiency and quality (e.g., customer satisfaction, customer complaints) are considered (see Gerhart et al., 2019, Chapter 7).

Second, Larkin also provides a nice discussion of competitive parity and competitive advantage and, unlike many, explicitly notes that achieving competitive parity can be a very important achievement. Third, he seeks to develop theory to describe what type of compensation system/strategy would work best under two different Porter competitive strategies: differentiation and cost leadership. Much work has already been done on this front. (For summaries of such research, see Gomez-Mejia and Balkin, 1992; Gomez-Mejia et al., 2016.) It would be helpful to begin with and build on this and related work. My sense is that work in this area may have tailed off both because generic strategy frameworks do not capture firm strategies all that well and because of the shift to studying broader HR systems, which include compensation, when studying contingency ideas.[4] Fourth, Larkin argues that "firms can . . . pay employees in non-monetary ways." Agreed. Again, much previous work has been done in this area, including the literature on not only compensation (e.g., Rynes et al., 2004) but also on fit (e.g., Kristof, 1996), recruiting (e.g., Rynes, 1991), and psychological contracts (Rousseau, 1995).

Finally, Larkin is concerned that compensation researchers have failed sometimes to "recognize that a dollar in increased pay is a dollar in increased costs" (p. 407). I think whether that is a concern depends on the dependent variable and whether it incorporates both cost and revenue. At each level of analysis, there are dependent variables (e.g., net revenue, profit) that inherently incorporate both and others that do not (performance rating, employee turnover). In the case of the latter variables, it may be of interest that there is a framework in the applied psychology literature, utility analysis, which does compare revenues and costs (e.g., Boudreau and Berger, 1985; Sturman et al., 2003; Gerhart et al., 2019, Chapter 7).

Nyberg and Reilly make the following additional points. First, as noted, they are focused on level of analysis issues, and wish to understand whether and how compensation (three forms, including PFP) processes at the individual level operate similarly at higher levels (e.g., unit, organizational). Second, they focus on how compensation influences HCRs. Here, I just wondered whether that focus was mostly limited to the "A" (ability) part of AMO (ability, motivation, and opportunity to contribute) logic. Certainly, the distinction between "HCR capacity and HR enactment" on p. 390 seems like the individual distinction between individual level ability and individual level performance, which presumably depends on M and O. Their subsequent discussion of "the complexities of employee motivation and behavior" on p. 390 seems to suggest they do wish to focus more on M. Not sure about O. I would encourage more attention to the M and O components. Third, Nyberg and Reilly observe that "psychology and economics researchers rarely exchange lessons" (p. 393). That seems hard to argue with.[5] Fourth, the discussion on p. 386 and p. 394 about the risk of incentives and/or PFP causing workers to ignore performance dimensions not included in the plan is important. I would just point out that this concern has been previously identified and nicely captured by Milgrom and Roberts as the equal compensation principle (Gerhart and Rynes, 2003).[6]

GOING FORWARD: TAKEAWAYS AND FUTURE RESEARCH

What are the takeaways and future research needs in compensation? Box 25.1 provides some brief answers, some of which relate to the chapters by Larkin and Nyberg and Reilly, and some of which come from a longer-term and broader perspective on the study of compensation.

Box 25.1, #1 argues that PFP has positive effects in general, consistent with my reading of Larkin and Nyberg and Reilly. Indeed, it is difficult to see how high performance at any level of analysis can be achieved without PFP (Gerhart, 2017). Shirking, free-riding, demotivation, and adverse sorting effects are more likely in the absence of PFP. It is difficult to identify many (there are always some exceptions) organizations, industries, or countries where competitive advantage or even competitive parity has been achieved without PFP (especially as defined here, which includes incorporation of promotion/advancement).

Box 25.1, #2 simply notes that execution, as well as design, of PFP matters. There are many things that can go wrong with PFP, and such risks increase with greater intensity of PFP. Consistent with both Larkin and especially Nyberg and Reilly, more research on how balancing different performance measures/plans, including at different levels of analysis (Nyberg and Larkin) and how that can improve performance (on average) and reduce risk (variance in performance), would be useful.

Box 25.1, #3 identifies what is a challenge in any research area: establishing causality. Nyberg and Reilly's work on intervening mechanisms is one way to make progress here (Gerhart and Milkovich, 1992). Use of longitudinal data is another. Again, Nyberg and Reilly's focus on how intervening mechanisms may not be homologous at different levels is important.

Box 25.1, #4 identifies what is another standard challenge in any research area: identifying moderators (also referred to as constraints, boundary conditions). For example, recent work by Fulmer and Shaw (2018) systematically addresses how person characteristics may moderate the effects of compensation. As another example, Larkin considered ideas about how competitive strategy may moderate the effect of compensation. Environment (e.g., within- or between-country differences in culture, form of capitalism, legal framework) is another potential moderator. The nature of other organizational characteristics such as other management systems (e.g., human resource systems more broadly) is another potential moderator (Gerhart and Rynes, 2003). My own perspective is that what appear to some to be obvious moderators of PFP (e.g., country differences, interdependence of work, how interesting/intrinsically motivating the work is) are not always supported by empirical evidence (e.g., Byron and Khazanchi, 2012; Cerasoli et al., 2014; Gerhart and Fang, 2015; Rabl et al., 2014; Trevor et al., 2012). Alternative logics may likewise question how obvious such moderator effects should have been.

Box 25.1, #5 is a call to acknowledge that PFP in the workplace is often very different than how PFP is operationalized in research, especially laboratory research. In the workplace, as noted, PFP unfolds over the course of a career. Most workers are not covered by individual incentive plans, despite that being one of the most researched forms of PFP.

Box 25.1, #6 is consistent with the call by Larkin and by Nyberg and Reilly to not study single dimensions of compensation in isolation. It also reflects Larkin's call to broaden study to better include nonmonetary rewards, and also relates to the literature on intrinsic motivation, which is a major source of concern about PFP among psychologists. An interesting development in psychology that warrants further study is the proposition that the quality of motivation produced by PFP depends on the nature of PFP, but that it is not as high as that produced by intrinsic sources of motivation (Gagné and Deci, 2005; Howard et al., 2017). Interestingly, there has been a recent major shift toward a more positive view of the role of PFP in encouraging creativity (Amabile and Pratt, 2016; Byron and Khazanchi, 2012; Gerhart and Fang, 2015).

CONCLUSION

The chapters by Larkin and Nyberg and Reilly complemented each other well, and reading them and comparing them is a helpful exercise in identifying what we know about compensation's effects as well as research needs on this topic.

CHAPTER SUMMARY

BOX 25.1 KEY TAKEAWAYS AND IMPLICATIONS FOR FUTURE RESEARCH

1. It only makes sense to pay everyone the same (i.e., not differentiate) if you cannot measure performance in a reasonably accurate and credible way. If the latter is possible, pay for performance (PFP) will generally yield positive effects via incentive and sorting effects.
2. Execution is at least as important as design in the success of PFP. Having accurate and credible performance measures, balancing different measures of performance to avoid unintended consequences, and actually paying for performance are just some of the necessary aspects of execution of PFP. Poor execution (and/or design) can result in serious, unintended consequences.
3. To make policy recommendations, we need to have confidence that associations between PFP and important outcomes are causal. Two steps toward inferring causality are using longitudinal data and documenting mechanisms (intervening/mediating variables, "opening the black box"). Although such recommendations have long been made, such work is still fairly rare. Level of analysis issues are also relevant here.
4. To make policy recommendations, we also need to know whether PFP effects depend on context, which can include person characteristics, organization, and environment characteristics.
5. The study of PFP should recognize that in organizations PFP unfolds largely over the course of a career, especially via promotion/advancement to higher job levels, which means higher base pay levels and higher variable pay opportunity.
6. The study of PFP should include more attention to not only studying it in the context of other dimensions of compensation and/or human resources, but also in the context of nonmonetary rewards, including intrinsically motivating work. Related to the latter, further work is needed on whether the quality of motivation produced by PFP is similar or different from that produced by intrinsically motivating work.

NOTES

1. Nonexempt in the United States means covered by the Fair Labor Standards Act. One necessary but not sufficient condition for being exempt from the Act is to have a salary of $455/week or more.
2. As Larkin (p. 418), observes, one might argue that there has been an over-emphasis on CEO pay. Gerhart and Rynes (2003, pp. 254–5) have made the same argument. One reason is that compensation data on the top five paid executives in public companies in the United States is publicly available.
3. This enactment seems to be unit performance or a closely related precursor to it.
4. Note that Nyberg and Reilly suggest that compensation may be sufficiently unique and important to study on its own.
5. As a sidebar, I would urge a bit of caution in Nyberg and Reilly's description of efficiency wage theories, which perhaps does not convey the fact that there are multiple versions. For example, on p. 393, they seem to say that that efficiency wage focuses only on sorting. (Note, this is often referred to as the adverse selection or sorting by ability version. See Gerhart and Rynes, 2003, Chapter 2.) It is useful to keep in mind that there are other versions, which focus on shirking/monitoring and gift exchange (Gerhart and Rynes, 2003), which have incentive effect mechanisms.
6. "If an employee's allocation of time or attention between two different activities cannot be monitored by the employer, then either the marginal rates of return to the employee must be equal, or the activity with the lower marginal rate of return receives no time or attention" (Milgrom and Roberts, 1992, p. 228).

REFERENCES

Amabile, T. M., and Pratt, M. G. (2016). The dynamic componential model of creativity and innovation in organizations: Making progress, making meaning. *Research in Organizational Behavior*, *36*, 157–83.

Boudreau, J. W., and Berger, C. J. (1985). Decision-theoretic utility analysis applied to employee separations and acquisitions. *Journal of Applied Psychology*, *70*(3), 581–612.

Brown, M. P., Sturman, M. C., and Simmering, M. J. (2003). Compensation policy and organizational performance: The efficiency, operational, and financial implications of pay levels and pay structure. *Academy of Management Journal*, *46*(6), 752–62.

Byron, K., and Khazanchi, S. (2012). Rewards and creative performance: a meta-analytic test of theoretically derived hypotheses. *Psychological Bulletin*, *138*(4), 809–30.

Cadsby, C. B., Song, F., and Tapon, F. (2007). Sorting and incentive effects of pay for performance: An experimental investigation. *Academy of Management Journal*, *50*(2), 387–405.

Cerasoli, C. P., Nicklin, J. M., and Ford, M. T. (2014). Intrinsic motivation and extrinsic incentives jointly predict performance: A 40-year meta-analysis. *Psychological Bulletin*, *140*(4), 980–1008.

Deci, E. L., Koestner, R., and Ryan, R. M. (1999). A meta-analytic review of experiments examining the effects of extrinsic rewards on intrinsic motivation. *Psychological Bulletin*, *125*(6), 627–68.

Fulmer, I. S., and Shaw, J. D. (2018). Person-based differences in pay reactions: A compensation-activation theory and integrative conceptual review. *Journal of Applied Psychology*, *103*(9), 939–58.

Gagné, M., and Deci, E. L. (2005). Self-determination theory and work motivation. *Journal of Organizational Behavior*, *26*, 331–62.

Gerhart, B. (2017). Incentives and pay for performance in the workplace. In A. J. Elliot (ed.), *Advances in Motivation Science*, vol. 4, 91–140. Cambridge, MA: Academic Press.

Gerhart, B., and Fang, M. (2014). Pay for (individual) performance: Issues, claims, evidence and the role of sorting effects. *Human Resource Management Review*, *24*(1), 41–52.

Gerhart, B., and Fang, M. (2015). Pay, intrinsic motivation, extrinsic motivation, performance, and creativity in the workplace: Revisiting long-held beliefs. *Annual Review of Organizational Psychology and Organizational Behavior*, *2*(1), 489–521.

Gerhart, B., and Milkovich, G. T. (1992). Employee compensation: Research and practice. In M. D. Dunnette and L. M. Hough (eds), *Handbook of Industrial and Organizational Psychology*, 481–569. Palo Alto, CA: Consulting Psychologists Press.

Gerhart, B., and Rynes, S. (2003). *Compensation: Theory, Evidence, and Strategic Implications*. Thousand Oaks, CA: Sage.

Gerhart, B., Newman, J. M., and Milkovich, G. T. (2019). *Compensation* (13th edn). New York: McGraw-Hill.

Gerhart, B., Rynes, S. L., and Fulmer, I. S. (2009). Pay and performance: Individuals, groups, and executives. *Academy of Management Annals*, *3*(1), 251–315.

Gerhart, B., Trevor, C. O., and Graham, M. E. (1996). New directions in compensation research: Synergies, risk and survival. In G. R. Ferris (ed.), *Research in Personnel and Human Resources Management*, vol. 14, 143–204. Greenwich, CT: JAI Press.

Gomez-Mejia, L. R., and Balkin, D. B. (1992). *Compensation, Organizational Strategy, and Firm Performance*. Cincinnati: South-Western.

Gomez-Mejia, L. R., Berrone, P., and Franco-Santos, M. (2016). *Compensation and Organizational Performance: Theory, Research, and Practice*. London: Routledge.

Howard, J. L., Gagné, M., and Bureau, J. S. (2017). Testing a continuum structure of self-determined motivation: A meta-analysis. *Psychological Bulletin*, *143*(12), 1346–77.

Jenkins Jr, G. D., Mitra, A., Gupta, N., and Shaw, J. D. (1998). Are financial incentives related to performance? A meta-analytic review of empirical research. *Journal of Applied Psychology*, *83*(5), 777–87.

Kristof, A. L. (1996). Person-organization fit: An integrative review of its conceptualizations, measurement, and implications. *Personnel Psychology*, *49*(1), 1–49.

Lazear, E. P. (2000). Performance pay and productivity. *American Economic Review*, *90*(5), 1346–61.

Milgrom, P., and Roberts, J. (1992). *Economics, Organization and Management*. London: Prentice Hall.

Nyberg, A. J., Pieper, J. R., and Trevor, C. O. (2016). Pay-for-performance's effect on future employee performance: Integrating psychological and economic principles toward a contingency perspective. *Journal of Management*, *42*(7), 1753–83.

Oyer, P., and Schaefer, S. (2011). Personnel economics: Hiring and incentives. In O. Ashenfelter and D. Card (eds), *Handbook of Labor Economics*, vol. 4, 1769–823. Amsterdam: North Holland.

Park, S., and Sturman, M. C. (2012). How and what you pay matters: The relative effectiveness of merit pay, bonuses and long-term incentives on future job performance. *Compensation and Benefits Review*, *44*(2), 80–85.

Pfeffer, J. (1998). Six dangerous myths about pay. *Harvard Business Review*, *76*, 108–20.

Pink, D. H. (2009). *Drive: The Surprising Truth About What Motivates Us*. New York: Riverhead.

Rabl, T., Jayasinghe, M., Gerhart, B., and Kühlmann, T. M. (2014). A meta-analysis of country differences in the high-performance work system–business performance relationship: The roles of national culture and managerial discretion. *Journal of Applied Psychology*, *99*(6), 1011–41.

Rousseau, D. (1995). *Psychological Contracts in Organizations: Understanding Written and Unwritten Agreements*. Thousand Oaks, CA: Sage.

Rynes, S.L. (1991). Recruitment, job choice, and post-hire consequences. In M. D. Dunnette and L. M. Hough (eds), *Handbook of Industrial and Organizational Psychology*. Palo Alto, CA: Consulting Psychologists Press.

Rynes, S. L., Gerhart, B., and Minette, K. A. (2004). The importance of pay in employee motivation: Discrepancies between what people say and what they do. *Human Resource Management*, *43*(4), 381–94.

Schwab, D. P., and Olson, C. A. (1990). Merit pay practices: Implications for pay-performance relationships. *Industrial and Labor Relations Review*, *43*(3), 237S–55S.

Shaw, J. D., and Gupta, N. (2015). Let the evidence speak again! Financial incentives are more effective than we thought. *Human Resource Management Journal*, *25*(3), 281–93.

Sturman, M. C., Trevor, C. O., Boudreau, J. W., and Gerhart, B. (2003). Is it worth it to win the talent war? Evaluating the utility of performance-based pay. *Personnel Psychology*, *56*(4), 997–1035.

Trevor, C. O., Gerhart, B., and Boudreau, J. W. (1997). Voluntary turnover and job performance: Curvilinearity and the moderating influences of salary growth and promotions. *Journal of Applied Psychology*, *82*(1), 44–61.

Trevor, C. O., Reilly, G., and Gerhart, B. (2012). Reconsidering pay dispersion's effect on the performance of interdependent work: Reconciling sorting and pay inequality. *Academy of Management Journal*, *55*(3), 585–610.

26. (Unavoidable) dynamics in incentive design

Tomasz Obloj and Todd Zenger

Implicitly scholars and practitioners alike view the design of incentives as an engineering exercise. A central actor with an envisioned path to value creation and a conception of the physical and human capital investments and actions required to compose it engineers a system of incentives and an accompanying organizational design deemed effective in composing the envisioned value. The central actor's aim is to compose and implement "optimal incentives" or the set of incentives that most efficiently generates the targeted behaviors strategically envisioned (Larkin, Chapter 24 this volume). The organizations that result from these efforts then compete both on the basis of their envisioned paths of value (Felin and Zenger, 2017) and on the skill with which these central actors engineer these incentives. More effective organizations are those that compose a better match between the behaviors sought and pay systems crafted.

Central to this matching calculus is defining the desired behavioral outcomes of employees and collections of employees. The designer must determine desired levels and forms of effort, the types and levels of talent to attract, the optimal levels of investment in skills and human capital, the desired forms of coordination, cooperation and communication, and the required patterns of knowledge transfer. With a clear understanding of these desired behaviors, the designer then selects among alternative incentive designs, calibrating incentive intensity, selecting performance measures, and determining optimal levels of performance aggregation. Much work in economics, management, and strategic human resources focuses on informing this matching exercise (e.g., Prendergast, 1999; Gibbons, 2005; Nyberg and Reilly, Chapter 23 this volume). However, throughout this literature, the fundamental design exercise is quite static – a central actor solves what amounts to an engineering exercise, dialing in incentives to achieve desired behaviors. While scholars recognize that incentive choices have intertemporal consequences related to their structure, for instance compensation may be deferred or rewards may be connected to tournament performance revealed over many years, such intertemporal influences merely add complexity to what otherwise remain static design choices. In other words, design choices today are selected with recognition of the intertemporal influence these choices will have on behavior.

In this chapter, we argue that this static engineering conception of incentive design is misguided, or at least quite incomplete, and not merely for the obvious reason that the central designer's beliefs about the optimal behaviors may change. Rather, we highlight important, frequently neglected, and inherently endogenous drivers of dynamics in incentive design. Our central claim is that even absent exogenous changes in what incentive systems ultimately seek to achieve, the central designer cannot statically engineer pay systems that achieve optimal outcomes, but rather must dynamically adjust their shape and form to achieve a desired outcome – even one that is quite static itself. We specifically highlight three endogenous drivers of these dynamics. First, complex complementarities among targeted behaviors and a fundamental multi-tasking problem create an unavoidable need to shift the short-term target of incentives, even if long-term targets remain constant. Incentive designers are generally constrained to selecting second-best contracts and the optimal second-best contract is dynamically changing. Second, individuals' responses to incentives are dynamic. They learn how to optimally respond to incentives in ways that are both productive and unproductive for the organization. While productive learning benefits the organization, adverse learning is destructive to envisioned outcomes, and prompts the need to shift incentives, triggering a new round of both productive and adverse learning. Third, incentives are distributed within a social community rife with social comparisons, and any adjustment to payouts received or to incentives imposed has a rippling effect on the organization whereby peers recalibrate perceptions of fairness and respond in ways that directly or indirectly shape incentives. All three of these unavoidable dynamics ensure that even in static environments with stable goals, "optimal incentives" are best viewed as a dynamic process rather than a static or stable composition. Anecdotal evidence also suggests that organizations recognize the need to approach incentive design dynamically, and periodically alter their design structures even absent any changes in the product-market competition or external environment space (Zoltners et al., 2001; Nickerson and Zenger, 2002; WorldatWork, 2008; Watson Wyatt, 2009).

In this chapter, we make the case for the inevitability of dynamics in incentive design. In the following section we articulate and briefly review the fundamentally static conception of optimal incentive design that permeates both the academic and popular literature. We then discuss and illustrate our three endogenous drivers of these unavoidable dynamics in composing incentives. We describe both the dynamic behavior and the dynamic outcomes prompted by a static incentive design, and then highlight how these endogenous drivers demand a dynamic approach to incentive design. In the final section we detail and discuss the broad workings and implications of a dynamic approach to incentive design. We debate as well how our theories of incentives both in economics and strategic human capital might incorporate these unavoidable dynamics.

ENGINEERING INCENTIVES

Pay systems across organizations are tremendously varied and in most organizations are complex and multi-faceted. Accordingly, they encompass a wide range of design choices. Central to designing incentives are choices about the construction of the performance metric based on which employees are rewarded, the portion of pay that is linked to performance, the slope of this relationship between measured performance and pay. For some pay systems, the relationship is quite steep, encouraging substantial attention to measures of performance, while for others the relationship is quite flat, encouraging greater attention to unmeasured attributes of performance. For some pay systems, the slope of the pay–performance relationship may be quite stable, while for others it may be convex or concave, prompting either heightened or sustained attention to particular performance measures. Some pay systems may also contain performance thresholds or incorporate discontinuities in the pay–performance relationship, further shaping the intertemporal attention of employees. Pay systems also vary in the type and form of performance measures to which pay is linked, as well as the correspondence between these measures and the nature of the work. Performance measures used in assigning pay may either be highly subjective or fully objective; and, if subjective, they may either be highly compressed or quite dispersed in form. These design choices shape attention to varying attributes of performance. Pay systems may also vary in the transparency of the formulas used in assigning pay (Ederer et al., 2018), and in the transparency of pay outcomes themselves. Transparency on pay formulas heightens attention to those performance measures visible in the formula, while opacity keeps employees focused on a broader set of performance attributes, including those unmeasured. Opacity about pay outcomes may diminish costly social comparison (Nickerson and Zenger, 2008), while transparency may for some underperformers prompt greater effort.

Compensation-related research in economics, strategic human resources, and management attempts to draw clear links between these features of incentive design and the individual and organizational behaviors that result. Much of this work assumes an equilibrium response by individuals to a given design solution. This is not surprising given that most theoretical models take a static form where the optimal incentive structure offered by the principal is backward induced conditional on an expected behavioral response to alternative contracts by employees (e.g. Gibbons, 2005; Holmstrom and Milgrom, 1991).[1] The dominant static paradigm thus assumes that employees observe any given pay system and respond to it in a predictable and stable way by optimizing their effort allocation across tasks and in time, in expectation of some performance and associated reward levels. While the response may involve intertemporal dynamics, these are known, anticipated, and calculated in advance. The role of the designer is then to engineer and choose the pay system that maximizes the value creation from the organization's perspective after taking into account the value captured by the employees.

This general approach has helped build an impressive body of theoretical and applied work in the economics of incentives and strategic human capital. At the same time, the approach has an important limitation in modeling optimal incentive designs because an implicit assumption is that employees or contractors fairly quickly converge to an expected behavioral response and then maintain that response with stability afterwards. The assumption would be unproblematic if a pay system's expected response was simply an average of various dynamic or changing response patterns. In other words, if such equilibrium outcomes were a close enough approximation of the actual observed behaviors, then a static, engineering solution to the incentive problem would be (from a designer's perspective) sufficient (cf. Becker, 1993). This, we argue, however is descriptively not true, and provides a constraining way to think about key levers that organizations have to affect the behaviors of their employees. In what follows, we discuss three distinct mechanisms through which behavioral responses or organizational performance dynamically and endogenously change in response to any given pay system, and then discuss how these dynamic responses in turn shape the dynamics of incentive design.

INCENTIVE DYNAMICS AND THE MULTI-TASKING PROBLEM

Composing efficient compensation systems in organizations often relies on a capacity to reduce the objectives set for each individual or collection of individuals to a single observable metric. For example, in a corporate setting this could be a composite measure of contributions to organizational performance, such as market capitalization of the firm;

or in an educational setting for students, the measure could be grade point average (GPA). Yet in many work settings, the value that the central actor envisions demands attention to a bundle of complementary and, in some cases, difficult to measure performance attributes. Thus, in many cases the role of the incentive system is not only to motivate effort but also to optimally allocate attention across such diverse tasks. For instance, the performance of a manufacturing organization may demand that employees attend to the quantity and cost of production, while simultaneously attending to product quality and overall safety. Overall performance is thus a composite result of executing a multitude of tasks that are often impossible to reduce to a single denominator, and where individual contributions are hard to measure (Arrow, 1951; Ethiraj and Levinthal, 2009). Recognition of this fundamental property of nearly all organizations' objectives has led to a vast theoretical literature – mostly conducted under an umbrella of multi-tasking principal-agent models (Holmstrom and Milgrom, 1991) – and is also reflected in an array of practitioner-oriented tools, such as Balanced Scorecard.

To solve this fundamental issue, an organizational designer must ensure that a compensation system steers efforts towards all requisite tasks, and that the relative attention paid to those tasks corresponds to their importance in a firm's objective function (for example, attention to safety may be more important for an infant toy manufacturer or nuclear power plant builder, while attention to quantity may be more central to a firm specializing in the production of single-use paper napkins). To achieve the requisite diverse and balanced attention, the designer may choose to separately attach rewards to measures of each performance dimension. But, if these dimensions vary in the accuracy with which they are measured, or if employees' capacity to influence each of these measures varies, then employees will weight their focus on those measured with greater precision or those most easily influenced (such as quantity), to the neglect of dimensions measured with less precision or where contributing efforts are less visible (such as quality).

The designer then has several options, but all of them are considered at most second-best solutions in the sense that they are inferior relative to a non-existent optimal solution that generates all the correct behaviors in precisely the right mix. An imperfect solution then has to be selected from among an array of suboptimal design choices. For instance, the designer can proceed to design a pay system that rewards all the desired performance dimensions, and simply endure the resulting distortions in effort. Alternatively, the designer can flatten incentives and essentially remove the distortionary effects of incentives, but then endure the resulting lower effort. The designer may choose to reward a more aggregated, comprehensive measure of performance (such as overall firm profitability), but again suffer the diminished motivation that accompanies rewarding a measure so distant from what the individual employee can influence as well as possibly an inappropriate relative distribution of effort across different tasks. A designer may also make the formula for rewarding performance more opaque and subjective, with the result of generating more balanced effort, but again with potentially compromised levels of effort.

In general, the implicit prescription for the designer is to sort through this array of potential "second-best solutions" with their respective advantages and disadvantages in search of the design choice that maximizes overall performance. Still, by definition, because of the very nature of complex, hard to measure and observe performance, all such incentive systems will invariably fall short of the productivity frontier. Although this is inevitable, we posit that this static approach locks an organization into a solution that is even more suboptimal than is possible if the designer dynamically adjusts the incentive design.

Our central point is that the optimal choice among these second-best alternatives is not static as the literature implicitly assumes, but instead is dynamically changing with time as the currently adopted design shapes organizational performance in ways that are not neutral to the targeted elements of performance. In other words, the second-best contract that you select today inevitably distorts behaviors relative to the productivity frontier in predictable ways, perhaps heightening attention to specific measures but neglecting others, or promoting more balanced attention while diminishing effort, or promoting cooperation and communication while diminishing independent initiative. Because these second-best solutions attend to some performance dimensions and tasks but neglect others, and overall performance is a reflection of attention to a complementary bundle of these dimensions, yesterday's second-best solution that highlights one performance dimension will likely be different from today's second-best choice.

In varying the selection of second-best contracts, firms achieve more balanced attention to the full complement of performance dimensions than can be achieved by making a static choice. Hence, firms' current performance problems and their alternative and relative disaggregation into distinct tasks (safety, quality, efficiency, production output, communication, etc.) arise in part endogenously in response to the previously selected incentive systems. Second-best incentive contracts never become first best, and, as a consequence of dynamic movement away from what a first-best contract could generate, what is second best dynamically changes. In these circumstances, therefore, a sequence of second-best choices may move the firm towards the efficient frontier more effectively than any single static choice. The task of the designer in a multi-tasking environment therefore is to understand the complementary pattern of performance dimensions required for overall performance, and to then dynamically compose a sequence of incentive designs that perpetuate progress. Skills in developing a conceptual model of the factors driving organizational performance or scorecard are essential. But, perhaps even more needful is an understanding of how alternative incentives drive differing behaviors and skills to then reshape incentives through effective organizational change and communication.

INCENTIVE DYNAMICS AND ADVERSE LEARNING

The need for incentive dynamics is not merely driven by multi-tasking, however. A second mechanism prompting dynamic adjustments to pay systems is employees' capacity for adverse learning. Such learning endogenously gives rise to what Obloj and Sengul (2012) call incentive life-cycles, where any given incentive structure first increases its effectiveness in inducing desired outcomes. This stage is followed by a reversal of trend as incentives lose their anticipated properties, become less effective at inducing intended responses, and hence are optimally changed in order to restart the productive cycle. This dynamic response pattern arises as a result of two concurrent micro-level processes – productive and adverse learning (Obloj and Sengul, 2012; Frank and Obloj, 2014). The first process – productive learning – is relatively well understood in the literature and can take many forms. A change in incentives is often accompanied by new tasks or procedures that take time and experience to learn (Kaplan and Henderson, 2005). Therefore, with time and accumulated experience, employees become more productive and generate more value for the focal organization. New incentive designs can also shift the structure of interdependencies across organizational units or departments, necessitating new collaborative patterns to be established, which also takes time and experimentation to compose. Imagine, for example, a business school that changes its incentive structure from entirely research-focused and decides to place greater emphasis (and condition compensation) on classroom performance. Such change is likely to trigger learning processes wherein professors invest greater amounts of time and effort into acquiring teaching skills, attending coaching sessions, and spending more time than before preparing for teaching. Such investments might also take the form of new collaborations with practitioners and firms in order to develop up-to-date teaching aids such as case studies. These efforts are likely to improve classroom performance. However, they are unlikely to fully materialize in the very short term; rather, this productive learning is expected to increase teaching performance of the focal university's faculty only over a period of months or years after the incentive change.

However, not all learning is organizationally productive. Employees are also likely to learn how to exploit a new incentive regime to their benefit through a process of adverse learning. There is a large literature showing that almost any high-powered incentive structure leads to gaming behaviors that generate harmful consequences unintended by the designers (Oyer, 1998; Pierce, 2012). Yet such responses are also unlikely to arise instantaneously and will become magnified over time as employees learn how to best shape their actions in ways that advantage them in value capture. Obloj and Sengul (2012) show evidence of such patterns in the banking context of sales of small personal loans. Using a field experiment in the setting of a Chilean beverage company, Brahm and Poblete (2018) show corroborating evidence of such adverse behaviors within a salesforce that withholds effort in response to recognizing evidence of goal ratcheting by management. Similarly, Lee and Puranam (2017) report that positive productivity and collaborative effort associated with incentive changes diminish over time, potentially due to adverse employee learning. In the case of a university changing its focus from research to teaching, faculty may figure out adverse ways to improve students' ratings by, for example, ending classes several minutes early, assigning less work, or inflating grades.

Taken together, these two learning processes give rise to incentive life-cycles. To prompt initial adaptation we suspect that for most incentive design choices, productive learning is likely to initially outpace adverse learning, but then over time be overtaken by the unintended accumulation and application of value-extracting skills or adverse learning. The precise trajectory and duration of these processes is likely to vary greatly from incentive system to incentive system, from organization to organization, and from individual to individual. Indeed, productive and adverse learning will be subject to the very same contingencies that are discussed more in depth in the chapters by Larkin and by Nyberg and Reilly in this volume. However, there is now solid evidence across a wide range of empirical contexts that both value-creating and value-extracting behaviors are to be expected to emerge in response to any incentive system, and that their dynamic nature should be seriously taken into account when thinking about incentive design and change. The net result is again that incentive design is a dynamic exercise, not a static one. Designers must monitor the dynamically changing individual responses to pay systems and make changes as productive responses wane and adverse learning accelerates.

INCENTIVE DYNAMICS AND SOCIAL COMPARISON

Traditional theorizing about pay systems assumes that individuals' actions in response to these pay systems play out in isolation. In particular, the implicit assumption is that employees respond individually to the incentives they confront, and that this response is quite independent of the incentives others receive. Yet there is overwhelming evidence that individuals have a natural propensity to socially compare their pay outcomes to those received by a relevant set of peers (Festinger, 1954; Möller and Marsh, 2013). This simple fact makes any organizational incentive system an intricate and complex mechanism wherein individual reward structures and associated outcomes are highly interrelated, fueled by individuals continuously comparing across individuals, departments, and even organizations. As a result of these comparisons, employees may take envy-fueled actions that are costly to the firm. Such actions then prompt organizations to react with further adjustments to pay outcomes or pay systems. These changes then prompt further reactions and the cycle continues.

That individuals assess and judge their own utility received from a given pay system by comparing their rewards received to those received by others has far-reaching consequences for the design of organizations and pay systems. Early work on social comparison processes originated from social psychology literature and focused on mechanisms through which individuals assess the fairness of relative inputs and outputs as well as alternative criteria that individuals use to select their set of peers to which they compare their own rewards (Festinger, 1954; Adams, 1963). A related stream of literature emerged in economics and focused on the broad implications of inequity aversion for utility theory (Fehr and Schmidt, 1999; Luttmer, 2005). These insights – that individuals are not solely motivated by their own material interest but also consider social goals when making decisions and choosing appropriate courses of action – imply that organizational members may respond to incentives in ways that go well beyond the traditional calculus of a rational actor model.

This aversion to perceptions of inequity also has important implications for the design of organizations and pay systems. Nickerson and Zenger (2008) propose a theory of the firm where limits to the scale and scope of firms arise as a consequence of increasing social comparison costs that emerge as organizational designers seek to motivate employees through pay for performance (PFP). Unless performance is precisely measured and is transparent to all, pay systems that link measured performance to pay often prompt perceptions of inequity and envy that generate costly behavioral responses that escalate in magnitude with increasing organizational scale and scope. Thus, constraints on firms' scale and scope arise because central designers cannot compose "optimal incentives" due to the influence of these social comparison costs. Design efficiency therefore often dictates that the composition of incentives be left to the market, where high-powered incentives are provided, triggering the high costs of social comparison. This theoretical effort has prompted a series of empirical papers that document negative productivity consequences of social comparison arising in response to various incentive structures, and highlighting the dynamic nature of these processes (e.g., Rawley and Simcoe, 2010; Larkin et al., 2012; Gartenberg and Wulf, 2017; Obloj and Zenger, 2017).

While these social comparison processes have important consequences for the design and shape of organizations, they also generate a need to dynamically manage pay systems. The fundamental logic is that any change to an incentive structure or to the realized and anticipated payouts received by organizational members generates a rippling effect in social comparisons through which peers recalibrate perceptions of fairness and respond in ways that directly or indirectly shape incentives. Similarly, any change to other organization design elements or adjustments to the workforce pool can, through these processes of social comparison, increase or diminish the effectiveness of a given incentive system. Imagine, for example, that a focal organization diversifies into a new activity and offers high-powered incentives to newly hired employees in a manner that is simply standard practice in this new industry. This strategic move generates an exogenous change to the social community and creates a new relevant set of peers against whom existing employees now reassess the fairness of their own rewards. This change may thus disrupt the current social equilibrium, necessitating a redesign of the incentive system for the whole organization, placing new constraints on the existing departments as well as the newly added one. This is akin to some of the limitations faced by large organizations pursuing corporate venture capital activities, and why they find it impossible to mirror the incentives offered by independent venture capitalists (Dushnitsky and Shapira, 2010). There is thus an important interdependency between organizational boundary decisions and incentive designs driven by these social comparison processes, and organizational designers must be cognizant of this interdependency as they dynamically compose organizations.

This dynamic interdependency of organizational and incentive design extends beyond boundary decisions, however. Any design changes that shape social comparison processes will shape perceptions of fairness, and consequently the effectiveness of pay systems. The outcomes of social comparison processes in organizations are crucially dependent on who the relevant peers are for each concerned individual. Individuals compare their relative inputs and outputs with other individuals they perceive as sufficiently proximate. As a consequence, organizational design decisions that shape the proximity of employees in ways that shape the choice of relevant peers will dynamically change fairness perceptions. Therefore, in response to changes in organizational design, incentive designers may adjust incentives; or, in response to changes in incentives, organizational designers may choose to adjust the proximity of peers. Empirical work provides evidence of this dynamic link. Obloj and Zenger (2017) empirically show that dimensions of distance in organizations – specifically social, structural, and physical distance – by shaping patterns of social comparison influence the effectiveness of incentives. Gartenberg and Wulf (2017) also consider hierarchical distance as an important predictor of the intensity of social comparison. For organizational designers, this has important implications in terms of the dynamics of incentive design. Any change to the fabric of a focal organization is likely to reshape the pattern of who relevant peers are, as well as perceptions of the fairness of pay systems. Thus, these social comparison processes affect the effectiveness of incentives and constrain broader choices of organizational design. Incentive designers must remain cognizant of social comparison effects, including these rippling dynamics that accompany changes, as they compose and craft pay systems and design organizations more broadly.

DYNAMIC INCENTIVE DESIGN

Our message in this chapter is not merely that incentive design is more complex than we might ordinarily assume. Nor is our message that the incentive design principles discussed in prior work are incorrect. Rather, our argument is that portraying organizational design as an engineering problem or a static optimization problem is misguided and may lead firms to fall into a trap of deteriorating performance and increasing misalignment between behaviors of organizational members and overall objectives. And, this is likely to be true even if the actual objectives of the organization remain quite static themselves. In other words, the mechanisms driving this need for dynamics are not only external to the focal firm – such as changes to the business environment, regulations, or competition – but rather arise endogenously and profoundly shape the need to think about design elements as unavoidably temporary and in need of dynamic reconfigurations. Though we believe design choices should be viewed as more temporary than permanent, our logic by no means negates the usefulness of prior work that links design choices regarding pay systems to desired outcomes. We merely advocate that these principles must be applied to design choices with greater repetition and frequency than perhaps scholars and practitioners have previously considered optimal.

But, our message goes beyond this. In particular, we have highlighted three endogenous drivers of dynamics in incentive design, and have articulated basic principles through which these drivers shape design choices dynamically. First, at an individual level, employees learn over time how to respond to pay systems. There are two concurrent learning processes – productive learning that increases the alignment of behavior with organizational objectives, and adverse learning that decreases this alignment. The relative pace of these alternative forms of learning gives rise to a dynamic phenomenon of incentive life-cycles. This means that although the effectiveness of any pay system is likely to take time to reach its maximum level, it is also likely to deteriorate after a certain period of time, necessitating a change to incentives in order to maintain performance levels.

Second, at a level of social groups that constitute any organization, individuals constantly engage in processes of social comparison – assessing the fairness of their rewards compared to relevant peers (relative to inputs) as well as the structure of the reward system they face. The structure of such social peer groups, and hence the reference point for comparison, constantly evolves as organizations change, grow, and re-focus. Consequently, processes of social comparison continually and differentially shape the effectiveness of incentive systems and the need for their re-design.

Finally, and at the more systemic level comprising how performance is measured and what is the nature of relevant tasks that define organizational objectives, we focus on the role of multi-tasking conflicts and complementarity in task bundles for the dynamics of incentive systems. Given that almost all feasible incentive systems are second best, in most settings no design can promote the optimal mix of behaviors with stability. Consequently, the necessarily distorted responses of organizational actors may move organizations further away from the productivity frontier, giving rise to a need to dynamically account for such processes with design changes. By varying the selection of suboptimal contracts, organizations can achieve a more balanced attention to all necessary tasks and ensure that complementarities between different performance dimensions are realized.

A central question then becomes: given these articulated dynamics in responses to pay systems, how must the central designer act in composing them? Rather than engineering an optimal incentive system, our argument is that incentive structures and organization design in general is about dynamically managing performance with incentives and structural levers, accepting a quasi-permanent state of being off-equilibrium. In other words, incentive systems are vehicles that enable organizational course corrections rather than solutions that permit an organization to be placed on auto-pilot. Organizational architects must thus continually closely attend to the evolving balance between tasks, changing proficiency with which employees seek and manage to create and capture value, and fully recognize the social nature of organizations and inherent inter-relatedness of responses to and evaluations of incentives. The resulting processes of dynamic incentive adjustments are likely to often result in imperfect configurations and require trial-and-error adaptation. Still, given that no pay system will be (or remain) a first best, vacillation between alternative forms, power, and structure of incentives is likely to result in greater value creation than settling for what – at some point in time – appeared to be the most efficient pay system.

CHAPTER SUMMARY

BOX 26.1 KEY TAKEAWAYS

1. Designing incentives	Our chapter argues against portraying and studying the design of incentive systems as an engineering practice. We argue instead that incentive systems are vehicles that enable organizational course corrections rather than solutions that permit an organization to be placed on auto-pilot. In other words, incentive design is a continuing process rather than an optimizing exercise.
2. Accepting second-best nature of incentives	Our chapter suggests that successful organizations are likely to employ a sequence of second-best contracts and design choices. Rather than striving for first best, organizational architects should accept and optimize the sequence and frequency of changes among imperfect solutions.
3. Understanding endogenous drivers of incentive dynamics	Our chapter discusses and provides examples for three endogenous drivers of incentive dynamics: a) Multi-tasking conflicts and complementarity in task bundles b) Employee learning c) Social comparison processes.

BOX 26.2 DIRECTIONS FOR FUTURE RESEARCH

1. Timing of incentive dynamics	Although prior research has extensively studied the issue of optimal timing of key strategic decisions (such as new product introduction, market entry, or FDIs), much less attention has been given to the timing of structural changes to organization design elements. Our chapter suggests that taking into account both exogenous and endogenous drivers of incentive effectiveness could help organizational architects better time the necessary adjustment to pay systems.
2. Sequence of incentive dynamics	Our chapter highlights a need to dynamically manage performance with incentives and structural levers in organizations. We have little to say, however, about the optimal sequencing of such necessary changes. Future work should investigate both benefits and costs of alternative sequencing patterns.

3.	Endogenous drivers of incentive dynamics	Our chapter discusses three endogenous drivers of dynamics in incentive design. Future research should fruitfully complement this list with other important mechanisms as well as study the interplay between endogenous and exogenous (e.g., environmental) drivers of incentive effectiveness.

NOTE

1. We abstract away here from "learning models" in labor economics where contracts are optimally re-designed once true type of agents is revealed (e.g., Laffont and Tirole, 1988; Baker et al., 1993).

REFERENCES

Adams, J. (1963). Towards an understanding of inequity. *Journal of Abnormal and Social Psychology*, *67*(5), 422–36.

Arrow, K. (1951). Alternative approaches to the theory of choice in risk-taking situations. *Econometrica*, *19*, 404–37.

Baker, G., Gibbs, M., and Holmstrom, B. (1993). Hierarchies and compensation. *European Economic Review*, *37*(2), 366–78.

Becker, G. S. (1993). Nobel Lecture: The economic way of looking at behavior. *Journal of Political Economy*, *101*(3), 385–409.

Brahm, F., and Poblete, J. (2018). Incentives and ratcheting in a multiproduct firm: A field experiment. *Management Science*, *64*(10), 4552–71. Retrieved from https://doi-org.ezproxy.hec.fr/10.1287/mnsc.2017.2861.

Dushnitsky, G., and Shapira, Z. (2010). Entrepreneurial finance meets organizational reality: Comparing investment practices and performance of corporate and independent venture capitalists. *Strategic Management Journal*, *31*(9), 990–1017.

Ederer, F., Holden, R., and Meyer, M. A. (2018). Gaming and strategic opacity in incentive provision. *RAND Journal of Labor Economics*, *49*(4), 819–54.

Ethiraj, S. K., and Levinthal, D. (2009). Hoping for A to Z while rewarding only A: Complex organizations and multiple goals. *Organization Science*, *20*(1), 4–21.

Fehr, E., and Schmidt, K. M. (1999). A theory of fairness, competition, and cooperation. *Quarterly Journal of Economics*, *114*(3), 817–68.

Felin, T., and Zenger, T. R. (2017). The theory-based view: Economic actors as theorists. *Strategy Science*, *2*(4), 258–71.

Festinger, L. (1954). A theory of social comparison processes. *Human Relations*, *7*, 117–40.

Frank, D. H., and Obloj, T. (2014). Firm-specific human capital, organizational incentives, and agency costs: Evidence from retail banking. *Strategic Management Journal*, *35*(9), 1279–301.

Gartenberg, C., and Wulf, J. (2017). Pay harmony? Social comparison and performance compensation in multibusiness firms. *Organization Science*, *28*(1), 39–55.

Gibbons, R. (2005). Incentives between firms (and within). *Management Science*, *51*(1), 2–17.

Holmstrom, B., and Milgrom, P. (1991). Multitask principal–agent analyses: Incentive contracts, asset ownership, and job design. *Journal of Law, Economics, and Organization*, *7*, 24–52.

Kaplan, S., and Henderson, R. (2005). Inertia and Incentives: Bridging Organizational Economics and Organizational Theory. *Organization Science*, *16*(5), 509–21.

Laffont, J. J., and Tirole, J. (1988). The dynamics of incentive contracts. *Econometrica*, *56*(5), 1153–75.

Larkin, I., Pierce, L., and Gino, F. (2012). The psychological costs of pay-for-performance: Implications for the strategic compensation of employees. *Strategic Management Journal*, *33*(10), 1194–214.

Lee, S., and Puranam, P. (2017). Incentive redesign and collaboration in organizations: Evidence from a natural experiment. *Strategic Management Journal*, *38*(12), 2333–52.

Luttmer, E. F. P. (2005). Neighbors as negatives: Relative earnings and well-being. *Quarterly Journal of Economics*, *120*(3), 963–1002.

Möller, J., and Marsh, H. W. (2013). Dimensional comparison theory. *Psychological Review*, *120*(3), 544–60.

Nickerson, J. A., and Zenger, T. R. (2002). Being efficiently fickle: A dynamic theory of organizational choice. *Organization Science*, *13*(5), 547–66.

Nickerson, J. A., and Zenger, T. R. (2008). Envy, comparison costs, and the economic theory of the firm. *Strategic Management Journal*, *29*(13), 1429–49.

Obloj, T., and Sengul, M. (2012). Incentive life-cycles learning and the division of value in firms. *Administrative Science Quarterly*, *57*(2), 305–47.

Obloj, T., and Zenger, T. (2017). Organization design, proximity, and productivity responses to upward social comparison. *Organization Science*, *28*(1), 1–18.

Oyer, P. (1998). Fiscal year ends and nonlinear incentive contracts: The effect on business seasonality. *Quarterly Journal of Economics*, *113*(1), 149–85.

Pierce, L. (2012). Organizational structure and the limits of knowledge sharing: Incentive conflict and agency in car leasing. *Management Science*, *58*(6), 1106–21.

Prendergast, C. (1999). The provision of incentives in firms. *Journal of Economic Literature*, *37*(1), 7–63.

Rawley, E., and Simcoe, T. S. (2010). Diversification, diseconomies of scope, and vertical contracting: Evidence from the taxicab industry. *Management Science*, *56*(9), 1534–50.

Watson, W. (2009). Current trends in sales force compensation and management. Willis Towers Watson. Retrieved from http://www.watsonwyatt.com/research/pdfs/WT-2009-13462.pdf.

WorldatWork (2008). Survey of the WorldatWork members. Retrieved from http://www.worldatwork.org/pub/E157963SI05.pdf.

Zoltners, A. A., Sinha, P., and Zoltners, G. A. (2001). *The Complete Guide to Accelerating Sales Force Performance*. New York: Amacom Books.

PART VIII

KEEPING STRATEGIC HUMAN CAPITAL RESOURCES: MOBILITY

27. Keeping strategic human capital resources: mobility

John P. Hausknecht

Employee mobility—generally defined as the movement of people from firms—is theorized as both a disruptive threat (e.g., Dess and Shaw, 2001; Hatch and Dyer, 2004; Shaw et al., 2005) and, under certain conditions, an enabling contributor (e.g., Somaya et al., 2008; Tzabbar and Kehoe, 2014) to unit performance and competitive advantage. Isolating the potential productive versus destructive consequences of mobility has proven challenging because most research on the topic (and on related turnover/retention concepts) adopts an undifferentiated view of leavers, one where each departing employee is treated the same as the next. Rarely do studies measure the actual human capital loss (or lack thereof) associated with employee departures. Indeed, only recently have studies begun to address talent loss associated with strategic or "core" roles (Hale et al., 2016), examine potential benefits of losing star employees (Tzabbar and Kehoe, 2014), or study human capital losses and additions over time (Reilly et al., 2014). In short, there is still much to learn about how, when, and why turnover and mobility matter for unit performance and competitive advantage.

The goal of this chapter is to provide a selective and critical review of the literature on human capital resources and collective turnover. The review is selective in that I do not consider the entire literature in either human capital resources or turnover/mobility. Not only have comprehensive reviews of these literatures appeared elsewhere (human capital: Nyberg et al., 2014; turnover/mobility: Hausknecht, 2017; Hausknecht and Trevor, 2011; Mawdsley and Somaya, 2016), but both literatures also have a long and rich history at micro and macro levels that falls well beyond the scope of this chapter. Instead, my aim is to consider the intersection of the two streams—i.e., to identify how human capital (resource) scholars think about and study mobility, and to comment on how turnover and mobility researchers consider and address human capital. The review is also critical in that I enumerate a number of key "observations" that are intended to spur further debate, discussion, and research.

RELEVANT CONSTRUCTS

Human Capital Constructs

Becker defined human capital in terms of the financial returns associated with investing in education, training, and related inputs. He delineated the systems and processes by which individuals build "talents required to succeed in the economic sphere" (1962: 45). Over time, human capital terminology expanded to encompass a variety of personal attributes (e.g., education, experience, knowledge, skills, or health), to refer to a range of employee types (e.g., professionals or top managers), and to signify "talent" at multiple levels of analysis (e.g., individual, group, and firm).

Along with the expansion of coverage has been a dilution in meaning, prompting researchers to clarify and refine the human capital lexicon. Ployhart et al. (2014) differentiated between related but distinct concepts including: *individual differences* (capacities that are heterogeneous across people); *KSAOs* (relatively stable knowledge, skills, abilities, and other characteristics); *human capital* (the subset of KSAOs that are relevant to economic ends); *human capital resources* (individual or unit capacities based on KSAOs that are accessible for unit-relevant performance); and *strategic human capital resources* (individual or unit capacities based on KSAOs that are accessible for unit-relevant competitive advantage).

To clarify these definitions, and to articulate relationships with other parts of their framework, Ployhart and colleagues state that:

1. individual KSAOs provide the foundations for human capital resources;
2. only a subset of individual KSAOs are relevant to producing economic outcomes and can thus constitute "human capital";
3. human capital resources can originate in individuals and/or emerge within units based on KSAOs that combine into distinct, collective-level resources that differ from their individual-level origins;
4. strategic human capital resources are those that are critical to building competitive advantage in a particular market (i.e., outperforming competitors), whereas human capital resources are those relevant to driving unit performance in general (and not necessarily in relation to any external competitive benchmark); and
5. human capital resources provide units with a certain level of "capacities"—reserves or supplies for potential to act toward a unit-relevant purpose.

Mobility-Related Constructs

Definitions of mobility vary, but all include the movement of employees out of firms (parallel to definitions of unit-level or collective turnover that involve aggregate employee departures from groups, units, or organizations; Hausknecht and Trevor, 2011). At macro levels, researchers commonly address mobility in terms of employees not only leaving firms, but also in terms of leaving one firm for another—e.g., "the interorganization movement of personnel" (Mawdsley and Somaya, 2016: 86); thus, many such studies adopt research designs that allow tracking of employee movement from source to destination firms. In contrast, at micro and meso levels, less attention is given to the post-exit destinations of employees (but see Hom et al., 2012), and researchers tend to focus on the proximal outcomes across multiple work units within a single organization rather than on the offsetting gains and losses associated with talent movement across firms (e.g., Call et al., 2015b; Hausknecht et al., 2009; Reilly et al., 2014). Given the separate treatment of macro views on mobility in this volume, I generally restrict this chapter to a discussion of micro/meso, single-firm contexts involving employee mobility/turnover, and use the latter terms interchangeably.

At the individual employee level, turnover involves "a time specific event marked by physical separation from the organization" (Mobley, 1982: 111). To capture the impelling cause of separations, departures may be recorded as either *voluntary* (employee-initiated) or *involuntary* (organization-initiated).[1] Individual-level studies dominated the turnover landscape for much of the 20th century (see Hom et al., 2017, for a review) until researchers began to conceptualize turnover in the aggregate (e.g., Terborg and Lee, 1984), therein drawing some of the earliest linkages between turnover rates and work unit characteristics. Turnover rates, often specified as the number of leavers over a given period divided by group size, provide the foundations for constructs that have been labeled *unit-level turnover*, *collective turnover*, *group turnover*, or *organizational turnover* (e.g., Hausknecht et al., 2009; Shaw et al., 2005). As discussed in subsequent sections, more recent treatments of collective turnover adopt this formulation to capture the quantity of leavers, but also add nuance to consider the *qualities* of departures so that the human capital resources available to the unit can be more accurately represented (Hausknecht and Holwerda, 2013; Nyberg and Ployhart, 2013).

Notions of "Capacity"

Integral to human capital-centric views on mobility is the notion of *capacity*, which, as noted above, Ployhart et al. (2014: 377) defined as "a reserve or supply for potential action directed toward a purpose." Similarly, Kraaijenbrink et al. (2010: 361) distinguished capacity from action or actual performance, suggesting that researchers should "theorize the distinctions between the building, acquiring, and possessing capacity (which includes resources and capabilities) versus the processes of deploying that capacity." Finally, Hausknecht and Holwerda (2013) proposed a collective turnover framework built mainly on the idea that unit departures constrain a unit's "productive capacity," or its ability to fully utilize its human and social capital resources. It seems an open question as to whether capacity is synonymous with resources (Ployhart et al., 2014), reflects a unit's current potential to perform based on member inputs and configurations (Hausknecht and Holwerda, 2013), or perhaps represents both. In any case, it is a key linking point that helps explain the manner in which turnover affects the stock and flow of human capital resources and its effects on unit performance.

RELATING HUMAN CAPITAL RESOURCES, TURNOVER, AND PERFORMANCE

Figure 27.1 provides a visual overview of several sample questions that are associated with the human capital resource and turnover literatures. The small area of overlap signals that each literature generally pursues its own agenda, yet there is clearly room for integration and application across domains. Some of this work is beginning to appear (Call et al., 2015a; Nyberg and Ployhart, 2013), but even a cursory review of the two literatures reveals limited crossover in terms of theories, constructs, research designs, and more. Nyberg and Ployhart (2013: 125) argued, "for too long human capital and turnover have been studied in relative isolation, as though they are independent phenomena." The turnover literature (particularly at the individual level) generally ignores the KSAOs or human capital associated with leavers, and instead is more focused on the psychological processes that underpin quit decisions among workers in general. Further, little or no attention is given to key employee groups (with exceptions, such as Siebert and Zubanov, 2009) or predicting quits of high-value talent such as stars or CEOs. On the human

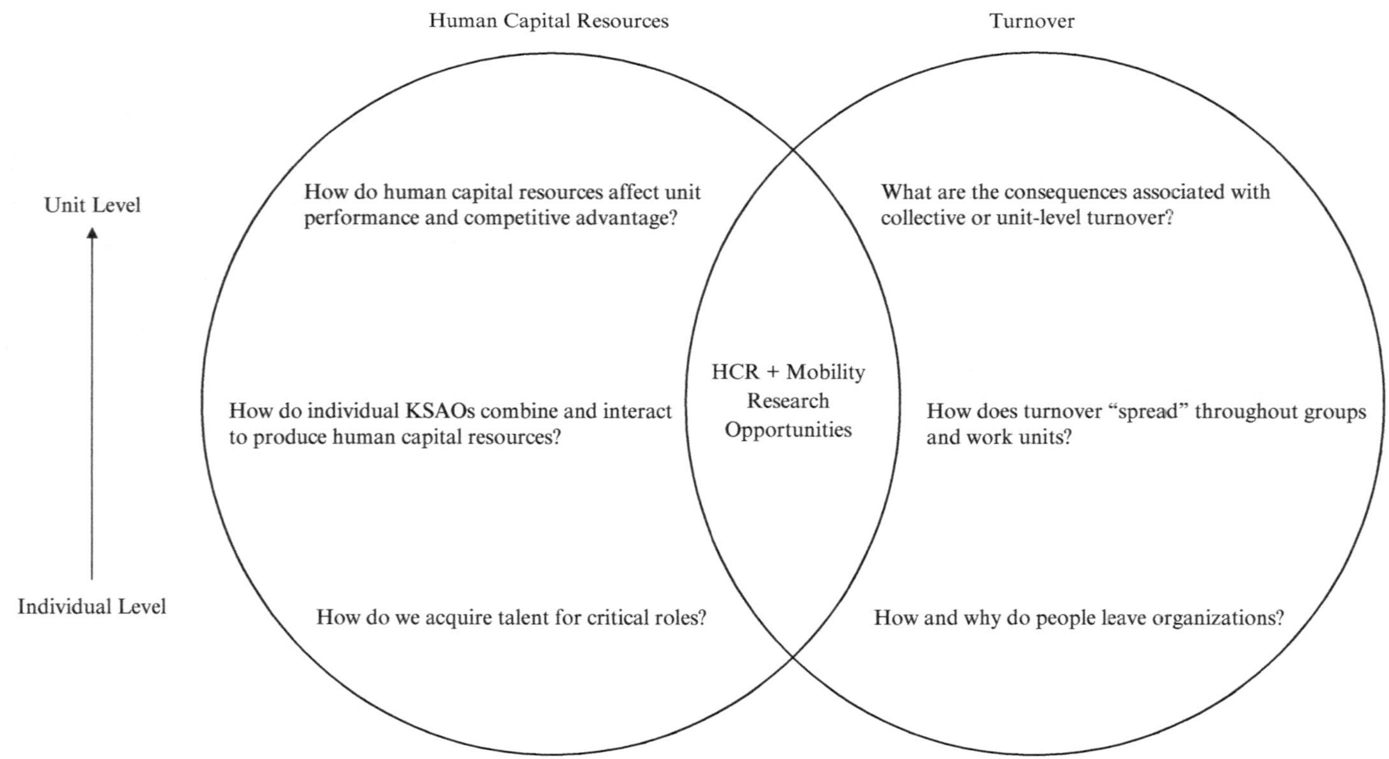

Figure 27.1 Comparison of human capital resource and turnover literatures

capital resource side, although resource loss via turnover and mobility is acknowledged, sometimes directly (Gardner et al., 2011; Nyberg and Ployhart, 2013), it often receives considerably less attention relative to understanding the determinants, emergence, and consequences of human capital resources.

Observation #1: With limited exceptions, the human capital resource and turnover literatures have developed in parallel. Researchers in the turnover domain rarely address the human capital associated with leavers; researchers in the human capital resource domain rarely consider the effects of mobility/turnover when linking HR practices, human capital resources, and unit performance.

If "human capital" is broadly conceived, one does find discussions of how collective turnover signifies human capital depletion and negatively affects unit or firm performance. For example, Dess and Shaw (2001: 447) stated, "because voluntary turnover diminishes human capital, productivity is weakened as turnover increases." Hatch and Dyer (2004: 1160) noted, "If, however, human capital is firm-specific, socially complex, path-dependent, and faces time compression diseconomies, firms with high turnover will suffer a significant competitive disadvantage relative to firms with more stable workforces where human capital can be developed and deployed." Thus, although the two literatures are largely independent, researchers have drawn linkages between turnover and human capital.

Observation #2: Traditionally, turnover has been viewed as synonymous with human capital loss.

As mentioned above, researchers are beginning to make (mostly theoretical) inroads into understanding how turnover and mobility might affect human capital *resources* and subsequent unit performance (Hausknecht and Holwerda, 2013; Nyberg and Ployhart, 2013). Nyberg and Ployhart introduced context-emergent turnover (CET) theory to draw parallels and distinctions between human capital resources and collective turnover. They specify the emergent nature of collective turnover, position it within the nomological network of strategic HRM research, and describe how timing and context influence turnover and its unit-level consequences. Collective turnover, defined as "the aggregate quantity and quality of employee knowledge, skills, abilities, and other characteristics (KSAOs) depleted from the unit" (109), is contrasted with human capital resources, or the "intangible unit-level constructs that can possess the characteristics needed to influence unit performance and competitive advantage" (113). Collective turnover is conceived in terms of both quantitative (proportion of departing employees from a unit) and qualitative elements (degree and type of KSAOs lost) and signals, functionally, the depletion of human capital resources. Notably, defining collective turnover in terms of KSAOs lost contrasts with "standard" unit-level turnover studies where turnover is defined solely in terms of the number of leavers where each departure is treated exactly the same as every other.

Observation #3: Turnover studies rarely address actual human capital resource loss.

An important point of emphasis within CET theory—and a notable departure from earlier human capital-turnover theorizing—is that collective turnover can yield positive, neutral, or negative effects on human capital resources depending on whether replacement quality and quantity exceeds, matches, or falls below that of leavers. This diverges from the view that employee turnover is a cost to be controlled, which is often found in individual-level studies aimed at justifying the importance of studying turnover and its antecedents. It also departs from familiar arguments that turnover of any amount signals human capital loss and disruption. Although there are often nontrivial separation, replacement, and training costs associated with turnover, there are also likely offsetting gains in terms of managing escalating wages, infusing units with new ideas, reducing conflict, and more (Staw, 1980). Further, as CET outlines, active management of collective turnover in terms of enhancing KSAOs of employees within the unit via replacements or removing members that interfere with the development of a trusting, supportive climate could be quite beneficial to human capital resource development and subsequent unit performance.

Observation #4: Turnover is almost universally viewed as a "negative"; rarely do researchers address conditions under which effects may be positive. This has produced a literature where negative performance effects dominate.

A final point stemming from CET theory and other turnover research (e.g., Batt and Colvin, 2011; Hausknecht and Trevor, 2011) is that the individual-level distinction between voluntary and involuntary turnover may be less appropriate at the unit level. That is, individual-level turnover distinguishes turnover types because voluntary turnover is less predictable and arguably more damaging than organization-initiated, involuntary turnover, which usually signals poor performer loss. The two types also have different antecedents, even at the unit level (Shaw et al., 1998). Nyberg and Ployhart (2014) argue that conceptualizing collective turnover as KSAO depletion already incorporates the level of "loss" associated with leavers, and is therefore a more parsimonious way to capture leaver value. Hausknecht and Holwerda (2013) make a similar point in suggesting that researchers should directly track the proficiencies of leavers, replacements, and remaining members—again, a method that is arguably more precise than a dichotomous indicator of leaver value.

Observation #5: If the aim is to understand how collective turnover affects human capital resources and unit performance, tracking KSAO/proficiency loss is more appropriate than tracking turnover voluntariness.

Hausknecht and Holwerda also conceptualized collective turnover as an emergent construct with meaning different from the simple aggregation of individual departures. They advanced five properties that should influence the productive capacity of a given unit:

1. leaver proficiencies (the extent to which leavers are experienced versus novice);
2. time dispersion (the extent to which departures are concentrated versus distributed over time);
3. positional distribution (the degree to which people leave from the same versus different positions);
4. remaining member proficiencies (the extent to which remaining members are proficient versus novice); and

5. newcomer proficiencies (the degree to which replacements are experienced versus novice).

As in CET theory, their argument is that turnover rates (of any given quantitative level) can refer to qualitatively different unit capacities depending on the timing of departures, the qualities of leavers, and characteristics of remaining members and replacements. Capacity is depleted to the extent that leavers are highly proficient, span multiple roles within units, and are concentrated in time. Capacity also suffers when remaining members themselves lack proficiency and when the level of human capital associated with replacements does not match or exceed that associated with leavers.

A central aspect of their theorizing—assuming some level of task interdependence is required for unit function—is that the departure and subsequent replacement of unit members effectively "resets" group development, meaning that some degree of coordination flux and disruption is expected following member exits. Moreover, even highly skilled replacements will require time to reach full proficiency, both in terms of their own role and their integration with remaining unit members. However, some of these challenges can be minimized if departures are spread over time, constrained to a small number of positions, or buffered by a stable core of proficient members, for instance. To this end, the measurement approach outlined by Hausknecht and Holwerda simultaneously accounts for the proficiencies of departing, remaining, and replacement members, as well as for the sequencing and distribution of departures across positions. Important to their theorizing, and consistent with CET theory, they contend that addressing turnover only as a "quantity" conceals the very dimensions that are expected to matter most for unit function and performance.

Observation #6: Turnover rates (as traditionally defined) are deficient indicators of collective turnover's actual effects on unit function.

Related to the previous point, across the collective turnover literature, researchers specify numerous group process factors that are presumably affected by turnover (and that transmit the effects of turnover to unit performance). Several examples are provided below:

> High overall turnover may raise transaction costs by requiring higher management-to worker ratios; undermining workplace rules that form the basis of organizational control (Price, 1977); shifting resources and experienced workers away from daily work to train and socialize novices (Staw, 1980); disrupting the social fabric and bonds of trust and social capital that have been shown to positively affect performance (Shaw [et al.], 2005); or lowering flexibility for internal redeployment or rotation across different jobs or skill sets. (Batt and Colvin, 2011: 700)
>
> Turnover impedes proficiency development and requires that remaining members engage in activities that do not directly contribute to productivity, such as socializing newcomers and compensating for their inexperience revising communication patterns, reconfiguring work flows, and so on. (Hausknecht and Holwerda, 2013: 214)

Although there are exceptions (Reilly et al., 2014; van der Vegt et al., 2010), the effects of turnover on coordination, communication, workload, tacit knowledge, transactive memory, and related process factors remain poorly understood. Further, when viewed from the perspective of human capital resource depletion, it is likely that different types of leavers (e.g., stars, CEOs, middle managers) would affect different characteristics of unit function differently.

Observation #7: The processes that turnover presumably affects are almost never measured; as such, we know little about turnover's effects on group dynamics; these effects probably depend on exactly who leaves.

Speaking of stars and CEOs, this literature primarily surfaced from macro researchers interested in understanding the *firm-level* consequences of CEO, top management team (TMT), and other "key talent" successions (e.g., Miller, 1993; Shen and Cannella, 2002). However, theories, designs, and data sources bear little resemblance to human capital or turnover theories as developed in the micro or meso literatures. Scholars are beginning to consider how the departure of single individuals (e.g., stars, leaders, and managers) has downstream consequences for turnover of remaining members as well as for unit performance (e.g., Ballinger and Schoorman, 2007; Call et al., 2015; Hale et al., 2016). This development is consistent with the view that human capital resources can stem from emergent, unit-level interactions as well as from the direct contributions of individuals (Ployhart et al., 2014). This said, there is ample room for integration of these literatures to understand the processes by which departure of key individuals affects unit function and performance. We also do not have ready theory that allows us to differentiate turnover content and processes for elite versus non-elite talent, but perhaps we should.

Observation #8: At present, there is little integration among the literatures on stars, CEO succession, collective turnover, and human capital resources.

FUTURE RESEARCH

As discussed throughout the review, the literatures on human capital resources and turnover have largely developed independently of one another. Although more recent studies have made conceptual and empirical inroads towards integration, there are many opportunities to advance the research agenda by crossing these two domains. Potentially valuable directions for future research include:

1. *Study human capital resources and turnover simultaneously*. As noted in the review, these are distinct constructs and yet both are important to forecasting unit performance.
2. *Identify conditions under which turnover creates value for units*. Although there is ample evidence of negative turnover–performance relationships, it is likely that studies have not been designed to reveal the conditions under which turnover benefits work unit function.
3. *Test and validate measures of collective turnover as human capital loss*. Consistent with CET and turnover capacity theories (Hausknecht and Holwerda, 2013; Nyberg and Ployhart, 2013), measures that better track actual human capital loss may better forecast unit performance.
4. *Study the group processes that turnover theoretically affects*. Valuable information can be gleaned from investigating the group processes that are thought to be disrupted

by turnover—this would allow for better understanding of *why* turnover matters and can direct practical interventions.

5. *Develop more comprehensive understanding of the unit-level impact of individual departures*. As discussed above, the CEO and star succession literatures often stem from macro/top-down theorizing and are aimed at predicting firm performance; much less is known about the departure of key talent at a more localized level (and its effects on unit function and performance).

As can be seen, there is ample room for integration of the human capital resource and turnover literatures. Although both areas have generally operated in parallel, recent theory and emerging empirical work reveals intriguing possibilities for better understanding of how the interplay of human capital resources and employee mobility jointly influence unit performance and, potentially, competitive advantage.

CHAPTER SUMMARY

BOX 27.1 KEY TAKEAWAYS

1. Defines human capital and turnover/mobility constructs and critically reviews the intersection of these literatures.
2. Argues that human capital and turnover are often studied in isolation even though departures of key employee groups, stars, and other key talent likely disrupt human capital resource development and deployment.
3. Suggests theoretical approaches and measurement/design strategies that would lead to better understanding of how human capital resources and mobility jointly influence capacity, performance, and competitive advantage.

BOX 27.2 DIRECTIONS FOR FUTURE RESEARCH

1. Pursue studies that develop theory (and contain measures) addressing both human capital *and* mobility constructs.
2. Examine conditions under which turnover/mobility has positive consequences for unit performance.
3. When appropriate for the setting, develop and validate measures of human capital loss that differ from traditional, quantity-based turnover measures.

NOTE

1. Such a practice dates back to at least 1926, when the Metropolitan Life Insurance Company formally reported factory workers' quit and discharge rates—a project undertaken "with a view chiefly to determining whether it was desirable and practicable to set up current, national index numbers of factory labor turnover experience" (Berridge, 1929: 62). Given the program's success, MetLife transferred national turnover rate reporting to the Bureau of Labor Statistics in July of 1929.

REFERENCES

Ballinger, G. A., and Schoorman, F. D. (2007). Individual reactions to leadership succession in workgroups. *Academy of Management Review*, *32*(1), 118–36.

Batt, R., and Colvin, A. J. (2011). An employment systems approach to turnover: Human resources practices, quits, dismissals, and performance. *Academy of Management Journal*, *54*(4), 695–717.

Becker, G. S. (1962). Investment in human capital: A theoretical analysis. *Journal of Political Economy*, *70*(5, Part 2), 9–49.

Berridge, W. A. (1929). Labor turnover in American factories. *Monthly Labor Review*, *29*, 62.

Call, M. L., Nyberg, A. J., and Thatcher, S. (2015). Stargazing: An integrative conceptual review, theoretical reconciliation, and extension for star employee research. *Journal of Applied Psychology*, *100*(3), 623–40.

Call, M. L., Nyberg, A. J., Ployhart, R. E., and Weekley, J. (2015). The dynamic nature of collective turnover and unit performance: The impact of time, quality, and replacements. *Academy of Management Journal*, *58*(4), 1208–32.

Dess, G. G., and Shaw, J. D. (2001). Voluntary turnover, social capital, and organizational performance. *Academy of Management Review*, *26*(3), 446–56.

Gardner, T. M., Wright, P. M., and Moynihan, L. M. (2011). The impact of motivation, empowerment, and skill enhancing practices on aggregate voluntary turnover: The mediating effect of collective affective commitment. *Personnel Psychology*, *64*, 315–50.

Hale, D., Ployhart, R. E., and Shepherd, W. (2016). A two-phase longitudinal model of a turnover event: Disruption, recovery rates, and moderators of collective performance. *Academy of Management Journal*, *59*(3), 906–29.

Hatch, N. W., and Dyer, J. H. (2004). Human capital and learning as a source of sustainable competitive advantage. *Strategic Management Journal*, *25*(12), 1155–78.

Hausknecht, J. P. (2017). Collective turnover. *Annual Review of Organizational Psychology and Organizational Behavior*, *4*, 527–44.

Hausknecht, J. P., and Holwerda, J. A. (2013). When does employee turnover matter? Dynamic member configurations, productive capacity, and collective performance. *Organization Science*, *24*(1), 210–25.

Hausknecht, J. P., and Trevor, C. O. (2011). Collective turnover at the group, unit, and organizational levels: Evidence, issues, and implications. *Journal of Management*, *37*(1), 352–88.

Hausknecht, J. P., Trevor, C. O., and Howard, M. J. (2009). Unit-level voluntary turnover rates and customer service quality: Implications of group cohesiveness, newcomer concentration, and size. *Journal of Applied Psychology*, *94*(4), 1068–75.

Hom, P. W., Lee, T. W., Shaw, J. D., and Hausknecht, J. P. (2017). One hundred years of employee turnover theory and research. *Journal of Applied Psychology*, *102*(3), 530–45.

Hom, P. W., Mitchell, T. R., Lee, T. W., and Griffeth, R. W. (2012). Reviewing employee turnover: focusing on proximal withdrawal states and an expanded criterion. *Psychological Bulletin*, *138*(5), 831–58.

Kraaijenbrink, J., Spender, J.-C., and Groen, A. J. (2010). The resource-based view: A review and assessment of its critiques. *Journal of Management*, *36*(1), 349–72.

Mawdsley, J. K., and Somaya, D. (2016). Employee mobility and organizational outcomes: An integrative conceptual framework and research agenda. *Journal of Management*, *42*(1), 85–113.

Miller, D. (1993). Some organizational consequences of CEO succession. *Academy of Management Journal*, *36*(3), 644–59.

Mobley, W. H. (1982). *Employee Turnover*. Reading, MA: Addison-Wesley.

Nyberg, A. J., and Ployhart, R. E. (2013). Context-emergent turnover (CET) theory: A theory of collective turnover. *Academy of Management Review*, *38*(1), 109–31.

Nyberg, A. J., Moliterno, T. P., Hale Jr, D., and Lepak, D. P. (2014). Resource-based perspectives on unit-level human capital: A review and integration. *Journal of Management*, *40*(1), 316–46.

Ployhart, R. E., Nyberg, A. J., Reilly, G., and Maltarich, M. A. (2014). Human capital is dead; long live human capital resources! *Journal of Management*, *40*(2), 371–98.

Reilly, G., Nyberg, A. J., Maltarich, M., and Weller, I. (2014). Human capital flows: Using context-emergent turnover (CET) theory to explore the process by which turnover, hiring, and job demands affect patient satisfaction. *Academy of Management Journal*, *57*(3), 766–90.

Shaw, J. D., Gupta, N., and Delery, J. E. (2005). Alternative conceptualizations of the relationship between voluntary turnover and organizational performance. *Academy of Management Journal*, *48*(1), 50–68.

Shaw, J. D., Delery, J. E., Jenkins, G. D., and Gupta, N. (1998). An organization-level analysis of voluntary and involuntary turnover. *Academy of Management Journal*, *41*(5), 511–25.

Shen, W., and Cannella, A. A. (2002). Revisiting the performance consequences of CEO succession: The impacts of successor type, postsuccession senior executive turnover, and departing CEO tenure. *Academy of Management Journal*, *45*(4), 717–33.

Siebert, W. S., and Zubanov, N. (2009). Searching for the optimal level of employee turnover: A study of a large UK retail organization. *Academy of Management Journal*, *52*(2), 294–313.
Somaya, D., Williamson, I. O., and Lorinkova, N. (2008). Gone but not lost: The different performance impacts of employee mobility between cooperators versus competitors. *Academy of Management Journal*, *51*(5), 936–53.
Staw, B. M. (1980). The consequences of turnover. *Journal of Occupational Behaviour*, *1*(4), 253–73.
Terborg, J., and Lee, T. (1984). A predictive study of organizational turnover rates. *Academy of Management Journal*, *27*, 793– 810.
Tzabbar, D., and Kehoe, R. R. (2014). Can opportunity emerge from disarray? An examination of exploration and exploitation following star scientist turnover. *Journal of Management*, *40*(2), 449–82.
Van Der Vegt, G. S., Bunderson, S., and Kuipers, B. (2010). Why turnover matters in self-managing work teams: Learning, social integration, and task flexibility. *Journal of Management*, *36*(5), 1168–91.

28. Retention is not a strategic imperative: on the pros and cons of employee turnover

Christopher I. Rider and David Tan

For many years, the study of employee mobility – primarily attrition and retention (i.e., turnover) – was the domain of micro organizational behavior (OB) researchers (e.g., Holtom et al., 2008). These researchers developed a large body of evidence on the conditions under which employees tend to depart an organization, producing many important insights on the psychological and social determinants of turnover as well as organizational factors that can reduce turnover rates (e.g., Griffeth et al., 2000; Lee et al., 2004). Given this voluminous literature's persistent emphasis on costly turnover, one might infer that organizations face a "retention imperative." That is, organizations must avoid or reduce employee attrition lest they incur excessive costs of recruiting, training, and socializing employees.

One might similarly infer a "retention imperative" from the literature on strategic human capital management. Building on the resource-based view (e.g., Wernerfelt, 1984; Peteraf, 1993; Barney, 2001), strategy research offers the insight that human capital is a valuable resource that can neither be bought nor owned (Coff, 1997). It follows that competitive advantages based on human capital are sustainable so long as organizations retain key employees (Campbell et al., 2012). This research implies that organizations can hire rivals' employees to gain competitive advantage but must also retain those employees to sustain any advantage gained. Much recent strategy research accordingly focuses on how firms can discourage rivals from offering jobs to their employees or dissuade employees from accepting such offers (e.g., Agarwal et al., 2009; Marx, 2011; Starr et al., 2018). As in the micro OB research, one might reasonably infer from this work that retention is imperative.

We note that other research suggests otherwise. Research on the pre-founding experiences of entrepreneurs documents that many entrepreneurs depart employers before founding new organizations (e.g., Freeman, 1986; Audia and Rider, 2005; Klepper, 2009; Sørensen and Fasiotto, 2011). Although there is some evidence, particularly in professional services, that entrepreneurship-related turnover is detrimental to departed employers (e.g., Phillips, 2002; Wezel et al., 2006; Campbell et al., 2012), many organizations survive and even prosper despite continually experiencing employee departures for entrepreneurship (e.g., Burton et al., 2002; Chatterji, 2009). For example, many semiconductor firms and auto manufacturers prospered for years despite employees regularly leaving to found new organizations – even competing ones (e.g., Freeman, 1986; Klepper, 2009). Employee retention, it seems, might not be a strategic imperative after all.

Macro OB research supports this position. Starting from the insight that organizations stratify society through the matching of people to jobs (e.g., Baron and Bielby, 1980; Baron, 1984), this work treats individuals' transitions from one employer to another as an important attainment mechanism that shapes inequality (e.g., Felmlee, 1982; Barnett et al., 2000). Two insights from this macro OB work inform our view on the "retention imperative." First, turnover that is detrimental to an employer often facilitates individual attainment (e.g., Phillips, 2002). Second, turnover viewed as detrimental to individuals is often considered beneficial to employers (e.g., Fligstein and Shin, 2007; Bidwell et al., 2013). In short, sometimes attrition is bad for an organization and sometimes it is not. A key challenge for researchers is identifying the conditions under which attrition is both good and bad for a focal organization.

With this objective in mind, we propose that a promising intellectual direction for future mobility research is to consider explicitly *where* employees go when they depart a focal organization. If the organizational costs of attrition are motivation for mobility research, then the question of *where* employees subsequently work after departing their employer is largely irrelevant. Yet, macro OB researchers have long recognized that the direction of mobility (i.e., upward or downward) is central to the attainment process and, therefore, theoretically relevant. Recent strategic human capital research also highlights how the subsequent employer of departed employees is consequential for employers (e.g., Somaya et al., 2008; Campbell et al., 2012; Carnahan and Somaya, 2013). So in many ways our suggestion is for research to continue in this direction, but in a more systematic fashion.

Our proposal is also relevant to researchers in the expanding literature on strategic human capital resources (SHCRs) (e.g., Schmidt and Hunter, 1998; Ployhart and Moliterno, 2011; Ployhart et al., 2014). This work extends traditional human capital research on individuals' knowledge, skills, abilities and other characteristics (KSAOs) by considering how KSAOs aggregate at the organizational level into SHCRs that shape organizational performance. While this work helpfully bridges the individual and organizational levels of analysis, we note that it does so by focusing internally at the individuals an organization currently employs. We specifically argue that employee departures shape how the departed organization is perceived in the labor market.

Based on this reasoning, we propose a "research imperative" for SHCR researchers: develop theories that consider how employee departures influence individuals not currently employed by an organization (i.e., prospective employees). We know that individuals want employment experiences that will help them construct rewarding inter-organizational careers (e.g., Bidwell and Briscoe, 2010; Bidwell et al., 2015; Tan and Rider, 2017). Seeking to gauge a prospective employer's prospects for helping them do so, the best information available to prospective employees is often the career transitions of departed employees. We, therefore, propose that SHCR researchers study how employee attrition and retention dynamics shape an organization's pool of prospective employees and, moreover, that focusing on *where* departing employees go after they leave will inform such work.

RELATED LITERATURE

Below, we review some macro OB, strategy, and entrepreneurship research focused on mobility in a highly targeted manner. We highlight key commonalities that have emerged from these large and growing research streams. Briefly, the macro OB literature highlights how the evolution of person–organization fit shapes the sequence of employment spells that constitute one's career. Strategic human capital management research highlights how firms can provide better person–organization fit to rivals' employees while also safeguarding against rivals doing the same to them. The entrepreneurship literature highlights how labor market frictions in person–organization matching shape entrepreneurial activity. After reviewing these literatures, we turn to recent work that nicely connects these literatures by examining post-departure employment destinations to understand individuals' competing career risks and the implications of such transitions for individuals. We build upon this work in elaborating a conceptual three-choice framework that offers promising directions for future macro-level research on SHCRs.

Macro OB: Inter-Organizational Careers

In the organizational theory literature, interest in mobility can be traced at least back to Weber (1947). Weber suggested that allowing employees to advance their careers entirely within a single bureaucracy promotes organizational rationality and employee specialization, both of which were thought to contribute to bureaucratic efficiency. Subsequent work accordingly investigated how organizations' "internal labor markets" govern the evolution of employees' careers through internal allocations of labor and rewards that promote the development of skills valued by employers (Doeringer and Piore, 1971).

Other work explored ways of characterizing the intra-organizational opportunity structure for career mobility, largely by examining how vacancy chains govern the movement of individuals among positions (White, 1970; Chase, 1991; Rosenfeld, 1992). Sociologists took a keen interest in these studies, subsequently finding ways to characterize how careers proceed differently for different groups of employees in ways that contribute to inequality in opportunities and rewards (e.g., Spilerman, 1977; Kalleberg and Sørensen, 1979; Baron, 1984; Barnett et al., 2000).

As these literatures are voluminous and reviewed extensively elsewhere, we focus our attention on how they have influenced recent mobility research. A key contribution of this broad body of work, at least for our purposes, is that understanding typical career mobility patterns is fundamental to our understanding of societally important phenomena like attainment, discrimination, and stratification. Individuals' career transitions consequently feature prominently in the organizational literatures on competition (e.g., Sørensen, 1999), change (e.g., Boeker, 1997), performance (e.g., Eisenhardt and Schoonhoven, 1990; Beckman, 2006; Briscoe and Rogan, 2015), survival (e.g., Phillips, 2002; Wezel et al., 2006; Bermiss and Murmann, 2015), knowledge transfer (e.g., Rosenkopf and Almeida, 2003; Groysberg et al., 2008), collaboration (e.g., Broschak, 2004; Rider, 2012; Rogan, 2014; Broschak and Block, 2014), inequality (e.g., Kronberg, 2013, 2014), and status (e.g., Bidwell et al., 2015; Rider and Tan, 2015; Rider and Negro, 2015; Tan and Rider, 2017).

In recent years, research on inter-organizational mobility has been largely motivated by two insights. First, the concept of "boundaryless careers" (Arthur and Rousseau, 1996) can be traced to the study of not only individuals' inter-organizational career transitions (e.g., Bidwell and Briscoe, 2010), but also to the study of individuals' transitions into alternative employment arrangements like freelancing or contracting (Barley and Kunda, 2006; Bidwell and Briscoe, 2010). As economy-wide research documents declining fluidity in U.S. labor markets over the past few decades (Molloy et al. 2016), this work suggests that high-wage professional workers are exceptions in the sense that they seem increasingly likely to enjoy mobility opportunities and to benefit from job mobility.

Second, and in contrast, the notion that work has become more precarious for many, and especially so for low-wage industrial workers, recurs in organizational work on the evolving employment relationship (e.g., Kalleberg, 2011; Cappelli, 1999). The upshot of these two research streams is that for a variety of reasons the long-term employment relationship that characterized much of the 20th century has given way to a 21st-century notion of inter-organizational careers in which people routinely move from one employer to another.

We note that, despite the ever-present notion of person–organization matching in this work, the study of inter-organizational careers typically focuses on either the supply or the demand side of the labor market – as opposed to the interface of the two market sides. For example, research on inter-organizational career ladders (Bidwell and Briscoe, 2010) attributes much mobility to individuals' desires to acquire skills training from some employers early in their careers and rewards for those skills from different employers later in their careers. In contrast, research on organizational innovation focuses on the demand side by highlighting how organizations recruit individuals away from other organizations to acquire resources that facilitate organizational change (e.g., Baty et al., 1971; Rao and Drazin, 2002; Rosenkopf and Almeida, 2003).

Whether starting from the perspective of the individual or the organization, the logical tie that binds these bodies of work is the notion of person–organization fit. More broad than theories of person–job matching commonly invoked in economics (e.g., Jovanovic, 1979), psychology (e.g., Caldwell and O'Reilly, 1990; Mitchell et al., 2001), or sociology (e.g., Burton and Beckman, 2007), "person–organization fit" generally refers to the extent to which an individual's values are congruent with the norms and values of an employing organization (Chatman, 1991). This notion of person–organization fit informs many accounts of individuals' transitions from one employer to another.

Organizational researchers generally infer that a focal individual moves from one organization to another because the second one offers better person–organization fit. In this work, the impetus for mobility is typically attributed to the individual, although the reasons for better fit often extend beyond the individual's values and the norms and values of their potential employers. For example, in their notion of inter-organizational career ladders, Bidwell and Briscoe (2010) characterize person–organization fit as the coincidence of individuals' skills and training needs and organizations' skill needs and their provision of training to their employees. Bidwell et al. (2015) imply that an individual's need to acquire quality signals and an organization's capability to provide such signals largely shape person–organization fit over the course of one's career. Rider and Tan (2015) focus on person–organization fit as shaped largely by individual values related to the balance of pecuniary and nonpecuniary employment benefits and organizations' capabilities to provide them based on financial resources and firm status. In such studies, mobility events occur as individual values evolve and organizations' capabilities to provide high fit positions do as well.

For our purposes, a key insight of this organizational work on mobility is that many individuals find themselves in positions where their current employer provides person–organization fit that is inferior to other alternatives. In short, this work largely focuses on how person–organization fit evolves with changes on the supply side of the labor market. As an informative contrast, we now review strategic human capital management research that places relatively greater emphasis on the demand side of the labor market.

Strategic Human Capital Management: Lateral Hiring

Strategic human capital management research builds on the insight that human capital is a valuable resource that can convey competitive advantage to employers (Coff, 1997; Campbell et al., 2012). In this work, organizations often hire another organization's employees to enhance their competitive position or weaken rivals' positions, occasionally leading to cycles of poaching and retaliation (Gardner, 2005). This work also informs us that departures to established firms and new firms exhibit differential effects on the departed firm's performance (Campbell et al., 2012).

In research on hiring from rivals, the impetus for mobility is typically positioned with the hiring organization and, specifically, its strategic needs for knowledge and/or capabilities. For example, Rosenkopf and Almeida (2003) argue that hiring technical workers away from other organizations can broaden an organization's technological search for knowledge beyond the knowledge stock of current employees. Internal human capital deficits are also cited in work that emphasizes how organizations often hire individuals away from other organizations, although evidence on the effectiveness of such human capital strategies is mixed (e.g., Groysberg et al., 2008; Dokko and Rosenkopf, 2010; Bidwell, 2011). Other research suggests that individuals are hired not for their human capital but, rather, their social capital. For example, Dokko and Rosenkopf argue that firms often hire to gain access to individuals' relationships to others within the industry. If such hires were not made, the hiring organizations would presumably be in a less advantageous position vis-à-vis rivals.

The important insight that we glean from this work is that, by extending the resource-based view of the firm, this work advances the idea that demand for other organizations' employees often induces mobility. In other words, even if individual needs do not evolve over time, some organizations might willingly provide better person–organization fit to individuals if doing so enhances their competitive advantage (or weakens rivals' positions). As a consequence, individuals with time invariant needs and skills might still engage in mobility – to other employers or to new firms – due to the competitive dynamics of markets and industries.

Because hiring from rivals is common, many organizations take steps both to encourage employee retention and to discourage rivals from hiring their employees. For example, some firms aggressively litigate potential patent infringements to discourage rivals from hiring their employees (e.g., Agarwal et al., 2009). Others require employees to sign non-compete agreements that create "mobility frictions" in the labor market and can be used specifically to restrict employment transitions to an organization's rivals (e.g., Marx, 2011; Starr et al., 2018; Starr et al., 2018). This research tells us that much mobility occurs despite organizational efforts both to enhance the person–organization fit of their current employees and to degrade the potential fit that might be achieved by changing employers (or starting a new organization).

An additional insight of this work is the finding that although employee departures generally exert negative effects on the performance of departed firm, this is not always so. Firms might benefit in terms of future business if an employee joins a potential customer (e.g., Carnahan and Somaya, 2013) and might experience enhanced labor market status if the employee's move is evidently career-advancing (e.g., Tan and Rider, 2017). This work draws our attention to the idea that the effect on the departed firm often depends on the employment destination of the departed employee, which might include established rivals of the departed firm or, alternatively, new entrants. The insights of strategic human capital management, then, direct our attention to work on entrepreneurship because new ventures represent both career options and subsequent employers of departed employees.

Entrepreneurship: Spinning Out

The entrepreneurship literature has also tackled the mobility phenomenon at both individual and organizational levels. At the individual level, prior research examines the conditions under which one is most likely to transition from employment to entrepreneurship (e.g., Dobrev and Barnett, 2005; Stuart and Ding, 2006; Sørensen, 2007). At the organization level, prior research examines the organizational characteristics that are most conductive to producing entrepreneurs (e.g., Freeman, 1986; Gompers et al., 2005). For the purposes of this chapter, this work essentially contributes the insight that many individuals depart their employers to become entrepreneurs who found new organizations (e.g., Freeman, 1986; Klepper and Sleeper, 2005; Audia and Rider, 2005, 2006; Burton et al., 2002; Elfenbein et al., 2010; Sørensen and Fasiotto, 2011).

An important contrast between entrepreneurship research and strategic human capital management research is the way in which retention is treated. While some strategy research views employee departures as potentially beneficial to firms (e.g., Carnahan and Somaya, 2013; Tan and Rider, 2017), relatively greater attention is paid by strategy researchers to what we refer to as a "retention imperative" – human capital is valuable and must, therefore, be retained. In entrepreneurship research, however, relatively greater attention is paid to the question of why employers let so many employees go (e.g., Freeman, 1986). That is, entrepreneurship researchers focus relatively more on the question of why retention is *not* a greater strategic priority.

Several influential entrepreneurship studies speak to the issue of firms' "failures" to retain employees who depart to start new organizations. Franco and Filson (2006), for example, develop a theory of how entrepreneurs use technological knowledge from their prior employers as the basis for new firms. Klepper (2009) and Klepper and Thompson (2010) attribute much entrepreneurship to disagreements among executives, managers, and rank-and-file employees about firm strategy, resulting in some employees departing to found new firms. Agarwal et al. (2004) develop the idea that firms with similarly strong technological and marketing capabilities produce entrepreneurs less often than firms with less balanced capabilities. These studies highlight the possibility that diseconomies of scope prevent firms from harnessing employees' business ideas, leading to employee departures and the production of entrepreneurs.

In our view, entrepreneurship research nicely bridges the work on inter-organizational careers and lateral hiring reviewed above. Like the work on inter-organizational careers, entrepreneurship research highlights how one's career objectives and transitions evolve over time. Like the work on strategic human capital management, entrepreneurship research highlights how the factors that drive people to leave their current employer might actually be orthogonal to the employment experience. Entrepreneurship research further calls our attention to career opportunities beyond the boundaries of established organizations. At least some career opportunities are to be realized by creating new organizations (Stinchcombe, 1965).

Some prior studies are explicitly designed to account for the empirical fact that many individuals move not between employers but, rather, from employment to entrepreneurship. For example, Campbell et al. (2012) theorize how employees at different points in the intra-organizational wage distribution differ both in their propensities to depart their employers and in their subsequent transitions between entrepreneurship and employment conditional on departure. Sørensen and Sharkey (2014) theorize how career advancement opportunities shape mobility events and model individual transitions to new employers and entrepreneurship based on one's earnings potential at their current employer. Rider et al. (2018) theorize how one's propensity to engage in entrepreneurial activity varies with two theorized costs that vary with one's career experience: (1) the costs to an individual of forming a new business and (2) the cost to an employer of absorbing the individual's human capital.

Work in this vein highlights what we believe to be a very promising avenue for future research – considering how an organization's labor market niche is shaped by employee mobility events. Specifically, we propose that future research on SHCRs consider how the composition of an organization's applicant pool varies as employees vary in their choices among: (1) continued employment with their current employer, (2) changing employers, and (3) entrepreneurship. Below, we elaborate how researchers might formalize arguments about these competing risks as a function of individual, organizational, and industrial characteristics. We then proceed to elaborate measurement and design considerations for organizational studies.

A FRAMEWORK FOR FUTURE RESEARCH

We propose a general framework for studying how employee mobility events influence an employer's labor market position. This framework specifically considers three choices that an individual will face as their career evolves: (1) remain with their employer, (2) change employers, or (3) enter entrepreneurship. Each of these choices is expected to exert some positive and negative effects on the employer's appeal to prospective employees, subsequently shaping the composition of the employer's applicant pool for open positions as well as the focal organization's costs of employing human capital resources. We, therefore, organize these potential pros and cons in a way conducive to systematic study.

In contrast to the internal labor markets era, modern careers often span multiple organizations (e.g., Cappelli, 1999). Individuals consequently expect their careers to evolve along "inter-organizational career ladders" as early employment experiences open up subsequent career opportunities with other employers (Bidwell and Briscoe, 2010; Bidwell et al., 2015). Consequently, individuals value an employment opportunity not only for its current period remuneration and other benefits, but also for its associated opportunities for future external mobility.

Consistent with this reasoning, in a study of lateral partner hiring by large U.S. law firms, we find that lawyer departures for evidently career-advancing opportunities at other firms contribute to their departed firm being viewed as higher status by other lawyers (Tan and Rider, 2017). In other words, there appear to be perceptual benefits of employee departures among prospective employees. Building on this insight, we outline a systematic approach to weighing such benefits against the costs of employee turnover to consider how employee departures influence a focal organization's competitive position in the labor market.

Consider two employees *i* and *j* of firm *A* who are observationally equivalent in terms of all relevant dimensions like qualifications, prior experience, current role, performance, etc. If *i* departs firm *A* to accept a position with a rival firm *B* and *j* continues working for firm *A*, then labor market observers must balance the information conveyed by their diverging career paths to update their impression of firm *A* as an employer.

On the one hand, the choices of *i* and *j* convey conflicting information about the appeal of the employment experience at firm *A*. Observers might infer that firm *A* is a good employer because *j* continues working for firm *A*. They might also infer that firm *A* is not a good employer because *i* moved to firm *B*. On the other hand, the departures also convey conflicting information about labor market frictions. Observers might infer that there are mobility-limiting frictions imposed on employees of firm *A* due to employee *j*'s continued employment with firm *A*, but might also infer that there are no such frictions based on *i*'s transition to firm *B*. How might a researcher draw inferences about a focal organization given such conflicting information, given such perceptual pros and cons?

We propose that researchers might take a systematic within-organization approach to examine how inter-temporal variation in the rates of employee departure types shape an organization's labor market position. Our proposed approach is subject to a few key assumptions. First, one must assume that organizations have baseline rates of employee departures and that organization-specific perceptions of labor market observers (e.g., prospective employees) are sensitive to variation around that baseline. Second, one must assume that such variation is visible to labor market observers. Third, one must assume that prospective employees share a general consensus around what constitutes upward and downward mobility in terms of career advancement (e.g., promotions and demotions are widely recognized). Of course, each assumption must be checked prior to applying our approach. Subject to these assumptions being maintained, researchers can utilize our approach. Figure 28.1 summarizes the possible departure types.

We relate specific types of employee departures to key organizational outcomes. In any given period, an employee can choose to: (a) continue in employment with the organization, (b) transition to another employer, or (c) transition to entrepreneurship. The organizational attrition rate is decreasing with the incidence of (a) and increasing with incidences

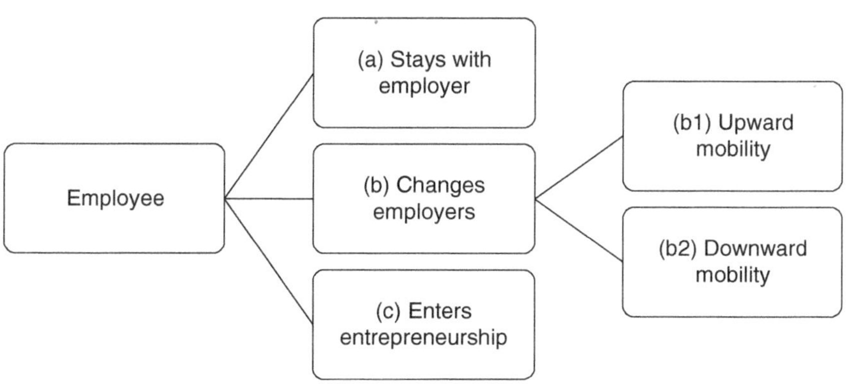

Figure 28.1 Departure types

of both (b) and (c); retention exhibits the opposite relationship with the incidence of each choice. Turnover costs are presumably increasing with both (b) and (c). Further disaggregating (b) into (b1) career-advancing transitions and (b2) career-hindering transitions based on employment titles or relevant employer status yields further insights.

Aggregating all such choices at the organizational level yields implications for how the focal organization is perceived by labor market observers (i.e., prospective employees). More specifically, an organization might be viewed as a provider of stable employment the higher is the incidence of (a); as a "stepping stone" the higher is the incidence of (b1); as a "dead end" the higher is the incidence of (b2); or as a "breeding ground" for entrepreneurs the higher is the incidence of (c). As the relative rates of these choices vary over time for a focal organization so, too, does its appeal among prospective employees. To the extent that such variance is visible to labor market observers, the characteristics of the applicant pool for organizational jobs should also vary.

We propose that research on SHCR develops theoretical expectations for how within-organization variation in (a), (b1), (b2), and (c) is related to measures of, broadly speaking, prospective employee quality for organizational jobs. For applicant pools, such measures might include applicant work experience, education (stratified both in terms of quantity and quality), and other productivity signals – e.g., exam scores, grade point average (GPA). For job candidates, such measures might include interviewer evaluations, expected duration of tenure, accepted offer rates, or acceptance rates conditional on offer terms (i.e., conditional yields). With such data researchers can identify both pros and cons of various employee departure types. Such efforts seem likely to enrich theories of strategic human capital management.

Our objective for this chapter has been to motivate an idea and to propose an approach to studying it. We acknowledge that we have not developed theoretical predictions, but we have highlighted and organized the relevant literature in a way that implies that maybe retention is not a strategic imperative. Our proposed framework is ideally applied to studying any organization – or a sample of organizations – for which specific longitudinal data are available. Researchers need data on not only organizational-level attrition and retention but, also on the career transitions of departed employees. Researchers must be able to distinguish employee departures for employment at other organizations from employee departures for entrepreneurship. Such data enable researchers to calculate retention and attrition rates, and to characterize individuals' transitions as upward or downward mobility in terms of career advancement, based on industry status hierarchies or position titles. Last, researchers need data on the applicant and/or candidate pools for organizational positions that enable one to measure the quality of prospective employees. From our perspective, such data enable researchers to examine how these different departures shape the organization's labor market appeal.

We think it important to note that SHCR researchers lacking such longitudinal, organizational data can still develop and test these ideas. Experimental methods also seem conducive to studying how employee departures shape an organization's appeal as an employer. For example, randomly varying the presentation of employee departures in recruitment materials and examining how such variation shapes applicant pools for open jobs is another way to push this research agenda forward. Applicant pools might differ along dimensions of quality or fit based on whether or not career-advancing departures to other employers are featured in recruitment materials. Alternatively, such materials might instead feature departures for entrepreneurship. In this way, SHCR researchers might be able to document perceptual benefits of employee turnover.

CLOSING COMMENTS

Much prior research implies a "retention imperative" – organizations must avoid or reduce employee attrition lest they incur excessive costs of recruiting, training, and socializing employees. But, recent research suggests a potential upside of employee departures. For example, firms might benefit when employees depart to customers or potential customers and steer business back to their former employer (e.g., Somaya et al., 2008; Carnahan and Somaya, 2013). Former employees might also transfer knowledge back to former colleagues (e.g., Corredoira and Rosenkopf, 2010). Furthermore, firms could benefit from hiring replacements for departed employees who bring new perspectives to the firm's business (e.g., McKendrick et al., 2009).

We focused on research that suggests how a firm's appeal as an employer might be enhanced when employees depart for higher-level positions with prominent rivals (Tan and Rider, 2017). In such cases, the opportunity to advance one's career through external mobility is presumably beneficial for attracting productive employees at reasonable cost (e.g., Bidwell et al. 2015). Strategic human capital management research offers the insight that human capital is a valuable resource and, like other valuable resources, it is competitively advantageous to utilize and therefore should be retained. We questioned this "retention imperative" with the intent of provoking macro mobility researches to develop a more extensive perspective on the pros and cons of employee mobility.

Absent such a general framework for studying mobility, macro research on the topic risks becoming compartmentalized into increasingly disconnected literatures that focus exclusively on specific outcomes (e.g., patenting, sales growth, reputation) related to employee mobility. As strategic management is fundamentally about making trade-offs, it seems to us that the "mobility imperative" for researchers is to develop a new literature that adequately characterizes mobility's trade-offs across a range of organizational outcomes.

To that end, as expanded availability of individual career history data enables more and more research on the movement of people across organizations, we propose that two specific changes in mobility research will be particularly fruitful. First, at the individual level, proper macro theories of mobility must account for three options that individuals face at all career points between labor market entry and retirement: (1) remaining with their employer, (2) changing employers, and (3) engaging in entrepreneurship.[1] Doing so will enable researchers to distinguish mobility events that are more or less favorable for individuals (e.g., by enabling career attainment) and for their employers (e.g., by retaining human capital).

Second, macro research on mobility must integrate the growing body of work on the potential pros and cons of employee departures into a theoretical framework that allows for strategic trade-offs across a broader range of organizational outcomes. Heeding these two suggestions and using websites like LinkedIn and/or national employee–employer data registries, macro mobility researchers are poised to produce important and novel insights about the evolution of modern careers and the role of human capital retention in sustaining competitive advantage. In doing so, retention is likely to become viewed as more "strategic" and, therefore, "elective" and no longer an "imperative."

NOTE

1. We acknowledge that unemployment and retirement are additional career options. We suggest that these options are less likely to overlap with the other three as such decisions are more closely associated with industry, occupation, and market conditions, or with the accumulation of experience, tenure, and age. We, therefore, omit these choices from our discussion.

REFERENCES

Agarwal, R., Ganco, M., and Ziedonis, R. H. (2009). Reputations for toughness in patent enforcement: Implications for knowledge spillovers via inventor mobility. *Strategic Management Journal*, *30*, 1349–74.

Agarwal, R., Echambadi, R., Franco, A. M., and Sarkar, M. B. (2004). Knowledge transfer through inheritance: Spin-out generation, development, and survival. *Academy of Management Journal*, *4*(4), 501–22.

Arthur, M. B., and Rousseau, D. M. (1996). *The Boundaryless Career: A New Employment Principle for a New Organizational Era*. New York: Oxford University Press.

Audia, P. G., and Rider, C. I. (2005). A garage and an idea: What more does an entrepreneur need? *California Management Review*, *48*, 6–28.

Audia, P. G., and Rider, C. I. (2006). Entrepreneurs as organizational products: Revisited. In. J. R. Baum, R. A. Baron and M. Frese (eds), *The Psychology of Entrepreneurship*. Hillsdale, NJ: Erlbaum.

Barley, S. R., and Kunda, G. (2006). Contracting: A new form of professional practice. *Academy of Management Perspective*, *19*, 1–19.

Barnett W. P., Baron, J. N., and Stuart, T. E. (2000) Avenues of attainment: Occupational demography and organizational careers in the California civil service. *American Journal of Sociology*, *106*, 88–144.

Barney, J. B. (2001). Resource-based theories of competitive advantage: A ten-year retrospective on the resource-based view. *Journal of Management*, *27*(6), 643–50.

Baron, J. N. (1984). Organizational perspectives on stratification. *Annual Review of Sociology*, *10*, 37–69.

Baron, J. N., and Bielby, W. T. (1980). Bringing the firms back in: Stratification, segmentation, and the organization of work. *American Sociological Review*, *45*, 737–65.

Baty, G. B., Evan, W. M., and Rothermel, T. W. (1971). Personnel flows as interorganizational relations. *Administrative Science Quarterly*, *16*, 430–43.

Beckman, C. M. (2006). The influence of founding team prior company affiliations on firm behavior. *Academy of Management Journal*, *49*, 741–58.

Bermiss, Y. S., and Murmann, J. P. (2015). Who matters more? The impact of functional background and top executive mobility on firm survival. *Strategic Management Journal*, *36*(11), 1697–716.

Bidwell, M. (2011). Paying more to get less: The effects of external hiring versus internal mobility. *Administrative Science Quarterly*, *56*, 369–407.

Bidwell, M. and Briscoe, F. (2010). The dynamics of interorganizational careers. *Organization Science*, *21*, 1034–53.

Bidwell, M., Briscoe, F., Fernandez-Mateo, I., and Sterling, A. (2013). The employment relationship and inequality: How and why changes in employment practices are reshaping rewards in organizations. *Academy of Management Annals*, *7*, 61–121.

Bidwell, M., Won, S., Barbulescu, R., and Mollick, E. (2015). I used to work at Goldman Sachs! How firms benefit from organizational status in the market for human capital. *Strategic Management Journal*, *36*(8), 1164–73.

Boeker, W. (1997). Strategic change: The influence of managerial characteristics and organizational growth. *Academy of Management Journal*, *40*, 152–70.

Briscoe, F., and Rogan, M. (2015). Coordinating complex work: Knowledge networks, partner departures, and client relationship performance in a law firm. *Management Science*, *62*(8), 2392–411.

Broschak, J. P. (2004). Managers' mobility and market interface: The effect of managers' career mobility on the dissolution of market ties. *Administrative Science Quarterly*, *49*, 608–40.

Broschak, J. P., and Block, E. S. (2014). With or without you: When does managerial exit matter for the dissolution of dyadic client-agency relationships? *Academy of Management Journal*, *57*(3), 743–65.

Burton, M. D., and Beckman, C. M. (2007). Leaving a legacy: Position imprints and successor turnover in young firms. *American Sociological Review*, *72*, 239–66.
Burton, M. D., Sørensen, J. B., and Beckman, C. M. (2002). Coming from good stock: Career histories and few venture formation. *Research in the Sociology of Organizations*, *19*, 229–62.
Caldwell, D. F., and O'Reilly, C. A. (1990). Measuring person-job fit with a profile comparison process. *Journal of Applied Psychology*, *75*, 648–57.
Campbell, B. A., Coff, R., and Kryscynski, D. (2012). Rethinking sustained competitive advantage from human capital. *Academy of Management Review*, *37*, 376–95.
Campbell, B. A., Ganco, M., Franco, A. M., and Agarwal, R. (2012). Who leaves, where to, and why worry? Employee mobility, entrepreneurship and effects on source firm performance. *Strategic Management Journal*, *33*, 65–87.
Cappelli, P. (1999). *The New Deal at Work: Managing the Market-Driven Workforce*. Boston: Harvard Business School Press.
Carnahan, S., and Somaya, D. (2013). Alumni effects and relational advantage: The impact on outsourcing when a buyer hires employees from a supplier's competitors. *Academy of Management Journal*, *56*, 1578–600.
Chase, I. (1991). Vacancy chains. *Annual Review of Sociology*, *17*, 133–54.
Chatman, J. A. (1991). Matching people and organizations: Selection and socialization in public accounting firms. *Administrative Science Quarterly*, *36*, 459–84.
Chatterji, A. K. (2009). Spawned with a silver spoon? Entrepreneurial performance and innovation in the medical device industry. *Strategic Management Journal*, *30*, 185–206.
Coff, R. (1997). Human assets and management dilemmas: Coping with hazards on the road to resource-based theory. *Academy of Management Review*, *48*, 374–402.
Corredoira, R. A., and Rosenkopf, L. (2010). Should auld acquaintance be forgot? The reverse transfer of knowledge through mobility ties. *Strategic Management Journal*, *31*, 159–81.
Dobrev, S. D., and Barnett, W. P. (2005). Organizational roles and transition to entrepreneurship. *Academy of Management Journal*, *48*, 433–49.
Doeringer, P. B., and Piore, M. J. (1971). *Internal Labor Markets and Manpower Analysis*. Lexington, MA: Heath Lexington.
Dokko, G., and Rosenkopf, L. (2010). Social capital for hire? Mobility of technical professionals and firm influence in wireless standards committees. *Organization Science*, *21*, 677–95.
Eisenhardt, K. M., and Schoonhoven, C. B. (1990). Organizational growth: Linking founding team, strategy, environment, and growth among U.S. semiconductor ventures, 1978–1988. *Administrative Science Quarterly*, *35*, 504–29.
Elfenbein, D. W., Hamilton, B. H., and Zenger, T. R. (2010). The small firm effect and the entrepreneurial spawning of scientists and engineers. *Management Science*, *50*(4), 659–81.
Felmlee, D. (1982). Women's job mobility processes within and between employers. *American Sociological Review*, *47*, 142–51.
Fligstein, N. and Shin, T. (2007). Shareholder value and the transformation of the U.S. economy, 1984–2000. *Sociological Forum*, *22*(4), 399–424.
Franco, A. M., and Filson, D. (2006). Spin-outs: Knowledge diffusion through employee mobility. *RAND Journal of Economics*, *37*(4), 841–60.
Freeman, J. (1986). Entrepreneurs as organizational products: Semiconductor firms and venture capital firms. *Advances in the Study of Entrepreneurship, Innovation, and Economic Growth*, *1*, 33–52.
Gardner, T. M. (2005). Interfirm competition for human resources: Evidence from the software industry. *Academy of Management Journal*, *48*, 237–56.
Gompers, P., Lerner, J., and Scharfstein, D. (2005). Entrepreneurial spawning: Public corporations and the genesis of new ventures, 1986 to 1999. *Journal of Finance*, *60*, 577–614.
Griffeth, R. W., Hom, P. W., and Gaertner, S. (2000). A meta-analysis of antecedents and correlates of employee turnover: Update, moderator tests, and research implications for the next millennium. *Journal of Management*, *26*(3), 463–88.
Groysberg, B., Lee, L.E., and Nanda, A. (2008). Can they take it with them? The portability of star knowledge workers' performance. *Management Science*, *54*, 1213–30.
Holtom, B. C., Mitchell, T. R., Lee, T. W., and M. Eberly, M. (2008). Turnover and retention research: A glance at the past, a closer review of the present, and a venture into the future. *Academy of Management Annals*, *2*, 231–74.
Jovanovic, B. (1979). Job matching and the theory of turnover. *Journal of Political Economy*, *87*, 972–90.
Kalleberg, A. L. (2011). *Good Jobs, Bad Jobs: The Rise of Polarized and Precarious Employment Systems in the United States, 1970s–2000s*. New York: Russell Sage Foundation.
Kalleberg, A. L., and Sørensen, A. B. (1979). Sociology of Labor Markets. *Annual Review of Sociology*, *5*, 351–79.
Klepper, S. (2009). Spinoffs: A review and synthesis. *European Management Review*, *6*, 159–71.

Klepper, S., and Sleeper, S. (2005). Entry by spinoffs. *Management Science*, *51*(8), 1291–306.
Klepper, S., and Thompson, P. (2010). Disagreements and intra-industry spinoffs. *International Journal of Industrial Organization*, *28*(5), 526–38.
Kronberg, A. (2013). Stay or leave? Externalization of job mobility and the effects on the U.S. gender earnings gap, 1979–2009. *Social Forces*, *91*(4), 1117–46.
Kronberg, A. (2014). Stay or leave? Race, education and changing returns to the external labor market strategy, 1976–2009. *Work and Occupations*, *41*(3), 305–49.
Lee, T. W., Mitchell, T. R., Sablynski, C. J., Burton, J. P., and Holtom, B. C. (2004). The effects of job embeddedness on organizational citizenship, job performance, volitional absences, and voluntary turnover. *Academy of Management Journal*, *47*, 711–22.
Marx, M. (2011). The firm strikes back: Non-compete agreements and the mobility of technical professionals. *American Sociological Review*, *76*, 695–712.
McKendrick, D. G., Wade, J. B., and Jaffee, J. (2009). A good riddance? Spin-offs and the technological performance of parent firms. *Organization Science*, *20*, 979–92.
Mitchell, T. R., Holtom, B. C., Lee, T. W., Sablynski, C. J., and Erez, M. (2001). Why people stay: Using job embeddedness to predict voluntary turnover. *Academy of Management Journal*, *44*, 1102–21.
Molloy, R., Trezzi, R., Smith, C. L., and Wozniak, A. (2016). Understanding declining fluidity in the U.S. labor market. *Brookings Papers on Economic Activity*, Spring, 183–259.
Peteraf, M. A. (1993). The cornerstones of competitive advantage: A resource-based view. *Strategic Management Journal*, *14*(3), 179–91.
Phillips, D. J. (2002). A genealogical approach to organizational life chances: The parent-progeny transfer among Silicon Valley law firms, 1946–1996. *Administrative Science Quarterly*, *47*, 474–506.
Ployhart, R. E., and Moliterno, T. P. (2011). Emergence of the human capital resource: A multilevel model. *Academy of Management Review*, *36*, 127–50.
Ployhart, R. E., Nyberg, A. J., Reilly, G., and Maltrich, M. A. (2014). Human capital is dead; long live human capital resources! *Journal of Management*, *40*, 371–98.
Rao, H., and Drazin, R. (2002). Overcoming resource constraints on product innovation by recruiting talent from rivals: A study of the mutual fund industry, 1986–94. *Academy of Management Journal*, *45*, 491–507.
Rider, C. I. (2012). How employees' prior affiliations constrain organizational network change: A study of U.S. venture capital and private equity. *Administrative Science Quarterly*, *57*(3), 453–83.
Rider, C. I., and Negro, G. (2015). Organizational failure and intraprofessional status loss. *Organization Science*, *26*(3), 633–49.
Rider, C. I., and Tan, D. (2015). Labor market advantages of organizational status: A study of lateral partner hiring by large U.S. law firms. *Organization Science*, *26*, 356–72.
Rogan, M. (2014). Executive departures without client losses: The role of multiplex ties in exchange partner retention. *Academy of Management Journal*, *57*, 563–84.
Rosenfeld, R. A. (1992). Job mobility and career processes. *Annual Review of Sociology*, *18*, 39–61.
Rosenkopf, L., and Almeida, P. (2003). Overcoming local search through alliances and mobility. *Management Science*, *49*, 751–66.
Schmidt, F. L., and Hunter, J. E. (1998). The validity and utility of selection methods in personnel psychology: Practical and theoretical implications of 85 years of research findings. *Psychological Bulletin*, *124*, 262–74.
Somaya, D., Williamson, I. O., and Lorinkova, N. (2008). Gone but not lost: The different performance impacts of employee mobility between cooperators and competitors. *Academy of Management Journal*, *51*, 936–53.
Sørensen, J. B. (1999). Executive migration and interorganizational competition. *Social Science Research*, *28*, 289–315.
Sørensen, J. B, and Fassiotto, M. A. (2011). Organizations as fonts of entrepreneurship. *Organization Science*, *22*, 1322–31.
Sørensen, J. B., and Sharkey, A. J. (2014). Entrepreneurship as a mobility process. *American Sociological Review*, *79*, 328–49.
Sørensen, M. (2007). How smart is smart money? A two-sided matching model of venture capital. *Journal of Finance*, *62*(6), 2725–62.
Spilerman, S. (1977). Careers, labor market structure, and socioeconomic achievement. *American Journal of Sociology*, *83*, 551–93.
Starr, E., Ganco, M., and Campbell, B. (2018). Strategic human capital management in the context of cross-industry and within-industry mobility frictions. *Strategic Management Journal*, *39*(8), 2226–54.
Starr, E., Prescott, J. J., and Bishara, N. (2018). Understanding noncompetition agreements: The 2014 Noncompete Survey Project. *Michigan State Law Review*, *2*, 369–64.
Stinchcombe, A. L. (1965). Organizations and social structure. Pp. 142–93 in J. G. March (ed.), *Handbook of Organizations*. Chicago, IL: Rand McNally.
Stuart, T. E. and Ding, W. W. (2006). When do scientists become entrepreneurs? The social structural antecedents of commercial activity in the academic life sciences. *American Journal of Sociology*, *112*(1), 97–144.

Tan, D. and Rider, C. I. (2017). Let them go? How losing employees to competitors can enhance firm status. *Strategic Management Journal*, *38*, 1848–74.

Weber, M. (1947). *The Theory of Social and Economic Organization*. New York: Oxford University Press.

Wernerfelt, B. (1984). A resource-based view of the firm. *Strategic Management Journal*, *5*(2), 171–80.

Wezel, F., Cattani, G., and Pennings, J. M. (2006). Competitive implications of interfirm mobility. *Organization Science*, *17*(6), 691–709.

White, H. C. (1970). *Chains of Opportunity: System Models of Mobility in Organizations*. Cambridge, MA: Harvard University Press.

29. A commentary on "Keeping strategic human capital resources: mobility"

Matthew Bidwell

Mobility, the process by which people move their employment from one organization to another, plays a critical role in determining the strategic human capital resources available to organizations. Where recruitment is how firms gain those strategic human capital resources, turnover is how they lose them again. Beyond its effects on organizations' stock of human capital, turnover can also disrupt organizations' performance through the disruptive effects of outflow, as social capital is lost, routines must be re-established with new workers, and knowledge must be rebuilt. Not surprisingly, turnover has therefore been a critical topic of study for scholars who are interested in how human capital resources affect firm performance (e.g. Coff 1997; Glebbeek and Bax 2004; Park and Shaw 2013; Reilly et al. 2014; Shaw et al. 1998, 2005).

The chapters by Hausknecht and Rider and Tan provide thoughtful and provocative analyses of the current state of research on mobility. Both chapters draw attention to the complex relationship between turnover and organizational performance, noting in particular that turnover may sometimes benefit performance. In this commentary, I commend their detailed analyses, although I do question their conclusions about the overall benefits of mobility. I also offer my own thoughts on the relationship between performance and turnover, drawing on some of the other ideas that the two chapters raise.

In particular, both chapters note how research on turnover tends to ignore the question of where the movers are going. Moreover, Rider and Tan note that research that follows movers across organizations often emphasizes the benefits of mobility to those movers because of the way it allows them to advance their careers. I develop these ideas to make three points: first, building on a long strand of existing literature, I note that in evaluating the costs and benefits of turnover we need to consider the costs of preventing that turnover. Second, I suggest that the costs of avoiding that turnover depend on where the mover is going. In particular, it will be much more costly to prevent socially "efficient" turnover that advances a mover's career than it is to prevent socially inefficient turnover that reflects poor working conditions or management practices. Third, I suggest that turnover may therefore in part reflect broader choices that organizations make about how to structure their organization and who to recruit. When it comes to reducing efficient turnover, lowering the costs of turnover may result in higher costs elsewhere. By attending to these differences in the causes of turnover, I suggest that we may gain more insight into how mobility relates to the broader strategic choices that firms make within the labor market, and how it should be evaluated within the framework of those strategies.

COMMENTS ON HAUSKNECHT AND RIDER AND TAN: DOES MOBILITY HAVE TO BE BAD?

The chapters by Hausknecht and Rider and Tan do an excellent job of synthesizing and advancing the wide range of different literatures that currently explore worker mobility. Hausknecht's chapter engages in the important work of bridging the well-developed micro literature on the causes of turnover (to which he is an important contributor) with perspectives from the literature on strategic human capital. He creates a lot of value through the thought that he puts into identifying the gaps in the intersection between the two literatures. He shows how viewing turnover as the loss of capacity rather than the loss of people is an important step in linking turnover research to firms' performance. Not all losses are equal, and focusing on who leaves is critical to our understanding of the impact on organizations.

Rider and Tan draw on very different literatures to develop a more comprehensive analysis of the different ways in which employee turnover can affect organizations. A core insight of their chapter is that it matters where the movers go next. Sometimes ex-employees benefit the organization by going on to become its customers (Somaya et al. 2008); sometimes, leavers' track records in going on to build successful careers may help the organization to gain status and attract others (Bidwell et al. 2015; Lehmberg et al. 2009; Rider and Tan 2015); sometimes movers may even return to the organization as boomerang employees, having gained valuable experience and knowledge elsewhere (Shipp et al. 2013; Swider et al. 2017).

A common and somewhat provocative theme across both chapters is the idea that the loss of human capital through turnover may not always be negative for the overall effectiveness of the firm's strategic human capital resources. Drawing on the micro literature, Hausknecht notes that not all turnover is negative; sometimes, it may allow organizations to replace a low performer with higher potential. While many people's decisions to leave may be met by their managers with alarm, in some cases those decisions may instead be accompanied by managerial sighs of relief. By promoting hiring, turnover also allows the organization to bring in new human capital with new knowledge and new perspectives. Moreover, as Rider and Tan note, movers may often be in a position to benefit their former employers once they have left. A particular strength of these well thought-out and worked-through arguments is in the way that they look beyond the immediate performance consequences of employee exit. Firms are complex social systems that are themselves embedded within complex social systems. As people move organizations, they free up new space for others to move in and rearrange relationships within the organization, creating ripples of change that may bring benefits as well as costs.

It is worth noting that these arguments have some similarities to earlier debates on the optimal level of turnover (Abelson and Baysinger 1984; Glebbeek and Bax 2004). Prior research speculated that just as turnover can be too high for optimal performance, it might also be possible for turnover to be too low. In particular, Abelson and Baysinger suggested that some separation of under-performing workers is probably a good thing in organizations, and that turnover rates that are too low may indicate a failure to clean house in this way. The implication they draw from this idea is that the performance effects of turnover vary with the level of turnover: too much turnover is disruptive; but too little suggests a failure to clear out underperforming employees, or too strenuous an effort on behalf of the organization to retain marginal human capital resources.

Despite the considerable intuitive appeal of these arguments, the question is whether they will survive contact with the data. Unfortunately, the initial evidence is not promising. Park and Shaw (2013) use a meta-analysis to synthesize research on how turnover affects organizational performance. The conclusion of that work is fairly clear: turnover harms organizations. Although there is some evidence that the marginal damage wrought by turnover increases at higher levels of turnover, scholars have largely failed to find evidence that too little turnover can also be damaging.

This is not to say that turnover cannot benefit organizations; nor, as Hausknecht suggests, that different research approaches might not be better placed to detect those benefits. My reading of the evidence, though, is that those benefits will usually act to lessen the overall damage that turnover does to organizational performance, rather than rendering turnover beneficial. While the benefits of turnover identified by the prior chapters are real, it is not clear that they are ever likely to outweigh the very tangible costs of recruitment, training, and business disruption that turnover engenders. While businesses might do well to maximize the benefits that turnover brings them, they would probably do even better to minimize that mobility in the first place.

Despite my sense that the negative effects of turnover tend to outweigh the positives, I do think that it is worth developing a second insight that Abelson and Baysinger offer. Beyond noting the sometimes positive effects of turnover, they also suggest that the costs of turnover should be set against the costs of retention. The exit of a given employee may usually be negative when compared to a counterfactual in which that person stays, with no other organizational changes. But that is not the long-run decision that organizations face. Instead, they need to compare the costs of that exit to the costs of any measures that the organization would have needed to take to retain that person. When compared to those retention costs, turnover may end up being the cheaper option.

The main implication that Abelson and Baysinger draw from their argument is that firms likely face diminishing costs to reducing turnover, so that some exit is inevitable. In the rest of this chapter, I want instead to take this argument in a different direction. An important point that Rider and Tan raise is that turnover is often good for the movers, allowing them to advance their careers by moving to a better job in another organization. I suggest that thinking about the benefits to the mover's career is important to thinking about the costs of preventing turnover: a move that has serious career advantages for the mover may be much harder to prevent than one undertaken for different reasons. Bringing those career-related aspects of mobility into our analyses may advance our understanding of the costs and benefits of turnover.

THE DIFFERENT CAUSES OF MOBILITY

My colleague Peter Cappelli once used a question on a doctoral qualifying exam that went something along the lines of: "a psychologist, a sociologist, and an economist walk into a bar and start arguing about mobility. What do they say?" As Rider and Tan note, each of those different disciplines has used different theoretical lenses to explore the same underlying phenomenon of mobility. Ultimately, those differences reflect the way that worker mobility has multiple different causes. While each of the disciplines is alive to those multiple causes, each discipline also ends up emphasizing some over others.

One important driver of mobility is uncertainty about how well a given job will fit a particular person, particularly in comparison to other alternatives. Economic approaches emphasize people's resulting search for the job that will fit them best as the cause of mobility. Those economic models tend to argue that people will choose the job that seems to be the best fit for them at the time. However, they may then leave that job, either because they learn that they are a less good fit for that job than they would like (e.g., Jovanovic 1979), or because they learn about the availability of other jobs that might be a better fit for them (e.g., Burdett and Mortensen 1998).

A second, related driver of mobility is employees' happiness with various different aspects of their job. These evaluations are central to many psychology-based theories of turnover. Core findings in this field relate to how workers' satisfaction with their job, relationship with their supervisor, and commitment to the organization shape their propensity to quit (Allen et al. 2010; Griffeth et al. 2000), while theoretical models have emphasized the violation of expectations about the relationship with the organization (Lee and Mitchell 1994) or the violation of psychological contracts to explain turnover (Rousseau 1995). Of course, poor evaluations of those jobs may simply reflect a basic lack of fit between the employee and the role. They may also reflect, though, failures by the organization to manage its human capital resources effectively.

A third driver of mobility which is particularly emphasized in sociological models is career progression. These models are based on the idea that careers tend to involve people climbing a ladder of jobs from lower-level to higher-level jobs as experience at one level makes them eligible for the next. Such moves are not just about finding a good fit, where someone may be as lucky about finding their first job as they are their fifth; instead those moves are about rising up through a structure of jobs from the less paid to the higher paid, where the jobs that someone can move into once they have accrued experience are very different to those available to them early in their career. Much sociological work on mobility was inspired by White's (1970) research on vacancy chains, which highlighted how promotion within organizations is often dependent on the creation of vacancies within higher-level jobs. Although such models are usually applied to mobility within organizations, they have also inspired research that explains moves across organizations, based on the idea that people move into better jobs as those roles become available to them over time (Haveman and Cohen 1994).

My goal in reviewing these approaches is not to help the next student that takes Peter's exam, but rather to emphasize that a single outcome – turnover – has a wide range of different causes. This multiplicity in the causes of turnover has important consequences for how we think about the costs of retention. In some cases, minor changes to how human capital resources are managed may be sufficient to increase retention. In other cases, such retention may be much harder. As a consequence, attending to the causes of turnover may help us to better understand how turnover relates to companies' broader business models.

EFFICIENT VS INEFFICIENT TURNOVER

Comparing across the multiple different causes of mobility highlighted above, I believe that it may be useful to distinguish two forms of turnover: that which is socially "efficient" and that which is "inefficient." In making this distinction, I am not taking the perspective of the firm being left. As outlined above, I think there are good reasons to believe that most, if not all, turnover is inefficient from the point of view of the employer. Instead, I am proposing that we assess efficiency in the economic sense of whether the sum of the costs and benefits experienced by all of the parties involved are positive, with the parties in this case being represented by the employer being left, the employer being joined, and the mover themselves. While the departed employer may usually suffer a loss from turnover, that loss may be outweighed by the gains experienced by the mover and their new employer. I also add a further tweak to the definition: the benefits to the mover are higher the worse they were managed initially. That might suggest that worse employers have higher efficient turnover. Because my goal is to differentiate turnover that is easy versus hard to prevent, I include the caveat that it should be evaluated given reasonable steps by the employer to prevent that turnover. Specifically, I define efficient turnover thus:

Efficient turnover can be defined as that turnover that maximizes the joint welfare of workers and both employers, even when the departed employer takes reasonable steps to optimize the conditions under which the mover labored.

I believe it makes sense to differentiate efficient versus inefficient turnover because of what it tells us about the ability of organizations to prevent such turnover. Abelson and Baysinger (1984) analogously define "functional turnover" as the loss of human capital resources that the firm prefers to retain on a cost adjusted basis. By focusing on the overall gains from turnover, I emphasize that what it costs to retain an employee depends heavily on what their alternative options look like. Where the employee is moving into a job that is a much better fit for them, the firm they are leaving may never be able to retain them for an acceptable cost.

In particular, the point of this definition is to differentiate between two fundamentally different causes of turnover. Inefficient causes essentially reflect bad management. Organizations may fail to pay market wages, fail to administer that pay fairly, fail to design jobs that will be satisfying as well as efficient, fail to select and train managers that can manage people effectively, or fail to fairly and judiciously manage psychological contracts. Inefficient turnover can also stem from firms' failure to effectively manage the initial fit between employees and the organization, either through inadequacies in their selection process or a lack of realistic job previews that would allow workers to make informed decisions about what jobs will best fit them. In those cases, workers do not move because the new role is inherently a better fit for them, but rather because of the failure of their prior employer to manage them effectively. Such inefficient turnover should be inherently preventable, and is likely to be value destroying.

Efficient turnover, by contrast, is caused by changes over time in the match between person and organization. This lack of match does not reflect a poor initial fit between the two; instead, where once the mover might have been best off working in the focal firm, that is no longer the case. Such changes in the fit between person and organization might happen because of demand-side changes in what the firm needs. Over time, organizations can change the kind of work they do for a wide variety of reasons, including changes in customer demand, changes in competitor actions, and internal and external innovations in technologies and business models. All of these changes can reduce the value that the firm places on the skills and abilities of its existing human capital resource. In some cases, that may lead the firm to lay people off. In other cases, the firm may no longer be willing to pay its human capital resources enough to lead them to stay.

The person–organization match might also change because of the kind of career-driven, supply-side shifts in the workers' skills, abilities, and preferences noted above. Most people change considerably over time, both in the skills they possess and in the kinds of rewards they prefer. A central source of human capital is on-the-job learning, which results in skills, productivity, and wages all growing as workers accrue experience (Becker 1993; Mincer 1970). Those increases in skills also affect the kinds of jobs that they will best fit, leading workers to be promoted along job ladders, moving from simpler to more complex jobs as they acquire the necessary skills (Doeringer and Piore 1971; Williamson et al. 1975). The accumulation of age and experience can also change the kinds of rewards that people most value (Cherrington et al. 1979; Tolbert and Moen 1998), further altering the extent to which workers will still match the job that they initially entered.

Whether these shifts in organizational demands and individual attributes lead to turnover depends on a variety of organizational factors. People may often change jobs within the firm, finding a better match within the internal labor market. My own research suggests that such internal mobility often yields better outcomes for both firms and workers than does matching through the external labor market (Bidwell 2011; Bidwell and Mollick 2015). Nonetheless, once the employee no longer matches the job they are in, there is no guarantee there will be another job within the same organization that provides a better match. In part, their inability to find a match with their employer may reflect changes in person–organization fit, as organization-level attributes such as structure, products and practices affect the extent to which the organization can deliver the rewards that the worker seeks (Bidwell and Briscoe 2010). In part, an inability to find a new match within the organization may reflect the set of jobs contained within that organization. If an employee is ready to move to a more skilled and more rewarding job but there is no vacancy available within the organization, then turnover may be necessary to find a better match.

THE DETERMINANTS OF EFFICIENT TURNOVER

The above discussion suggests that levels of turnover may vary across organizations for two reasons. They may vary in their levels of inefficient turnover, based on the extent to which they effectively manage their strategic human capital resources at all levels of the organization. They may also vary in their levels of efficient turnover. Unlike inefficient turnover, the levels of efficient turnover will be rooted in basic characteristics of the organization, including its business strategy, its growth rate, its structure and employment strategy.

As I argued above, levels of efficient turnover depend on the balance between the rate of change of both the organization's needs and its employees' capacities and preferences on the one hand, and on the ability of the organization to accommodate those changes internally on the other hand. On the demand side, levels of efficient turnover should be greater when organizations are undergoing more rapid changes in technology or business model, and when the organization's business is sufficiently focused that there are very limited opportunities to redeploy human capital resources to other areas.

When it comes to supply-side changes, the biggest determinant of how much people change is likely to be the age at which they are hired. People go through the most rapid change in interests and capacities earlier in their career, with the majority of lifetime wage growth taking place in the first ten years of the career (Bernhardt et al. 2001; Topel and Ward 1992). It is also well established that younger employees are more likely to quit their jobs (Griffeth et al. 2000). The extent to which that mobility will reflect efficient turnover (rather than, for example, the challenges of selecting the right younger workers or managing them effectively) will depend on how able the organization is to accommodate that growth in skills through opportunities for internal promotion.

The capacity to accommodate those changes is likely to reflect the structure of the organization. Research in the vacancy chain literature highlights how opportunities for promotion depend on the basic ratio of lower-level, less-skilled jobs and the higher-level jobs into which people can be promoted (Stewman 1986; Stewman and Konda 1983). The higher the ratio between those lower-level jobs and the higher-level jobs in the grade above, the harder it is for somebody in one of those lower-level jobs to find an experienced role to grow into. Where such organizations seek to fill those lower-level jobs with inexperienced workers, they are likely to experience high levels of efficient turnover, as employees must turn to the outside labor markets to find better jobs to move up into. Organizational growth can also create opportunities for internal development, with more opportunities created as organizations grow and add positions. Similarly, the vacancy chain literature emphasizes that exits from a higher level of the organization create opportunities for upward mobility out of the level below (Stewman and Konda 1983; White 1970). Levels of efficient turnover may therefore be negatively correlated across levels in organizations – the lower the turnover out of one level, the greater the efficient turnover out of the level below as employees must look elsewhere for opportunities to exploit their growing skills.

SUMMARY AND IMPLICATIONS

The value of retention is a central issue in managing strategic human capital resources, and one that is explored in the chapters by Hausknecht and Rider and Tan. Arguably, the literature on turnover implicitly views retention as the norm, with turnover a failure to be avoided. Research on careers, though, suggests that mobility across jobs, particularly for less experienced workers, is highly desirable and almost inevitable. No matter how strong the initial match between person and job, and how well the person is managed, jobs change and people change. Where people face strong returns to moving jobs, the question is not whether they will move, but rather whether those moves will take place within the same organization or into a different one.

Viewing much turnover as efficient, and therefore difficult to avoid, has implications for debates about the performance effects of mobility. I have suggested that all turnover may well be disruptive to performance; but, following Abelson and Baysinger (1984), I note that the appropriate benchmark is the cost of avoiding that turnover. Those costs, though, will vary with the reasons that people are leaving. Where turnover is inefficient, and driven by a failure to manage human capital resources properly rather than an underlying lack of fit between person and job, then steps to reduce turnover should have a positive effect on performance. For efficient turnover, though, the costs that the organization would need to incur to prevent a move are likely to outweigh the benefits. No doubt organizations would benefit from lower inefficient turnover; but they are unable to achieve it for a reasonable price.

Differentiating efficient versus inefficient kinds of turnover also sheds light on the way that turnover can be an inevitable consequence of other structural and employment decisions. The extent to which firms are able to retain workers will depend on both the rate at which those firms change strategies and the extent to which their hierarchical structure allows them to continue to absorb people into higher levels as those people gain experience. Those basic strategy and structure decisions will usually reflect many factors other than retention, including the nature of the industry, technology, competition and so on. Hence, we should see at least some component of retention as reflecting broader decisions that the organization makes about what to do and what kinds of human capital to staff itself with. For at least some organizations, a higher level of turnover may be an acceptable price for the strategy and structure that they have chosen.

These arguments have clear practical implications. In seeking to address the effects of turnover, managers should consider how much of that turnover is efficient versus inefficient. Inefficient turnover should be promptly dealt with through improvements to hiring processes, management practices, employment conditions and job design. They must then decide how much they can and should try to reduce efficient turnover. Efficient turnover can be reduced, for example, by increasing the number of experienced versus inexperienced positions so that fewer young employees are hired and more opportunities are created for existing employees as they grow in their jobs. In many cases, though, firms may find that it is more profitable to have a high level of efficient turnover than it is to reshape their structure so as to prevent that turnover.

In terms of future research, I think there are two related areas that might bear fruit. First, while turnover research has long acknowledged that debates about performance ought to pay attention to the costs of preventing turnover, those retention costs have been little developed in either theoretical or empirical work. I think that attending to those costs could enrich our understanding of the turnover–performance link. Second, Hausknecht and Rider and Tan all note that turnover research has tended to pay relatively little attention to where people go after they leave. Drawing on ideas about careers, I have suggested that understanding those destinations is critical for understanding what those companies could have done to avoid their turnover. Taking a more nuanced approach to where people go and the underlying causes of their turnover may therefore enrich our understanding of the fundamental question of how mobility affects organizational performance.

CHAPTER SUMMARY

BOX 29.1 KEY TAKEAWAYS

1. Career progression requires people to change jobs. Turnover happens when those changes cannot take place without people also moving employers.
2. Mobility can be socially efficient or socially inefficient. Socially inefficient mobility is due to poor management. Socially efficient mobility reflects organizations' structural inability to offer employees' sufficient opportunities for career development.
3. Although socially efficient turnover is likely damaging to organizational performance, it may be less costly than the steps needed to prevent it. We therefore need to evaluate the costs of turnover within the broader set of strategic and structural decisions that shape the possible career paths within organizations.

BOX 29.2 DIRECTIONS FOR FUTURE RESEARCH

1. What are the sources and determinants of retention costs, and how do they compare to the costs of turnover?
2. How do the levels and costs of turnover relate to the different strategic and structural decisions that organizations make that shape their overall sets of career opportunities?

REFERENCES

Abelson, M. A., and Baysinger, B. D. (1984). Optimal and dysfunctional turnover: Toward an organizational level model. *Academy of Management Review 9*(2), 331–41.

Allen, D. G., Bryant, P. C., and Vardaman, J. M. (2010). Retaining talent: Replacing misconceptions with evidence-based strategies. *Academy of Management Perspectives 24*(2), 48–64.

Becker, G. S. (1993). *Human Capital: A Theoretical and Empirical Analysis with Special Reference to Education* (third edn). Chicago, IL: University of Chicago Press.

Bernhardt, A., Morris, M., Handcock, M. S., and Scott, M. A. (2001). *Divergent Paths: Economic Mobility in the New American Labor Market*. New York: Russell Sage Foundation.

Bidwell, M. J. (2011). Paying more to get less: Specific skills, incomplete information and the effects of external hiring versus internal mobility. *Administrative Science Quarterly 56*(3), 369–407.

Bidwell, M. J., and Briscoe, F. S. (2010). The dynamics of inter organizational careers. *Organization Science 21*(5), 1034–53.

Bidwell, M. J., and Mollick, E. (2015). Shifts and ladders: Comparing the role of internal and external mobility in executive careers. *Organization Science 26*(6), 1629–45.

Bidwell, M. J., Won, S., Barbulescu, R., and Mollick, E. (2015). I used to work at Goldman Sachs! Status, careers and competitive advantage. *Strategic Management Journal 36*(8), 1164–73.

Burdett, K., and Mortensen, D. T. (1998). Wage differentials, employer size, and unemployment. *International Economic Review 39*(2), 257–73.

Cherrington, D. J., Condie, S. J., and England, J. L. (1979). Age and work values. *Academy of Management Journal 22*(3), 617–23.

Coff, R. W. (1997). Human assets and management dilemmas: Coping with hazards on the road to resource-based theory. *Academy of Management Review 22*(2), 374–402.

Doeringer, P. B., and Piore, M. J. (1971). *Internal Labor Markets and Manpower Analysis*. Lexington, MA: Heath.

Glebbeek, A. C., and Bax, E. H. (2004). Is high employee turnover really harmful? An empirical test using company records. *Academy of Management Journal 47*(2), 277–86.

Griffeth, R. W., Hom, P. W., and Gaertner, S. (2000). A meta-analysis of antecedents and correlates of employee turnover: Update, moderator tests, and research implications for the next millenium. *Journal of Management 26*(3), 463–88.
Haveman, H. A., and Cohen, L. E. (1994). The ecological dynamics of careers: The impact of organizational founding, dissolution, and merger on job mobility. *American Journal of Sociology 100*(1), 104–52.
Jovanovic, B. (1979). Job matching and the theory of turnover. *Journal of Political Economy 87*(5), 972–90.
Lee, T. W., and Mitchell, T. R. (1994). An alternative approach: The unfolding model of voluntary employee turnover. *Academy of Management Review 19*(1), 51–89.
Lehmberg, D., Rowe, W. G., White, R. E., and Phillips, J. R. (2009). The GE paradox: Competitive advantage through fungible non-firm-specific investment. *Journal of Management 35*(5), 1129–53.
Mincer, J. (1970). The distribution of labor incomes: A survey with special references to the human capital approach. *Journal of Economic Literature 8*, 1–26.
Park, T. Y., and Shaw, J. D. (2013). Turnover rates and organizational performance: A meta-analysis. *Journal of Applied Psychology 98*(2), 268–309.
Reilly, G., Nyberg, A. J., Maltarich, M., and Weller, I. (2014). Human capital flows: Using context-emergent-turnover (CET) theory to explore the process by which turnover, hiring, and job demands affect patient satisfaction. *Academy of Management Journal 57*(3), 766–90.
Rider, C. I., and Tan, D. (2015). Labor market advantages of organizational status: A study of lateral partner hiring by large U.S. law firms. *Organization Science 26*(2), 356–72.
Rousseau, D. M. (1995). *Psychological Contracts in Organizations: Understanding Written and Unwritten Agreements*. Thousand Oaks, CA: Sage.
Shaw, J. D., Gupta, N., and Delery, J. E. (2005). Alternative conceptualizations of the relationship between voluntary turnover and organizational performance. *Academy of Management Journal 48*(1), 50–68.
Shaw, J. D., Delery, J. E., Jenkins Jr, G. D., and Gupta, N. (1998). An organization-level analysis of voluntary and involuntary turnover. *Academy of Management Journal 41*(5), 511–25.
Shipp, A. J., Furst-Holloway, S., Harris, B. T., and Rosen, B. (2013). Gone today but here tomorrow: Extending the unfolding model of turnover to consider boomerang employees. *Personnel Psychology 67*(2), 421–62.
Somaya, D., Williamson, I. O., and Lorinkova, N. (2008). Gone but not lost: The different performance impacts of employee mobility between cooperators versus competitors. *Academy of Management Journal 51*(5), 936–53.
Stewman, S. (1986). Demographic models of internal labor markets. *Administrative Science Quarterly 31*(2), 212–47.
Stewman, S., and Konda, S. L. (1983). Careers and organizational labor markets: Demographic models of organizational behavior. *American Journal of Sociology 88*(4), 637–85.
Swider, B. W., Liu, J. T., Harris, T. B., and Gardner, R. G. (2017). Employees on the rebound: Extending the careers literature to include boomerang employment. *Journal of Applied Psychology 102*(6), 890–909.
Tolbert, P. S., and Moen, P. (1998). Men and women's definitions of "good" jobs: similarities and differences by age and across time. *Work and Occupations 25*(2), 168–94.
Topel, R. H., and Ward, M. P. (1992). Job mobility and the careers of young men. *Quarterly Journal of Economics 107*(2), 439–79.
White, H. C. (1970). *Chains of Opportunity: System Models of Mobility in Organizations*. Cambridge, MA: Harvard University Press.
Williamson, O. E., Wachter, M. L., and Harris, J. E. (1975). Understanding the employment relation: The analysis of idiosyncratic exchange. *Bell Journal of Economics 6*(1), 250–78.

30. Human enterprise*

Rajshree Agarwal

The knowledge-based view of the firm (Grant, 1996: 112) explicitly notes: "firms exist . . . because they can create conditions under which multiple individuals can integrate their specialist knowledge." Human capital resources, unlike other resources owned by the firm, though, are subject to individuals' freedom to quit at will (Coff, 1997). Rich literature streams in employee mobility and entrepreneurship have accordingly developed implications for the opportunities and challenges for firms to create and capture value based on human capital resources. Mobility and entrepreneurship are important conduits of knowledge diffusion through individuals' human capital, including those embedded in relationships (Agarwal et al., 2004; Almeida and Kogut, 1999; Campbell et al., 2017; Mawdsley and Somaya, 2018). Moreover, the implications of mobility and entrepreneurship extend well beyond competitive interaction among firms, and scholars have highlighted their important role in the evolution of industries and economies (Agarwal et al., 2007; Klepper, 2015).

The predominant focus of literature streams on human capital resources and employee mobility and entrepreneurship has been on the *capabilities* of individuals, and the *pecuniary incentives/returns* to individuals and firms for investment in capability development. This is not surprising given their base of human capital theory drawing primarily from an economics lens. In this thought piece, I integrate across some recent work to propose these literature streams may benefit from expanding our conceptualization of individuals at work beyond "human capital" to "human enterprise."

ECONOMIC ORIGINS OF HUMAN CAPITAL THEORY

When revisiting classical work on human capital theory (Becker, 1962; Mincer, 1958; Schultz, 1961), it is illuminative that Schultz (1961: 2) started his presidential address by noting the "deep seated moral and philosophical issues" in treating individuals as "property or marketable assets" resulting in "the mere thought of investment in human beings [as] offensive." Becker (1994: 16) similarly recalled his hesitation with the term human capital, given some academic thinking "around the belief in the exploitation of labor by capital" could result in problematic interpretations that "human capital exploits labor too . . . with skilled workers and unskilled workers pitted against each other in the alleged class conflict between labor and capital."

Nonetheless, the pioneering scholars resisted mainstream thinking, with Schultz (1961: 3) noting: "the failure to treat human resources explicitly as a form of capital, as a produced means of production, had fostered the classical notion of labor as a capacity to do manual work requiring little knowledge and skill, a capacity . . . laborers are endowed about equally." Rejecting this notion, Schultz (1961: 3) underscored the link between human capital and productivity of nations: "acquisition of knowledge and skill that have economic value . . . are in great part the product of investment, and combined with other human investment, predominantly account for the productivity superiority of technically advanced countries." At the individual level, Mincer's (1958) seminal life-cycle model built on a positive correlation between individuals' learning ability and their investment in training to explain income differentials.

Such a focus on *investment* naturally led to decades of human capital scholarship within economics, where the predominant lens has been on the cost-benefit calculus of *pecuniary* returns to education, training and experience in enhancing productivity of individuals with different *abilities*, including across demographic groups and over time (Ben-Porath, 1967; Becker, 1994; Hanushek and Woessmann, 2008; Heckman, 2000). Economic models explicitly relate compensation schemes such as pay for performance (PFP) to productivity (e.g. Fama, 1991; Lazear, 1986, 2000), and additionally examine incentive compatibility in light of potential principal-agent concerns (e.g. Holmstrom and Milgrom, 1994). Moreover, even when nonpecuniary drivers (e.g. motivation, self-esteem, preferences) are incorporated, they are either cast as non-cognitive abilities in models of human capital formation (e.g. Cunha and Heckman, 2007) or modeled as compensating differentials—paying for non-pecuniary motivations because they substitute for pecuniary rewards (e.g. Hamilton, 2000). Models of firms' investment in training similarly focus on the efficiency of investments and the division of pecuniary costs and benefits among firms and individuals (cf. review in Leuven, 2005). Salient in these models are transactions costs of contracting between firms and individuals, and the threat of turnover in the presence of asymmetric information in human capital markets (Acemoglu and Pischke, 1999; Hashimoto, 1981; Kahn and Huberman, 1988; Rubinstein, 1982; Stevens, 1994; Topel, 1986).

DOMINANT PERSPECTIVES IN MANAGEMENT AND ENTREPRENEURSHIP ON HUMAN CAPITAL (RESOURCES)

Within management, many of the theoretical perspectives on strategic human capital management developed from the above economics base (Wright and McMahan, 1992), and share the focus on pecuniary returns (to individuals and firms) of investment in human capabilities. Resource- and knowledge-based views—the dominant perspective—focus on how firms may create sustainable competitive advantage (superior profitability) through their human resource practices (Barney and Wright, 1998; Lepak and Snell, 1999; Wright et al., 1994). Utilizing the valuable, rare, imitability and organization (VRIO) framework, for example, Barney and Wright (1998) suggest human capital resources may serve as a basis for firm competitive advantage if firms focus training activities on firm-specific skills, create team-based rather than individual-based competencies, and focus on human resource systems rather than single practices.

Within entrepreneurship, literature streams emphasize the critical role of founders' human capital because their knowledge context shapes new venture capabilities, access to complementary assets, strategies and performance (cf. review in Agarwal and Shah, 2014). As an example, the literature on spinouts—new ventures created by ex-employees of incumbent organizations—documents the "inheritance" of capabilities and knowledge transfer through founding teams for superior performance of spinouts relative to other entrants in the industry (Agarwal et al., 2004; Klepper and Sleeper, 2005; Phillips, 2002; Wezel et al., 2006).

While the human capital resource-based view examines competitive dynamics in product markets, other scholars have employed an agency/transaction costs perspective for examining competitive interaction between firms and individuals (and within individuals in the same firm) in resource markets. For example, Coff (1997) cautions against superior profitability stemming from human capital, given individuals can appropriate rents with a threat of mobility. Further, literature streams in employee mobility and entrepreneurship explicitly invoke agency theory, opportunism and economic cost-benefit calculus for individuals' decisions regarding staying, moving to a competitor, or starting a new venture (Anton and Yao, 1995; Ganco et al., 2015; Hellmann, 2007). Motivations for mobility and entrepreneurship are thus largely pecuniary in nature (e.g. Carnahan et al., 2012).

Non-pecuniary factors have been examined to some extent, but these are largely related to *negative* motivations and drivers, such as strategic disagreements and managerial conflict (Amason, 1996; Pelled et al., 1999; Klepper and Thompson, 2010), envy and jealousy through social comparison (Nickerson and Zenger, 2008), and the quest for power and control (Greve and Mitsuhashi, 2007; Pfeffer and Salancik, 1978; Pfeffer and Cohen, 1984; Smith et al., 2006; Wasserman, 2012).

QUESTIONING SOME (IMPLICIT) ASSUMPTIONS OF LITERATURE ON HUMAN CAPITAL RESOURCES, MOBILITY AND ENTREPRENEURSHIP

The above brief literature review is deliberately stylized to draw attention to two foundational foci in the literature—on capabilities and on pecuniary incentives—and the associated assumptions regarding individuals at work. In this section, I elaborate on two of my recent papers relaxing these assumptions, often ones I personally made in my earlier research.

Motivations and Team-Building Processes of Employee Founders

The burgeoning literature on spinouts noted above has largely adopted a knowledge-based view perspective, linking human capital to the founding and growth of new ventures (Agarwal et al., 2004; Anton and Yao, 1995; Gambardella et al., 2014; Klepper and Sleeper, 2005). As excellently summarized by Kaul et al. (2018), the literature privileges *entrepreneurial ideas or innovation projects* as the genesis—drawing largely on agency or knowledge spillover models. Indeed, Agarwal et al. (2004) conforms to this perspective: in this paper, my coauthors and I implicitly assumed innovation projects create opportunities, and individuals or teams working on these projects access the knowledge to form new ventures. With each firm that operated in the disk drive industry during the 1977–97 period as the unit of analysis, we showed that incumbent firms with underutilized knowledge are more likely to spawn new ventures. We theorized and documented that incumbent firms with higher levels of either technological or market pioneering knowledge are more likely to spawn entrepreneurial ventures than incumbents with higher levels of both types of knowledge. We also showed the inheritance of these capabilities from incumbent to spinout firms—spinout firms with superior capabilities were associated with incumbent firms with superior capabilities in a within-group comparison. Moreover, these capabilities had beneficial effects on spinout performance relative to all other entrants in the industry. Based on secondary data at the firm level, we inferred that pre-existing teams working together at incumbent firms would leave when incumbents choose not to pursue their projects.

I recently had the opportunity to revisit these inferences in Shah et al. (2018). We appended the quantitative data on disk-drive spinouts with qualitative information from our interviews with their founders to examine founder motivations and building of the founding teams. The triangulation of quantitative and qualitative data continued to support the Agarwal et al. (2004) relationships between capabilities and performance of the spinout firms; but the qualitative insights revealed motivations and processes inconsistent with inferences and dominant assumptions, both in Agarwal et al. (2004) and in the received literature. First, the genesis of spinouts was neither innovation projects nor their pre-existing teams. Spinout teams were created *after* a "ringleader" chose to venture out, and purposefully sought cofounders. Second, money was the reward (commensurate with efforts), but not the reason for creating the new venture. The desire to create in the presence of fertile opportunities in a growing industry was a common "pull" motivation in both ringleaders and cofounders, as was the desire for equity (fairness). However, ringleaders exhibited additional "push" motivations—these included strategic disagreements, bureaucratic hurdles and interpersonal/ethical frictions with managers. Third, remarkable in their *absence* was any flavor of opportunistic behavior or agency-based motivations. In the few instances when ringleaders had formed innovative ideas (though never fully formed technologies) in the incumbent firm, they first actively sought to pursue them internally rather than enter into a cost-benefit calculus of exploiting them outside incumbent firm boundaries. Fourth, team-building processes complemented the underlying motivations. Ringleaders actively built their founding team by seeking complementary human capital to ensure functional comprehensiveness, but this was only a baseline consideration. The more successful spinouts additionally exhibited *complementarity*—the matching of "best in class" talent across functional areas, and a willingness to problem-solve and "get the job done." Founding teams of high-performing spinouts paid deliberate attention to alignment of values and aspirational goals, often to ensure the "push" factors leading to spinout formation were not repeated in the new venture. These efforts were critical to building trust and strong cohesion among the more successful spinout teams. These teams demonstrated mutual respect and a focus on delivering on aligned aspirations rather than blame-games, which in turn ensured an empowered ability to meet the challenges of innovation and growth. As a result, not only did founder motivations and attention to selection in team-building processes endogenously create superior opportunities; their success also signaled the presence of fertile opportunities to other aspiring and enterprising individuals.

Stable and Shared Leadership for Growth of Firms

Within both economics and management, decades of evolutionary research seeking to explain growth of firms and industries has devoted considerable attention to firm characteristics such as pre-entry experience, first-mover advantage, scale economies, and increasing returns to innovation (Bayus and Agarwal, 2007; Braguinsky et al., 2012; Chen et al., 2012; Helfat and Lieberman, 2002; Jovanovic and MacDonald, 1994; Klepper, 1996; Klepper and Simons, 2000). Though several scholars in this tradition, including myself, have parallel research relating individual-level capabilities to strategy and to mobility and entrepreneurship decisions for performance consequences, Felin et al. (2015: 581) astutely note: "evolutionary arguments in strategy . . . are fundamentally silent about individuals." This is in spite of classic work by Schumpeter (1949), Penrose (1959) and Chandler (1977), who extol the importance of entrepreneurial and managerial talent as critical determinants of firm growth.

In part, the missing focus on individuals stems from a lack of linked micro-macro data tracing the census of firms within evolving industries to examine their growth consequences. In my own research on firm and industry evolution, this was certainly the case, and I often found my aspirations for undertaking such a study stymied by lack of data. Evolutionary data on firms and industries already require painstaking assembly and triangulation across various sources through years of scholarly effort and dedication (e.g. Agarwal et al., 2002; Klepper and Sleeper, 2005; Klepper, 2015), so acquiring additional comprehensive, individual-level information is often prohibited by availability and time/cost factors.

Thanks to the treasure trove of rich data collected by Serguey Braguinsky and a dedicated team of scholars on the Japanese cotton spinning industry, I was fortunately able to embark on a study examining what characteristics of top management teams (TMTs) determined firm growth within an evolving industry (Agarwal et al., 2018). The historical context of the study is during the unique window wherein Japan's ascension from a pre-industrial autarky to a developed economy was enabled by simultaneous human capital (through newly developed educational systems) evolution and industrial evolution.

Triangulation of quantitative and qualitative panel data for the census of 125 cotton spinning firms operating in the 1883–1914 period with detailed information on TMTs, physical, financial and human capital, and firm productivity yielded several important insights. First, stable and shared TMT leadership was at the crux of the seven entrepreneurial firms that emerged as "centers of gravity," accounting for the majority of innovations, 70 percent of industry output and 80 percent of the university-educated engineers in the industry. Second, a deep dive into the "stable and shared leadership" construct revealed that shared leadership addressed the Penrosian managerial diseconomies of scale to help achieve growth, but maintaining its stability was a very difficult endeavor. Third, business histories of the "center of gravity" firms, when contrasted with other firms that were similar in timing of entry, initial human capital and size, revealed that stability of shared leadership depended on factors beyond the classic emphasis on human capabilities and focus on pecuniary incentives. At root was not the *lack* of discord, but the *manner* in which discord in TMT was addressed. The center of gravity firms enjoyed disproportionately greater periods of stable shared leadership because they ensured strategic alignment on long-term firm development, even as they experienced discord. Fourth, and most importantly, several interlocking strategies underpinned the virtuous spiral between stable, shared leadership and growth. These consisted of joint buy-in of leadership and shareholders for growth initiatives in spite of short-term costs, adoption of merit-based promotions in spite of cultural "glass ceilings" for engineering talent, and a focus on honorable resolution in situations of conflicts and ethical breaches. In contrast, other firms encountering similar circumstances responded with politics and power struggles, and prioritized short-term value appropriation over long-term value creation for a negative spiral of repeated discord and lackluster performance.

The Relevance of Psychological Theories of Human Behavior

In aspiring to understand the causal mechanisms for the genesis and growth of firms and industries, I became increasingly aware of parallel literature streams on psychological and philosophical factors influencing individuals at work, and their decisions to engage in entrepreneurship (Baum et al., 2014; Gartner et al., 1992; Locke and Baum, 2007; Shane et al., 2003). Particularly useful was the review by Gartner et al., who note the need to examine questions at the interface of the questions "what do persons in organizations do?" and "why do they do what they do?" Their review builds on the classification of motivation theories by Landy and Becker (1987), which include *expectancy* (Vroom, 1964), *reinforcement* (Skinner, 1971), *equity* (Goodman, 1977), *need* (Maslow, 1954), and *goal-setting* (Locke, 1968). Based on this review, Gartner et al. encourage research in entrepreneurial settings not only because it helps answer the question of entrepreneurial motivations, but also because such research is relevant to questions regarding how entrepreneurs may motivate other individuals who have capabilities critical for their organization's success.

For sure, in both of the above papers, the founder and historical TMT narratives uncovered the relevance of these theories. Among them, expectancy and reinforcement theories seem closest to economic calculus models of optimization in the presence of rewards and punishments because they seek to explain decisions to join, stay, or create a new venture based on thoughtful consideration of each option's costs and benefits. In Shah et al. (2018), a growing industry and prior successful spinouts signaled fertile opportunities that beckoned employees, particularly those with high human capital, towards entrepreneurship. In Agarwal et al. (2018), "center of gravity" firms' willingness to promote engineers in top management teams in spite of cultural norms beckoned fresh graduates with technical backgrounds to join them. Equity theory applied in Shah et al. not only because founders with high human capital sought monetary rewards commensurate with efforts, but also because many ringleaders ventured out due to perceived lack of justice in the organization's treatment of all employees (not just themselves). In Agarwal et al. (2018), the attention to justice in resolution of ethical infractions of top management teams was critical to restoring stability in shared leadership, and thus sustained periods of growth for "center of gravity" firms.

Perhaps more than the other three theories, though, the two research papers jointly show the relevance of need and goal-setting theories, when taken in conjunction. Both theories place primacy on human *agency and aspiration*. Maslow's hierarchy of needs emphasizes the quest for self-esteem and self-actualization as an important driver of human behavior, and Locke's goal-setting theory relates the setting of conscious goals, particularly those that are daring and difficult, to higher levels of achievement. In Shah et al. (2018), the founder narratives provide rich evidence of the desire to create as a key driver unifying ringleaders and cofounders. Moreover, the more successful spinouts had founder teams that matched with each other based on their reputation of being "best in class" talent and ability to problem-solve; and, as noted above, these founders never wavered in the effort they invested in ensuring the achievement of their ambitious, shared goals. In Agarwal et al. (2018) similarly, we saw that leaders with high human capital in top management teams of center of gravity firms shared a lofty vision and aligned painstaking efforts in complementary tasks to attain high growth. Remarkable in the latter study was the role of such shared and stable leadership in attracting fresh talented engineers and promoting their upward mobility for firm- and industry-level growth.

CONCEPTUALIZING HUMAN ENTERPRISE

> In times of change, learners inherit the earth, while the learned find themselves beautifully equipped to deal with a world that no longer exists.
> We are told that talent creates its own opportunities. But it sometimes seems that intense desire creates not only its own opportunities, but its own talents. (Eric Hoffer)

In charting my above (perhaps idiosyncratic) journey of a scholar who started in evolutionary economics and increasingly appreciated the role of psychological and philosophical drivers, I claim neither sole nor first-mover status. For sure, I stand on the shoulders of giants as I continue my research quest in conceptualizing human enterprise (Rand, 1957). I note also the emphasis on "non-hedonic" motivations by economists who have had a foundational impact on the role of human action, and thereby human capital and entrepreneurship. Schumpeter (1934: 93–4) extolled the joy experienced by the entrepreneur "of creating, for getting things done, or simply of exercising one's energy and ingenuity." Similarly, von Mises (1949: 139) noted: "For the pioneering genius to create is the essence of life. To live means for him to create." Even Adam Smith (1790 [1976]: 23) emphasized the critical role of moral sentiments, and the notion of self-command "of the passions which subjects all the movements of our nature to what our own dignity and honor, and the propriety of our own conduct require."

In light of these quotes, it is perhaps a puzzle that our current (macro) models linking human capital resources, employee mobility and employee entrepreneurship to firm-level strategies and performance do not centrally feature individuals' aspirations and purpose, and often abstract entirely from these critical drivers of both human capital investments and their performance outcomes. The literature on scientific human capital is perhaps an exception, where several contemporary scholars have been studying non-pecuniary motivations and preferences, and their interactions with human capital (Agarwal and Ohyama, 2013; Gagliardi and Mariani, 2016; Gambardella et al., 2016; Giarratana et al., 2018; Roach and Sauermann, 2010; Sauermann, 2017; Stern, 2004). Of particular note is the excellent tabulation of RandD personnel's extrinsic, intrinsic and social incentives by Cohen and Sauermann (2007), and their call for research examining the management of multiple motives and alignment of firms' goals with those of their innovative personnel.

Armed with these insights, I develop some preliminary thoughts regarding the concept of human enterprise, drawing upon its distinction from the concept of human capital to provide additional clarity (see Box 30.1). Human capital, as noted above, is defined as the knowledge, experiences, and skills of an individual that shape their abilities. However, the concept of human capital *does not* encompass human aspiration, which provides an individual the motive power for achievement of a (long-term) hope, goal, or desire.[1] Human enterprise is defined as systematic, purposeful activity that may be daring or difficult, based on the combination of an individual's abilities and aspirations. Though entrepreneurial settings such as new venture creation represent fertile ground for the flourishing of human enterprise, they are by no means the only context within which individuals may exhibit or pursue enterprise. Existing organizations, particularly those engaging in strategic renewal (Agarwal and Helfat, 2009), also provide opportunities for individuals to exercise their human enterprise and attain upward mobility—in economic *and* in intellectual and psychological realms. While the concept of human capital focuses on individuals' accumulated stock of *past investments* in capabilities, human enterprise also incorporates drivers of current and future investments (flows) of activity that may potentially result in human capital, and capitalize upon it. The focal question for human capital relates to *what* are the capabilities embodied in an individual. For human enterprise, the focal questions are *why* do individuals pursue different activities, and *how* does this shape and benefit from human capabilities? In doing so, human enterprise has to draw upon not just economics—the primary theoretical base for human capital—but also psychology and philosophy.

The above conceptual distinctions also imply differences in the sources for individual heterogeneity. Building on human capital differences in innate abilities and past investments in gaining knowledge and skills, human enterprise additionally acknowledges the main and interaction role of individual motivations and purpose. Such heterogeneity has implications for both firm- and individual-level strategies and performance. At the firm level, human capital heterogeneity has been used to examine how organizational structures and strategies may create and capture value from its human capital resources, including coordination routines and training programs for complementary human capital. Incorporating heterogeneity in human enterprise refocuses attention to creating and capturing value by maximizing human potential through organizational structures and strategies aimed at both human capital development *and* achievement/alignment of purpose. Similarly, at the individual level, heterogeneous human capital has been related to (internal and external) mobility and entrepreneurship decisions, with a primary focus on pecuniary motives to capture rents from past human capital investments, including innovation projects. Heterogeneity in human enterprise permits the expansion of the lens to include non-pecuniary motives, including the achievement of ambitious and aligned goals within an organization.

IMPLICATIONS FOR FUTURE RESEARCH

Based on the above conceptualization, this section sketches an incomplete list of research questions related to the study of human enterprise, and some thoughts on opportunities and challenges encountered in research designs for undertaking such studies (see Summary Box 30.2).

Embracing Selection in Team and Organizational Formation Literature

The first set of research questions center on the need to embrace selection in our theories of team and organizational formation, and of employee mobility and entrepreneurship. When undertaking recent research projects (Lazar et al., 2018; Shah et al., 2018),

I was struck by relative paucity of research on selection of individuals into teams and organizations, particularly in the context of the voluminous body of macro- and micro-literature streams on team characteristics—processes—outcomes. This is not only true for entrepreneurial team formation (cf. review in Lazar et al., 2018), but also in the organizational behavior (OB) literature on teams of individuals in established organizations (Bell and Kozlowski, 2012; Cohen and Bailey, 1997; Mathieu et al., 2008, 2017). OB scholars have focused largely on team socialization rather than team selection, perhaps due to the assumption that teams are pre-formed by managers higher in the organizational hierarchy who exogenously select team members. Accordingly, selection—particularly self-selection—of members is understudied. Macro studies have recently recognized the importance of *controlling* for selection in light of endogeneity concerns when examining "treatment" relationships between characteristics and outcomes (Camuffo et al., 2018; Dahl and Sorenson, 2012; Rocha et al., 2018). However, selection is not studied extensively in and of itself for theoretical linkages to individual mobility and entrepreneurship, formation of team characteristics, and subsequent effects on organizational strategies and performance. Moreover, the little research that exists on *criteria* used in selection or matching of individuals is often within disciplinary silos (Lazar et al., 2018). Scholars use an economics lens to privilege resource seeking, and search for complementary human capital using instrumental rationality (Kamm and Nurick, 1993), the social psychology lens to focus on similarity and interpersonal attraction (Byrne, 1997), and the sociology lens to examine the role of social capital within networks (Aldrich and Kim, 2007).

A study of human enterprise in examining selection for team and organizational formation requires a disciplined integration of these lenses, with careful attention to the compensatory or reinforcing causes and effects of individual aspiration, human capital, and network access to other individuals. Future research may examine how selection—particularly based on aspirations—may impact team and organizational characteristics, processes, and outcomes.[2] For example, (self)-selection of individuals into teams and organizations need not be on capabilities alone (e.g. Lazear, 2000 focuses on entrepreneurs possessing generalist vs. specialist human capital). It may also be critically dependent on the manner in which the opportunities within the team, organization, or venture match with individual aspirations (e.g. systematic differences in aspirations that lead individuals with similar human capital to different pathways).

Embracing Aspirations into Human Capital Models of Individual, Firm and Industry Evolution

At an individual level, a study of human enterprise opens up important questions regarding evolutions of careers. The acquisition of human capital over time itself is conditional on human aspirations, not merely on the pecuniary incentives for such investment. Indeed, individual aspirations may often reinforce the quest for economic rewards (e.g. Agarwal and Ohyama, 2013; Shah et al., 2018) rather than substitute for them (e.g. Stern, 2004; Hamilton, 2000). Moreover, past decisions and their outcomes shape future aspirations and investments in human capital. Decades of human capital research has examined the causes and consequences of investments in gaining knowledge, skills and experience. Future research that revisits these relationships by integrating the role of human aspiration has the potential to yield important insights on the sources and performance outcomes of individuals' investments in human capital.

At the firm level, a study of human enterprise puts the primacy on *people* in examining firm evolution and growth, similar to the call by Felin et al. (2015). Important research topics include the evolution of characteristics and processes of teams and organizations as they encounter challenges and opportunities for growth. While there is some research on managing conflict within entrepreneurial and top management teams (Boeker, 1992; Boeker and Karichalil, 2002; Eisenhardt and Bourgeios, 1988), many issues remain understudied. For example, what are the factors important for *maintaining* an alignment of aspirations and purpose, both within founding teams that evolve to become top management teams and within an expanding employee talent pool for organizations that scale up operations? Do organizations recover, and if so, how, from negative shocks to such alignment? How important are key individuals in developing the ethos of an organization, and how do the leaders' and their successors' aspirations matter in maintaining the ethos?

Particularly relevant in this vein is budding research examining the "engineered social process anchored by an overarching aspiration and a paradoxical strategic intent that unfolds over time" (Tushman et al., 2015: 252). In addition to the mainstream examination of firm evolution based on capabilities and product sequencing (Helfat and Lieberman, 2002; Helfat and Raubitschek, 2000), this requires strategy scholars to examine organizational identity and aspiration as touchstones for leading strategic change, as noted by Mike Tushman in a recent interview (Euchner, 2015). The literature on strategic renewal of organizations (e.g. Agarwal and Helfat, 2009) is becoming increasingly cognizant of emotional and cognitive frames (Eggers and Kaplan, 2013; Eisenhardt, 2000; Raffaelli et al., 2018), and may further benefit from incorporating insights from literature on leader–member exchange (e.g. Graen and Uhl-Bien, 1995). In doing so, future research may also shed light on integrated human resource management systems for fostering human enterprise, rather than having views in silos that privilege *either* strategic and economic incentives *or* psychological causes and consequences of individuals at work. In this vein, research could examine not just the presence of complementarities in human enterprise within firms, but also factors that create dis-complementarities, such as agonistic relationships (Brymer and Hitt, Chapter 15 this volume).

Rich literature streams on industry evolution, harking back to Schumpeter's (1942) concept of creative destruction, have focused on innovative entry and incumbent exit when examining competitive dynamics among firms as industries evolve from inception to maturity (e.g. Gort and Klepper, 1982; Tushman and Anderson, 1986). The dominant focus is on firm capabilities, and transfer of these capabilities across firms through employee mobility and entrepreneurship (Klepper, 2002; Mostafa and Klepper, 2017). However, as in Agarwal et al. (2018) above, there is a need to examine the role of human enterprise in shaping firm-level attributes such as pre-entry experience, first-mover advantage, scale economies, and increasing returns to innovation. Our study of the Japanese cotton spinning industry is but one case study, and many more such deep dives are necessary for uncovering how human enterprise research on individual and firm evolution noted earlier in this section may contribute to industry-level dynamics. Continuing with the above thread on leader–member exchange, for example, budding research has begun to integrate organizational behavior, strategy, and entrepreneurship literature where subordinates reassess their organizational attachment in light of leader departure (Shapiro et al., 2016). Accordingly, alongside existing work examining the relationships between capabilities of source and recipient firms due to team mobility and entrepreneurship, there exist opportunities for examining how *relationships* per se matter, and cause team mobility or entrepreneurship for endogenous growth of opportunities within industries (Shah et al., 2018).

Studying Institutions that Foster Human Enterprise

Using macro-economic and sociological lenses, management researchers have also examined inter-regional and cross-country differences in institutions that foster entrepreneurship (cf. review in Bjørnskov and Foss, 2016; Terjesen et al., 2016). As Bjørnskov and Foss note, psychological factors are often absent. The primary focus is on entrepreneurial activity as a mechanism or "economy-level capability" for economic growth given the "lure of profit," similar to the above focus on human capabilities in the quest for economic returns. Accordingly, studies have focused attention on institutions that foster economic freedom—through upward mobility and through immigration of talent across firms, regions and economies (Saxenian, 1996, 2007; Terjesen et al., 2016).

However, rich opportunities for research exist for studying institutions that help develop and sustain human aspirations or hinder them, particularly in examining the philosophical (or ethical) premises underpinning institutions. Similar to work examining the impact of education and training on developing human capital, future research could examine the impact of education and training programs that foster human enterprise through a holistic examination of the interaction of human abilities and aspirations. Within this context, it is important to note that a pragmatic focus in business school courses on profit or earnings maximization devoid of any discussion of how this may relate to aspirations results in students being torn between pursuing "profit" or "purpose" in their own lives. The implicit assumption many students carry is that a pursuit of monetary rewards is at odds with being virtuous—accordingly, they often believe they have to make tradeoffs between material and moral values. The dominant notion is that trade helps achieve human needs for material consumption (economic needs and luxuries), but it is at best irrelevant for, and at worst in conflict with, achieving ethical values, a sense of community, and psychological eudaimonia. Similar dichotomies seem to prevail regarding reason vs. emotion and self vs. others. Research examining whether such assumptions of dichotomies are indeed justified, and the effect on human action when these assumptions are challenged, will help further our understanding of factors that foster human enterprise.

Other opportunities may include the integration of insights from historical studies of economies and technologies to understand the role of institutions in enabling human enterprise. For example, in according a central role to economic incentives, Rosenberg (1992) notes that Marx ignored other, more distinctive features of capitalist institutions for increasing human productivity through investments in science and technology—these include the exercise of *autonomy* in the presence of wide *diversity* of human potential. Rosenberg stressed the virtues of markets as being the arbiter across multiple actors engaging in experimentation in the presence of uncertainty, which Knight (1921) defined as arising from partial knowledge. In contrast to central planning models that derive "first best solutions" under assumptions of omniscience and infallibility, actual decision-making by individuals requires the exercise of judgment under uncertainty (Foss and

Klein, 2012; Knight, 1921), the creation of knowledge and opportunities through effectuation (Saraswathy, 2001), and interactions with other productive individuals consistent with the trader principle (Rand, 1964). These scholars are calling to our attention that central planning and entrepreneurial theories make fundamentally different assumptions about the epistemology of knowledge, and accordingly result in important differences in socio-political institutions for governing individual interaction and crucial divergence in fostering and benefiting from human enterprise. To a point, future research may begin to address the concerns noted in the quotes by Schultz (1961) and Becker (1994) above that the concept of human capital may not pay enough attention to the underlying "deep-seated moral and philosophical issues," including the perception of exploitation of labor by those with human capital.

Opportunities and Challenges for Conducting Empirical Research in Human Enterprise

Some may appropriately note the above research agenda is not only very extensive, but also all-encompassing—spanning levels of analysis and across entire disciplines, let alone single literature streams. However, this is merely reflective of the causes and consequences of human behavior, which defy singular assumptions made within disciplinary silos. The opportunities and challenges for management scholars lie precisely in our ability to integrate across disciplines when studying individuals at work and devise research designs to capture interactions of human ability and aspirations.

Empirically, decades of careful scholarship has provided us substantial knowledge regarding the concept of human capital, and the same potential exists for the concept of human enterprise. The examinations of human capital causes and consequences have relied on the creation of novel datasets that are comprehensive in the included variables and longitudinal in design—e.g. the National Longitudinal Survey of Youth (NLSY), Scientists and Engineers Statistical Data System (SESTAT). In addition, linked micro-macro data across multiple countries (e.g. Denmark, the United States) have enabled the study of employee mobility and entrepreneurship. These datasets may potentially lend themselves to a study of human enterprise. As an example, the SESTAT database contains rich panel data on individuals graduating from US universities, and the survey questions pertain to both human capital investments and to psychological motivations (Agarwal and Ohyama, 2013; Sauermann and Cohen, 2010).

More importantly, there exists significant potential for the creation of altogether new datasets that measure various human abilities and aspirations, and the manner in which organizations and institutions affect alignment through human capital resource management systems. Some enterprising scholars have already begun such data development, providing important insights on research design for future scholars (Prescott et al., 2016; Sauermann and Roach, 2013). Moreover, increased digitization and advances in information systems and data science have substantially increased availability of data and reduced the costs of compiling qualitative and quantitative data from multiple sources for comprehensiveness. While not a trivial task, the ability and willingness of future scholars to engage in such undertakings will be critical to the development of scholarly insights on human enterprise.

Methodologically, a study of human enterprise will need a triangulation of insights—within and across studies—that harness the power of datasets that comprise of qualitative, quantitative, and longitudinal information. Both studies described above (Agarwal et al., 2018; Shah et al., 2018) use a multi-method design. In each, we leveraged secondary or archival data to discern associations between attributes and outcomes, and primary data to provide answers to research questions that examined motivations and processes. Thus, multiple methods are particularly relevant for studies seeking to examine the processes that underlie observed characteristics–outcome relationships, or seeking to shed light on evolutionary pathways (Kaplan, 2016). Many of the research questions important to the study of human enterprise focus on path-dependence, and are ill suited to strict causal interpretations. Instead of devising identification strategies to control for endogeneity, they require research designs that embrace the inherent endogeneity in relationships, as for example through the use of historical methods (Braguinsky and Hounshell, 2016; Ingram et al., 2012) or matching models (Honore and Ganco, 2016; Mindruta et al., 2016).

Finally, the study of human enterprise will need more abduction, not just induction or deduction. Abduction enables scholars to start with "surprising facts or puzzles," particularly those that cannot be explained through singular disciplinary lenses or existing theories (Heckman and Singer, 2017). Rather than having to deduce theories (and sometimes develop post hoc hypotheses) or induce theories, abduction enables scholars to choose the "best" explanation among many alternatives, including explanations that integrate across alternatives.

CONCLUSION

Studying individuals at work—whether in established organizations or in their efforts at creating new ventures—through an integrated lens of human enterprise is itself a systematic, purposeful activity that may be daring or difficult. Our knowledge of the various ways in which human abilities and aspirations may interact to explain individual, team, and organizational behavior for important consequences across levels of analysis is at an incipient stage of evolution. The landscape is thus characteristic of Knightian uncertainty, requiring us as scholars to exercise thoughtful effort and judgment in creating new knowledge through experimentation and building on each other's shared insights. Nonetheless, in our quest we may well be armed by our own introspection and aspirations—knowing we are defined by more than our capabilities, and we are motivated by more than just monetary incentives.

CHAPTER SUMMARY

BOX 30.1 KEY TAKEAWAYS: HUMAN CAPITAL AND HUMAN ENTERPRISE

Concepts	Human capital	Human enterprise
Definition	Knowledge, experiences and skills of an individual	Systematic, purposeful activity that may be daring or difficult; combines both capabilities and aspirations of an individual

Static vs. dynamic	Accumulated stock of *past investments* in knowledge, experience and skills	*Current and future* investments (flows) of activity that can potentially result in human capital
Focal question	*What* are the capabilities that comprise human capital?	*Why* do individuals pursue different activities, and *how* does this shape and benefit from human capabilities?
Theoretical base	Primarily economics	Economics, psychology, and philosophy (ethics and epistemology)
Sources of individual heterogeneity	Differences in innate abilities, and past investments (e.g. education, job experience) in gaining knowledge and skills	Differences in human capital, motivations, and purpose
Implications for firm strategy and performance	Creating and capturing value by harnessing human capital resources through firm structures and strategies, including training and coordination of complementary human capital	Creating and capturing value by maximizing human potential through firm structures and strategies, for human capital development, *and* achievement/alignment of purpose
Implications for individual mobility and entrepreneurship	Mobility and entrepreneurship decisions primarily driven by desire to capture rents from past investments in human capital, including innovation projects	Mobility and entrepreneurship decisions driven not only for rent capture from past human capital investments, but also to achieve non-pecuniary goals and ensure alignment of purpose

BOX 30.2 DIRECTIONS FOR FUTURE RESEARCH

Future research in	Potential directions
Theory development	Greater emphasis on theories of matching and selection, by individuals and by firms
	Need to incorporate drivers related to individual aspirations and abilities in theories of individual, firm and industry evolution
	Systematic and disciplined integration of theories in psychology (cognitive and social), philosophy (ethics and epistemology) with existing economics and management theories of human capital for the nature of work, and determinants of individual decision-making and performance differentials
	Study of institutions that foster human enterprise and enable upward mobility in economic, psychological, and intellectual realms
Data development	Identify and compile datasets that enable answering both "what" and "why" questions
	Primacy on longitudinal or panel data development where variables may measure both "stocks" of human capital and "flows" of human enterprise
Research design and methods	Embrace selection and endogeneity, not just control for it
	Greater use of multi-method research design, historical analysis, matching models, and abduction

NOTES

* I have benefited enormously from conversations, co-authorships, and advisor–advisee relationships with the following people, listed alphabetically: Serguey Braguinsky, Heejung Byun, Ben Campbell, Seth Carnahan, Gilad Chen, Pao-lien Chen, Joonkyu Choi, Raj Echambadi, Miriam Erez, Justin Frake, April Franco, Martin Ganco, Alfonso Gambardella, Shweta Gaonkar, Brent Goldfarb, Michael Gort, Brad Greenwood, Connie Helfat, David Kirsch, Steven Klepper, Moran Lazar, Najoung Lim, Denisa Mindruta, Ella Miron-Spektor, Mahka Moeen, Anthony Nyberg, Atsushi Ohyama, Dan Olson, Lihong Qian, MB Sarkar, Henry Sauermann, Sonali Shah, Brian Silverman, Steve Sonka, Evan Starr, Charlie Williams, and Audra Wormald. They represent the enterprising individuals who have fueled my personal growth in aspirations and ability. Additionally, John Allison, Rudy Lamone, Rob Posner, and Ed Snider embody for me the alignment of purpose and high human capital. All errors are mine.

1. Motivations and aspirations are deeply intertwined concepts and provide answers to the question of *why*. Aspiration refers to a strong desire to achieve something high or great. Motivation is the reason for an action or behavior. Thus, an aspiration may be driven and underpinned by multiple motives acting in conjunction, and it includes the element of a (moral) purpose.
2. John Allison, former CEO of BBandT, recounted his guest experience in a Finance course on the topic of opportunistic behavior in the workplace. The professor illustrated the issue with the *Peanuts* cartoon series analogy of Lucy van Pelt repeatedly snatching the football away as Charlie Brown tried to kick it, providing various "treatment" options that Charlie Brown may have to reduce the impact of Lucy's behavior. When the professor asked John for his opinion on the matter, John said simply: "We would not hire Lucy in the first place." Interesting also in this context is Schulmiller's (2014) analysis of Lucy's motives and the physiological, psychological, and philosophical justifications for the repeat Fall drama in the series.

REFERENCES

Acemoglu, D., and Pischke, J. S. (1999). Beyond Becker: Training in imperfect labor markets. *Economic Journal*, *109*(453), 112–42.

Agarwal, R., and Helfat, C. E. (2009). Strategic renewal of organizations. *Organization Science*, *20*(2), 281–93.

Agarwal, R., and Ohyama, A. (2013). Industry or academia, basic or applied? Career choices and earnings trajectories of scientists. *Management Science*, *59*(4), 950–70.

Agarwal, R., and Shah, S. K. (2014). Knowledge sources of entrepreneurship: Firm formation by academic, user and employee innovators. *Research Policy*, *43*(7), 1109–33.

Agarwal, R., Audretsch, D., and Sarkar, M. B. (2007). The process of creative construction: Knowledge spillovers, entrepreneurship, and economic growth. *Strategic Entrepreneurship Journal*, *1*(3–4), 263–86.

Agarwal, R., Braguinsky, S., and Ohyama, A. (2018). Centers of gravity: The effect of stable shared leadership in top management teams on firm growth and industry evolution. Working paper.

Agarwal, R., Sarkar, M. B., and Echambadi, R. (2002). The conditioning effect of time on firm survival: A life cycle approach. *Academy of Management Journal*, *45*(5), 971–94.

Agarwal, R., Echambadi, R., Franco, A., and Sarkar, M. (2004). Knowledge transfer through inheritance: Spin-out generation, development and performance. *Academy of Management Journal*, *47*(4), 501–22.

Aldrich, H. E., and Kim, P. H. (2007). Small worlds, infinite possibilities? How social networks affect entrepreneurial team formation and search. *Strategic Entrepreneurship Journal*, *1*(1–2), 147–65.

Almeida, P., and Kogut, B. (1999). Localization of knowledge and the mobility of engineers in regional networks. *Management Science*, *45*(7), 906–17.

Amason, A. C. (1996). Distinguishing the effects of functional and dysfunctional conflict on strategic decision making: Resolving a paradox for top management teams. *Academy of Management Journal*, *39*(1), 123–48.

Anton, J. J., and Yao, D. A. (1995). Start-ups, spin-offs, and internal projects. *Journal of Law, Economics and Organization*, *11*(2), 362–78.

Barney, J. B., and Wright, P. M. (1998). On becoming a strategic partner: The role of human resources in gaining competitive advantage. *Human Resource Management*, *37*(1), 31–46.

Baum, J. R., Frese, M., and Baron, R. A. (2014). *The Psychology of Entrepreneurship*. New York: Psychology Press.

Bayus, B., and Agarwal R. (2007). The role of pre-entry experience, entry timing, and product technology strategies in explaining firm survival. *Management Science*, *53*(12), 1887–902.

Becker, G. S. (1962). Investment in human capital: A theoretical analysis. *Journal of Political Economy*, *70*(5, Part 2), 9–49.

Becker, G. S. (1994). *Human Capital: A Theoretical and Empirical Analysis with Special Reference to Education* (3rd edn). Chicago: University of Chicago Press.
Bell, B. S., and Kozlowski, S. W. (2012). Three conceptual themes for future research on teams. *Industrial and Organizational Psychology*, *5*(1), 45–8.
Ben-Porath, Y. (1967). The production of human capital and the life cycle of earnings. *Journal of Political Economy*, *75*(4, Part 1), 352–65.
Bjørnskov, C., and Foss, N. J. (2016). Institutions, entrepreneurship, and economic growth: What do we know and what do we still need to know? *Academy of Management Perspectives*, *30*(3), 292–315.
Boeker, W. (1992). Power and managerial dismissal: Scapegoating at the top. *Administrative Science Quarterly*, *37*(3), 400–21.
Boeker, W., and Karichalil, R. (2002). Entrepreneurial transitions: Factors influencing founder departure. *Academy of Management Journal*, *45*(4), 818–26.
Braguinsky, S., and Hounshell, D. A. (2016). History and nanoeconomics in strategy and industry evolution research: Lessons from the Meiji-era Japanese cotton spinning industry. *Strategic Management Journal*, *37*(1), 45–65.
Braguinsky, S., Klepper, S., and Ohyama, A. (2012). High-tech entrepreneurship. *Journal of Law and Economics*, *55*(4) 869–900.
Byrne, D. (1997). An overview (and underview) of research and theory within the attraction paradigm. *Journal of Social and Personal Relationships*, *14*(3), 417–31.
Campbell, B. A., Krycynski, D., and Olson, D. M. (2017). Bridging strategic human capital and employee entrepreneurship research: A labor market frictions approach. *Strategic Entrepreneurship Journal*, *11*(3), 344–56.
Camuffo, A., Cordova, A., and Gambardella, A. (2018). A scientific approach to entrepreneurial decision-making: Evidence from a randomized control trial. *Management Science*. https://ssrn.com/abstract=3295625.
Carnahan, S., Agarwal, R., and Campbell, B. A. (2012). Heterogeneity in turnover: The effect of relative compensation dispersion of firms on the mobility and entrepreneurship of extreme performers. *Strategic Management Journal*, *33*(12), 1411–30.
Chandler, A. D. (1977). *The Visible Hand: The Managerial Revolution in American Business*. Cambridge, MA: Harvard University Press.
Chen, P.-L., Williams, C., and Agarwal, R. (2012). Growing pains: Pre-entry experience and the challenge of transition to incumbency. *Strategic Management Journal*, *33*(3), 252–76.
Cohen, S. G., and Bailey, D. E. (1997). What makes teams work: Group effectiveness research from the shop floor to the executive suite? *Journal of Management*, *23*(3), 239–90.
Cohen, W. M., and Sauermann, H. (2007). Schumpeter's prophecy and individual incentives as a driver of innovation. In F. Malerba and S. Brusoni (eds), *Perspectives on Innovation*, 73–104. Cambridge: Cambridge University Press.
Coff, R. W. (1997). Human assets and management dilemmas: Coping with hazards on the road to resource-based theory. *Academy of Management Review*, *22*(2), 374–402.
Cunha, F., and Heckman, J. (2007). The technology of skill formation. *American Economic Review*, *97*(2), 31–47.
Dahl, M. S., and Sorenson, O. (2012). Home sweet home: Entrepreneurs' location choices and the performance of their ventures. *Management Science*, *58*(6), 1059–71.
Eggers, J. P., and Kaplan, S. (2013). Cognition and capabilities: A multi-level perspective. *Academy of Management Annals*, *7*(1), 295–340.
Eisenhardt, K. M. (2000). Paradox, spirals, ambivalence: The new language of change and pluralism. *Academy of Management Review*, *25*(4), 703–5.
Eisenhardt, K. M., and Bourgeois III, L. J. (1988). Politics of strategic decision making in high-velocity environments: Toward a midrange theory. *Academy of Management Journal*, *31*(4), 737–70.
Euchner, J. (2015). The challenges of ambidextrous leadership: An interview with Michael Tushman. *Research Technology Management*, *58*(3), 16.
Fama, E. F. (1991). Time, salary, and incentive payoffs in labor contracts. *Journal of Labor Economics*, *9*(1), 25–44.
Felin, T., Foss, N. J., and Ployhart, R. E. (2015). The microfoundations movement in strategy and organization theory. *Academy of Management Annals*, *9*(1), 575–632.
Foss, N. J., and Klein, P. G. (2012). *Organizing Entrepreneurial Judgment: A New Approach to the Firm*. Cambridge: Cambridge University Press.
Gagliardi, L., and Mariani, M. (2016). Work motivations and sorting into compensation schemes in industrial research. Working paper.
Gambardella, A., Ganco, M., and Honore., F. (2014). Using what you know: Patented knowledge in incumbent firms and employee entrepreneurship. *Organization Science*, *26*(2), 456–74.
Gambardella, A., Khashabi, P., and Panico, C. (2016). Managing innovation in the industrial context: A project-level investigation of autonomy. Working paper.
Ganco, M., Ziedonis, R. H., and Agarwal, R. (2015). More stars stay, but the brightest ones still leave: Job hopping in the shadow of patent enforcement. *Strategic Management Journal*, *36*(5), 659–85.

Gartner, W. B., Bird, B. J., and Starr, J. A. (1992). Acting as if: Differentiating entrepreneurial from organizational behavior. *Entrepreneurship Theory and Practice*, *16*(3), 13–32.
Giarratana, M. S., Mariani, M., and Weller, I. (2018). Rewards for patents and inventor behaviors in industrial research and development. *Academy of Management Journal*, *61*(1), 264–92.
Goodman, P. S. (1977). Social comparison process in organizations. In B. M. Staw and G. R. Salancik (eds), *New Directions in Organizational Behavior*, 97–132. Chicago: St. Clair.
Gort, M., and Klepper, S. (1982). Time paths in the diffusion of product innovations. *Economic Journal*, *92*(367), 630–53.
Graen, G. B., and Uhl-Bien, M. (1995). Relationship-based approach to leadership: Development of leader-member exchange (LMX) theory of leadership over 25 years: Applying a multi-level multi-domain perspective. *Leadership Quarterly*, *6*(2), 219 47.
Grant, R. M. (1996). Toward a knowledge-based theory of the firm. *Strategic Management Journal*, *17*(Winter special issue), 109–22.
Greve, H. R., and Mitsuhashi, H. (2007). Power and glory: Concentrated power in top management teams. *Organization Studies*, *28*(8), 1197–221.
Hamilton, B. H. (2000). Does entrepreneurship pay? An empirical analysis of the returns to self-employment. *Journal of Political Economy*, *108*(3), 604–31.
Hanushek, E. A., and Woessmann, L. (2008). The role of cognitive skills in economic development. *Journal of Economic Literature*, *46*(3), 607–68.
Hashimoto, M. (1981). Firm-specific human capital as a shared investment. *American Economic Review*, *71*(3), 475–82.
Heckman, J. J. (2000). Policies to foster human capital. *Research in Economics*, *54*(1), 3–56.
Heckman, J. J., and Singer, B. (2017). Abducting economics. *American Economic Review*, *107*(5), 298–302.
Helfat, C. E., and Lieberman, M. B. (2002). The birth of capabilities: Market entry and the importance of pre-history. *Industrial and Corporate Change*, *11*(4), 725–60.
Helfat, C. E., and Raubitscheck, R. S. (2000). Product sequencing: Co-evolution of knowledge, capabilities and products. *Strategic Management Journal*, *21*(10–11), 961–79.
Hellmann, T. (2007). When do employees become entrepreneurs? *Management Science*, *53*(6), 919–33.
Holstrom, B., and Milgrom, P. (1994). The firm as an incentive system. *American Economic Review*, *84*(4), 972–91.
Honore, F., and Ganco, M. (2016). Entrepreneurial teams' acquisition of talent: A two-sided approach. US Census Bureau Center for Economic Studies Paper CES-WP-16-45.
Ingram, P., Rao, H., Silverman, B. S. (2012). History in strategy research: What, why, and how? In Steven J. Kahl, Brian S. Silverman, and Michael A. Cusumano (eds), *History and Strategy*, 241–73. Bingley, UK: Emerald.
Jovanovic, B., and MacDonald, G. M. (1994). The life cycle of a competitive industry. *Journal of Political Economy*, *102*(2), 322–47.
Kahn, C., and Huberman, G. (1988). Two-sided uncertainty and up-or-out contracts. *Journal of Labor Economics*, *6*(4), 423–44.
Kamm, J. B., and Nurick, A. J. (1993). The stages of team venture formation: A decision-making model. *Entrepreneurship Theory and Practice*, *17*(2), 17–27.
Kaplan, S. (2016). Mixing quantitative and qualitative research. In and K. D. Elsbach and R. M. Kramer (eds), *Handbook of Qualitative Organizational Research: Innovative Pathways and Ideas*, 423–33. London: Routledge.
Kaul, A., Ganco, M., and Raffiee, J. (2018). A general theory of employee entrepreneurship: a knowledge-based view. University of Wisconsin working paper, Presented at Academy of Management Meetings.
Klepper, S. (1996). Entry, exit, growth, and innovation over the product life cycle. *American Economic Review*, *86*(3), 562–83.
Klepper, S. (2002). The capabilities of new firms and the evolution of the US automobile industry. *Industrial and Corporate Change*, *11*(4), 645–66.
Klepper, S. (2015). *Experimental Capitalism: The Nanoeconomics of American High-Tech Industries*. Princeton: Princeton University Press.
Klepper, S., and Simons, K. L. (2000). Dominance by birthright: Entry of prior radio producers and competitive ramifications in the U.S. television receiver industry. *Strategic Management Journal*, *21*(10/11), 997–1016.
Klepper, S., and Sleeper, S. (2005). Entry by Spinoffs. *Management Science*, *51*(8), 1291–306.
Klepper, S., and Thompson, P. (2010). Disagreements and intra-industry spinoffs. *International Journal of Industrial Organization*, *28*, 526–38.
Knight, F. H. (1921). *Risk, Uncertainty and Profit*. New York: Hart, Schaffner and Marx.
Landy, F. J., and Becker, W. S. (1987). Motivation theory reconsidered. *Research in Organizational Behavior*, *9*, 1–38.
Lazar, M., Miron-Spektor, E., Agarwal, R., Erez, M., Goldfarb, B., and Chen, G. (2018). Entrepreneurial team formation: An integrative review and a proposed research agenda. University of Maryland working paper, Presented at Academy of Management Meetings.

Lazear, E. P. (1986). Salaries and piece rates. *Journal of Business*, *59*(3), 405–31.
Lazear, E. P. (2000). Performance pay and productivity. *American Economic Review*, *90*, 1346–61.
Lepak, D. P., and Snell, S. A. (1999). The human resource architecture: Toward a theory of human capital allocation and development. *Academy of Management Review*, *24*(1), 31–48.
Leuven, E. (2005). The economics of private sector training: A survey of the literature. *Journal of Economic Surveys*, *19*(1), 91–111.
Locke, E. A. (1968). Toward a theory of task motivation and incentives. *Organizational Behavior and Human Performance*, *3*(2), 157–89.
Locke, E. A., and Baum, J. R. (2007). Entrepreneurial motivation. In J. R. Baum, M. Frese, and R. A. Baron (eds), *The Organizational Frontiers: The Psychology of Entrepreneurship*, 93–112. Mahwah, NJ: Erlbaum.
Maslow, A. (1954). *Motivation and Personality*. New York: Harper & Row.
Mathieu, J. E., Hollenbeck, J. R., van Knippenberg, D., and Ilgen, D. R. (2017). A century of work teams in the *Journal of Applied Psychology*. *Journal of Applied Psychology*, *102*(3), 452–67.
Mathieu, J., Maynard, M. T., Rapp, T., and Gilson, L. (2008). Team effectiveness 1997–2007: A review of recent advancements and a glimpse into the future. *Journal of Management*, *34*(3), 410–76.
Mawdsley, J. K., and Somaya, D. (2018). Demand-side strategy, relational advantage, and partner-driven corporate scope: The case for client-led diversification. *Strategic Management Journal*, *39*(7), 1834–59.
Mincer, J. (1958). Investment in human capital and personal income distribution. *Journal of Political Economy*, *66*(4), 281–302.
Mindruta, D., Moeen, M., and Agarwal, R. (2016). A two-sided matching approach for partner selection and assessing complementarities in partners' attributes in inter-firm alliances. *Strategic Management Journal*, *37*(1), 206–31.
Mostafa, R., and Klepper, S. (2017). Industrial development through tacit knowledge seeding: Evidence from the Bangladesh garment industry. *Management Science*, *64*(2), 613–32.
Nickerson, J. A., and Zenger, T. R. (2008). Envy, comparison costs, and the economic theory of the firm. *Strategic Management Journal*, *29*(13), 1429–49.
Pelled, L. H., Eisenhardt, K. M., and Xin, K. R. (1999). Exploring the black box: An analysis of work group diversity, conflict and performance. *Administrative Science Quarterly*, *44*(1), 1–28.
Penrose, E. (1959). *The Theory of the Growth of the Firm*. Oxford: Oxford University Press.
Pfeffer, J., and Cohen, Y. (1984). Determinants of internal labor markets in organizations. *Administrative Science Quarterly*, *29*(4), 550–72.
Pfeffer, J., and Salancik, G. R. (1978). *The External Control of Organizations: A Resource Dependence Perspective*. New York: Harper & Row.
Phillips, D. J. (2002). A genealogical approach to organizational life chances: The parent-progeny transfer among Silicon Valley law firms, 1946–1996. *Administrative Science Quarterly*, *47*(3), 474–506.
Prescott, J. J., Bishara, N. D., and Starr, E. (2016). Understanding noncompetition agreements: The 2014 Noncompete Survey Project. *Michigan State Law Review*, *2*, 369–464.
Raffaelli, R. L., Glynn, M. A., and Tushman, M. (2018). Flexing the frame: The role of cognitive and emotional framing in innovation adoption by incumbent firms. Working paper.
Rand, A. (1957). *Atlas Shrugged*. New York: Dutton.
Rand, A. (1964). *The Virtue of Selfishness*. New York: Penguin.
Roach, M., and Sauermann, H. (2010). A taste for science? PhD scientists' academic orientation and self-selection into research careers in industry. *Research Policy*, *39*(3), 422–34.
Rocha, V., Van Praag, M., Folta, T. B., and Carneiro, A. (2018). Endogeneity in strategy-performance analysis: An application to initial human capital strategy and new venture performance. *Organizational Research Methods*, doi: 10.1177/1094428118757313.
Rosenberg, N. (1992). Economic experiments. *Industrial and Corporate Change*, *1*(1), 181–203.
Rubinstein, A. (1982). Perfect equilibrium in a bargaining model. *Econometrica*, *50*, 97–110.
Sauermann, H. (2017). Fire in the belly? Employee motives and innovative performance in start-ups versus established firms. *Strategic Entrepreneurship Journal*, *12*, 423–54.
Sauermann, H., and Cohen, W. M. (2010). What makes them tick? Employee motives and firm innovation. *Management Science*, *56*(12), 2134–53.
Sauermann, H., and Roach, M. (2013). Increasing web survey response rates in innovation research: An experimental study of static and dynamic contact design features. *Research Policy*, *42*(1), 273–86.
Saxenian, A. (1996). *Regional Advantage: Culture and Competition in Silicon Valley and Route 128*. Cambridge, MA: Harvard University Press.
Saxenian, A. (2007). *The New Argonauts: Regional Advantage in a Global Economy*. Cambridge, MA: Harvard University Press.
Schulmiller, E. (2008). All your life, Charlie Brown. All your life. Slate, 8 October. https://slate.com/culture/2014/10/the-history-of-lucys-pulling-the-football-away-from-charlie-brown-in-peanuts.html, accessed 26 December 2018.

Schultz, T. W. (1961). Investment in human capital. *American Economic Review*, *51*(1), 1–17.
Schumpeter, J. A. (1934). *The Theory of Economic Development*. Cambridge, MA: Harvard University Press.
Schumpeter, J. A. (1942). *Capitalism, Socialism and Democracy*. New York: Harper & Brothers.
Schumpeter, J. A. (1949). Economic theory and entrepreneurial history. In R. R. Wohl (ed.), *Change and the Entrepreneur: Postulates and the Patterns for Entrepreneurial History*. Cambridge, MA: Harvard University Press.
Shah, S. K., Agarwal, R., and Echambadi, R. (2018). Jewels in the crown: Exploring motivations and team building processes of employee entrepreneurs. Working paper.
Shane, S., Locke, E. A., and Collins, C. J. (2003). Entrepreneurial motivation. *Human Resource Management Review*, *13*(2), 257–79.
Shapiro, D. L., Hom, P., Shen, W., and Agarwal, R. (2016). How do leader departures affect subordinates' organizational attachment? A 360-degree relational perspective. *Academy of Management Review*, *41*(3), 479–502.
Skinner, B. F. (1971). *Contingencies of Reinforcement*. East Norwalk, CT: Appleton-Century-Crofts.
Smith, A. (1790) [1976]. *The Theory of Moral Sentiments*. Oxford: Oxford University Press.
Smith, A., Houghton, S. M., Hood, J. N., and Ryman, J. A. (2006). Power relationships among top managers: Does top management team power distribution matter for organizational performance? *Journal of Business Research*, *59*(5), 622–9.
Stern, S. (2004). Do scientists pay to be scientists? *Management Science*, *50*(6), 835–53.
Stevens, M. (1994). Labor contracts and efficiency in on-the-job training. *Economic Journal*, *104*, 408–19.
Terjesen, S., Hessels, J., and Li, D. (2016). Comparative international entrepreneurship: A review and research agenda. *Journal of Management*, *42*(1), 299–344.
Topel, R. (1986). Job mobility, search, and earnings growth: A reinterpretation of human capital earnings functions. *Research in Labor Economics*, *8*, 199–233.
Tushman, M. L., and Anderson, P. (1986). Technological discontinuities and organizational environments. *Administrative Science Quarterly*, *31*(3), 439–65.
Tushman, M. L., O'Reilly, C. A., and Harreld, J. B. (2015). Leading proactive punctuated change. In R. Henderson, R. Gulati, and M. Tushman (eds), *Leading Sustainable Change: An Organizational Perspective*. Oxford: Oxford University Press.
Von Mises, L. (1949). *Human Action: A Treatise on Economics*. New Haven: Yale University Press.
Vroom, V. (1964). *Work and Motivation*. New York: Wiley.
Wasserman, N. (2012). *The Founder's Dilemmas: Anticipating and Avoiding the Pitfalls that Can Sink a Startup*. Princeton: Princeton University Press.
Wezel, F. C., Cattani, G. and Pennings, J. M. (2006). Competitive implications of interfirm mobility. *Organization Science*, *17*(6), 691–709.
Wright, P. M., and McMahan, G. C. (1992). Theoretical perspectives for strategic human resource management. *Journal of Management*, *18*(2), 295–320.
Wright, P. M., McMahan, G. C., and Williams, A. (1994). Human resources and sustained competitive advantage: A resource-based perspective. *International Journal of Human Resource Management*, *5*(2), 301–26.

CONCLUSION

31. Human capital resources: a convergence of questions but divergence of answers

Anthony J. Nyberg, Robert E. Ployhart, and Thomas P. Moliterno

The chapters in this volume demonstrate that scholarly interest in human capital resources (HCR) is vibrant and growing. This volume unites 51 scholars steeped in sociology, economics, strategy, labor economics, human resources, organizational behavior, and psychology. The range of experience contributes to differing views about HCR: what they are, what they do, and how they are formed. When looking across chapters, one may wonder how we can reach an understanding of HCR when leading scholars have such different views. How can there be scientific advancement of HCR if there is such a broad diversity of expert opinion?

We argue such a view is unnecessarily pessimistic and misses the point of this book, and the efforts of so many extraordinary researchers. We are encouraged to see researchers exploring the nuances of HCR from a variety of scholarly domains, theoretical perspectives, and academic disciplines. It is through the variability and diversity of these different perspectives that we can understand the multiple dimensions of the HCR construct. Moreover, this volume demonstrates commonalities in the types of questions scholars ask: how human capital (HC) becomes a human capital resource (HCR); how an HCR becomes strategic human capital resource (SHCR); the factors that shape the process of HCR formation; and how HCRs affect outcomes across organizational levels.

One often writes a book to provide answers, and in this regard the current volume perhaps comes up short. However, the objective of this book was to identify the important questions that need answers. While each section included both *starter* and *commentary* chapters for each topic, in reality the entire book is a starter because it encourages answers to a common set of questions raised by the HCR scholarly community. In this final chapter we seek to provide additional commentary, and especially highlight the common questions and themes, identify some tentative conclusions, and make specific recommendations for future research.

COMMON THEMES

The chapter authors addressed eight topics thoughtfully, creatively, and provocatively. We do not restate what is in those chapters, and instead encourage interested readers to go directly to the chapters that address their topic of interest. Rather, we focus our attention on integration across the chapters to highlight five common themes (see Table 31.1).

Table 31.1 Common themes across the chapters

Common theme	Explanation	Relevant chapters
1. Interconnectedness of HCR structure and emergence	The structure of HCR will influence the value of HCR, and the intended structure of HCR will influence the emergence process. Additionally, relationships among members of the HCR (and between HCR and others) will influence the emergence and the performance of the HCR.	1, 2, 3, 4, 5, 6, 9, 12, 13, 14, 15, 18, 19, 20, 21, 22, 23, 24, 25, 26, 27, 28, 29, 30, 31
2. HCR complexity	HCR research generally underestimates the complexity of emergence process.	5, 6, 7, 25
3. Exogenous forces on HCRs	HCRs are influenced by endogenous and exogenous factors. This includes the systems that influence the emergence of HCR.	5, 6, 8, 9, 10, 11, 13, 17, 18, 19, 20, 21, 22, 23, 24, 25, 26, 27, 28, 29, 30, 31
4. Motivating HCRs	HCRs form unique contexts that require substantially greater investigation to understand the manner and boundary conditions that exist when thinking about motivating HCR.	8, 10, 12, 13, 14, 15, 16, 17, 19, 20, 21, 22, 23, 24, 25, 26, 27, 31
5. HCR retention	HCRs are complex, and thus thinking about how to attract, retain, and motivate HCRs also necessarily involves more complex tools than are generally studied.	17, 18, 19, 20, 21, 22, 23, 24, 25, 26, 27, 28, 29, 30

1. HCR Structure and HCR Emergence are Interconnected

Throughout the book, the authors challenged common approaches to thinking about how HCRs are structured and how the structure affects the value of a particular HCR. These authors noted that both the formation and the structure of HCRs influence how they perform and how organizations capture value from them (Barney and Mackey; Bridoux and Stoelhorst; Bermiss and Darnell; Camuffo and De Stefano; Cannella and Sy; Chadwick and Coff; Conroy; Eckardt and Jiang; Kehoe and Bentley; Kozlowski; Ployhart and Chen; Porter et al.). Together, these authors showcase that the configuration of HCR influences both the inputs and the outputs of the HCR.

2. HCRs and the Emergence Process are Complex

Closely related to the interconnectedness of HCR structure and emergence is the recognition that the emergence of HCR is extremely complex (Cannella and Sy; Eckardt and Jiang: Kozlowski). As discussed in the book, the structure (and the intended structure) of HCRs influences the emergence process, and likewise the emergence process influences the structure (Cannella and Sy; Echardt and Jiang; Kozlowski). Similarly, authors emphasize that emergence is more complex theoretically and empirically than is often acknowledged, in part because it is necessarily a dynamic process that takes different forms (Cannella and Sy; Kozlowski). Further, when considered in the HCR context, there may be emergence aspects that are unknowable or unmeasurable (Cannella and Sy). Although not explicitly mentioned, the role of complexity was also central to ideas regarding value capture and teams (Bridoux and Stoelhorst; Bermiss and Darnell; Cannella and Sy; Chadwick and Coff; Conroy; Eckardt and Jiang; Kozlowski; Ployhart and Chen; Porter et al.).

3. Exogenous Forces Influence HCRs

Many authors also invoke the role of exogenous forces in developing HCRs and shaping HCR effectiveness. This included thinking about systems (Campbell and Kryscynski; Cannella and Sy; Kozlowski; Lewin and Teece), the relationship with social capital (Crocker; Morris and Snell; Wright and Essman), and the degree of alignment between HCRs and the organization's intended outcomes (Brymer and Hitt; Campbell and Kryscynski; Delery and Roumpi; Weller). Further, these influences, along with some degree of path-dependence, can help general human capital to become firm-specific SHCRs (Crocker; Campbell and Kryscynski; Cannella and Sy; Weller).

4. Motivating HCRs is Important but Poorly Understood

After thinking about the emergence and the structure of HCR, scholars also noted the importance of motivating HCR. For instance, Porter et al. and Ployhart and Chen use lessons from the teams literature to highlight challenges that organizations have in forming and motivating HCR. Similarly, authors discussed unique motivation requirements that exist when considering HCR in teams (Porter et al.) and entrepreneurs (Agarwal). Other views considering the role of HCR motivation included thinking about how we mobilize (Bermiss and Darnell; Ployhart and Chen; Porter et al.; Wiersema) and compensate HCRs (Gerhart; Larkin; Nyberg and Reilly; Obloj and Zenger). Additionally, through considering the unique context (e.g., Bermiss and Darnell; Wiersema), systems and practices (e.g., Gerhart; Larkin; Lewin and Teece; Nyberg and Reilly; Obloj and Zenger; Porter et al.), structure (e.g., Barney and Mackey; Camuffo and De Stefano; Delery and Roumpi; Kehoe and Bentley; Weller), and social pressures (e.g., Agarwal; Brymer and Hitt; Crocker; Morris and Snell; Porter et al.; Wright and Essman) researchers provided insight into how to motivate HCR.

5. Retaining HCRs Remains Critical

A seminal insight in the literature is that HCRs are the resource where we must worry about voluntary self-depletion (Coff, 1997). While a few authors focused specifically on this topic (Bidwell; Hausknecht; Rider and Tan), concerns about retention were also raised as critical outcomes of building HCRs (Barney and Mackey; Camuffo and De Stefano; Kehoe and Bentley), and as key outcomes resulting from incentive systems (Gerhart; Larkin; Nyberg and Reilly: Obloj and Zenger) and social influences (Brymer and Hitt; Crocker; Morris and Snell; Porter et al.; Wright and Essman). In a unique twist on the traditional turnover literature, both Bidwell's and Rider and Tan's chapters highlight the *benefits* of HCR turnover both in the short and long term, and the importance of thinking about the individual leavers when we consider HCR turnover. Similarly, Brymer and Hitt expounded on the destructive effects, including HCR depletion, that can emanate from social capital.

In sum, these five common themes provide evidence that the field of SHCR is advancing to recognize a core set of principles, assumptions, and shared terms. Although different authors and different chapters may refer to these five themes in different ways, the fact that they recognize them as important and worthy of scholarly attention signals some convergence in the HCR space. This, by itself, is a significant advancement: consider that the last handbook of human capital, published in 2011 by Burton-Jones and Spender, scarcely addressed any of these topics. Specifically, the concept of HCR emergence and the notion of individual knowledge, skills, abilities, and other characteristics (KSAOs) are not even mentioned in that earlier book. Thus, in the span of roughly one decade, we see simultaneously an expanded HCR universe (in terms of the scholarly community) and a contracted HCR universe (in terms of the core assumptions adopted in this community).

There was once a debate about whether individual-level KSAOs form the basis of the HCR; we believe that debate is over. There may be many ways that HCRs may be built, developed, created, bundled, and so on. Moreover, these processes may occur at multiple organizational levels: Ployhart and Moliterno (2011) build on the resource theoretic logic to discuss this as an organizational dynamic capability (Helfat et al., 2007; Helfat and Martin, 2015). Somewhere in that complex organizational capability lies KSAOs, individually and collectively. KSAOs then are the atoms that comprise the broader HCR universe.

FUTURE RESEARCH

The chapter authors provide extraordinary insight into the state of the HCR literature and offer numerous suggestions for fruitful future directions. With the benefit of seeing across all the chapters, we highlight six areas where we believe HCR research should build on the common themes noted above. These six areas for future research are described below and summarized in Table 31.2.

1. Bridging Great Divides

Calls to bridge micro–macro divides have been made for decades (e.g., Hitt et al., 2007; Nyberg, Moliterno et al., 2014; Wright et al., 2014; Nyberg and Wright, 2015; Eckardt et al., 2018), yet here we are again making this call fully recognizing that "the divide" remains stubbornly resilient and will likely be here for the foreseeable future. But just because the challenge is daunting does not mean we should avoid addressing it. And so we once again urge scholars to bridge these divides, knowing that the journey is difficult but also the one that is likely to produce the greatest insight.

For instance, the microfoundations literature is one such area that has been working to bridge these divides. However, one of the interesting aspects of the long-running debate about microfoundations is the frequency with which the call to study them does not include the researchers steeped in those very microfoundations (for one exception, see Felin et al., 2015). Even though this entire book is founded on the premise that there is value in bridging these conversations, and even though the chapter authors did that better here than in most places, there was still a strong tendency within sections for authors to focus on their respective topics from within their traditional domains (i.e., micro vs. micro). For example

Table 31.2 Six suggestions for future research

Main idea	Explanation
1. Bridging great divides	We need much more cross-level and cross-discipline research. This research is necessarily challenging (due to a lack of common language) and risky (it remains difficult to get reviewers and editors that understand how such a paper should work).
2. Incorporate time and change	HCR research must account for and use time when thinking about the emergence process. We also need to examine the changes in HCRs more carefully because HCRs are necessarily always changing, and thus examining static or cross-sectional slices of an HCR is unlikely to capture the true nature of HCRs.
3. Complementarities/ matching	HCRs do not exist in isolation, and we need to know how matching and complementarities both influence the performance of each individual within the unit and the performance of the overall unit.
4. Measurement: think of the organization holistically and measure specifically	We need to find better ways to measure our HCR constructs and their effects. Focusing on such methodological issues may be an effective mechanism to unite micro and macro perspectives. After all, an equation is an operationalization of a theory, and the precision of an equation lays bare assumptions and theoretical differences.
5. Social capital/HCR convergence	What is the difference between social capital and HCR? Is there any meaningful difference; should we integrate these concepts into a new more inclusive type of resource?
6. Practitioner implications	The study of HCRs is the study of how an organization leverages the individuals in the organization to achieve unit-/organizational-level outcomes. This issue is of broad importance in industry. Is our research consistent with the key challenges in industry? Is our research providing meaningful, specific, and actionable guidance for practice?

(and not surprisingly), starter chapter authors frequently approached topics with a strong focus based in their core research domains, and commentary authors appeared to be more likely to focus disproportionate attention on the chapters that were also based in the same literature (e.g., micro commentaries focused more energy on micro starter chapters than on the macro starter chapter of the same topic). This is inevitable as we should write about the topics that we know best; but it should be clear that we can learn a great deal from a broader spectrum of perspectives (Eckardt et al., 2018). For this reason, this volume offers sections with chapters spanning micro and macro perspectives on a particular topic. We hope this is how readers of this handbook will approach the scholarship herein: reading an entire section rather than only the chapters that speak to their a priori micro or macro perspective. Doing so will provide the reader with opportunities for greater clarity. Reading research on HCRs from a different discipline is often enlightening and lays bare one's assumptions and bounded understanding of the topic. Ployhart (2012: 64) invoked Nietzsche to explain this:

> one may say there is an abyss that divides micro and macro theory and research. Looking into this abyss, as the philosopher Nietzsche said, also looks back into us. The 'abyss that looks into us' causes one to revisit some fundamental truths of our own literature and to question some assumptions that have to date been unquestioned.

One of the primary challenges of crossing a great divide involves the art of translating language differences (Eckardt et al., 2018). If the HCR construct is to have a lasting role in management scholarship and practice, then there must be a common understanding of what this resource is and what it does. For instance, while there have been thousands of micro-level studies, over more than seven decades, on "turnover" (Hom et al., 2017), that scholarship rarely informs the macro-level research conducted on "mobility" (e.g., employees leaving a firm to start new businesses) or turnover in the top management team. Similarly, and compounding the problem, the micro research on turnover rarely integrates findings from the macro-level mobility literature.

Of course, it is extremely difficult to learn new languages and new areas of research, and this difficulty gets greater with experience and deeper expertise. Yet we have a simple solution: conduct research with author teams that involve multiple perspectives. Examples abound, including in this book (e.g., Chadwick and Coff; Eckardt and Jiang; Lewin and Teece; Moliterno and Nyberg; Nyberg and Reilly). Along these lines, we would all benefit from being more receptive and developmental when reviewing, such that when we see authors stray into our territory, rather than get upset about their ignorance of our work, we should help educate them to help develop better-grounded science (Eckardt et al., 2018).

2. Time and Change

Throughout this volume, authors highlighted the need to better understand how time works to influence HCR formation and effectiveness; this was a particular focus in the emergence process section of the book (Cannella and Sy; Eckardt and Jiang; Kozlowski). A few ideas that stand out are the reminder that HCRs will be better understood through combining a dynamic capabilities approach with a strategic human resource systems approach (Lewin and Teece). Similarly, Obloj and Zenger focus on the role of time in thinking about the inevitable fluidity of HCR, and hence the challenges associated with research examining HCRs in a static manner. Yet there are also specific challenges raised by Cannella and Sy, Kozlowski, and Obloj and Zenger about the need to theorize and examine change. The fluidity of HCRs creates challenges rarely embraced by researchers who generally focus on static resources. However, change is a window for seeing into dynamic responses that provide insight into both the phenomenon and the causal mechanisms influencing the phenomenon. Additionally, methodological tools—e.g., random coefficient growth modeling (RCGM), discontinuous random coefficient growth modeling (DRCGM), and survival analysis—are sufficiently common that we ought to strive to use time and change more regularly and effectively in HCR research.

However, from our reading of the chapters in this volume and the literature more broadly, we are encouraged by the manner in which empirical HCR research has considered temporal issues. The dynamic capability perspective offered in early HCR research (Ployhart and Moliterno, 2014) necessarily suggests a temporal component to HCR development. We might go so far as to say that HCR research may be ahead of other areas in the study of change. There is research on HCR inflows and outflows, talent mobility, talent pipelines, path-dependence, dynamic capabilities, resource orchestration, industry dynamism and growth, and so on (Ployhart et al., 2011; Helfat and Peteraf, 2003; Reilly et al., 2014). Yet in all these studies, time and change are largely a backdrop—a context or a metric—rather than a focal part of the theorizing and analysis. Giving temporal issues prominence will change the conversation. For example, how does the value of HCRs change over time? What is the "shelf life" of HCR value capture? Does the rate of change in HCR quality or quantity influence performance change? Does it matter whether HCR quality or quantity lags or leads relative to competitor HCRs? At the end of the day, firms invest in HCRs because they expect them to produce change in operational and strategic outcomes; thus to study change processes is to align theory with practice (more on this later).

3. Complementarities/Matching

A number of authors in the volume discussed complementarities or matching and how it affects HCR value (e.g., Campbell and Kryscynski; Weller). For instance, Kehoe and Bentley and Delery and Roumpi highlight the importance of matching when thinking about the potential value-add of HCRs and the necessity for thinking about how to optimize HCRs; similar arguments have recently been made in Weller et al. (2019). Through considering complementarities and matching we can investigate how HCRs emerge and how emergence process differences affect the quality of the resultant HCRs. In addition to thinking about how components within an HCR are matched, we should also be asking: what should the HCR be matched with (e.g., a job, a set of HR practices, a strategy, etc.)?

We argue that we ought to be pushing further to think about how matching and complementarities influence the performance of each individual within the unit and the performance of the overall unit. That is, how does matching affect both the individual- and unit-level HCR (Ployhart et al., 2014)? Along these lines, in a recently published article, Wolfson and Mathieu (2018) provide a template for thinking about how HCR research can go further to examine interactions across teams, individuals, and situations. As suggested by Porter et al., Wolfson and Mathieu test the effects that collective competencies have on individual performance. By coupling insights from competencies and teams research, the Wolfson and Mathieu article provides a blueprint for thinking about when HCRs will be more or less beneficial and how we may look at HCRs across levels from the individual through the team, department, business unit, and organization.

Of course, the idea here is that we would do well to break away from thinking of complementarity as a static state, and think about the *potential* for complementarities. For example, one may think of factors that vary within the contextual environment (e.g., industry demands, firm's culture), and question whether complementarities exist for different types of HCRs in those different contexts. Alternatively, one might consider how different types of HCRs are complementary with different types of leaders (e.g., leader–member exchange, LMX, theory) or team members (e.g., group composition). The point is that most HCR research has focused on HCRs in isolation from other resources, and thus research needs to understand how complementarities and matching *among* resources may contribute to greater/lesser value creation and capture. Such an approach could require a dramatic shift in future research because it would change the question of aligning HCRs to firm strategy to a question of first aligning HCR to other resources, and only then the combination to firm strategy.

4. Measurement: Think of the Organization Holistically and Measure Specifically

We have more tools to analyze more complex data than ever before. Additionally, multilevel and longitudinal data are ever more prevalent. Data that links employee attitudes with behaviors and higher-order outcomes are increasingly available around the world. Additionally, as data becomes easier for organizations to collect, even the largest organizations appear to be increasing their appreciation for the need to engage in greater scientific discovery regarding management practices and HCR development. We appear to be in a golden age where organizations are looking for data-driven answers that fall right into the skillset of academic researchers. As obvious as it sounds, we all need to be striving to incorporate more sophisticated data into our research, and we should be stronger about holding ourselves and others accountable for using data that appropriately answers the questions investigated. Today's research conclusions are the foundations for future research. However, when conclusions are built on poor proxies, the foundation is unstable and can lead later generations to waste considerable energy.

Given the availability of data that speaks to the heart of HCR topics, we believe that methods may be used to drive new questions that theory has not yet considered. Further, this method-driven approach may be more effective in uniting micro-macro areas than many theoretical efforts. Obviously, one cannot divorce theory from methods, and we learn the most when theory and method form a symbiotic relationship. But our point is that data wins arguments, and it is oftentimes easier for scholars trained in different disciplines to come to a common understanding and a shared world view when focusing on methods and empirical research. Although there are also methodological differences among micro-macro scholars (e.g., construct validity vs. endogeneity; Wright et al., 2014), data can be analyzed in multiple ways and results across methods can be compared. Oddly enough, this means that attempts to integrate micro-macro perspectives on HCRs might advance more quickly if scholars converge on the types of data and datasets they analyze. Indeed, we see this happening now, as more micro scholars are looking at firm-level outcomes and more macro scholars are looking at individual-level inputs to those outcomes.

5. Social Capital/HCR Convergence

Authors in this book (e.g., Crocker; Hitt and Brymer; Morris and Snell; Wright and Essman) raised great questions about the relationship between social capital and HCR. This relationship is elementary to the functioning of HCRs in that they often involve human interaction and there are strong connections between a person's human capital and social capital. This relationship is also one that has received stunningly little attention, given its inextricable connection. The lack of attention is likely due, in part, to the fact that much social capital research is published in the social network literature—and this is not a literature that HCR researchers tend to focus attention on (see our comments above). We argue that understanding how social capital and HCRs are related will help propel great progress in understanding how HCRs are formed and how effective they can be.

In fact, we question whether there is much of a meaningful distinction between social capital and HCR—both are resources based on and among people. When we talk about the unit-level HCR, necessarily we are talking about social capital since the unit-level HCR comprises individuals and there is some relational (i.e., social) capital that emerges at the same as the HCR. So is the value that the unit-level HCR creates owing to the individuals it comprises or the social capital that inheres in the relational space embedded in the HCR? And if the answer is "both" (as we suspect it is), how do we decompose this value? Minimally, how is social capital different from an HCR complementarity? Is HCR matching just an element of social capital? The social capital construct comes mainly from sociology and thinking on HCRs comes mainly from economics, but they clearly overlap in significant ways. It is probably time to move past these old distinctions and move on to understanding where they are the same, if they are different, and maybe even replace the old labels with new, more inclusive, constructs.

6. Practitioner Value

There is obviously a great deal of research interest in HCRs, but is any of this work influencing practice? How much of this work is guided by practice? In general, to what extent is the thought and attention devoted to HCRs having any measurable impact on the world it claims to understand?

It is not surprising that only a few chapters included relevant practical implications (e.g., Gerhart) given that authors were not asked to address such issues. However, to the extent that we can help organizations understand that there are useful lessons that can be drawn from HCR research, and to the extent that researchers can help answer questions that are truly plaguing organizations, we will have greater access to data and will be able to make greater contributions to both research and practitioners (Kryscynski and Ulrich, 2015). We argue that HCR research is fundamentally a research topic that involves the biggest problems that organizations face—namely, how do they attract, retain, organize, and motivate their talent in ways that optimize individual and organizational performance? So, then, where are the specific actionable guidelines for what we should prescribe to managers? Which actions should we tell managers they should do, and which actions should we tell managers they should not do? It would be very interesting to have a group of managers comment on the field of HCR research: what questions are we not considering and how well are we answering their most important questions?

CONCLUSION

From micro to macro perspectives, and from multiple scholarly disciplines, researchers are advocating that we learn more about how organizations can use people to compete in the marketplace. Whether they are taking a bottom-up perspective or a top-down perspective, scholars are converging on the importance of examining people as the common element that influences organizational outcomes. However, this convergence does not imply that answers to these shared questions will be simple. In contrast, this will be an extremely complicated journey that requires expanding the literatures we read; trying to appreciate, while maintaining respect for, alternative perspectives and different traditions; and substantially greater cross-discipline and cross-level collaboration. This book provides a starting point on this journey because the authors in this book, who are paragons in the burgeoning HCR field, provide insights and suggestions that create a strong foundation for future multilevel and interdisciplinary HCR research. We look forward to the road ahead.

REFERENCES

Burton-Jones, A., and Spender, J.-C. (eds) (2011). *The Oxford Handbook of Human Capital*, Oxford: Oxford University Press.

Coff, R. W. (1997). Human assets and management dilemmas: Coping with hazards on the road to resource-based theory. *Academy of Management Review*, *22*(2), 374–402.

Eckardt, R., Crocker, A., Ahn, Y., Floyd, S. W., Boyd, B. K., Hodgkinson, G. P., Kozlowski, S. W. J., Moliterno, T. P., and Starbuck, W. H. (2018). Reflections on the micro-macro divide: Ideas from the trenches and moving forward. *Strategic Organization*. https://doi.org/10.1177/1476127018770048.

Felin, T., Foss, N. J., and Ployhart, R. E. (2015). The microfoundations movement in strategy and organization theory. *Academy of Management Annals*, *9*(1), 575–632.

Helfat, C. E., and Martin, J. A. (2015). Dynamic managerial capabilities: Review and assessment of managerial impact on strategic change. *Journal of Management*, *41*(5), 1281–312.

Helfat, C. E., and Peteraf, M. A. (2003), The dynamic resource-based view: Capability lifecycles. *Strategic Management Journal*, *24*(10), 997–1010.

Hitt, M. A., Beamish, P. W., Jackson, S. E., and Mathieu, J. E. (2007). Building theoretical and empirical bridges across levels: Multilevel research in management. *Academy of Management Journal*, *50*(6), 1385–99.

Hom, P. W., Lee, T. W., Shaw, J. D., and Hausknecht, J. P. (2017). One hundred years of employee turnover theory and research. *Journal of Applied Psychology*, *102*, 530.

Kryscynski, D. and Ulrich, D. (2015). Making strategic human capital relevant: A time-sensitive opportunity. *The Academy of Management Perspectives*, *29*, 357–69.

Nyberg, A. J., and Wright, P. M. (2015). 50 years of human capital research: Assessing what we know, exploring where we go. *Academy of Management Perspectives*, *29*(3), 287–95.

Nyberg, A. J., Moliterno, T. P., Hale, D. H., and Lepak, D. P. (2014). Resource-based perspectives on unit-level human capital: A review and integration. *Journal of Management*, *40*(1), 316–46.

Ployhart, R. E. (2012). The psychology of competitive advantage: An adjacent possibility. *Industrial and Organizational Psychology*, *5*(1), 62–81.

Ployhart, R. E., and Moliterno, T. P. (2011). Emergence of the human capital resource: A multilevel model. *Academy of Management Review*, *36*(1), 127–50.

Ployhart, R. E., Van Iddekinge, C. H., and MacKenzie, W. (2011). Acquiring and developing human capital for sustained competitive advantage: The interconnectedness of generic and specific human capital resources. *Academy of Management Journal*, *54*(2), 353–68.

Ployhart, R. E., Nyberg, A. J., Reilly, G., and Maltarich, M. A. (2014). Human capital is dead; long live human capital resources! *Journal of Management*, *40*(2), 371–98.

Reilly, G., Nyberg, A. J., Maltarich, M., and Weller, I. (2014). Human capital flows: Using context-emergent turnover (CET) theory to explore the process by which turnover, hiring, and job demands affect patient satisfaction. *Academy of Management Journal*, *57*(3), 766–90.

Weller, I., Hymer, C., Nyberg, A. J., and Ebert, J. (2019). How matching creates value: Cogs and wheels for human capital resources research. *Academy of Management Annals*, *13*(1), 188–214.

Wolfson, M. A. and Mathieu, J. E. (2018). Sprinting to the finish: Toward a theory of human capital resource complementarity. *Journal of Applied Psychology*, *103*, 1165.

Wright, P. M., Coff, R., and Moliterno, T. P. (2014). Strategic human capital: Crossing the great divide. *Journal of Management*, *40*(2), 353–70.

Index